The Complete Works of
WASHINGTON
IRVING

Richard Dilworth Rust
General Editor

MISCELLANEOUS WRITINGS
1803-1859

Volume I

Washington Irving
1805

WASHINGTON IRVING

MISCELLANEOUS WRITINGS

1803-1859

Volume I

Edited by
Wayne R. Kime

Twayne Publishers
Boston
1981

Published by Twayne Publishers

A Divison of G. K. Hall & Co.

The Complete Works of Washington Irving

Volume XXVIII

CENTER FOR EDITIONS OF
AMERICAN AUTHORS

AN APPROVED TEXT

MODERN LANGUAGE
ASSOCIATION OF AMERICA

®

Library of Congress Cataloging in Publication Data

Irving, Washington, 1783–1859.
Miscellaneous writings, 1803–1859.

(The complete works of Washington Irving; v. 28–29)
Includes bibliographical references and indexes.
I. Kime, Wayne R.
PS2072.M57   1981   818′.209   80–19108
ISBN 0–8057–8520–5 (set)

Manufactured in the United States of America

For my mother, Betty Kime Wendt

CONTENTS

TEXTS

Early Prose Writings, 1803–1815

ACKNOWLEDGMENTS

I am grateful to my fellow Irving editors and also to a knowledgeable corps of librarians and colleagues for the assistance they have given me during the preparation of this edition. Professors Richard Beale Davis, Bruce Granger, Andrew B. Myers, and Walter A. Reichart, and Mrs. Betty Husting kindly answered my queries on specific points, and Professors Ralph M. Aderman, Edwin T. Bowden, and Dahlia Terrell on many occasions shared information, exchanged opinions, and offered advice in a generous manner that places me in their particular debt. In supervising a series of machine collations of the various editions and impressions of Irving's *Spanish Papers*, the late Professor Henry A. Pochmann made an important contribution to the task of research which subsequently became my own responsibility. The late Professor Herbert L. Kleinfield was helpful as a sounding board and advisor on topics general and specific connected with the *Miscellaneous Writings*. And I am especially grateful to Professor Lewis Leary for his timely encouragement and unfailing cooperation.

This project could hardly have been completed without financial assistance from the Center for Editions of American Authors of the Modern Language Association of America, which through its grant from the National Endowment for the Humanities furnished funds for materials, travel, and free working time. The Canada Council provided the further assistance of a Leave Fellowship in 1974–1975. By far the most significant practical help, however, has been given me by my mother, Mrs. Betty Kime Wendt, who though at a distance of 2,500 miles has served with remarkable efficiency as a typist, file clerk, proofreader, and critic.

Last, I thank my wife, Alicia, and my son, Evan, for their inspiriting presence, their help, and their patience.

W. R. K.

Fairmont State College, West Virginia

ILLUSTRATIONS

York *Morning Chronicle* in December, 1803, and extending to his revised biographical sketch of Thomas Campbell in the *Analectic Magazine* for March, 1815, afford a fairly comprehensive sampling of his youthful talents and enthusiasms. His lifelong interest in the drama—not merely in dramatic literature but in actors, acting, and stagecraft as well—is foreshadowed in his first series of publications, the nine "Letters of Jonathan Oldstyle" (1802–1803), and also in his subsequent contributions to the *Morning Chronicle* under the name of "Dick Buckram." His formidable skills as a political satirist, to be given fullest expression in *A History of New York* (1809), are apparent in his contributions in 1804 to two other New York newspapers, *The Corrector* and the *Evening Post*. His sociable taste for preparing anonymous literary works in collaboration with friends, in which manner the piquant *Salmagundi* papers (1807–1808) were produced, he indulged once more in March, 1809, when, as one of the reigning local literati, in the *New-York Review* he helped verbally to annihilate an individual who had dared to question in public the authority of his influential coterie.

As editor of the *Analectic Magazine* in 1813 and 1814 Irving enjoyed a ready outlet for his current literary interests and had access to a continuous flow of contemporary European literature which played a significant part in his developing new ones. The early promise of his achievements in American history and biography, chiefly in the *Life and Voyages of Christopher Columbus* (1828) and the *Life of George Washington* (1855–1859), is to be discerned in the biographical sketches of American naval heroes he contributed to the *Analectic Magazine*. Similarly his active interest in the American Indian, years afterward to result in the three "Western" books, *A Tour on the Prairies* (1835), *Astoria* (1836), and *The Adventures of Captain Bonneville, U.S.A.* (1837), is documented in "Traits of Indian Character" (February, 1814) and "Philip of Pokanoket" (June, 1814), which two sketches were incorporated in *The Sketch-Book* (1819–1820). His future activities as a mediator between Europe and the United States—an interpreter of European culture to his countrymen and an adapter of foreign literary models to native themes and settings—are incipient in his biographical sketches of Thomas Campbell and Lord Byron, the passages he reprinted from the recent works of Walter Scott, Thomas Moore, and others, and the articles he included in the *Analectic Magazine* on subjects as diverse as the Spanish peasantry and the legendary lore of Germany. By May, 1815, when at the age of thirty-two he sailed for Europe to begin a seventeen-year sojourn there, Irving had developed the interests he was to continue exploring for the more than forty years of his subsequent career. Moreover, he had adopted a literary role, as what George S. Hellman termed an "Ambassador" from the New World to the Old,[1] which was to earn him a unique position in the history of American literature. Irving's early prose works thus occupy an important place in the canon of his writings. They foreshadow the breadth and variety of his achievement as America's first professional man of letters.

The opening of New York's Park Theater in 1798 and the beginning of performances there by William Dunlap's Old American Company together quickly confirmed Irving's early taste for plays and playgoing. He began his career as an author in November, 1802, when, adopting the pseudonym "Jonathan Oldstyle," he addressed to his brother Peter Irving's daily newspaper, the New York *Morning Chronicle,* the first in a series of nine letters detailing the manifold shortcomings of the city as a center of culture, especially as these were revealed in performances at the theater. The ribaldry and unruliness of the audience, the silly and trite musical accompaniments, the gimcrack stage arrangements, the trivial "afterpieces," even the personal appearances of some of the actors, all received treatment.[2] According to William Dunlap, the "irritation caused" by these comments was at first "excessive,"[3] but the ill feeling was not long-lived. The pseudonym notwithstanding, Irving's authorship of the "Oldstyle" letters was an open secret, and he frankly declared himself "a friend to the theatre,"[4] if not to all its shortcomings. He gained more friends and admirers than enemies in his youthful exercises as a theater critic; he was already on friendly terms with Dunlap, the actors Thomas A. Cooper and Joseph Tyler, and no doubt others.

The "Oldstyle" series proper ended in April, 1803, but Irving's two contributions to the *Morning Chronicle* on December 24 and 30 of that year may be regarded virtually as addenda to it. The format of the "Oldstyle" letters, a communication to the editor of the newspaper by the fictitious author, interspersed with letters to that personage by his friend

1. Irving's roles as an interpreter of European culture to Americans, and while in Europe a distinguished representative of the contemporary United States, are emphasized by Hellman in his biographical study, *Washington Irving, Esquire, Ambassador at Large from the New World to the Old* (New York, 1925).

2. Prior to their being included in the *Oldstyle and Salmagundi* volume of the present edition, edited by Bruce I. Granger and Martha Hartzog, the "Letters of Jonathan Oldstyle" had never been reprinted in full. Eight of the nine (omitting the first) appeared in *Letters of Jonathan Oldstyle, Gent.* (New York: William H. Clayton) in 1824, and in an English edition of the same year; five (the first through the fifth in the *Morning Chronicle*) were included in the posthumous *Spanish Papers and Other Miscellanies,* ed. Pierre M. Irving, 2 vols. (New York, 1866), II, 11–36; hereafter cited as *Spanish Papers.*

3. Dunlap, *History of the American Theatre,* 3 vols. (1832; reprint New York, 1963), II, 167.

4. Irving to William Irving, Genoa, December 20, 1804 (Yale).

"Andrew Quoz," is adopted in the later sketches with only minor vari-
ation: here "Quoz" is the recipient of letters addressed to him by one
of the actors, "Dick Buckram." Like the "Oldstyle" letters, those from
"Buckram" to "Quoz" were the youthful Irving's burlesque report on an
actual sequence of events: the recent nine-week season in Albany, New
York, of a contingent of players from the Old American Company. After
an ambitious but financially disappointing season at the Park Theater,
on July 15, 1803, the company began to give further performances in
Mount Vernon Gardens, an amusement park whose bills of entertainment they shared with Signior Manfredi, a popular acrobat.[5] However,
summer theater in New York was brought to a halt shortly thereafter
by an epidemic of yellow fever which raged throughout August and
part of September. At the end of July or early in August, fifteen regular
members of Dunlap's company, under the leadership of the veteran
Lewis Hallam (ca. 1740–1808), made their way to Albany. There, hiring
a suitable hall, they advertised in a local newspaper their intention to
present a series of performances, thus offering the citizenry of the state
capital its first opportunity since 1785 to witness serious drama performed by a theatrical troupe of acknowledged stature. Despite minor
problems occasioned by their necessarily makeshift arrangements, the
players enjoyed a successful stay in Albany, performing thrice weekly
between August 22 and October 28 before their return to New York,
where they opened at the Park Theater for the 1803–1804 season on
November 14.[6]

Coincidentally, some of Irving's movements during the summer of
1803 paralleled those of the actors under Lewis Hallam. On July 30, in
company with his employer, Josiah Ogden Hoffman, and several other
members, friends, and associates of the Hoffman family, the twenty-
year-old author sailed up the Hudson River from New York on the first
leg of an extended tour which was to take him as far north as Montreal.
The Hoffman entourage arrived in Albany on August 1, and the next
day Irving accompanied the ladies of the party to the nearby resort
town of Ballston Spa, where they remained for two more days before

5. Dunlap, *History of the American Theatre*, II, 198; Oral S. Coad, *William
Dunlap* (1917; reprint New York, 1962), pp. 77–78; George C. D. Odell, *Annals
of the New York Stage*, 15 vols. (New York, 1927–1949), II, 179–85; New York
Evening Post, July 11, 1803, p. 2, col. 1; July 25, 1803, p. 2, col. 2.

6. Albany *Register*, August 19, 1803, p. 2, col. 1; New York *Morning Chronicle*,
November 11, 1803, p. 3, col. 2; November 16, 1803, p. 2, col. 5; "The Albany
Theatre," in *Collections on the History of Albany*, ed. Joel Munsell, 4 vols. (Albany,
1865–1871), II, 32; Arthur Hornblow, *A History of the Theatre in America*, 2 vols.
(New York, 1919), I, 285–86. In his *History of the American Theatre*, William
Dunlap summarized the activities of his company laconically: "During this
summer [1803], the performers of the New-York theatre played at Mount Vernon
Gardens for a short time, and afterwards at Albany, with some success" (II, 200).

setting out again on their journey. It is possible that while in Albany Irving fell in with members of the Old American Company, but the journal he kept at the time affords no hint of such a meeting. It may also be that at some time afterward, passing through the city on his way home with the Hoffmans, he met some of the actors or even saw them perform a play. Unfortunately, his journal of 1803 breaks off abruptly with him in the remote village of Osgewatchie on August 30, and we have no evidence of his precise whereabouts for several weeks after that date.[7] In any case, he had almost certainly been aware in July that the Hallam contingent was considering a removal from New York, even though he may not have learned the results of their visit to Albany until after he had himself returned from Canada. He could hardly have failed at that time to hear accounts of the actors' recent experiences, for during their absence from the Shakespeare Gallery, the headquarters of the Old American Company, the premises had been occupied by Peter Irving as the editorial office of the New York *Morning Chronicle*.[8] Whether from firsthand experience, through conversation with friends, or from reading the three newspapers published in Albany in 1803—the *Centinel*, the *Gazette*, and the *Register*—Irving eventually gathered a substantial amount of information about the expedition.[9] The literary fruits of his inquiries, the two letters from "Dick Buckram" to "Andrew Quoz," must thus have amused informed readers not only by their comic extravagance but by their recognizable foundation in fact.

Irving's contributions a few months later to the short-lived newspaper called *The Corrector* derive from a set of circumstances almost entirely different from those which surround his *Morning Chronicle* articles. As the editor of the *Morning Chronicle* since its inception in October, 1802, Peter Irving had firmly supported the aspirations of that enigmatic figure Aaron Burr, who in 1804 was attempting to recoup his political fortunes as a candidate for the governorship of New York. In March of that year Peter resolved to establish and edit anonymously a second Burrite organ. The avowed purpose of the new publication, *The Corrector*, was re-

---

7. *Journals and Notebooks*, vol. 1, ed. Nathalia Wright (Madison, 1969), pp. 5–6; hereafter cited as *Journals*, I. The scanty evidence available concerning Irving's activities after August 30, 1803, is in Pierre M. Irving, *The Life and Letters of Washington Irving*, 4 vols. (New York, 1862–1863), I, 59—hereafter cited as PMI, and in Stanley T. Williams, *The Life of Washington Irving*, 2 vols. (New York, 1935), I, 33–34, 387, n. 55—hereafter cited as STW. See also Irving to William Irving, Nice, September 20, 1804, and Irving to Sarah Storrow, Sunnyside, September 19, 1853 (Yale).

8. New York *Morning Chronicle*, August 9, 1803, p. 3, col. 1; October 31, 1803, p. 3, col. 1.

9. See Wayne R. Kime, "An Actor Among the Albanians: Two Rediscovered Sketches of Albany by Washington Irving," *New York History*, 56 (October, 1975), 409–25, esp. 415–16; see also below, pp. 280–81.

luctantly to chastise the enemies of Burr's cause for their "flagitious conduct" in mounting a one-sided campaign of slanderous abuse against the editor of the *Morning Chronicle* and his associates. "The task is hateful," Peter wrote in an early issue of *The Corrector* under the pseudonym of "Toby Tickler, Esq.," "but the good of society requires its execution, and it shall be faithfully performed."[10] Doubtless a supplementary motive for this moral crusade was, by denigrating the opponents of Aaron Burr, to strengthen his candidacy in the forthcoming state elections. At any rate, upon announcing his intention to establish *The Corrector* Peter seems to have found a willing coadjutor in his younger brother Washington. Irving was not at that time a supporter of Burr, but he was firmly opposed to the policies favored by Burr's implacable enemies, the Jeffersonian Democrats. He was incensed, moreover, at the unmerited insults being directed at Peter, whose polite demeanor and inoffensiveness of speech were proverbial. Irving thus began anonymously to publish satirical articles in *The Corrector*; and as Pierre M. Irving expressed it in a manuscript narrative of the incident, the author was "by no means lenient when he undertook to apply the lash. Some of the severest sarcasms in the Corrector came from his pen, and more than one of the epithets stuck to the parties through life." Pierre's further remark that "there was ever more of wit than malice in his effusions" may require qualification in light of the obvious exuberance of the articles which have been attributed to Irving.[11] It is known, after all, that he held a low opinion of Peter's enemies—in particular of James Cheetham, the editor of the New York *American Citizen*, who supported the gubernatorial candidacy of the Democratic incumbent, Morgan Lewis, and who had led his adherents in a shrill campaign of abuse against the Burrites.[12] Still it is probably true that, as Pierre M. Irving put it, Irving "had not the least relish for the asperities of party strife" and did regard his compositions as more than simply hostile volleys in an acrimonious political skirmish.[13]

10. *The Corrector*, no. 3 (April 4, 1804), p. 11, col. 2.

11. On the basis of a stylistic study of Irving's early writings, Martin Roth has identified forty-five of the anonymous articles published in *The Corrector* as his and has edited them as *Washington Irving's Contributions to The Corrector* (Minneapolis, 1968). For further discussion of Roth's methods of attribution, and of the procedures adopted in selecting the fourteen items included in this volume as Irving's, see pp. 281–87.

12. Irving to William Irving, Bordeaux, August 1, 1804 (Yale); an extract in a hand not Irving's.

13. Pierre M. Irving's manuscript summary of *The Corrector* episode is in the Berg Collection, New York Public Library. The greater part of it is included in Wayne R. Kime, "Pierre M. Irving's Account of Peter Irving, Washington Irving, and the *Corrector*," *American Literature*, 43 (March, 1971), 108–14. For a sum-

"*We Will Rejoice! ! !*," Irving's contribution to the New York *Evening Post* for May 14, 1804, was an outgrowth of the same political campaign as prompted his articles in *The Corrector*. Peter Irving's immediate motivation for conducting the latter newspaper was removed on April 26, when the polls for the three-day state elections were closed; and on that date he published its tenth and final issue. Although he had failed to win the governorship for Aaron Burr, who had irremediably undermined his own prospects by a series of questionable activities, Peter had at least been successful in arousing public indignation at the practices of James Cheetham, the intemperate journalistic mouthpiece of the party in power. Thus vindicated, he retired from the battlefield and concentrated his efforts upon editing the *Morning Chronicle*, whose relatively sedate tone was better attuned to his character than the cantankerousness of *The Corrector*. Meanwhile, the Democrats enjoyed their resounding victory unmolested, and Irving found himself deprived of the customary outlet for the productions of his now active pen. Under these circumstances, his natural recourse was to submit any further writings to William Coleman's *Evening Post*, the Federalist newspaper in the city. Coleman, who had been an ally of *The Corrector* during the campaign, was both a cordial enemy of the Democrats and an acquaintance of Irving; a versatile man of a literary turn himself, he would in all likelihood be receptive to anti-Democratic contributions from the young author.[14] Thus Irving's only real difficulty in the aftermath of the election was probably that no news was occurring to stimulate the renewed exercise of his satiric talents.

Before many days elapsed, a suitable opportunity arose. On the morning of May 11, James Cheetham's *American Citizen* published a "General Plan of Arrangements for the Celebration of the Acquisition of Louisiana by the United States," an article setting forth the details of an elaborate commemorative ceremony to be held in the city on the following day, and to include, among other observances, a formal procession of militia, fraternal societies, and civic officers.[15] The Louisiana Purchase, the object of the proposed festival, had been agreed upon by treaty one year before—on April 30, 1803—and was rightly regarded by supporters of Jefferson throughout the United States as a major political victory for the Democratic party; for the Federalists, their only con-

---

mary of New York state politics during this period, see Dixon Ryan Fox, *The Decline of Aristocracy in the Politics of New York* (New York, 1918), pp. 61–68.

14. William Coleman (1766–1829) was the editor and owner of the *Evening Post* from its inception in 1801 until his death, when his assistant William Cullen Bryant assumed the editorship. For Irving's subsequent dealings with him, see *Letters of Washington Irving to Henry Brevoort, Jr.*, ed. George S. Hellman (New York, 1918), pp. 329–30.

15. *American Citizen*, May 11, 1804. p. 2, cols. 1–2.

siderable opponents, had been opposed to the measure, condemning it as a wasteful folly. Thus the celebration in New York City, timed as it was to follow the elections in which the Democrats had won an easy victory over the Burrites and the Federalists, seemed certain to become a partisan celebration of the Democratic ascendancy rather than a demonstration of unanimous patriotic pride. William Coleman was understandably ironical when he alluded, in the Federalist *Evening Post* for May 11, to "the enthusiasm which must surely take possession of every American on this occasion."[16] Coleman may now have enlisted Irving's aid in rendering the planned celebration ridiculous, or Irving may have taken up the task independently; neither can have overlooked the possibilities for satire in the announcement of the self-gratulatory ceremonial.

On Saturday, May 12, the celebration was held as scheduled, and Irving set out to travesty it in a burlesque account of the procession of troops, societies, and dignitaries. "*WE WILL REJOICE!!!*," his report of the parade, was published in the *Evening Post* two days later. Not surprisingly, the cast of characters prominent in the article included some of the personages whom he had attacked in his contributions to *The Corrector*: Cheetham, the Democratic hatchet man; De Witt Clinton, the Democratic mayor of New York City; Samuel Latham Mitchill, the dryasdust pedant; and others. Likewise Irving employed the same devices of literary billingsgate as had appeared in his writings for the Burrite newspaper, such as derisive sobriquets and asterisks or dashes to fill in the omitted portions of his victims' names—names which, as annotated copies of *The Corrector* reveal, were easily recognizable to informed contemporary readers.[17] Finally, unifying his account within a single conceit, Irving drew upon the newspaper advertisements

---

16. *Evening Post*, May 11, 1804, p. 2, col. 4.

17. The copy of *The Corrector* owned by the Beinecke Library, Yale University (which lacks issues 8 and 10) includes the following marginal identifications in an unknown hand (identifications in parentheses): p. 3: Candidate Bob (Robt Livingston); Joseph Surface (present sherriff); p. 6: Daniel (D^l Ludlow); Maturin (M Livingston); Ourang-Outang (Tunis Wortman Clark of the Mayors Cort &c); Sylvanus (Conl Hunting); F——— (Major Fairley); p. 7: Billy Luscious (W. L. Rose an attorney); Ambrose (Ambrose Spencer a NY Gent); p. 8: C——m (Cheetham); D—— W—— C—— (De Witt Clinton); S——O (Saml Osgood); J—— F——— (Ja^s Fairley); M——L (M Lewis); p. 11: Captain Skunk (Dewit Clinton who fought a duel with Swartwout); [friend of Captain Skunk] (Mr. Ryker his second); Ourang-Outang (Tunis Wortman); Knight (Cheetham); Maryland Apothecary (Tillotson one of our Senators); p. 34: J——R——— (John R. Livingston); R—— R——— (Riker); T——s W——n (Wortman).

The copy of *The Corrector* owned by the Library of Congress includes the following identifications by an unknown hand: p. 27: Ourang-Outang (Wortman); p. 34: R—— R——— (Richard Riker); T——s W———n (Wortman); ——— of Plandome, Esq. (Sylvanus); p. 39: M.L. (Maturin Livingston).

for two local theaters, the Park and the Grove, to portray the Democratic procession as itself a hilarious theatrical entertainment.[18]

The *Evening Post* article won praise from the judges whose opinions Irving valued most highly, the anti-Democratic intelligentsia of the city; but even by the time the work was published his attention had probably been diverted from literary and political concerns, for he was busy making final preparations for a voyage on May 19 from New York to Bordeaux. Under the sponsorship of two elder brothers, William and Ebenezer, he was about to begin a two-year residence in the Old World during which, as they hoped, he would devote himself to studying at firsthand the monuments of ancient and modern civilization. These hopes, orthodox among American parents and elder brothers of the era, were to be disappointed. Irving was sensible of his brothers' generosity, however, and upon his arrival in Europe he wrote letters home which revealed an attempt at least to keep up appearances. Thus, after almost a year of desultory wandering through France, Greece, and Italy, in April, 1805, he wrote to William Irving from Rome, informing him that he was about to leave there, in company with a genial friend, for Paris, where he planned to "pay attention to several branches of art and science into which I wish to get a little insight." "In fact," he gravely reflected in another letter written at about this time, "there is no place in Europe where a young man, who wishes to improve himself, and is determined to act with prudence, can spend a certain space of time to more advantage than at Paris."[19] But William was able to estimate his brother's protestations at their true value. In a testy reply, he took accurate measure of what was to remain one of Irving's primary instincts. "I have no doubt," he wrote, "that Mr. Cabell, who is to be your fellow-traveller, is a very estimable fellow ... as his excellence has induced you to give up, for the momentary pleasure of his society in Paris, all the advantages of a patient and leisurely journey through Italy.... Good company, I find, is the grand desideratum with you; good company made you stay eleven weeks at Genoa, where you needed not to have stayed there more than two, and good company drives you through all Italy in less time than was necessary for your stay at Genoa."[20] Indeed,

18. For a discussion of Irving's use of the theatrical advertisements, see Wayne R. Kime, "Washington Irving and the 'Extension of the Empire of Freedom': An Unrecorded Contribution to the *Evening Post*, May 14 1804," *Bulletin of the New York Public Library*, 76 (1972), 225–27; see also below, pp. 287–88.

19. Washington Irving to William Irving, Rome, [April, 1805]; PMI, I, 139, 141. In his reply (see note 20), William Irving referred to Irving's "letter, dated Rome, 4th April." Although Pierre M. Irving separated the two fragmentary passages from Irving's correspondence quoted here, they may both have formed parts of the letter of April 4.

20. William Irving to Washington Irving, New York, July 8, 1805; PMI, I, 140.

even as he had sailed for Europe Irving would almost have traded the experiences awaiting him, simply to be reunited with his family and friends at home. As late as January 25, 1805, he confessed himself to William "famishing for want of intelligence about the little world of my acquaintances."[21] Yet whatever William and Ebenezer may have concluded as to the wisdom of their joint expenditure, Irving's visit to Europe was far from lost time. Inevitably he acquired a certain sophistication which, upon his return to New York in March, 1806, conferred upon him a special distinction in the fashionable circles of the town. More importantly, he formed the habit of faithfully recording in his travel journals notes of the sights and persons he encountered along his way. In later years Irving's journals were often to prove useful to him as budgets of material to be drawn upon for use in his published writings.

Although in 1806 he resumed the study of law in the New York law office of Josiah Ogden Hoffman, Irving's real interests at that time would seem still to have been social and literary. Together with his brother Peter, Gouverneur Kemble, Henry Brevoort, Henry Ogden, James Kirke Paulding, and other companions he amused himself at Dyde's, a genteel tavern near the theater, ate what the group called "blackguard suppers" at a less pretending porter house nearby, talked politics and gossiped in the sociable home of William Irving, or rusticated at "Cockloft Hall," a rambling house a few miles outside the city, which Kemble had inherited from a deceased uncle. Known variously among themselves as "the Nine Worthies," the "true lads of Kilkenny," or the "SAD DOGS," these young gentlemen formed an elite coterie, both social and literary. As Pierre M. Irving explained in the *Life and Letters*, in the early nineteenth century "literati and men of intellect entered . . . into [New York] society, and gave it something of their own tone and character."[22]

Out of this carefree comradeship grew the *Salmagundi* papers in which, with witty insouciance, Irving, William Irving, and Paulding under several pseudonyma amused their fellow citizens by portraying them in caricature. "Like all true and able editors," they announced in the first number, "we consider ourselves infallible; and therefore, with the customary diffidence of our brethren of the quill, we shall take the liberty of interfering in all matters either of a public or a private nature." *Salmagundi* was a great popular success in local circles, even though, as Evert A. Duyckinck later observed, for the pungency of its satire it it was also "the mild terror of the town."[23] It firmly consolidated Irving's

21. Washington Irving to William Irving, Ship Matilda, December 25, 1804–January 25, 1805 (Yale).

22. PMI, I, 165.

23. *Salmagundi; or, The Whim-Whams and Opinions of Launcelot Langstaff, Esq., and Others*, ed. Evert A. Duyckinck (New York, 1860), p. 14; "Editor's Preface," p. xiii.

local status, not only as a humorous observer of manners, but as an arbiter of fashionable taste.

At the end of 1808 or early in 1809, James Ogilvie (ca. 1775–1820), a Scottish pedagogue, orator, and cultural visionary who had come to the United States several years before, arrived in New York to offer a series of public lectures. Together with other members of his circle—notably Gulian C. Verplanck, Paulding, and David C. Colden—Irving became a warm supporter of the orator, exerting his influence to promote Ogilvie's interests and introducing him, despite his eccentric habits, into New York society. However, certain of the pious, in particular those who had reason to be irritated at the general complacency of the Irving circle, professed themselves indignant that this "uncouth infidel" should frequent genteel drawing rooms. One John Rodman (1775–1847), an amateur man of letters, seized the occasion not only to attack Ogilvie rather savagely, but probably also to pay back old scores against Irving and his friends. These aims he realized in a pamphlet entitled *Fragment of a Journal of a Sentimental Philosopher Found during his Residence in the City of New-York* (1809).

In a preliminary "Advertisement" to the *Fragment*, Rodman, posing as an anonymous "Editor," solemnly warned his readers against the immoral influence of Ogilvie and of those who supported him:

> Against the itinerant propagators of infidelity—the insiduous [*sic*] pretenders to philanthropy and benevolence, it is the duty of every father of a family to be vigilant. By allowing them free access to our houses, they have numberless opportunities of instilling the poison of their principles into the very bosom of domestic life.... They give us the cold-blooded, atheistical system of Godwin for the cheering, mild, and benevolent doctrines of Christ....Let those gentlemen who have taken pains to introduce a certain wandering orator into the domestic circles of this city, seriously reflect on the consequences that may result to society; and particularly to that portion of it who constitute the charm and the blessing of life....[24]

In the "journal' 'which follows—supposedly picked up in a hostelry room after the departure of a guest—Ogilvie is made out the complete humbug; and as Richard B. Davis has noted, "there is more than a grain of truth in the depiction."[25] The orator reveals more of himself through his comments in the fictional journal upon each new acquaintance he makes. John Rodman does not name these individuals, but he char-

24. Rodman, *Fragment* (New York, 1809), pp. 3–4.
25. Davis, "James Ogilvie and Washington Irving," *Americana*, 35 (July, 1941), 441.

acterizes them in such a way that the persons alluded to are unmistake-
able; annotations in extant copies of the *Fragment* reveal that the
victims of his attack were readily identified.[26] Irving is "Young T.":

> *Saturday.* Young T. came to see me—had a letter to him from Mr. C.
> a true Godwinian, and friend of Mr. Jefferson's—T. interesting
> young man—has genius—wrote a book, which I took care to praise—
> has read a good deal in the authors of the new school, and a little
> tinged with their notions—don't admire Dr. Johnson—like him for
> that—much thought of here—must have his good opinion—will go
> far with the public—asked his advice about an oration—even altered
> it to please his taste—[27]

However they may have viewed its telling references to James Ogilvie's slovenliness, weakness for women, addiction to laudanum, and other
foibles,[28] as arbiters of New York's literary fashions Irving and his
friends were not prepared to allow the *Fragment* to pass unnoticed;
such reflections upon themselves were not to be borne. Probably with
Irving as the guiding spirit and principal author, for the nonce they
created the *New-York Review; or Critical Journal*, published by Inskeep
& Bradford, a journal in which, as "good natured critics," they might
conveniently annihilate Rodman at one stroke. In the single issue of the
New-York Review, dated March, 1809, they executed the task with
awesome efficiency. First answering his charges point-for-point with
unremitting irony, they then attacked him for his "pitiful forgeries" and
his "invention" in the *Fragment* "of incidents which never occurred"—
branding his purported "defence of religion or morality" as no more than
an "impertinence." Finally, they offered him a "friendly hint" to "abstain
from pen, ink, and paper," and to "keep in doors, like a good little man,"
adding the caveat that if "we ever catch him, hawking his hard ware
about the purlieus of Parnassus, we will most certainly straddle him over
a rail, and ride him round the premises, to the great amusement and
laughter of the muses, and the eternal terror of all interlopers in like
case offending."[29] John Rodman had met his match. Henceforward, at
least as a critic of Irving and his friends, he was silent.

In the spring of 1809 Irving published *A History of New York*, his
most ambitious literary work to date, which immediately won him renewed local notoriety and gradually brought him wider recognition as
one of the most promising young authors in the United States. After that

26. See the Textual Commentary on the *New-York Review*, p. 289, n. 72.
27. *Fragment*, pp. 11–12.
28. *Ibid.*, pp. 8, 9, 19, 28, 31–32.
29. *New-York Review*, pp. 108, 118–19.

event, however, a combination of circumstances severely curtailed his literary productivity for more than three years. During the period he remained a fixture in New York society, often making excursions as well to Philadelphia, which boasted its own literary circle, and to Washington D.C., where William Irving was serving with distinction as a congressman. Early in 1812 he managed to bring out a second, thoroughly revised edition of the *History*, but his activities did not become very purposeful until June of that year, when war broke out against Great Britain and he was dispatched to Washington in order to lobby on behalf of the endangered interests of P. & E. Irving & Co., the family importing firm. As the United States hastily mobilized itself to combat its powerful foe, Irving's own energies were stirred. He was impressed by the stories of American military exploits then coming into circulation,[30] and as a friend of the naval leaders Stephen Decatur and William Bainbridge he began to think seriously of enlisting. In December, 1812, he attended a public dinner in New York to honor three naval heroes. "It was the most splendid entertainment of the kind I ever witnessed," he reported with patriotic fervor to Peter Irving, who was then living in Europe. "I never in my life before felt the national feeling so strongly aroused."[31]

Before the war was over Irving was in fact to serve as aide-de-camp to Daniel D. Tompkins, the governor of New York and commander of the state militia, but at the close of 1812 he took up an occupation appropriate both to his patriotic sentiments and also to his literary talents. Moses Thomas, a Philadelphia bookseller who had recently purchased a monthly magazine entitled *Select Reviews*, proposed that he edit the work for an annual fee of 1,500 dollars. Although he had almost no experience as an editor, Irving readily agreed. "I have undertaken to conduct the Select Reviews," he reported with satisfaction to Henry Brevoort, who was then also in Europe, "for the sake of pastime & employment of idle hours. I am handsomely paid & the work is no trouble."[32] The responsibilities of editing soon grew much more demanding than he had bargained for, but during the next two years Irving continued to conduct this cultural miscellany—which, after consultation with Thomas, he renamed the *Analectic Magazine*.

He had at first understood that his sole duty as editor would be to make judicious selections of articles from the leading journals of Europe for reprinting in the *Analectic Magazine*. However, it developed not

30. See *Letters of Washington Irving to Henry Brevoort*, p. 20.

31. Irving to Peter Irving, New York, December 30, 1812; PMI, I, 293. See also I, 292, 295, 296; and STW, I, 135.

32. *Letters of Washington Irving to Henry Brevoort*, pp. 90–91. In regularized form this passage from Irving's letter dated January 2, 1813, appears in PMI, I, 294; for a similarly worded announcement to Peter Irving, see *ibid.*, I, 291.

long afterward that Thomas intended him to depart from that format, which had defined *Select Reviews*. On December 18, 1812, Irving wrote to his friend James Renwick from Washington, confessing his consternation upon learning of Thomas' previously unmentioned plans:

> ... my publisher ... has been advertising, every day or two, some addition and improvement ... of which I have known nothing until I saw the advertisements. At one time there is to be a series of portraits of our naval commanders, with biographical sketches. At another a history of the events of our maritime war, &c., on the plan of–the British Naval chronicle! and here am I–poor I ... most wickedly made the editor of a vile farrago, a congregation of heterogeneous articles, that have no possible affinity to one another.[33]

Thomas wished not only for the *Analectic Magazine* to include original and contemporaneous matter, but for some of it to come from Irving. Yet, taking an interest in his new duties, the author decided to go along with most of these proposals.[34] He thus prepared several unsigned articles on topics which interested him; Paulding and Verplanck—especially the former—generously supplied him with further copy; and no doubt other acquaintances offered suggestions for items to be reprinted or else provided bits of information for the monthly collection of "Literary Intelligence." Irving assumed full responsibility for the contents of the magazine; but as he was to do throughout his career, he actively sought the aid of interested friends in pursuance of the project.

Existing as it did in the atmosphere of strong national sentiment which accompanied the war with England, the *Analectic Magazine* became under Irving's editorship an instrument to express and influence the opinions of Americans, toward both themselves and their enemy. From first to last, Irving maintained a consistent editorial stance with regard to the present and future relations between the United States and England: despite the hostilities, he warned against a total severing of ties between the two countries. In his biographical sketch of Thomas Campbell he wrote: "Whatever may be the occasional collisions ... which will inevitably take place between two great commercial nations ... whatever may be the clamorous expressions of hostility vented at such times by our unreflecting populace, or rather uttered in their name by a host of hireling scribblers ... it is certain, that the well-educated and well-informed class of our citizens entertain a deep-rooted good will, and a rational esteem, for Great Britain." More particularly, he em-

33. PMI, I, 290.
34. See the passage from Irving's letter to Charles Prentiss, New York, April 4, 1814 (American Antiquarian Society); in STW, I, 136.

phasized the influence for international friendship of the "writers of
Great Britain," who through our "long habit and . . . affection" have
become "the adopted citizens of our country." But to these statesmanlike
remarks he added a quiet warning—to be reiterated in *The Sketch-Book*
—lest the mother country should alienate the affection of her already
powerful young offspring.[35] "Surely," he wrote, "it cannot be to the
interest of Great Britain to trifle with such feelings."[36]

While he discouraged an attitude of continuing antagonism toward
England once the fighting should end, Irving sought in the *Analectic
Magazine* to promote self-esteem among Americans on the basis of their
nation's achievements in the War of 1812. In pursuit of this aim he
adopted editorial policies remarkably similar to those of *The Port-Folio*,
the other most influential literary monthly in the contemporary United
States. *The Port-Folio*, which before the war had identified itself with
a genteel conception of literary pursuits as proper to one's hours of
"elegant leisure,"[37] sought during the conflict to become instead "a
repository of every thing that may tend to give character to our country,
and to cherish in the breasts of our fellow citizens, the holy flame of
genuine patriotism." Hence this magazine solicited from its readers
"original articles of American biography, accompanied with well-ex-
ecuted portraits of the personages described," and often featured them
as the leading items in its successive issues.[38] Similarly, Irving encouraged in the *Analectic Magazine* the compilation of what *The Port-
Folio* grandly termed a *"Biographia Americana,"* publishing numerous
sketches of military figures, including four of his own—of Captain
James Lawrence (August, 1813), Lieutenant William Burrows (November, 1813), Commodore Oliver H. Perry (December, 1813), and Captain
David Porter (September, 1814).

The Port-Folio sought not only to foster collective self-esteem among
Americans, but also to to stimulate a vigorous national literature which
would reflect the auspicious new spirit. Thus in several of its issues
it published collections of patriotic lyrics, and in May, 1814, it offered
a cash prize for the best national song, which would be introduced

35. In the urbanely polemic essay entitled "English Writers on America."
36. "A Biographical Sketch of Thomas Campbell," *Analectic Magazine*, 5
(March, 1815), 245–46.
37. Ironically, *The Port-Folio* had employed this very term to describe Irving's
mode of life prior to assuming the editorship of the *Analectic Magazine*. See Irving
to James Renwick, Washington, December 18, 1812; PMI, I, 290.
38. "To the Patrons of the Port Folio," *Port-Folio*, n.s. 3, no. 5 (May, 1814),
395–97. As instances of *The Port Folio*'s adherence to this policy, see the articles
entitled "Life of Captain William Henry Allen" (January, 1814), 1–23; "On the
Naval Resources of the United States" (January, 1814), 62–81; "Life of Commodore Perry" (March, 1814), 203–19; "Life of Commodore Murray" (May,
1814), 399–409; "Biographical Memoir of Commodore Dale" (June, 1814), 500–15.

amid the celebrations on Independence Day, July 4.[39] Irving organized
no contests in the *Analectic Magazine,* but as its editor he expressed
views about the national literature distinctly similar to those held by
the editors of *The Port-Folio.* For example, in his review of Edwin C.
Holland's *Odes, Naval Songs, and Other Occasional Poems* (March,
1814), he praised the South Carolina poet for avoiding the habit, prevalent among contemporary versifiers, of "composing" verses in praise
of American military prowess merely by making a few judicious changes
to British songs. "We would rather hear our victories celebrated in the
merest doggrel that sprang from native invention," he wrote, "than
beg, borrow or steal from others, the thoughts and words in which
to express our exultation."[40] In the issue for December, 1814, he found
space to introduce and reprint Francis Scott Key's lyric written after
the unsuccessful British bombardment of Fort McHenry near Baltimore,
subsequently to be adopted as the United States national anthem.

Meanwhile, Irving kept up the reputation of the *Analectic Magazine*
as a monthly collection of European periodical literature. Upon assuming the editorship he had asked Peter to send along to him from
Europe "any periodical work...which you may think of importance"
and also "copies of new works that appear, that are not of a local or
too expensive nature, fit for republication in this country"; and he made
a similar request of Brevoort.[41] He was thus assured of a steady supply
of potential copy with which to instruct his readers, and at the same
time a convenient source of gratuitous amusement to himself. As the
months passed he reprinted excerpts from the recent poetry of Byron
(of whom he wrote a biographical sketch, published in July, 1814),
Moore, and Scott, and also political speculations, narratives of travel,
and essays in natural history. His interest in the productions of American authors, apparent in the review of Holland's *Odes,* was also re-

39. "To Readers and Correspondents," *Port-Folio,* n.s. 3 (May, 1814), 497.
An authoritative discussion of the relationship between politics and belles lettres
in magazines during the War of 1812 is by Frank L. Mott, *A History of American
Magazines,* 5 vols. (New York, 1930–1968), I, 177–78, 183–90. Mott's commentary
on the *Analectic Magazine* is in the same volume, pp. 279–83.

40. "*Odes, Naval Songs, and other occasional Poems. By Edwin C. Holland,
Esq. Charleston,*" *Analectic Magazine,* 3 (March, 1814), 245. In the "Preface" to
his *Odes,* Holland had expressed his own enthusiastic awareness of the literary
implications of the war. "The late GLORIOUS NAVAL VICTORIES," he wrote,
"achieved under the Flag of the *United States,* have afforded a brilliant theme to the
labors of the Historian, the pencil of the Painter, and the Genius of the Poet" (p. vi).

41. Irving to Peter Irving, New York, December 30, 1812; PMI, I, 292. On
December 9, 1812, Brevoort wrote to Irving from Edinburgh that he had prevailed upon a friend "to use his utmost endeavors in procuring and forwarding
to New York the different periodicals of France, as well as those of note published
on the continent, such, for instance, as Kotzebue's, &c." (PMI, I, 298).

vealed in his notices of Robert Treat Paine's *Works* (March, 1813) and the anonymous *Lay of the Scottish Fiddle* (September, 1813)—according to its title page "Supposed to be written by *Walter Scott, Esq.*," but in fact the work of James Kirke Paulding.

In December, 1814, owing to the sudden failure of its publishers and the consequent financial ruin of its proprietor, Moses Thomas, the *Analectic Magazine* sank into deep difficulties and Irving promptly "signed off whatever was due" to him.[42] He felt sympathy for Thomas, who on the whole had treated him honorably, and he assisted him in effecting an arrangement through which the magazine might be continued; but he did not resume the editorship. Probably, in fact, he was relieved to be able to sever his connection with the *Analectic Magazine* in so uninvidious a way. As Pierre M. Irving summarized the situation, the "conduct of this Magazine, which he had hoped to find a mere pastime, proved to be an irksome business. He had a great repugnance to periodical labor of every description, and to one branch of it, criticism, his aversion was pointed, for he wished to be just, and could not bear to be severe."[43] But at least, with the other benefits it conferred, his stint as editor of the *Analectic Magazine* had taught him a useful lesson about his own temperamental limitations. "I . . . would never again undertake the editorship of that or any other periodical work," he wrote to Verplanck on January 17, 1815;[44] and he was as good as his word. Despite Sir Walter Scott's willingness a few years later to secure an editorship for him at a handsome salary, he would not consider the proposition. He avoided regular association with any periodical for twenty-five years, until, due to financial difficulties, in 1839 he agreed to contribute articles to the *Knickerbocker Magazine*—thus forcing himself once more temporarily to perform a "monthly recurring task"[45] uncongenial to his nature.

His final publication in the *Analectic Magazine,* the biographical sketch of Thomas Campbell, was actually a "revised, corrected, and materially altered" version of a text he had prepared five years earlier. At that time Archibald Campbell, a brother of the poet who was living in New York, had just received the manuscripts of *Gertrude of Wyoming* and *O'Connor's Child,* and had solicited Irving's aid in securing an American publisher for them. The latter managed to locate a suitable person, Charles I. Nicholas of Philadelphia, who agreed to undertake the work provided Irving would make a selection of Campbell's earlier poems to be included with these latest ones, and that in addition he

---

42. Irving to Gulian C. Verplanck, Philadelphia, January 17, 1815; quoted in STW, I, 141.

43. PMI, I, 299.

44. STW, I, 141.

45. Irving to Pierre M. Irving, n.p., April, 1840; PMI, III, 152.

would write a biographical introduction. He agreed to do so, and making full use of the scanty materials supplied him for the purpose by Archibald Campbell,[46] he hastily wrote out the desired commentary. Although *The Poetical Works of Thomas Campbell*, with its sketch "By a Gentleman of New-York," sold widely in the United States, Irving was dissatisfied with his own contribution—which, as he later remarked, had been "written against the vein."[47] Meanwhile Peter Irving, who also had reservations about the essay, made the acquaintance of Thomas Campbell, grew to admire him, took up his interest, and urged Irving to assist him in the United States in any way possible.[48] This proved impracticable, but on the basis of fuller information Irving did in 1815 revise the biographical sketch in a manner pleasing to himself and, no doubt, to Peter as well. In the next few years, moreover, he was able effectively to promote Campbell's fortunes in the United States.[49]

The revised "Biographical Sketch of Thomas Campbell" brought to an appropriate close Irving's association with the *Analectic Magazine*, in which as editor he had sought to promote among Americans an enlightened respect for England, in particular for the talents of her authors. The sketch stands also as a fitting conclusion to Irving's formative period as a writer. Having by 1815 risen from the status of a bright young man-about-town to that of a respected literary personality with a national reputation, he was about to begin a new era in his career. As he set sail aboard the ship *Mexico* on May 25, 1815, to undertake what he assumed would be a brief mission in Liverpool of untangling the financial difficulties of P. & E. Irving & Co., he quite possibly looked forward to meeting face to face the poet whom he had recently portrayed as best he could at secondhand. But he could not have guessed that he was about to begin a seventeen-year sojourn in Europe, during which he was not only to meet Thomas Campbell but was to become the friend of Scott, Moore, Rogers—the men whose works he had avidly sought out as a youth—and was himself to win international fame.

POEMS, 1803–1855

Washington Irving was in a double sense an occasional poet: he wrote verse rarely and, in most instances, at times when according to the conventions of his era the composition of suitable lines was a

46. A clear notion of the sort of information Archibald Campbell was able to provide may be derived from entries in a notebook Irving compiled in 1810. See Barbara D. Simison, "Washington Irving's Notebook of 1810," *Yale University Library Gazette*, 24 (July, 1949), 11–15.

47. PMI, I, 253.

48. See *ibid.*, I, 303–6.

49. *Letters of Washington Irving to Henry Brevoort*, pp. 124, 151, 239, 251–58.

desirable observance. Drafts of brief poems scattered through his travel journals reveal that from time to time Irving amused himself by casting his thoughts into verse, but he seldom paid further attention to these casual jottings.[50] A few completed poems may be found elsewhere among his miscellaneous writings—in *The Corrector* contributions (1804) and the two plays (1823)—but with those exceptions the twelve pieces included here represent Irving's total output as a writer of verse. Of the twelve, which were written over more than half a century, only three— the "Address of Cooper on Assuming the Management of the Park Theatre," "*Passaic—A Tradition*," and "The Dull Lecture"—were clearly intended for publication, public recitation, or even "public" display in manuscript form. The rest were essentially private performances, written for the amusement of friends, offered as complimentary gifts or as con- tributions to the personal albums of his hosts, prompted by visits to places of interest, or else prepared simply as exercises in composition.

The frequent quotations from English and American poets in Irving's early works, his well-filled commonplace books containing passages copied from the writings of English, French, German, Spanish, and Italian poets and dramatists he admired, and other details including his practical efforts on behalf of William Cullen Bryant in England and Thomas Campbell in the United States, or his friendships with Scott, Moore, and Rogers, suggest together that he was widely read in poetry, both past and present. His own poems reveal an ability to write com- petently in several verse forms, such as the expository discourse in heroic couplets, the literary ballad, and the sentimental love lyric. However, it cannot be said that Irving's manner as a poet "developed" in any significant way, that he ever achieved a poetic style distinctively his own, or indeed that he ever sought to do so. He was, at need, a competent versifier within patterns already well established, and he pretended to be no more than that.

Inevitably, some of Irving's most notable characteristics as a prose writer may be discerned in his poems as well. His pleasant talents as a humorist are well illustrated, for example, by two works of light verse written at opposite ends of his career, "Signs of the Times" (ca. 1810) and "The Lay of the Sunnyside Ducks" (1855). The former poem, unpublished during his lifetime, is a product of the years of irresponsible good fellowship he enjoyed in New York as one of the "SAD DOGS" who, as *Salmagundi* expressed it, "riot at Dyde's on im- perial champagne, / And then scour our city—the peace to maintain...."[51] Pierre M. Irving recounted in the *Life and Letters* an anecdote, told him by the author years afterward, which was apparently representa-

50. See, for example, *Journals,* I, 397, 581.
51. *Salmagundi,* ed. Duyckinck, p. 64.

tive of these bibulous entertainments. Henry Ogden, a friend of Irving's, was on his way home after a riotous gathering when, being tipsy, he fell "through a grating, which had been carelessly left open, into a vault beneath. The solitude, [Ogden] said, was rather dismal at first, but several other of the guests fell in, in the course of the evening, and they had on the whole quite a pleasant night of it."[52] A similarly unedifying incident served in part as the occasion for "Signs of the Times." While on his way home with various companions from another celebration at Dyde's Tavern, the fashionable meeting place in Park Row, one Morris Ogden—possibly a relative of Henry—took down the sign of a local merchant, Cheesbrough & Co., and ran off with it on his shoulder. The next day he and Irving, who had witnessed the theft, attended church together and heard a sermon in which, reflecting upon the ominous "signs of the times," the preacher unwittingly made several remarks which applied to the recent adventure. Irving is said thereupon to have written on the leaf of a Psalm book his impromptu account of Morris Ogden's comeuppance.[53]

"The Lay of the Sunnyside Ducks," another account of the humorous discomfiture of a friend, is Irving's latest known effort in verse. Upon his return home in 1846 after four years' service as the United States' minister to Spain, the author began an extensive campaign of improvements to "Sunnyside," his estate on the east bank of the Hudson River about twenty miles north of New York City. One of his projects was to dam up a small brook which ran across his property into the river. The necessary operations proved successful and resulted in a handsome pond, nicknamed "The Little Mediterranean," which gave him much satisfaction. Encircled by footpaths and shaded by trees, this picturesque pond became the year-round home of a flock of ducks and geese and a stopping-off-place for many other species.[54] In 1855, shortly after purchasing a residence just uphill from Irving's property, Edward S. Jaffray, Jr., a prominent New York merchant, sought repeatedly to dam the brook which supplied "The Little Mediterranean"; he hoped to divert some of the water for use in his own home. Irving followed Jaffray's project with interest, and as it proceeded he made friends with his new neighbor's five-year-old daughter, Florence. At last, after Jaffray had abandoned his plans as impracticable, Irving addressed to Florence "The Lay of the Sunnyside Ducks," in which he playfully portrayed her

52. PMI, I, 165; see also STW, I, 76.
53. The poem was first published, with a note explaining the circumstances of its composition, by Gabriel Harrison in *The Life and Writings of John Howard Payne* (Albany, 1875), p. 398. According to Harrison, the poem was found in an album of Payne's after the death of the actor.
54. Harold Dean Cater, "Washington Irving and Sunnyside," *New York History*, 38 (Summer, 1957), 146–55.

father as having almost robbed the Sunnyside ducks of their home. Obviously with Jaffray's assistance, Florence then wrote a "Reply to the Lay of the Sunnyside Ducks," cast in the meter of Longfellow's *Hiawatha* (1855), which began:

> Much beloved Mr. Irving
> I received your charming letter,
> All about the Indian streamlet—
> All about the top-knot ducklings—
> How my Papa, very selfish,
> Tried to dam up all the water,
> Tried to keep more than he ought to....

Neither "The Lay of the Sunnyside Ducks" nor the reply to it was published until 1886, when Jaffray included them both in a letter he contributed to James T. Scharf's *History of Westchester County, New York.*[55]

Two examples of a second sort of occasional poem, verses Irving wrote at the specific request of other persons, are included here: the "Address of Cooper on Assuming the Management of the Park Theatre" (1807) and "The Dull Lecture" (1827). Irving greatly admired the acting ability of Thomas A. Cooper (1776–1849), and throughout his lifetime he was fond of comparing Cooper's performances in various roles with those by other tragedians of the day, such as Kean, Kemble, and Cooke.[56] He and Cooper had become good friends by 1806, when the latter became the lessee and manager of New York's Park Theater and set out, with uncertain hopes of success, on this adventuresome new phase of his career. As a personal favor, Cooper asked Irving to prepare a rhymed address for him to recite at the first performance at the Park under the new managership. The latter attempted to do so, but for some reason he was unable to complete the task in time. One year later, therefore, at the beginning of the 1807–1808 season, Cooper renewed his request; and "to oblige,"[57] the author finished off the verses. Although the completed poem was thus not precisely an address on Cooper's "assuming the management," it did mark a perhaps equally important event in the actor's association with the Park Theater. Following the season of 1806–1807 the interior of the building had at great

55. Scharf, *History of Westchester County, New York*, 2 vols. (Philadelphia, 1886), 239–40.

56. For the comparisons see *Letters of Washington Irving to Henry Brevoort*, pp. 46–47, 56, 150; PMI, IV, 420. Cooper in 1812 married Irving's vivacious friend Mary Fairlie, the "Sophy Sparkle" of *Salmagundi*; see *Letters to Brevoort*, pp. 78–79.

57. PMI, I, 204.

expense been extensively rebuilt and redecorated. On August 28, 1807, the New York *Evening Post* commented enthusiastically on the result, concluding that the theater now "unites more of taste, grandeur, room, convenience, and elegance than any one in the United States."[58] And a few days later, on September 9, Cooper began the new season by reciting to a crowded house Irving's lines. His versified promise to the occupants of the gallery that, thanks to the redesigned stage machinery, "Shifters of scenes no more shall act amiss / Nor jumbling seas with towns provoke your hiss" was apparently made good that night, for in their review of the performance the authors of *Salmagundi* praised "particularly the gentlemen who shifted the scenes, who acquitted themselves with great celerity, dignity, pathos, and effect."[59] Irving, as a contributor both to the performance and to the review of it in *Salmagundi,* had obviously done all he could to promote the ambitious efforts of his friend Cooper. However, according to Pierre M. Irving he "put no value" on his verses in themselves. They remained unpublished until Pierre included them in the *Life and Letters,* with the enigmatic prefatory remark that they constituted "the longest piece of versification into which [the author] was ever tempted."[60]

"The Dull Lecture," the other of Irving's poems written "to oblige," was first published in *The Atlantic Souvenir; Christmas and New Year's Offering. 1828* (1827). These few lines served as a literary accompaniment to an engraving of a painting by his friend G. S. Newton (1794–1835) which appeared as the frontispiece to the volume. Upon meeting Newton, in 1818, Irving had at once liked him and recognized his promise as an artist. According to William Dunlap, he was actually responsible in part for stimulating Newton to cultivate the variety of painting which eventually won him widest recognition: the portrayal of humorous scenes from domestic life, often based upon literary models.[61] Certainly Irving followed the artist's career with special interest, kept in regular contact with him, and promoted his interests whenever possible. Whether in fact he arranged for the publication in *The Atlantic Souvenir* of the engraving from Newton's painting is not known, but the fact that he supplied the verses at the artist's request suggests that he was associated in some way with the use of the engraving by Carey, Lea, & Carey, his sometime publishers.[62] His verses took their title from the painting, which depicts an old philosopher

58. Quoted in Odell, *Annals of the New York Stage,* II, 291.

59. *Salmagundi,* ed. Duyckinck, p. 299.

60. PMI, I, 204.

61. Dunlap, *History of the Rise and Progress of the Arts of Design in the United States* (1834; reprint New York, 1965), III, 84.

62. Carey and Lea had published the first American edition of *Tales of a Traveller* (1824) and were in 1828 to lease from Irving the copyright to four of

reading aloud from a folio volume as the light of a summer day streams through the casement of his cell; his auditor, a beautiful young girl seated on the other side of a small table, is fast asleep. The scene was of the sort which, to Irving's thinking, Newton was especially well qualified to portray.

The largest group of Irving's completed poems consists of verses commemorating incidents in his travels: visits to sites of historical or picturesque interest, residences in the homes of his hosts, and personal reflections as he moved from place to place. The earliest of these, written during his tour to Canada in the summer of 1803, is a mocking couplet he is said to have scratched above the fireplace of "The Temple of Dirt," an especially unkempt tavern in upstate New York where he and his companions once stayed overnight.[63] Another is *"Passaic—A Tradition,"* the poem by which he was probably best known during his lifetime, and which he apparently composed in the spring of 1806 as an album contribution. At the turn of the nineteenth century the falls of the Passaic River, an abrupt drop of ninety feet into a narrow chasm through which the river dashed and foamed before resuming its usual broad and placid course, was a leading tourist attraction.[64] In 1775 a Mr. Godwin had constructed a public house near the falls to accommodate visitors from New York City, which was less than twenty miles away; and a few years later his successor, Abraham Godwin, had installed on the premises what quickly became known as "Godwin's Album," a register for the written impressions of his patrons. Although the album itself has not survived, what purported to be a copy of Irving's contribution to it was published in the New York *Weekly Visitor* in September, 1806; and during the next eight years three other magazines, two of which acknowledged Godwin's Album as their source, published slightly varying texts of their own. According to Eugene L. Huddleston, Irving's legendary account of the place "Where the torrent leaps headlong embosomed in foam" was the most popular product of a contemporary fad for verses celebrating the falls of the Passaic.[65]

---

his back works. Shortly before the publication of *The Atlantic Souvenir*, in October, 1827, Irving and Newton were in correspondence; the author was then living in Madrid, the painter in London. See Andrew B. Myers, "Washington Irving and Gilbert Stuart Newton: A *New-York Mirror* Contribution Identified," *Bulletin of the New York Public Library*, 76 (1972), 240. Myers reprints in this article "Newton the Painter," a bit of literary journalism about the artist which Irving wrote in 1835; see below, Vol. II, p. 88.

63. See *Journals*, I, 16–17; PMI, I, 51.

64. Oral S. Coad, " 'A Pleasant Place to See,' " *Journal of the Rutgers University Library*, 25 (June, 1962), 11–13.

65. Huddleston, "Washington Irving's 'On Passaic Falls,' " *American Notes & Queries*, 4 (1965), 51–52. A holograph manuscript text of the poem, dated May

A less pretending poem, written at a place of wider renown, is the quatrain Irving composed in October, 1821, upon his second visit to Shakespeare's birthplace at Stratford.[66] In these lines he reiterated a central theme of Shakespeare's sonnets, that the imaginative life inherent in the writings of a genuine poet renders him in a sense immortal. The theme had been implicit in "Stratford-on-Avon," one of the essays in *The Sketch-Book* (1819–1820).

A few of the poems Irving wrote in the course of his travels reveal an introspective or even confessional dimension which sets them apart from all his other verses. The untitled lines he wrote in April, 1805, while crossing the Lake of Lucerne in company with his friend Joseph C. Cabell, are of interest in this regard. Having squandered the past few months in Italy rather than exploring its principal cities in the deliberate manner his elder brothers William and Ebenezer had expected him to do, at that time he was en route to Paris to begin belatedly a strenuous course of study more acceptable to his long-suffering sponsors.[67] The opposition in his verses between the sweet, almost luxurious sleep of the present, upon "the placid bosom of the Lake," and the "Aching Back and labored sweating Brow" to be endured while at "the Plow" the next morning in "the Vineyard and Garden of the Lord" neatly typifies his probable sense of his own situation. Unpublished during the author's lifetime, the verses were copied by Cabell into one of his own journals.[68]

Irving's contribution to the album of Thomas Hope at that gentleman's country residence, Deep Dene, dated June 24, 1822, is the most explicitly autobiographical poem he ever wrote. After seven years of absence from the United States, during which *The Sketch-Book* and *Bracebridge Hall* had been published, in June, 1822, he was riding the crest of literary popularity both in England and at home. From Deep

---

26, 1806, and owned by the Library of Congress, is adopted as the copy-text for this edition.

66. The poem was first published in *The Albion*, n.s. 1 (March 2, 1833), 72; it appeared in print on two further occasions during the nineteenth century, and a fuller text was provided by John H. Birss, "New Verses by Washington Irving," *American Literature*, 4 (November, 1932), 296. A description by Irving of his third visit to Stratford, in 1832, when he discovered that he had himself become part of the legendary history of the place, is in PMI, II, 466.

67. See above, pp. xxiii–xxiv. In fact, though he apparently expected to become at Paris a more serious and studious traveler than heretofore, no such transformation occurred; his four months in that city were perhaps even gayer than those which preceded them. See PMI, I, 144–51.

68. A thorough account of the relationship between these two young Americans on their European travels is by Richard B. Davis, "Washington Irving and Joseph C. Cabell," in *English Studies in Honor of James Southall Wilson* (Charlottesville, 1951), pp. 7–22. Irving's poem was published for the first time in Davis' study.

Dene, where he was Hope's guest, he wrote to his elder sister Mrs. Catherine Paris that he was "sensible of the extreme kindness and hospitality that is lavished on me by all ranks," especially by his present host, "one of the richest and most extraordinary men in England." Yet he went on to say that, amid all the attention he was receiving in this foreign country, what gave him still greater satisfaction was the hope that "I can enjoy the affection of my relatives while living, and leave a name that may be cherished by the family when my poor wandering life is at an end."[69] From year to year his ties to his family and friends in New York had gradually loosened, and in some moods he felt with lonely regret that the hospitality of strangers in Europe was an empty substitute for the life he had forsaken at home. When he described himself in the Deep Dene album verses as the "Strange tenant of a thousand homes, / And friendless, with ten thousand friends!" Irving was giving frank expression to this home feeling.[70] The poem sounded a keynote for the solemn sentiments he was to express in a speech to his countrymen upon his return to the United States in 1832.[71]

"¡Ay Dios de mi alma!," Irving's one known poem in Spanish, was apparently another album contribution. The manuscript text in which it survives is dated "London. Sept. 9th 1830," during the period of his service as secretary to the United States legation at the Court of St. James. He had come to England a few months previously, after a memorable residence of more than three years in Spain, and at the time he wrote "¡Ay dios ..." he was swamped both with minor diplomatic duties and with burdensome social obligations. Earlier in 1830, he had complained in a letter to an acquaintance in Spain, Don Juan Wetherell, of "the thousand distractions which beset me in London. . . . How often I look back with regret to the tranquil life of literary liesure [sic] that I passed in Andalusia, under such serene skies; and in the enjoyment of such a delicious climate!"[72] The contrast between his memory of Spain and his present harried existence probably lent personal significance to the exclamatory refrain of the Spanish verses, "¡Ay! que Inglaterra / Ya no es para mi" ("Oh! England is no longer for me").

One of two further poems, both of which are addressed to ladies, affords a final example of Irving's writing verse more or less explicitly

69. Irving to Catharine Paris, The Deep Dene, Surry [sic], June 21, 1822; PMI, II, 83–84.

70. The verses were first published after his death, in the *Cornhill Magazine*, 1 (May, 1860), 582.

71. See below, Vol. II, pp. 59–60.

72. Quoted by Richard E. Peck in "An Unpublished Poem by Washington Irving," *American Literature*, 39 (May, 1967), 206. The manuscript text of "¡Ay Dios . . . ," which is owned by the University of Virginia, was first published in Peck's note.

as a vehicle for his own sentiments and moods. So far as can be determined, the "Song" dated "Oct. 1810," which was unpublished during his lifetime,[73] is addressed to no one in particular and is simply a set of rhymes on a traditional theme: the swain's proposal to his loved one that she come live with him in his rural home. On the other hand, the complimentary lines Irving sent to Miss Emily Foster on her nineteenth birthday, May 4, 1823, are a veiled expression of his genuine feelings. Irving had met this young English lady shortly after his arrival in Dresden, Germany, in December 1822, and in frequent meetings thereafter he had become a valued friend of the Foster family. As the weeks passed, moreover, his regard for Emily Foster had steadily grown. His birthday poem, with its conventional praise of her "innate worth," "gentle virtues," and "generous gifts of heart and mind," was thus more than a polite compliment. Probably sensing the wistful affection felt for her by this kind American gentleman more than twice her age, Emily wrote in her private journal: "*My Birthday, that good dear nice Mr Irving sent me delightful verses the first almost he ever wrote I hope it is not vain to transcribe them I do it more for his sake than for the partial* COMPLIMENTS (*are a cold word*) *to me.*"[74] Irving's lines, punctiliously enclosed with a covering note addressed to her mother, were probably as direct a statement as he ever made to Emily Foster of his admiration for her.[75]

His candid admission at the close of the note to Mrs. Foster, that "I have no confidence in my rhymes,"[76] was certainly more than polite self-deprecation. While he was diffident of all his literary efforts upon their first apearance, Irving advanced no claims whatever for any of his poems—few of which, as we have seen, he ever intended to publish. Since he not only assisted Pierre in gathering materials for the *Life and Letters* but also indicated to him something of his wishes for the collection of miscellaneous writings which was to appear posthumously as *Spanish Papers,* it is probably significant that Pierre included his uncle's poems not in the latter work, among his uncollected literary produc-

73. It was first published by Gabriel Harrison in *The Life and Writings of John Howard Payne,* p. 397.

74. *The Journal of Emily Foster,* ed. Stanley T. Williams and Leonard B. Beach (New York, 1938), pp. 130–31.

75. The poem was first published in PMI, II, 152–53. For discussions of the relationship between Irving and Emily Foster, see George S. Hellman, *Washington Irving, Esquire* (New York, 1925), pp. 53–57; STW, I, 233–54; and Walter A. Reichart, *Washington Irving and Germany* (Ann Arbor, 1957), pp. 93–101. A further account of Irving's relationship with the Fosters while in Dresden is given below, pp. xlii–xliv.

76. PMI, II, 152.

tions,[77] but in the *Life and Letters,* as documents of interest to students of his life history. Irving would never have agreed with *The Port-Folio's* characterization of him in 1814 as "a favourite of the Nine—one of the chosen and legitimate sons of song."[78]

PLAYS, 1823

In the summer of 1822, shortly after the publication of *Bracebridge Hall,* Washington Irving left London for the Continent with a dual purpose in mind. First, he was anxious to cure a nervous complaint causing painful irritation of the skin, a condition recently aggravated by the strain of composition. Second, he planned as he traveled to begin filling his journals with material for use in a future literary work. He looked forward in particular to exploring Germany, the repository of "all those supernatural tales" which had fascinated English and American readers for the past two decades.[79] "I mean to get into the confidence of every old woman I meet with in Germany," he wrote to his friends the Storrows, "and get from her, her budget of wonderful stories."[80] At some point in his travels he hoped to settle down, devote himself amid congenial surroundings to the study of German, and in good time produce a collection of tales and sketches on European themes. After visits of varying length to Frankfurt, Heidelberg, Munich, Salsburg, and Vienna, on November 28 he entered Dresden, the capital of the Kingdom of Saxony, and sensed at once that he had reached the place he was looking for. His ensuing winter and spring in this lively city, with its intelligent and accessible royal family, its diplomatic community, its excellent theater and, with Carl Maria von Weber as

77. Irving's poems, or those believed at the time to be his, were first collected by William R. Langfeld, "The Poems of Washington Irving," *Bulletin of the New York Public Library,* 34 (November, 1930), 763–79. Langfeld included selections from the two plays, *Abu Hassan* and *The Freyschütz,* and also two brief poems (p. 773), both of which have since been identified as transcriptions of lines in Joseph Addison's "A Letter from Italy"; see *Journals,* I, 258, 263. Langfeld included in his collection one other poem (p. 775), drawn from Irving's journals, which is omitted here because it is not a completed work; it is included in *Journals,* I, 581.

78. "To Readers and Correspondents," *The Port-Folio,* n.s. 3, no. 6 (June, 1814), 610.

79. Reichart, *Washington Irving and Germany,* pp. 41–42. The quotation in Reichart's definitive study of Irving's German experiences is from "The Spectre Bridegroom," one of the tales in *The Sketch-Book* in which the author had drawn upon the legendary lore of Germany. See H. A. Pochmann, "Irving's German Sources in *The Sketch Book*," *Studies in Philology,* 27 (1930), 477–507.

80. Irving to Thomas W. Storrow, Haerlem, July 11, 1822; *Washington Irving and the Storrows: Letters from England and the Continent 1821–1828,* ed. Stanley T. Williams (Cambridge, Mass., 1933), p. 17.

director, its even more distinguished opera, were to produce few of the professional results Irving had intended. But they were to yield other compensations, for he enjoyed in Dresden what Walter A. Reichart has described as "one of the gayest periods of his life."[81]

A few days after his arrival, Irving struck up a friendship with Barham John Livius (1786?–1865), a dramatist and composer who himself had arrived only recently.[82] Livius had come to Dresden in order to purchase from Weber the score of the German composer's famous opera, *Der Freischütz* (1821), and the right to adapt it for production on the English stage. The London theaters were extremely popular at this time, and their managers were hard put to satisfy the insistent demands of the audiences for a steady supply of new plays. The hack writers, of whom Livius was one, welcomed the literary opportunity thus afforded them. According to Allardyce Nicoll, they "wrote plays, as a cobbler makes shoes, for the purpose of bringing in a few pence or a few pounds, and consequently they sought in Paris, not for what was new and vital, but for what was old and sure to please."[83] In this manner, before his journey to Dresden Livius had adapted a French comedy which he retitled *Maid or Wife: or, The Deceiver Deceived* (1821) and had also composed the music for some of the adaptations of the popular playwright James R. Planché.[84]

Shortly after meeting Livius, whose familiarity with London greenrooms gave them much in common, Irving was introduced by him to his cousin Mrs. Amelia Morgan Foster, an English lady who had been living in Dresden since 1820 with her two daughters Emily and Flora, now eighteen and sixteen years of age, and three younger sons. Beginning on December 19, when he and Livius were dinner guests of the Fosters, Irving was a frequent visitor in their home. That he quickly

81. Reichart, *Washington Irving and Germany*, p. 64. The other most useful composite accounts of the Dresden period are in PMI, II, 125–60, and STW, I, 215–54. An indispensable primary source is Irving's *Journals and Notebooks*, vol. 3, ed. Walter A. Reichart (Madison, 1970), II, 92–154; hereafter cited as *Journals*, III.

82. Livius' background, and his working relationship with Irving, are best set forth by Walter A. Reichart, "Washington Irving's Friend and Collaborator: Barham John Livius, Esq.," *PMLA*, 56 (June, 1941), 513–21; hereafter cited as "Irving and Livius." See also Reichart, *Washington Irving and Germany*, pp. 81–102, 121–36 passim; and Percival R. Kirby, "Washington Irving, Barham Livius, and Weber," *Music and Letters*, 31 (April, 1950), 133–47.

83. Nicoll, *A History of the Early Nineteenth Century Drama 1800–1850*, 2 vols. (Cambridge, 1930), I, 81. Nicoll spells "Livius" both thus and "Levius"; see I, 144, and II, 335.

84. Reichart, *Washington Irving and Germany*, pp. 122–23. For further discussion of Livius' relationship with Planché, see the Textual Commentary to *The Freyschütz*, pp. 342–59.

became a valued friend of the family is suggested by an entry in Emily Foster's private journal, written probably in late December. "Mr Irving is very interesting with his stories about his handsome Indians painting & pluming themselves, & strutting ... before their cabin doors," she wrote; "... he is neither tall nor slight, but most interesting, dark, hair of a man of genius waving, silky, & black, eyes full of varying feeling, & an amiable smile."[85] Irving's reputation as an author had preceded him to Dresden, and through the good offices of his old friend John P. Morier, the British envoy extraordinary, he had an immediate entrée both to intellectual circles and to the social whirl of the city. However, he always valued his access to the homes of hospitable relatives or friends, and from December until May 20, 1823, when he set out from Dresden on a tour of Bohemia and Silesia, few days passed when he did not see the Fosters. Picnics, visits at court, excursions to places of historic interest or to the royal wild boar chase, studies in Italian and German with Emily, the devising of "tableaux," dancing, and evenings of conversation diversified the time he spent with members of this accomplished family.

A pastime which repeatedly occupied Irving, Livius, and the Fosters was the rehearsal and presentation, using rented scenes and costumes, of amateur theatricals. With a few friends, the little group first produced an adapted version of Fielding's *Tom Thumb*, with Irving as King Arthur opposite Mrs. Foster's Dollalolla, but at Livius' instance they presently formed more ambitious plans for presenting his own musical comedy, *Maid or Wife*. Livius had a high opinion of his own talents, and as the director of this enterprise he apparently assumed a manner of arrogant authority that was irritating to some. As Irving wrote in a letter to his brother Peter, he proved "so much of a martinet" that the rehearsals were unsatisfactory "from being so much managed." Irving went on to describe how a few of Livius' "theatrical subjects" therefore conspired to get up a different play, independent of his "managerial discipline":

> We pitched upon the little comedy of *Three Weeks after Marriage*, which I altered and arranged so as to leave out two or three super-fluous characters. I played the part of Sir Charles Rackett; Miss Foster, Lady Rackett; Miss Flora Foster, Dimity; Mrs. Foster, Mrs. Druggett; and a young officer by the name of Corkran, the part of Mr. Druggett. You cannot imagine the amusement this little theatrical plot furnished us. We rehearsed in Mrs. Foster's drawing-room, and as the whole was to be kept a profound secret,

85. *The Journal of Emily Foster*, pp. 110–11. The most reliable sources of information about the Foster family are STW, I, 232–43 and notes; Reichart, *Washington Irving and Germany*, pp. 80–102.

and as Mrs. Foster's drawing-room is a great place of resort, and
as especially our dramatic sovereign, Colonel Livius, was almost an
inmate of the family, we were in continued risk of discovery, and
had to gather together like a set of conspirators. . . . The colonel
had ordered a dress rehearsal of his little opera; the scenery was
all prepared, the theatre lighted up, a few amateurs admitted: the
colonel took his seat before the curtain, to direct the rehearsal.
The curtain rose, and out walked Mr. and Mrs. Druggett in proper
costume. The little colonel was perfectly astonished, and did not
recover himself before the first act was finished; it was a perfect
explosion to him. We afterwards performed the little comedy
before a full audience of the English resident in Dresden, and of
several of the nobility that understood English, and it went off
with great spirit and success.[86]

Subsequently the amateur troupe presented Susannah Centlivre's
The Wonder! A Woman Keeps a Secret, which Irving had pruned to
suit the strengths of the company.

However, amid all the high-jinks Irving was uneasily aware that
"continual procrastination, and too much distraction and dissipation
of mind"[87] were keeping him from the task of authorship he had set
himself. "I have done nothing with my pen since I left you," he wrote
in March to Charles Leslie, the painter, "absolutely *nothing!* I have
been gazing about, rather idly, perhaps, but yet among fine scenes of
striking character, and I can only hope that some of them may stick
to my mind, and furnish me with materials in some future fit of
scribbling."[88] As a matter of fact, his pen had not been entirely idle.
Livius, recognizing his aptitude for adapting plays, probably impressed
with his considerable knowledge of stagecraft and wide reading in
the English drama, and perhaps sensing as well the potential future
usefulness of his contacts in London,[89] had suggested that they collaborate in preparing *Der Freischütz,* with its accompanying libretto by

86. Irving to Peter Irving, Dresden, March 10, 1823; PMI, II, 141–42. Emily
Foster noted in her journal that, "Mr Irving at the last moment [before Livius'
discomfiture] almost relented it seemed giving the manager's consequential dignity
such a fatal blow, however the fun overcame the remorse" (*The Journal of Emily
Foster,* p. 118).

87. Irving to Peter Irving, Dresden, March 10, 1823; PMI, II, 138.

88. Irving to Leslie, Dresden, March 15, 1823; *Autobiographical Recollections.
By the Late Charles Robert Leslie, R. A.,* ed. Tom Taylor (Boston, 1860), p. 252.

89. Despite the absence of explicit evidence, in an article entitled "Washington
Irving's Librettos," *Music and Letters,* 29 (October, 1948), 348–55, George R.
Price strongly imputes this motive to Livius. That the suggestion is not far from
accurate is suggested by Livius' shameless toadying, string-pulling, and name-
dropping; see especially Reichart, "Irving and Livius," pp. 522–25.

Friedrich Kind, for presentation in England. Irving, who was not only
at a loss for present literary occupation but was already an enthusiastic
admirer of Weber's music,[90] was easily persuaded to undertake this
task of adaptation in a genre that had always fascinated him. In
January, therefore, he had become "Busy with Col Livius about the
songs & music of the Freischutz."[91]

Owing to his feeble German, Irving's capacity for assistance was at
first severely limited; but as the weeks passed the two men gradually
came to work together on an equal basis. Frequent consultations, sometimes at Irving's rooms, sometimes at a cottage in the country where
Livius was not very discreetly keeping a mistress, sometimes with
Weber himself present, brought the project to a temporary conclusion
on April 12. A few days afterward the two began an even more concentrated campaign of adaptation, this time addressing themselves to
an earlier opera by Weber, *Abu Hassan* (1811), with libretto by Franz
Karl Hiemer. They completed their work on May 18, only two days
before Irving left Dresden with another acquaintance, Lieutenant John
Cockburn, on his six-week tour. At Prague, to occupy himself while
Cockburn lay ill with scarlet fever, Irving pored once again and at
length over the adaptation of *Der Freischütz*. In all probability he and
Livius discussed these independent contributions to the collaboration
at some time between late June, when he returned to Dresden, and
July 12, when he departed thence permanently.[92]

During his thirteen-month residence in Germany Irving had thus
helped to prepare English versions of *Der Freischütz* and *Abu Hassan*
and had become "tolerably well supplied with German localities, manners, characters, &c.";[93] but the tales and sketches he wished to fashion
from that accumulated fund of observation and lore had not yet begun
to take shape. Moreover, despite his eagerness to press forward with
the latter project, upon taking up residence in Paris early in August
he was distressed to find himself utterly incapacitated for writing.
"I am aware," he explained in a letter to Peter, "that this is all an affair
of the nerves . . . produced [in part] by the anxious feeling on resuming
literary pursuits." He felt the need to scrape together a "regular income,
however moderate," from his combined literary property, but "a dread

90. Reichart, *Washington Irving and Germany*, p. 123. By July, 1824, Irving
had seen *Der Freischütz* performed at least six times. A list of "Dramatic and
Musical Performances which Washington Irving Attended During His German
Travels" is given as an Appendix in *Washington Irving and Germany*, pp. 193–98.

91. Irving, *Journals*, III, 112.

92. He accompanied the Fosters, who were returning to England, as far as
Rotterdam, where he bade them farewell on July 30; see *The Journal of Emily
Foster*, pp. 167–68; PMI, II, 129; IV, 386.

93. Irving to Peter Irving, Paris, September 4, 1823; PMI, II, 166.

of future evil—of failure in future literary attempts" left him "wretchedly out of spirits."[94] Happily, by September 4 this mood had passed, and he summarized his circumstances to Peter on a more hopeful note. He had "been thinking over the German subjects," he said, and felt confident that, "when I once get to work ... I shall be able to spin them out very fluently." In the meantime, "I am busy on a slight literary job which I hope will put some money in my pocket without costing much time or trouble, or committing my name."[95]

A few weeks before he had fallen in with John Howard Payne, the actor and playwright, his companion at intervals since 1807 both in New York and London.[96] Payne's chronic improvidence had rendered it unsafe for him to remain in England, within reach of his creditors, and he had thus decided to continue his association with the London theaters at an expedient distance, by joining the corps of journeyman playwrights who were busy adapting French plays for the English stage. With his customary infectious enthusiasm, Payne had urged Irving to assist him in altering A. V. P. Duval's *La Jeunesse du duc Richelieu* (1796), and to divide the profits once the new version should be disposed of.[97] Irving felt an indulgent regard for his erratic friend, having long been persuaded of his genuine talent as an actor. He needed money, he was at present incapable of preparing a worthy sequel to *The Sketch-Book* and *Bracebridge Hall*, and his appetite for play adaptation had been whetted by his collaboration in recent months with Livius. He readily agreed to Payne's proposal, but with one stern proviso: his participation in the joint venture must remain a close secret. Evidently he regarded the translation and altering of plays as a sort of slumming, an activity not creditable to a man of his considerable, if not yet firmly established repute in the literary world.[98] Payne, no stranger to the merits and means of self-protective anonymity, readily accepted the condition, and so in September, 1823, the two began their work. The "slight literary job" Irving had mentioned to Peter consisted of rewriting Payne's rough translation of *Richelieu*.

94. Irving to Peter Irving, Paris, [August 5?], 1823; [August 20?], 1823; PMI, II, 164–65. For the dates, see *Journals*, III, 206, 214.

95. Irving to Peter Irving, Paris, September 4, 1823; PMI, II, 166–67.

96. The most important sources of information on Irving's relationship with Payne are Gabriel Harrison, *John Howard Payne* (Philadelphia, 1885), passim; Thatcher T. Payne Luquer, "Correspondence of Washington Irving and John Howard Payne [1821–1828]," *Scribner's Magazine*, 48 (October, 1910), 461–82; (November, 1910), 597–616; STW, I, 265–72, 282–90, and the index.

97. PMI, II, 167.

98. Irving often reiterated to Payne his wish to remain nameless as a collaborator. See Luquer, "Correspondence of Irving and Payne," pp. 472, 477, 478, 480; and STW, I, 269.

From September through November Irving worked steadily, retouching the plays on which Payne was then engaged—*Richelieu, Charles II, Married and Single, The Waggoner,* and *Azendai.* A letter he wrote early in October to Peter, whom he had enlisted in some capacity as a third partner in the venture, affords a glimpse of the manner in which he and Payne were cooperating: "Payne is busy upon Azendai, making a literal translation. I am looking over it as he translates, and making notes where there must be alterations, songs, choruses, &c. It will have to be quite re-written, as the dialogue is flimsy and pointless; still the construction will answer, and that is the main point."[99]

Payne, formerly the lessee and manager of Sadler's Wells Theatre, was an experienced practical dramatist and was familiar with the tastes of contemporary English audiences. He was quite capable of creating creditable adaptations by himself, but he valued Irving, not only as a coreviser of texts but as the possessor of a keen and sympathetic critical intelligence. In a letter to Mary W. Shelley he defined the value to himself of the close working relationship:

> An hours conversation has given an entirely new direction to the ideas of both, and done more service than a month's meditation or than either could have rendered the other apart—He often begins by not agreeing with me but always ends by thinking much better of my plans than I myself do.... Since chance threw me among pens, ink and paper, he and his elder brother are the only persons who have ever boldly and unhesitatingly encouraged me with the hopes of ultimate success and prosperity ... it is a very agreeable thing to be impelled by the enthusiasm of such a mind.[100]

As Irving labored over the several French plays, he was also occasionally in correspondence with Livius, then living in Berlin, about the songs for *Der Freischütz,* which the former was still attempting to improve.[101] He had entered with relish into his covert career of dramatic authorship and he was in hopes, not only of earning a decent wage, but perhaps also of achieving a success sufficiently great to warrant disclosure of his activities. On October 24, Payne set out incognito for London, to offer the completed plays to the theaters and inform them of the others to come; Irving remained in Paris at work on *Azendai, The Waggoner,* and *Charles II,* planning to send them along as soon as he could.

99. PMI, II, 169.

100. From a draft of a letter by Payne to Mrs. Shelley [n.p., 1825]; quoted in STW, I, 268.

101. Reichart, "Irving and Livius," p. 522; Irving, *Journals,* III, 235. Williams' statement (STW, I, 270) that Irving was composing "songs for Payne's version of *Der Freischütz"* is an error; Payne wrote no such play.

His evident facility in this species of composition, perhaps reinforced by the deference both Livius and Payne paid to his suggestions, was arousing in Irving a seductive theme for speculation: why should he not set aside mere adaptations and declare himself an independent dramatist, an author of original works for Covent Garden and Drury Lane? He had been only half-ironical when, amid the season of amateur theatricals at Dresden, he had avowed to Charles Leslie that, "I had no idea of this fund of dramatic talent lurking within me."[102] With the volume of European sketches still sadly in abeyance, the notion of himself as a professional playwright assumed a fine plausibility. On October 23, the day before Payne's departure, he remarked in his journal that he had conceived an idea for a new play, dealing with the youth of Shakespeare. Three days later he "arranged the plot," and on November 13, still full of his scheme, he wrote in the journal that he "felt greatly excited about the Shakespearean aim": "My Idea is to make him a varied character beloved by his wild associates for his joyous social character—by Ann H however unlike any other of his acquaintance—so novel—talks so freely—His own aspirings after something better—when in presence of nature his feelings expand—he longs for what he knows not what[—]feels as if he could embrace the landscape—The Stars the Moon delight him—chime of bells by midnight &c &c...."[103] Quite likely the view of himself as potentially a legitimate dramatist rather than a furtive hack lay behind an arch comment he made to Payne in late November. Payne had reported that, after some delay, Charles Kemble of Covent Garden had accepted *Richelieu,* but that the fortunes of other pieces, including *Azendai,* appeared to hang in the balance. Irving replied: "I don't care which theatre takes Azendai—nor do I care much if either of them takes it—I beg you will let it be understood I ask nothing as a favor, and by no means advise their accepting a piece, as extending a kind of patronage. I feel perfectly independent of the theatre—tho' I feel more and more that I have dramatic stuff within me."[104] He was piqued to learn that Kemble was aware of his role as coadapter of *Azendai.*

Payne was waging his sales campaign on behalf both of himself and Irving and also of Irving and Livius: he had received instructions to offer the English versions of *Der Freischütz* and *Abu Hassan* "as

102. Irving to Leslie, Dresden, March 15, 1823; Leslie, *Autobiographical Recollections,* p. 252.

103. *Journals,* III, 233, 235, 242.

104. Irving to Payne, Paris, November 22, 1823; Luquer, "Correspondence of Irving and Payne," p. 475. For the difficulties with *Azendai,* which Kemble thought too long, see Luquer, "Correspondence," pp. 472–77.

from Livius."[105] On November 7 he reported that Kemble had definitively refused the latter piece unless, to satisfy the popular taste for
animals onstage, "horses could be put in it!!!!"[106] Irving twice inquired
later in the month concerning the two German operas, but by December 17 he seems to have abandoned hope that either of them could
be placed by proxy.[107]

Beginning about December 1, in fact, his enthusiasm for playwriting
appears gradually to have been supplanted by a resolute determination
to piece together a new prose work. John Murray, his publisher in
London, was anticipating a new Irving title for publication in the
spring,[108] and he was anxious to oblige. On December 5 he labored
over his "History of an Author," a manuscript that had occupied him
intermittently since before the publication of *Bracebridge Hall*; on
December 10 he at last "began Germ[an] work," but got nowhere; on
December 17 he was "enlivend" by a sudden "thot"—he would "arrange
the Mss on hand so as to make 2 vols of Sketch Book."[109] During the
remainder of the month he pursued these ideas and began other
sketches, chiefly of France and the French character, several of which
were to remain unpublished until years later.[110] Late in December he
received from the delighted Payne an offer to share the proceeds from
the recent sale to Covent Garden of *Charles II* and *Married and Single*,
but half of this he refused. He had had "nothing to do" with the former
play, he claimed—"it is entirely your own." He now wished *Azendai* to
be offered to none of the theaters, for "as my name has been committed
with it to C. Kemble I wish to withdraw the piece."[111]

Irving was fast coming to realize that the remuneration he could

105. Irving to Payne, Paris, November 12, 1823; Luquer, "Correspondence of
Irving and Payne," p. 472.

106. Payne to Irving, London, November 7, 1823; PMI, II, 171. For a discussion
of the rage for theatrical animals, see Nicoll, *A History of the Early Nineteenth
Century Drama*, I, 24–28.

107. Luquer, "Correspondence of Irving and Payne," pp. 472, 477; Reichart,
Washington Irving and Germany, p. 126.

108. Murray to Irving, London, November 8, 1823; PMI, II, 177. See also
Irving, *Journals*, III, 261; Ben H. McClary, ed., *Washington Irving and the House
of Murray* (Knoxville, 1969), pp. 47–49.

109. *Journals*, III, 253, 255–56, 258. For the genesis of his "History of an
Author," see STW, II, 289–92. As late as February 8, 1824, Irving wrote Leslie
from Paris that he was preparing "a couple more volumes of the 'Sketch Book'"
(Leslie, *Autobiographical Recollections*, p. 260). See also McClary, *Irving and
the House of Murray*, p. 49.

110. See *Journals*, III, 259–60. The four "Sketches in Paris in 1825 [*sic*]," first
published in the *Knickerbocker Magazine* in 1840 and reprinted in *Wolfert's Roost*
(1855), were written at this time.

111. Irving to Payne, Paris, December 29, 1823; Luquer, "Correspondence of
Irving and Payne," p. 478.

anticipate from writing plays was far less than what he stood to earn by continuing as a writer of prose. For example, Payne had disposed of the two plays together for two hundred guineas; *Bracebridge Hall* by itself had brought a thousand. Further thought along these lines led Irving to the conclusion that, for prudence sake, he should abandon his incipient dramatic career. On January 31, 1824, in a letter to Payne announcing his decision, he put the case clearly:

> I am sorry to say I cannot afford to write any more for the theatres. The experiment has satisfied me that I never should in any wise be compensated for my time and trouble. I speak not with any reference to my talents; but to the market price my productions will command in other departments of literature. . . .
>
> My long interval of travelling, and the time expended in these dramatic experiments have thrown me quite behindhand, both as to pecuniary and literary affairs: & I am now applying myself to make up for it, but I shall run low in purse before I can get a work ready for publication.[112]

From time to time during the next two years Irving continued to assist both Payne and Livius in various ways, almost always requesting that his anonymity be preserved, but the letter to Payne marks the effective conclusion of his own writing for the theaters.[113] During the next few months he devoted his energies primarily to completing *Tales of a Traveller,* a miscellany which he substituted for the abandoned collection of German sketches, and which was published on August 25, 1824.

During the fall of 1823, while Payne was in England attempting to market the literary merchandise on hand, Livius was also conducting negotiations with the London managers. On December 28 he wrote to Carl August Böttiger, director of the Museum of Classical Art in Dresden, that " '*Abu Hassan*'—not having been deemd '*strong enough*' (to employ the technical term of the Theatre), for one of the *great Houses* and the small theatres in London *being very ill mounted for operas*—I have determined to *lay it by*. . . ."[114] Although it might have served as a spritely and, according to Allardyce Nicoll, a not unconventional "afterpiece,"[115] *Abu Hassan* was in fact never produced, at least in the version Livius and Irving had prepared.[116] Early in 1824 Livius came to London to promote at firsthand the claims of the other

112. Luquer, "Correspondence of Irving and Payne," p. 480.

113. Reichart, *Washington Irving and Germany,* pp. 135–36; STW, I, 272.

114. Reichart, "Irving and Livius," pp. 523–24.

115. See Nicoll, *A History of the Early Nineteenth Century Drama,* I, 144–46.

116. Walter A. Reichart suggests that their version was "probably the basis" of a play entitled *Abu Hassan* which appeared at Drury Lane on April 4, 1825, and was credited to William Dimond (*Washington Irving and Germany,* p. 135).

collaborative effort, which he called *The Freyschütz,* and his exertions on its behalf were more successful. The lasting fame of Weber's *Der Freischütz* of course rests upon its music, but its contemporary popularity derived in large part from Kind's libretto, with its story of a man who sells his soul to the Devil in exchange for supernatural aid, in the form of magic bullets. The varied attractions of *Der Freischütz*—quaint folk melodies, a plot portraying the trials of two appealing lovers, and lavish scenic effects to represent the mysterious supernatural presence— gave great satisfaction. After its initial success in Berlin the opera was produced throughout Germany, and during the next few years it was presented in London, Paris, and New York as well.[117] Little wonder, then, that Charles Kemble was interested in Livius' adaptation. "M. Kemble has written to me in the most kind & flattering way," Livius had informed Böttiger on December 28, "respecting the piece which I sent him, founded on the Freyshüts, and expressed an *anxious wish 'to venture it.'* "[118]

The play was accepted by Covent Garden in February, and on May 24 Livius wrote to Irving that it would be performed early in the coming season—that is, in the fall. By August, when the two men came together at Paris after a year apart, Livius had learned that *The Freyschütz* would be presented in October, and "with great Splendor."[119] Irving could not be persuaded to join his friend's most recent undertaking, an adaptation of *Abu Hassan* for the French stage, but he willingly assisted him in preparing a final manuscript of *The Freyschütz* for publication by the London firm of John Miller.[120] His journal entries for early October reveal that he served Livius as critic and perhaps as incidental coreviser of this text.[121] Moreover, surviving fragments of his hastily written suggestions for a preface to the published play demonstrate that his opinions still carried considerable weight.[122] Whether he received a share of the profits from the stage presentation of *The Freyschütz,* which began its successful run on October 14, or from the published play, which appeared a few weeks later and in a second edition in 1825, is unknown. Probably his agreement to assist Livius had been less carefully defined than with Payne, and almost certainly Irving would have refused payment rather than commit his name to the work, which was produced and published as that of Livius alone.

117. Reichart, *Washington Irving and Germany,* p. 124.

118. Reichart, "Irving and Livius," p. 523.

119. Reichart, "Irving and Livius," p. 525; *Journals,* III, 385–86.

120. *The Freyschütz; or, the Wild Huntsman of Bohemia . . . Adapted from the German by Barham Livius, Esq.* (London, 1824).

121. See *Journals,* III, 401–2.

122. For a comparison of Irving's notes with the corresponding passages in Livius' preface to *The Freyschütz,* see the Textual Commentary to Irving's version of the play, pp. 352–53.

In the preface to *The Freyschütz* Livius preserved his friend's anonymity, merely stating his obligation to a person "whose name, were he permitted, it would be his pride and his pleasure to declare, for various valuable hints and emendations."[123] At least for a time, Payne also followed Irving's injunctions. In the preface to *Charles II*, which had been produced in May, 1824, and was published soon afterward, he professed himself "indebted" to an unnamed literary acquaintance "for invaluable touches."[124] However, a few months later he submitted for Irving's approval a draft of a dedicatory letter to be published with *Richelieu*. In the dedication he identified his friend as the contributor to *Charles II*, adding with gratitude that the assistance had been "repeated to such an extent in the present work, as to render it imperative upon me to offer my thanks publicly." It is safe to say that Irving regarded the acknowledgment as far from "imperative," but he nevertheless accepted the compliment graciously. "I have nothing to object to the Dedication," he wrote in reply on January 3, 1825; "... it is a matter of feeling and your own feelings must govern you in it."[125]

Probably because he continued to regard his interlude of writing for the theaters as at best unseemly for an author of his stature, in subsequent years Irving had little to say of his collaborations with Livius and Payne and his temporary flirtation with the idea of becoming a playwright. The aim he expressed in August, 1823, to achieve through authorship "a regular income, however moderate," was more than two decades in the realization; and it was achieved not through covert hack work but through hard labor on his Spanish volumes, his Western narratives, and at last his mutually advantageous bargain with George Putnam in 1848 to produce a revised edition of his complete writings. He never put to the test his sense of himself as a potentially successful writer of plays. Thus the small space allotted in the delegated *Life and Letters* to the period of dramatic authorship was owing not only to the secondary importance of the experiment in the context of Irving's long career, but also to the limited supply of information he had made available to his nephew and biographer, Pierre M. Irving.[126] No plays were included in *Spanish Papers*, the delegated posthumous collection

123. *The Freyschütz*, p. viii.

124. Quoted in PMI, II, 177. According to W. R. Langfeld and P. C. Blackburn, *Washington Irving: A Bibliography* (New York, 1933), p. 60, *Charles the Second; or, The Merry Monarch* was first published in 1824 by the London firm of Longman, Hurst, Rees, Orme, Brown, and Green.

125. Luquer, "Correspondence of Irving and Payne," pp. 597–98. The full text of Payne's dedication to *Richelieu: A Domestic Tragedy, Founded on Fact* (New York, 1826) is reprinted in PMI, II, 174–75.

126. What Pierre termed "this theatrical episode in the author's life" is described in PMI, II, 166–76. A striking instance of Irving's apparent reluctance to

of the miscellaneous writings, at least in part because, as editor, Pierre had no access to texts which could properly be called Irving's own. The published *Richelieu* and *The Freyschütz* could not be regarded as of his sole authorship any more than could, say, the *Salmagundi* papers of 1807–1808; and Pierre possessed no manuscript evidence of Irving's independent input into the collaborations with Livius and Payne.

The two Irving manuscripts discovered in England years afterward by George S. Hellman, and subsequently edited by him for publication in 1924 as *The Wild Huntsman* and *Abu Hassan*,[127] were thus doubly of interest to students of Irving and his career. Not only was their existence previously unsuspected, but their character as virtually complete texts representing the author's own contributions to the joint effort with Livius warranted their being considered, in a limited sense, "his." As one might expect, both manuscripts include notations and emendations by Livius in which Irving apparently acquiesced, thus revealing their function as working texts, bases provided to facilitate a continuing collaboration.[128] Prepared as they were for an audience of one, and that individual a coauthor, the manuscripts naturally pose some problems for the modern reader: for example, they include cryptic abbreviations, references to passages in other drafts of the plays which are no longer known to exist, and punctuation that must be termed slovenly. Nevertheless, unlike Irving's later cooperative productions with Payne, some of whose manuscripts are also extant,[129] these two texts are neither incidental revisions nor mere transcriptions of his collaborator's previous efforts; they are independent creations which Irving prepared for scrutiny by Livius and himself. The two working drafts, representing the author's latest traceable contributions to the cooperative enterprise,

discuss his activities as a playwright is afforded by the notes taken in 1859 by Pierre, then at work on the biography, concerning his uncle's recollections of Payne. In full, and somewhat regularized, they are as follows: "Payne: successful in *Junius Brutus*, brought his creditors upon him who threw him in limbo; in prison wrote *Teresa, or the Orphan of Geneva*, another success which got him out. Then went over to Paris, where W.I. fell in with him. Was once manager of Sadler's Wells. Took a walk with W.I. in Pere la Chaise and sat on a tomb; slim, and told of his management which W.I. incorporated in 'Buckthorne' " (Pierre M. Irving, "Journal, 1859"; in the Berg Collection, New York Public Library). The agreement to write plays, and the collaboration that followed it, go unmentioned.

127. *The Wild Huntsman, by Washington Irving* (*hitherto unpublished*), ed. Hellman (Boston: The Bibliophile Society, 1924); *Abu Hassan, by Washington Irving* (*hitherto unpublished*), ed. Hellman (Boston: The Bibliophile Society, 1924).

128. The collaboration between Irving and Livius is discussed in detail in the Textual Commentaries to the two plays, pp. 342–59, 359–70.

129. At the Henry E. Huntington Library. See STW, I, 270.

provide us the best evidence available to assess the validity of his belief for a time that, in other circumstances, he might have become a
successful dramatist.

PROSE WRITINGS, 1829–1855

Between 1829 and 1855 the reputation of Washington Irving grew from
that of an established prose writer, known internationally yet somewhat
out of touch with his own countrymen, to that of an American culture-
hero—what an anonymous citizen once termed "a national property."[130]
He continued throughout this period to perform the function he had
defined for himself in editing the *Analectic Magazine* (1813–1814), as
a mediator between the cultures of the New World and the Old. However, as the years passed he gradually assumed for his contemporaries an
additional role, as a source of reminiscences concerning the famous
personages and events of an earlier era, a means of communication with
the past. Moreover, the miscellaneous writings of his later career bespeak his perception that, to American readers, the portrayed scenes of
his own early life had become of interest in themselves. Interwoven as
they were with the early history of the United States, the events of his
youth were legendary.

In November, 1828, then living at Seville, Irving learned with alarm
that a "literary pirate" in the United States was busy preparing an
abridgment of his three-volume *Life and Voyages of Christopher Columbus,* published earlier that year.[131] He had intended eventually to bring
out his own condensed version of the biography, regarding it as potentially a profitable undertaking, and he therefore set about at once
to forestall this "paltry poacher."[132] Within a month of intense effort
he had completed the task, and at that time he prepared a public statement of his sentiments upon learning of the attempt to supersede him,
and additionally of his intention to make available at once his own
abridgment. In that announcement, which appeared in the New York
American for April 4, 1829, he did not attempt to deny his financial
motive, but he laid stress upon a quite different consideration. He had
been "hurt" to learn of the intended piracy, he wrote, for he had regarded
his biography of the discoverer of America "as a peculiar offering to

130. John Esten Cooke, "Irving at Sunnyside in 1858," *Hours at Home,* 1 (October, 1865), 509.
131. The American edition (New York: G. &. C. Carvill, 1828) was in three
volumes; the English (London: John Murray, 1828) in four. See Langfeld and
Blackburn, *Washington Irving: A Bibliography,* pp. 27–28.
132. Irving to Peter Irving, Seville, November 19, 1828; PMI, II, 352.

my countrymen, whose good opinion...has never ceased to be the leading object of my ambition, and the dearest wish of my heart."[133] Though ostensibly self-serving, this claim was sincere. More than thirteen years had passed since Irving's departure from the United States on a supposedly temporary mission to Liverpool in 1815, and now, at the age of forty-five, he was distressed at the thought that his ties to family and homeland were inevitably weakening. He was aware that anonymous enemies in the United States had spread rumors calling into question his attachment to his home country,[134] and he was anxious to demonstrate in whatever way possible his real sentiments. Happily, his announcement of the forthcoming abridgment met with every sort of success he could have wished. It was introduced sympathetically in the New York *American*, whose editor urged the still-nameless pirate to abandon his enterprise; that individual did so; and when the condensed biography was published, on June 9, 1829, it found an undisputed field.[135]

Nevertheless, Irving's concern over his reputation in the United States was not dispelled until May, 1832, when at last he returned home. He was welcomed in New York City by tumultuous crowds of old friends and admiring strangers whose obvious good feelings left him, as he confessed to his brother Peter, "as happy as mortal being can be."[136] On May 30 a public dinner was held in his honor, and the New York *Morning Courier* described this celebration as a great success, a rare instance of "spontaneous homage" accorded to a public figure. "The toasts and addresses," the reporter wrote in summing up his detailed account, "were all appropriate, spirited, talented, complimentary, witty, and sarcastic." Touched by the demonstrations in his honor, in his own address Irving frankly alluded to the doubts he had felt as to his standing among his countrymen. Betraying a deep emotion which rarely overtook him in public, he pronounced the evening "the proudest, the happiest of my life."[137] Henceforward, he was to enjoy the affection of Americans in a manner so nearly continuous and unanimous as to render him almost unique among contemporary personalities.

133. Irving, "Advertisement," New York *American*, April 4, 1829, p. 2, col. 4.
134. See PMI, II, 253; STW, I, 315–17.
135. For the introductory comments in the New York *American*, see the Textual Commentary, Vol. II, p. 373 below. On April 14, 1829, the *American* reported that G. &. C. Carvill of New York had undertaken to publish the abridgment and also a "new edition, in a cheaper and smaller form, of the large work. For both enterprises, we are persuaded, they will find in the public demand, abundant reward" (p. 2, col. 2). The abridgment was favorably reviewed in the issue for June 16, p. 2, col. 4.
136. Irving to Peter Irving, New York, May 30, 1832; PMI, II, 486.
137. "Dinner to Washington Irving," New York *Morning Courier*, June 2, 1832, p. 2, cols. 1–7.

The three years which had intervened between his statement in 1829 concerning the abridgment of *Columbus* and his return to the United States were filled with literary activity, within which two interrelated features are of particular interest in a survey of his miscellaneous writings. These are, first, his generous services as a promoter in England of the recent productions of American talent; and second, his steadily eroding relationship with John Murray II, the "Prince of Booksellers" whose London firm had published the English editions of his last several works. The latter trend dates from April, 1829, when Irving discovered that through an unauthorized tampering with the title page of *A Chronicle of the Conquest of Granada*, then just published, Murray had invited serious misconceptions as to the historical accuracy of the work. Upon completing his manuscript, the author had directed that the *Conquest of Granada* was to appear as the work of Fray Antonio Agapida, a fictitious historical personage whose style exemplified the pious zeal and unabashed bigotry of the early historians of Spain. However, when he received a copy of the published volumes he discovered with consternation that Murray had instead printed "By Washington Irving" on the title page. On May 9, he protested to the publisher in strong terms. "I presume you have done this to avail yourself of whatever attraction my name might have," he wrote, ". . . but this might have been effected in some other way, without meddling with the work itself, which ought never to be touched without the knowledge and consent of the author."[138] A few months later, having arrived in London to assume duties as secretary of the United States legation there, Irving recurred to the subject in an interview with Murray. Evidently recognizing that his interference with the nettled author's "experiment in literature" had obscured its real nature,[139] and perhaps had also decreased its sales potential, the publisher invited him to prepare for a fee an anonymous explanation of his aims in the *Conquest of Granada*, to be published in the Murray house organ, the *Quarterly Review*. Mollified, Irving accepted the offer. His self-review—one of the most lucid critical statements he ever wrote—duly appeared in the *Quarterly Review* for May, 1830.[140]

Not long after his relations with Murray had thus been restored to their usual uneasy harmony, Irving received from Lieutenant Alexander

138. Irving to John Murray II, Granada, May 9, 1829; McClary, *Washington Irving and the House of Murray*, p. 124. See also PMI, II, 376.

139. The quoted phrase is Irving's. See Irving to Prince Dolgorouki, Seville, January 10, 1829; PMI, II, 366.

140. For an authoritative summary of the circumstances which resulted in Irving's writing the article see Earl N. Harbert, "Irving's *A Chronicle of the Conquest of Granada*: An Essay in the History of Publication, Revision, and Critical Reception," *Bulletin of the New York Public Library*, 80 (Summer, 1976), 400–415, esp. pp. 404–7.

Slidell, a young American with whom he had become acquainted at Madrid in 1826, a request for assistance in securing an English publisher for *A Year in Spain*, a travel account he had published at Boston in 1829.[141] Although his responsibilities at the legation and his attention to three of his own literary projects then in progress—*Voyages and Discoveries of the Companions of Columbus* (1831), *The Alhambra* (1832), and a biography of Mahomet—left him little time to spare, he undertook the task. John Murray expressed willingness to bring out the work, provided he would retouch it for the British market, correct the proofsheets, and write a notice of it for the *Quarterly Review*. To these forbidding conditions—no payment was offered, nor ever received—Irving again agreed. The review of *A Year in Spain*, which he eventually prepared from proofsheets, was discriminating but not surprisingly favorable.[142] In his view Slidell's youthful enthusiasm and good nature, and also his painterly eye for colorful detail, rendered the book far superior to the run of pedestrian travel accounts then so prevalent; and he intended his critical notice to serve primarily as a frame for quotations from the work which would exemplify these engaging qualities. However, prior to its publication in February, 1831, the article underwent considerable revision, almost certainly by John G. Lockhart, the editor of the *Quarterly Review*. In the published version some of the quotations Irving had wished to include were missing, and others were considerably abbreviated; moreover, a distinct and again unauthorized note of condescension toward Slidell, as "our young American," had crept into the article.[143] This marked a disappointing conclusion to his several months' stewardship on behalf of *A Year in Spain*.[144]

As an American writer anxious not to alienate his countrymen, in 1830 and 1831 Irving was uneasily conscious that adverse inferences

141. (Boston: Hilliard, Gray, Little, and Wilkins, 1829). A second, enlarged American edition (New York: G. &. C. &. H. Carvill, 1830) was the work for which Slidell hoped to find a market in England.

142. *A Year in Spain* was to remain throughout Irving's lifetime one of his favorite books; see PMI, IV, 312.

143. "ART. 1.—*A Year in Spain* . . . ," *Quarterly Review*, 44, no. 88 (February, 1831), 341. Irving's practices in editing the Slidell volume have been described by Ben H. McClary in "Washington Irving's British Edition of Slidell's *A Year in Spain*," *Bulletin of the New York Public Library*, 73 (June, 1969), 368–74. Lockhart's revisions to the manuscript of Irving's review are described and listed in part by the same author in "Irving, Lockhart, and the *Quarterly Review*," *Bulletin of the New York Public Library*, 76 (1972), 231–36.

144. Interestingly, despite Irving's regard for the book, his published review of it was not included by Pierre M. Irving in *Spanish Papers*. It seems quite possible that Pierre had been informed that the *Quarterly Review* text was so far at variance from his uncle's wishes as not properly to have a place among his collected writings. The text of the review in the present edition derives from the author's manuscript, which is in the archives of John Murray, Ltd., London.

might be drawn from his contributing articles to the high-Tory *Quarterly Review*. Indeed, at one point he had himself condemned the magazine as "so hostile to our country that I cannot bear to lift my pen in its service."[145] Thus on September 1, 1831, forwarding to Lockhart a review of a second American work he had managed to place with the house of Murray, his friend Henry Wheaton's *History of the Northmen*, he felt compelled to plead to the editor for "fair play." "The touch of republicanism in the prelude is more for my own sake than for the sake of the author [i.e., Wheaton]," he noted. "I am vehemently suspected from the company I keep, and the Tory review in which I occasionally write." Revealing some of the irritation he felt at the cavalier manner in which his review of *A Year in Spain* had been handled, he urged Lockhart "not to lop down this article in your cursed bid of Precaution as you did its predecessors."[146] In the event, Irving's concern for "fair play" toward his commentary on the *History of the Northmen* proved needless, for the article was never to appear in the *Quarterly Review*. Shortly after sending the manuscript to Lockhart, he fell into a dispute with John Murray II which resulted in the suspension of his business relationship with the firm for several years. In the midst of this falling-out Murray may well have directed Lockhart to return the review of Wheaton's *History*.[147] At any rate, when Irving returned to the United States he had some form of the text in his possession, for the article was published in the prestigious yet suitably republican *North American Review* for October, 1832.

While in England Irving performed one further duty as an agent for American literary wares, securing a publisher for the *Poems* of William Cullen Bryant. Even though he had recently broken off relations with the firm, in January, 1832, he inquired of John Murray II whether he might be interested; but Murray's antipathy to verse was pronounced, and his reply was not encouraging.[148] Presently, however, Irving hit upon John Andrews, "a fashionable bookseller,"[149] who agreed to publish the volume provided he edit it and write a dedication. Once again, he assented; and the result of the ensuing project was *Poems, by William Cullen Bryant, An American*, with a dedicatory letter to Samuel

145. Irving to Alexander Everett, Puerto Sta. Maria, October 21, 1828; PMI, II, 347.

146. Ben H. McClary, "Washington Irving's Amiable Scotch Friends: Three Unpublished Letters to the John Gibson Lockharts," *Studies in Scottish Literature*, 4 (October, 1966), 103. The circumstances surrounding Irving's authorship of the review of Wheaton's *History of the Northmen* are described in PMI, III, 267; STW, II, 22; McClary, *Washington Irving and the House of Murray*, pp. 150–62.

147. McClary speculates thus in *Washington Irving and the House of Murray*, p. 162, n. 9.

148. John Murray III to Irving, London, January 30, 1832; PMI, II, 474.

149. The phrase is Pierre M. Irving's in *ibid*.

Rogers. In his letter Irving took occasion both to comment on the merits of Bryant's poetry and to praise Rogers for his exemplary services to such as Bryant, his "kind disposition to promote the success of American talent."[150] On that note of unassuming tribute to the English poet for good offices akin to what he had himself performed for Bryant, Wheaton, and Slidell, the history of Irving's miscellaneous writings prior to his return to the United States concludes.

Beginning in May, 1832, he entered with zest into the process of renewing acquaintances, not only with old friends but with the United States itself, which as he had repeatedly heard had changed so dramatically during his long absence. He made a six-month tour of the West and South; he observed the congressional debates at Washington; he thought about investing in Western land, and about buying a house. It was not until April, 1835, that he brought out *A Tour on the Prairies*, his account of an interlude in the Western journey of 1832. *A Tour*, the first volume he had published on an "American" topic—or indeed on any topic—since his return, was followed in 1836 by another Western writing, *Astoria; or, Anecdotes of an Enterprise Beyond the Rocky Mountains*, and the following year by *The Rocky Mountains*, more familiarly known as *The Adventures of Captain Bonneville, U. S. A.* With these three works he made clear his commitment to the United States, not merely as a place of residence but as a rich source of material for literary treatment.

Meanwhile, even as he sought out specifically "national" themes he continued in his role as a cosmopolitan, a promoter of transatlantic intercommunication. Thus, writing anonymously in the *New-York Mirror* for March 1, 1834, he recounted a humorous anecdote in a letter he had received from a friend in England concerning Charles Mathews, the celebrated English comedian who had visited the United States twelve years before. On March 21, 1835, the *New-York Mirror* published a similar anonymous communication derived from a letter he had recently received, this time an account of "our countryman" the artist Gilbert Stuart Newton, who was then in poor health and living in England.[151] In 1835 Irving also contributed two short pieces to popular gift-books, one published in England, the other in the United States. To the countess of Blessington, editoress of the elegant *Heath's Book of Beauty*, he forwarded a "nautical anecdote" of a New England sea

---

150. Irving, "To Samuel Rogers, Esq.," in *Poems, by William Cullen Bryant, An American* (London, 1832), p. [iii].

151. "Newton the Painter," *New-York Mirror*, 12, no. 38 (March 21, 1835), 303. Irving had also supplied a biographical sketch of Newton to William Dunlap which the latter included in his *History of the Rise and Progress of the Arts of Design in the United States*, II, 302–4. That sketch may be found in the *Letters* volumes of the present edition.

captain. In a covering letter he expressed hope that "The Haunted Ship" would prove satisfactory to Lady Blessington, adding that "a tarpaulin story may present an acceptable contrast to others more sentimental and refined."[152] Interestingly, he sent his second gift-book contribution, "An Unwritten Drama of Lord Byron," not to her ladyship, who took a particular interest in Byron and had recently edited a volume of his Conversations,[153] but to the Philadelphia publishers of The Gift: A Christmas and New Year's Present for 1836.[154] For American readers, still caught up in their fascination with the flamboyant personality of the late poet, he selected from his notebooks a suggestive bit of information about a play Byron "did not write" but thought of writing. For the English, he drafted a Yankee ghost story.

From youth to age Irving possessed the happy faculty of remaining on good terms with persons of all temperaments and from all walks of life. He was not of a disputatious nature; and since as a mature author he was moreover somewhat jealous of his privacy, probably the last sort of public prominence he could have wished was that to be gained through involvement in the often rancorous newspaper controversies that characterized American journalism of the era. Nevertheless, in the early months of 1837 he repeatedly found his name placed before the public in ways which necessitated his preparing statements for the press. The first of these incidents grew out of what he had thought an innocuous remark in "The Creole Village," a sketch he contributed to a gift-book entitled The Magnolia for 1837, that among the Old World customs and traditions still extant in the New, in the state of Virginia there might be found "peculiarities characteristic of the days of Elizabeth and Sir Walter Raleigh."[155] Coincidentally, The Magnolia was published shortly before an acidulous debate began, in letters to the New York American, over the cultural peculiarities bequeathed by English colonists to the inhabitants of contemporary Virginia and North Carolina. One of the controversialists, Professor George Tucker of the University of Virginia, quoted Irving's observation in a letter supporting the claims of his state as the primary repository of surviving transatlantic customs. In response, Joseph Seawell Jones, a historian of North Carolina and

152. Irving to [Edward Bulwer?], Newhall, May 2, 1835; R. R. Madden, The Literary Life and Correspondence of The Countess of Blessington (London, 1855), III, 309.

153. Conversations of Lord Byron with the Countess of Blessington (London: H. Colburn, 1834). The first American edition of this work was published by Carey and Hart of Philadelphia in 1836.

154. Irving, "An Unwritten Drama of Lord Byron," in The Gift: A Christmas and New Year's Present for 1836 (Philadelphia, [1835]), p. 166.

155. Irving, "The Creole Village: A Sketch from a Steamboat," in Wolfert's Roost and Other Papers, Now First Collected (New York, 1855), pp. 38–39.

an advocate of his own state's pretensions, accused Tucker of "blundering arrogance and ignorance" and for good measure attacked Irving as well.[156] The author's rejoinder, which appeared in the *American* for January 7, 1837, included a disclaimer of any disposition to take sides in the matter, together with an ironic wish that his verbal assailant would soon enjoy a restoration of good sense and good temper.

A few days after he had extricated himself from the battle of the local historians, Irving found himself the target of another public attack, one which he was unable to view with such detached good nature. In an editorial entitled "Mutilating Books" which appeared in *The Plaindealer* for January 14, 1837, William Leggett, formerly assistant editor of the New York *Evening Post* under William Cullen Bryant, accused Irving on two counts of "deficiency of manliness" as an author. The first alleged offense referred to a revision he had made to one of Bryant's poems when editing the London edition of 1832. In a display of what Leggett termed "literary pusillanimity," he had altered in a poem entitled "Marion's Men" a line which reflected adversely on the courage of English soldiers, revising it to one which "might be more soothing to an Englishman's ears." The second imputed misdemeanor, which carried a strongly implied charge of hypocrisy, pertained to a preface he had included in the American edition of *A Tour on the Prairies*. This statement, in effect an expanded restatement of his sentiments in the address at the welcoming dinner of 1832,[157] Leggett described as "full of *amor patriae* and professions of American feeling." Noting, however, that "for the London market" Irving had "studiously omitted" all those "professions," Leggett suggested that they were hollow, and calculated simply to win over the American audience, while their omission from the English edition was to avoid alienating that cherished clientele.[158]

Apparently Irving had not yet entirely overcome the concern he had felt five years before as to his reputation in the United States, for he seemed to consider the intemperate attack in *The Plaindealer* as a genuine threat to his good name. He drafted a stern reply in which he

156. Jones' letter was dated December 27, 1836 (New York *American*, January 7, 1837, p. 2, col. 6).

157. As a representative example, the following sentences from Irving's "Introduction" to *The Crayon Miscellany . . . No. 1. Containing A Tour on the Prairies* (Philadelphia, 1835), p. xi, may be compared to their earlier counterparts in Irving's 1832 address (Vol. II, p. 60 below): "At length the long anticipated moment arrived. I again saw the 'blue line of my native land' rising like a cloud in that horizon where, so many years before, I had seen it fade away. I again saw the bright city of my birth rising out of its beautiful bay; its multiplied fanes and spires, and its prolonged forests of masts, proclaiming its augmented grandeur. My heart throbbed with pride and admiration as I gazed upon it—I gloried in being its son."

158. Leggett, "Mutilating Books," *The Plaindealer*, 1, no. 7 (January 14, 1837), 102.

vindicated himself against Leggett's charges. His letter to *The Plain-dealer*, which appeared in the issue for January 28, 1837, included an explanation both of his reasons for omitting comments addressed specifically to Americans from the London edition of *A Tour* and of the circumstances which had led him to consent to the revision of "Marion's Men." He effectively rebutted Leggett's demeaning accusa-tions, but in the process—as often occurs in such interchanges—he un-wittingly offended a third party, William Cullen Bryant.

At the close of the portion of his letter relating to his methods in editing Bryant's *Poems*, Irving noted that, since the poet had himself thanked him by letter for his services, "I was therefore, I confess, but little prepared to receive a stab from his bosom friend"—namely, Leg-gett.[159] Bryant thought he discerned here a suggestion that he was himself in some measure responsible for Leggett's comments. Nor, it would seem, was he alone in forming this interpretation, for in a letter published in *The Plaindealer* for February 11, 1837, he observed that "many of the friends of [Irving] are still determined to make me, in some way or other, the instigator of an attack upon him."[160] In an arch tone, Bryant went on to deny having influenced his former colleague in any way. And Irving, upon reading this latest public letter, at once addressed to Bryant a shocked disclaimer of "the remotest intention" to suggest that he had played a part in the original attack.[161] This letter of apology, which he pointedly forwarded to the New York *American* rather than to *The Plaindealer*, dispelled the misunderstanding and, to his relief, ended the incident.

Only one further public charge was made during Irving's lifetime which he saw fit to answer in print. This came in 1851, and ironically it occurred in the *Personal Memoirs* of his friend and admirer Henry Rowe Schoolcraft, the pioneering ethnologist. In the course of preparing *Astoria*, his account of the epic undertaking in commerce and explora-tion conceived by John Jacob Astor and intended by him to secure for the United States a fur-trading empire on the Northwest coast, Irving came to admire Astor and formed a friendship with him. At the time he had agreed to undertake the book, he had stipulated firmly that whatever profit he might derive from it would be from sales alone; he

159. Irving, in "Washington Irving," *The Plaindealer*, 1, no. 9 (January 28, 1837), 131.

160. Bryant, in "Mr. Irving's 'Poetick License,'" *The Plaindealer*, 1, no. 11 (February 11, 1837), 165.

161. *"To Mr. William Cullen Bryant, Esq.,"* New York *American*, February 17, 1837, p. 2, col. 6. The progress and resolution of this unpleasant affair are described in full in PMI, III, 102–12. Bryant also gives an account of the mis-understanding in his *Discourse on the Character and Genius of Washington Irving* (New York, 1860), pp. 33–34.

would accept no other remuneration. Astor had heeded his wishes, but as the years passed and their friendship deepened the old merchant attempted to reward him in some tangible way for his literary assistance and his later attentive good will, always to be refused. Astor was fertile in expedients, however, and at last he managed virtually to force money on Irving: for by naming him as an executor of his will he delegated to him a duty—and a statutorily determined remuneration—which as a gentleman he could scarcely refuse. Thus, following Astor's death in January, 1848, Irving began two years' service as an executor, whose value was calculated upon its completion at the substantial sum of $10,592.66.[162]

To the suspicious, notably the porcupinish James Fenimore Cooper, Irving's cordial relations with Astor over more than a decade had been an unmistakable sign of his sycophancy and greed. Upon learning that his fellow author had been named an executor, Cooper wrote his wife that rumor spoke of a $50,000 legacy for Irving. "What an instinct that man has for gold!" Cooper scoffed. "He is to be Astor's biographer! Columbus and John Jacob Astor. I dare say Irving will make the last the greatest man."[163] For his part, Irving was aware that bits of unflattering misinformation such as Cooper's were in circulation, just as they had been in the months after the publication of *Astoria*. To some persons, even physical proximity to the wealthy man seemed reprehensible, no matter how honorable to either party it might in fact have been. Had not the author closeted himself with Astor on numerous occasions since 1835, and were not his visits especially frequent in the months just preceding Astor's death? The inevitable stories spawned by such ruminations as these disturbed him, but he chose to make no public statement on the matter until a suitable tale should surface in public, lest he should appear overeager to explain himself.

The first slur to reach print about his relations with Astor was in Schoolcraft's *Personal Memoirs*. In that prosy work, and apparently without the slightest intention to offend, Schoolcraft recounted an "instructive" conversation he had held in 1838 with Albert Gallatin, wherein the statesman had made the following comments:

> Several years ago J[ohn] J[acob] A[stor] put into my hands the journal of his traders on the Columbia, desiring me to use it. I put it in the hands of Malte Brun, at Paris, who used the geographical facts in his work, but paid little respect to Mr. Astor, whom he

162. Kenneth W. Porter, *John Jacob Astor, Business Man* (Cambridge, Mass., 1931), II, 1055.

163. *The Letters and Journals of James Fenimore Cooper*, ed. James F. Beard (Cambridge, Mass., 1968), V, 330.

regarded merely as a merchant seeking his own profit.... Astor
did not like it. He was restive several years, and then gave Washington Irving $5,000 to take up the MSS. This is the history of
"Astoria."[164]

Upon reading Schoolcraft's report of the allegation by Gallatin, Irving
acted swiftly. He wrote out a detailed and dignified rebuttal and sent it
to Evert A. Duyckinck for insertion in the influential *Literary World*,
which Duyckinck edited; and when galley proofs were returned he
corrected them with unusual care, elaborating the statement at several
points. In the published text, which appeared as a letter to Schoolcraft
in the *Literary World* for November 22, 1851, Irving affirmed in rather
stern tones his admiration for the late merchant and firmly denied the
rumor that he was Astor's hack. Their intimacy, he wrote, "was sought
originally on [Astor's] part, and ... was drawn closer when... I became
acquainted... with the scope and power of his mind, and the grandeur
of his enterprises." As to a financial arrangement, he stated categorically
that Astor "was too proverbially rich a man for me to permit the shadow
of a pecuniary favor to rest on our intercourse."[165] For the remainder
of his lifetime this statement achieved its desired effect by silencing
speculation, in public at least, about his relationship with Astor.

Notwithstanding his dislike of controversy or recrimination of any
kind, Irving was thus at need, and in self-defense, an effective controversialist. The same may be said of his infrequent performances as a
public speaker. He regularly declined requests to speak before audiences
large or small, pleading as his excuse "insuperable diffidence";[166] yet
on occasions when a brief speech was clearly necessary and not to be
avoided, he managed to acquit himself creditably. His remarks at the
welcoming dinner in 1832 reveal that, at what he recognized to be an
epochal moment in his career, he could rise even to eloquence. On March
30, 1837, he contributed his mite to the proceedings of "The Booksellers' Dinner," a lavish entertainment in honor of American authors,
sponsored by the publishers and booksellers of New York, Philadelphia,
and Boston. The order of the evening at the City Hotel in New York
included dinner, followed by comments from the toastmaster, and then
thirteen regular toasts, the singing of several "airs," and the sentiments
of many dignitaries present, of whom Irving was one. In his remarks

164. Schoolcraft, *Personal Memoirs of a Residence of Thirty Years with the
Indian Tribes on the American Frontier* (Philadelphia, 1851), pp. 624–25.

165. Irving, "Correction of a Misstatement Respecting 'Astoria,'" *Literary World*,
9, no. 251 (November 22, 1851), 408.

166. See, for example, David E. Sloane, "Washington Irving's 'Insuperable Diffidence,'" *American Literature*, 43, no. 1 (March, 1971), 114–16. See also PMI, II,
486–91.

before this gathering dedicated to the progress of American authorship
and publishing, he took as his theme the importance of Anglo-American
cooperation. As he had done in the dedicatory letter to Bryant's *Poems*,
he praised Samuel Rogers as "an enlightened and liberal friend of
America and Americans," this time citing his admiration of another
American poet, Fitz-Greene Halleck. According to the New York *American*, in which a full account of the proceedings appeared on April 3,
Irving's toast to "Samuel Rogers—the friend of American genius" was
so warmly received that "the company all rose, and drank the health
standing, with the greatest enthusiasm."[167]

Irving's miscellaneous writings include only one other speech—his
remarks, or rather his apology for having prepared no remarks, at a
meeting convened in honor of the late James Fenimore Cooper on
February 24, 1852. Having served as chairman of the Committee of
Arrangements for this memorial observance, Irving had already paid a
tribute of time and effort to the author; the notion that in addition he
intended to address the audience was an unfortunate misunderstanding.[168]
Nevertheless, the brevity of his comments in turning over the meeting to
the master of ceremonies, Daniel Webster, is ironic in light of the
strained relations which had existed between him and Cooper during the
latter's lifetime. Irving had always made it a point to speak generously
of Cooper, but he was well aware of the latter's ill-concealed dislike
of him.[169] Once, when the two men had both happened to be standing
in George Putnam's bookshop, the publisher had almost as an act of
courage introduced them. To his surprise, they had chatted together
quite amiably. "Mr. Irving afterwards frequently alluded to the incident,"
Putnam recalled in a memoir, "as being a very great gratification to him.
He may have recalled it with new satisfaction, when, not many months
afterwards, he sat on the platform at the Cooper Commemoration, and
joined in Bryant's tribute to the genius of the departed novelist."[170]

Early in 1839 a combination of circumstances led Irving to set aside
his long-confirmed dislike of professional magazine writing and become
a contributor to the *Knickerbocker Magazine*. His most recent literary
project, a history of the conquest of Mexico, had come to grief the
previous December when, upon learning that William H. Prescott was
at work on the same topic, he had at once surrendered his own prior

167. "The Booksellers' Dinner," New York *American*, April 3, 1837, p. 1, col.
5–p. 2 col. 5.

168. See *Memorial of James Fenimore Cooper* (New York, 1852), pp. [v, 7].

169. See, for example, "Desultory Thoughts on Criticism," *Knickerbocker Magazine*, 14 (August, 1839), 177; Vol. II, p. 122 below. See also STW, II, 210, and index,
s.v. "Cooper."

170. Putnam, "Recollections of Irving. By His Publisher," *Atlantic Monthly*,
6 (July, 1860), 608.

claim to it. Prescott was delighted and relieved at that development, but as Irving later observed to Pierre M. Irving, "I doubt whether [he] was aware of the extent of the sacrifice I made" thus impulsively. "When I gave it up to him, I in a manner gave him up my bread, for I depended upon the profit of it to recruit my waning finances."[171] Having purchased the country estate near Tarrytown, New York, to which he was later to assign the famous name "Sunnyside," and having invested heavily in stocks and in land speculation, Irving was hard hit by the Great Panic of 1837 which swept away thousands of his dollars and reduced the flow of dividends from his still-solvent investments. To complicate matters, owing primarily to the Panic his rural home became a temporary residence for several suddenly dependent members of his family. Without a literary undertaking to substitute for the history of the conquest of Mexico, and with a diminished inflow of cash, Irving had no real choice but to make what bargain he could in return for his services as a magazinist. On February 4, 1839, he signed an agreement with Lewis Gaylord Clark, the editor of the *Knickerbocker Magazine*, to supply monthly contributions in consideration of a $2,000 annual fee.[172]

Thus in his initial article, published in the March issue under the pseudonym of "Geoffrey Crayon," he announced his intention henceforth to "bestow my wisdom and tediousness upon the world" in periodical instalments;[173] and over the next two years he adhered faithfully to the pact with Clark, making the best of his temporary occupation. From the outset, it is true, he gave himself no more trouble in preparing copy than was absolutely necessary. Clark, who recognized the value to the already prosperous *Knickerbocker Magazine* of an article by "Geoffrey Crayon" as one of its regular features, was willing to make allowances for the often hastily prepared copy he received; and several of the extant manuscripts of Irving's articles are liberally besprinkled with corrections in the editor's bright-blue ink.[174] Even though in April, 1840, Irving avowed to Pierre his wish to resume writing as a free agent and so escape the onus of "a monthly recurring task,"[175] his connection with the *Knickerbocker Magazine* was sufficiently comfortable that he did not sever it until nearly a full year later.

171. Irving to Pierre M. Irving, Madrid, March 24, 1844; PMI, III, 143.

172. PMI, III, 147; Lewis Gaylord Clark, "Recollections of Washington Irving," *Lippincott's Magazine*, 3 (May, 1869), 552.

173. Irving, "To the Editor of the Knickerbocker," *Knickerbocker Magazine*, 13 (March, 1839), 206.

174. On occasion Irving also made use of his nephew Pierre, for whom he had recently exerted his influence to secure employment in New York City. Pierre served as copyeditor, as unofficial courier between the author and Clark, and perhaps in other capacities.

175. Irving to Pierre M. Irving, n.p., April, 1840; PMI, III, 152.

The majority of his acknowledged articles for the magazine, as "Geoffrey Crayon" or under other recognizable pseudonyms, were collected in 1855 as parts of a miscellaneous volume entitled *Wolfert's Roost*. However, the twelve acknowledged contributions not so collected, and thus included in the present volume, afford by themselves a representative sampling of the material he supplied to the *Knickerbocker Magazine*. In a manner quite satisfactory to Clark, ordinarily he avoided breaking new ground in style or theme, elaborating instead on the well known material that had won him fame. Thus in his initial letter as "Geoffrey Crayon," he descanted upon the happy appropriateness of his writing for a magazine named after Diedrich Knickerbocker,[176] his teacher and dear friend in youth. In a subsequent article, "Sleepy Hollow" (May, 1839), he recalled the days when he had accompanied Diedrich Knickerbocker as that personage pursued the researches which eventually resulted in his *History of New York* and other writings. In two further contributions, "Communipaw" (September, 1839) and "Conspiracy of the Cocked Hats" (October, 1839), using pen names coined for the nonce he portrayed a sleepy Dutch village along the Hudson River much as Diedrich Knickerbocker had done for the colony of New Netherlands at large, as an enchanting yet unheralded region of "poetry and romance."[177] For other *Knickerbocker Magazine* articles Irving sketched scenes from the history of Spain, the notes for which narratives had lain almost untouched since the days in Madrid when he had pursued his research for the *Columbus*. These included "Pelayo and the Merchant's Daughter" (January, 1840) and "Abderahman" (May, 1840), two samples of romantic biography drawn from lengthier narratives he planned to complete at some indefinite date.[178] In the "Letter from Granada" (July, 1840) he added an account, reminiscent of *The Alhambra*, of the picturesque local traditions among the peasantry of Spain.

A few of Irving's articles for the *Knickerbocker Magazine* dealt with matters which had long been of interest to him but which he had not previously singled out for separate treatment. Such a work was "National Nomenclature" (August, 1839), wherein his fascination with place-names, expressed in works as diverse as the *History of New York, Colum-*

176. See Irving, "To the Editor of the Knickerbocker," pp. 207–8. In the initial issue of what was then entitled the *Knickerbacker*, the editors explained in January, 1833, that they had adopted the name of "the Dutch Herodotus" for their magazine "as good catholics when they take the cowl sometimes adopt that of their tutelar saint" ("Introduction," 1, no. 1, p. 6).

177. Irving, "Conspiracy of the Cocked Hats," *Knickerbocker Magazine*, 14 (October, 1839), 305.

178. See p. lxxxi, and the Textual Commentaries to "The Chronicle of Pelayo" and "Chronicle of the Ommiades," Vol. II, pp. 452–55, 474–77.

bus, and *Astoria*, came to fruition in a plea that locations of "sublimity and beauty" within the United States should be marred no further by "trite, poverty-stricken names." Thus, as a national name drawn from one of the grandest physical features of the American continent, and employing as well the nomenclature of the land's aboriginal inhabitants, he recommended "The United States of Alleghania" as one which might also be adopted without the necessity of altering "our old national cypher of U. S. A."[179]

In its concern for euphonious and distinctive American place-names, "National Nomenclature" touched upon an issue which had more than once in recent years received comment in the *Knickerbocker Magazine*.[180] The same coincidental conjunction between the editorial concerns of the magazine and Irving's own interests occurred in two other of his articles. He had never relished playing the role of literary critic—according to Pierre M. Irving he "wished to be just, and could not bear to be severe"[181]—and moreover he doubted the usefulness of published critical commentary to anyone, except perhaps the critic himself. In "Desultory Thoughts on Criticism" (August, 1839) he set forth the latter view in relation to a central concern of the *Knickerbocker Magazine*, the fostering of a healthy national literature. American literature, he suggested, would be best served if permitted to flourish "for some time longer, in the freshness and vigor of native vegetation," rather than subjected as at present to the "excess of criticism" which impedes its natural growth.[182] On a similar note, in a public letter on the desirability of an international copyright agreement (January, 1840), he pointed out that in the absence of an enforceable law to protect the financial interests of publishers, the very survival of professional authorship in the United States was in jeopardy. Together with a few brief departures from the subjects traditionally associated with his writings, such as "The Taking of the Veil, and the Charming Letoriéres" (June, 1840) and "American Researches in Italy" (October, 1841), his major contributions to the *Knickerbocker Magazine* made up a diverse yet characteristic collection of articles.

179. Irving, "National Nomenclature," *Knickerbocker Magazine*, 14 (August, 1839), 159, 162.

180. See, for example, Lydia M. H. Sigourney, "Indian Names," *Knickerbocker Magazine*, 2 (October, 1833), 264–65; Anon., "Our Last Article for 1833," 2 (December, 1833), 490–91; S. L. K., "Our Struggle for Independence," 5 (February, 1835), 117–23; Anon., "Language," 7 (January, 1836), 102–4; A. B. C., "Names of Towns in the United States," 9 (January, 1837), 19–25; "Editor's Table," 9 (January, 1837), 98–99; "Editor's Table," 9 (June, 1837), 630; H. R. Schoolcraft, "Mohegan Language and Geographical Names," 10 (September, 1837), 214–16.

181. PMI, I, 299.

182. Irving, "Desultory Thoughts on Criticism," p. 175.

From the enthusiastic public reception of his offerings as a magazinist it is clear that Irving had lost neither his keen sensitivity to prevailing tastes nor his ability to satisfy them. His monthly productions were not, however, without their detractors, including even so frankly admiring an acquaintance as Henry W. Longfellow. In July, 1839, the poet wrote regretfully to G. W. Greene that Irving was "writing away *like fury,* in the Knickerbocker;—*he had better not*; old remnants—odds and ends,— about Sleepy Hollow, and Granada. What a pity."[183] Irving's friend Charles A. Davis once recalled him describing his authorship of the *Knickerbocker Magazine* articles in a similarly slighting way, as "'only hammering over some ores which having years before been drawn up to the mouth of the mine had been left there by him as not worth *smelting.*'" Nevertheless, Davis added as his own contrary opinion that "some of those productions were very amusing and characteristic."[184]

In addition to his acknowledged articles, most of which appeared beneath a collective title, "The Crayon Papers," Irving contributed to the *Knickerbocker Magazine* several brief items which were published either anonymously or under pseudonyms not associated with his proper name. In a memoir, Lewis Gaylord Clark recalled that on a visit he had made to Irving's home during this period, the author had handed to him a packet of manuscripts with the remark: "'There is an *omnium gatherum* of literary stores and quaint excerpts, intermixed with personal anecdotes of distinguished men and women whom I met during my residence abroad. Perhaps you may find some "good things" for your "Editor's Table."... But don't mention my name in connection with them.'"[185] It is quite possible that Irving published in the "Editor's Table" section of the *Knickerbocker Magazine* a larger collection of brief notes than has thus far been identified. However, those pieces which, through surviving manuscripts and other evidence, can certainly be ascribed to him do reveal that he prepared them casually and intended them to serve a variety of purposes. Some, such as his anecdote of Admiral Sir Eliab Harvey's experience among the Quaker families of Long Island (February, 1840), and the seriocomic anecdote of the French Revolution (April, 1840), were similar in kind to the anonymous *New-York Mirror* contributions of a few years before: they afforded glimpses of famous personalities or events, using information he had gleaned from transatlantic acquaintances. These brief narratives may originally have formed parts of "private" letters Irving had addressed to Clark, with the mutual understanding that the editor was welcome

183. H. W. Longfellow to G. W. Greene, Cambridge, July 23, 1839; in STW, II, 107.

184. Charles A. Davis to Pierre M. Irving, New York, June, 1863 (Berg Collection, New York Public Library).

185. Clark, "Recollections of Irving," p. 559.

to use selected passages in print if so inclined.[186] Another letter, from a fictitious "Hiram Crackenthorpe, of St. Louis" (May, 1839), served as a comic pendant to Charles A. Davis' popular sketch, "The First Locomotive," which had appeared in the *Knickerbocker Magazine* the month before.[187]

Perhaps the most interesting—and also least characteristic—of Irving's anonymous writings in the "Editor's Table" section of the magazine was one entitled "The 'Empire of the West'" (March, 1840). In this commentary, prompted by an essay on the progress of discovery, trade, and settlement in the Far West recently published in the *North American Review*,[188] the author of *Astoria* and *The Adventures of Captain Bonneville* took occasion to insist, in terms much stronger than he had employed in those works, on the critical importance of the West to the future welfare of the United States. Here he frankly appealed to nationalistic sentiments in favor of territorial expansion, referring to the region between the Rocky Mountains and the Pacific Ocean as "our empire." At the same time, he portrayed the English fur-trading concerns then in competition with their American counterparts for control of that vast territory in bold terms, as embodiments of "wily Commerce" extending its "meshes" over land belonging to the United States by "indefeasible right."[189] Irving's researches in preparing his Western writings had convinced him that American sovereignty from coast to coast must be asserted at once. In "The 'Empire of the West'" he therefore sought in an unusually partisan manner to advance his views on this internationally sensitive topic. However, to avoid giving offense to his acquaintances on either side of the Atlantic, he published the article anonymously.

Not long after he had severed his connection with the *Knickerbocker Magazine*, Irving was notified of his appointment as the United States minister to Spain. Assuming that the diplomatic duties in Madrid would leave him ample time to pursue work on the biography of George

186. Such an understanding was clearly behind Clark's publishing in the issue for April, 1840 (vol. 15, pp. 349–50) a passage which, as manuscript evidence reveals, was drawn from a letter Irving had addressed to the editor. For the original text see Irving to Lewis G. Clark, Greenburgh, March 17, 1840, in the *Letters* volumes of the present edition.

187. Davis, "The First Locomotive," *Knickerbocker Magazine*, 13 (April, 1839), 343–48.

188. Anon., "Discovery beyond the Rocky Mountains," *North American Review*, 50 (January, 1840), 75–144.

189. Irving, "The 'Empire of the West,'" *Knickerbocker Magazine*, 15 (March, 1840), 260. For a more thorough discussion of this article in relation to Irving's other writings on the West, see Wayne R. Kime, "Washington Irving and the 'Empire of the West': An Unacknowledged Review," *Western American Literature*, 5 (Winter, 1971), 277–85.

Washington for which he was then gathering material, he accepted the position with little hesitation. However, his more than four years' service in Spain proved to be much more demanding than he had anticipated, and when he returned to Sunnyside in October, 1846, the biography was virtually untouched. Nevertheless, on this homecoming from Europe he was vexed by far fewer anxieties and uncertainties than on his earlier return, fourteen years before. After a series of reunions he began an ambitious campaign of renovations and additions to his cottage, and with the assistance of Pierre M. Irving—now his unofficial comptroller and financial counselor—began negotiations with various publishers who had come forward with proposals to bring out, in fitting style, a collective edition of his revised works. The notion of poring over the entire corpus of his writings to prepare such an edition was not in itself very attractive, but Pierre reminded him that performing the task was his surest means to the financial independence he desired. "Make all despatch with the preparation of your uniform edition," Pierre advised him in April, 1847, "and then to work to complete your Life of Washington, and take your ease forever after."[190]

On July 26, 1848, Irving signed an agreement with George P. Putnam to cooperate in producing an "Author's Revised Edition" of his back works. The contract promised to provide him financial security for the remainder of his lifetime, but once signed it also carried a responsibility to complete the revision of his writings. Thus far that process of "'fagging" labor had gone slowly,[191] once having been interrupted by a therapeutic diversion to the still uncompleted histories of medieval Spain in which he took special interest, and more than once simply abandoned. Henceforward, however, Irving set himself in harness; and for the next two years he devoted his literary energies solely to the Author's Revised Edition and to projects associated with it. That task complete, he resumed work on what he now regarded as the "crowning effort" of his career,[192] the *Life of George Washington,* whose fifth and final volume he managed to complete only a few months before his death in 1859.

Throughout the 1850's, owing both to his achievements over the past five decades and to the increased circulation given his works by George Putnam's handsome new edition, Irving was known in the United States as a presiding genius of the national literature—in a common phrase,

190. Pierre M. Irving to Washington Irving, [New York, April 14, 1847]; PMI, IV, 16.

191. The term "fagging" was habitual with Irving in reference to unexciting literary jobwork; see, for example, PMI, IV, 52.

192. Irving, "Preface," *Life of George Washington,* vol. 5 (New York, 1859), [v].

"the Patriarch of American Letters."[193] As John Esten Cooke put it, he "had outlived the generation which witnessed his early struggles, and those who thus looked on him as the head of our literature were a sort of posterity."[194] Despite his various connections with contemporary life, Irving came to be regarded in some measure as already a relic of the past, a personality of interest not only in himself but as a source of vicarious contact with bygone personalities and events. His miscellaneous writings published within the final decade of his career were well calculated to satisfy the expectations aroused by this prevailing attitude. Always a modest man, he was "utterly incapable," as Donald Grant Mitchell testified, "of being lionized" as a literary hero.[195] Nevertheless, as if in tacit recognition of the stature he had attained, in his fugitive writings he tended to dwell upon himself—his early experiences and opinions, his memories of deceased acquaintances.

Thus in 1850, at the request of the New York publishing firm of Harper and Brothers, he supplied a brief memoir of Thomas Campbell as an introduction to the first American edition of William Beattie's *Life and Letters* of the late author.[196] In these recollections of his meetings with Campbell, he lent an autobiographical dimension to the bibliographical record of his association with the Scottish poet, whose verse he had helped introduce to American readers four decades before. In 1852 he contributed to Putnam's lavishly produced volume, *The Home Book of the Picturesque*, an essay entitled "The Catskill Mountains" in which he recounted a voyage he had made when a boy up the Hudson River, in continual view of the Catskills, "the great poetical region of our country." The "magical influences" of the mountains, and the "marvellous legends" he had heard about them in the course of the journey, he recalled, had begotten in his mind "a host of fanciful notions . . . which have haunted it ever since."[197] In 1855, piecing together an article for *The Knickerbocker Gallery*, a gift-book prepared as a tribute to Lewis Gaylord Clark, he drew from his notebooks the material for another sketch associated with his earlier wanderings. "Conversations with Talma," an account of his acquaintance with the great French tragedian while at Paris in 1821 and in 1823–1824, included as

193. George Ripley, "Washington Irving," *Harper's New Monthly Magazine*, 2 (April, 1851), 580.

194. Cooke, "Irving at Sunnyside," p. 511.

195. Mitchell, "A New Preface," *Dream-Life: A Fable of the Seasons* (New York, 1863), pp. v–vi.

196. The original edition of Beattie's *Life and Letters of Thomas Campbell* was published in 1849 in three volumes (London: E. Moxon); a second English edition, also in three volumes, appeared in 1850 (London: Hall, Virtue).

197. Irving, "The Catskill Mountains," *The Home Book of the Picturesque* (New York, 1852), pp. 72, 74.

well a previously unpublished essay he had written in the latter year,
and which had grown out of his interchanges with the actor. In 1855
he also contributed to Evert A. and George L. Duyckinck's *Cyclopædia
of American Literature* the last miscellaneous writing of his lifetime,
a memoir of his late friend the painter Washington Allston. Here he
described, with a hint of nostalgia, a few memorable weeks he had
spent in company with Allston in 1805, touring the galleries of Rome
under the tutelage of his enthusiastic and already accomplished elder
countryman. Adding a revealing insight into his own subsequent career
as that desultory sketcher "Geoffrey Crayon," he portrayed himself as
suddenly struck while with Allston in Rome by the thought, " 'Why
might I not remain here and turn painter?' "[198]

In view of the suggestiveness and variety even of these scattered
recollections, it is little wonder that Irving was repeatedly urged during
the 1850's to prepare an autobiography. George Putnam, who became
a close friend of the elderly author and to whom he often confided his
memories, ventured more than once to suggest—"not professionally,"
he claimed—" 'I hope you have taken time to make a note of these.' "[199]
Irving's only reply was a humorous negative shake of the head. Aside
from the scattered glimpses he offered to those who encountered his
miscellaneous writings, the only autobiographical recollections he left
behind him were those included by Pierre M. Irving in *The Life and
Letters of Washington Irving* (1862–1863).

Finally, beyond their autobiographical import and their appeal to
an American public to whom his career had assumed an almost legendary character, the fugitive writings of Irving's last decade suggest
strong threads of continuity running through the diverse events and
enthusiasms of his lifetime. The role as mediator between the cultures
of England and the United States he reaffirmed in introducing to
American readers the British biography of Thomas Campbell. His taste
for legendary tales associated with the picturesque regions along the
Hudson River became itself a subject for treatment in "The Catskill
Mountains." His lifelong attraction to the drama, whether in printed
form or as presented onstage, was confirmed in "Conversations with
Talma," with its shrewd comments on the French adaptations of
Shakespeare's plays. And in his memoir of Washington Allston he bore
testimony to that early affinity for pictorial art which he expressed
later in life both in his writings and in his friendships with artists
such as Gilbert Stuart Newton, Sir David Wilkie, and Charles Leslie.
Retaining in his last years many of the interests he had displayed in

198. Irving, "Washington Allston," in *Cyclopædia of American Literature*, ed.
Evert A. and George L. Duyckinck (New York, 1855), II, 15.
199. Putnam, "Recollections of Irving," p. 604.

youth, Irving had come to serve not merely as a bridge between nations but as a link between generations as well.

NARRATIVES OF SPANISH HISTORY LEFT
. UNPUBLISHED AT IRVING'S DEATH

The effective beginning of Washington Irving's career as a student of Spanish history was January 30, 1826, when he received from the United States minister to Spain, Alexander Hill Everett, an invitation to translate into English the monumental study by Don Martín Fernández de Navarrete, *Colección de los viages y descubrimientos, que hicieron por mar los españoles desde fines del siglo XV.*[200] Everett's proposal, with which he enclosed a passport and a letter of appointment as attaché to the American legation at Madrid, came at an opportune time. For the past fourteen months, while living in Paris and casting about inconclusively for a successor to his most recent work, *Tales of a Traveller* (1824), Irving had also been pursuing independently a rather intensive course of study in the language and literature of Spain, having no more specific an aim than to see that country, in which he had long felt an interest, and perhaps to write a book about it.[201] He required almost no time to weigh the merits of his opportunity. "I am on the wing for Madrid!" he wrote on February 7 to his friend John Howard Payne,[202] and within a few days he and his brother Peter, who intended to assist in the translation, reached their destination. With Everett's assistance they rented rooms at the home of Obadiah Rich, the American consul and the possessor of a magnificent library of Spanish history and literature. Irving could hardly believe his good fortune. "The Books," he wrote to Thomas W. Storrow not long after commencing his study of Navarrete's *Colección,* "which Robertson was years in collecting are all within my reach."[203]

The compilation of Navarrete, he found, "presented rather a mass

200. STW, I, 296, 303. Two volumes of the five-volume compilation (1825–1837) by Navarrete (1765–1844) had appeared thus far.

201. For a succinct account of Irving's early interest in Spain and his study of Spanish beginning in December, 1824, see STW, I, 297–98; see also PMI, II, 245–49. For an authoritative survey of the author's seven-year residence in Spain and interests in things Spanish, see Stanley T. Williams, *The Spanish Background of American Literature,* 2 vols. (New Haven, 1955), II, 12–45.

202. Irving to Payne, Bordeaux, February 7, 1826; STW, I, 296.

203. Irving to Storrow, Madrid, April 14, 1826; *Washington Irving and the Storrows,* p. 79. Irving's allusion is to William Robertson (1721–1792), whose historical writings, including the *History of Charles V* (1769) and *History of America* (1777), he was to use in preparing his own new work. For a capsule biography of Irving's generous host Obadiah Rich (1783–1850), see STW, I, 471, n. 40.

of rich materials for history, than a history itself."[204] But he was not discouraged by his assessment. He grew convinced that, despite his sketchy background as a serious historian, he himself was a proper person to write the narrative of Columbus' life for which Navarrete had provided in part a documentary foundation. "It will require great attention hard study & hard work," he told Storrow, "but I feel stimulated to it, and encouraged by the singular facilities which are thrown in my way." Peter would be helpful as an assistant, but "I mean to look into every thing myself, to make myself master of my subject."[205] During the next few months Irving worked harder than he ever had before. By June he was "fagged and exhausted," but for two months longer he labored "incessantly . . . sometimes all day & a great part of the night."[206] Again and again, in the year that was to elapse from the latter date before he could complete *The Life and Voyages of Christopher Columbus* (1828), he lamented to friends and relatives the number of minor points still to be established and disputed facts to be settled; but he pushed on. "I find there is nothing keeps up my spirits more than hard work," he told Storrow in July, adding in the next month that he had begun "a trial of skill in an entirely new line, in which I had to satisfy both the public and myself."[207]

Inevitably, in preparing the biography of Columbus he consulted records relating to the contemporaneous siege and conquest of Granada, the Moorish capital of Spain, by the navigator's patrons the monarchs Ferdinand and Isabella. These collateral researches opened up to him a wide range of inviting topics in Spanish and Moorish history. In August, 1826, probably as a respite from the exacting labor he had performed thus far on the *Columbus,* he began work on a second historical narrative, one possessing its own firm documentary basis but incorporating as well the qualities of credulous zeal which characterized some of the early Spanish chroniclers. During the next two months he became "so deeply interested" in his embryonic *Chronicle of the Conquest of Granada* (1829), with its imaginary author the pious monk Fray Antonio Agapida, that he "wrote out the heads of chapters for

204. "Preface," *The Life and Voyages of Christopher Columbus;* see also *Washington Irving and the Storrows,* p. 67.

205. Irving to Thomas W. Storrow, Madrid, April 4, 1826; *Washington Irving and the Storrows,* p. 80. The entire letter, pp. 78–81, is an important statement of the author's aims for the *Columbus.*

206. Irving to Thomas W. Storrow, Madrid, June 12, 1826; *Washington Irving and the Storrows,* p. 83.

207. Irving to Storrow, Madrid, July 9, 1826; *Washington Irving and the Storrows,* pp. 89, 94. For further references by Irving to his difficulties in establishing the factual outline of *Columbus,* see pp. 97, 100, 105, 108–9; PMI, II, 255, 257, 263; McClary, *Washington Irving and the House of Murray,* pp. 86, 89, 92.

the whole work" before returning to the perplexities of the *Columbus*.[208]
He proposed to enlist his nephew Pierre M. Irving, who was then
concluding a youthful tour of Europe, as proofreader for the English
edition of the biography; but his continual discovery of new sources
of information, his difficulties in gaining access to unpublished documents, and his languorous, inaccurate copyists conspired to frustrate
the plan. "I had no idea of what a complete labyrinth I had entangled
myself in when I took hold of the work," he confessed ruefully to
Pierre in February, 1827.[209]

Nevertheless, even before he completed the biography six months
later he had set to work on other topics, in addition even to the
Granada, which he had encountered during his strenuous initiation as
a historian of Spain. Irving's journals testify to his enthusiasm as he
began these undertakings, later summarized by Pierre M. Irving as
"a suite of works ... illustrative of the domination of the Arabs in
Spain, and also ... a Conquest of Mexico, a theme upon which he had
been brooding."[210] Among his subjects for research in the latter months
of 1827 were El Cid and Amerigo Vespucci—for both of which biographies his notes have been lost; "Don Roderick" the Goth—subsequently
to be included as "The Legend of Don Roderick" in *Legends of the
Conquest of Spain* (1835); the story of the Abencerrage, from Monte-
mayor's *Diana* (1542); Pelayo (d. 738), Fernan Gonzalez (910–ca.
970), and Fernando the Saint (ca. 1200–1252);[211] a series of biographies,
drawn chiefly from Conde's *Historia de la Dominación de los Arabes
en España* (1820–1821), which in his journals he abbreviated variously
as "Arabian MS," "Omeya," "Moorish Hist," and "Chronicles"; and the
conquest of Mexico, using information from Fray Bernardino de
Sahagún's *Historia general de las Cosas de Nueva España*.[212] He pursued his studies in the mornings, at the stately library of the Jesuits'
College of St. Isidoro, not far from his rooms. "You cannot think what

208. Irving, Autobiographical Notes, Madrid, January 10, 1843; STW, I, 313.
209. PMI, II, 257.
210. *Ibid.*, II, 270.
211. In addition to these early Spanish heroes, Irving took notes on the tenth-
century figures Don Garcia Fernandez, Ruy Velasquez, and the "Seven Sons of
Lara," the latter family being a popular topic in Spanish balladry. The manuscripts
he prepared on the basis of his studies of these personages are owned, respectively,
by the Berg Collection, New York Public Library; the University of Virginia; and
the University of Texas at Austin. See William J. Scheick, ed., " 'The Seven Sons
of Lara': A Washington Irving Manuscript," *Resources for American Literary
Studies*, 2 (1972), 208–17.
212. Andrew B. Myers, ed., "Washington Irving's Madrid Journal 1827–1828
and Related Letters," *Bulletin of the New York Public Library*, 62 (May–August,
1958), 301–8, 407–12. Irving's loose translation of a portion of Sahagún's *History*
is owned by the Manuscript Division, New York Public Library.

a delight I feel," he once wrote to his friend the Russian diplomat Prince Dolgorouki, "in passing through its galleries filled with old, parchment-bound books. It is a perfect wilderness of curiosity to me. What a deep-felt quiet luxury there is in delving into the rich ore of these old, neglected volumes."[213] Irving had discovered a body of material both congenial to his tastes and, he believed, promising as the contents of future literary productions. On December 31 he wrote in his journal: "So ends the year 1827—tranquilly—It has been a year of labor, but much more comfortable than most I have passed in Europe, and leaves me in a state of moderate hope as to the future."[214]

In March, 1828, following two months of preliminary research for still another new project, a life of Mahomet, Irving left Madrid, his baggage laden with works in progress, on a tour southward through Spain. Late in April, having explored with interest some of the Moorish monuments which had figured in his as yet fragmentary chronicle of the Ommiades dynasty (752–1030 A.D.),[215] he settled in a cottage outside Seville and began another period of writing, as concentrated yet tranquil as those in Madrid. Here he exulted over the "quiet and deep enjoyment in sitting out in the air in the still serenity of the country, and passing one of these balmy summer nights in gazing at the stars,"[216] but his activities in the daylight hours were no less purposeful than his evenings were serene. By late October the manuscript of the two-volume *Granada* was complete, copied, and dispatched to John Murray, his publisher in London, and amid his composition of that work he had agonized over the proper treatment for "The Legend of Don Roderick" and made excursions into Seville to pursue further enquiries concerning Columbus in the Archives of the Indies. Irving's work on *Granada* approximated what a few years later he was to describe to Peter as his ideal for authorship—"not to *drudge* at literary labor, but to use it as an agreeable employment."[217] However, in 1828 such a luxury was one he could not yet afford for very long. Thus as the year drew to a close he allowed most of the works he had begun so auspiciously at Madrid to remain untouched. Instead, to put money in his purse at once, in nineteen days of virtually continuous writing he prepared a one-volume abridgment of *Columbus* for sale to a general audience—

213. Irving to Dolgorouki, Madrid, January 22, 1828; PMI, II, 273.

214. *Ibid.*, II, 271; see also Myers, ed., "Irving's Madrid Journals," p. 411.

215. See *Journal of Washington Irving 1828 and Miscellaneous Notes on Moorish Legend and History*, ed. Stanley T. Williams (New York, 1937), pp. 9, 11, and passim.

216. Irving to Mlle. Antoinette Bolviller, Seville, July 20, 1828; PMI, II, 328–29.

217. Irving to Peter Irving, [London, Spring, 1831]; PMI, II, 423. See also Irving's letter to Henry Brevoort, April 4, 1827, in *Letters of Washington Irving to Henry Brevoort*, pp. 410–11.

especially schoolchildren, and at other times he made progress on a sequel to the full biography which was to be published in 1831 as *Voyages and Discoveries of the Companions of Columbus.*

Irving recognized that the *Granada* was "something of an experiment" and might not at once win favor; but at least, he told his agent in London Colonel Thomas Aspinwall, he had written it with a clear aim in mind. It was a narrative compiled from "old chronicles, embellished, as well as I am able, by the imagination, and adapted to the romantic taste of the day—something . . . between a history and a romance."[218] His persistent difficulties in shaping the account of "Don Roderick," a similar work, had turned upon the problem of giving free expression to the imaginative and apocryphal "romance" elements of the story without sacrificing its claims as a veracious history. On March 3, 1829, he wrote to Peter, who took particular interest in "Don Roderick," that after much thought he had worked out an appropriate method of treatment.

> You will probably be disappointed in the manner in which the work will be executed. I throw out a great deal, and reduce the whole to a chronicle or legend that will take up perhaps but part of a volume. . . . The original plan would be too much like a transcript of the old chronicle by the Moor Rasis, and would probably be stigmatized as such; at the same time the material of the chronicle was too coldly extravagant and flimsy to please as romance, and could possess no merit as history. . . . A large work, therefore, resting upon such materials, would run a risk of being a literary failure. A story condensed into a short chronicle or legend, containing the most striking scenes at full length and with full effect, appears to me more likely to be successful, and may be supported by succeeding chronicles of Don Pelayo, &c., so that the entire two volumes will contain a variety, part of which shall be entirely new to the British public.

The life of Roderick the Goth had "seemed to want substance in my hand," he said, but he had now "brought it to a sound, substantial form, which I can expand, and ornament, and render attractive." Having formulated a working principle, Irving looked forward to arranging his notes for the several chronicles which would accompany "Don Roderick," "so as to have materials to work upon for some few months without the necessity of much invention or planning."[219]

On May 12, 1829, he began his memorable residence in the governor's

218. Irving to Aspinwall, Seville, April 4, 1829; STW, I, 344.
219. Irving to Peter Irving, Seville, March 3, 1829; PMI, II, 371–73.

quarters of that stately relic of Moorish civilization, the Alhambra. Peter Irving had "set his heart"[220] on his brother's completing a full history of the Moors in Spain under the pseudonym Fray Antonio Agapida, and the author himself was ready to begin. On May 30 he wrote Peter that he was "anxious before I leave to put other manuscripts in order,"[221] and within two weeks he had completed drafts of "The Legend of Don Roderick," "Legend of the Subjugation of Spain," "Legend of Count Julian and His Family," and "The Legend of Pelayo." However, his admiration for the Alhambra had stimulated in Irving a desire, as he said, "to get some writings under way connected with the place, and that shall bear the stamp of real intimacy with the charming scenes described."[222] Until his departure on July 29 to assume the secretaryship of the United States legation at London, he lived quietly, visiting with a few friends and beginning in a desultory way to prepare his "Spanish *Sketch-Book*," *The Alhambra* (1832). Optimistically, as he prepared to leave he convinced himself that his diplomatic duties need not make a serious inroad into the time he wished to devote to authorship. "My Spanish materials I can work up in England," he assured Peter, "where I can have all the necessary works, and where you will be within reach to consult with."[223]

This confident expectation was to be disappointed. Reunions with friends, the duties at the legation under the indifferent leadership of Louis McLane, the United States minister, and what he termed "the hurry and scurry, and heartless bustle of London"[224] left him little time for writing; and the time he did have was occupied by preparations for the publication of the *Companions of Columbus* and by *The Alhambra*. Early in 1831 he escaped to the home of his sister, Sarah Van Wart, and her family at Birmingham, intending to turn a few days "to advantage in a literary way." But, as he later confessed to Peter, his own mood betrayed him: "I came down prepared for the purpose, with my trunk half filled with manuscripts; but though I had every convenience and facility . . . I have been visited by one of the most inveterate fits of mental inertness that I have ever experienced. It is excessively provoking. . . ."[225] Thus, when he repacked his trunks in April, 1832, for his eagerly awaited return to the United States, among his papers were the notes and drafts of the Spanish chronicles which he had begun with such enthusiasm five years before.

220. *Ibid.*, II, 388; see also IV, 14.
221. Irving to Peter Irving, Alhambra, May 30, 1829; PMI, II, 390.
222. Irving to Peter Irving, Alhambra, June 13, 1829; PMI, II, 391.
223. Irving to Peter Irving, Alhambra, July 18, 1829; PMI, II, 399. Peter Irving was then living at Rouen.
224. Irving to Peter Irving, London, October 19, 1830; PMI, II, 437.
225. Irving to Peter Irving, Birmingham, February 3, 1831; PMI, II, 448–49.

In the three-volume *Crayon Miscellany* (1835), which he described to Peter as a deliberately varied gathering of "single volumes which would not be of sufficient importance to stand by themselves, and which would otherwise lie dormant in my trunk, as they have already done,"[226] Irving at last brought into print some of the unused Spanish material. *Legends of the Conquest of Spain,* the third number of the series, included three of the four narratives he had drafted during his stay in the Alhambra. As late as July 8, "The Legend of Pelayo" was also to form part of the volume. It had in fact been stereotyped by that date, but for some reason—quite possibly because it would have swollen *Legends* to a size that far exceeded *A Tour on the Prairies* and *Abbotsford and Newstead Abbey,* its two predecessors, "Pelayo" was at the last moment withheld.[227] In the preface to the published volume Irving explained, somewhat as he had to Peter in 1829, that in preparing its contents he had "ventured to dip more deeply into the enchanted fountains of old Spanish chronicle than has usually been done ... but ... he trusts he will illustrate more fully the character of the people and the times. He has thought proper to throw these records into the form of legends, not claiming for them the authenticity of sober history, yet giving nothing that has not historical foundation."[228] The *Legends* achieved a popular success beyond the author's expectations, and late in 1835 he set his nephew Pierre to work as a research "pioneer" for another blending of history and romance, a narrative of the Spanish conquest of Mexico. However, when Pierre decided to leave New York to make his fortune in Western real estate, Irving set aside that project. His work on the Spanish narratives was deferred once more as he completed his two major "Western" books, *Astoria* (1836) and *The Adventures of Captain Bonneville* (1837).

Irving naturally associated his unpublished Spanish chronicles with the hopeful periods of tranquil yet demanding labor in Madrid and in the Alhambra when he had first worked on them. Like the shelf of "venerable, parchment-bound tomes" he had brought home from Spain for his personal library, these manuscripts served him as "mental tonics,"[229] quickeners of his instincts for authorship. Nor could he forget his brother Peter's confidence that the chronicles were peculiarly well suited to his talents. In the fall of 1838, "feeling the want of something to arouse and exercise" his mind after "a fit of deep depression" brought

226. Irving to Peter Irving, New York, January 8, 1835; PMI, III, 65.

227. *Ibid.*, III, 74, 76.

228. "Preface," *The Crayon Miscellany, No. 3, Containing Legends of the Conquest of Spain* (Philadelphia, 1835), pp. viii–ix.

229. Irving, "Spanish Romance," in *Spanish Papers,* I, 456. This sketch was first published in the *Knickerbocker Magazine,* 14 (September, 1839), 225–31; see n. 232.

on in part by the sudden death of Peter not long before,[230] he resumed
work on the history of the conquest of Mexico. Early in December,
however, he abandoned this project upon being informed that William
H. Prescott was engaged on the identical topic.[231] Shortly afterward,
to make ends meet, he began his two years' association with the
Knickerbocker Magazine, during which period he published selections
from two of his Spanish works, "Pelayo and the Merchant's Daughter"
(January, 1840) and "Abderahman; Founder of the Dynasty of the
Ommiades in Spain" (May, 1840).[232] But when he severed his relationship with the magazine in 1841, to resume writing "in my former independent way,"[233] he had chiefly in mind preparing a collective edition
of his works and continuing to gather material for a biography of
George Washington, another project he had conceived years before.
Upon his appointment as the United States minister to Spain in 1842,
he was determined to continue work while in Madrid on those two
undertakings, especially the latter;[234] and he busily gathered together
the papers and printed volumes he thought would prove necessary.
The Spanish narratives he left untouched.

Over four years later, when he returned home from his diplomatic
mission in October, 1846, he plunged, not into writing, but into an
ambitious program of renovations and additions to "Sunnyside," his
country home. "I am growing a sad laggard in literature," he confessed
at the end of the year to Pierre, on whose advice and assistance he
had come increasingly to rely, "and need some one to bolster me up
occasionally."[235] Pierre's efforts to that end were successful, and not
long afterward Irving informed his nephew, who was then living in
New York, that the spell of literary indolence was broken. "I must tell

230. Irving to William H. Prescott, New York, January 18, 1839; PMI, III, 138.
Peter Irving, who had returned to the United States in 1836 and was living at
his brother Washington's home, died June 27, 1838.

231. For a surviving fragment of Irving's abandoned history see below, Vol. II,
pp. 339–41.

232. The following additional sketches in the *Knickerbocker Magazine* derived
from Irving's years in Spain: "Recollections of the Alhambra" (June, 1839),
"Spanish Romance" (September, 1839), "Legend of the Engulphed Convent"
(March, 1840), "Letter from Granada" (July, 1840)—see below, Vol. II, pp. 148–52,
and "Don Juan: A Spectral Research" (March, 1841). Except for "Letter from
Granada," all these articles were reprinted in *Wolfert's Roost* (1855).

233. Irving to Pierre M. Irving, [Greenburgh], April, 1840; PMI, III, 152.

234. Pierre M. Irving, who was with Irving as he considered whether to accept
the appointment, was "persuaded he would have declined it, but for a confident
belief that a diplomatic residence at Madrid need work no interruption to his
Life of Washington, the literary task upon which he had now set his heart" (PMI,
III, 176–77).

235. Irving to Pierre M. Irving, [Sunnyside, December 31], 1846; PMI, III,
396–97.

you," he wrote with satisfaction, "that I have lately been working up some old stuff which had lain for years lumbering like rubbish in one of my trunks, and which, I trust, will more than pay the expense of my new building."[236] Irving had refreshed his creative faculties by returning to his "mental tonics," the chronicles of early Spain.

Pierre, who was thoroughly devoted to his uncle's interests and ordinarily a paragon of tact, was anxious at this time to see Irving at work revising his earlier publications. As Irving's attorney and financial adviser, he had received generous offers from various publishers to sponsor a collected edition of the revised works, and he knew that the time was ripe for the author to win permanent financial security by striking a good bargain for the edition. "You lost the Conquest of Mexico by not acting upon the motto of *Carpe diem*," he warned in reply to his uncle's note, "and I am a little afraid you may let slip the present opportunity." This advice produced an explanation in which, adopting a tone of patient forbearance, Irving summarized the inception and interrupted progress of the project which, "somehow or other," he had allowed to "grow cool":

> I am apt to get out of conceit of anything I do; and I suffered the manuscript of these Chronicles to lie in my trunks like waste paper. About four or five weeks since, I was tired, one day, of muddling over my printed works, and yet wanted occupation. I don't know how the idea of one of these chronicles came into my head. It was the Chronicle of Count Fernan Gonzalez, one of the early Counts of Castile.... I took it up, was amused with it, and found I had hit the right vein in my management of it. I went to work and rewrote it, and got so in the spirit of the thing, that I went to work, *con amore*, at two or three fragmentary Chronicles, filling up the chasms, rewriting parts. In a word, I have now complete, though not thoroughly finished off, The Chronicle of Pelayo; The Chronicle of Count Fernan Gonzalez; the Chronicle of the Dynasty of the Ommiades in Spain ... also the Chronicle of Fernando the Saint, with the reconquest of Seville. I may add others to the series; but if I do not, these, with additions, illustrations, &c., will make a couple of volumes; and I feel confident that I can make the work a taking one—giving a picture of Spain at various periods of the Moorish domination, and giving illustrations of the places of noted events, from what I myself have seen in my rambles about Spain. Some parts of these Chronicles run into a quiet, drolling vein, especially in treating of miracles and miraculous events; on which occasions Fray Antonio Agapida comes to my assistance,

236. Irving to Pierre M. Irving, [Sunnyside, early April], 1847; PMI, III, 402.

with his zeal for the faith, and his pious hatred of the infidels. You see, all this has cost me but a very few weeks of amusing occupation, and has put me quite in heart again, as well as in literary vein. The poring over my published works was rather muddling me, and making me feel as if the true literary vein was extinct. I think, therefore, you will agree with me that my time for the last five weeks has been well employed.[237]

Irving had abandoned the plan of a full history of early Spain in favor of a less pretending "picture . . . at various periods," but he had performed his task with the same concentration and quiet satisfaction the legends had previously inspired in him.

Unfortunately, before Pierre received his uncle's firm self-vindication he decided to write him a second note, urging a speedy return to the back works. Having learned from a relative who had been staying with Irving that he was engaged on his "old Moorish Chronicles," Pierre selected the term "skimmings" to denote the very compositions in which his uncle took such pride. He had an "agreeable though indistinct" recollection of those "skimmings," he blandly wrote, but felt that the reading public was impatient for something a bit more substantial. "Make all haste with the preparation of your uniform edition," he counseled, "and then to work to complete your Life of Washington, and take your ease forever after." In this letter Pierre had formulated Irving's long-term wishes almost to a tee, but the manner in which he did so was soon to cause him consternation.

The next day Irving replied, roundly informing his nephew that he "could know nothing of the work":

> The whole may be mere "skimmings," but they pleased me in the preparation; they were written when I was in the vein, and that is the only guide I go by in my writings, or which has led me to success. Besides, I write for pleasure as well as profit; and the pleasure I have recently enjoyed in the recurrence, after so long an interval, of my old literary vein, has been so great, that I am content to forego any loss of profit it may occasion me by a slight postponement of the republication of my old works. . . .
>
> However, I'll say no more on the subject, but another time will ride my hobby privately, without saying a word to anybody.[238]

Once he discovered what had happened (Irving's first letter arrived in New York two days after the one just quoted), Pierre sought as best he could to recant, but to no practical purpose. The misunderstanding had

237. PMI, IV, 14–15; Irving's letter was dated April 14.
238. PMI, IV, 16–17. Pierre wrote his second note on April 14; Irving replied to it the next day.

disconcerted Irving, and he could not be persuaded to resume work on the manuscripts. Instead, he returned fitfully to the uninspiring yet prospectively remunerative task of "muddling" over his back works.

With Pierre's assistance in drafting an agreement, in July, 1848, Irving authorized George P. Putnam to begin publishing the Author's Revised Edition of the collected works; and thus he began the more than two years of labor necessary to make good his side of the bargain. To divert himself during this period he prepared thorough revisions of works on two topics he found especially attractive, a life of Goldsmith he had prepared in 1842 for Harper's Family Library, and a life of Mahomet he had submitted to John Murray in 1831 but which that publisher had refused. Yet he failed to derive the satisfaction he had anticipated from rewriting the biographies. As he told Pierre of the *Goldsmith* (1849), he "had no time to finish it off as he wished."[239] Perhaps to ensure that the special appeal of his Spanish narratives should be spared from adulteration by this habit of hurry, Irving omitted *Legends of the Conquest of Spain* from the revised edition. He planned at some indefinite date to reprint them, together with the manuscripts that had engaged his attention in 1847, in a separate publication.[240]

Once he had at last fulfilled his obligation to George Putnam, Irving turned to the work which he had come over the years to envision as "the crowning effort" of his career, *The Life of George Washington*.[241] In 1854 he secured the full-time assistance of Pierre, and thereafter he devoted himself single-mindedly to that "long task."[242] He made steady progress, but the protracted strain of his efforts exacted a heavy toll. In October, 1858, then at work on the fifth and final volume, he confided to Pierre the fear that he "might have injured himself seriously" by his devotion to the *Washington*, "that the pitcher might have gone once too often to the well."[243] He completed the biography in February, 1859, and by then, afflicted with asthma and extreme nervousness, and suffering from an enlarged heart, he knew that the surmise had been accurate. On April 3, his seventy-sixth birthday, he called Pierre into his study and showed him the still unpublished Spanish chronicles. Pierre did not record the substance of their conversation,[244] but there can be

239. PMI, IV, 53. Pierre is apparently reporting Irving's conversation from notes taken at the time.

240. PMI, III, 76.

241. "Preface," *The Life of George Washington*, V, [iii].

242. Irving to Sarah Storrow, Sunnyside, January 13, 1852; PMI, IV, 102.

243. PMI, IV, 255. Pierre is reporting his uncle's conversation on the basis of notes taken at the time.

244. His summary account of it in PMI, IV, 278, is virtually identical to the entry in his private journal for 1859, p. [21] (Berg Collection, New York Public Library).

little doubt that Irving expressed or strongly implied to his literary executor and delegated biographer his wish that the works might eventually
appear in print, should he not live to publish them.

Pierre's initial duties after Irving's death on November 28, 1859, were
as executor of his late uncle's estate and as the author of the four-volume
Life and Letters; but from the first he intended, in accordance with the
author's wishes, to edit a collection of the miscellaneous writings which
would include the *Legends of the Conquest of Spain* and those which
in 1847 had been left "complete, though not thoroughly finished off."
Soon after publication of the second volume of the biography, in which
he had alluded to the Spanish narratives begun in 1827, in October,
1862, Pierre received from Henry Coppée, afterward himself a historian
of Spain,[245] a request for further information about the "valuable materials" Irving had "amassed" at that time. In his reply, Pierre assured
Coppée that his uncle's preparations for a series of chronicles which
would interlink *Legends of the Conquest of Spain, Mahomet and His
Successors*, and the *Granada* and so form "a wild and varied, but compact
and complete department of history," were "altogether fragmentary."
He planned, he added, "eventually to publish . . . such of the intermediate
chronicles as received from him something approaching to a final
handling."[246]

The works selected by Pierre for posthumous publication in *Spanish
Papers* (1866)—"The Legend of Pelayo," "Abderahman: Founder of the
Dynasty of the Ommiades in Spain," "Chronicle of Fernan Gonzalez,
Count of Castile," and "Chronicle of Fernando the Saint"—had been
subjected by Irving to varying degrees of revision,[247] but they did represent nearly all the material he had brought near to completion. Pierre
intended to include a fairly substantial portion of the fragmentary
"Chronicle of the Ommiades" and even transcribed as printer's copy the
passages in Irving's manuscript which had been so extensively revised
as to be almost illegible. However, probably owing to limitations of
space, he was unable to include more than the first three chapters,
which had been revised from the account of Abderahman in the *Knickerbocker Magazine*.[248] In a terse preface to these narratives, Pierre ex-

245. Coppée (1821–1895) was the author of *A History of the Conquest of Spain
by the Arab Moors*, 2 vols. (1881); the work was first published in 1873 in *The
Penn Monthly*.

246. Pierre M. Irving to Rev. H. Coppée, Irvington, October 20, 1862 (Historical Society of Pennsylvania).

247. The stages through which these works passed during Irving's lifetime, and
the manner in which they were prepared by Pierre for publication in *Spanish
Papers*, are described in the Textual Commentary.

248. For an account of Pierre's careful study of the "Ommiades" manuscript,
see the Textual Commentary for that work.

plained that he had chosen them "because they bore the impress of being most nearly, though not fully, prepared for the press, and because they had for [Irving] a special fascination, arising in part, perhaps, from his long residence" in Spain.[249] With tact and intelligent respect for his late uncle's wishes, Pierre thus brought partially to fruition a project which Irving had conceived almost four decades before.

The Spanish legends and chronicles included in the present edition of Irving's miscellaneous writings represent a selection only slightly larger than what Pierre M. Irving published in *Spanish Papers*. The texts of "The Chronicle of Pelayo," "Chronicle of Fernan Gonzalez, Count of Castile," and the "Chronicle of Fernando the Saint" are derived almost entirely from the identical manuscripts which served as printer's copy for the original collection.[250] The portion of the "Chronicle of the Ommiades" included here, comprising the reigns of Abderahman, Hixem, and Alhakem, the first three monarchs in that dynasty, duplicates the one Pierre intended to publish before he was obliged to omit most of it; however, the text is derived from Irving's own surviving manuscripts rather than from his nephew's transcriptions (which are also extant). "The Successors of Pelayo: Favila," previously unpublished, is an apparently representative example of the brief accounts Irving thought of employing to link up the more extended narratives in his selective survey of early Spanish and Moorish history. Taken together, these works afford us a reasonably clear notion of the series of historico-legendary "chronicles" Irving might have produced, had he lived to realize his aim.

OTHER PROSE WRITINGS LEFT UNPUBLISHED AT IRVING'S DEATH

Washington Irving's habits as an author were throughout his career somewhat erratic. In creative periods, as during his residence in Madrid in 1827–1828, he devoted a large proportion of his energy to the tasks of research, composition, and revision. At other times, as in the three years following his return to the United States in 1832, his attention to literary affairs was minimal. As the years passed Irving gradually accumulated a substantial backlog of manuscript material—research notes, early drafts, and miscellaneous jottings—which he had set aside but intended at some time to prepare for publication. Yet, owing both to fortuitous circumstances and to his own shrewd prudence in managing

---

249. "Preface by the Editor," in *Spanish Papers*, I, iv.

250. For a few brief passages where Irving's manuscripts have been lost, it is necessary to supply the missing text from the corresponding passages in *Spanish Papers*, for which publication Irving's own manuscripts served as printer's copy. The points at which this recourse to the posthumous text is necessary are specified in the Textual Commentary.

his literary resources, he managed during his lifetime to complete all but one of the major undertakings thus deferred. The exception, of course, was his suite of narratives portraying scenes in the early history of Spain, selections from which were included by Pierre M. Irving in the posthumous collection of fugitive writings, *Spanish Papers and Other Miscellanies, Hitherto Unpublished or Uncollected*.[251]

In his later years Irving found a variety of convenient outlets for his miscellaneous prose writings. For example, as a contributor to the *Knickerbocker Magazine* (1839–1841) he drew upon his notebooks, his early drafts, and on occasion even his correspondence in order to supply monthly copy; and in preparing the Author's Revised Edition of his works (1848–1850) he enriched some of the volumes—notably *The Sketch-Book* and *The Alhambra*—by incorporating in them material long on hand but withheld from earlier editions. Moreover, in 1855 he fashioned a popular volume, *Wolfert's Roost*, out of miscellaneous items which had previously appeared in print. Thereafter he intended to bring out still another collection of reprinted works, which would have included many of those in the present volumes; but according to Pierre M. Irving his preparations for the purpose were "slight."[252]

As his uncle's delegated biographer and literary executor, Pierre M. Irving was in an ideal position to bring to fruition Irving's unfulfilled wishes for that final miscellany. He had access to all Irving's papers, and he was probably as familiar as anyone before or since with the extent and variety of his complete writings. However, as the editor of *Spanish Papers* Pierre did not attempt to provide an exhaustive compilation of the previously uncollected works. In compliance with Irving's own wishes, and probably also in the belief that the author's memory would not be well served by an aggregation of often unrelated fragments,[253] he omitted from *Spanish Papers* several of the completed prose writings, both published and unpublished.

In accordance with the general purpose of the present edition of Irving's *Complete Works*—to make available for study as full a record of the author's literary achievements as possible—this final section of the *Miscellaneous Writings* brings together a group of writings which he completed but apparently did not publish during his lifetime.[254] The

---

251. A somewhat fuller selection from the medley of Spanish narratives than Pierre M. Irving included in *Spanish Papers* forms the contents of part 5 in the present work, Vol. II, pp. [179]–328.

252. "Preface by the Editor," in *Spanish Papers*, I, [iii].

253. See *Spanish Papers*, I, [10]; Pierre M. Irving to the Reverend Henry Coppée, New York, October 20, 1862 (Historical Society of Pennsylvania).

254. Irving's essay on Sir David Wilkie in Spain apparently was published during the author's lifetime, but according to his own testimony it appeared in a garbled Spanish translation of the English original; see below, pp. xxxix–xc.

gathering includes selections diverse in content, some fragmentary and others surviving in full, whose probable dates of original composition are scattered within the period 1820–1851.

"My Uncle," the text of which untitled work survives in a manuscript owned by Yale University, is probably the earliest in the collection. A few possibly autobiographical details have been pointed out,[255] but it seems clear nonetheless that the narrator of the piece is not Irving himself but a fictional character, an Englishman, giving an account of a relation he knew when a child in the ancestral residence he terms "the Hall." Irving's published writings include the portrayal of no character who resembles the uncle described here, but the sketch does include several details whose similarities to features of his works published between 1820 and 1824 suggest that it was composed within that period.

In the sections of *The Sketch-Book* (1820) describing Geoffrey Crayon's Christmas visit to the rural home of his friend Frank Bracebridge, the latter is represented as providing his guest with information distinctly similar to some of the material in "My Uncle."[256] However, the primary focus of this group of sketches is the Bracebridges' traditional Christmas celebration, and Frank Bracebridge does not dwell upon any of his relations—such as a deceased uncle—who are absent from the annual family gathering. *Bracebridge Hall* (1822), wherein Irving portrays at much greater length a subsequent visit by Geoffrey Crayon to the Hall, would seem to provide a more likely frame for "My Uncle." Early in the work, for example, Crayon notices with interest "long rows of portraits" hanging in the family home, thus suggesting the possibility of some further account of the personages represented therein.[257] Yet subsequent chapters in *Bracebridge Hall* include no capsule biographies of characters not on the scene; nor, indeed, is Frank Bracebridge ever once quoted at length in the manner of the unpublished sketch. Similarities may also be noted between "My Uncle" and the extended first-person narrative entitled "Buckthorne" in *Tales of a Traveller* (1824). Both works, for example, portray the literary world of London, with attention to its caste system and its hungry tribe of "poor-devil authors."[258]

---

255. See Barbara D. Simison, ed., "Washington Irving's 'My Uncle,'" *Yale University Library Gazette*, 38 (October, 1963), 86, and nn. 2, 5, 10, 12.

256. See especially, in "Christmas Eve" and "Christmas Day," the brief "history" of his eccentric relation Master Simon, the recollections of his boyhood at the Hall, and the characterization of his father, the Squire.

257. The portraits are described in "Family Relics." The emphasis upon childish superstitions in "My Uncle" finds several rough counterparts in *Bracebridge Hall*. See especially "St. Mark's Eve," "Gypsies," and "Popular Superstitions."

258. See also in *Tales of a Traveller* the articles entitled "A Literary Dinner" and "The Poor-Devil Author."

Taken together, the varied suggestions of continuity between "My Uncle" and passages in *The Sketch-Book, Bracebridge Hall,* and *Tales of a Traveller* indicate that an account of a gentle, eccentric relative whom the narrator had known in childhood, who had been a favorite of the family, and who had dabbled in literature might well have been in Irving's mind as a possible theme between 1820 and 1824. "My Uncle," which textual evidence reveals to be a fragment of a longer work,[259] seems most probably a passage which, though drafted and revised with care, was for some reason rejected from *Bracebridge Hall.*

Unlike the foregoing piece, Irving's essay on Sir David Wilkie in Spain is readily identifiable as to its purpose and approximate date of origin. While living in Madrid during the winter of 1827–1828 the author was a frequent companion of Wilkie, who was then immersed in study of the great Spanish painters and in experiments with his own painting while under the influence of their distinctive style.[260] The following spring, at the close of a tour southward through Spain, Irving chanced to meet Wilkie once again in Seville. On April 15, expressing to Alexander H. Everett his pleasure at the event, he added that "I . . . promise myself much gratification in visiting the masterpieces of Murillo in company with him."[261] Over the next few days this anticipation was fully realized as he and Wilkie toured together the chapels, monasteries, and private collections of the city.[262]

A full year later, after Wilkie had returned to England and won enthusiastic recognition of the paintings he had completed while abroad, Irving informed him that he had "scribbled an article for a newspaper at Seville, on the subject of your visit to Spain." It "was hastily done," he wrote on May 15, 1829, "and some blunders were made by the editor in translating it: altering here & there the force and the exact meaning of my expressions. I thought it would have a good effect in awakening

259. See the Textual Commentary to "My Uncle," Vol. II, pp. 513–14.

260. See Leslie, *Autobiographical Recollections,* p. 279; Andrew B. Myers, ed., "Washington Irving's Madrid Journal 1827–1828 and Related Letters," *Bulletin of the New York Public Library,* 62 (July, 1958), 407–16.

261. PMI, II, 309; see also Irving to Henry Brevoort, Jr., Madrid, February 23, 1828, in *ibid.,* II, 283.

262. See *Washington Irving Diary Spain 1828–1829,* ed. Clara L. Penney (New York, 1926), pp. 9–14; PMI, II, 314–15. Shortly after the death of Wilkie in 1841, Viscount Mahon recalled thus the friendship of the late artist and Irving while together in Spain: "I saw two men of such great, yet such different genius, employed in the observance and delineation of that most beautiful and most interesting country; the one with a keen eye to discern, and a powerful pen to describe, all the traits of national manners; the other ever and anon stopping amid some lovely landscape to consider how he might best transfer its beauties and its tints to his own as glowing but more permanent canvas" ("Appendix C. Wilkie Statue," in Allan Cunningham, *The Life of Sir David Wilkie* [London, 1843], III, 521).

kind feelings not merely towards yourself, but towards British artists
& amateurs in general."[263] The Seville newspaper in which the translated text of Irving's account appeared has not yet been identified; but
it is virtually certain that a manuscript owned by Yale University includes the original English text from which the garbled Spanish version
was made. In subject matter and apparent intention the manuscript
essay conforms neatly to Irving's description of the published article.
Thus, even though the dating of the manuscript remains in some doubt,
with April, 1828, and May, 1829, the extreme limits of possibility, it
seems clear that the version included here represents the author's wishes
for the English text of the essay.

Owing to a want of evidence, the date and circumstances under
which Irving composed "The Village Curate," the manuscript of which
is owned by Washington University, must remain conjectural. However,
as an account of an incident in rural Spain, introduced by general comments on the "Spanish peasantry," the tale seems quite possibly one of
the several which, as he later testified, Irving was obliged to set aside
from the first edition of The Alhambra (1832).[264] That the work was
written prior to 1832 with an eye to including it in The Alhambra,
rather than at a later date for the expanded Author's Revised Edition
of that work (1850), seems clear from the handwriting in the manuscript,
which is free from the abrupt and nervous slurring of the elderly Irving's
hand. Moreover, as an anecdote only generally localized, in "a lonely
part of the country at some distance from Seville," the tale is appropriate
to the 1832 edition wherein Irving does not confine himself to sketches
and legends associated specifically with the Alhambra and its immediate
neighborhood, as he does in the Author's Revised Edition. The same
variance of intention might furthermore account for the omission of the
tale from the revised version, as being no longer harmonious with the
author's aims. Tentatively, therefore, "The Village Curate" may be
dated at some time prior to the spring of 1832, when Irving gave his
last hurried attentions to The Alhambra as he made preparations for
his return to the United States.

"The Log House Hotel," which survives in manuscript form at Washington University, is a sketch based upon an incident in the author's
extended tour of the West in the fall of 1832. On September 16, the
second day of their journey southwestward from St. Louis to the U.S.
Army post at Fort Gibson, where they arrived on October 8, Irving's

---

263. Irving to David Wilkie, Alhambra–Granada, May 15, 1829 (Sleepy Hollow
Restorations).

264. See below, pp. xciv–xcv.

party stopped for dinner at a small house on the Boon's Lick Road.[265] Irving did not record his impressions of this scene in the extant journals he compiled during the tour, but his companion Charles J. Latrobe wrote a brief account of it in his own journal; and at the appropriate point in *The Rambler in North America* (1835), a two-volume work describing his travels, he introduces a more detailed portrayal of such a western farm.[266] That the "hotel" in Irving's sketch is identical with the one described by Latrobe in his journal and in *The Rambler in North America* is evident from the numerous details common to the three texts. The date on which he composed "The Log House Hotel" is uncertain, but a fragment of a letter on the reverse side of one of its pages— "Washington. Jan. 18th, 1833 / Gentlemen, / It is with"—affords at least a general indication.

A Tour on the Prairies (1835), the major literary fruit of Irving's Western journey, is a narrative of events which occurred several weeks after the one portrayed in "The Log House Hotel." Unless his plans for *A Tour* underwent considerable revision—and the known facts of the work's genesis give no such indication—his comic sketch of the earlier experience was never intended to form a part of that volume. Perhaps, like "The Creole Village," another product of the Western tour,[267] "The Log House Hotel" was intended to stand by itself as a contribution to a magazine or gift-book. But if so, a suitable occasion for its publication apparently never arose.

As we have seen, the inception of Irving's work on a history of the Spanish conquest of Mexico was in 1827; but as he once told Pierre M. Irving, the splendid topic of Cortez's exploits in the New World had

---

265. A map of Irving's route on his Western tour following the departure from St. Louis is in *The Western Journals of Washington Irving*, ed. John F. McDermott (1944; reprint Norman, Okla., 1966), opposite p. 176.

266. The pertinent passage from Latrobe's diary, given by John F. McDermott in "An Unpublished Washington Irving Manuscript," *Papers in English Language and Literature*, 1 (Autumn, 1965), 370, follows: "the pretty family—the negro caterer for our dinners—which are chased for a good quarter of an hour before killed—the negro—his style, appearce & Conversation, his hope & aspirations after pleasure in manumission." See also Latrobe, *The Rambler in North America, MDCCCXXXII–MDCCCXXXIII* (London, 1835), I, 121–23; the published passage is given by McDermott, pp. 370–71, from the second edition of 1836. Other published accounts of the Western journey written by Irving's companions include Henry L. Ellsworth, *Washington Irving on the Prairie or A Narrative of a Tour of the Southwest in the Year 1832*, ed. Stanley T. Williams and Barbara D. Simison (New York, 1937), and *On the Western Tour with Washington Irving: The Journal and Letters of Count de Pourtalés*, ed. George F. Spaulding, trans. Seymour Feiler (Norman, Okla., 1968).

267. "The Creole Village. A Sketch from a Steamboat," in *The Magnolia for 1837* (New York, [1836]), pp. 315–26. This sketch was reprinted in *Wolfert's Roost* (New York, 1855), pp. 38–48.

excited his imagination since childhood.[268] On December 12, 1827, he noted in his journal that he had written "all day on Friar Sahaguns conquest of Mexico"; and for several days thereafter, he noted further attentions to a work he called "Montezuma."[269] Probably these studies consisted of digesting facts and copying important passages from source material—research duties he customarily performed in the early stages of work on his historical writings. The following year, then at Seville, he apparently performed further preliminary research. On October 21, 1828, he recorded reading in Don Antonio de Solis' *Historia de la Conquista de Mexico* (1771), and the next day he began his journal entry "Write at Mexican story"[270]—suggesting both that he was drawing upon Solis, and possibly also that the conception of the Spanish conquest was beginning to take shape in his mind as a narrative. Nevertheless, from this date the projected history lay untouched until December, 1835, when he enlisted his nephew Pierre, who had just completed duties as a research assistant gathering materials for *Astoria* (1836), to undertake a similar "pioneering" task for the conquest of Mexico. For a few weeks Pierre complied with his uncle's wishes; but in February, 1836, he left New York for Toledo, Ohio. Irving was too busy to take up the project himself, and so it was again postponed.

In the fall of 1838, "fearing that, if I waited to collect materials, I should never take hold of the theme," Irving at last set to work in earnest on his history. Having refamiliarized himself with the standard published accounts, "and kindled myself into a heat by exercise of drafting the story,"[271] for three months he worked almost daily on his new book. By December he had completed a rough draft of the first volume when, busy one day in the New York Society Library, he was informed by the librarian, his friend Joseph Green Cogswell, that William H. Prescott was then occupied on the identical topic. Prescott, who had recently won recognition with his three-volume *History of the Reign of Ferdinand and Isabella the Catholic* (1838), had long been a frank admirer of

268. Irving to Pierre M. Irving, Madrid, March 24, 1844; PMI, III, 143, See also above, p. lxxvi.

269. Myers, "Irving's Madrid Journals," pp. 410–11. In his first day's work, with Fray Bernardino de Sahagún's monumental manuscript account, *Historia general de las cosas de Nueva España,* Irving may have fashioned a part of the 86-page translation and adaptation from Sahagún's text which survives in the Manuscript Division, New York Public Library. For further commentary on these holograph research notes, see Myers, "Irving's Madrid Journals," p. 417, n. 100. Irving also reported to William H. Prescott in 1839 that while in Madrid he "had a few chapters of Padre Sahagun copied out for me, relating merely to some points of the Spanish invasion" (PMI, III, 139).

270. Penney, *Washington Irving Diary,* p. 75.

271. Irving to William H. Prescott, New York, January 18, 1839; PMI, III, 138.

Irving's Spanish histories.[272] He hoped as his next project to write a narrative of the conquest of Mexico, but he was unwilling to take the field against Irving should the more popular author have laid claim to the subject. He had thus prevailed upon Cogswell to sound Irving upon what work he was then engaged.

Irving was distressed at the unexpected information given him by the librarian; yet immediately, and in a manner so gracious that it became legendary even during his lifetime, he relinquished his claim to the theme of the conquest. He asked Cogswell to convey his good wishes to Prescott, volunteering to the latter whatever assistance he might be able to offer as the result of his researches in Spain. And thus, by a single courtly gesture, he abandoned a long-deferred undertaking which in recent months had aroused in him the "vein" of literary enthusiasm—"the first," he confessed to his sister Sarah, "I had had for a long time."[273] Pierre M. Irving recalled in the *Life and Letters* that, on the same day when Irving had first informed him of the decisive conversation with Cogswell, "he mentioned . . . that he had been looking over some papers in the morning, and had come across his commencement of the Conquest of Mexico; that he read over what he had written, and, in a fit of vexation at having lost the magnificent theme, destroyed the manuscript."[274]

Such a conclusion to the affair seems fitting in light of Irving's frustrated regret at being displaced by Prescott, and there is no reason to doubt either his testimony to his nephew or Pierre's intended veracity in recounting it. Nevertheless, in 1915, a passage which purported to be a fragment of the abandoned history was published by Joseph F. Taylor, together with a facsimile manuscript page, in Irving's hand, which corresponded to a portion of the printed text.[275] The passage thus presented is a condensed, recast translation of part of a chapter in Solis' *Historia*, describing one of the mysterious omens observed by the Aztecs as signifying the imminence of a conquering army which would lay waste their grand yet corrupt civilization.[276] The present whereabouts of the original

---

272. See, for example, *The Papers of William Hickling Prescott*, ed. C. Harvey Gardiner (Urbana, 1964), p. 67; *The Correspondence of William H. Prescott, 1833–1847*, ed. Roger Walcott (Boston, 1925), pp. 48, 204; and "Irving's Conquest of Granada," in Prescott's *Biographies and Critical Miscellanies* (New York, 1845), pp. 88–122.

273. Irving to Mrs. Sarah Van Wart, [Greenburgh], December 1, 1838; PMI, III, 132. The fullest accounts of Irving's abandonment of his history are in *ibid.*, III, 133–34, 143; George Ticknor, *Life of William Hickling Prescott* (Boston, 1864), pp. 166–73; STW, II, 104–6.

274. PMI, III, 134.

275. Joseph F. Taylor, "Washington Irving's Mexico: A Lost Fragment," *The Bookman*, 41 (1915), 665–69.

276. See the Textual Commentary to "[History of the Conquest of Mexico]," Vol. II, pp. 518–19.

manuscript is unknown, but the facsimile page provided by Taylor is drafted and revised with sufficient care to make it clear that Irving's text was not casually written. Whether or not he actually intended it to form part of his own history,[277] the text first published in 1915 is the sole specimen extant in any form which *may* be a fragment of that work.

In his preface to the Author's Revised Edition of *The Alhambra*, Irving wrote that several of the papers he had "roughly sketched out" while a resident of the Alhambra, in the spring of 1829, were "thrown aside as incomplete" three years later, when he hurriedly assembled the contents of the first edition. "In the present edition," he went on, "I have revised and re-arranged the whole work, enlarged some parts, and added others, including the papers originally omitted."[278] The "Legend of Prince Ahmed el Kamel; or the Pilgrim of Love," which first appeared in the Author's Revised Edition, was thus one of the papers excluded in 1832, or else it was composed specifically for the expanded edition of 1850. In view of the tale's considerable length and of Irving's exhaustion at the time he was revising *The Alhambra*, the former possibility seems by far the more likely. However, on the basis of textual evidence the "Illustration to the Legend of Prince Ahmed" included in the present collection, and obviously intended to serve as a pendant to the legend, appears to derive from the period when the Author's Revised Edition was being prepared.[279] The handwriting in the manuscript text, owned by Princeton University, is hasty, angular, nervous, and slurred—generally characteristic of the later period. Moreover, while Irving might not have wished to compose from the beginning a work of such length as the "Legend of Prince Ahmed," he could well have been content to do so for the much briefer "Illustration," which is little more than a condensed adaptation of a chapter in George Sale's translation of *The Koran*. The reasons why he decided to omit it from the enlarged *Alhambra* remain in doubt. Possibly he realized that, as rearranged and expanded,

277. That Irving did intend to include in his history some account of the mysterious omens observed among the Aztecs at the time of the Spanish invasion is suggested by four pages of holograph notes owned by the University of Virginia, entitled "Mexican Portents" and including information summarized from Antonio de Herrera y Tordesillas, *Historia General de los Castellanos* (1601). Also owned by the University of Virginia are seven pages of notes, numbered 98–104, which describe events during the conquest of Mexico.

278. "Preface to the Revised Edition," *The Alhambra* (New York, 1850), pp. [vii]–viii.

279. On the other hand, Howard C. Horsford takes the "Illustration" to be one of the works Irving describes in the Author's Revised Edition as having been "roughly sketched out" years before; Horsford specifies 1826–1832 as the likely range of dates. See his "'Illustration to the Legend of Prince Ahmed': An Unpublished Sketch by Washington Irving," *Princeton University Library Chronicle*, 14 (1952–1953), 30–31.

the volume had swollen to so great a length that some of its contents must once again be withheld.

Irving's two accounts of youthful journeys in remote regions of New York State, unpublished during his lifetime, were included by Pierre M. Irving in the *Life and Letters*; the manuscripts of both works are now lost. According to Pierre, the recollections of a voyage up the Hudson River in 1800 formed part of an "unfinished article" the author began in June, 1851, intending it for publication in *The Home Book of the Picturesque* (1852 [1851]), but then threw aside in favor of "The Catskill Mountains," which eventually appeared as his contribution to the volume.[280] Comparison of the passage published in the *Life and Letters* with "The Catskill Mountains" reveals that in slightly revised form several sentences in the earlier text made their way into the autobiographical sections of the essay to which it gave place.[281] Especially noteworthy is the shared tone of nostalgia for what, in the rejected fragment, Irving recalls as "the good old times."

The narrative of a journey in 1814 from Utica to Sackett's Harbor, on Lake Ontario, recounts part of an incident in Irving's brief military career, as aide-de-camp to Daniel D. Tompkins, the governor of New York and commander in chief of the state militia.[282] Upon his arrival in Albany from New York in September, "Colonel Irving" heard rumors that Sackett's Harbor was threatened with a British attack both by land and by water. Eager to be on the scene, he requested of Tompkins some mission to the lines and was accordingly sent there, with discretionary powers to order out more militia should that prove necessary. The passage reproduced in the *Life and Letters* describes the latter portion of his journey to the place of anticipated conflict, where, as it happened, the British attack failed to materialize. The account is of interest as including a *tour de force* of landscape description, a verbal panorama which evokes the benign grandeur of the wilderness scene perhaps as effectively as any other among Irving's writings.

That Pierre M. Irving should have published in the delegated *Life and Letters* his uncle's recollections of the youthful journeys in 1800 and 1814 has a distinct appropriateness. Both pieces, the former certainly and the latter evidently productions of Irving's later years, are in their autobiographical nature characteristic of his miscellaneous writings of that period. Having achieved the status almost of a legendary figure, and recognizing the keen public curiosity about his life history, from time

280. PMI, I, 40. For "The Catskill Mountains," see below, Vol. II, pp. 163–67.

281. See the Textual Commentary to "[A Voyage up the Hudson River in 1800]," Vol. II, p. 521.

282. According to Pierre M. Irving, the manuscript pages on which Irving wrote his account "evidently form pages of an article, which he had prepared for the press" (PMI, I, 316).

to time during the 1850's he sketched in for publication a few scattered scenes from his own early career.[283] He would thus have thought it fitting that the two fragmentary sketches should prove useful to his nephew in fashioning a full biography. In this way, as in many others, he helped make it possible for Pierre to compile in the *Life and Letters* a work wherein, as Pierre put it, "the author, in every stage of his career, [was] as far as possible, his own biographer."[284]

283. See Introduction, pp. lxxi–lxxiii.
284. "Preface," PMI, I, 6.

EARLY PROSE WRITINGS
1803-1815

[CONTRIBUTIONS TO THE
NEW YORK *MORNING CHRONICLE*]

TO MR. ANDREW QUOZ

Dear Sir,

The lively interest you appeared to take in Dramatic concerns, last winter, and your friendly vindication of the "Rights of Actors" encourages me to presume, that a brief account of the manner in which your theatric friends passed the summer, would not be unacceptable.

Feeling, in common with my professional brethren, a high sense of the obligations we are under, to you, I have thought it "writ down in my duty," to furnish you, from the pages of my Journal, with a slight sketch of our unfortunate manoeuvres.

Having been disconcerted in our plans, and driven out of our nest, at Mount Vernon Garden, by the Epidemic; we called together a meeting of several of the company, to determine which way we should direct our movements.

Emboldened by the approbation bestowed upon us, in the provincial town of New-York; we determined to repair to the METROPOLIS of the State, though not without great apprehensions of ill-success, in a place that was no doubt the standard of taste and refinement.

Having among our acquaintance, several *Gentlemen of the Law*, whom we were apprehensive might *arrest* us in our departure, and detain us in town with their *friendly importunities*, we determined to retreat without ceremony in the *cool* of the Evening, and happily succeeded in the attempt.

We now looked forward with impatience, anticipating the attention and curiosity we should attract on our arrival in Albany—Albany! the very name had music in our ears, that seat of opulence and splendor, of elegance and hospitality; there the Muses have fixed their abode! There the Arts and Sciences are encouraged, and there the man of genius receives the reward of his labours.

Such, Mr. Quoz, were the fond ideas that floated in our imaginations! We looked forward to a golden harvest, when our temples should be bound with bays, and our pockets lined with the gifts of Albanian munificence. How can I describe our emotions when the majestic domes and tin steeples of the metropolis slowly rose to view from the bosom of the

Hudson. Each breast swelled with joyous expectation, the tear of extacy trembled in every eye.

We found the city spacious and elegant, the people smiling, courteous and hospitable. An old assembly room was chosen for our exhibitions, and we immediately went to work to prepare the stage and scenery. From the limited state of our funds, we were obliged to make shift with few scenes. One therefore, sufficed for parlor, kitchen and hall; another for grove or garden, forest or street; a white sheet represented the sea, and a dark blue baize curtain hung with red cloaks, the infernal regions. These I must confess were rather meagre contrivances, but to make up for the deficiency, we carried with us a ball of a twelve pounder, and as rosin was cheap we could afford to give them plenty of thunder and lightning!

Thus, Mr. Quoz, did we make shift to get every thing arranged; our prospect of success was truly flattering—during our preparations the Citizens were continually running in and out, and appeared to be very curious about our proceedings; generous patrons, thought we, how impatient must you be for the time when you may flock to the theatre and reward our talents and ingenuity!

The important night big with our fate arrived, we made a striking display of the riches of our wardrobe; as I had to act the part of a Lover, I was arrayed in superior style, having on a sky colored silk coat, red jacket, green small clothes, and shoes decorated with large plated buckles; understanding that the Albanians were of Dutch extraction, I made my *debut* in a deliberate manner smoking a tobacco pipe.

I own, I felt a little aukward in my dress, having never acted the fine gentleman before, but I am since told, that I acquitted myself extremely well, except that I turned in my toes, and was rather stiff in the joints.

My fellow performers were tricked out in equal splendor with myself, and the lady to whom I was to urge my tender suit appeared in all the loveliness of red ribbons and brocade. The candles were close snuffed, the fiddle strings rosined, the thunder bolts ready to roll, and the lightning to flash at a moment's warning, in short every thing was prepared to astonish the good people of Albany into approbation; think then Mr. Quoz what must have been our chagrin, when amongst a numerous audience we could scarcely recognize the bright countenance of a single substantial Albanian. Some of our old patrons who had fled from New-York; a few strangers from different parts of the country and an inconsiderable number of the younger people of the metropolis composed the whole of our auditors.

Our mortification at this neglect from a people so celebrated for patronizing elegant amusements cannot be conceived. The next morning however disclosed the cause. Unfortunately for us, the day before had presented a remarkably fine fish market and the good people were so busily engaged in feasting on sturgeon, that they had no time to attend to any other diversion. With this reason we were perfectly satisfied; had the cause been an assembly, a concert or an oratoria, our chagrin would have been almost insurmountable; but certainly we could not have the egregious vanity to think of rivalling a *sturgeon feast*.

A call to rehearsal interrupts my narration for the present, but I will resume it the first leisure moment.

Your humble servant,
DICK BUCKRAM.

TO MR. ANDREW QUOZ

Dear Sir,

I concluded my former letter, with an account of our melancholy lack of auditors, on our first evening of performance, in consequence of a miraculous draught of Sturgeon.

Fully convinced, however, that it was not through want of *taste* that the Albanians did not attend, we immediately went to work with renewed spirit, and determined to melt them with tragedy on the next exhibition.

An army was equipped, equal in number and splendor, to those who generously tag at the heels of our theatric warriors in New-York; our military music consisted of a drum, fife and two pot lids by way of cymbals, and for want of a trumpeter, the *entree* of our heroes was announced by a ferry-man with his conk-shell.—Our orchestra was in a style equally superb and consisted of three most inveterate fiddlers. Their music was much admired, being a selection of *veteran symphonies*, from the ancient stock of the New-York leader, that had *grown grey* in the service.

For a few days we succeeded happily.—The novelty of a theatre was attractive; our sceneries were admired; the citizens were pleased to express their approbation of our operas, because "we sung *without warbling*, that defect common to modern singers!!" and as to our *dunder and blixum*, it gave universal satisfaction. Indeed, we found our thunder of most material service, for whenever any of us were out in our parts, or an actor was tardy in making his appearance, we had but to wink to the prompter, and a peel of thunder came happily to our assistance; the audience clapped their hands, encored, and pronounced the gentleman who roll'd the thunder ball, a most promising performer.

Ah happy days! Ah prosperous times of hearty dinners and hot suppers, why was your date so short! why were your enjoyments so transient! Poor dogs that we were, no sooner had we begun to get familiar with our new patrons, and to display our talents with confidence, but we had the misfortune to experience a general defection.

Far be it, from me, Mr. Quoz, to question the taste of the good people of Albany; their love of sturgeon and hatred of warbling, place that far beyond the reach of dispute. Unfortunately, however, they were too much engaged in more *solid* and *profitable* pursuits to pay us that attention they doubtless would otherwise have shewn. Of course, the number of citizens who attended our exhibitions, was rather circumscribed, and their curiosity was unluckily diverted into another channel.

An eminent Artist, arrived from New-York, loaded to the muzzle with fire works; his bills blazed conspicuously at every corner; his rockets soared over the city and dazzled every eye.—The honest folks gaped at them with astonishment, "they swore in faith 'twas strange! 'twas passing strange!" and then, so cheap—wondrous cheap; at our place they had to pay a dollar admittance, while here, it was but climbing on a fence, and they might see the work *"free gratis"* for nothing at all!! In vain we essayed every art to draw them back; in vain we re-inforced our orchestra with a music grinder, and advertized an extra storm of *Dunder and blixum*—all would not do—the artist still kept his ground. To be sure, he sometimes got out of gun powder, but then he always gave them *plenty of brimstone*.

How long, fire-works would have been the rage, I cannot say, had not brimstone disagreed as much with their nerves, as it did with those of the honest citizens of New-York, on a certain fourth of July exhibition; we should therefore most probably have experienced a return of their patronage, had not, as ill luck would have it, a company of wooden puppets arrested their attention. To see a number of persons, act a play, even though they did it tolerably well, was nothing remarkable; for what could be more natural or easy, than for a man to walk and talk in his own manner and language; but to see several little sticks of wood, strutting about, squeaking thro' the nose, and hopping a hornpipe like men and women—lord! it was so strange, so queer, so out of the way, every lady was in raptures.

In a short time, however, their surprise wore off, and they began to look upon us with returning complacency, when who should arrive in town, but another formidable enemy—the *learned pig!* There was new matter for astonishment and admiration! A pig that understood one and one made two, and could cast up a sum according to Cocker or Dilworth, was not to be passed over with neglect, by a mercantile people. Every one was for seeing the remarkable animal—every one was for having some of the breed to stock their counting rooms. For some time we kept the field against the pig, with unequal success, when fortunately we advertised a play for the benefit of Mr. Hogg. Here then, the match stood, Hogg against Pig, the bets ran high in favor of pig, when as a desperate resource we promised in the bills a dissertation between the play and the farce, on the art to grow rich, to be spoken in the character of *Major Sturgeon.* The plan succeeded, Hogg beat the Pig all hollow, and the knowing ones were finely taken in.

Thus, Mr. Quoz, were the honest people of the metropolis, distracted with a variety of amusements, and their judgements continually undetermined, on which they should bestow their patronage—good souls! how do I wonder, that possessed of such a flow of spirits, such volatile imagination, you managed to keep your senses in such a confused medley of plays, puppets, pigs and brimstone!

Satisfied with the meagre success of our expedition, we determined to return once more to our old situation in New-York, and henceforth be content with the humble honors of a *provincial* theatre. We accordingly took our leave of Albany, *sans drum, sans trumpet, a la mode Francaise,* and arrived safely in this city, where we have always found the inhabitants not too refined to relish our performances, but indulgent to our faults, and sensible of our merits. Happy were we, to meet once more our fellow performers who had not once accompanied us in our unfortunate excursion, and infinitely more so were we on our first evening's exhibition, to behold once more the smiling faces of our patrons, and receive their kind and friendly salutations.

We found the theatre in some little derangement on our return, having been converted during the sickly season, into a printing office.— This change, however, was not material in its nature, as the place had still been devoted to the instruction and amusement of the public; things were much in the state we left them except the robes of Dr. Last, which were considerably worn by the Editor, during his medical lucubrations.

This reminds me of an observation I have somewhere seen, *"sic tempora mutantur et* trumpery *mutantur idem."*

Your humble servant,
DICK BUCKRAM.

[March 31–April 26, 1804]

[CONTRIBUTIONS TO *THE CORRECTOR*]

BEWARE OF IMPOSTORS!!

—

TWENTY YEARS PRACTICE!!

—

JAMES CHEETHAM—QUACK-DOCTOR

—

Has *on hand,* at his ſhop No. 136 Pearl-ſtreet, a variety of *drugs* of his own invention, which he will difpofe of at the loweſt rates, as he wiſhes to ſell off his ſtock. Among the number are his famous ſoporific doſes entitled, VIEW, NARRATIVE, NINE LETTERS, &c. which are power-ful promoters of ſleep; if however, they are taken in too large quantities, they are apt to excite a naufea at the ſtomach. The patient will find it difficult to ſwallow them at firſt, they generally have to be crammed down the throat by force, and the patient beaten over the head with a club called *the Citizen,* if he refuſes to take them.

Likewise on hand, a large quantity of that celebrated medicine en-titled, A REPLY TO ARISTIDES. This has been ſtigmatized by ſeveral with the name of a compoſition of *opium and lead.* Dr. Cheetham, however, afſures the public that it is compounded of a *variety* of drugs, and that he was afſiſted in preparing it by the OURANG OUTANG, a creature forming "the very link that joins the animal to the human race."

This *beaſt* had been troubled with a *bad habit* for ſome time, but, in confequence of the *pills of Aristides,* he made a defperate effort, and relieved himfelf in the famous reply.

For the above, and ſundry other *Physics,* apply either to Doctor Cheetham, or to his Jack Pudding, the Baboon and Surrogate. It has been reported that the Jack Pudding was afflicted with the *hydrophobia;* this is A FALSEHOOD, and muſt have originated from his known averſion to *clean water.* To do away the report, notice is hereby given, that he will be publicly waſhed on the firſt day of April next, at the pump, oppoſite St. Paul's, after which, he will be ſhaved and dreſſed in a *clean ſhirt.* He will then be delivered to ſuch of his friends as can recol-lect him in the difguife of *cleanlineſs.* As this Jack Pudding is peculiarly diverting, from a faculty of making queer faces and playing monkey tricks, he affords much diverſion to the Quack Doctor and his friends—by making himfelf ridiculous for their amufement or advantage. He has made up ſome trifling articles of phyſic himfelf, entitled Joe Gumption, Homeſpun, &c. &c. They do not produce the effect he contemplated, but are admirably efficacious in exciting *yawning.* He intends, the next he iſſues, to have his handſome, queer phiz, engraved and affixed to the doſe.

BILLY LUSCIOUS.

"One of those unmeaning things *which nature makes by the* groce— *then sends them forth ashamed of her own work, and puts no stamp upon them."*

As every movement of a *great man* is interesting, I cannot but notice the important biography of *Billy Luscious*——
      "A Rose by any other name would smell as sweet."
This two legged creature being extremely desirous of notice, I shall steal a moment from tickling brutes of a higher grade, and endeavor to pierce through the "clouds and thick darkness" that involve his *obſcurity.*

Like a cypher, when placed by himself, he is *naught*, but thrown among more important figures he serves to *swell a number*. He does well enough to shout in the tatter-de-malion train of our political jugglers, a convenient ass of burden to do their drudgery, and carry their handbills into the country.

The first attempt of this *muffin faced meddler*, to become notorious, was when he commenced the practice of the law, and a dirty *debut* did he make. His name appeared on painted boards at the fly-market, bull's-head, &c. &c. &c. Handbills were stuck up in every grog-shop, where *assault and battery* occurrences were likely to take place. On his boards and bills, were his rates and charges for bonds, mortgages, writs, &c. at *half price*. For the first time in this city, perhaps in the world, was the profession of the law, advertised at *wholesale and retail*. The consequence was, Billy's *law shop* was crowded by the fag ends of humanity; wherever he went he had at his heels a ragged regiment, of drunken negroes, six-penny sharpers, bruising sailors and bum bailiffs.

Another way to gain employment was, the practice of going on board of vessels, just arrived, and exciting the men to sue their Captain, for any chastisement he had (most probably with reason) inflicted. After some time, however, his face became so familiar, and his motives so well known among the tars, that *rope's-ends* were prepared for his reception. An old wag of a sea captain, it is said, undertook to regale the unfortunate LUSCIOUS with a round dozen at the gangway.

The application *tickled* him so much, that in his extacy, he danced over the side of the vessel. Having a heavy head, he would doubtless, for once in his life, have descended below the *surface* of things, had not a *dung boat* fortunately laid along side of the vessel, and received him on the kindly soil from which he sprung.

By manœuvres such as these, has the ingenious Luscious rendered himself contemptible to a proverb among the professors of the law; and he forms to this day a *butt* at which the young students aim their little witticisms.

Having amassed some property by such *honorable* means, Billy began to sigh for some *office* that might yield him some degree of consequence, and serve as a cloak to cover past meannesses. He accordingly turned his attention to politics. For a time he served as a humble drudge among the lower orders of the federal party. But with Riker, Spencer, and many other *worthies* he thought it *expedient* to turn flaming republican, when that side of the political scale preponderated. Like candidate Bob, who will pardon us for placing him in such despicable company, any office will do for him, and he for any office. At first he made an attempt among the illustrious candidates for the shrievalty. Here, however, he was disappointed, that office being decreed as a reward for the *brilliant talents*, the uniform republicanism, and the great *political influence* of Joseph Surface, Esq. From the office of sheriff, he turned to that of master in chancery; still, however, he was doomed to disappointment. No matter, if neither sheriff nor master in chancery was to be obtained, he'd e'en try for *justice of the ten pound court*, and this, at present, is the object he has in view, the grand stimulus of his political labors.*

* P. S. Since writing the above I am informed, that Billy is difappointed alfo in his expectations of being appointed a *juft-afs;* he must therefore remain contented with *half* of the title.

ARISTIDEAN GALLERY of PORTRAITS.

The amateurs of the fine arts, will find in this collection a rich fund of amusement. The moralist may here contemplate the vanity and short lived greatness of an imbecile, arrogant and wicked faction.

Number I,

Is the portrait of Captain Skunk, as he was dubbed by a wag of the day; it arose from the following circumstances: This gallant gentleman went once a privateering, and fell in with an enemy of equal force; they exchanged five broadsides; his antagonist behaved with cool bravery, and shewed a determination to continue the fight, although disabled in his lower timbers. Our hero took advantage of this circumstance, and determined to sheer off—he immediately put before the wind, and fired from his stern ports such discharges as effectually secured his retreat; he resolved never more to have any thing to do with such a bloody business.

NUMBER II,

Is the portrait of the intimate friend and partner in iniquity of our noble Captain Skunk; this is a half length drawing, and dressed in a *spencer;* the object of the painter by this appears to have been to shew that this worthy personage wanted bottom—it is said, that owing to two unlucky occasions, he took such an aversion to a cow-skin and a horse-whip, that the sight or noise of either always threw him into a tremor.

NUMBER III,

Is the drawing of an animal, very much resembling an Ourang-Outang; he has been put in this collection merely from the partiality Captain Skunk had for him, as he frequently amused him and his company by dancing on a table in boots, &c. For those tricks and other humiliating services, the Captain procured him, nominally, a handsome appointment, because says he, although he is a scoundrel, he must be rewarded. It is true a certain portion of this office was to be shared with this *Tunisian,* by Brother George, and a certain Bull-faced notary.

NUMBER IV.

This Knight of the burning house, as he was called in England, having been regularly installed at Manchester, began his career in that country, and would certainly have finished it there; for immediately after his Manchester honors, a more *elevated* mark of distinction was intended him, and which he most certainly merited and would have enjoyed, had it not been for his mother's advice, who was afraid that the collar of this new order might hurt his respiration; for, says she, he has always had such a tickling about the weason, that I think it ominous, and therefore in the utmost trepidation and hurry actually packed him in a chest with old hats, and shipped him for New-York, with the rest of her hopeful sons. If we can't *cheat'em* here, says she, we'll *cheat'em* there. The knight, on his arrival, received the fraternal hug of Captain Skunk and his associates; and these are strong grounds to believe he will die in the full fruition of that *elevated* rank which his mother was so solicitous he should avoid.

NUMBER V.

This scraggy looking figure was a Maryland apothecary, whose patrimony was so small that it required a chevalier of industry to profit from it. Tom, says his father to him, just before he died, you are not born to be a gentleman, I have but little to leave you, and that little very poor soil, by industry alone, can you derive any benefit from it; therefore, *Till it son, Till it son,* which advice became afterwards proverbial for a dirty beginning.

There are a number of other well drawn portraits in the collection, which will perhaps be noticed hereafter.

AN AMATEUR.

THE CONGRESSIONAL FRACAS,
A TRUE STORY.

—

To be said and sung.

—

The following anecdote of *Cheetham's confederate*, the *worthy* D——
W—— C——, needs no testimony to support it. It is a "round unvarnished tale" composed of *notorious facts*, all which, if necessary,
can be clearly proved in a *court of justice*. In relating it I shall for
variety sake avail myself alternately of prose and rhyme. I care not
if either of them are very polished; it is the *matter*, not the *manner* I
consult; and this is certain, the more despicable or barbarous my rhyme
may prove, the more worthy will it be of the *hero* it celebrates.

The *illustrious* political vagabond D—— W—— C——, having been
appointed mayor of the city of New-York, in compliance with the
general *wishes* of the inhabitants, he thought it *prudent* to keep his
precious carcass clear of the city while yet afflicted with the epidemic.
To kill time he repaired to Washington, where he exhibited his *modest*
countenance in the senate chamber, and displayed his *persuasive* eloquence on the proposed amendment of the constitution. In the contest
about closed or open doors, it is said his *bravery* was peculiarly
evidenced.

> His head on high the hero rear'd,
>   And fiercely ſcowl'd around, ſir—
> Ye gods, how awful he appear'd!
>   How terrible he frown'd, ſir!

> Not Cheetham's face at dead of night,
>   Such terror could command, ſir,
> Though that ſame gallows-looking wight
>   Had *dagger* in his hand, ſir.

> Not *tender-hearted Iſaac's* brow,
>   Inſpir'd ſuch awful dread, ſir,
> When with a cudgel's gentle blow,
>   He bruiz'd the German's head, ſir.

> Loudly the gallant ſtateſman cried,
>   While all with wonder whiten,
> That "none his brave and ſteadfaſt ſoul
> "From duty's path ſhould *frighten!*"

This manly intrepidity, as may be supposed, occasioned a general stare of astonishment. To be sure no body *had attempted* to frighten the orator, but then there was great bravery in *anticipating* the attempt. Had D—— W—— rested here, he might have come off with flying colors; but it is the nature of some kind of curs never to stop barking till they get themselves in a scrape. General Dayton rose and spoke on the subject of debate in a temperate and rational manner; but our hero was *touchwood;* he had assumed the bully, and nothing could keep him from bouncing out.

> The *brave* D—— W—— again caught fire,
>   Boldly he roſe to view, ſir,
> And loud pronounc'd with manly ire
>   The general's words *untrue,* ſir.

> So tickled was he with the ſpeech,
>   He ſaid it *twice,* report adds,
> Then wink'd around, as if to ſay,
>   "Dam'me, a'nt I the ſort, lads?"

To this the General replied, and observed, that as to the expressions of Mr. C——, he would notice them at a proper place, and in a proper manner; and then proceeded to answer the previous observations of D—— W—— on the question under consideration. Thus far our hero's *bravery* was displayed, and now for his *prudence.*

After senate had adjourned, D—— W—— was waited on by Major P. Butler, a gallant officer, who loves the smell of gunpowder, and is well versed in those little ceremonies which occasionally take place between gentlemen. The Major opened his business with all appropriate etiquette, and with the most punctilious politeness informed D—— W—— that General Dayton expected him to eat his words by way of supper that night, or else requested the honor of cracking a pistol for breakfast in the morning. The very idea of a pistol, turned the stomach of our hero: it is said ever to have had that effect since he surfeited himself at an entertainment given him by S——t, and there is nothing he more nauseates to this day than the noise of fire-arms, or smell of gunpowder. Butler's mention of a *pistol,* I am told, absolutely threw him into a cold sweat, and occasioned the most violent distortion of countenance.

Not *Yahoo** Miller, when a bowl
  Of water meets his ſight, ſir,
Doth up his glaſſy blinkers roll
  With more amuſing fright, ſir.

Not Spencer when in guilty dreams
  He ſees the well-earned gibbet,
And feels his neck in hempen plight,
  More horror could exhibit.

Nor warrior Purdy felt his ſoul
  With wilder terror ſwelling
When from the field of Mars, he ſtole
  A *rogue's march* to his dwelling.

Ned Ferris too, that greaſy rogue
  Ne'er in ſuch fever fried, ſir,
When for his knaviſh impudence
  The Burrite drumm'd his hide, ſir.

In ſhort, no bridewell bird e'er ſeem'd
  More horribly affrighted;
Not e'en the Ourang-Outang, when
  For perjury indicted.

His ſpirits ſought, the *lower port,*
  From whence *of yore* they ſallied,
But thrice he ſmote upon his breaſt,
  And the deſerters rallied.

Yet ſtill he blink'd, and puff'd, and gaſp'd,
  And ſeem'd in wondrous fluſter,
And begg'd the ſmall ſpace of two hours
  His ſcatter'd thoughts to muſter.

As this request was but reasonable, the Major very civilly assented, and politely took his leave. During the two hours, D. W. is said to have remained in a state of great irresolution, till fortunately he happened

---

* "*And this countrie is greeviouſly afflicted with a loathſome animal the which theye do call Yahoo. This creture is of the monkie kynd, and withall, very troubleſome and miſchevious. It is full of filthie tricks, and will voide its ordure on paſſengers, from the trees on the which it is perched. In truthe, it is a marvelous naſtie beeſte.*"—Snigger's Travels.

to cast his eyes on Falstaff's soliloquy on *honor;* struck with the force of the argument it contained, he was immediately convinced that the better part of valor is *discretion.* Checking therefore his courageous spirit that urged him to fight, he determined *prudently* to evade the combat. At the expiration of the term, the Major, punctual to a minute, made his appearance, and requested to know which of the two alternatives Mr. C—— had adopted.

> "That I'm a man of mighty pluck,"
>   He anſwer'd, "is well known, ſir,
> How quick I can a ſhot *digeſt,*
>   In Sw——t's fight was ſhewn, ſir.

> But now I really have no time:
>   To York I muſt repair, ſir,
> At four o'clock to-morrow morn
>   To be inſtalled Mayor, ſir."

> "Let not that vex you," Butler cries,
>   "The moon ſhines clear and bright, ſir,
> And ſurely your young eyes can ſee
>   *Ten paces* by its light, ſir.

> But if you ſhould object to this,
>   Another hour we'll take, ſir;
> You ſay the ſtage ſets off at *four*—
>   This is a ſlight miſtake, ſir.

> Sıx is the hour it means to ſtart,
>   So we can ride ahead, ſir,
> And do the buſineſs by *day-light,*
>   E'er folks are out of bed, ſir.

> Still, if both theſe you diſapprove,
>   You muſt ſign a confeſſion,
> That all you ſaid 'gainſt Dayton was
>   A palpable tranſgreſſion.

> This explanation muſt be read
>   In full aſſembled ſenate,
> And you may travel on to York
>   As ſoon as you ſhall pen it.

At this D. W————'s eyes ſparkle up,
    And joy his mind bewitches:
"Dam'me," thinks he, "I yet ſhall ſave
    My bacon, and my *breeches!*"

The writing ſign'd, moſt joyfully
    To ſweet New-York he fagg'd, ſir,
In four-wheel'd waggon call'd a ſtage
    By four ſtarved cattle dragg'd, ſir.

And when he ſafe arriv'd in town,
    And told of this affair, ſir;
To ſee the joy of all *the gang*—
    Good lord! 'twould make you ſtare, ſir.

To Jemmy Cheetham's longing arms
    He flew in eager haſte, ſir,
And ſnout to ſnout thoſe *boſom friends*
    In ecſtacy embrac'd, ſir.

And Wortman too, that man of gall,
    With fond emotions ſmitten,
Did ſlaver o'er his *gallant* friend,
    Juſt like a cat her kitten.

And Yahoo Miller far renown'd
    For *gumption*, and for dirt, ſir,
In very joy his muzzle ſcrap'd,
    And hoiſted a CLEAN SHIRT, ſir!!!

Thrice Monkey Riker bow'd his head,
    Till his noſe ſwept the floor, ſir,
Proteſting on his honor, he
    Was ne'er ſo glad before, ſir.

In ſhort, the whole *Clintonian gang*
    Pour'd in from each direction,
Until they form'd a ſtinking throng,
    Enough to breed infection.

Now let us ſing, long live D————t,
    That man that fights ſo well, ſir;
And when he next doth take the field,
    May you be there to ſmell, ſir.

EBENEZER.

I have feen the man, nay, I know him. "But to fay I know any good of him, were to fay more than I know."

The *honorable* Ebenezer ———, is a man whofe folly renders him unfit for any thing, but to be the tool of a knave. Ignorant, conceited, and empty, he would be utterly unworthy of my notice, were it not that through his "feven-fold fhield of tough bull hide" I may perhaps hit fome of his employers who fhelter themfelves behind the brick and mortar of his compofition. I bear *him* no enmity—Heaven forbid I fhould!

"The lion preys not upon carcafes."

But it was through the iron and brafs armor of the hero of old, that a paffage was atchieved to his heart. It is through the iron and brafs of fuch mad, malignant ideots as Cheetham, and fuch thick-fkulled blockheads as Ebenezer, Billy Lufcious, and others, that we muft penetrate, to reach the finews of a faction, more wildly depraved than ever before difgraced this country—more weak and malicious than ever difgraced the world.

Every body knows that Ebenezer was a gallant fupporter of the rights of his country during the revolutionary war. Like the brave Jean Bon St. André, he would indeed occafionally run away; but what of that?— he always ordered his men to fight to the laft extremity. It was there-fore perhaps not a little owing to his valor that he gained "the affections and favors" of De Witt, who is himfelf more valiant than "St. George—and the dragon to boot."

Ebenezer was fome years ago tranflated moft miraculoufly from his farm-yard to a feat on the bench, and from a judge of horfe-flefh, became a judge of right and wrong, by virtue of his office. Our "moft righteous judge," our "fecond Daniel," now began to fancy him a man of no fmall ability. He dealt out law indeed with a fparing hand, but then again he adminiftered juftice, with a vengeance, in fuch quantities that every man, woman, and child was fatisfied to their heart's content, and went away, as honeft Lithgow fays, "rejoicing in an extraordinary forrow of delights."

In this fituation, where his fame fpread not beyond the narrow limits of his fphere of action, he continued for fome time, and might perhaps have continued ftill, had not the valiant De Witt difcovered him. This great political quack-doctor and chymift, who can tranfmute lead into gold, and for whom has been probably reſerved the honor of diſcovering the philoſopher's ſtone, ſaw immediately, in him, a man formed in the very avarice of nature, without one qualification to attract the eſteem of men of honor, and hugged himſelf in the fortunate diſcovery. He ſaw that Ebenezer might be made, or rather that nature had already made him, a tool, a beaſt of burthen, a fawning ſpaniel, who would fetch and carry, and think himſelf rewarded by "the crumbs which fall from the great man's table." He took him by the hand, and was not diſappointed; for he had looked into a congenial heart.

Ebenezer now acting a part on a more wide, extended, and various theatre, exhibited a chaos of blunders and ſtupidity. He was the clown, the ſcaramouch of the play, and the jeſt of the audience. But he was ſtill the ſtedfaſt, humble dependant, who always anſwered to the whiſtle of his maſter, and licked the duſt at his feet.

For theſe good ſervices he is now about to receive his reward, in again diſgracing the high ſtation of ſenator, and immeaſurably diſgracing his conſtituents.

Power of Omnipotence! that *ſuch* a man ſhould aſpire to *ſuch* a ſtation!

> "I had rather be a toad,
> And live upon the vapor of a dungeon,"

than be *his colleague*. I ſhould bluſh for myſelf,—I ſhould bluſh for *him*;—and above all, I ſhould bluſh for my country!

"So much for Buckingham!"

RODERICK.

TO TOBY TICKLER, ESQ.

Dear Sir,

Our countrymen have been ſo frequently reproached by foreigners, not only with an inſenſibility to the merits and productions of literature, but with a total abſence of the talents and genius requiſite for the execution of any work of ſcience, of taſte, or imagination; that I feel a pride, grateful to the ſpirit of my patriotiſm, in announcing to the public, under your auſpices, an undertaking which ought forever to ſilence the malignant calumnies of European critics.

Mons. H. Carritat, *Libraire and Bibliothécaire*, at Fenelon's Head, Broadway, has lately iſſued propoſals for publiſhing by ſubſcription "New and intereſting publications by native and living authors." Many of theſe works have already appeared at periodical ſeaſons, and more are now in preparation for the preſs. In order, therefore, to afford your readers ſome idea of their ſeveral merits, I ſhall from time to time tranſmit to you a ſhort account of each performance in the form of a *Catalogue Raiſonnée*; and I have now taken the liberty of encloſing a notice of thoſe numbers which have already been preſented to the public.

I am, Dear Sir,
Your affectionate Couſin,
TOUCHSTONE TICKLER.

"New and Intereſting Publications by Native and Living Authors."
Catalogue Raiſonnée, &c.

No. 1. "The Coalition, or the Conſtitution violated and a Bank deſtroyed," a Tragedy now performing with unbounded applauſe at the *Theatre Legiſlatif*, Albany; the principal characters by Meſſrs. C——n, L——n, L——s, S——r, and P——y. With an appendix, containing a ſevere criticiſm upon the whole by the Hon. W——m D——g, and J——n W——h. A pamphlet ſlightly ſtitched.

No. 2. "The character of the worſhipful Jeremiah Sneak, Mayor of Garratt, vindicated from the miſ-repreſentations of Mr. Samuel Foote. by D—— W——t C——n, Eſq. &c. &c. &c." This work tho' not lettered, is bound in genuine Calf.

No. 3. "An Eſſay on the art of Toad-Eating," in which the firſt principles of lying, ſhuffling, cutting and *miſ*-dealing, are traced from actual experience. By M——n L——n, toad-eater to the honorable the C——f J——e and director of the M——n C——y.

No. 4. "Memoirs of the Brag-Club," containing ſecret anecdotes of celebrated members, with annotations and comments, by ladies of the ſociety. To which is added a ſhort treatiſe upon the moſt approved methods of breeding, rearing, feeding and fighting game cocks. By Miſter R——t L——n, ſtanding candidate to the family. The orthography executed by his loving brother M——n and aſſiſtants. *In ſheets*.

No. 5. "The Redemptioners, or the innocence of Frederic, and the perjury of his maſter," a tragic comedy, founded upon facts proven at a trial at Oyer and Terminer in 1801. By I——c C——n, late German convict, but now director of the M——n C——y. This work is bound in *Sheep* with a hollow back, richly gilt and totally unlettered.

No. 6. "Modern gratitude or mere matter of moon-ſhine," a farce, by D—— L——, Eſq. P. M. C. and A. S. S.

No. 7. "An arithmetical treatiſe upon the value of ſtripes, with compendious tables, ſhewing the market price of floggings, horſe-whippings, kickings, cuffings and canings, at any given period," *a compoſition*, by Mr. J——s A——n, director of M——n C——y. *With corrections*, by Capt. P——e, D. P——r, and Mr. H. N. C——r. (Sheep gilt and hot preſſed.)

No. 8. "The Beauties of Deformity," *a viſion*. Anonymous. MOTTO,
  "Argus poſſeſſed an hundred eyes 'tis true,
  But ⸺ looks an hundred ways with two;
  Gimblets they are, and bore you thro' and thro'."
        (To be Continued.)

TO TOBY TICKLER, ESQ.

Dear Toby,
  I have heard with infinite pleaſure, that the intereſt and attention
of a generous public have been promptly excited and irreſiſtibly attracted by thoſe learned labors of our countrymen, which, with your
friendly aſſiſtance, I had the honor, in the former part of the week,
of announcing to the world.
  The ingenious productions of our native authors, have been the only
themes of converſation in all our polite aſſemblies ſince your notice
of their publication; and the diverſity of their ſeveral merits has afforded
conſtant topics for diſcuſſion amongſt men of judgment in ſcience,
and taſte in criticiſm, ever ſince they firſt received the ſanction of your
approbation.
  I feel myſelf, therefore, in a high degree encouraged, not only to
proceed in the execution of my plan to the fartheſt limits of its firſt
conception, but even to extend the original bounds of its propoſal, ſo
far as to recommend, the infant exertions of our fellow-citizens for the
cultivation of the *Fine Arts*, to the ſame encouragement and patronage.
For this purpoſe I have encloſed for publication, two ſeveral catalogues
which have been handed to me by a young artiſt of great taſte and
genius:—The one, containing an account of the late valuable additions
to the Shakeſpeare Gallery; and the other, a liſt of thoſe original pictures which have been collected and eſtabliſhed as the foundation of
a ſimilar inſtitution.
  If the Academy of Arts already afford (as a director diſtinguiſhed
for his improved taſte, and practical experience, has frequently aſſerted)
the beſt ſchool for *ſculpture* beyond the precincts of Paris, the capital
of modern Europe; you will eaſily be convinced, my dear ſir, by an
attentive peruſal of the originals of the Shakeſpeare collection, and the
Pandemonian Gallery, that the "American Academy" will, before the
revolution of many years, diſpute the palm of excellence in *painting*,
with the ſchools of London, of Paris, and of Rome.
                          I am, dear Couſin,
                          Your's moſt courteouſly,
                          TOUCHSTONE TICKLER.

CHARACTERISTIC PORTRAITS,
Lately added to the Shakeſpeare Gallery.

No. 1. The Ariſtocratic Compact, an allegorical painting in water colours. The background and drapery, executed by D. W. C., the figures by that promiſing artiſt, Morgan Rattler.

> "——————Shall fall,
> And like the baſeleſs fabric of a viſion,
> Leave not a wreck behind."

"We are joined with none but nobility; ſuch as will ſtrike ſooner than drink, and drink ſooner than pray: and yet I lie, for they pray continually to their ſaint, the commonwealth; or rather, not *pray to her*, but *prey on her*; for they ride up and down on her, and make her their booty."—Hen. IV.

No. 2. A ſtriking likeneſs of that celebrated comedian, Mr. Lewis, as Autolicus.—— "I am known to be humorous, and to love a glaſs *of hot wine* without one drop of allaying Tiber in it."

N. B. The laſt and beſt editor of Shakeſpeare is inclined to expunge the words *hot wine*, and ſubſtitute champaign—the laſt is certainly more in character.

No. 3. An expounder of the prophecies, in the robes of a Turkiſh Mufti.

> "And ſee a prayer-book in his hand,
> True ornament to know a holy man."

> " 'Tis a very fine thing to be father-in-law
> To a very magnificent three-tail'd Baſhaw—
> On perquiſites I lay my paw, &c."

No. 4. A highly colored portrait of his honor, the Mayor of Garratt, as he appeared in the character of Capt. Bobadil, in the tragi-comedy of the *bloody buſineſs*, lately performed with unbounded applauſe at a private theatre in the neighborhood of this city.

> "And telling me 'twas great pity, ſo it was,
> This villainous ſalt-petre ſhould be digg'd
> Out of the bowels of the harmleſs earth—
> And but for theſe vile guns
> He would himſelf have been a warrior."

"Why he ſtalks up and down, like a peacock, bites his lip with a politic regard, as who ſhould ſay, there were wit in his head; and ſo perhaps there is, but it lies coldly in him, as fire does in flint which will not ſhew without knocking."

No. 5. A medallion containing the L——n arms; ſupporters, two judges; creſt, a ſhip in diſtreſs; motto, *Spero meliora*, i. e. more offices and better ones.

No. 6. An ourang-outang painted by a right learned clerk.

> "—Beware of yonder beaſt—
> Look, when he fawns, he bites, and when he bites,
> His venom tooth will rankle to the death;
> Sin, death, and hell have ſet their marks upon him."

"I'll not meddle with conſcience, it is a dangerous thing—a man cannot lie, but it accuſeth him; a man cannot *ſwear*, but it checks him."

No. 7. A remarkably fine head of Julian the apoſtate, by Sir A. S. F. R. S.

> "The high permiſſion of all-ruling Heaven,
> Left him at large to his own black deſigns
> That with reiterated crimes he might
> Heap on himſelf deſtruction; while he ſought
> Evil to others."

No. 8. Mr. R. R——r, in the character of Gratiano. "Gratiano ſpeaks an infinite deal of nothing—his reaſons are as two grains of wheat hid in two buſhels of chaff; you may ſearch all day ere you find them; and then they are not worth the ſearch."

No. 9. The ſame ludicrous performer as Dicky Goſling.—"I likes to go out ven I'm dreſſed in my maſter's cloaths—caſe vy, I looks a little like him, and every body thinks I'm ſome great man."

No. 10. A Maryland quack doctor, intended as a companion print to that of the Scribe, by T——n, F. R. S.

> "I do remember an apothecary—
> Culling of ſimples, meagre were his looks,
> Sharp miſery had worn him to the bone—
> And if a man did need a poiſon now,
> Here lives a caitiff wretch, would ſell him one.
> Being holiday the beggar's ſhop is ſhut."

—

ORIGINAL PICTURES,

By American artiſts, lately eſtablished and collected as the foundation of an inſtitution, to be denominated the PANDÆMONIAN GALLERY.

No. 1. Is a ſuperb painting of the Arch Fiend, ſeated upon his royal throne at the opening of the Council. From the youthful hand and promiſing pencil of D———— W———t C————n.

> "High on the throne of royal ſtate,—
> Satan exalted ſat, by merit raiſ'd
> To that bad eminence; and from deſpair
> Thus high uplifted beyond hope, aſpires
> Beyond thus high, inſatiate to purſue
> Vain war with heav'n, and by ſucceſs untaught,
> His proud imaginations ſtill diſplay'd."

There is one objection that the connoiſſeurs have made in this piece, in which we feel ſome diſpoſition to concur, namely, that Mr. C———n's repreſentation of the arch enemy is deficient in *ſpirit* and in majeſty; but in the expreſſion, he has been univerſally allowed to have excelled, if poſſible, the malignity of the devil himſelf.

No. 2. Moloch ſpeaking in the Council. By Mr. A———e S———r, an artiſt who has exhibited in many rival academies.

> "————Moloch, ſcepter'd king,
> Stood up, the ſtrongeſt and the fierceſt ſpirit
> That fought in *hell*, now fiercer by deſpair:
> His truſt was with his leader to be deem'd
> Equal in ſtrength, and rather than be leſs,
> Car'd not to be at all; ————"

"The character of Moloch is admirably preſerved in all its circum-ſtances; and the expreſſion full of that fire and fury which diſtinguiſh this ſpirit from his compeers. It may be worth while to obſerve, that Milton has repreſented this violent impetuous ſpirit as the *firſt* that riſes in the council. All the ſentiments with which he ſupplies him, are raſh, audacious and deſperate—becoming the bitterneſs of this im-placable fiend."—Addiſon on Milton.

No. 3. An admirably well finiſhed full length portrait of Belial. By the hon. J———— A———g, an artiſt of much experience and conſider-able practice in foreign ſchools.

> "————On *th' other ſide* uproſe
> Belial, in act more graceful and humane;
> A fairer perſon loſt not heaven; he ſeem'd
> For dignity compoſ'd and high exploit;
> But all was falſe and hollow; though his tongue
> Dropt manna, and could make the worſe appear
> The better reaſon, to perplex and daſh

> Matureſt counſels: for his thoughts were low;
> To vice induſtrious, but to nobler deeds
> Timorous and ſlothful: yet he pleaſ'd the ear."

No. 4. "The loweſt ſpirit of Hell," an exact copy of the ineſtimable original. By T——s W————.

> "————The leaſt erected ſpirit that fell
> From heav'n, for e'en in heav'n his looks and thoughts
> Were always downcaſt bent, admiring more
> The riches of heav'n's pavement, trodden gold,
> Than ought divine or holy elfe enjoy'd
> In viſion beatific:————"
> "————than whom a ſpirit more lew'd
> Breath'd not in hell, or more groſs to love
> Vice for itſelf:————"

No. 5. Repreſents the ſerpent biting the heel of the woman's ſeed. By J——s C————m, a foreign artiſt of great notoriety, chiefly celebrated for his ſkill in *head-pieces*. This branch of his art he has however totally neglected, having reſolved to confine himſelf, for the future, to allegorical ſubjects in the *horrid* ſtyle.

> "———— A ſerpent arm'd
> With mortal ſting: about his middle round
> A cry of hell-hounds never ceaſing bark'd,
> A hideous peal; yet, when they lift, would creep,
> If aught diſturb'd their noiſe, into his breaſt,
> And kennel there, yet there ſtill bark'd and howl'd
> Within unſeen."

No. 6. Beelzebub's remonſtrance at the breaking up of Pandemonium. By a veteran artiſt, who deſires his name henceforward to be conceal'd.

> "Which, when Beelzebub perceived, than whom
> *Satan except*, none higher ſat, with grave
> Aſpect he roſe, and in his riſing ſeem'd
> A pillar of ſtate; deep on his front engraven
> Deliberation ſat and public care;
> And princely counſel in his face yet ſhone,
> Majeſtic though in ruin."

CHARACTERISTIC PORTRAITS,

Lately added to the Shakeſpeare Gallery.

(Continued.)

No. 11. Scene, the Witches' Cave. Enter Hecate and the Three Weird Sifters. This painting is the joint production of eminent artifts. Hecate by D. W. C. the Witches by Meffrs. L——w——s, R. and M. L——n.

> "By the pricking of my thumbs
> Something wicked this way comes.
> Why, how now, Hecate, you look angry.
> *Hecate.* Have I not reaſon? Beldams as you are,
> Saucy and overbold. How did you dare
> To trade and traffic with this bank—
> And I the miftrefs of your charms,
> The clofe contriver of all harms,
> Was never call'd to bear my part
> Or ſhew the glories of our art."

No. 12. Mr. I——c C——n, a much admired tragedian of the German fchool, as Dogberry in *Much ado about nothing*.

"Thou art damned like an ill roaft egg, all on one fide.—Oh that I had been written down an afs—though it be not written down, yet forget not that I am an afs—I am a wife fellow—and which is more, an elder—and which is more, a houfeholder—and which is more, as pretty a piece of flefh as any in Meffina; and a rich fellow go to, and a fellow that hath had loffes, and one that hath two gowns and every thing handfome about him.—Oh that I had been writ down an afs."

No. 13. Another fcene from the fame piece, by Jofeph Surface, Efq.

"You are thought to be the moft fenfelefs and difartlefs man to be conftable of the watch.—Therefore bear you the lantern."

No. 14. a young fportfman, painted *a la quafh*, by Morgan Rattler. Young Adam L——s, he that fhot fo true.

"— But 'twas a ftrange fancy to take aim at a partridge, and bring down an afs."

No. 15. The independent magiftrate, a companion to the above, by Mr. Juftice T——n.

"1ft *Judge*. Do you fee yonder cloud that's almoft in the fhape of a camel? 2d *Judge*. By the mafs, and 'tis like a camel indeed. 1ft *Judge*. Methinks 'tis like a weafel. 2d *Judge*. Very like a weafel. 1ft *Judge*. Or like a whale. 2d *Judge*. Very like a whale."

No. 16. Solemn Stupidity, a ftudy from nature, by G——t L——n, Efq. of Poughkeepfie.

"There are a ſet of men, whoſe viſages
Do cream and mantle, like a ſtanding pool—
With purpoſe to be dreſs'd in an opinion
Of wiſdom, gravity, profound conceit,
As who ſhould ſay—I am, Sir, oracle,
And when I ope my mouth, let no dog bark."

No. 17. Verges in *Much ado about nothing*, a ſketch, by Edgaronka, a Canadian ſavage.

"Yes, I thank God, I am as honeſt as any man living, that is an old man, and no honeſter than I."

N. B. This laſt and No. 14 have been much injured by the injudicious application of a thick coat of varniſh, by one I. Ch——m, an itinerant ſign-painter.

ISAAC.

Orthoëpy. Conſiderable diverſity exiſts among our *literati*, reſpecting the true pronunciation of ARISTIDES, whether the accent ſhould be laid on the penultima or antepenult. "Who ſhall decide when doctors diſagree." Ainſworth, Lempriere and Walker concur in accenting the penultima. American *erudition* diſdains, however, an appeal to foreign umpires. Fortunately the citizens of New-York need not traverſe the Atlantic for authorities; as our city can boaſt the moſt correct ſtandard of pronunciation in the United States. A celebrated *orthoëpiſt* who lives, not many miles from Trinity Church, and nearly oppoſite an eminent *preſident* of *ſoft-horned** pedigree, has effectually ſettled all doubts concerning this conteſted word; he invariably pronounces it, *Harry-Strides*, which we beg may, hereafter, paſs current throughout the Union. Of the correctneſs of this pronunciation there can be no diſpute, when the public is informed that this renowned Orthoëpiſt ſuperintended, during our revolutionary war, an academy, vulgarly yclep'd *ſchool*. Whether it was a grammar ſchool or a common Engliſh ſchool, fame has not recorded. From his accurate acquaintance with the rules of proſody and his extenſive trading in claſſical lore, we preſume the former; and that he muſt have been ſomething more than a mere *Abecedarian*. In the exerciſe of the birch, it is inſinuated, that this quondam *bum-bruſher* and *gerund-grinder* acquired that conſummate ſkill in handling the *Argumentum Baculinum* which has, ſince, rendered him ſo notorious. Many a trembling wight has he laid his cruel

*Soft in the horn and hard in the hoof, like the Devil's Jack Aſs.
Spaniſh Proverb.

Claws on. Their dolorous ditty, chaunted to the lugubrious notes of *miſericordia,* ſtill reſounds in my ear.

> Hic, Hæc, Hoc,
> Lay him on the block;
> Noun, Pronoun,
> Pull his Galligaſkins down;
> Verb, Participle,
> *Now the rod begins to tickle.*
> ALAS POOR ISAAC! ! !

COL. BLUBBER.

"What have we here? A man or a fiſh? A fiſh; he ſmells like a fiſh; a very ancient and fiſh-like ſmell. A ſtrange fiſh. Were I in England now and had but this fiſh painted, not an holiday fool there but would give me a piece of ſilver—Legg'd like a man! and his fins like arms! I do now let looſe my opinion, this is no fiſh."

Col. Blubber that well known FAT-HEADED FOOL, has juſt gone down to Suffolk to electioneer. He had ſome weeks ſince arrived thus far on his expedition, but was recalled, *by his maſters,* to aid in deſtroying the Merchant's Bank, which was one *precious* buſineſs of the laſt legiſlative ſeſſion. His travels up were ludicrous enough, had I time to tell them. He was benighted, and beſtormed, and bewildered, the ſtage could not proceed—but COL. BLUBBER was on *meritorious* buſineſs, that admitted not of delay. The Bank executioners were bellowing for aſſiſtance. Accordingly, BLUBBER, ſought ſome other conveyance, and with his uſual good ſenſe, being in a hurry, chartered a heavy country waggon. Here he was met riding through a tremendous ſhower of rain, in all the majeſty of dirt, with ſome gude wife's yellow flannel petticoat tied round his big head.

People ſuppoſed him a huge LAND PORPOISE, carrying round the country for a ſhew.

The poor BLUBBER, with all his *rapidity* of journeying, did not get in at the death. He found at his arrival that he had come on a fool's errand, for the Merchant's Bank had been already *ſmothered* by its enemies. BLUBBER had nothing to do, but pack himſelf up again, and away for Suffolk: where he promiſes to effect great things. He conſiders the independent citizens of Suffolk county as a ſet of ignorant beings, and is eternally boaſting of his great influence over them—how he ſplutters and bullies at the polls—and how he leads them all by the noſe.

He ſtill preaches up his new doctrine—that the legiſlature has a right to make a governor for the ſtate! That the people are *bound* to vote for Morgan Lewis. That any bank not owned by the ariſtocratic faction ought to be deſtroyed—becauſe the caſh of the ſtate ſhould all go into the pockets of the GREAT FAMILIES, and their obſequious friends. He ſtill aſſerts THAT MORGAN LEWIS NEVER WAS A FEDERALIST!!!

"Thou lieſt, moſt ignorant monſter, why thou debaſed fiſh thou!— Wilt thou tell a monſtrous lie, being but half a fiſh, and half a monſter!"

TO TOBY TICKLER, ESQ.

Nephew Toby,

Thou graceleſs dog—thou impudent raſcal; and canſt thou ever have the audacity to look your old uncle in the face again, after playing him ſuch an abominable prank.—But this I ſuppoſe is what you call quizzing the old fellow. Yet, perhaps I am too violent.—Well, well, publiſh this ſhort account of my misfortunes, and I forgive you all: but have a care how you treſpaſs again.

You recollect, that laſt evening, when, after having told me a great many long rigmarole ſtories, you finally prevailed upon me to attend the Clintonian meeting (for which the Lord forgive you) I left you abruptly, and ran, or rather hobbled home with all the eagerneſs of expectation.

Already feaſting in idea upon the delicious repaſt of republican eloquence which awaited me; I was all impatience—ſtalked acroſs my parlour—looked at my watch a hundred times—threw down a dozen pipes—ſwore at the ſervants, and flew into a paſſion with your ſiſter for not giving me my tea. At length the tea was ready. I ſwallowed down two or three cups (not, however, without burning my mouth as many times) and hurried off to the Union Hotel. I found the room almoſt full; eager to get a good place, with ſome difficulty I crowded on, till I got nearly oppoſite to the orcheſtra in which the chairman and ſecretary were placed. While the introductory buſineſs of the meeting was going on, and the tickets intended to be ſupported at the enſuing election, were reading, I had time to make a few remarks on the audience, as well as on my own *comfortable* ſituation. You well know, Toby, the delicacy of my noſe; but never did I ſo fervently wiſh that I had been born without one: for ſuch a congregation of peſtilent vapours—ſuch a foul compound of nauſeous ſmells, were ſurely never before collected. I did not dare to ſpeak, laugh, or cough—nay, ſcarcely did I venture to breathe, for fear of letting the foul air into my mouth.

The room was crowded with a ſhabby ſet of all nations, and all colours. To give you ſome idea of this reſpectable aſſemblage, I muſt deſcribe to you my own neighbors.—A little ugly Jew ſtood juſt before me, and every now and then, yawning full in my face, saluted me with such an abominable blast as almost turns my stomach to think of it.— Foh, foh, an ounce of civit, good apothecary, to sweeten my imagination. At my right hand was posted a greasy fellow whom I recollect to have somewhere seen in the capacity of a quack doctor—on my left, a tall French Creole, and behind me to my inexpressible torment, a gigantic raw-boned Irishman, who coolly rested his sharp elbow upon my back, and amused himself with shaking the ashes of a lighted segar into the curls of my wig; I ventured to remonstrate, but "Och my jewel, and can't you be aisy," was the only answer I received.

Near the wall was stationed the great Cheetham; and by his side, that ugly baboon-faced fellow, whom cousin Touchstone calls the Ourang-outang. A hundred times did I wish myself comfortably seated at home, smoaking my pipe, and reading the Corrector. But wishes were idle, and to attempt to force my way out would have been ridiculous.

At length a young man mounted a table; he began in a pretty audible whisper to detail all the so-often refuted calumnies against Col. Burr. He called upon the *ghost* of young Behrens to haunt the slumbers of every lazy republican—he invoked the goddess of liberty, and the genii of the constitution—he asserted (in the true aristocratic slang) that Mr. Burr was supported only by a ragamuffin crew.—Here some of his auditory cast a look at their own shabby apparel, and began something like a hiss.—He talked about political consistency, and Arnold, and Catiline, and at last boldly declared that there was more true liberty in Virginia than in any other state in the union. In good truth, the youth was fluent enough, and in any other place, and on any other subject, I might have listened to him with some pleasure. At every pause, Cheetham and his friends cheered the speaker with a clap; the baboon-faced gentleman sickened with envy, and Billy Luscious clasped his hands in ecstacy, and exclaimed, "Astonishing young man!—Wonderful youth!"

At length, the harangue was finished, the meeting adjourned, and I thought my misfortunes at an end. But no, a man had taken his stand at the door, presented a ragged hat, and demanded a shilling of every citizen for the use of the room. I had not provided myself with change— I was abused for a spy—damned for an impudent Burrite—kicked for a federal intruder, and at last was tumbled down stairs by a drunken sailor. After losing the heel of one shoe, and the buckle of the other, I got with some difficulty to the door. Here I was accosted by a pert jackanapes, who asked me, how many freeholders I supposed there might have been in the room? Perhaps an hundred and twenty (and between you and I, Toby, this was a pretty liberal allowance). Here was another bone of contention; however, I put on a bold face, and the puppy walked off.

Well how long have I been in purgatory? I put my hand to my fob—my watch was gone. And fo ended the difaftrous adventures of

Your unfortunate Uncle,
BICKERSTAFFE TICKLER.

P. S. I had almoft forgot to tell you, that the Irifhman's curfed fegar, fet fire to my wig, and totally ruined 13 curls.

ORIGINAL PICTURES
For the Pandemonian Gallery.
(Continued.)

No. 7. Satan entering into the ferpent. This piece is the joint production of D. W. C. and J——s Ch——m.

> "Satan,
> With narrow fearch, and with infpection deep,
> Confider'd every creature, which of all
> Moft opportune might ferve his wiles, and found
> The ferpent, vileft beaft of all the field;
> Him, after long debate, irrefolute
> Of thoughts revolved, his final fentence chofe,
> Fit veffel, fitteft imp of fraud, in whom
> To enter, and his dark defigns to hide
> From fharpeft fight."

Connoiffeurs have remarked, that Mr. C——n in his reprefentation of Satan, has foftened down the ferocity and defpair fo confpicuous in No. 1. into an expreffion of malignant cunning.

N. B. That due juftice may be done to every exertion of genius, it muft be obferved that the ferpent, is the fole and unaided production of J. C——m.

No. 8. Satan, after his arrival at Pandemonium relates the fuccefs of his expedition; but, inftead of the applaufe which he expected, is received with a univerfal hifs, by the worfhipful Jeremiah Sneak.

> "So having fpoke, a while he ftood, expecting
> Their univerfal fhout, and high applaufe
> To fill his ear, when contrary he hears
> On all fides, from innumerable tongues
> A difmal univerfal hifs, the found
> Of univerfal fcorn."

No. 9. The devil aſſuming the form and garb of an angel, by S——— O———.

> "Hypocriſy, the only evil that walks
> Inviſible except to God alone,
> By his permiſſive will, thro' heaven and earth."

Candid criticiſm muſt allow, that this is the worſt picture in the Gallery. The angel form is ſo aukwardly delineated, and the colours laid, or rather plaiſtered on, without taſte or diſcrimination. The traits of villainy are ſtill too apparent, amidſt all the affectation of angelic innocence. When Mr. O. next attempts the repreſentation of hypocriſy, he ſhould take a few leſſons from his youthful relation, D. W. C.

No. 10. The devil ſtarting up in his own native deformity, on being touched by the ſpear of truth, by the author of the *romances* of Poor Behrens and Honeſt Morgan.

> "Him thus intent, Ithuriel with his ſpear
> Touch'd lightly; for no falſehoods can endure
> Touch of celeſtial temper; but returns
> Of force to its own likeneſs. Up he ſtarts
> Diſcovered and ſurpriſed."

This is a very ſpirited performance, every circumſtance is forcibly impreſſed on the mind of the ſpectator; and the unbluſhing confidence of the *father of lies* is admirably depicted.

No. 11. Niſroch, receiving his orders from Satan, a companion to No. 5. by the ſame artiſt, the well known J. Ch———m.

> "———Upſtood
> Niſroch, of lying fiends the prime;
> As one he ſtood, eſcap'd from cruel fight,
> Sore toil'd, his riv'n arms to havoc hewn.
> To him, in aſpect cloudy Satan ſpake,
> Be this thy choſen taſk—
> To be a liar in four hundred mouths;
> For lying is thy ſuſtenance, thy food,
> But ſtill pretend to truth."

Although Mr. Ch———m claims the whole merit of this painting, connoiſſeurs pretend to diſcover many ſtrokes of the ſublimely horrid pencil of D. W. C.

No. 12. The devils tranformed into ſerpents entwining the imagined tree of government, by the friends of the combined families.

"They fondly thinking to allay
Their appetite with guſt, inſtead of fruit
Chew'd bitter aſhes. Oft they aſſay'd,
Hunger and thirſt conſtraining, drug'd as oft
With hatefulleſt diſreliſh writh'd their jaws
With ſoot and cinders fill'd."

This is an unfiniſhed piece, but it is hoped will be in readineſs for public inſpection in a few days.

TO TOBY TICKLER, ESQ.

——

A very ſingular diary was found under a dining table, about three weeks ago, by one of the lateſt gueſts, and handed to me with per-miſſion to ſhew it to whom I pleaſed. As the whole world will ſee it ſooner or later (for I cannot keep it to myſelf) it may as well make its appearance in your very excellent paper. It ſeems to me to be altogether without connection; and written only for the amuſement of its illuſtrious author, is almoſt unintelligible to any one elſe. Publiſh the following extract as a ſpecimen, and if it afford as much amuſement to the public as it has to me, I will endeavor to decypher the remainder, and add occaſionally an explanatory note, where the ſenſe is moſt uncommonly obſcure. There are no dates, and the ſlips of paper upon which this intereſting journal is written, are ſo mixed and confuſed, and jumbled together, that it will be the work of an age to reduce them to any ſort of order.

1. Began to prepare for circuit—deviliſh troubleſome—wiſh I could get ſomething better. Gun out of order—no flints—pointer lame—muſt wait a day for him. Mem. to buy two pair of ſilk ſtockings—muſt take Bob and Mat along.

2. Bought a tweezer-caſe—met D——— C———n, C———m, and E———r, (Mat and Bob too) about my election—all a farce—can't get in—D W———t grum ſpoke croſs to C———m, don't know why, R———r ſupple as uſual, crack'd a joke upon his leg, didn't mind it, good na-tured little dog; dined at Mats, beef tough, we all wondered why gud-geons had ſuch large mouths, D. W———t wiſhed the people had as big, for he could'nt make 'em ſwallow any thing now a days; D——— W———t told ſome ſtories about Burr, believe he lied, for C———m ſaid he'd ſwear to 'em; ſnuffed up my noſe when I paſſed D——— W———t; couldn't help it, muſt have ſome fun, he got in a paſſion—call'd my *back bob* to ſet *next* to me, walk'd out, D——— W———t and I good friends again; boys huzza for Burr, C———m whipt 'em away, went home, Mat and Bob got two pigeons, had a good ſet at

brag, Mat at his *old tricks* again.—Croſſed to Long-Iſland, remembered what D——— W——t told me, and ſhook a greaſy butcher by the hand, Faugh! dirty work, neck or nothing tho', loft poor Quirk ſwimming over the river; dined at White's—ſheep's-head not half boil'd; Mat's red champaigne ropy. N. B. went to bed ſober as a judge.

Charged Jury in Kings County, Bob's cock got the pip; no buſineſs; poor Bob, ſent him ten miles for a bottle good champaigne; lock'd up jury, made Mat call a meeting to nominate governor—ſtay'd at home to pick my eyebrows; D——— W——t pop'd in upon me, (lives cloſe by) call'd me coxcomb and aſs; bawl'd out for Bob, (forgot I'd ſent him for champaigne) frighten'd half to death; Bob came back empty; went to bed ſeven o'clock.

Sick all day—lay abed—D——— W——t bored me.

Roſe at nine; ſhot a cock before breakfaſt; Bob bullied a fellow who wouldn't let me walk over his wheat field; uſeful fellow Bob; muſt give him a place; do any dirty work—dined at D——— W——t's; D——— W——t's ſoup never ſalt enough; went to Queens; got chamber maid to waſh my feet; pretty girl; mum.—

Had ſuch a cold couldn't charge jury; no matter, caſe of murder; Dick promiſed to wake me when they began to ſum up—Starve him! he forgot it.—

Man beat his wife, bruiſed her piteouſly; but did'nt uſe a *ſtick thicker* than his *thumb*, directed jury to bring in verdict *not guilty*; they brought him in *guilty*, ſent 'em out again, they returned *guilty* a ſecond time; wouldn't obey me; ſo I rode 'em round the country in a *cart*, aye, in a *cart!* rare ſport—ſo I uſe the power that the law gives me, dam'me.

Here my confuſion begins, Mr. Tickler; however make the beſt of it:

Adjourn'd court; went to J——n W——t's. Mem. to try and find out what J——n is; aſked Dick, but he "proteſted on his honor" he could not tell (little monkey) a grum looking fellow aſked me how the wind was; J——n keeps good madeira tho'; he talked to me about conſiſtency; what right has he to ſay any thing about it; muſtn't ſay ſo tho'; aſked me if I got a good price for my butter; old quiz, put him under the table for't.

My dear Toby, I can get no farther, I'm loft in a maze of perplexities; but you ſhall hear from me again.

Your loving friend,
RIGDUMFUNNIDOS.

TO TOBY TICKLER, ESQ.

——

Dear Coufin,

The patronage which has been fo liberally extended to the new and interefting performances of our native authors, has induced the proprietors to enlarge their plan beyond the limits of their firft intention; and the candor and indulgence of a generous public has ftimulated our learned countrymen to fo beneficial an emulation in their labors, and to fo extraordinary an exertion of their talents, that I am now enabled to prefent to you for publication, a catalogue of no lefs than ten numbers of a work undertaken with fingular fpirit, and conducted with uncommon ability.

The productions which I firft had the honor of ufhering to the favor of the public, have been fought after with avidity, and read with intereft. The names of the ingenious authors have been called forth from obfcurity, or refcued from oblivion, whilft their characters, perhaps not duly appreciated before my notice of their merits, have been vindicated from mifconception, preferved from mifapprehenfion, and placed in the jufteft and trueft lights before the eyes of their admiring countrymen.

There has occurred, however, one melancholy circumftance, which, as it tends to mortify the pride of genius, ferves alfo to deprefs the delight which I have hitherto experienced in the profecution of my tafk. Soon after the publication of my firft letter, the celebrated author of the "Redemptioners" difcovered the moft alarming and diftreffing fymptoms of mental derangement, which feem to threaten in the end a total deftruction of his intellectual powers. The cafe of this tragi-comic poet is as remarkable as it is lamentable. Ever fince the commencement of his malady, his mind feems to have dwelt upon no other fubject, than the drama which was mentioned in the laft catalogue, and which was received with fo much applaufe by the public; this feems "the mafter ftring which makes harmony or difcord with him." He does not, however, as might reafonably be expected, dwell with rapture on its merits, or appear intoxicated with the approbation which mark'd its reception. But with a fingularity which ever diftinguifhes the madnefs of men of genius, he complains of the libellous nature of his own performance, and has actually prevailed upon his friends to inftitute a profecution againft his printer for publifhing the productions of his own imagination.

"Great genius fure to madnefs is alli'd,
And thin partitions do their bounds divide."

In the lift of thofe works which compofe the fubject of my prefent enclofure you will find a variety of excellence, calculated for the amufement and inftruction of readers of all taftes and of every defcription. The lovers of comedy and farce will find much entertainment in "the Knight of the Burning Peftle," and "the Humors of Contradiction;" the admirers of poefy will be moved, by the Doric fimplicity of ——— and enraptured with the fublime devotion of the heavenly mufe of Mr. O———d: whilft the experimental philofopher and natural hiftorian will reap a rich harveft of materials from the labors of that *great man* whofe "fame has traverfed the ocean, and circumnavigated the globe," and whofe name is celebrated from the peak of Teneriffe to the foot of the Dunderberg—from the head of the Penobfcot to the mouth of the Michillimachinac—from Cape Cod to Little-Egg-Harbour—from the Antipodes to the centre of the earth.

I am, dear Sir,
your affectionate
relation and friend,
TOUCHSTONE TICKLER.

P. S. In a future communication it is my intention to furnifh you with copious extracts from feveral of thefe works, with an impartial criti-cifm upon their general merits and execution.

————

"*New and interesting publications by native and living Authors.*"

No. 9. "The Knight of the Burning Peftle; or a voyage to the Promon-tory" a pantomimical farce by J———n B———me Efq. S. and C. A. M.
"*Non cuicunque datum eft habere nafum.*"
No. 10. "He wou'd or he wou'd not; or the humours of contradiction," a Burletta, by J——— W———s Efq. F. I. C. W.
No. 11. "The way to wealth, an experimental treatife on the art of faving a fortune" reduced to fyftem and arranged under two diftinct heads, viz.
Part 1ft. Stopping payment in *feafon*.
Part 2d. Paying piftareens for pounds.
By J——— R. ——— Gent.

"———*Rem facias rem,*
Si poffis recte, fi non, quocunque modo rem."

No. 12. "The fpecious fycophant or the biography of a parafite," in which it is clearly demonftrated that a fop and a fool by the conftant practice of *boo*-ing, fawning, cringing, flattering and lying, will inevit-ably attain the firft honors of his profeffion, and the moft lucrative offices of the ftate—written for the edification of the promifing youth of the faction—by R——— R———, Efq. A. G. S. D. Printed upon a *vellum* paper and bound in the form of a fmall pocket volume.

No. 13. "The Loves of Tygers," a comico, politico, philofophico, mifanthropical poem, imitated from Dr. Darwin—by G———— C———— jun. and T——s W——n Efqs. This piece was fet to mufic by a frantic fidler, and will be fung after the election by the leaders of the coalition in full chorus, with a grand accompaniment of *guns, drums, trumpets, marrow bones and cleavers.*

No. 14. "Experiments and obfervations upon Soap Suds, for the benefit of S——s M——r, Efq. with an appendix in 2 vols folio, containing, 1. A treatife upon the manufacture of words to be derived from all languages. 2. Microfcopic examinations of the pineal glands of a loufe. 3. A memoir concerning the natural hiftory of the *porcus doctus,* vulgarly called the learned pig", by ——————— ——————— of Plandome, Efq. M. D. L. L. D. *nuper* Proff. Chym. Hift. Nat. et Agrie. Theor. et Prac. et Chowcol. Proff. in Col. Coll. *nunc* Cent. V. Fredon. Sec. Agrie. Soc. A. P. S. S. F. R. S. Lond. et Ed. *nec non* Sos. Hon. Acad. Heid. Phys. Hofp. Nov. Eber, *A. S. S.* &c. &c. &c. &c. &c. &c.

No. 15. A new edition of the fame work, to which is prefixed a life of the learned author, written by himfelf, embellifhed with a portrait of the doctor, efteemed a ftriking likenefs, and accompanied by a fupplementary appendix, in royal quarto, containing an accurate lift of all his offices, titles, honors and dignities, as well thofe he enjoys at prefent, as thofe he enjoyed lately, and thofe which he never did enjoy, ftrongly bound in calf. Motto—"There is no man more free than myfelf from the defpicable vice of vanity: but without paffing the bounds of modefty, I may venture to affert, that wherever fcience is cultivated, and genius revered, there is the name of M———— honored, and his labors acknowledged with gratitude. My fame is not confined within the limits of Fredonia, vaft as they are.—No, it has traverfed the ocean—it has circumnavigated the globe, and now fills and pervades every region of the civilized world."—*Extracted from the anfwer to the addrefs of the Medical ftudents of Columbia College.*

No. 16. "The hymn of the hypocrites," by S———— O————, Efq. S. R. et N. O. N. Y. D.—*Extract.*

> "Praife ye, D. W. all ye who hope for fame,
> Or boaft the *royal* blood, and *Clinton* name;
> Praife him, each *Livingfton,* or fool or knave,
> And your cropt-heads in fign of worfhip wave."

RARE FUN ! ! !

The ariftocratic faction have fpared no pains or manœuvres to pleafe the populace and attract them to the polls. The Clintonian *menage* was opened yefterday, and its collection of queer animals exhibited to the public in every ward. MONKEY DICK being troubled with a lamenefs in one of his ſcrapers, was carried out to the ſeventh ward in a coach. Here he peep'd out, and ſmirk'd and nodded, and bobb'd his head about like Punch in a puppet-box, to the great amuſement of ſpectators.

The OURANG OUTANG was ſtationed at the eighth ward. He, however, was mute, and ſupported his cauſe merely by *making faces*. It is ſaid an overflowing of the bile occaſioned the peculiar deadlineſs of aſpect for which he has been remarked theſe two days paſt. If this continues, I would recommend an *oath* to him, to purge away the *bad humor* with which he is afflicted. I fancy he would not ſtrain at the preſcription.

The YAHOO put on a *clean* ſhirt, and for ſome time walked about *incog*; he was at length ſmell'd out, notwithſtanding his *diſguiſe*, and at the cry of YAHOO! he made a precipitate retreat. We adviſe the *Yahoo* not to confine the *temporary* ſyſtem of cleanlineſs he has adopted merely to his face and hands, but to ſuffer the reſt of his body to partake of the *uncommon* refreſhment. Perhaps a little ſmoking would be adviſable in a caſe of ſuch inveterate ſtench and filthineſs.

The GREASY PORPOISE, *Ferris*, puff'd and blow'd about the eighth ward poll. He was attended by a conſtable at each elbow to protect his carcaſe from being drumm'd. To this prudent precaution he was indebted for not getting a ſound drubbing from a gentleman whom he inſulted by his impertinence. *Ned* trembles and turns pale when even he ſees a Burrite; he always walks peculiarly faſt through the ſtreets, with his face turned backward.

Young SLABSIDES, the *unlicked ſuccubus*, ran about on *Monkey Dick*'s errands. As this youth however does but retail the remnants of Cheetham's and Wortman's miſerable ſpeeches, I will not damn him into notice.

BILLY LUSCIOUS ſneaked about as uſual with his pockets full of handbills. This *muffin face meddler* not having brains enough to connect many words together, chuſes rather to read a handbill than make a ſpeech. He is ſerviceable to electioneer among his old clients in dram ſhops, &c. &c. &c. It is obſerved he ſtill ſmells of the *dung-hill*.

(*To be continued.*)

[May 14, 1804]

"WE WILL REJOICE ! ! !"

Duane's Jubilee—On Saturday last was celebrated in the Lanes and Highways of our city, a grand Democratic Pantomimic Fete, got up at the command of William Duane, the Irish *Dictator*, managed by Citizen Mooncalf, and entitled, *"Extension of the Empire of Freedom,"* or LOUISIANA CONQUERED *by an Ass—laden with gold!"*

Harlequin Herald,   *Citizen V——— Z——t*
Clown,   *Mooncalf*
Scaramouch,   *by an Officer of distinction*
Pantaloon,   *by an Indian Native,*
(being his first appearance on any stage)
Other characters, by gentlemen *without character*. The principal scene
in this entertaining *farce*, was a

GRAND PROCESSION.

This was opened by a ragged regiment of sweeps, negroes, and tatter-
de-malion boys, bearing old hats, shoes, dishclouts and dead cats, on
the ends of broomsticks. These young gentlemen certainly made a very
respectable and truly formidable appearance—a faithful specimen of
what was to follow. To these succeeded a few *well mounted* horsemen,
escorting what at first was taken for the Ostrich which is advertised to
be seen at Savages' Museum. It was stuck, in an aukward attitude, upon
a light grey horse, and fantastically tricked out, partly in uniform and
partly in ribbons and cocks' tails. Viewed at a little distance in one of
its paws seemed placed a standard, on which was painted *"Extension
of the Empire of Freedom,"** &c. It was amusing to hear the observations of the croud as it approached: one declared it to be the real
Ostrich, carrying about for a shew; another remarked, that if the
feathers on its head were stuck in its tail, he should have taken it for
that kind of bird vulgarly called *****poke*; a third insisted it must
be the Yahoo, lately imported from Louisiana, where *Sniggers*, the
traveller, observes "Theye do abounde most abundantlie, and do ramble
about with featheres stucke sometymes in theyre heades and sometymes
in theyre rumpes, and afforde much divertisement and pleasantrie."
Here a grave looking man, who had been obstructed by the croud, and
was waiting till the mob got by, observed, with much solemnity of
manner, that it reminded him of the verse in the Revelations—"And I
looked and beheld a *pale horse*, and his name that sat on him was
Death, and *Hell followed with him.*"
One part of the procession was composed of the respectable order of
catchpoles, parading two and two, with their *staves of office*. When
these came along, a little boy pulled my sleeve and asked me if these

---

*The truly sapient Dr. Septon, Centum Vir. A.S.S. &c. &c. &c. ad infin. who is
said to have dictated the inscription, was very desirous to have this printed
"Extension of the empire of *Fredon*." As the Doctor is a man of political importance, it was thought adviseable to indulge his whim, but the painter, who was a
stupid elf, supposed it was false spelling, and therefore changed *n* into *m*. The
Doctor was conspicuous in one part of the procession, floundering along with a
pretty buck's tail in his hat, inflated with literary and political *gas*, and sweltering
under the load of titles daily heaped upon him.

were not the Judges? But his mother silenced him by a nod of her head, and saved me the trouble of answering. Next to them came a few genuine members of the honorable the corporation; his honor the *Mayor*, and his *vice* honor the sheriff, walking among them arm in arm. Notwithstanding the natural assurance of the former of these gentlemen, he appeared completely ashamed of his situation: as he passed the Coffee House his face was a glowing cinder. His companion shewed his perturbation in a different style; a faintish paleness occupied his countenance the whole way. Their eyes were bent upon the ground, as if afraid to encounter the broad grin of ridicule and contempt that was visible in the countenance of every spectator. In one part of the procession was displayed a huge map of *Louisiana*, the New Canaan, flowing with *buttermilk* and *molasses*, and with a huge mountain of salt in the centre. A great bargain! price *only* Fifteen Millions! This *raree show* was supported on one side by little citizen Cowdry, the carpenter, father of master Sammy, of certificate memory; and on the other, by citizen Soap-suds, a knight of the comb, while between them "Lo! the poor Indian," with his eyes cast down on the earth, and looking for all the world like a prisoner going to execution. The rear of this tag-rag and bobtail exhibition was brought up by seven or eight *genuine republican* officers of the brigade of the city and county of New-York, preceded by Bully Lowther, the carman, in uniform without epaulets. If the reader wishes to learn their respectability, it will suffice to inform him that Captain JAMES DAGGERMAN was one of the foremost, and best looking among them.

Any comments on this pantomimic farce are unnecessary—Suffice it to say that it has afforded a sufficient fund of laughter to supply the city for a fortnight to come, and was truly of a piece with the *Mammoth Loaf* frolic of our worthy President, at Washington.

THE NEW-YORK REVIEW; OR, CRITICAL JOURNAL. TO BE CONTINUED AS OCCASION REQUIRES. MARCH 1809. CONTAINING *STRICTURES ON A PAMPHLET ENTITLED "FRAGMENT OF A JOURNAL OF A SENTIMENTAL PHILOSOPHER"*

> *Fragment of a Journal of a Sentimental Philosopher, during his residence in the city of New-York. To which is added, a Discourse upon the nature and properties of Eloquence as a Science, delivered to his disciples previous to his departure.—New-York—Sargeant, 8vo. pp. 38.*

Among our painful duties, as faithful reviewers, it is not the least, that we have occasionally to toil through the muddy volumes of blundering stupidity, or to skim over the frothy pages of conceited impertinence. When, however, in the course of our thankless labours, we encounter

a work, which is suggested by sound morality, and conducted with ingenuity and candour; we sit down to it with a double relish, from the
novelty of the regale.

Such was the case when we opened the erudite little pamphlet before
us—which, if we may judge from the rhapsodical connection of its parts,
must have been written by some windy genius, just sublimated by a
plentiful bladder of nitrous oxyd.

This very original and witty performance, is an attack upon a certain
literary gentleman, here designated by the name of a *Sentimental Philosopher*. It is on the very original plan of a Journal, in which the
Philosopher is made to describe himself and his friends; tell the world
what a wicked infidel he was; what ridiculous pranks he played, and
what marvellous foul linen he wore. In the course of this, our champion
takes occasion, with a single back-stroke, to demolish some score or so
of infidel writers, such as Southey, Holcroft, Darwin, Smith, and Minshull, and delivers sundry dozen of distressed damsels from the dungeons
of these wicked giants—which done, he wipes his sword, makes a
flourishing speech on eloquence, borrowed from some friendly author
for the occasion, smirks, smiles, makes a profound bow to the ladies, and
retires behind a stinking little French proverb.

It has too long been the fate of substantial, orthodox principles, to
be defended by ponderous champions, who wield nothing but the cumbrous weapons of reason, religion and common sense; but we may now
expect wonderful effects, since that irresistible weapon, nonsense, is
enlisted in the cause—and we congratulate all our fellow lodgers in the
temple of morality, that we have a brisk little cur at the door, who will
fly out, and snap and yelp, at every suspicious passenger. While we
heartily condemn the disorganizing principles inculcated by Godwin
and his fellow apostates; we cannot but lament, that our advocates for
the true faith, have hitherto confined themselves to the puny measures of
refuting their doctrines, exposing the fallacy of their opinions, and
demonstrating their evil tendency to corrupt and subvert the order of
society. The true way to abolish the flimsy doctrines of modern philosophy, is now and then to knock one if its disciples on the head. Such
also is the opinion of the lively author of the work we are now reviewing—who has bent all his talents, not to refute opinions, but to extermi-
nate an individual—reminding us forcibly of one of our bustling little
firemen, who scampers about the streets, with his leather hat—sets all
the bells ringing and throws the whole city in a hubbub—to put out a
chimney on fire.

Among the most amusing portions of the labour of a reviewer, is that
of enquiring into the character of the author of any work before him, and
of introducing him to the reader. And indeed this part of gentleman-
usher is not only agreeable, but useful; inasmuch as it gives no little

insight into the intention of the writer, and his abilities for the work he has undertaken. Having, as we freely own, this harmless propensity to pry into the affairs of authors, our very hearts leaped when we first opened this strange and original little book; and it was unanimously resolved, that one of our most inquisitive colleagues should be forthwith dispatched, to gather all the particulars possible, concerning this unaccountable adventurer into the fairy land of literature. He returned, however, with no positive account, but a very considerable rumour. Were it not that in this goose quill age, every body can write, whether he can read or not, it might peradventure create some little astonishment, that this unheard of author is said to be a certain brisk, dapper little Ironmonger; who has long been beating the bushes of literature, without starting any game, and rapping at the door of several professions, without gaining admittance into any.

A journeyman shoemaker once wrote a poem in England, a blacksmith's son another, a madman composed tragedies, and a cow prophesied during the war;—but that a dealer in coffee mills and pepper boxes should, in a fit of enthusiasm, jump over his counter, climb the heights of Parnassus, and attempt to retail his pot-hooks and trammels among the muses, is a prodigy almost beyond our belief.

Be this as it may, we almost fancy we can see the author, striding along the broad road of fame like a pair of his own tongs; or receiving the first rudiments of literature, by the profound study of HL hinges, while an apprentice to some pains-taking ironmonger—who, rest his soul! perhaps never lived to see his aspiring shop-boy turn author.

From his constant sarcasms at the dingy appearance of the Philosopher, we portray him to ourselves a well dressed, smirking little man, well shaven and shorn; who makes genius consist in clean linen, who carries morality in the plaits of his shirt, and whose creed, like that of the Mahometan, consists in frequent ablutions. A smart, vapouring little Pharisee, who judges of a Christian by the cut of his garment; and who, happily for the good cause, has just whisked into the house of faith, time enough to slap the door in the Philosopher's face, and spit at him through the key hole. We can see him, picking his teeth, and paring his nails between every sentence, and at the end of a paragraph, starting up and running to his ever-ready looking glass, to admire the head that could produce such a wonderful concatenation of ideas.

Having thus formed to ourselves, what we consider a probable likeness of the author, and which should have been prefixed to his work, like the portrait of Noah Webster to his spelling book, or Jack the giant-killer to his far-famed chronicle; we will now proceed to consider the work itself.

The following is the flourish of trumpet, with which, like a doughty knight our author enters the lists. "In publishing the following pages, the editor is persuaded, that he renders a very important service to the community."

This is something like commencing an acquaintance by reminding us of a debt, or rather, claiming our gratitude in advance, before we have received any services. In paying two shillings for the pamphlet, we had ignorantly supposed ourselves at clear accounts with the author; and he should at least have suffered us to read his work through, before he insisted that we ought to thank him into the bargain. One thing, however, is certain, that from this introductory paragraph we learn the author is highly satisfied with himself: this to good natured reviewers like ourselves is a most acceptable piece of information; as we are certain we run the less chance of hurting his feelings, by any accidental blow we may happen to give in the course of our strictures.

In the execution of his work, our author has shewn a most praise-worthy ingenuity in the construction of his sentences; by the means of dashes parcelling out his ideas into pennyworths; and saving the expence and labour of long periods. He has demolished the Philosopher, not by contesting his opinions, and exposing the fallacy of his doctrines; but like a terrier ferreting out rats, has dogged him from house to house, pimped among servants for anecdotes of what passed in the parlour, and even (we stop our noses, while we record the humble labours of this industrious layman) rummaged over the archives of a certain temple, to search for fragments of his letters or memorandums. He has roundly proved *(by assertion)* that the various eccentricities of conduct, and benevolent actions of the Philosopher were plain proofs of his heretical opinions and detestable hypocrisy; that the eye of devout Christianity was outraged by his wearing dirty linen, and the whole bulwark of morality suffered violence by his opening his snuff box with a case knife! These and a variety of similar facts about laudanum phials, cow tail wigs, &c. jumbled together without attending to the formal shackles of rule or order, are admirably suited to the excursive genius of our retailer of hardware, and prove that he has found out a method of making books, as the Israelites of yore did of manufacturing bricks, out of chaff and stubble.

While our valiant little author is in full yelp at the heels of the Phi-losopher; he now and then turns aside to give a most fearful snap at Godwin, Southey, and Holcroft, and the other marauders on morality. In noticing these authors he is careful always to speak of them in the very same terms used by the author of "The Pursuits of Literature;" and which have regularly been worn threadbare by all such anti-Jacobin and anti-Godwinian writers, as would rather figure in their neighbour's clothes, than in their own ragged garments.

Indeed "The Pursuits of Literature" seems to be a standing text book of our exceedingly well-read author, and as it contains abundance of light and pleasant reading, we would recommend it to the perusal of all literary young women, who are not engaged in the profounder studies of Moore's Poems.

But while our author is busily employed in hunting down "small deer," it is a matter of infinite astonishment to us, that wielding, as he does, such ponderous weapons, he has not assayed his prowess, in the pursuit of higher game. This however like good natured critics, we are inclined to attribute to his modesty, and it is really with pleasure we acknowledge our obligation to him, for this one display of a quality, so little to be expected from a dealer in brass and iron.

To this singular and uncommon modesty, we ascribe his not having noticed the abominable and truly censurable hypocrisy of the Philosopher, in his public orations; where, with all the close disguise of a designing innovator, he carefully abstained from disclosing a single sentiment, or uttering a single argument, calculated to corrupt the hearts, or undermine the principles of his auditors. That an advocate for Godwinism, should thus have the unparalleled effrontery, to keep from the public those very opinions, which according to our authentic little author, he set out on purpose to propagate; is an instance of the most singular and deliberate hypocrisy, that ought to have been proclaimed to the world, by the sound of the largest tin trumpet in the shop of our journalist.

But the indefatigable apostle of infidelity, insidiously neglected the opportunities offered him, in six or seven public lectures, of instilling his sceptical doctrines into the minds of crowded and enthusiastic audiences, and insolently dared to declaim on the "deep toned" heroes of duelling, the fatal and inexorable consequences of gaming, the incalculable advantages of education, and the divine virtues of charity and universal benevolence. Infamous hypocrisy! and no less infamous than original; for upon the honour of reviewers this is the first instance of the kind we have seen, heard or read of. This is the very man, according to the logic of our author, who we ought to guard against, who having a dagger in his bosom, keeps it concealed, and throws his purse into the lap of society.

Another instance of his detestable hypocrisy, and his insidious attempts on the morals of society, and which our quill valiant hero has equally neglected to notice, is the pretensions of our Philosopher to charity. That a man who does not believe in the Christian religion, should dare to practise any of its doctrines, is downright blasphemy. That he should appropriate the proceeds of some of his public orations, amounting to several hundred dollars, to the assistance of charitable institutions, is a base attempt to hurt the feelings of numbers of our most strenuous professors of religion, who are content to talk about the virtue, which the Philosopher has the effrontery to practise. It is one of those hyperbolical exertions of charity, which our author, judging from that infallible standard, his own heart, should at once have placed to the score of hypocrisy.

These and several other enormities, in the hurry of his zeal, he has forgotten to mention, but we trust he will notice them in the continuation of his journal, should his researches in the temple enable him to furnish any further fragments.

We cannot but observe the excessive caution with which our journalist has abstained from all quotations from infidel or pagan writers; excepting such as have been sanctified by immemorial use since the days of honest old Burton, of quoting memory. By this prudent precaution, these little ornaments of composition, which give such grace and dignity to a work, and so slyly convey an idea of the profound learning of the author, are, in him, as blameless as they are erudite. Our author, who doubtless has been accustomed from his childhood to the vending of *old saws*, (we assure him upon the honour of reviewers that we mean no pun) perceived that fifty years of constant wear and tear in the literary world had completely worn out all power of doing harm from *nil desperandum—risum teneatis amici*, and *fas ab hoste doceri*—quotations which had become so exceedingly current, that he might have picked them up from among the inscriptions of tea-boards, tobacco-boxes, and *ne plus ultra* razors.

Such is the exuberance of our author's ideas, that finding he has more than enough to overwhelm the Philosopher, he has most civilly thrown a handful in the face of his friends. Certain presumptuous gentlemen of this city, who, without waiting to ask a dispensation from our little Boniface, dared, like some hundreds of their ignorant and apostate fellow-citizens, to be pleased with the eloquence of the orator, and even to visit him in private, have received the chastisement their horrible iniquities demanded. Our shrewd writer of journals, who seems to have a peculiar faculty at diving into the hearts of men, and discovering opinions, hidden even from themselves; has plainly proved (*by assertion*) that they could visit this man of science and letters, for no other purpose, than because they were thorough-paced Godwinians. We are only surprised that he stopped here, and did not, according to the same rule, prove that all those crowded audiences, who thronged to hear his eloquence, were downright apostates, and deserved to be burned, without benefit of clergy. Surely those who admire the eloquence, or fancy of a man, must likewise believe in all his opinions; in the same manner, that all who admire the binding and gilding of a book, are converts to the doctrines it contains. Such at least is the ingenious syllogism, upon which our author has founded most of his sturdy assertions.

After trotting briskly, in little broken-winded sentences, over the field of science and morals; after having ransacked all the parlour mantlepieces for cards, and cellar-kitchens for anecdotes, of the hapless Philosopher and his friends; our doughty little knight-errant, at length pounces upon game more worthy of his prowess. These are no other than those hapless wights Dr. S——— and Mr. M———. Whether any literary rivalship had anciently subsisted between the venerable orator and physician, the jocular author and man milliner, and the learned hardware man and satirist, is matter of much suspicion: certain it is, these tottering followers of the muses, are for ever swept away, by the very wind and whiff of his fell sword. Shame, that men, who embodied together might have formed a constellation of kindred genius, sufficient to set a tinder-box in a blaze, should thus let out the dangerous secret that authors are but men; and that even Dr. S——— and Mr. M———, and our thrice-valiant Journalist, are afflicted with mere human passions. But the triumvirate of Rome sunk beneath the arm of Cæsar, so doth this of New-York, beneath our dictatorial retailer of the small wares of Birmingham and Parnassus.

It is singular what ludicrous ideas will sometimes intrude themselves into the brain, and with their frisking overset and dissipate the gravest speculations of the philosopher, and the most profound researches of the critick.—We will honestly confess that though engaged in a conflict equal in danger with any recorded in chivalry or song, we could not separate the idea of our author and his warlike equipments, from that of the renowned Knight of La Mancha.—We fancied we saw him mounted on his Rosinante, saluting the morning sun in the far famed field of Montoil, and anticipating the renown of those exploits that were fermenting in his brain, and turning it topsy-turvy.—At other times we beheld him in imagination opening the cage of the lions and provoking his fate with all the headlong impetuosity of mental derangement. Again our fancy portrayed him metamorphosing giants into wind-mills, attacking them in spite of the sage remonstrances of his squire, and getting soundly drubbed for his pains.—Lastly he appeared to our diverted imagination, returning to his home like the poor Knight of the woful countenance, bruised, battered, and disconsolate in the disastrous termination of his misadventures.

While we gaze with fond admiration on this wonderful production of human genius, thus rich with various lore; thus gay with fancy, and sparkling with wit; and reflect on the very short time which, we are told, intervened between its first conception and its glorious entrance into the world, we are lost in astonishment. We stand staring in stupid wonder, as if we had seen one of the fairy palaces of eastern fable rise up before us in a single night, from amid the barren sands of a desert, and the sturdy little yeoman standing like a dwarf at the portal. Incredible as it may appear, we assure our readers (and we have taken much pains to ascertain the fact) that this admirable performance was planned, the necessary facts collected, and the whole thrown into that happy form which it now bears, in the short space of four months, three weeks and five days—not to mention odd hours and minutes.

Seven cities were said to have contended for the honour of having given birth to Homer. This in ancient times was, doubtless, thought no small compliment to the Iliad; but scarcely had this formidable pamphlet been five days in the world, before nine cities, thirteen villages, and forty-seven post towns, presented their claims to the honour of being its birth place. The cause of this wrangling, we understand, on diligent enquiry, is that the author becoming impregnated with wit, in New-York; ran cackling and scratching from thence to Philadelphia; from Philadelphia to Baltimore; from Baltimore to Washington, and thence back again; searching for some convenient spot, where he might lay his egg with comfort and decency. At length he pitched upon Albany— Albany! the Athens of America—the seat of the Muses—the metropolis of fashion.—Albany! whose lofty spires glitter with tin, and whose hospitable boards smoak with sturgeon! Here the egg was safely laid, and forthwith transported to New-York to be hatched. We mention these particulars, not to gratify any idle curiosity of the present day, but to prevent the effusion of ink and hard words among the learned of some future age, who may think this subject worthy of controversy.

But the most important service which this mighty pamphlet has done to society is, that it has, at one blow, accomplished the death of Tom Paine; who was found dead in his room on Friday last, with this pamphlet in his hand, and his thumb on the very passage that makes such contemptuous mention of his name. Thus this arch champion of infidelity, who, like a second Goliah, had set at naught the armies of Israel, and bearded certain of its stoutest heroes, was at length, while he reared his head aloft like a blazing sun in the midst of the firmament, brought low like his prototype of yore, by a pigmy slinger of pebbles.

And now having sufficiently amused ourselves, and flattered the vanity of our author, it behoves us to have a little serious chat with him before we part. We are fully assured, that if this sturdy little man should have the ill nature to mistake all that we have already said for sheer irony, and should have the hardihood to appeal from our decisions, he will not fail to charge us with being the disciples of that terrible innovator Godwin. This is the usual weapon of a testy author; who commonly solaces his chagrin in the indiscriminate condemnation of all those unfortunate caitiffs, who have not taste enough to admire his writings. It is like raising the cry of mad dog; in which case there are always a host of officious and charitable byestanders, ready to throw stones at the accused, without enquiring into the justice of the accusation.

But we seriously assure this testy little gentleman, that we have long held the principles and opinions of Godwin in detestation; and often had occasion to regret the importance which has been given to the speculations of this preacher of immorality and infidelity. However dangerous we acknowledge these doctrines, it is with pain we are forced to confess, that the interests of society have suffered equally from the indiscreet zeal of those, who have undertaken to confute them, without talents or ingenuity for the task; and who have supplied their deficiencies by crying out *murder*, or *fire*, instead of resorting to the exertions necessary to prevent the one, or to extinguish the other.

It is to be hoped, and we most sincerely believe, that the foundations of morality and religion are laid too firmly in the human heart, to be easily shaken by the mere cavils of an ingenious sophist. It is the un-founded alarms which are continually sounded by the well meaning opposers of the false and hollow principles of the Godwinians, which are, in our opinion, most calculated to impair religious and moral prin-ciples, in minds where they have taken but superficial root; or where, as is the case with perhaps the majority of mankind, they have been re-ceived, without scrutiny, as the immutable laws of the divinity. These impotent alarms startle us to danger, without guarding us against it; and often point out to the careless and indifferent the paths of infidelity, which they could never otherwise have thought of. A weak defence of the Christian religion, is infinitely more pernicious, than the empty attacks of Paine or Godwin, and is calculated to awaken doubts of an institution, which is not better defended. Superficial believers are led to imagine, that there are no stronger evidences of its truth, because none more convincing are adduced; and thus the best of causes is in-jured, by the imbecility of its advocates.

Such being our opinions, while we look with pride to the dignified and substantial defences of a Butler and a Watson, we could not forbear treating the frivolous attempts of this puny defender of the faith, with the contempt they merited. Besides, we imagined we could see some more questionable incentive than religious zeal, at the bottom of this frothy vapouring. It is too often, under the guise of some amiable or honourable motive, that the selfish heart takes occasion to discharge its malignity. Covering under the sacred mantle of religion those passions, which he dares not own, the envious man gives vent to his spleen; and pretending to defend Christianity from attacks which have never been made, darts his venom at the object of his ill humour. In the holy char-acter of an advocate of a most amiable and pure religion, he outrages its precepts; secure that there will be a host of worthy, but zealous and unthinking people, ready to accept his pretended motive, as an apology for the illiberality of his conduct. Such is the case with the writer before us, who has dragged, with all his puny and diminutive force, into public view, an individual who, whatever may be his faults, has none to answer for to this community. A man who while here, conducted himself with unblemished innocence; whose foibles were such as often cling to the most amiable characters; and whose benevolence was exerted, in a manner that might serve as an example to those few, who have cruelly attempted to blacken his character.

What were the private opinions of Mr. O———, we will not pretend to say—as we do not arrogate to ourselves, like our author, the supreme power of judging of the hearts of men. But the lectures that he publicly delivered, and the whole tenor of his conversation, as far as it has reached our ears, were free from harm or reproach. We consider him, in fact, a mere amusing, philosophical Quixote; who had not wickedness to devise, nor artfulness enough to execute, the mischiefs our windy alarmist has asserted—and whose harmless eccentricities and visionary speculations, might have excited the smile of the gay, or the compassion of the charitable; but could never deserve the unfeeling and personal lash of the censorious. Neither do we think the orator is to be cut up by piece-meal, because a few enthusiastic individuals were dazzled and enraptured by his figures, his quotations and his hyperbole, any more than our worthy lecturers on chemistry are to be personally lampooned, because some dozens of dabblers in science, have chosen to bewilder their brains by inhaling nitrous oxyd.—Multitudes of our fellow citizens, of all descriptions thronged to hear him, yet we do not find that our churches are the less attended, the order of society subverted, or infidelity more prevalent than formerly.—True it is, that some unlucky females have amused themselves with the science of chemistry; but as we have ever considered, that the study of nature, is calculated to lead the student "from nature up to nature's God," we entertain very little fears for their orthodoxy on that account.

But if Mr. O———'s opinions were really as pernicious and as insidiously instilled, as our journalist would fain have us believe, why were they not attacked before? Why was he suffered to remain several weeks in this city, and no assault made until his back was turned, and his power of doing injury had ceased? Why also was not the attack generously confined to his opinions, and his orations? The latter were certainly open to discussion; and though abounding with beauties, yet we think both his compositions and elocution were marked with defects, which would have afforded abundant food for candid criticism. Why did the writer resort to pitiful forgeries of conversations which never passed; to the invention of incidents which never occurred? Why did he wreak his impertinence on every gentleman, who for amusement or any other innocent motive, visited Mr. O———, and ascribe to them opinions which they never avowed, nor ever entertained? Was it necessary for the reputation of Mr. O———'s *secret* opinions that he should be unfeelingly derided for being the victim to an unhappy attachment to laudanum, which is its own relentless punisher? Was it necessary also to the defence of religion or morality, that Mr. O———'s wig should be pulled from his head, or that he should be stripped to his shirt and exposed to public view? that his occasional neglect of his person should be made the subject of paltry ribaldry? If it was, then all the defenders of that good cause have mistaken the weapons they were to employ; and instead of foolishly resorting to argument, ought to have attacked the hats, coats, wigs and breeches of their adversaries, and hung up the dirty shirts of infidels, in terrorem to their accomplices.

And now we conclude, seriously and solemnly, by informing this strenuous advocate for morality and clean linen; who seems to have the interests of the church and the washerwoman so much at heart—that for once we suffer him to escape without chastisement. We advise him to abstain from pen, ink, and paper; to write no more criticisms upon his own work in the Commercial Advertiser, or any other newspaper—to wince and vapour in no more pamphlets—but to return to his home and keep in doors, like a good little man, until this singular delirium with which he is afflicted is happily subsided; assuring him that the world is likely to revolve regularly, as it has ever done heretofore, without his leaving his business to run and put it in order. But if, notwithstanding this friendly hint, we ever catch him, hawking his hardware about the purlieus of Parnassus, we will most certainly straddle him over a rail, and ride him round the premises, to the great amusement and laughter of the muses, and the eternal terror of all interlopers in like case offending.

P. S. Just as our work was going to press, we received the important intelligence that Paine is not dead, as was erroneously stated; he was only stunned, by the mighty journal, but by the application of timely medical aid he was fortunately restored.

[March, 1813]

[REVIEW OF *THE WORKS . . . OF ROBERT TREAT PAINE*]

The Works, in verse and prose, of the late ROBERT TREAT PAINE, *jun. Esq. with Notes. To which are prefixed Sketches of his Life, Character, and Writings.* 8vo. pp. 464. Belcher. Boston, 1812.

In reviewing the work before us, criticism is deprived of half its utility. However just may be its decisions, they can be of no avail to the author. With him the fitful scene of literary life is over; praise can stimulate him to no new exertions, nor censure point the way to future improvement. The only benefit, therefore, to be derived from an examination of his merits, is to deduce therefrom instruction for his survivors, either as to the excellencies they should imitate, or the errors they should avoid.

There is no country to which practical criticism is of more importance than this, owing to the crude state of native talent, and the immaturity of public taste. We are prone to all the vices of literature, from the casual and superficial manner in which we attend to it. Absorbed in politics, or occupied by business, few can find leisure, amid these strong agitations of the mind, to follow the gentler pursuits of literature, and give it that calm study, and meditative contemplation, necessary to discover the true principles of beauty and excellence in composition. To render criticism, therefore, more impressive, and to bring it home, as it were, to our own bosoms, it is not sufficient merely to point to those standard writers of Great Britain, who should form our real models, but it is important to take those writers among ourselves who have attained celebrity, and scrutinize their characters. Authors are apt to catch and borrow the faults and beauties of neighbouring authors, rather than of those removed by time or distance; as a man is more apt to fall into the vices and peculiarities of those around him, than to form himself on the models of Roman or Grecian virtue.

This is apparent even in Great Britain, where, with all the advantages of finished education, literary society, and critical tribunals, we see her authors continually wandering away into some new and corrupt fashion of writing, rather than conforming to those orders of composition which have the sanction of time and criticism. If such be the case in Great Britain, and if even her veteran literati have still the need of rigorous criticism to keep them from running riot; how much more necessary is it in our country, where our literary ranks, like those of our military, are rude, undisciplined, and insubordinate. It is for these reasons that we presume with freedom, but, we trust, with candour, to examine the relics of an American poet; to do justice to his merits; but to point out his errors, as far as our judgment will allow, for the benefit of his cotemporaries.

The volume before us commences with a biography of the author written by two several hands. The style is occasionally overwrought, and swelling beyond the simplicity proper to this species of writing, but on the whole creditable to the writers. The spirit in which it is written is both friendly and candid. We cannot but admire the generous struggle between tenderness for the author's memory, and a laudable determination to tell the whole truth, which occurs whenever the failings of the poet are adverted to. We applaud the frankness and delicacy with which the latter are avowed. If biography have any merit, it consists in presenting a faithful picture of the character, the habits, the whole course of living and thinking of the person who is the subject—for, otherwise, we may as well have a romance, and an ideal hero imposed on us, for our wonder and admiration.

The biography of Mr. Paine presents another of those melancholy details, too commonly furnished by literary life. Those gleams of sunshine, and days of darkness—those moments of rapture, and periods of lingering depression—those dreams of hope, and waking hours of black despondency: such is the rapid round of transient joys and frequent sufferings, that form the "be all and the end all, here" of the unlucky tribe that live by writing. Surely, if the young imagination could ever be repressed by sad example, these gloomy narratives would be sufficient to deter it from venturing into the fairy land of literature—a region so precarious in its enjoyments, and fruitful in its calamities.

We find that Mr. Paine started on his career, full of ardour and confidence. His collegiate life was gay and brilliant. His poetic talents had already broken forth, and acquired him the intoxicating, but dangerous meed of early praise. The description given of him by his biographer, at this time, is extremely prepossessing.

> "He was graduated with the esteem of the government and the regard of his cotemporaries. He was as much distinguished for the opening virtues of his heart, as for the vivacity of his wit, the vigour of his imagination, and the variety of his knowledge. A liberality of sentiment and a contempt of selfishness are usual concomitants, and in him were striking characteristics. Urbanity of manners and a delicacy of feeling imparted a charm to his benignant temper and social disposition."

After leaving college, we begin to perceive the misfortunes which his early display of talents had entailed upon him. He had tasted the sweets of literary triumph, and, as it is not the character of genius to rest satisfied with past achievements, he longed to add fresh laurels to those he had acquired. With this strong inclination towards a literary life, we behold him painfully endeavouring to accustom himself to mercantile pursuits, and harness his mind to the diurnal drudgery of a counting-house. The result was such as might naturally be expected. He neglected the monotonous pages of the journal and the ledger, for the magic numbers of Homer and Horace. His fancy, stimulated by restraint, repeatedly flashed forth in productions that attracted applause: he was more frequently found at the theatre than on 'change; delighted more in the society of scholars and men of taste and fancy, than of "substantial merchants," and at length abandoned the patient, but comfortable realities of trade, for the splendid uncertainties of the muse.

Our limits will not permit us to go into a minute examination of his life, which would otherwise be worthy of attention; for the habits and fortunes of an author, in this country, might yield some food for curious speculation. Unfitted for business, in a nation where every one is busy; devoted to literature, where literary leisure is confounded with idleness; the man of letters is almost an insulated being, with few to understand, less to value, and scarcely any to encourage his pursuits. It is not surprising, therefore, that our authors soon grow weary of a race which they have to run alone, and turn their attention to other callings of a more worldly and profitable nature. This is one of the reasons why the writers of this country so seldom attain to excellence. Before their genius is disciplined, and their taste refined, their talents are diverted into the ordinary channels of busy life, and occupied in what are considered its more useful purposes. In fact, the great demand for rough talent, as for common manual labour, in this country, prevents the appropriation of either mental or physical forces to elegant employments. The delicate mechanician may toil in penury, unless he devote himself to common manufactures, suitable to the ordinary consumption of the country; and the fine writer, if he depend upon his pen for a subsistence, will soon discover that he may starve on the very summit of Parnassus, while he sees herds of newspaper editors battening on the rank marshes of its borders.

Such is most likely to be the fate of authors by profession, in the present circumstances of our country. But Mr. Paine had certainly nothing of the kind to complain of. His early prospects were extremely flattering. His productions met with a local circulation, and the poet with a degree of attention and respect, highly creditable to the intelligent part of the union where he resided.

> "The qualities," says his biographer, "which had secured him esteem at the university were daily expanding, and his reputation was daily increasing. His society was eagerly sought in the most polished and refined circles; he administered compliments with great address; and no *beau* was ever a greater favourite in the *beau monde!*"

Having now confided to his pen for a support, Mr. Paine undertook the editorship of a semi-weekly paper, devoted to Federal politics. It was conducted without diligence, and, if we may judge from the effects, without discretion; for it drew upon him the vengeance of a mob, which attacked the house where he resided, and the resentment of a young gentleman, whose father he had satirized. This youth, with an impetuosity hallowed by his filial feeling, demanded honourable satisfaction— it was denied, and the consequence was, that, in a casual rencounter, he took it, in a more degrading manner, on the person of Mr. Paine.

This was a deadly blow to the reputation of our author; and his standing in society was still more impaired by his subsequent marriage

with an actress, which produced a rupture with his father, and a deser-
tion by the fashionable world. This last is mentioned in terms of useless
reprehension by his biographer. It is idle to rail at society for its laws
of rank and gradations of respect. These rise, of themselves, out of
the nature of things, and the moral and political circumstances in which
that society is placed; and the universal acquiescence in them by the
soundest minds, is a sufficient proof that they are salutary and correct.
Mr. Paine should have foreseen the inevitable consequences of his
union, in a society so rigid and religious, and where theatrical exhibitions had been considered so improper as for a long time to have been
prohibited by law. Having foreseen the consequences, and willingly encountered them, it would have been a proof of his firmness and good
sense, to have submitted to them without repining.

Unfortunately, Mr. Paine seems to have been deficient in that true
kind of pride, which draws its support from the ample sources of conscious worth and integrity; which bears up its possessor against unmerited neglect, and induces him to persist in doing well, though
certain of no approbation but his own. The moment the world neglected
him, he began to neglect himself, as if he had theretofore acted right
from the love of praise, rather than the love of virtue.

He contracted habits of intemperance, which, added to his natural
heedlessness, and want of application, rendered all the remainder of his
life a scene of vicissitude. His newspaper establishment, from want of
his personal attention, proved unfortunate; at the end of eighteen
months he disposed of it, and became master of ceremonies of the
Boston Theatre; an anomalous office which we do not understand, but
which for a time produced him a present means of subsistence. Notwithstanding the irregularity of his habits, it seems that he never exerted
his talents without ample success. He was occasionally called on for
orations, odes, songs, and addresses, which not only met with public
applause, but with a pecuniary remuneration that is worthy of being
recorded in our literary history. For his "Invention of Letters," a poem
of about three hundred lines, we are told he received *fifteen hundred
dollars*, exclusive of expense; and *twelve hundred* by the sale of his
"Ruling Passion," a poem of about the same length. The political song
of "Adams and Liberty" produced him also a profit of *seven hundred
and fifty dollars*. These are sevenfold harvests, that have rarely been
equalled even in the productive countries of Europe.

After a few years passed in this manner, having in some measure
reformed his habits, his friends began to entertain hopes of rescuing
him from this precarious mode of subsistence. They urged him to study
the law, and offered him pecuniary assistance for the purpose. He
listened to their advice; abandoned the theatre; applied himself diligently to legal studies; was admitted, and became a successful advocate.

Business poured in upon him—his reputation rose—prospects of ease, of affluence, of substantial respectability, opened before him—but he relinquished them all with his incorrigible recklessness of mind, and relapsed into his former self-abandonment. From this time the springs of his mind seem to have been rapidly broken down—invention languished—literary ambition was almost at an end; at the same time, an inordinate appetite for knowledge was awakened, but it was that kind of appetite which produces indigestion, rather than an invigoration of the system.

> "During these last years of his life," says his biographer, "without a library, wandering from place to place, frequently uncertain where, or whether he could procure a meal; his thirst and acquisition of knowledge astonishingly increased. Though frequently tormented with disease, and beset by duns and 'the law's staff-officers,' from whom, and from prison, he was frequently relieved by friendship; neither sickness nor penury abated his love of a book, and of instructive conversation."

It is painful to trace the concluding history of this eccentric, contradictory, but interesting man. Broken down by penury and disease; disheartened by fancied, perhaps real, but certainly self-brought neglect; debilitated in mind, and shattered in reputation, he languished into that state of nervous irritability and sickliness of thought, when the world ceases to interest and delight; when desire sinks into apathy, and "the grasshopper becomes a burden."

We cannot refrain from recurring to the picture given of him by his faithful biographer, at the outset of his career, with all the glow of youth and fancy, and the freshness of blooming reputation that graced his opening talents, and contrasting it with the following, taken in his day of premature decay and blighted intellect. The contrast is instructive and affecting—a few pages present the sad reverse of years.

> "He was fed and lodged in an apartment at his father's; and in this feeble and emaciated state, walked abroad, from day to day, looking like misery personified, and pouring his lamentations into the ears of his friends, who were happy to confer those little acts of kindness which afforded to him some momentary consolation."

Even "during this period of unhoused and disconsolate wretchedness," when the taper was fast sinking in the socket, he was still capable of poetical excitement. At the request of the "Jockey Club," he undertook to write a song for their anniversary dinner. His enfeebled imagination faltered at the effort, until, spurred on by the last moment, he aroused himself into a transient glow of composition, executed the task, and then threw by the pen for ever.

It is worthy of mention, that under all this accumulation of penury, despondency and sickness, the passion still remained for one species of amusement, which addresses itself chiefly to the imagination; or rather, perhaps, the habit remained, after the passion had subsided. He attended the theatre but two evenings before his death. This was the last gleam of solitary pleasure—on the following day, feeling his end approaching, he crawled to an "attic chamber in his father's house," as to one of those retreats

"Where lonely want retires to die."

Here he languished until the next evening, when, in the presence of his family and friends, he expired without a struggle or a groan.

Such is a brief sketch of the biography of Robert Treat Paine: a man, calculated to flourish in the sunshine of life, but running to waste and ruin in the shade. We have been beguiled into a more particular notice of this part of the work, from the interest which it excited, and the strong moral picture which it presented. And indeed the biography of authors is important in another point of view, as throwing a great light upon the state of literature and refinement of a nation. In a country where authors are few, any tract of literary anecdote, like the present, is valuable, as adding to the scanty materials from which future writers will be enabled to trace our advancement in letters and the arts. Hereafter, curiosity may be interested to gather information concerning these early adventurers in literature, not because they may have any great merit in their works, but because they were the first to adventure; as we are curious about the early settlers of our country, not from their eminence of character, but because they were the first that settled.

In looking back upon the life of Mr. Paine, we scarcely know whether his misfortunes are to be attributed so much to his love of literature, as to his want of discretion and practical good sense. He was a man that seemed to live for the moment; drawing but little instruction from the past, and casting but careless glances towards the future. So far as relates to him, his country stands acquitted in its literary character; for certainly, as far as he made himself useful in his range of talents, he was amply remunerated.

The character given of him by his last biographer is highly interesting, and evinces that quick sensibility and openness to transient impressions, incident to a man more under the dominion of the fancy than the judgment.

"To speak of Mr. Paine as a man; *hic labor, hoc opus est.* In his intercourse with the world, his earliest impressions were rarely correct. His vivid imagination, in his first interviews, undervalued or overrated almost every individual with whom he came in contact; but when a protracted acquaintance had effaced early impressions, his judgment recovered its tone, and no man brought his associates to a fairer scrutiny, or could delineate their characteristics with greater exactness.

Nullius addictus jurare, in verba, magistri;

and when he had once formed a deliberate opinion, without a change of circumstances, it is not known that he ever renounced it. Studious to please, he was only impatient of obtrusive folly, impertinent presumption, or idle speculation. His friendships were cordial, and his good genius soon rectified the precipitance of his enmities. To conflicting propositions he listened with attention; heard his own opinions contested with complacency, and replied with courtesy. No root of bitterness ever quickened in his mind. If injured, he was placable; if offended, he

——— showed a hasty spark,
And straight was cold again.

Parcere subjectis et debellare superbos,

was in strict unison with the habitual elevation of his feelings. Such services as it was in his power to render to others he performed with manly zeal; and their value was enhanced, by being generally rendered where they were most needed; and through life he cherished a lively gratitude towards those from whom he had received benefits."

On his irregular habits, his biographer remarks in palliation—"He sensibly felt, and clearly foresaw the consequences of their continuous indulgence, and passed frequent resolutions of reformation; but daily embarrassments shook the resolves of his seclusion, and reform was indefinitely postponed. He urged as an excuse for delaying the Herculean task, that it was impossible to commence it while perplexed with difficulty and surrounded with distress. Instead of rising with an elastic power, and throwing the incumbent pressure from his shoulders, he succumbed under its accumulating weight, until he became insuperably recumbent; and vital action was only precariously sustained, by administering 'the extreme medicine of the constitution for its daily food.' "

We come now to the most ungracious part of our undertaking; that of considering the literary character of the deceased. This is rendered the more delicate, from the excessive eulogiums passed on him, in the enthusiasm of friendship, by his biographers, and which make us despair of yielding any praise that can approach to their ideas of his deserts.

We are told that Dryden was Mr. Paine's favourite author, and in some measure his prototype; but he appears to have admired, rather than to have studied him. Like all those writers who take up some particular author as a model, a degree of bigotry has entered into his devotion, which made him blind to the faults of his original; or, rather, these faults became beauties in his eyes. Such, for instance, is that propensity to far-sought allusions, and forced conceits. Had he studied Dryden in connexion with the literature of his day, contrasting him with the poets who preceded him, and those who were his cotemporaries—Mr. Paine would have discovered that these were faults which Dryden reprobated himself. They were the lingering traces of a taste which he was himself endeavouring to abolish. Dryden was a great reformer of English poetry; not merely by improving the versification, and taming the rude roughness of the language into smoothness and harmony; but by abolishing from it those metaphysical subtleties, those strange analogies and extravagant combinations, which had been the pride and study of the old school. Thus struggling to cure others and himself of these excesses, it is not surprising that some of them still lurked about his writings; it is rather a matter of surprise, that the number should be so inconsiderable.

These, however, seem to have caught the ardent and ill-regulated imagination of Mr. Paine, and to have given a tincture to the whole current of his writings. We find him continually aiming at fine thoughts, fine figures, and epigrammatic point. The censure that Johnson passes on his great prototype, may be applied with tenfold justice to him: "His delight was in wild and daring sallies of sentiment—in the irregular and eccentric violence of wit. He delighted to tread upon the brink of meaning, where light and darkness begin to mingle; to approach the precipice of absurdity, and hover over the abyss of unideal vacancy." His verses are often so dizened out with embroidery, that the subject matter is lost in the ornament—the idea is confused by the illustration; or rather, instead of one plain, distinct idea being presented to the mind, we are bewildered with a score of similitudes. Such, for instance, is the case with the following passage, taken at random, and which is intended to be descriptive of misers:

"In life's dark cell, pale burns their glimmering soul:
A rush-light warms the winter of the pole.

To chill and cheerless solitude confined,
No spring of virtue thaws the ice of mind.
They creep in blood, as frosty streamlets flow,
And freeze with life, as dormice sleep in snow.
Like snails they bear their dungeons on their backs,
And shut out light—to save a window tax!"

His figures and illustrations are often striking and beautiful, but too often far-fetched and extravagant. He had always plenty at command, and, indeed, every thought that he conceived drew after it a cluster of similies. Among these he either had not the talent to discriminate, or the self-denial to discard. Every thing that entered his mind was transferred to his page, trope followed trope, illustration was heaped on illustration, ornament outvied ornament, until what at first promised to be fine, ended in being tawdry.

Of his didactic poems one of the most prominent is the "Ruling Passion." It contains many passages of striking merit, but is loaded with epithet, and distorted by constant straining after epigram and eccentricity. The author seems never content unless he be sparkling; the reader is continually perplexed to know what he means, and sometimes disappointed, when he does find out, to discover that he means so little. It is one of the properties of poetic genius to give consequence to trifles. By a kind of magic power, it swells things up beyond their natural dimensions, and decks them out with a splendour of dress and colouring that completely hides their real insignificance. Pigmy thoughts that crept in prose, start up into gigantic size in poetry; and strutting in lofty epithets, inflated with hyperbole, and glittering with fine figures, are apt to take the imagination by surprise, and dazzle the judgment. The steady eye of scrutiny, however, soon penetrates the glare; and when the thought has shrunk back to its real dimensions, what appeared to be oracular, turns out to be a truism.

As an instance of this we will quote the following passage:

"Heroes and bards, who nobler flights have won
Than Cæsar's eagles, or the Mantuan swan,
From eldest era share the common doom;
The sun of glory shines but on the tomb.
Firm as the Mede, the stern decree subdues
The brightest pageant of the proudest muse.
Man's noblest powers could ne'er the law revoke,
Though Handel harmonized what Chatham spoke;
Though tuneful Morton's magic genius graced
The Hyblean melody of Merry's taste!

"Time, the stern censor, talisman of fame,
With rigid justice portions praise and shame:
And, while his laurels, reared where genius grew,
'Mid wide oblivion's lava bloom anew;
Oft will his chymic fire, in distant age
Elicit spots, unseen on ancient page.

So the famed sage, who plunged in Ætna's flame,
'Mid pagan deities enshrined his name;
'Till from the iliac mountain's crater thrown,
The Martyr's sandal cost the God his crown." P. 187.

Here the simple thought conveyed in this gorgeous page, as far as we can rake it out from among the splendid rubbish, is this, that fame is tested by time; a truth, than which scarcely any is more familiar, and which the author, from the resemblance of the fourth line, and the tenor of those which preceded it, had evidently seen much more touchingly expressed in the elegy of Gray.

The characters in this poem, which are intended to exemplify a ruling passion, are trite and commonplace. The pedant, the deluded female, the fop, the old maid, the miser, are all hackneyed subjects of satire, and are treated in a hackneyed manner. If these old dishes are to be served up again, we might at least expect that the sauces would be new. It is evident Mr. Paine drew his characters from books rather than from real life. His fop flourishes the cane and snuff-box as in the days of Sir Fopling Flutter. His old maid is sprigged and behooped, and hides behind her fan according to immemorial usage; and in his other characters we trace the same family likeness that marks the descendants of the heroes and heroines of ancient British poetry.

The following description of the Savoyard is sprightly and picturesque, though, unfortunately for the author, it reminds us of the Swiss peasant of Goldsmith, and forces upon us the contrast between that sparkling poetry which dazzles the fancy, and those simple, homefelt strains, which sink to the heart, and are treasured up there.

"To fame unknown, to happier fortune born,
The blithe Savoyard hails the peep of morn;
And while the fluid gold his eye surveys,
The hoary glaciers fling their diamond blaze;
Geneva's broad lake rushes from its shores,
Arve gently murmurs, and the rough Rhone roars.
'Mid the cleft Alps, his cabin peers from high,
Hangs o'er the clouds, and perches on the sky.
O'er fields of ice, across the headlong flood,

From cliff to cliff he bounds in fearless mood.
While, far beneath, a night of tempest lies,
Deep thunder mutters, harmless lightning flies;
While, far above, from battlements of snow
Loud torrents tumble on the world below;
On rustic reed he wakes a merrier tune,
Than the lark warbles on the 'Ides of June.'
Far off let glory's clarion shrilly swell;
He loves the music of his pipe as well.
Let shouting millions crown the hero's head,
And pride her tessellated pavement tread,
More happy far, this denizen of air
Enjoys what nature condescends to spare;
His days are jocund, undisturbed his nights,
His spouse contents him and his mule delights." P. 184.

The conclusion of this very descriptive passage partakes lamentably
of the bathos. We cannot but smile at the last line, where he has paid
the conjugal feelings of his hero but a sorry compliment, making him
more delighted with his mule than with the wife of his bosom.

The "Invention of Letters" is another poem, where the author seems
to have exerted the full scope of his talents. It shows that adroitness in
the tricks of composition, that love for meretricious ornament, and at
the same time that amazing store of imagery and illustration, which
characterize this writer. We see in it many fine flights of thought, and
brave sallies of the imagination, but at the same time a superabundance
of the luscious faults of poetry; and we rise from it with augmented
regret, that so rich and prolific a genius had not been governed by a
purer taste. The following eulogium of Faustus is a fair specimen of the
author's beauties and defects.

"Egyptian shrubs, in hands of cook or priest,
A king could mummy, or enrich a feast;
Faustus, great shade! a nobler leaf imparts,
Embalms all ages, and preserves all arts.

The ancient scribe, employed by bards divine,
With faltering finger traced the lingering line.
So few the scrivener's dull profession chose,
With tedious toil each tardy transcript rose;
And scarce the Iliad, penned from oral rhyme,
Grew with the bark that bore its page sublime.

But when the press, with fertile womb supplies
The useful sheet, on thousand wings it flies;

Bound to no climate, to no age confined,
The pinioned volume spreads to all mankind.

No sacred power the Cadmean art could claim,
O'er time to triumph, and defy the flame:
In one sad day a Goth could ravage more
Than ages wrote, or ages could restore.

The Roman helmet, or the Grecian lyre,
A realm might conquer, or a realm inspire;
Then sink, oblivious, in the mouldering dust,
With those who blessed them, and with those who curst.
What guide had then the lettered pilgrim led
Where Plato moralized; where Cæsar bled?
What page had told, in lasting record wrought,
The world who butchered, or the world who taught?

Thine was the mighty power, immortal sage!
To burst the cerements of each buried age.
Through the drear sepulchre of sunless Time,
Rich with the trophied wrecks of many a clime,
Thy daring genius broke the pathless way,
And brought the glorious relics forth to day."   Pp. 165–66.

Of the lyrical poetry of Mr. Paine we can but give the same mixed opinion. It sometimes comes near being very fine, at other times is bombastic, and too often is obscure by far-fetched metaphors. The enthusiasm, which is the life and spirit of this kind of poetry, certainly allows great license to the imagination, and permits the poet to use bolder figures and stronger exaggerations than any other species of serious composition; but he should be wary that he be not carried too far by the fervour of his feelings, and that he run not into obscurity and extravagance. In listening to lyrical poetry, we have to depend entirely on the ear to comprehend the subject; and as verse follows verse without allowing time for meditation, it is next to impossible for the auditor to extricate the meaning, if it be entangled in metaphor. The thoughts, therefore, should be clear and striking, and the figures, however lofty and magnificent, yet of that simple kind that flash at once upon the mind.

The following stanza is one of those that come near being extremely beautiful. The versification is swelling and melodious, and captivates the ear with the luxury of sound; the imagery is sublime, but the meaning a little obscure.

"The sea is valour's charter,
   A nation's wealthiest mine:
His foaming caves when ocean bares,
   Not pearls, but heroes shine;
Aloft they mount the midnight surge,
   Where shipwrecked spirits roam,
And oft the knell is heard to swell,
   Where bursting billows foam.
Each storm a race of heroes rears,
   To guard their native home."   P. 275.

The ode entitled "Rise Columbia," possesses more simplicity than most of his poems. Several of the verses are deserving of much praise, both for the sentiment and the composition.

"Remote from realms of rival fame,
   Thy bulwark is thy mound of waves;
The sea, thy birthright, thou must claim,
   Or, subject, yield the soil it laves.

Nor yet, though skilled, delight in arms;
   Peace and, her offspring, Arts be thine;
The face of Freedom scarce has charms,
   When on her cheeks no dimples shine.

While Fame, for thee, her wreath entwines,
   To bless, thy nobler triumph prove;
And, though the eagle haunts thy pines,
   Beneath thy willows shield the dove.

*   *   *   *   *

Revered in arms, in peace humane,
   No shore, nor realm shall bound thy sway;
While all the virtues own thy reign,
   And subject elements obey!"

The ode of "Spain, Commerce and Freedom," is a mere conflagration of fancy. What shall we say to such a "melting hot—hissing hot" stanza as the following:

"Bright Day of the world! dart thy lustre afar!
   Fire the north with thy heat! gild the south with thy
      splendour!
With thy glance light the torch of redintegrant war,

Till the dismembered earth effervesce and regender!
Through each zone may'st roll,
'Till thy beams at the Pole,
Melt Philosophy's Ice in the sea of the soul!

We have unwarily exceeded our intended limits in this article, and must now bring it to a conclusion. From the examination which we have given Mr. Paine's writings, we can by no means concur in the opinion, that he is an author on whom the nation should venture its poetic claims. His natural requisites were undoubtedly great, and had they been skilfully managed, might have raised him to an enviable eminence. He possessed a brilliant imagination, but not great powers of reflection. He thinks often acutely, seldom profoundly—indeed, there was such a constant wish to be ingenious and pungent, that he was impatient of the regular flow of thought and feeling, and seemed dissatisfied with every line that did not contain a paradox, a simile, or an apothegm. There appears also to have been an indistinctness in his conceptions: his mind teemed with vague ideas; with shadows of thought, which he could not accurately embody, and the consequence was a frequent want of precision in his writings. He had read much, and miscellaneously; and having a tenacious memory, was enabled to illustrate his thoughts by a thousand analogies and similies, drawn from books; and often to enrich his poems with the thoughts of others. Indeed, his acquired treasures were often a disadvantage; not having a simple discriminating taste, he could not select from among them; and being a little ostentatious of his wealth, was too apt to pour it in glittering profusion upon his page.

If we have been too severe in our animadversions on this author's faults, we can only say, that the high encomiums of his biographers, and the high assumptions of the author himself, which are evident from the style of his writings, obliged us to judge of him by an elevated standard. Mr. Paine ventured in the lofty walks of composition, and appears continually to have been measuring himself with the masters of the art. His biographers have even hinted at placing him "on the same shelf with the prince of English rhyme," and thus, in a manner, have invited a less indulgent examination than, perhaps, might otherwise have been given.

If, however, we are unjust in our censures, a little while will decide their futility. To the living every hour of reputation is important, as adding one hour of enjoyment to existence; but the fame of the dead, to be valuable, must be permanent; and it is in nowise impaired, if for a year or two the misrepresentations of criticism becloud its lustre.

We assure the biographers of Mr. Paine, that we heartily concur with them in the wish to see one of our native poets rising to equal excellence with the immortal bards of Great Britain; but we do not feel any restless anxiety on the subject. We wait with hope, but we wait with patience. Of all writers a great poet is the rarest. Britain, with all her patronage of literature, with her standing army of authors, has, through a series of ages, produced but a very, very few who deserve the name. Can it, then, be a matter of surprise, or should it be of humiliation, that, in our country, where the literary ranks are so scanty, the incitements so small, and the advantages so inconsiderable, we should not yet have produced a master in the art? Let us rest satisfied—as far as the intellect of the nation has been exercised, we have furnished our full proportion of ordinary poets, and some that have even risen above mediocrity; but a really great poet is the production of a century.

[August, 1813]

BIOGRAPHY

OF

CAPTAIN JAMES LAWRENCE

To speak feelingly, yet temperately, of the merits of those who have bravely fought and gloriously fallen in the service of their country, is one of the most difficult tasks of the biographer. Filled with admiration of their valour, and sorrow for their fate, we feel the impotency of our gratitude, in being able to reward such great sacrifices with nothing but empty applause. We are apt, therefore, to be hurried into a degree of eulogium, which, however sincere and acknowledged at the time, may be regarded as extravagant by the dispassionate eye of after years.

We feel more particularly this difficulty, in undertaking to give the memoirs of one, whose excellent qualities and gallant deeds are still vivid in our recollection, and whose untimely end has excited, in an extraordinary degree, the sympathies of his countrymen. Indeed, the popular career of this youthful hero has been so transient, yet dazzling, as almost to prevent sober investigation. Scarce had we ceased to rejoice in his victory, before we were called on to deplore his loss. He passed before the public eye like a star, just beaming on it for a moment, and falling in the midst of his brightness.

Captain James Lawrence was born on the 1st of October, 1781, at Burlington, in the state of New-Jersey. He was the youngest son of John Lawrence, Esq. an eminent counsellor at law of that place. Within a few weeks after his birth his mother died, and the charge of him devolved on his sisters, to whom he ever showed the warmest gratitude for the tender care they took of his infant years. He early evinced that excellence of heart by which he was characterized through life; he was a dutiful and affectionate child, mild in his disposition, and of the most gentle and engaging manners. He was scarce twelve years of age when he expressed a decided partiality for a seafaring life; but his father disapproving of it, and wishing him to prepare for the profession of the law, his strong sense of duty induced him to acquiesce. He went through the common branches of education, at a grammar school, at Burlington, with much credit to himself, and satisfaction to his tutors. The pecuniary misfortunes of his father prevented his receiving a finished education, and between the age of thirteen and fourteen he commenced the study of the law with his brother, the late John Lawrence, Esq. who then resided at Woodbury. He remained for two years in this situation, vainly striving to accommodate himself to pursuits wholly repugnant to his taste and inclinations. The dry studies of statutes and reporters, the technical rubbish, and dull routine of a lawyer's office, were little calculated to please an imagination teeming with the adventures, the wonders, and variety of the seas. At length, his father being dead, and his strong predilection for the roving life of a sailor being increased by every attempt to curb it, his brother yielded to his solicitations, and placed him under the care of Mr. Griscomb, at Burlington, to acquire the principles of navigation and naval tactics. He remained with him for three months, when, his intention of applying for a situation in the navy being generally known, several of the most distinguished gentlemen of the state interested themselves in his behalf, and wrote to the navy department. The succeeding mail brought him a midshipman's warrant; and between the age of sixteen and seventeen he entered the service of his country.

His first cruise was to the West Indies in the ship Ganges, commanded by Captain Thomas Tingey. In this and several subsequent cruises, no opportunity occurred to call forth particular services; but the attention and intelligence which he uniformly displayed in the discharge of his duties, the correctness of his deportment, and the suavity of his manners, gained him the approbation of his commanders, and rendered him a favourite with his associates and inferiors.

When the war was declared against Tripoli, he was promoted to a lieutenancy, and appointed to the command of the schooner Enterprise. While in this command he volunteered his services in the hazardous exploit of destroying the frigate Philadelphia, and accompanied Decatur as his first lieutenant. The brilliant success of that enterprise is well known; and for the gallantry and skill displayed on the occasion, Decatur was made post captain, while Lawrence, in common with the other officers and crew, were voted by congress two months' extra pay—a sordid and paltry reward, which he immediately declined.

The harbour of Tripoli appears to have been the school of our naval heroes. In tracing the histories of those who have lately distinguished themselves, we are always led to the coast of Barbary as the field of their first experience and young achievement. The concentration of our little navy at this point, soon after its formation, has had a happy effect upon its character and fortunes. The officers were most of them young in years, and young in arms, full of life, and spirits, and enthusiasm. Such is the time to form generous impressions and strong attachments. It was there they grew together in habits of mutual confidence and friendship; and to the noble emulation of so many young minds newly entering upon an adventurous profession, may be attributed that enterprising spirit and defiance of danger that has ever since distinguished our navy.

After continuing in the Mediterranean about three years and a half, Lawrence returned to the United States with Commodore Preble, and was again sent out on that station, as commander of Gun boat No. 6, in which he remained for sixteen months. Since that time he has acted as first lieutenant of the Constitution, and as commander of the Vixen, Wasp, Argus and Hornet. In 1808 he was married to a daughter of Mr. Montaudevert, a respectable merchant of New-York, to whom he made one of the kindest and most affectionate of husbands.

At the commencement of the present war he sailed in the Hornet sloop of war, as part of the squadron that cruised under Commodore Rodgers. While absent on this cruise Lieutenant Morris was promoted to the rank of post captain, for his bravery and skill as first lieutenant of the Constitution in her action with the Guerriere. This appointment, as it raised him two grades, and placed him over the heads of older officers, gave great offence to many of the navy, who could not brook that the regular rules of the service should be infringed. It was thought particularly unjust, as giving him rank above Lawrence, who had equally distinguished himself as first lieutenant of Decatur, in the destruction of the frigate Philadelphia, and who, at present, was but master and commander.

On returning from his cruise Captain Lawrence, after consulting with Commodores Rodgers and Bainbridge, and with other experienced gentlemen of the navy, addressed a memorial to the senate, and a letter to the secretary of the navy, wherein, after the fullest acknowledgments of the great merits and services of Captain Morris, he remonstrated in the most temperate and respectful, but firm and manly language, on the impropriety of his promotion, as being contrary to the rules of naval precedence, and particularly hard as it respected himself. At the same time, he frankly mentioned that he should be compelled, however reluctant, to leave the service, if thus improperly outranked.

The reply of the secretary was singularly brief; barely observing, that if he thought proper to leave the service without a cause, there would still remain heroes and patriots to support the honour of the flag. There was a laconic severity in this reply calculated to cut a man of feeling to the heart, and which ought not to have been provoked by the fair and candid remonstrance of Lawrence.

Where men are fighting for honour rather than profit, the utmost delicacy should be observed towards their high-toned feelings. Those complaints which spring from wounded pride, and the jealousy of station, should never be regarded lightly. The best soldiers are ever most tenacious of their rank; for it cannot be expected that he who hazards every thing for distinction, will be careless of it after it is attained. Fortunately, Lawrence had again departed on a cruise before this letter arrived, which otherwise might have driven from the service one of our most meritorious officers.

This second cruise was in company with Commodore Bainbridge, who commanded the Constitution. While cruising off the Brazils they fell in with the Bonne Citoyenne, a British ship of war, having on board a large amount of specie, and chased her into St. Salvadore. Notwithstanding that she was a larger vessel, and of a greater force in guns and men than the Hornet, yet Captain Lawrence sent a challenge to her commander, Captain Green, pledging his honour that neither the Constitution nor any other American vessel should interfere. Commodore Bainbridge made a similar pledge on his own part; but the British commander declined the combat, alleging that though perfectly satisfied that the event of such a rencounter would be favourable to his ship; "yet he was equally convinced that Commodore Bainbridge could not swerve so much from the paramount duty he owed his country as to become an inactive spectator, and see a ship belonging to the very squadron under his orders, fall into the hands of the enemy."

To make him easy on this point, Commodore Bainbridge left the Hornet four days together off the harbour in which the Bonne Citoyenne lay, and from which she could discover that he was not within forty miles of it. He afterwards went into the harbour and remained there three days, where he might at any time have been detained twenty-four hours, at the request of Captain Green, if disposed to combat the Hornet. At length the Constitution went off altogether, leaving Lawrence to blockade the Bonne Citoyenne, which he did for nearly a month, Captain Green not thinking proper to risk an encounter. It is possible that having an important public trust in charge, and sailing under particular orders, he did not think himself authorized to depart from the purpose of his voyage, and risk his vessel in a contest for mere individual reputation. But if such were his reasons, he should have stated them when he refused to accept the challenge.

On the 24th of January Captain Lawrence was obliged to shift his cruising ground, by the arrival of the Montagu 74, which had sailed from Rio Janeiro for the express purpose of relieving the Bonne Citoyenne and a British packet of 12 guns, which likewise lay at St. Salvadore. At length, on the morning of the 24th February, when cruising off Demarara, the Hornet fell in with the British brig Peacock, Captain Peake, a vessel of about equal force. The contest commenced within half pistol shot, and so tremendous was the fire of the Americans, that in less than fifteen minutes the enemy surrendered, and made signal of distress, being in a sinking condition. Her mainmast shortly went by the board, and she was left such an absolute wreck, that, notwithstanding every exertion was made to keep her afloat until the prisoners could be removed, she sunk with thirteen of her crew, and three brave American tars, who thus nobly perished in relieving a conquered foe. The slaughter on board of the Peacock was very severe; among the slain was found the body of her commander, Captain Peake. He was twice wounded in the course of the action; the last wound proved fatal. His body was wrapped in the flag of his vessel, and laid in the cabin to sink with her, a shroud and sepulchre worthy so brave a sailor.

During the battle the British brig L'Espeigle, mounting 15 two and thirty pound carronades and 2 long nines, lay at anchor, about six miles inshore. Being apprehensive that she would beat out to the assistance of her consort, the utmost exertions were made to put the Hornet in a situation for action, and in about three hours she was in complete preparation, but the enemy did not think proper to make an attack.

The conduct of Lawrence towards his prisoners was such, as, we are proud to say, has uniformly characterized the officers of our navy. They have ever displayed the liberality and scrupulous delicacy of generous minds towards those whom the fortune of war has thrown in their power; and thus have won by their magnanimity those whom they have conquered by their valour. The officers of the Peacock were so affected by the treatment they received from Captain Lawrence, that on their arrival at New-York they made a grateful acknowledgment in the public papers. To use their own expressive phrase, "they ceased to consider themselves prisoners." Nor must we omit to mention a circumstance highly to the honour of the brave tars of the Hornet. Finding that the crew of the Peacock had lost all their clothing by the sudden sinking of the vessel, they made a subscription, and from their own wardrobes supplied each man with two shirts, and a blue jacket and trowsers. Such may rough sailors be made, when they have before them the example of high-minded men. They are beings of but little reflection, open to the impulse and excitement of the moment; and it depends in a great measure upon their officers, whether, under a Lawrence, they shall ennoble themselves by generous actions, or, under a Cockburn, be hurried away into scenes of unpremeditated atrocity.

On returning to this country Captain Lawrence was received with great distinction and applause, and various public bodies conferred on him peculiar tokens of approbation. While absent the rank of post captain had been conferred on him, and shortly after his return he received a letter from the secretary of the navy, offering him the command of the frigate Constitution, provided neither Captains Porter or Evans applied for it, they being older officers. Captain Lawrence respectfully declined this conditional appointment, for satisfactory reasons which he stated to the secretary. He then received an unconditional appointment to that frigate, and directions to superintend the navy-yard at New-York in the absence of Captain Ludlow. The next day, to his great surprise and chagrin, he received counter orders, with instructions to take command of the frigate Chesapeake, then lying at Boston, nearly ready for sea. This appointment was particularly disagreeable to him. He was prejudiced against the Chesapeake, both from her being considered the worst ship in our navy, and from having been in a manner disgraced in the affair with the Leopard. This last circumstance had acquired her the character of an unlucky ship—the worst of stigmas among sailors, who are devout believers in good and bad luck; and so detrimental was it to this vessel, that it has been found difficult to recruit crews for her.

The extreme repugnance that Captain Lawrence felt to this appointment induced him to write to the secretary of the navy, requesting to be continued in the command of the Hornet. Besides, it was his wish to remain some short time in port, and enjoy a little repose in the bosom of his family: particularly as his wife was in that delicate situation that most calls forth the tenderness and solicitude of an affectionate husband. But though he wrote four letters successively to the secretary, he never received an answer, and was obliged reluctantly to acquiesce.

While lying in Boston roads, nearly ready for sea, the British frigate Shannon appeared off the harbour, and made signals expressive of a challenge. The brave Lawrence immediately determined on accepting it, though conscious at the time of the great disparity between the two ships. The Shannon was a prime vessel, equipped in an extraordinary manner, for the express purpose of combating advantageously one of our largest frigates. She had an unusually numerous crew of picked men, thoroughly disciplined and well officered. She was commanded by Captain Broke, one of the bravest and ablest officers in the service, who fought merely for reputation.

On the other hand, the Chesapeake was an indifferent ship: with a crew, a great part of whom were newly recruited, and not brought into proper discipline. They were strangers to their commander, who had not had time to produce that perfect subordination, yet strong personal attachment, which he had the talent of creating wherever he commanded. His first lieutenant was sick on shore; the other officers, though meritorious, were young men; two of them mere acting lieutenants; most of them recently appointed to the ship, and unacquainted with the men.

Those who are in the least informed in nautical affairs, must perceive the greatness of these disadvantages.

The most earnest endeavours were used, by Commodore Bainbridge and other gentlemen of nice honour and sound experience, to dissuade Captain Lawrence from what was considered a rash and unnecessary exposure. He felt and acknowledged the force of their reasons, but persisted in his determination. He was peculiarly situated: he had formerly challenged the Bonne Citoyenne, and should he decline a similar challenge, it might subject him to sneers and misrepresentations. Among the other unfortunate circumstances that attended his ill-starred battle, was the delay of a written challenge from Captain Broke, which did not arrive until after Captain Lawrence had sailed. It is stated to have been couched in the most frank and courteous language; minutely detailing the force of his ship: and offering, if the Chesapeake should not be completely prepared, to cruise off and on until such time as she made a specified signal of being ready for the conflict. It is to be deeply regretted that Captain Lawrence did not receive this gallant challenge, as it would have given him time to put his ship in proper order, and spared him the necessity of hurrying out in his unprepared condition, to so formal and momentous an encounter.

After getting the ship under way, he called the crew together, and having ordered the white flag to be hoisted, bearing the motto, "Free trade and sailors' rights," he, according to custom, made them a short harangue. While he was speaking several murmurs were heard, and strong symptoms of dissatisfaction appeared in the manners and countenances of the crew. After he had finished, a scoundrel Portuguese, who was boatswain's mate, and acted as spokesman to the murmurers, replied to Captain Lawrence in an insolent manner, complaining, among other things, that they had not been paid their prizemoney, which had been due for some time past.

The critical nature of the moment, and his ignorance of the dispositions and characters of his crew, would not allow Captain Lawrence to notice such dastardly and mutinous conduct in the manner it deserved. He dared not thwart the humours of men, over whose affections he had not had time to acquire any influence, and therefore ordered the purser to take them below and give them checks for their prizemoney, which was accordingly done.

We dwell on these particulars to show the disastrous and disheartening circumstances under which Captain Lawrence went forth to this battle—circumstances which shook even his calm and manly breast, and filled him with a despondency unusual to his nature. Justice to the memory of this invaluable officer, requires that the disadvantages under which he fought should be made public.*

It was on the morning of the 1st of June that the Chesapeake put to sea. The Shannon, on seeing her come out, bore away, and the other followed. At 4 P. M. the Chesapeake haled up and fired a gun; the Shannon then hove to. The vessels manœuvred in awful silence, until within pistol shot, when the Shannon opened her fire, and both vessels almost at the same moment poured forth tremendous broadsides. The execution in both ships was terrible, but the fire of the Shannon was peculiarly fatal, not only making great slaughter among the men, but cutting down some of the most valuable officers. The very first shot killed Mr. White, sailing master of the Chesapeake, an excellent officer whose loss at such a moment was disastrous in the extreme. The fourth lieutenant, Mr. Ballard, received also a mortal wound in this broadside, and at the same moment Captain Lawrence was shot through the leg with a musket ball; he however supported himself on the companion-way, and continued to give his orders with his usual coolness. About three broadsides were exchanged, which, from the closeness of the ships, were dreadfully destructive. The Chesapeake had three men shot from her helm successively, each taking it as the other fell; this of course produced irregularity in the steering, and the consequence was, that her anchor caught in one of the Shannon's after ports. She was thus in a position where her guns could not be brought to bear upon the enemy, while the latter was enabled to fire raking shots from her foremost guns, which swept the upper decks of the Chesapeake, killing or wounding the greater portion of the men. A hand grenade was thrown on the quarter-deck, which set fire to some musket cartridges, but did no other damage.

In this state of carnage and exposure about twenty of the Shannon's men, seeing a favourable opportunity for boarding, without waiting for orders, jumped on the deck of the Chesapeake. Captain Lawrence had scarce time to call his boarders, when he received a second and mortal wound from a musket ball, which lodged in his intestines. Lieutenant Cox, who commanded the second division, rushed up at the call for the boarders, but came just in time to receive his falling commander. He was in the act of carrying him below, when Captain Broke, accompanied by his first lieutenant, and followed by his regular boarders, sprang on board the Chesapeake. The brave Lawrence saw the overwhelming danger; his last words, as he was borne bleeding from the deck, were, "don't surrender the ship!"

Samuel Livermore, Esq. of Boston, who from personal attachment to

---

*The particulars of this action are chiefly given from a conversation with one of the officers of the Chesapeake; and we believe may be relied on as authentic.

Captain Lawrence had accompanied him in this cruise as chaplain, attempted to revenge his fall. He shot at Captain Broke, but missed him: the latter made a cut at his head, which Livermore warded off, but in so doing received a severe wound in the arm. The only officer that now remained on the upper deck was Lieutenant Ludlow, who was so entirely weakened and disabled by repeated wounds, received early in the action, as to be incapable of personal resistance. The comparatively small number of men, therefore, that survived on the upper decks, having no officer to head them, the British succeeded in securing complete possession, before those from below could get up. Lieutenant Budd, who had commanded the first division below, being informed of the danger, hastened up with some men, but was overpowered by superior numbers and cut down immediately. Great embarrassment took place, in consequence of the officers being unacquainted with the crew. In one instance in particular, Lieutenant Cox, on mounting the deck, joined a party of the enemy through mistake, and was made sensible of his error by their cutting at him with their sabres.

While this scene of havoc and confusion was going on above, Captain Lawrence who was lying in the wardroom in excruciating pain, hearing the firing cease, forgot the anguish of his wounds: having no officer near him, he ordered the surgeon to hasten on deck and tell the officers to fight on to the last, and never to strike the colours; adding, "they shall wave while I live." The fate of the battle, however, was decided. Finding all further resistance vain, and a mere waste of life, Lieutenant Ludlow gave up the ship; after which he received a sabre wound in the head from one of the Shannon's crew, which fractured his skull and ultimately proved mortal. He was one of the most promising officers of his age in the service, highly esteemed for his professional talents, and beloved for the generous qualities that adorned his private character.

Thus terminated one of the most remarkable combats on naval record. From the peculiar accidents that attended it, the battle was short, desperate and bloody. So long as the cannonading continued, the Chesapeake is said to have clearly had the advantage; and had the ships not ran foul, it is probable she would have captured the Shannon. Though considerably damaged in her upper works, and pierced with some shotholes in her hull, yet she had sustained no injury to affect her safety; whereas the Shannon had received several shots between wind and water, and, consequently, could not have sustained the action long. The havoc on both sides was dreadful; but to the singular circumstance of having every officer on the upper deck either killed or wounded, early in the action, may chiefly be attributed the loss of the Chesapeake.

There have been various vague complaints circulated of the excesses of the victors, and of their treatment of our crew after the surrender. These have been, as usual, dwelt on and magnified, and made subjects of national aspersion. Nothing can be more illiberal than this. Where the scene of conflict is tumultuous and sanguinary, and the struggle desperate, as in the boarding of a ship, excesses will take place among the men which it is impossible to prevent. They are the inevitable incidents of war, and should never be held up to provoke national abhorrence or retaliation. Indeed, they are so liable to be misrepresented by partial and distorted accounts, that very little faith is ever to be placed in them. Such, for instance, is the report, that the enemy discharged several muskets into the cockpit after the ship had been given up. This, in fact, was provoked by the wanton act of a boy below, who shot down the sentinel stationed at the gangway, and thus produced a momentary exasperation, and an alarm that our men were rising. It should be recollected, likewise, that our flag was not struck, but was haled down by the enemy; consequently, the surrender of the ship was not immediately known throughout, and the struggle continued in various places, before the proper orders could be communicated. It is wearisome and disgusting to observe the war of slander kept up by the little minds of both countries, wherein every paltry misdeed of a paltry individual is insidiously trumpeted forth as a stigma on the respective nation. By these means are engendered lasting roots of bitterness, that give an implacable spirit to the actual hostility of the times, and will remain after the present strife shall have passed away. As the nations must inevitably, and at no very distant period, come once more together in the relations of amity and commerce, it is to be wished that as little private animosity may be encouraged as possible; so that though we may contend for rights and interests, we may never cease to esteem and respect each other.

The two ships presented dismal spectacles after the battle. Crowded with the wounded and the dying, they resembled floating hospitals sending forth groans at every roll. The brave Broke lay delirious from a wound in the head, which he is said to have received while endeavouring to prevent the slaughter of some of our men who had surrendered. In his rational intervals he always spoke in the highest terms of the courage and skill of Lawrence, and of "the gallant and masterly style" in which he brought the Chesapeake into action.

The wounds of Captain Lawrence rendered it impossible to remove him after the battle, and his cabin being very much shattered, he remained in the wardroom. Here he lay, attended by his own surgeon, and surrounded by his brave and suffering officers. He made no comment on the battle, nor indeed was heard to utter a word, except to make such simple requests as his necessities required. In this way he lingered through four days, in extreme bodily pain, and the silent melancholy of a proud and noble heart, and then expired. His body was wrapped in the colours of his ship and laid on the quarter-deck of the Chesapeake, to be conveyed to Halifax, for interment.

At the time of his death he was but thirty-two years of age, nearly sixteen of which had been honourably expended in the service of his country. He was a disciplinarian of the highest order, producing perfect obedience and subordination without severity. His men became zealously devoted to him, and ready to do through affection what severity would never have compelled. He was scrupulously correct in his principles, delicate in his sense of honour; and to his extreme jealousy of reputation he fell a victim, in daring an ill-matched encounter, which prudence would have justified him in declining. In battle, where his lofty and commanding person made him conspicuous, the calm collected courage, and elevated tranquillity, which he maintained in the midst of peril, imparted a confidence to every bosom. In the hour of victory he was moderate and unassuming; towards the vanquished he was gentle, generous and humane. But it is on the amiable qualities that adorned his private character, that his friends will hang with the fondest remembrance—that bland philanthropy that emanated from every look, that breathed forth in every accent, that gave a grace to every action. His was a general benevolence, that, like a lambent flame, shed its cheering rays throughout the sphere of his influence, warming and gladdening every heart, and lighting up every countenance into smiles. But there is one little circle on whose sacred sorrows even the eye of sympathy dares not intrude. His brother being dead, he was the last male branch of a family, who looked up to him as its ornament and pride. His fraternal tenderness was the prop and consolation of two widowed sisters, and in him their helpless offspring found a father. He left, also, a wife and two young children to whom he was fervently attached. The critical situation of the former was one of those cares which preyed upon his mind at the time he went forth to battle. The utmost precautions have been taken by her relatives, to keep from her the knowledge of her husband's fate; their anxiety has been relieved by the birth of a son, who, we trust, will inherit the virtues, and emulate the actions of his father. The unfortunate mother is now slowly recovering from a long and dangerous confinement; but has yet to learn the heart-rending intelligence, that the infant in her arms is fatherless.

There is a touching pathos about the death of this estimable officer, that endears him more to us than if he had been successful. The prosperous conqueror is an object of admiration, but in some measure of envy: whatever gratitude we feel for his services, we are apt to think them repaid by the plaudits he enjoys. But he who falls a martyr to his country's cause excites the fulness of public sympathy. Envy cannot repine at laurels so dearly purchased, and gratitude feels that he is beyond the reach of its rewards. The last sad scene of his life hallows his memory; it remains sacred by misfortune, and honoured, not by the acclamations, but the tears of his countrymen. The idea of Lawrence, cut down in the prime of his days, stretched upon his deck, wrapped in the flag of his country—that flag which he had contributed to ennoble, and had died to defend—is a picture that will remain treasured up in the dearest recollections of every American. His will form one of those talismanic names which every nation preserves as watchwords for patriotism and valour.

Deeply, therefore, as every bosom must lament the fall of so gallant and amiable an officer, there are some reflections consoling to the pride of friendship, and which may sooth, though they cannot prevent, the bitter tear of affection. He fell before his flag was struck. His fall was the cause, not the consequence, of defeat. He fell covered with glory, in the flower of his days, in the perfection of mental and personal endowment, and the freshness of reputation; thus leaving in every mind the full and perfect image of a hero. However we may deplore the stroke of death, his visits are occasionally well timed for his victim: he sets a seal upon the fame of the illustrious, fixing it beyond the reach of accident or change. And where is the son of honour, panting for distinction, who would not rather, like Lawrence, be snatched away in the brightness of youth and glory, than dwindle down to what is termed a good old age, wear his reputation to the shreds, and leave behind him nothing but the remembrance of decrepitude and imbecility.

With feelings that swell our hearts do we notice the honours paid to the remains of the brave Lawrence at Halifax. When the ships arrived in port, a generous concern was expressed for his fate. The recollection of his humanity towards the crew of the Peacock was still fresh in every mind. His funeral obsequies were celebrated with appropriate ceremonials, and an affecting solemnity. His pall was supported by the oldest captains in the British service that were in Halifax; and the naval officers crowded to yield the last sad honours to a man who was late their foe, but now their foe no longer. There is a sympathy between gallant souls that knows no distinction of clime or nation. They honour in each other what they feel proud of in themselves. The group that gathered round the grave of Lawrence presented a scene worthy of the heroic days of chivalry. It was a complete triumph of the nobler feelings over the savage passions of war. We know not where most to bestow our admiration—on the living, who showed such generous sensibility to departed virtue, or on the dead, in being worthy of such obsequies from such spirits. It is by deeds like these that we really feel ourselves subdued. The conflict of arms is ferocious, and triumph does but engender more deadly hostility; but the contest of magnanimity calls forth the better feelings, and the conquest is over the affections. We hope that in such a contest we may never be outdone; but that the present unhappy war may be continually softened and adorned by similar acts of courtesy and kindness on either part, thus sowing among present hostilities the quickening seeds of future friendship.

As to the event of this battle, deeply as we mourn the loss of so many valuable lives, we feel no further cause of lamentation. Brilliant as the victory undoubtedly was to the conquerors, our nation lost nothing of honour in the conflict. The ship was gallantly and bloodily defended to the last, and was lost, not through want of good conduct or determined bravery, but from the unavoidable chances of battle.* It was a victory "over which the conqueror mourned—so many suffered." We will not enter into any mechanical measurement of feet and inches, or any nice calculation of force; whether she had a dozen men more or less, or were able to throw a few pounds more or less of ball, than her adversary, by way of accounting for her defeat; we leave to nicer calculators to balance skill and courage against timber and old iron, and mete out victories by the square and the steelyard. The question of naval superiority, about which so much useless anxiety has been manifested of late, and which we fear will cause a vast deal of strife and ill blood before it is put to rest, was in our opinion settled long since, in the course of the five preceding battles. From a general examination of these battles, it appears clearly to us that, under equal circumstances of force and preparation, the nations are equal on the ocean; and the result of any contest, between well-matched ships, would depend entirely on accident. This, without any charge of vanity, we may certainly claim: the British, in justice and candour, must admit as much, and it would be arrogant in us to insist on any thing more.

Our officers have hitherto been fighting under superior excitement to the British. They have been eager to establish a name, and from their limited number, each has felt as if individually responsible for the reputation of the navy. Besides, the haughty superiority with which they have at various times been treated by the enemy, had stung the feelings of the officers, and even touched the rough pride of the common sailor. They have spared no pains, therefore, to prepare for contest with so formidable a foe, and have fought with the united advantages of discipline and enthusiasm.

An equal excitement is now felt by the British. Galled by our suc-

---

* In this we speak of the loyal, and really American part of the crew. We have, it is true, been told of treacherous conduct among the murmurers, a number of whom, headed by the dastardly Portuguese boatswain's mate, are said to have deserted their commander at the moment of most need. As this matter will come under the scrutiny of the proper tribunal, we pass it over without further notice. If established, it will form another of the baleful disadvantages under which this battle was fought, and may serve to show the policy of admitting the leaven of foreign vagabonds among our own sound-hearted sailors.

cesses, they begin to find that we are an enemy that calls for all their skill and circumspection. They have therefore resorted to a strictness of discipline, and to excessive precautions and preparations that had been neglected in their navy, and which no other modern foe has been able to compel. Thus circumstanced, every future contest must be bloody and precarious. The question of superiority, if such an idle question is still kept up, will in all probability be shifting with the result of different battles, as either side has superior advantages, or superior good fortune.

For our part, we conceive that the great purpose of our navy is accomplished. It was not to be expected that with so inconsiderable a force, we should make any impression on British power, or materially affect British commerce. We fought, not to take their ships and plunder their wealth, but to pluck some of their laurels wherewith to grace our own brows. In this we have succeeded; and thus the great mischief that our little navy was capable of doing to Great Britain, in showing that her maritime power was vulnerable, has been effected, and is irretrievable.

The British may now swarm on our coasts—they may infest our rivers and our bays—they may destroy our ships—they may burn our docks and our ports—they may annihilate every gallant tar that fights beneath our flag—they may wreak every vengeance on our marine that their overwhelming force enables them to accomplish—and after all what have they effected? redeemed the pre-eminence of their flag? destroyed the naval power of this country?—no such thing. They must first obliterate from the tablets of our memories, that deep-traced recollection, that we have repeatedly met them with equal force and conquered. In that inspiring idea, which is beyond the reach of mortal hand, exists the germ of future navies, future power, and future conquest. What is our navy? —a handful of frigates; let them be destroyed; our forests can produce hundreds such. Should our docks be laid in ruins, we can rebuild them— should our gallant band of tars be annihilated, thanks to the vigorous population of our country, we can furnish thousands and thousands of such—but so long as exists the moral certainty that we have within us the spirit, the abilities, and the means of attaining naval glory—so long the enemy, in wreaking their resentment on our present force, do but bite the stone which has been hurled at them—the hand that hurled it remains uninjured.

[September, 1813]

CAPTAIN LAWRENCE

Since the publication of our biographical sketch of this lamented officer, a letter has been put in our hands, from Commodore Bainbridge, contradicting the statement of his having dissuaded Captain Lawrence from encountering the Shannon; and mentioning that he did not see Captain Lawrence for several days previous to his sailing. The hasty manner in which the biography was written, though it is a poor apology for incorrectness, may account for any errors that may occur. In fact, we did but consider ourselves as pioneers, breaking the way for more able and wary biographers who should come after us: who might diligently pursue the path we had opened, profit by the tracks we had left, and cautiously avoid the false steps we had made.

The facts respecting the battle were almost all taken from notes of a conversation with one of the officers of the Chesapeake, which were afterwards revised and acknowledged by him. Some, it is true, were cautiously selected from the current reports of the day, according as they bore the stamp of probability, and were supported by the concurrence of various testimony. These may occasionally be somewhat misstated, but we believe that in general they are materially correct. That any blame could ever attach for a moment to the conduct of Captain Lawrence, in encountering the Shannon, though superior in equipment, we never insinuated, or supposed. On the contrary, we admired that zeal for the honour of his flag, and that jealousy of his own reputation, that led him, in the face of obvious disadvantages, to a battle, which men of less heroism would have declined without disgrace. The calculating, cautious-spirited commander, who warily measures the weapons, and estimates the force of his ópponent, and shuns all engagements, where the chances are not in his favour, may gain the reputation of prudence, but never of valour. There were sufficent chances on the side of Lawrence to exculpate him from all imputation of rashness, and sufficient perils to entitle him to the highest character for courage. He who would greatly deserve, must greatly dare, for brilliant victory is only achieved at the risk of disastrous defeat, and those laurels are ever brightest, that are gathered on the very brink of danger.

[September, 1813]

THE LAY OF THE SCOTTISH FIDDLE:

A TALE OF HAVRE DE GRACE

A little work, "supposed to be written by Walter Scott, Esq." with the above title, has just issued from the press, under the fashionable modern form of a poem *with notes:* the late period at which it was put in our hands prevents us from entering into a particular account of it. The writer appears to have more than one object in view. At first, his intention seems to be merely to satirize and parody the writings of Walter Scott, which have lately had such an all pervading circulation in the fashionable world; but in the course of all his work, he seems disposed to extend his lash to the follies and errors of his countrymen; to advocate the present war; and to retaliate, in a good-humoured way, on the British invaders in the Chesapeake, for their excesses at Havre de Grace. But though ridicule and merriment appear to be the leading features, the work is occasionally diversified by little passages of pathos and feeling; the descriptions of American scenery, and American manners, are touched off with much truth of pencil and felicity of manner, and there are several veins of thought, that would do credit to a work of a more elevated and sober character.

There are, however, some traces of political satire discernible in this volume, which, though managed with great good nature, we regret that the revising hand of the author had not expunged; as they are calculated to awaken angry feelings in some bosoms, and to injure the interests of a work, which would otherwise be read with pleasure and approbation throughout the union.

We subjoin à few extracts, hastily made, as specimens of the nature and merits of the work.

The introduction is somewhat of a parody on the introduction to Mr. Scott's Lay of the Last Minstrel; instead of a harper, we are presented with a fiddler.

> "THE way was long, though 'twas not cold,
> But the poor bard was weak and old,
> And carried scor'd upon his front
> Of many a year the long account.
> His *Fiddle*, sole remaining pride,
> Hung dangling down his ragged side,
> In faded bag of flannel green,
> Through which the well carv'd head was seen
> Of gaping lion, yawning wide,
> In regal pomp of beastly pride.

The last of all the race was he,
Who charm'd the ear with tweedle dee.
For lack-a-day! full well I ween
The happy times he once had seen,
When in the merry capering days
Of olden time he tun'd his lays,
'Mong gallant lads, or jolly sailors,
And play'd 'the de'el amang the tailors,'
Had given place to other glee,
And different strains of harmony.
'The bigots of this iron time
Had call'd his harmless art a crime;'
And now, instead of dance and song
Pricking the night's dull pace along,
And sprightly gambols deftly play'd
By rustic lad and gleeful maid,
And all that decks the cheek of toil
With nature's warm and heartfelt smile:
No sound is heard borne on the gale,
In village lone or rural dale,
But canting, whining, nasal notes,
Twanging through hoarse and foggy throats,
Ascending up the startled sky,
Mocking the ear of deity
With nonsense blasphemous and wild;
While wretches, of their peace beguil'd,
Scare the dull ear of drowsy night
With screams that boding screech owls fright,
And hollow moans, that seem to flow
From damned souls in shades below.
Love-feasts are held at midnight's hour,
When fancy wields her potent power,
And to the trembling wretch's eyes
Sepulchres ope, and spectres rise,
Gaunt forms, and grisly shapes appear,
And sweet religion turns to fear.
A fiddler now (no wight so poor)
May beg his bread from door to door,
Nor tune to please a peasant's ear,
Those notes that blithe King Cole might hear.

"A little dog with gentle speed,
Though not of black St. Hubert's breed,
Led by a string this man of wo,

Whose faltering steps, all sad and slow,
Seem'd hastening towards that long, long home,
Where rich and poor at last must come.
Why did'nt that puppy walk behind?
Alas! the fiddler was stone blind,
And might not find his way alone,
Ev'n though meridian sun had shone.
Betide him weal, betide him wo,
In summer heat or winter snow,
Or when the cutting midnight blast
Around the leafy forest cast,
And withering frost launch'd on the air
Laid the sweet face of nature bare;
When man and nature seem'd combin'd
With biting frost and whistling wind,
To waste his poor remains of life
In anxious toil and fruitless strife;
Still that same dog ne'er shrunk the while
From nature's frown, or woo'd her smile;
But faithful to his wonted trust,
More true than man, than man more just,
He led the wight, from day to day,
Unharm'd through all his darksome way.
In lonely shed, at brightning blaze,
In dewy fields, or hard highways,
Or under branch of spreading tree,
Where'er his lodgings chanc'd to be,
Still that same little faithful guide,
Stretch'd at his feet or by his side,
While the poor houseless wanderer slept,
His guardian watch for ever kept."   P. 13–17.

The following description of American scenery is given on the enemy's
entering the Susquehanna.

X.

"And now they came in gallant pride,
Where Susquehanna's noble tide,
In silent pomp, is seen to pay
Its tribute to the lordly bay.
And on its beauteous margin spied
The little town, in rural pride,
Reposing in the folded arms

Of peace, nor dreaming of those harms,
Which fortune, in her fitful spite,
Decreed should come that fatal night.

XI.

"The sun low in the west did wane,
And cross the level of the plain;
The shadow of each tree the while,
Seem'd lengthen'd into many a mile;
The purple hue of evening fell
Upon the low sequester'd dell;
And scarce a lingering sunbeam play'd
Around the distant mountain's head.
The sweet south wind sunk to a calm,
The dews of evening fell like balm;
The night-hawk, soaring in the sky,
Told that the twilight shades were nigh;
The bat began his dusky flight,
The whip-poor-will, *our* bird of night,
Ever unseen, yet ever near,
His shrill note warbled in the ear;
The buzzing beetle forth did hie,
With busy hum and heedless eye;
The little watchman of the night,
The fire-fly, trimm'd his lamp so bright,
And took his merry airy round
Along the meadow's fragrant bound,
Where blossom'd clover, bath'd in dew,
In sweet luxuriance blushing grew.

XII.

"O Nature! Goddess ever dear,
What a fair scene of peace was here!
What pleasant sports, what calm delights,
What happy days, what blameless nights,
Might in such gentle haunts be spent
In the soft lap of bland content!
But vain it is that bounteous heav'n
To wretched man this earth has given;
Vain, that its smiling face displays
Such beauties to his reckless gaze,
While this same rash malignant worm

Raises the whirlwind and the storm,
Pollutes her bosom with hot blood,
Turns to rank poison all her good,
And plays before his maker's eyes,
The serpent of this paradise." P. 71–73.

The following picture is admirably descriptive of a country bumpkin
in love; the scenery is delightfully managed.

VII.

"Close in a darksome corner sat
A scowling wight, with old wool hat,
That dangled o'er his sun-burnt brow,
And many a gaping rent did show;
His beard in grim luxuriance grew;
His great toe peep'd from either shoe;
His brawny elbow shown all bare;
All matted was his carrot hair,
And in his sad face you might see,
The withering look of poverty.
He seem'd all desolate of heart,
And in the revels took no part.
Yet those who watch'd his blood-shot eye,
As the light dancers flitted by,
Might jealousy, and dark despair,
And love detect, all mingled there.

VIII.

"He never turn'd his eye away
From one fair damsel passing gay;
But ever, in her airy round,
Watch'd her quick step, and lightsome bound;
Wherever in the dance she turn'd,
He turn'd his eye, and that eye burn'd
With such fierce spleen, that sooth to say,
It made the gazer turn away.
Who was the damsel passing fair,
That caus'd his eyeballs thus to glare?
It was the blooming Jersey maid,
That our poor wight's tough heart betray'd.

IX.

"By Pompton stream, that silent flows,
Where many a wild flower heedless blows
Unmark'd by any human eye,
Unpluck'd by any passer by,
There stands a church, whose whiten'd side
Is by the traveller often spied,
Glittering among the branches fair
Of locust trees, that flourish there.
Along the margin of the tide,
That to the eye just seems to glide,
And to the list'ning ear ne'er throws
A murmur to disturb repose,
The stately elm majestic towers,
The lord of Pompton's fairy bowers.
The willow, that its branches waves
O'er neighbourhood of rustic graves,
Oft, when the summer south wind blows,
Its thirsty tendrils playful throws
Into the river rambling there,
The cooling influence to share,
Of the pure stream, that bears imprest
Sweet nature's image in its breast.

X.

"Sometimes, on sunny sabbath day,
Our ragged wight would wend his way
To this fair church, and lounge about
With many an idle sun-burnt lout,
And stumble o'er the silent graves;
Or where the weeping willow waves,
His listless length would lay him down,
And spell the legend on the stone.
'Twas here, as ancient matrons say,
His eye first caught the damsel gay,
Who in the interval between
The *services*, oft tript the green,
And threw her witching eyes about,
To great dismay of bumpkin stout,
Who felt his heart rebellious beat,
Whene'er those eyes he chanc'd to meet.

XI.

"As our poor wight all listless lay,
Dozing the vacant hours away,
Or watching with his half shut eye,
The buzzing flight of bee or fly,
The beauteous damsel pass'd along,
Humming a stave of sacred song.
She threw her soft blue eyes askance,
And gave the booby such a glance,
That quick his eyes wide open flew,
And his wide mouth flew open too.
He gaz'd with wonder and surprise
At the mild lustre of her eyes,
Her cherry lips, her dimpled cheek,
Where Cupids play'd at hide and seek,
Whence, many an arrow well, I wot,
Against the wight's tough heart was shot.

XII.

"He follow'd her where'er she stray'd,
While every look his love betray'd;
And when her milking she would ply,
Sooth'd her pleas'd ear with Rhino-Die,
Or made the mountain echoes ring
With the great feats of John Paulding;
How he, stout moss-trooper bold,
Refus'd the proffer'd glittering gold,
And to the gallant youth did cry,
'One of us two must quickly die.'

XIII.

"On the rough meadow of his cheek,
The scythe he laid full twice a week,
Foster'd the honours of his head,
That wide as scrub-oak branches spread,
With grape-vine juice, and bear's grease too,
And dangled it in eel-skin queue.
In short, he tried each gentle art
To anchor fast her floating heart;
But still she scorn'd his tender tale,
And saw, unmov'd, his cheek grow pale,

Flouted his suit with scorn so cold,
And gave him oft the bag to hold." P. 88–94.

[November, 1813]

BIOGRAPHICAL NOTICE

OF THE LATE LIEUTENANT BURROWS

It is the laudable desire of every brave man to receive the praises of his countrymen: but there is a dearer and more cherished wish that grows closer to his heart; it is to live in the recollections of those he loves and honours; to leave behind him a name, at the mention of which the bosom of friendship shall glow, the eye of affection shall brighten; which shall be a legacy of honest pride to his family, causing it to dwell on his worthy deeds, and glory in his memory. The bravest soldier would not willingly expose himself to certain danger, if he thought that death were to be followed by oblivion; he might rise above the mere dread of bodily pain, but human pride shrinks from the darkness and silence of the grave.

It is the duty, and it is likewise the policy, therefore, of a nation, to pay distinguished honour to the memories of those who have fallen in its service. It is, after all, but a cheap reward for sufferings and death; but it is a reward that will prompt others to the sacrifice, when they see that it is faithfully discharged. The youthful bosom warms with emulation at the praises of departed heroes. The marble monument that bears the story of a nation's admiration and gratitude, becomes an object of ambition. Death, the great terror of warfare, ceases to be an evil when graced with such distinctions; and thus one hero may be said, like a phœnix, to spring from the ashes of his predecessor.

In the gallant young officer who is the subject of the present memoir, we shall see these observations verified; he fought with the illustrious example of his brethren before his eyes, and died with the funeral honours of Lawrence fresh in his recollection.

Lieutenant William Burrows was born in 1785, at Kinderton, near Philadelphia, the seat of his father, William Ward Burrows, Esq. of South Carolina. He was educated chiefly under the eye of his parent, who was a gentleman of accomplished mind and polished manners. It is not known whether he was intended for any particular profession; but great pains were taken to instruct him in the living languages; and at the age of thirteen he was as well acquainted with the German as with his mother tongue; he was likewise kept rigidly at the study of the French, for which, however, he showed a singular aversion. The dawning of his character was pleasing and auspicious; to quickness of intellect he added an amiable disposition and generous sensibility of heart. His character, however, soon assumed more distinct and peculiar features; a shade of reserve began gradually to settle on his manners. At an age when the feelings of other children are continually sallying forth, he seemed to hush his into subjection. He appeared to retire within himself: to cherish a solitary independence of mind, and to rely as much as possible on his own resources. It seemed as if his young imagination had already glanced forth on the rough scene of his future life, and that he was silently preparing himself for its vicissitudes. Nor is it improbable that such was the case. Though little communicative of his hopes and wishes, it was evident that his genius had taken its bias. Even among the gentle employments and elegant pursuits of a polite education, his family was astonished to perceive the rugged symptoms of the sailor continually breaking forth: and his drawing master would sometimes surprise him neglecting the allotted task, to paint the object of his silent adoration—a gallant ship of war.

On finding that such was the determined bent of his inclinations, care was immediately taken to instruct him in naval science. A midshipman's warrant was procured for him in November, 1799, and in the following January he joined the sloop of war Portsmouth, commanded by Captain M'Neale, in which he sailed to France. This cruise, while it confirmed his predilection for the life he had adopted, made him acquainted with his own deficiencies. Instead of the puerile vanity and harmless ostentation which striplings generally evince when they first put on their uniform, and feel the importance of command, it was with difficulty he could be persuaded to wear the naval dress, until he had proved himself worthy of it by his services. The same mixture of genuine diffidence and proud humility was observed in the discharge of his duties towards his inferiors; he felt the novelty of his situation, and shrunk from the exercise of authority over the aged and veteran sailor, whom he considered his superior in seamanship. On his return home, therefore, he requested a furlough of some months, to strengthen him in the principles of navigation. He also resumed the study of the French language, the necessity for which he had experienced in his late cruise, and from his knowledge of grammatical elements, joined to vigorous application, he soon learned to use it with fluency.

He was afterwards ordered on duty, and served on board of various ships until 1803, when he was ordered to the frigate Constitution, Commodore Preble. Soon after the arrival of that ship in the Mediterranean, the commodore, noticing his zeal and abilities, made him an acting lieutenant. In the course of the Tripolitan war he distinguished himself on various occasions by his intrepidity; particularly in one instance, when he rushed into the midst of a mutinous body, and seized the ringleader, at the imminent hazard of his life. After his return to the United

States, in 1807, he was in different services, and among others, as first lieutenant of the Hornet. While in this situation, he distinguished himself greatly during a violent and dangerous gale, insomuch that his brother officers attributed the preservation of the ship entirely to his presence of mind and consummate seamanship.

The details of a sailor's life are generally brief, and little satisfactory. We expect miraculous stories from men who rove the deep, visit every corner of the world, and mingle in storms and battles; and are mortified to find them treating these subjects with provoking brevity. The fact is, these circumstances that excite our wonder, are trite and familiar to their minds. He whose whole life is a tissue of perils and adventures, passes lightly over scenes at which the landsman, accustomed to the security of his fireside, shudders even in imagination. Mere bravery ceases to be a matter of ostentation, when every one around him is brave; and hairbreadth 'scapes are common-place topics among men whose very profession consists in the hourly hazard of existence.

In seeking, therefore, after interesting anecdotes concerning those naval officers whose exploits have excited public enthusiasm, our curiosity is continually baffled by general accounts, or meager particulars, given with the technical brevity of a log-book. We have thus been obliged to pass cursorily over several years of Burrows' seafaring life, though doubtless chequered by many striking incidents.

From what we can collect, he seems to have been a marked and eccentric character. His peculiarity, instead of being smoothed and worn down by mingling with the world, became more and more prominent, as he advanced in life. He had centered all his pride in becoming a thorough and accomplished sailor, and regarded every thing else with indifference. His manners were an odd compound of carelessness and punctilio, frankness and taciturnity. He stood aloof from the familiarity of strangers, and in his contempt of what he considered fawning and profession, was sometimes apt to offend by blunt simplicity, or chill by reserve. But his character, when once known, seemed to attach by its very eccentricities, and though little studious of pleasing, he soon became a decided favourite. He had an original turn of thought and a strong perception of every thing ludicrous and characteristic. Though scarcely ever seen to laugh himself, he possessed an exquisite vein of dry humour which he would occasionally indulge in the hours of hilarity, and, without moving a muscle of his own countenance, would set the table in a roar. When under the influence of this lurking drollery, every thing he said and did was odd and whimsical. His replies were remarkably happy, and, heightened by the peculiarity of his manner, and the provoking gravity of his demeanour, were sources of infinite merriment to his associates. It was his delight to put on the dress of the common sailor, and explore the haunts of low life, drawing from thence traits of character and comic scenes with which he would sometimes entertain his messmates.

But with all this careless and eccentric manner, he possessed a heart full of noble qualities. He was proud of spirit, but perfectly unassuming; jealous of his own rights, but scrupulously considerate of those of others. His friendships were strong and sincere; and he was zealous in the performance of secret and important services for those to whom he was attached. There was a rough benevolence in his disposition that manifested itself in a thousand odd ways; nothing delighted him more than to surprise the distressed with relief, and he was noted for his kindness and condescension towards the humble and dependent. His companions were full of his generous deeds, and he was the darling of the common sailors. Such was the sterling worth that lay encrusted in an unpromising exterior, and hidden from the world by a forbidding and taciturn reserve.

With such strong sensibilities and solitary pride of character, it was the lot of Burrows to be wounded in that tender part where the feelings of officers seem most assailable. In his promotion to a lieutenancy he had the mortification to find himself outranked by junior officers, some of whom he had commanded in the Tripolitan war. He remonstrated to the navy department, but without redress. On Mr. Hamilton's going into office, he stated to him his claims, and, impatient of the slight which he conceived he had suffered, offered to resign his commission, which, however, was not accepted. Whether the wrongs of which he complained were real or imaginary, they preyed deeply on his mind. He seemed for a time to grow careless of the world and of himself; withdrew more than ever from society, and abandoned himself to the silent broodings of a wounded spirit. Perhaps this morbid sensibility of feeling might in some measure have been occasioned by infirmity of body, his health having been broken by continual and severe duty; but it belongs to a saturnine character, like that of Burrows, to feel deeply and sorely. Men of gayer spirits and more mercurial temperament, may readily shake off vexation, or bustle it away amid the amusements and occupations of the world; but Burrows was scanty in his pleasures, limited in his resources, single in his ambition. Naval distinction was the object of all his hope and pride; it was the only light that led him on and cheered his way, and whatever intervened left him in darkness and dreariness of heart.

Finding his resignation was not accepted, and feeling temporary disgust at the service, he applied for a furlough, which, with some difficulty, he obtained. He then entered as first officer on board the merchant ship Thomas Penrose, Captain Ansley, and sailed on a commercial voyage to Canton. On his return passage he was captured and carried into Barbadoes, but permitted to come home, on parole. Immediately on his being exchanged, in June, 1813, he was appointed to the command of the brig Enterprise, at Portsmouth.

This appointment seemed to infuse new life and spirits into Burrows, and to change his whole deportment. His proper pride was gratified on having a separate command; he no longer felt like an unimportant individual, but that he had rank and station to support. He threw off a great deal of his habitual reserve, became urbane and attentive; and those who had lately looked upon him as a mere misanthrope, were delighted with the manly frankness of his manners.

On the first of September, the Enterprise sailed from Portsmouth on a cruise. On the fifth, early in the morning, they espied a brig inshore getting under way. They reconnoitred her for a while to ascertain her character, of which they were soon informed by her hoisting three British ensigns, and firing a shot as a challenge. The Enterprise then haled upon a wind, stood out of the bay, and prepared for action. A calm for some time delayed the encounter; it was succeeded by a breeze from the S. W. which gave our vessel the weather-gage. After manœuvring for a while to the windward in order to try her sailing with the enemy, and to ascertain his force, the Enterprise, about 3 P.M., shortened sail, hoisted three ensigns, fired a gun, tacked, and ran down with an intention to bring him to close quarters. When within half pistol shot the enemy gave three cheers, and commenced the action with his starboard broadside. The cheers and the broadside were returned on our part, and the action became general. In about five minutes after the battle had commenced, the gallant Burrows received a musket ball in his body and fell; he however refused to be carried below, but continued on deck through the action. The active command was then taken by Lieutenant M'Call, who conducted himself with great skill and coolness. The enemy was out manœuvred and cut up: his maintopmast and topsail-yard shot away; a position gained on his starboard bow, and a raking fire kept up, until his guns were silenced and he cried for quarters, saying that as his colours were nailed to the mast he could not hale them down. The prize proved to be his Britannic majesty's brig Boxer of 14 guns. The number of her crew is a matter of conjecture and dispute. Sixty-four prisoners were taken, seventeen of whom were wounded. How many of the dead were thrown into the sea during the action it is impossible to say;* the British return only four as killed; courtesy forbids us to question the veracity of an officer on mere presumption; but it is ever the natural wish of the vanquished to depreciate their force; and, in truth,

---

* In a letter from Captain Hull to Commodore Bainbridge he describes the state of the Boxer when brought into port: and observes, "We find it impossible to get at the number of killed; no papers are found by which we can ascertain it. I however counted ninety hammocks which were in her netting with beds in them, besides several beds without hammocks; and she had excellent accommodations for all her officers below in state-rooms, so that I have no doubt that she had one hundred men on board."

we have seen with regret various instances of disingenuousness on the part of the enemy, in their statements of our naval encounters. But we will not enter into disputes of this kind. It is enough that the enemy entered into the battle with a bravado at the mast head, and a confidence of success; this either implied a consciousness of his own force, or a low opinion of his antagonist; in either case he was mistaken. It is a fruitless task to vindicate victories against the excuses of the vanquished —sufficient for the victor is the joy of his triumph, he should allow the enemy the consolation of accounting for it.

We turn gladly from such an idle discussion to notice the last moments of the worthy Burrows. There needs no elaborate pencil to impart pathos and grandeur to the death of a brave man. The simple anecdotes given in simple terms by his surviving comrades, present more striking pictures, than could be wrought up by the most refined attempts of art. "At 20 minutes past three P. M." says one account, "our brave commander fell, and while lying on the deck, refusing to be carried below, raised his head and requested that *the flag might never be struck*." In this situation he remained during the rest of the engagement, regardless of bodily pain; regardless of the life-blood fast ebbing from his wound; watching with anxious eye the vicissitudes of battle; cheering his men by his voice, but animating them still more by his glorious example. When the sword of the vanquished enemy was presented to him, we are told that he clasped his hands and exclaimed, "I am satisfied, I die contented!" He now permitted himself to be carried below, and the necessary attentions were paid to save his life, or alleviate his sufferings. His wound, however, was beyond the power of surgery, and he breathed his last within a few hours after the victory.

The commander of the Boxer, Captain Samuel Blythe, was killed early in the action by a cannon ball; had he lived he might have defended his ship more desperately, but it is not probable with more success. He was an officer of distinguished merit; having received a sword from government for his good conduct under Sir James L. Yeo, in the capture of Cayenne. He was also one of the pall-bearers to our lamented Lawrence, when buried at Halifax. It was his fate now to receive like courtesy at the hands of his enemy. His remains, in company with those of the brave Burrows, were brought to Portland, where they were interred with military honours. It was a striking and affecting sight, to behold two gallant commanders, who had lately been arrayed in deadly hostility against each other, descending into one quiet grave, there to mingle their dust peacefully together.

At the time of his decease Lieutenant Burrows was but in his twenty-ninth year; a most untimely death, as it concerned the interests of his country, and the fulness of his own renown. Had he survived there is little doubt that his great professional merits, being rendered conspicuous by this achievement, would have raised him to importance, and enlarged the sphere of his usefulness. And it is more than probable that those rich qualities of heart and mind, which, chilled by neglect, had lain almost withering in the shade, being once vivified by the quickening rays of public favour, would have sprung forth in full luxuriance. As it is, his public actions will live on the proud page of our naval history, and his private worth will long flourish in the memory of his intimates, who dwell with honest warmth on the eccentric merits of this generous and truehearted sailor. For himself he was resigned to his premature fate: life seems never to have had much value in his eyes, and was nothing when weighed with reputation. He had attained the bright object of his wishes, and died in the full fruition of the warrior's hope, with the shouts of victory still sounding in his ears.

[December, 1813]

BIOGRAPHICAL MEMOIR

OF

COMMODORE PERRY

In taking up the pen to commemorate another of our naval victories, we solicit the patience of our readers if we indulge in a few preliminary reflections, not strictly arising out of the subject of this memoir, though, we trust, not wholly irrelevant.

Indeed, we do not pretend to the rigid precision and dispassionate coolness of historic narrative. Excited as we are by the tone and temper of the times, and the enthusiasm that prevails around us, we cannot, if we would, repress those feelings of pride and exultation, that gush warm from the heart, when the triumphs of our navy are the theme. Public joy is at all times contagious; but in the present lowering days of evil, it is a sight as inspiring as it is rare, to behold a whole nation breaking forth into gladness.

There is a point, however, beyond which exultation becomes insulting, and honest pride swells into vanity. When this is exceeded even success proves injurious, and, instead of begetting a proper confidence in ourselves, produces that most disgusting of all national faults, boastful arrogance. This is the evil against the encroachments of which we would earnestly caution our countrymen; it comes with such an open and imposing front of worthy patriotism, and at such warm and incautious moments, that it is apt to take possession of us before we are aware. We have already noticed some symptoms of its prevalence. We have seen many of our papers filled with fulsome and extravagant paragraphs, echoing the vulgar joy and coarse tauntings of the rabble: these may be acceptable to the gross palates of the mean minded; but they must grieve the feelings of the generous and liberal; and must lessen our triumphs in the eyes of impartial nations. In this we behold the striking difference between those who fight battles, and those who merely talk about them. Our officers are content modestly to announce their victories; to give a concise statement of their particulars, and then drop the subject: but then the theme is taken up by a thousand vaunting tongues and vaunting pens; each tries to outvie the other in extravagant applause, until the very ear of admiration becomes wearied with excessive eulogium.

We do not know whether, in these remarks, we are not passing censure upon ourselves, and whether we do not largely indulge in the very weakness we condemn: but of this we are sure, that in our rejoicings no feelings enter insulting to the foe. We joy, indeed, in seeing the flag of our country encircled with glory, and our nation elevated to a dignified rank among the nations of the earth; but we make no boastful claims to intrinsic superiority, nor seek to throw sneer or stigma on an enemy, whom, in spite of temporary hostility, we honour and admire.

But, surely, if any impartial mind will consider the circumstances of the case, he will pardon our countrymen for overstepping, in the flush of unexpected and repeated success, the modest bounds of propriety. Is it a matter of surprise that, while our cheeks are yet scarce cool from the blushes—the burning blushes—of wounded pride and insulted patriotism, with which we have heard our country ridiculed and set at naught by other nations—while our ears still ring with the galling terms in which even British statesmen have derided us, as weak, pusillanimous and contemptible—while our memories are still sore with the tales of our flag insulted in every sea, and our countrymen oppressed in every port— is it a matter of surprise that we should break forth into transports at seeing these foul aspersions all suddenly brushed away—at seeing a continued series of brilliant successes flashing around the national standard, and dazzling all eyes with their excessive brightness? "Can such things be, and overcome us, like a summer cloud," without, not merely our "special wonder," but our special exultation? He who will cast his eye back, and notice how, in little more than one short year, we have suddenly sprung from peaceful insignificance to proud competition with a power whose laurels have been the slow growth of ages, will easily excuse the temporary effervescence of our feelings.

For our parts we truly declare that we revere the British nation. One of the dearest wishes of our hearts is to see a firm and well grounded friendship established between us. But friendship can never long endure, unless founded on mutual respect, and maintained with mutual independence; and however we may deplore the present war, this double good will spring out of it, we will learn our own value and resources, and we will teach our antagonist and the world at large to know and estimate us properly. There is an obsequious deference in the minds of too many of our countrymen towards Great Britain, that not only impairs the independence of the national character, but defeats the very object they would attain. They would make any sacrifices to maintain a precarious, and patched up, and humiliating, connexion with her; but they may rest assured that the good opinion of Great Britain was never gained by servile acquiescence; she never will think the better of a people for thinking despicably of themselves. We execrate that lowliness of spirit that would flatter her vanity, cower beneath her contumely, and meanly lay our honours at her feet. We wish not her friendship gratuitously; but to acquire it as a right; not to supplicate it by forbearance and long-suffering, but gallantly to win and proudly to maintain it. After all, if she will not be a friend, she must be content to become a rival; she will be obliged to substitute jealousy for contempt, and surely it is more tolerable, at any time, to be hated than despised.

Such is the kind of feeling that we avow towards Great Britain—equally removed, we trust, from rancorous hostility on the one side, and blind partiality on the other.

Whatever we may think of the expediency or inexpediency of the present war, we cannot feel indifferent to its operations. Whenever our arms come in competition with those of the enemy, jealousy for our country's honour will swallow up every other consideration. Our feelings will ever accompany the flag of our country to battle, rejoicing in its glory—lamenting over its defeat. For there is no such thing as releasing ourselves from the consequences of the contest. He who fancies he can stand aloof in interest, and by condemning the present war, can exonerate himself from the shame of its disasters, is wofully mistaken. Other nations will not trouble themselves about our internal wranglings and party questions; they will not ask who among us fought, or why we fought—but *how* we fought. The disgrace of defeat will not be confined to the contrivers of the war, or the party in power, or the conductors of the battle; but will extend to the whole nation, and come home to every individual. If the name of American is to be rendered honourable in the fight, we shall each participate in the honour; if otherwise, we must inevitably support our share of the ignominy. For these reasons do we watch, with anxious eye, the various fortunes of this war; a war awfully decisive of the future character and destinies of the nation. But much as we are gladdened by the bright gleams that occasionally break forth amid the darkness of the times, yet joyfully, most joyfully, shall we hail the period, when the "troubled night" of war shall be passed, and the "star of peace" again shed its mild radiance on our country.

We have seized this opportunity to express the foregoing sentiments, because we thought that if of any value, they might stand some chance of making an impression, when accompanied by the following memoir. And, indeed, in writing these naval biographies, it is our object not merely to render a small tribute of gratitude to these intrepid champions of our honour; but to render our feeble assistance towards promoting that national feeling which their triumphs are calculated to inspire.

Oliver Hazard Perry is the eldest son of Christopher Raymond Perry, Esq. of the United States navy. He was born at Newport, Rhode Island, in August, 1785, and being early destined for the navy, he entered the service in 1798, as midshipman, on board the sloop of war General Greene, then commanded by his father. When that ship went out of commission he was transferred to a squadron destined to the Mediterranean, where he served during the Tripolitan war. His extreme youth prevented his having an opportunity of distinguishing himself; but the faithfulness and intelligence with which he discharged the duties of his station, recommended him greatly to the favour of his superior officers; while his private virtues, and the manly dignity of his deportment, commanded the friendship and respect of his associates.

On returning from the Mediterranean he continued sedulously attentive to his profession, and though the reduction of the navy, and the neglect into which it fell during an interval of peace, disheartened many of the officers, and occasioned several to resign, yet he determined to adhere to its fortunes, confident that it must at some future period rise to importance. It would be little interesting to enumerate the different vessels in which he served, or to trace his advances through the regular grades. In 1810, we find he was ordered to the United States schooner Revenge, as lieutenant commandant. This vessel was attached to the squadron of Commodore Rodgers, at New London, and employed in cruising in the Sound, to enforce the embargo act. In the following spring he had the misfortune to lose the Revenge on Watch Hill Reef, opposite Stoney Town. He had sailed from Newport, late in the evening, for New London, with an easterly wind, accompanied by a fog. In the morning he found himself enveloped in a thick mist, with a considerable swell going. In this situation, without any possibility of ascertaining where he was, or of guarding against surrounding dangers, the vessel was carried on the reef, and soon went to pieces. On this occasion Perry gave proofs of that admirable coolness and presence of mind for which he is remarkable. He used every precaution to save the guns and property, and was in a great measure successful. He got off all the crew in perfect safety, and was himself the last to leave the wreck. His conduct in respect to this disaster underwent examination by a court of inquiry, at his own request, and he was not merely acquitted of all blame, but highly applauded for the judgment, intrepidity, and perseverance he had displayed. The secretary of the navy, Mr. Hamilton, also wrote him a very complimentary letter on the occasion.

Shortly after this event he returned to Newport, being peculiarly attracted thither by a tender attachment for Miss Mason, daughter of Dr. Mason, and niece of the Hon. Christopher Champlin of the United States senate; a lovely and interesting young lady, whom he soon after married.

At the beginning of 1812 he was promoted to the rank of master and commander, and ordered to the command of the flotilla of gun-boats stationed at the harbour of New-York. He remained on this station about a year; during which time he employed himself diligently in disciplining his crew to serve either as landsmen or mariners; and brought his flotilla into an admirable state of preparation for active operations.

The gun-boat service, however, is at best but an irksome employ. Nothing can be more dispiriting for ardent and daring minds than to be obliged to skulk about harbours and rivers, cramped up in these diminutive vessels, without the hope of exploit to atone for present inconvenience. Perry soon grew tired of this inglorious service, and applied to the secretary of the navy to be ordered to a more active station, and mentioned the Lakes as the one he should prefer. His request was immediately complied with, and he received orders to repair to Sackett's Harbour, Lake Ontario, with a body of mariners to reinforce the squadron under Commodore Chauncey. So popular was he among the honest tars under his command, that no sooner was the order known than nearly the whole of the crews volunteered to accompany him.

In a few days he was ready to depart, and tearing himself from the comforts of home, and the endearments of a young and beautiful wife and blooming child, he set off at the head of a large number of chosen seamen, on his expedition to the wilderness. The rivers being completely frozen over, they were obliged to perform the journey by land, in the depth of winter. The greatest order and good humour, however, prevailed throughout the little band of adventurers, to whom the whole expedition seemed a kind of frolic, and who were delighted with what they termed a land cruise.

Not long after the arrival of Perry at Sackett's Harbour, Commodore Chauncey, who entertained a proper opinion of his merits, detached him to Lake Erie, to take command of the squadron on that station, and to superintend the building of additional vessels. The American force at that time on the Lake consisted but of several small vessels; two of the best of which had recently been captured from the enemy in a gallant style by Captain Elliot, from under the very batteries of Malden. The British force was greatly superior, and commanded by Commodore Barclay, an able and well tried officer. Commodore Perry immediately applied himself to increase his armament, and having ship carpenters from the Atlantic coast, and using extraordinary exertions, two brigs of twenty guns each were soon launched at Erie, the American port on the Lake.

While the vessels were constructing, the British squadron hovered off the harbour, but offered no molestation. At length, his vessels being equipped and manned, on the fourth of August Commodore Perry succeeded in getting his squadron over the bar at the mouth of the harbour. The water on the bar was but five feet deep, and the large vessels had to be buoyed over: this was accomplished in the face of the British, who fortunately did not think proper to make an attack. The next day he sailed in pursuit of the enemy, but returned on the eighth, without having encountered him. Being reinforced by the arrival of the brave Elliot, accompanied by several officers and eighty-nine sailors, he was enabled completely to man his squadron, and again set sail on the twelfth, in quest of the enemy. On the fifteenth he arrived at Sandusky Bay, where the American army under General Harrison lay encamped. From thence he cruised off Malden, where the British squadron remained at anchor, under the guns of the fort. The appearance of Perry's squadron spread great alarm on shore; the women and children ran shrieking about the place, expecting an immediate attack. The Indians, we are told, looked on with astonishment, and urged the British to go out and fight. Finding the enemy not disposed to venture a battle, Commodore Perry returned to Sandusky.

Nothing of moment happened until the morning of the tenth of September. The American squadron were, at that time, lying at anchor in Put-in-Bay, and consisted of

Brig Lawrence,	Commodore Perry,	20 guns.
Niagara,	Captain Elliot,	20
Caledonia,	Purser M'Grath,	3
Schooner Ariel,	Lieutenant Packet,	4
Scorpion,	Sailing-Master Champlin,	2
Somers,	Almy,	2 and 2 swivels.
Tigress,	Lieutenant Conklin,	1
Porcupine,	Midshipman G. Senat,	1
Sloop Trippe,	Lieutenant Smith,	1

54 guns.

At sunrise they discovered the enemy, and immediately got under way and stood for him with a light wind at southwest. The British force consisted of

Ship Detroit,	19 guns,	1 on pivot, and 2 howitzers.
Queen Charlotte,	17	1 on pivot.
Schooner Lady Prevost,	13	1 do.
Brig Hunter,	10	
Sloop Little Belt,	3	
Schooner Chippeway,	1	2 swivels.

63 guns.

At 10 A.M. the wind haled to the southeast and brought our squadron to windward. Commodore Perry then hoisted his Union Jack, having for a motto, the dying words of the valiant Lawrence, "Don't give up the ship!" It was received with repeated cheerings by the officers and crews. And now having formed his line he bore for the enemy; who likewise cleared for action, and haled up his courses. It is deeply interesting to picture to ourselves the advances of these gallant and well-matched squadrons to a contest, where the strife must be obstinate and sanguinary, and the event decisive of the fate of almost an empire.

The lightness of the wind occasioned them to approach each other but slowly, and prolonged the awful interval of suspense and anxiety that precedes a battle. This is the time when the stoutest heart beats quick, "and the boldest holds his breath;" it is the still moment of direful expectation; of fearful looking out for slaughter and destruction; when even the glow of pride and ambition is chilled for a while, and nature shudders at the awful jeopardy of existence. The very order and regularity of naval discipline heighten the dreadful quiet of the moment. No bustle, no noise prevails to distract the mind, except at intervals the shrill piping of the boatswain's whistle, or a murmuring whisper among the men, who, grouped around their guns, earnestly regard the movements of the foe, now and then stealing a wistful glance at the countenances of their commanders. In this manner did the hostile squadrons approach each other, in mute watchfulness and terrible tranquillity; when suddenly a bugle was sounded from on board the enemy's ship Detroit, and loud huzzas immediately burst forth from all their crews.

No sooner did the Lawrence come within reach of the enemies' long guns, than they opened a heavy fire upon her, which, from the shortness of her guns, she was unable to return. Commodore Perry, without waiting for his schooners, kept on his course in such gallant and determined style that the enemy supposed it was his intention to board. In a few minutes, having gained a nearer position, he opened his fire. The length of the enemies' guns, however, gave them vastly the advantage, and the Lawrence was excessively cut up without being able to do any great damage in return. Their shot pierced her sides in all directions, killing our men on the birth deck and in the steerage, where they had been taken down to be dressed. One shot had nearly produced a fatal explosion; passing through the light room it knocked the snuff of the candle into the magazine; fortunately the gunner happened to see it, and had the presence of mind to extinguish it immediately with his hand.

Indeed, it seemed to be the enemies' plan to destroy the commodore's ship, and thus throw the squadron into confusion. For this purpose their heaviest fire was directed at the Lawrence, and blazed incessantly upon it from their largest vessels. Finding the hazard of his situation, Perry made sail, and directed the other vessels to follow for the purpose of closing with the foe. The tremendous fire, however, to which he was exposed, soon cut away every brace and bowline, and the Lawrence became unmanageable. Even in this disastrous plight she sustained the action for upwards of two hours, within canister distance, though for a great part of the time he could not get more than three guns to bear upon her antagonists. It was admirable to behold the perfect order and regularity that prevailed among her valiant and devoted crew, throughout this scene of horror. No trepidation, no confusion occurred, even for an instant; as fast as the men were wounded they were carried below and others stept into their places; the dead remained where they fell until after the action. At this juncture the fortune of the battle trembled on a point, and the enemy believed the day their own. The Lawrence was reduced to a mere wreck; her decks were streaming with blood, and covered with mangled limbs and the bodies of the slain; nearly the whole of her crew was either killed or wounded; her guns were dismounted, and the commodore and his officers helped to work the last that was capable of service.

Amidst all this peril and disaster the youthful commander is said to have remained perfectly composed, maintaining a serene and cheerful countenance, uttering no passionate or agitated expression, giving out his orders with calmness and deliberation, and inspiriting every one around him by his magnanimous demeanour.

At this crisis, finding the Lawrence was incapable of further service, and seeing the hazardous situation of the conflict, he formed the bold resolution of shifting his flag. Giving the ship, therefore, in charge to Lieutenant Yarnall, who had already distinguished himself by his bravery, he haled down his union, bearing the motto of Lawrence, and taking it under his arm, ordered to be put on board of the Niagara, which was then in close engagement. In leaving the Lawrence he gave his pilot choice either to remain on board, or accompany him; the faithful fellow told him "he'd stick by him to the last," and jumped into the boat. He went off from the ship in his usual gallant manner, standing up in the stern of the boat, until the crew absolutely pulled him down among them. Broadsides were levelled at him, and small arms discharged by the enemy, two of whose vessels were within musket shot, and a third one nearer. His brave shipmates who remained behind, stood watching him, in breathless anxiety; the balls struck around him and flew over his head in every direction; but the same special providence that seems to have watched over the youthful hero throughout this desperate battle, conducted him safely through a shower of shot, and they beheld with transport his inspiring flag hoisted at the mast head of the Niagara. No sooner was he on board than Captain Elliot volunteered to put off in a boat and bring into action the schooners which had been kept astern by the lightness of the wind; the gallant offer was accepted, and Elliot left the Niagara to put it in execution.

About this time the commodore saw, with infinite regret, the flag of the Lawrence come down. The event was unavoidable; she had sustained the whole fury of the enemy, and was rendered incapable of defence; any further show of resistance would but have been most uselessly and cruelly to have provoked carnage among the relics of her brave and mangled crew. The enemy, however, were not able to take possession of her, and subsequent circumstances enabled her again to hoist her flag.

Commodore Perry now made signal for close action, and the small vessels got out their sweeps and made all sail. Finding that the Niagara was but little injured, he determined, if possible, to break the enemy's line. He accordingly bore up and passed ahead of the two ships and brig, giving them a raking fire from his starboard guns, and also to a large schooner and sloop from his larboard side at half pistol shot. Having passed the whole squadron, he luffed up and laid his ship along side the British commodore. The smaller vessels under the direction of Captain Elliot having, in the mean time, got within grape and canister distance, and keeping up a well directed fire, the whole of the enemy struck excepting two small vessels which attempted to escape, but were taken.

The engagement lasted about three hours, and never was victory more decisive and complete. The captured squadron, as has been shown, exceeded ours in weight of metal and number of guns. Their crews were also more numerous; ours were a motley collection, where there were some good seamen, but eked out with soldiers, volunteers and boys, and many were on the sick list. More prisoners were taken than we had men to guard. The loss on both sides was severe. Scarcely any of the Lawrence's crew escaped unhurt. Among those slain was Lieutenant Brooks of the marines, a gay and elegant young officer, full of spirit, of amiable manners, and remarkable for his personal beauty. Lieutenant Yarnall, though repeatedly wounded, refused to quit the deck during the whole of the action. Commodore Perry, notwithstanding that he was continually in the most exposed situations of the battle, escaped uninjured; he wore an ordinary seaman's dress, which, perhaps, prevented him from being picked off by the enemies' sharp shooters. He had a younger brother with him, on board the Lawrence as midshipman, who was equally fortunate in receiving no injury, though his shipmates fell all round him. Two Indian chiefs had been stationed in the tops of the Detroit to shoot down our officers, but when the action became warm, so panic struck were they with the terrors of the scene, and the strange perils that surrounded them, that they fled precipitately to the hold of the ship, where they were found after the battle in a state of utter consternation. The bodies of several other Indians are said to have been found the next day on the shores of the Lake, supposed to have been slain during the engagement and thrown overboard.

It is impossible to state the number of killed on board the enemy. It must, however, have been very great, as their vessels were literally cut to pieces; and the masts of their two principal ships so shattered that the first gale blew them overboard. Commodore Barclay, the British commander, certainly did himself honour by the brave and obstinate resistance which he made. He is a fine looking officer, of about thirty-six years of age. He has seen much service, having been desperately wounded in the battle of Trafalgar, and afterwards losing an arm in another engagement with the French. In the present battle he was twice carried below, on account of his wounds, and had the misfortune to have his remaining hand shot away. While below the second time, his officer came down and told him that they must strike, as the ships were cut to pieces, and the men could not be kept to their guns. Commodore Barclay was then carried on deck, and after taking a view of their situation, and finding all chance of success was over, reluctantly gave orders to strike.

We have thus endeavoured to lay before our readers as clear an account of this important battle as could be gathered from the scanty documents that have reached us; though sketched out, we are sensible, with a hand but little skilled in naval affairs. The leading facts, however, are all that a landsman can be expected to furnish, and we trust that this glorious affair will hereafter be recorded with more elaborate care and technical precision. There is, however, a distinctness of character about a naval victory, that meets the capacity of every mind. There is such a simple unity in it; it is so well defined; so complete within itself; so rounded by space; so free from those intricacies and numerous parts that perplex us in an action on land, that the meanest intellect can fully grasp and comprehend it. And then, too, the results are so apparent; a victory on land is liable to a thousand misrepresentations; retreat is often called falling back, and abandoning the field called taking a new position; so that the conqueror is often defrauded of half the credit of his victory; but the capture or destruction of a ship is not to be mistaken, and a squadron towed triumphantly into port, is a notorious fact that admits of no contradiction.

In this battle, we trust, incontrovertible proof is given, if such proof were really wanted, that the success of our navy does not arise from chance, or superiority of force; but from the cool, deliberate courage, the intelligent minds and naval skill of our officers, the spirit of our seamen, and the excellent discipline of our ships; from principles, in short, which must insure a frequency of prosperous results, and give permanency to the reputation we have acquired. We have been rapidly adding trophy to trophy, and successively driving the enemy from every excuse in which he sought to shelter himself from the humiliation of defeat; and after having perfectly established our capability of fighting and conquering in single ships, we have now gone further and shown that it is possible for us to face the foe in squadron, and vanquish him even though superior in force.

In casting our eye over the details of this engagement, we are struck with the prominent part which the commander takes in the contest. We realize in his dauntless exposure and individual prowess, what we have read in heroic story, of the warrior, streaming like a meteor through the fight, and working wonders with his single arm. The fate of the combat seemed to rest upon his sword; he was the master spirit that directed the storm of battle, moving amid flames, and smoke, and death, and mingling wherever the struggle was most desperate and deadly. After sustaining in the Lawrence the whole blaze of the enemy's cannonry; after fighting until all around him was wreck and carnage; we behold him, looking forth from his shattered deck, with unruffled countenance, on the direful perils that environed him, calculating with wary eye the chances of the battle, and suddenly launching forth on the bosom of the deep, to shift his flag on board another ship, then in the hottest of the action. This was one of those master strokes by which great events are achieved, and great characters stamped, as it were, at a single blow— which bespeak the rare combination of the genius to conceive, the promptness to decide, and the boldness to execute. Most commanders have such glorious chances for renown, some time or another, within their reach; but it requires the nerve of a hero to grasp the perilous opportunity. We behold Perry following up his daring movement with sustained energy—dashing into the squadron of the enemy—breaking their line—raking starboard and larboard—and in this brilliant style achieving a consummate victory.

But if we admire his presence of mind and dauntless valour in the hour of danger, we are no less delighted with his modesty and self command amidst the flush of triumph. A courageous heart may carry a man stoutly through the battle, but it argues some strong qualities of head, to drain unmoved the intoxicating cup of victory. The first care of Perry was to attend to the comfort of the suffering crews of both squadrons. The sick and wounded were landed as soon as possible, and every means taken to alleviate the miseries of their situation. The officers who had fallen, on both sides, were buried on Sunday morning, on an island in the lake, with the honours of war. To the surviving officers he advanced a loan of one thousand dollars, out of his own limited purse—but, in short, his behaviour in this respect is best expressed in the words of Commodore Barclay, who, with generous warmth and frankness, has declared, that "the conduct of Perry towards the captive officers and men, was sufficient, of itself, to immortalize him!"

The letters which he wrote announcing the intelligence were remarkably simple and laconic. To the secretary of the navy he observes, "It has pleased the Almighty to give to the arms of the United States a signal victory over their enemies on this lake. The British squadron, consisting of two ships, two brigs, one schooner, and one sloop, have this moment surrendered to the force under my command, after a sharp conflict." This has been called an imitation of Nelson's letter after the battle of the Nile; but it was choosing a noble precedent, and the important national results of the victory justified the language. Independent of the vast accession of glory to our flag, this conquest insured the capture of Detroit—the rout of the British armies—the subjugation of the whole peninsula of Upper Canada, and, if properly followed up, the triumphant success of our northern war. Well might he say "it had pleased the Almighty," when, by this achievement, he beheld immediate tranquillity restored to an immense extent of country. Mothers no longer shrunk aghast, and clasped their infants to their breasts, when they heard the shaking of the forest or the howling of the blast—the aged sire no longer dreaded the shades of night, lest ruin should burst upon him in the hour of repose, and his cottage be laid desolate by the firebrand and the scalping knife—Michigan was rescued from the dominion of the sword, and quiet and security once more settled on the harassed frontiers, from Huron to Niagara.

But we are particularly pleased with his subsequent letter giving the particulars of the battle. It is so chaste, so moderate and perspicuous; equally free from vaunting exultation and affected modesty; neither obtruding himself upon notice, nor pretending to keep out of sight. His own individual services may be gathered from the letter, though not expressly mentioned; indeed, where the fortune of the day depended so materially upon himself, it was impossible to give a faithful narrative without rendering himself conspicuous.

We are led to notice these letters thus particularly, because that we find the art of letter writing is an accomplishment as rare as it is important among our military gentlemen. We are tired of the valour of the pen and the victories of the inkhorn. There is a common French proverb, "Grand parleur, mauvais combattant," which we could wish to see introduced into our country, and engraven on the swords of our officers. We wish to see them confine themselves in their letters to simple facts, neither swaggering before battle, nor vaunting afterwards. It is unwise to boast before, for the event may prove disastrous—and it is superfluous to boast afterwards, for the event speaks for itself. He who promises nothing, may with safety perform nothing, and will receive praise if he perform but little; but he who promises much will receive small credit unless he perform miracles. If a commander have done well, he may be sure the public will find it out, and their gratitude will be in proportion to his modesty. Admiration is a coin which, if left to ourselves, we lavish profusely, but we always close the hand when dunned for it.

Commodore Perry, like most of our naval officers, is yet in the prime of youth. He is of a manly and prepossessing appearance; mild and unassuming in his address, amiable in his disposition, and of great firmness and decision. Though early launched among the familiar scenes of naval life, (and nowhere is familiarity more apt to be licentious and encroaching,) yet the native gentility and sober dignity of his deportment, always chastened, without restraining, the freedom of intimacy. It is pleasing thus to find public services accompanied by private virtues; to discover no drawbacks on our esteem; no base alloy in the man we are disposed to admire; but a character full of moral excellence, of high-minded courtesy, and pure unsullied honour.

Were any thing wanting to perpetuate the fame of this victory, it would be sufficiently memorable from the scene where it was fought. This war has been distinguished by new and peculiar characteristics. Naval warfare has been carried into the interior of a continent, and navies, as if by magic, launched from among the depths of the forest. The bosoms of peaceful lakes which, but a short time since, were scarcely navigated by man, except to be skimmed by the light canoe of the savage, have all at once been ploughed by hostile ships. The vast silence that had reigned for ages on those mighty waters, was broken by the thunder of artillery, and the affrighted savage stared with amazement from his covert, at the sudden apparition of a seafight amid the solitudes of the wilderness.

The peal of war has once sounded on that lake, but probably will never sound again. The last roar of cannonry that died along her shores, was the expiring note of British domination. Those vast internal seas will, perhaps, never again be the separating space between contending nations; but will be embosomed within a mighty empire; and this victory, which decided their fate, will stand unrivalled and alone, deriving lustre and perpetuity from its singleness.

In future times, when the shores of Erie shall hum with busy population; when towns and cities shall brighten where now extends the dark and tangled forest; when ports shall spread their arms, and lofty barks shall ride where now the canoe is fastened to the stake; when the present age shall have grown into venerable antiquity, and the mists of fable begin to gather round its history; then will the inhabitants of Canada look back to this battle we record, as one of the romantic achievements of the days of yore. It will stand first on the page of their local legends, and in the marvellous tales of the borders. The fisherman, as he loiters along the beach, will point to some half buried cannon, corroded with the rust of time, and will speak of ocean warriors that came from the shores of the Atlantic—while the boatman, as he trims his sail to the breeze, will chant in rude ditties the name of Perry—the early hero of Lake Erie.

[March, 1814]

ODES, NAVAL SONGS, AND OTHER OCCASIONAL POEMS. BY EDWIN C. HOLLAND, ESQ. CHARLESTON

A small volume, with the above title, has been handed to us, with a request that it might be criticised. Though we do not profess the art and mystery of reviewing, and are not ambitious of being either wise or facetious at the expense of others, yet we feel a disposition to notice the present work, because it is a specimen of one branch of literature at present very popular throughout our country, and also, because the author, who, we understand, is quite young, gives proof of very considerable poetical talent, and is in great danger of being spoiled.

We apprehend, from various symptoms about his work, that he has for some time past received great honours from circles of literary ladies and gentlemen, and that he has great facility at composition—we find, moreover, that he has written for public papers under the signature of Orlando; and above all, that a prize has been awarded to one of his poems, in a kind of poetical lottery, cunningly devised by an "eminent bookseller."

These, we must confess, are melancholy disadvantages to start withal; and many a youthful poet, of great promise, has been utterly ruined by misfortunes of much inferior magnitude. We trust, however, that in the present case they are not without remedy, and that the author is not so far gone in the evil habit of publishing, as to be utterly beyond reclaim. Still we feel the necessity of extending immediate relief, from a hint he gives us on the cover of his book, that the present poems are "presented merely as specimens of his manner, and comprise but a *very small portion*" of those he has on hand. This information really startled us—we beheld in imagination a mighty mass of odes, songs, sonnets and acrostics, impending in awful volume over our heads, and threatening every instant to flutter down, like a theatrical snow-storm of white paper. To avert so fearful an *avalanche* have we hastened to take pen in hand, determined to risk the author's displeasure, by giving him good advice, and to deliver him, if possible, uninjured out of the hands both of his admirers and his patron.

The main piece of advice we would give him is, to lock up all his remaining writings, and to abstain most abstemiously from publishing for some few years to come. We know that this will appear very ungracious counsel, and we have not very great hope that it will be adopted. We are well aware of the eagerness of young authors to hurry into print, and that the muse is too fond of present pay, and "present pudding," to brook voluntarily the postponement of reward. Besides, this early and exuberant foliage of the mind is peculiar to warm sensibilities and lively fancies, in which the principles of fecundity are so strong as to be almost irrepressible. The least ray of popular admiration sets all the juices in motion, produces a bursting forth of buds and blossoms, and a profusion of vernal and perishable vegetation. But there is no greater source of torment to a writer, than the flippancies of his juvenile muse. The sins and follies of his youth arise in loathsome array, to disturb the quiet of his maturer years, and he is perpetually haunted by the spectres of the early murders he has perpetrated on good English and good sense.

We have no intention to discourage Mr. Holland from his poetic career. On the contrary, it is in consequence of the good opinion we entertain of his genius, that we are solicitous that it should be carefully nurtured, wholesomely disciplined, and trained up to full and masculine vigour, rather than dissipated and enfeebled by early excesses. We think we can discern in his writings strong marks of amiable, and generous, and lofty sentiment, of ready invention, and great brilliancy of expression. These are as yet obscured by a false, or rather puerile taste, which time and attention will improve, but it is necessary that time and attention should be employed. Were his faults merely those of mediocrity we should despair, for there is no such thing as fermenting a dull mind into any thing like poetic inspiration; but we think the effervescence of this writer's fancy will at a future day settle down into something substantially excellent. Rising genius always shoots forth its rays from among clouds and vapours, but these will gradually roll away and disappear, as it ascends to its steady and meridian lustre.

One thing which pleases us in the songs in this collection, is, that they have more originality than we commonly meet with in our national songs. We begin to think that it is a much more difficult thing to write a good song than to fight a good battle; for our tars have achieved several splendid victories in a short space of time; but, notwithstanding the thousand pens that have been drawn forth in every part of the union, we do not recollect a single song of really sterling merit, that has been written on the occasion. Nothing is more offensive than a certain lawless custom which prevails among our patriotic songsters, of seizing upon the noble songs of Great Britain, mangling and disfiguring them, with pens more merciless than Indian scalping knives, and then passing them off for American songs. This may be an idea borrowed from the custom of our savage neighbours, of adopting prisoners into their families, and so completely taking them to their homes and hearts, as almost to consider them as children of their own begetting. At any rate, it is a practice worthy of savage life, and savage ideas of property. We have witnessed such horrible distortions of sense and poetry—we have seen the fine members of an elegant stanza so mangled and wrenched, in order to apply it to this country, that our very hearts ached with sympathy and vexation. We are continually annoyed with the figure of poor Columbia, an honest, awkward, dowdy sort of dame, thrust into the place of Britannia, and made to wield the trident, and "rule the waves," and play off a thousand clumsy ceremonies before company, as maladroitly as a worthy tradesman's wife, enacting a fine lady or a tragedy queen.

Besides, there is in this a pitifulness of spirit, an appearance of abject poverty of mind, that would be degrading, if it really belonged to the nation. Nay more, there is a positive dishonesty in it. We may, if we choose, plunder the bodies of our enemies, whom we have fairly conquered in the field of battle; and we may strut about, uncouthly arrayed in their garments, with their coats swinging to our heels, and their boots "a world too wide for our shrunk shanks," but the same privilege does not extend to literature; and however our puny poetasters may flaunt for a while in the pilfered garbs of their gigantic neighbours, they may rest assured, that if there should be a tribunal hereafter to try the crimes of authors, they will be considered as mere poetical highwaymen, and condemned to swing most loftily for their offences.

It is really insulting to tell this country, as some of these varlets do, that she "needs no bulwarks, no towers along the steep," when there is a cry from one end of the union to the other for the fortifying our seaports and the defence of our coast, and when every post brings us intelligence of the enemy depredating in our bays and rivers; and it is still more insulting to tell her that "her home is on the deep," which, if it really be the case, only proves that at present she is turned out of doors. No, if we really must have national songs, let them be of our own manufacturing, however coarse. We would rather hear our victories celebrated in the merest doggrel that sprang from native invention, than beg, borrow, or steal from others, the thoughts and words in which to express our exultation. By tasking our own powers, and relying entirely on ourselves, we shall gradually improve and rise to poetical independence; but this practice of appropriating the thoughts of others, of getting along by contemptible shifts and literary larcenies, prevents native exertion, and produces absolute impoverishment. It is in literature as in the accumulation of private fortune; the humblest beginnings should not dishearten; much may be done by persevering industry, or spirited enterprise; but he who depends on borrowing will never grow rich, and he who indulges in theft will ultimately come to the gallows.

We are glad to find that the writer before us is innocent of these enormous sins against honesty and good sense; but we would warn him against another evil, into which young writers, and young men, are very prone to fall—we mean bad company. We are apprehensive that the companions of his literary leisure have been none of the most profitable, and that he has been trifling too much with the fantastic gentry of the Della Cruscan school, revelling among flowers, and hunting butterflies, when he should have been soberly walking, like a duteous disciple, in the footsteps of the mighty masters of his art. We are led to this idea from seeing in his poems the portentous names of "the blue eyed Myra," and "Rosa Matilda," and from reading of "lucid vests veiling snowy breasts," and "satin sashes," and "sighs of rosy perfume," and "trembling eve-star beam, through some light cloud's glory seen," (which, by the by, is a rhyme very much like that of "muffin and dumpling,") and

> —"The sweetest of perfumes that languishing flies
> Like a kiss on the nectarous morning tide air."

Now all this kind of poetry is rather late in the day—the fashion has gone by. A man may as well attempt to figure as a fine gentleman in a pea-green silk coat, and pink satin breeches, and powdered head, and paste buckles, and sharp toed shoes, and all the finery of Sir Fopling Flutter, as to write in the style of Della Crusca. Gifford has long since brushed away all this trumpery.

We think also, the author has rather perverted his fancy, by reading the amatory effusions of Moore; which, whatever be the magic of their imagery and versification, breathe a spirit of heartless sensuality, and soft voluptuousness, beneath the tone of vigorous and virtuous manhood.

This rhapsodising about "brilliant pleasures," and "hours of bliss," and "humid eyelids," and "ardent kisses," is, after all, mighty cold-blooded, silly stuff. It may do to tickle the ears of love-sick striplings and romantic milliners; but one verse describing pure domestic affection, or tender innocent love, from the pen of Burns, speaks more to the heart than all the meretricious rhapsodies of Moore.

We doubt if in the whole round of rapturous scenes, dwelt on with elaborate salacity by the modern Anacreon, one passage can be found,

combining equal eloquence of language, delicacy of imagery, and im-
passioned tenderness, with the following picture of the interview and
parting of two lovers.

> "How sweetly bloom'd the gay, green birk,
>   How rich the hawthorn's blossom;
> As underneath their fragrant shade
>   I clasp'd her to my bosom!
> The golden hours, on angel wings,
>   Flew o'er me and my dearie:
> For dear to me, as light and life,
>   Was my sweet Highland Mary.
>
> "Wi' mony a vow, and lock'd embrace,
>   Our parting was fu' tender;
> And pledging oft to meet again,
>   We tore oursels asunder;
> But O! fell death's untimely frost,
>   That nipt my flower sae early!
> Now green's the sod, and cauld's the clay,
>   That wraps my Highland Mary.
>
> "O pale, pale now those rosy lips,
>   I aft hae kiss'd sae fondly!
> And clos'd for ay the sparkling glance
>   That dwelt on me sae kindly!
> And mouldering now in silent dust
>   That heart that lo'ed me dearly!
> But still within my bosom's core,
>   Shall live my Highland Mary."

Throughout the whole of the foregoing stanzas we would remark the
extreme simplicity of the language, the utter absence of all false colouring, of those "roseate hues," and "ambrosial odours," and "purple mists,"
that steam from the pages of our voluptuous poets, to intoxicate the
weak brains of their admirers. Burns depended on the truth and tenderness of his ideas, on that deep toned feeling which is the very soul of
poetry. To use his own admirably descriptive words,

> "His rural loves are nature's sel,
> Nae bombast spates o' nonsense swell;
> Nae *snap conceits*, but that *sweet spell,*
>   *O' witchin love,*

> *That charm, that can the strongest quell,*
> *The sternest move."*

But the chief fault which infests the style of the poems before us, is a passion for hyperbole, and for the glare of extravagant images and flashing phrases. This taste for gorgeous finery, and violent metaphor, prevails throughout our country, and is characteristic of the early efforts of literature. Our national songs are full of ridiculous exaggeration, and frothy rant, and commonplace bloated up into fustian. The writers seem to think that huge words, and mountainous figures, constitute the sublime. Their puny thoughts are made to sweat under loads of cumbrous imagery, and now and then they are so wrapt up in conflagrations, and blazes, and thunders and lightnings, that, like Nick Bottom's hero, they seem to have "slipt on a brimstone shirt, and are all on fire!"

We would advise these writers, if they wish to see what is really grand and forcible in patriotic minstrelsy, to read the national songs of Campbell, and the Bannock-Burn of Burns, where there is the utmost grandeur of thought conveyed in striking but perspicuous language. It is much easier to be fine than correct in writing. A rude and imperfect taste always heaps on decoration, and seeks to dazzle by a profusion of brilliant incongruities. But true taste always evinces itself in pure and noble simplicity, and a fitness and chastness of ornament. The muses of the ancients are described as beautiful females, exquisitely proportioned, simply attired, with no ornaments but the diamond clasps that connected their garments; but were we to paint the muse of one of our popular poets, we should represent her as a pawnbroker's widow, with rings on every finger, and loaded with borrowed and heterogeneous finery.

One cause of the epidemical nature of our literary errors, is the proneness of our authors to borrow from each other, and thus to interchange faults, and give a circulation to absurdities. It is dangerous always for a writer to be very studious of cotemporary publications, which have not passed the ordeal of time and criticism. He should fix his eye on those models which have been scrutinized, and of the faults and excellencies of which he is fully apprized. We think we can trace, in the popular songs of the volume before us, proofs that the author has been very conversant with the works of Robert Treat Paine, a late American writer of very considerable merit; but who delighted in continual explosions of fancy and glitter of language. As we do not censure wantonly, or for the sake of finding fault, we shall point to one of the author's writings, on which it is probable he most values himself, as it is the one which publicly received the prize in the Bookseller's Lottery. We allude to THE PILLAR OF GLORY. We are likewise induced to notice this particularly, because we find it going the rounds of the union; strummed at pianos, sung at concerts, and roared forth lustily at public dinners. Having this universal currency, and bearing the imposing title of *Prize Poem*, which is undoubtedly equal to the Tower Stamp, it stands a great chance of being considered abroad as a prize production of one of our universities, and at home as a standard poem, worthy the imitation of all tyros in the art.

The first stanza is very fair, and indeed is one of those passages on which we found our good opinion of the author's genius. The last line is really noble.

> "Hail to the heroes whose triumphs have brighten'd
>   The darkness which shrouded America's name!
> Long shall their valour in battle that lighten'd,
>   Live in the brilliant escutcheons of fame!
>   Dark where the torrents flow,
>   And the rude tempests blow,
> The stormy-clad Spirit of Albion raves;
>   Long shall she mourn the day,
>   When in the vengeful fray,
> Liberty walk'd, like a God, on the waves."

The second stanza, however, sinks from this vigorous and perspicuous tone. We have the "halo and lustre of story" *curling* round the "wave of the ocean;" a mixture of ideal and tangible objects wholly inadmissible in good poetry. But the great mass of sin lies in the third stanza, where the writer rises into such a glare and confusion of figure as to be almost incomprehensible.

> "The pillar of glory the sea that enlightens,
>   Shall last till eternity rocks on its base!
> The splendour of fame its waters that brightens,
>   Shall follow the footsteps of time in his race!
>   Wide o'er the stormy deep,
>   Where the rude surges sweep,
> Its lustre shall circle the brows of the brave!
>   Honour shall give it light,
>   Triumph shall keep it bright,
> Long as in battle we meet on the wave!"

We confess that we were sadly puzzled to understand the nature of this ideal pillar, that seemed to have set the sea in a blaze, and was to last "till eternity rocks on its base," which we suppose is, according to a vulgar phrase, "forever and a day after." Our perplexity was increased by the cross light from the "splendour of fame," which, like a footboy with a lantern, was to jog on after the footsteps of time; who it appears was to run a race against himself on the water—and as to the other lights and gleams that followed, they threw us into complete bewilderment. It is true, after beating about for some time, we at length landed on what we suspected to be the author's meaning; but a worthy friend of ours, who read the passage with great attention, maintains that this pillar of glory which enlightened the sea, can be nothing more nor less than a light-house.

We do not certainly wish to indulge in improper or illiberal levity. It is not the author's fault that his poem has received a prize, and been elevated into unfortunate notoriety. Were its faults matters of concernment merely to himself, we should barely have hinted at them; but the poem has been made, in a manner, a national poem, and in attacking it, we attack generally that prevailing taste among our poetical writers for excessive ornament—for turgid extravagance, and vapid hyperbole. We wish in some small degree to counteract the mischief that may be done to national literature by eminent booksellers crowning inferior effusions as prize poems, setting them to music, and circulating them widely through the country. We wish also, by a little good-humoured rebuke, to stay the hurried career of a youth of talent and promise, whom we perceive lapsing into error, and liable to be precipitated forward by the injudicious applauses of his friends.

We therefore repeat our advice to Mr. Holland, that he abstain from further publication until he has cultivated his taste, and ripened his mind. We earnestly exhort him rigorously to watch over his youthful muse; who, we suspect, is very spirited and vivacious, subject to quick excitement, of great pruriency of feeling, and a most uneasy inclination to breed. Let him in the mean while diligently improve himself in classical studies, and in an intimate acquaintance with the best and simplest British poets, and the soundest British critics. We do assure him that really fine poetry is exceeding rare, and not to be written copiously nor rapidly. Middling poetry may be produced in any quantity —the press groans with it—the shelves of circulating libraries are loaded with it—but who reads merely middling poetry? Only two kinds can possibly be tolerated, the very good, or the very bad; one to be read with enthusiasm, the other to be laughed at.

We have in the course of this article quoted him rather unfavourably, but it was for the purpose of general criticism, not individual censure; before we conclude, it is but justice to give a specimen of what we consider his best manner. The following stanzas are taken from elegiac lines on the death of a young lady. The comparison of a beautiful female to a flower is obvious, and frequent in poetry, but we think it is managed here with uncommon delicacy and consistency, and great novelty of thought and manner.

"There was a flow'r of beauteous birth,
   Of lavish charms, and chasten'd die,
It smil'd upon the lap of earth,
   And caught the gaze of ev'ry eye.

"The vernal breeze, whose step is seen
   Imprinted in the early dew,
Ne'er brush'd a flow'r of brighter beam,
   Or nurs'd a bud of lovelier hue!

"It blossom'd not in dreary wild,
   In darksome glen, or desert bow'r,
But grew, like Flora's fav'rite child,
   In sun-beam soft, and fragrant show'r.

"The graces lov'd with chasten'd light,
   To flush its pure, celestial bloom,
And all its blossoms were so bright,
   It seem'd not form'd to die so soon.

"Youth round the flow'ret ere it fell,
   In armour bright was seen to stray,
And beauty said, *her* magic spell
   Should keep its perfume from decay.

"The parent-stalk from which it sprung,
   Transported as its halo spread,
In holy umbrage o'er it hung,
   And tears of heav'n-born rapture shed.

"Yet, fragile flow'r! thy blossom bright,
   Though guarded by a magic spell,
Like a sweet beam of evening light,
   In lonely hour of tempest fell,

"The death-blast of the winter air,
   The cold frost and the night-wind came,
They nipt thy beauty once so fair!—
   It shall not bloom on earth again!"

From a general view of the poems of Mr. Holland, it is evident that he has the external requisites for poetry in abundance; he has fine images, fine phrases, and ready versification; he must only learn to think with fulness and precision, and he will write splendidly. As we have already hinted, we consider his present productions but the blossoms of his genius, and like blossoms they will fall and perish—but we trust that after some time of silent growth and gradual maturity, we shall see them succeeded by a harvest of rich and highly flavoured fruit.

[July, 1814]

LORD BYRON

Among the cluster of poets that have lately sprung up in Great Britain, the most fashionable, at the present day, is Lord Byron. Independent of his literary merits, his popularity may be attributed, in some degree, to his rank, youth, and the eccentric and romantic cast of his private character. He is descended from a noble and illustrious family, that may be traced back to the reign of William the Conqueror. Two of his ancestors fell in the field of Cressy, another fought under the banner of Earl Richmond at the battle of Bosworth, and several lost their lives in the armies of Charles I.

Lord Byron inherited the title at an early age, in immediate succession from his granduncle William. He passed several of his youthful years in Scotland, but received the chief part of his education at the celebrated school of Harrow, and finished it at the university of Cambridge. While at school, he evinced those peculiar traits of character, and that poetical talent, which have since distinguished him. He was independent, and rather haughty in his manners; limited in his friendships; eccentric in his opinions; and of a proud reserve that approached to misanthropy. Still he does not seem to have been unpopular; his schoolmates, though they were repelled from his intimacy, yet gave him credit for high and generous qualities, and strong sensibilities; he was accounted an apt student and a good scholar, and was remarked as excelling in poetical exercises. Shortly after leaving school, and before he was of age, he published a volume of miscellaneous poems, entitled "Hours of Idleness, by Lord Byron, *a minor*." This volume fell under the lash of the Edinburgh reviewers, who animadverted upon it in a strain of coarse but highly ludicrous satire. Their strictures, though severe, were in general just, and though their ridicule may have been galling to the individual, yet if it could operate in any degree to restrain that fatal eagerness to rush into notoriety, which is the misfortune of so many young writers, we cannot but think it highly beneficial. Still we consider their censure of the poems as too unqualified—many passages in the volume are stamped with considerable poetical merit; several of the poems, which, from their date, must have been written when his lordship was but fifteen years of age, are surprising productions for such early youth, and, indeed, the whole collection, as the writings of "a minor," certainly bore the air of very great promise.

One of the best of the poems is an elegy on Newstead Abbey, the family seat of the Byrons. Here his lordship dwells on the former power and feudal grandeur of his ancestors, recounts their gallant exploits, and pours forth, in elevated language, the feelings of a high-born soul, meditating on the ruins of past magnificence. The concluding stanzas apply immediately to himself, and are selected as being characteristic of the poet.

"Newstead! what saddening change of scene is thine!
    Thy yawning arch betokens slow decay;
The last and youngest of a noble line
    Now holds thy mouldering turrets in his sway.

"Deserted now, he scans thy gray worn towers;
    Thy vaults, where dead of feudal ages sleep;
Thy cloisters, pervious to the wintry showers;
    These, these he views, and views them but to weep.

"Yet are his tears no emblem of regret,
    Cherish'd affection only bids them flow;
Pride, Hope, and Love, forbid him to forget,
    But warm his bosom with impassion'd glow.

"Yet, he prefers thee to the gilded domes,
    Or gewgaw grottoes of the vainly great;
Yet lingers mid thy damp and mossy tombs,
    Nor breathes a murmur 'gainst the will of fate.

"Haply thy sun, emerging, yet may shine,
    Thee to irradiate with meridian ray;
Hours, splendid as the past, may still be thine,
    And bless thy future, as thy former day."

It is worthy of remark, that in one of the poems in this collection, he seems to have anticipated the castigation of criticism, and even to have acquiesced in its justice:

"Still I must yield those worthies merit,
Who chasten with unsparing spirit,
    Bad rhymes, and those who write them;
And though myself may be the next
By critic sarcasm to be vext,
    I surely will not fight them.

"Perhaps they would do quite as well
To break the rudely sounding shell
   Of such a young beginner;
He who offends at pert nineteen,
At thirty may become, I ween,
   A very hardened sinner."

But with all this apparent meekness, and professed submission to the rod, Lord Byron possessed the inseparable irritability of an author, and retorted upon the Edinburgh critics in the well-known satire of "English Bards and Scotch Reviewers." The success of this poem at once stamped his reputation; it met with vast circulation, and universal applause. The million were delighted with it, from the relish that almost every one has for any thing pungent and satirical; some authors extolled it, because they had formerly suffered under the lash of the critics themselves, and rejoiced in any thing that could reach their feelings, or prove their fallibility: while many others joined in the plaudits, by way of making favour with the poet, least they should at some future time suffer under the satire of his excursive muse.

The poem, indeed, was intrinsically excellent, possessing much of the terseness and vigour of Roman satire; and though he lay about him with an unsparing hand, and often cut down where he should merely have lopped off, still, we think, the garden of poetry would be wonderfully benefited by frequent visitations of the kind. The most indifferent part of the poem is that where the author meant to be most severe; his animadversions on the critics have too much of pique and anger; the heat of his feelings has taken out the temper of his weapon; and when he mentions Jeffrey he becomes grossly personal, and sinks beneath the dignity of his muse. Whatever may have been the temporary pain of the application, we think Lord Byron was benefited by the caustic of criticism. He was entering into literature with all the lulling advantages of a titled author; a strong predisposition on the part of society to admire; and none of those goads to talent that stimulate poor and obscure aspirers after fame, whose only means of rising in society is by the vigorous exertion of their talents. His lordship might, therefore, have slipped quietly into the silken herd of "persons of quality," who have from time to time scribbled volumes of polite, spindle-shanked poetry, in their nightgowns and slippers, had not the rough critic of the north given a salutary shake to his nerves, and provoked him to the exertion of full and masculine talent.

On coming of age, Lord Byron, after taking his seat in the house of peers, went abroad and spent some time in the south of Europe, and among the Grecian islands. He appears to have trod those classic regions with the enthusiasm of a scholar, and to have stored his mind and exalted his imagination with the relics of departed taste and grandeur, and the luxurious scenes and gorgeous imagery of the east. He returned to England in 1811, and in the spring of 1812 published "Childe Harold's Pilgrimage." The limits of this brief article will not allow us to enter into any examination of the merits of this poem, which, indeed, has been thoroughly scrutinized by every periodical publication of the times. In the notes appended to it, his lordship again took occasion to indulge in a few hits of no great force against his old adversaries, the Edinburgh reviewers. These writers, in reviewing his "Childe Harold," spoke of it with great candour and applause, and in the conclusion of their criticism, adverted, in terms of manly moderation, to his lordship's determined hostility. This unexpected liberality touched the generous feelings of the poet, and in a letter, which he immediately wrote to Mr. Jeffrey, he lamented the literary feud that had arisen between them, expressed his sense of the fair and candid criticism of Childe Harold, and regretting that his resentments had led him to the publication of his satire, declared, that as an atonement, he would endeavour to suppress its circulation, and banish it from print. His lordship has faithfully observed the promise, and the consequence is, that a copy of "English Bards and Scotch Reviewers" is not to be procured at present in any of the bookshops of Great Britain.

The subsequent writings of Lord Byron are too well known to need recapitulation. He has published a succession of brilliant little eastern tales, decorated with appropriate and splendid imagery. These are in every one's hands, and are the hackneyed subjects of every review. The profits of these writings have been liberally dispensed by his lordship to various persons; for, though by no means very affluent in his circumstances, he considers it a point of pride not to receive pecuniary emolument from the inspirations of his muse. In the introduction to his last poem he expresses a determination not to publish again for several years; and we understand he is about once more to depart on his poetic rambles in the east. We hope he may keep to his determination, and give time for that poetical genius, which has hitherto manifested itself in brilliant sparks and flashes, to kindle up into a fervent and a lasting flame.

[September, 1814]

BIOGRAPHICAL MEMOIR

OF

CAPTAIN DAVID PORTER

David Porter, the eldest son of Captain David Porter, was born in Boston on the 1st February, 1780. His father was an officer in our navy during the revolutionary war, and distinguished himself on various occasions by his activity, enterprise, and daring spirit. Being necessarily absent from home for the greater part of his time, the charge of his infant family devolved almost entirely on his wife. She was a pious and intelligent woman; the friend and instructor of her children, teaching them not merely by her precepts, but by her amiable and virtuous example.

Soon after the conclusion of the war, Captain Porter removed with his household to Baltimore, where he took command of the revenue cutter the Active. Here in the bosom of his family he would indulge in the veteran's foible of recounting past scenes of peril and adventure, and talking over the wonders and vicissitudes that chequer a sea-faring life. Little David would sit for hours and listen and kindle at these marvellous tales, while his father, perceiving his own love of enterprise springing up in the bosom of the lad, took every means to cherish it, and to inspire him with a passion for the sea. He at the same time gave him all the education and instruction that his limited means afforded, and being afterwards in command of a vessel in the West-India trade, proposed to take him a voyage by way of initiating him into the life of a sailor. The constitution of the latter being feeble and delicate excited all the apprehensions of a tender mother, who remonstrated with maternal solicitude, against exposing the puny stripling to the dangers and hardships of so rude a life. Her objections, however, were either obviated or overruled, and at the age of sixteen he sailed with his father for the West Indies, in the schooner Eliza. While at the port of Jeremie, in the island of St. Domingo, a pressgang endeavoured to board the vessel in search for men: they were bravely repelled with the loss of several killed and wounded on both sides; one man was shot down close by the side of young Porter. This affair excited considerable attention at the time. A narrative of it appeared in the public papers, and much praise was given to Captain Porter for the gallant vindication of his flag.

In the course of his second voyage, which he performed as mate of a ship, from Baltimore to St. Domingo, young Porter had a further taste of the vicissitudes of a sailor's life. He was twice impressed by the British, and each time effected his escape, but was so reduced in purse as to be obliged to work his passage home in the winter season, destitute of necessary clothing. In this forlorn condition he had to perform duty on a cold and stormy coast, where every spray was converted instantaneously into a sheet of ice. It would appear almost incredible that his feeble frame, little inured to hardship, could have sustained so much, were it not known how greatly the exertions of the body are supported by mental excitement.

Scarcely had he recovered from his late fatigues when he applied for admission into the navy; and on receiving a midshipman's warrant, immediately joined the frigate Constellation, Commodore Truxton. In the action with the French frigate the Insurgent, Porter was stationed in the foretop, and distinguished himself by his good conduct. Want of friends alone prevented his promotion at the time. When Commodore Barron was appointed to the command of the Constellation, Porter was advanced to the rank of lieutenant solely on account of his merit, having no friends or connexions capable of urging his fortunes. He was ordered to join the United States schooner Experiment under Captain Maley, to be employed on the West-India station. During the cruise they had a long and obstinate engagement with a number of brigand barges in the Bite of Leogane, which afforded him another opportunity of bringing himself into notice. He was also frequently employed in boat expeditions to cut out vessels, in which he displayed much coolness and address. Commodore Talbot, who commanded on that station, gave him charge of the Amphitrite, a small pilot boat prize schooner mounting five small swivels taken from the tops of the Constellation, and manned with fifteen hands. Not long after taking this command he fell in with a French privateer mounting a long twelve pounder and several swivels, having a crew of forty men, and accompanied by a prize ship and a large barge with thirty men armed with swivels. Notwithstanding the great disparity of force, Porter ordered his vessel to be laid alongside the privateer. The contest was arduous, and for some time doubtful, for in the commencement of the action he lost his rudder, which rendered the schooner unmanageable. The event, however, excused the desperateness of the attack, for after an obstinate and bloody resistance the privateer surrendered with the loss of seven killed and fifteen wounded. Not a man of Porter's crew was killed; several, however, were wounded, and his vessel was much injured. The prize was also taken, but the barge escaped. The conduct of Lieutenant Porter in this gallant little affair was highly applauded by his commander.

Shortly after his return to the United States he sailed, as first lieutenant, in the Experiment, commanded by Captain Charles Stewart. They were again stationed in the West Indies, and afforded great protection to the American commerce in that quarter. They had several engagements with French privateers, and were always successful, insomuch that they became the terror of those marauders of the ocean, and effectually controlled their rapacity and kept them quiet in port. The gallant and lamented Trippe was second lieutenant of the Experiment at the time.

When the first squadron was ordered for the Mediterranean, Porter sailed as first lieutenant of the schooner Enterprise, Captain Stewart. In this cruise they encountered a Tripolitan corsair of very superior force; a severe battle ensued in which the enemy suffered great slaughter, and was compelled to surrender, while our ship received but little injury. In this brilliant action Porter acquired much reputation from the conspic-

uous part he acted. He afterwards served on board of different ships in
the Mediterranean station and distinguished himself by his intrepidity
and zeal whenever an opportunity presented. On one occasion he commanded an expedition of boats sent to destroy some vessels laden with
wheat, at anchor in the harbour of old Tripoli; the service was promptly
and effectually performed; in the engagement he received a musket ball
through his left thigh.

Shortly after recovering from his wound he was transposed from the
New-York to the Philadelphia, Captain Bainbridge, as first lieutenant.
The frigate was then lying at Gibraltar, when he joined her in September,
1803. She soon after sailed for the blockade of Tripoli. No event took
place worthy of mention until the 31st of October. Nearly a week previous to this ill-fated day, the weather had been tempestuous, which
rendered it prudent to keep the ship off the land. The 31st opened with
all the splendour of a Sicilian morning: the promise of a more delightful
day never appeared. The land was just observed, when a sail was
descried making for the harbour, with a pleasant easterly breeze. It was
soon ascertained to be an armed ship of the enemy, and all sail was set
in chase. After an ineffectual pursuit of several leagues, Captain Bainbridge had just given orders to hale off, when the frigate grounded. Every
expedient that skill or courage could devise to float or defend her, was
successively resorted to, but in vain. The particulars of this unfortunate
affair are too generally known to need a minute recital; it is sufficient to
add that this noble ship and her gallant crew were surrendered to a
barbarous and dastardly enemy, whose only motive in warfare is the
hope of plunder. Throughout the long and dreary confinement, which
ensued, in the dungeons of Tripoli, Porter never suffered himself for a
moment to sink into despondency; but supported the galling indignities
and hardships of his situation with equanimity and even cheerfulness.
A seasonable supply of books served to beguile the hours of imprison-
ment, and enabled him even to turn them to advantage. He closely
applied himself to the study of ancient and modern history, biography,
the French language, and drawing; in which art, so useful to a seaman,
he has made himself a considerable proficient. He also sedulously cultivated the theory of his profession, and improved the junior officers by
his frequent instructions; representing the manoeuvres of fleets in battle
by means of small boards ingeniously arranged. He was active in promoting any plan of labour or amusement that could ameliorate the
situation or dispel the gloomy reflections of his companions. By these
means captivity was robbed of its heaviest evils, that dull monotony that
wearies the spirits, and that mental inactivity that engenders melancholy
and hypochondria.

An incident which occurred during his confinement deserves to be
mentioned, as being highly creditable to Lieutenant Porter. Under the

rooms occupied by the officers was a long dark passage, through which the American sailors, who were employed in public labour, frequently passed to different parts of the castle. Their conversation being repeatedly heard as they passed to and fro, some one made a small hole in the wall to communicate with them. For some days a constant intercourse was kept up, by sending down notes tied to a string. Some persons, however, indiscreetly entering into conversation with the seamen, were overheard, and information immediately carried to the Bashaw. In a few minutes the bolts of the prison door were heard to fly back with unwonted violence, and Sassi (chief officer of the castle) rushed furiously in. His features were distorted, and his voice almost inarticulate with passion. He demanded in a vehement tone of voice by whom or whose authority the wall had been opened; when Porter advanced with a firm step and composed countenance, and replied, "I alone am responsible." He was abruptly and rudely hurried from the prison, and the gate was again closed. This generous self-devotion, while it commanded the admiration of his companions, heightened their anxiety for his fate; apprehending some act of violence from the impetuous temper and absolute power of the Bashaw. Their fears, however, were appeased by the return of Porter, after considerable detention; having been dismissed without any further severity through the intercession of the minister Mahomet Dghies, who had on previous occasions shown a friendly disposition towards the prisoners.

It is unnecessary here to dwell on the various incidents that occurred in this tedious captivity, and of the many ingenious and adventurous plans of escape, devised and attempted by our officers, in all which Porter took an active and prominent part. When peace was at length made, and they were restored to light and liberty, he embarked with his companions for Syracuse, where a court of inquiry was held on the loss of the Philadelphia. After an honourable acquittal he was appointed to the command of the United States brig Enterprise, and soon after was ordered by Commodore Rodgers to proceed to Tripoli, with permission to cruise along the shore of Bengazi, and to visit the ruins of Leptis Magna, anciently a Roman colony. He was accompanied in this expedition by some of his friends, and after a short and pleasant passage, anchored near the latter place. They passed three days in wandering among the mouldering remains of Roman taste and grandeur; and excavated in such places as seemed to promise a reward for their researches. A number of ancient coins and cameos were found, and, among other curiosities, were two statues in tolerable preservation; the one a warrior, the other a female figure, of beautiful white marble and excellent workmanship. Verde antique pillars, of large size, formed of a single piece, and unbroken, were scattered along the shores. Near the harbour stood a lofty and elegant building, of which Lieutenant Porter took a drawing:

from its situation and form it was supposed to have been a Pharos. The awning under which the party dined was spread on the site, and among the fallen columns of a temple of Jupiter, and a zest was given to the repast, by the classical ideas awakened by surrounding objects.

While in command of the Enterprise, and at anchor in the port of Malta, an English sailor came alongside and insulted the officers and crew by abusive language; Captain Porter overhearing the scurrilous epithets he vociferated, ordered a boatswain's mate to seize him and give him a flogging at the gangway. This well merited chastisement excited the indignation of the Governor of Malta, who considered it a daring outrage, and gave orders that the forts should not permit the Enterprise to depart. No sooner was Captain Porter informed of it, than he got his vessel ready for action, weighed anchor, and with lighted matches and every man at his station, with the avowed determination of firing upon the town if attacked, sailed between the batteries and departed unmolested.

Shortly after this occurrence, in passing through the Straits of Gibraltar, he was attacked by twelve Spanish gun boats, who either mistook, or pretended to mistake, his vessel for a British brig. The calmness of the weather, the weight of their metal, and the acknowledged accuracy of their aim, made the odds greatly against him. As soon, however, as he was able to near them, they were assailed with such rapid and well directed volleys as quickly compelled them to shear off. This affair took place in sight of Gibraltar, and in presence of several ships of the British navy; it was, therefore, a matter of notoriety, and spoken of in terms of the highest applause.

After an absence of five years, passed in unremitted and arduous service, Captain Porter returned to the United States, and shortly after was married to Miss Anderson, daughter of the member of congress of that name, from Pennsylvania. Being appointed to the command of the flotilla, on the New Orleans station, he discharged, with faithfulness and activity, the irksome duty of enforcing the embargo and non-intercourse laws. He likewise performed an important service to his country, by ferreting out and capturing a pirate, a native of France, who, in a small well-armed schooner, had for some time infested the Chesapeake; and who, growing bolder by impunity, had committed many acts of depredation, until his maraudings became so serious as to attract the attention of government.

While commanding on the Orleans station, the father of Captain Porter died, an officer under his command. He had lived to see the wish of his heart fulfilled, in beholding his son a skilful and enterprising sailor, rising rapidly in his profession, and in the estimation of his country.

The climate of New Orleans disagreeing with the health of Captain

Porter and his family, he solicited to be ordered to some other station, and was, accordingly, appointed to the command of the Essex frigate, at Norfolk.

At the time of the declaration of war against England, the Essex was undergoing repairs at New-York, and the celerity with which she was fitted for sea reflected great credit on her commander. On the 3d of July, 1812, he sailed from Sandy Hook on a cruise, which was not marked by any incident of consequence, excepting the capture of the British sloop of war Alert, Captain Laugharne. Either undervaluing the untried prowess of our tars, or mistaking the force of the Essex, she ran down on her weather quarter, gave three cheers and commenced an action. In a few minutes she struck her colours, being cut to pieces, with three men wounded, and seven feet of water in her hold. To relieve himself from the great number of prisoners, taken in this and former prizes, Captain Porter made a cartel of the Alert, with orders to proceed to St. Johns, Newfoundland, and thence to New-York. She arrived safe, being the first ship of war taken from the enemy, and her flag the first British flag sent to the seat of government during the present war.

Having returned to the United States and refitted, he again proceeded to sea, from the Delaware, on the 27th of October, 1812, and repaired, agreeably to instructions from Commodore Bainbridge, to the coast of Brazil, where different places of rendezvous had been arranged between them. In the course of his cruise on this coast he captured his Britannic majesty's packet Nocton, and after taking out of her about 11,000 pounds sterling in specie, ordered her for America. Hearing of Commodore Bainbridge's victorious action with the Java, which would oblige him to return to port, and of the capture of the Hornet by the Montague, and learning that there was a considerable augmentation of British force on the coast, and several ships in pursuit of him, he abandoned his hazardous cruising ground, and stretched away to the southward, scouring the coast as far as Rio de la Plata. From thence he shaped his course for the Pacific Ocean, and, after suffering greatly from want of provisions, and heavy gales off Cape Horn, arrived at Valparaiso, on the 14th of March, 1813. Having victualled his ship, he ran down the coast of Chili and Peru, and fell in with a Peruvian corsair, having on board twenty-four Americans, as prisoners, the crews of two whaling ships, which she had taken on the coast of Chili. The Peruvian captain justified his conduct on the plea of being an ally of Great Britain, and the expectation likewise of a speedy war between Spain and the United States. Finding him resolved to persist in similar aggressions, Captain Porter threw all his guns and ammunition into the sea, liberated the Americans, and wrote a respectful letter to the viceroy explaining his reasons for so doing, which he delivered to the captain. He then proceeded to Lima, and luckily recaptured one of the American vessels as she was entering the port.

After this he cruised for several months in the Pacific, inflicting immense injury on the British commerce in those waters. He was particularly destructive to the shipping employed in the spermaceti whale fishery. A great number with valuable cargoes were captured; two were given up to the prisoners; three sent to Valparaiso and laid up; three sent to America; one of them he retained as a storeship, and another he equipped with twenty guns, called her the Essex junior, and gave the command of her to Lieutenant Downes. Most of these ships mounted several guns, and had numerous crews; and as several of them were captured by boats or by prizes, the officers and men of the Essex had frequent opportunities of showing their skill and courage, and of acquiring experience and confidence in naval conflict.

Having now a little squadron under his command, Captain Porter became a complete terror in those seas. As his numerous prizes supplied him abundantly with provisions, clothing, medicine, and naval stores of every description, he was enabled for a long time to keep the sea, without sickness or inconvenience to his crew; living entirely on the enemy, and being enabled to make considerable advances of pay to his officers and crew without drawing on government. The unexampled devastation achieved by his daring enterprises, not only spread alarm throughout the ports of the Pacific, but even occasioned great uneasiness in Great Britain. The merchants, who had any property afloat in this quarter, trembled with apprehension for its fate; the underwriters groaned at the catalogue of captures brought by every advice, while the pride of the nation was sorely incensed at beholding a single frigate lording it over the Pacific, roving about the ocean in saucy defiance of their thousand ships; revelling in the spoils of boundless wealth, and almost banishing the British flag from those regions, where it had so long waved proudly predominant.

Numerous ships were sent out to the Pacific in pursuit of him; others were ordered to cruise in the China seas, off New Zealand, Timor and New Holland, and a frigate sent to the River La Plata. The manner in which Captain Porter cruised, however, completely baffled pursuit. Keeping in the open seas, or lurking among the numerous barren and desolate islands that form the Gallipagos groupe, and never touching on the American coast, he left no traces by which he could be followed; rumour, while it magnified his exploits, threw his pursuers at fault; they were distracted by vague accounts of captures made at different places, and of frigates supposed to be the Essex hovering at the same time off different coasts and haunting different islands.

In the mean while Porter, though wrapped in mystery and uncertainty himself, yet received frequent and accurate accounts of his enemies, from the various prizes which he had taken. Lieutenant Downes, also, who had convoyed the prizes to Valparaiso, on his return, brought advices of the expected arrival of Commodore Hillyar in the Phœbe frigate rating thirty-six guns accompanied by two sloops of war. Glutted with spoil and havoc, and sated with the easy and inglorious captures of merchantmen, Captain Porter now felt eager for an opportunity to meet the enemy on equal terms, and to signalize his cruise by some brilliant achievement. Having been nearly a year at sea, he found that his ship would require some repairs, to enable her to face the foe; he repaired, therefore, accompanied by several of his prizes, to the Island of Nooaheevah, one of the Washington groupe, discovered by a Captain Ingraham of Boston. Here he landed, took formal possession of the island in the name of the government of the United States, and gave it the name of Madison's Island. He found it large, populous and fertile, abounding with the necessaries of life; the natives in the vicinity of the harbour which he had chosen received him in the most friendly manner, and supplied him with abundance of provisions. During his stay at this place he had several encounters with some hostile tribes on the island, whom he succeeded in reducing to subjection. Having calked and completely overhaled the ship, made for her a new set of water casks, and taken on board from the prizes provisions and stores for upwards of four months, he sailed for the coast of Chili on the 12th December, 1813. Previous to sailing he secured the three prizes which had accompanied him, under the guns of a battery erected for their protection, and left them in charge of Lieutenant Gamble of the marines and twenty-one men, with orders to proceed to Valparaiso after a certain period.

After cruising on the coast of Chili without success, he proceeded to Valparaiso, in hopes of falling in with Commodore Hillyar, or, if disappointed in this wish, of capturing some merchant ships said to be expected from England. While at anchor at this port Commodore Hillyar arrived, having long been searching in vain for the Essex, and almost despairing of ever meeting with her. Contrary to the expectations of Captain Porter, however, Commodore Hillyar, beside his own frigate, superior in itself to the Essex, was accompanied by the Cherub sloop of war, strongly armed and manned. These ships, having been sent out expressly to seek for the Essex, were in prime order and equipment, with picked crews, and hoisted flags bearing the motto "God and country, British sailors' best rights: *traitors offend both.*" This was in opposition to Porter's motto of "Free trade and sailors' rights," and the latter part of it suggested doubtless, by error industriously cherished, that our crews are chiefly composed of English seamen. In reply to this motto Porter hoisted at his mizen, "God, our country, and liberty: tyrants offend them." On entering the harbour the Phœbe fell foul of the Essex in such manner as to lay her at the mercy of Captain Porter; out of respect, however, to the neutrality of the port, he did not take advantage of her exposed situation. This forbearance was afterwards acknowledged by Commodore Hillyar, and he passed his word of honour to observe like conduct while they remained in port. They continued therefore, while in harbour and on shore, in the mutual exchange of courtesies and kind offices that should characterize the private intercourse between civilized and generous enemies. And the crews of the respective ships often mingled together and passed nautical jokes and pleasantries from one to the other.

On getting their provisions on board the Phœbe and Cherub went off the port, where they cruised for six weeks, rigorously blockading Captain Porter. Their united force amounted to 81 guns and 500 men, in addition to which they took on board the crew of an English letter of marque lying in port. The force of the Essex consisted of but 46 guns, all of which, excepting six long twelves, were 32 pound carronades, only serviceable in close fighting. Her crew, having been much reduced by the manning of prizes, amounted to but 255 men. The Essex junior being only intended as a storeship, mounted ten 18 pound carronades and ten short sixes with a complement of only 60 men.

This vast superiority of force on the part of the enemy prevented all chance of encounter, on any thing like equal terms, unless by express covenant between the commanders. Captain Porter, therefore, endeavoured repeatedly to provoke a challenge, (the inferiority of his frigate to the Phœbe not justifying him in making the challenge himself,) but without effect. He tried frequently also to bring the Phœbe into single action; but this Commodore Hillyar warily avoided, and always kept his ships so close together as to frustrate Captain Porter's attempts. This conduct of Commodore Hillyar has been sneered at by many, as unworthy a brave officer: but it should be considered that he had more important objects to effect than the mere exhibition of individual or national prowess. His instructions were to crush a noxious foe, destructive to the commerce of his country; he was furnished with a force competent to this duty; and having the enemy once within his power, he had no right to waive his superiority, and, by meeting him on equal footing, give him a chance to conquer, and continue his work of destruction.

Finding it impossible to bring the enemy to equal combat; and fearing the arrival of additional force, which he understood was on the way, Captain Porter determined to put to sea the first opportunity that should present. A rendezvous was accordingly appointed for the Essex junior, and having ascertained by repeated trials that the Essex was a superior sailer to either of the blockading ships, it was agreed that she should let the enemy chase her off; thereby giving the Essex junior an opportunity of escaping.

On the next day, the 28th March, the wind came on to blow fresh from the southward, and the Essex parted her larboard cable and dragged her starboard anchor directly out to sea. Not a moment was lost in getting sail on the ship; but perceiving that the enemy was close in with the point forming the west side of the bay, and that there was a possibility of passing to windward, and escaping to sea by superior sailing, Captain Porter resolved to hazard the attempt. He accordingly took in his top gallant sails and braced up for the purpose, but most unfortunately on rounding the point a heavy squall struck the ship and carried away her main top mast, precipitating the men who were aloft into the sea, who were drowned. Both ships now gave chase, and the crippled state of his ship left Porter no alternative but to endeavour to regain the port. Finding it impossible to get back to the common anchorage, he ran close into a small bay about three quarters of a mile to leeward of the battery, on the east of the harbour, and let go his anchor within pistol shot of the shore. Supposing the enemy would, as formerly, respect the neutrality of the place, he considered himself secure, and thought only of repairing the damages he had sustained. The wary and menacing approach of the hostile ships, however, displaying their motto flags and having jacks at all their masts' heads, soon showed him the real danger of his situation. With all possible despatch he got his ship ready for action, and endeavoured to get a spring on his cable, but had not succeeded, when, at 54 minutes past 3 P.M. the enemy commenced an attack.

At first the Phœbe lay herself under his stern and the Cherub on his starboard bow; but the latter soon finding herself exposed to a hot fire, bore up and ran under his stern also, where both ships kept up a severe raking fire. Captain Porter succeeded three different times in getting springs on his cables, for the purpose of bringing his broadside to bear on the enemy, but they were as often shot away by the excessive fire to which he was exposed. He was obliged, therefore, to rely for defence against this tremendous attack merely on three long twelve pounders, which he had run out of the stern ports; and which were worked with such bravery and skill as in half an hour to do great injury to both the enemy's ships and induce them to hale off and repair damages. It was evidently the intention of Commodore Hillyar to risk nothing from the daring courage of his antagonist, but to take the Essex at as cheap a rate as possible. All his manœuvres were deliberate and wary; he saw his antagonist completely at his mercy, and prepared to cut him up in the safest and surest manner. In the mean time the situation of the Essex was galling and provoking in the extreme; crippled and shattered, with many killed and wounded, she lay awaiting the convenience of the enemy, to renew the scene of slaughter, with scarce a hope of escape or revenge. Her brave crew, however, in place of being disheartened, were aroused to desperation, and by hoisting ensigns in their rigging and jacks in different parts of the ship, evinced their defiance and determination to hold out to the last.

The enemy having repaired his damages, now placed himself with both his ships, on the starboard quarter of the Essex, out of reach of her carronades, and where her stern guns could not be brought to bear. Here he kept up a most destructive fire, which it was not in Captain Porter's power to return; the latter, therefore, saw no hope of injuring him without getting under way and becoming the assailant. From the mangled state of his rigging he could set no other sail than the flying jib; this he caused to be hoisted, cut his cable, and ran down on both ships, with an intention of laying the Phœbe on board.

For a short time he was enabled to close with the enemy, and the firing on both sides was tremendous. The decks of the Essex were strewed with dead, and her cockpit filled with wounded; she had been several times on fire, and was in fact a perfect wreck; still a feeble hope sprang up that she might be saved, in consequence of the Cherub being compelled to hale off by her crippled state; she did not return to close action again, but kept up a distant firing with her long guns. The disabled state of the Essex, however, did not permit her to take advantage of this circumstance; for want of sail she was unable to keep at close quarters with the Phœbe, who, edging off, chose the distance which best suited her long guns, and kept up a tremendous fire, which made dreadful havoc among our crew. Many of the guns of the Essex were rendered useless, and many had their whole crews destroyed: they were manned from those that were disabled, and one gun in particular was three times manned; fifteen men were slain at it in the course of the action, though the captain of it escaped with only a slight wound. Captain Porter now gave up all hope of closing with the enemy, but finding the wind favourable, determined to run his ship on shore, land the crew, and destroy her. He had approached within musket shot of the shore, and had every prospect of succeeding, when in an instant the wind shifted from the land and drove her down upon the Phœbe, exposing her again to a dreadful raking fire. The ship was now totally unmanageable; yet as her head was toward the enemy, and he to leeward, Captain Porter again perceived a faint hope of boarding. At this moment Lieutenant Downes of the Essex junior came on board to receive orders, expecting that Captain Porter would soon be a prisoner. His services could be of no avail in the deplorable state of the Essex, and finding from the enemy's putting his helm up, that the last attempt at boarding would not succeed, Captain Porter directed him, after he had been ten minutes on board, to return to his own ship, to be prepared for defending and destroying her in case of attack. He took with him several of the wounded, leaving three of his boat's crew on board to make room for them. The Cherub kept up a hot fire on him during his return. The slaughter on board of the Essex now became horrible, the enemy continued to rake her, while she was unable to bring a gun to bear in return. Still her commander, with an obstinacy that bordered on desperation, persisted in the unequal and almost hopeless conflict. Every expedient that a fertile and inventive mind could suggest was resorted to, in the forlorn hope that they might yet be enabled by some lucky chance to escape from the grasp of the foe. A halser was bent to the sheet anchor, and the anchor cut from the bows, to bring the ship's head round. This succeeded; the broadside of the Essex was again brought to bear; and as the enemy was much crippled and unable to hold his own, Captain Porter thought she might drift out of gunshot before she discovered that he had anchored. The halser, however, unfortunately parted, and with it failed the last lingering hope of the Essex. The ship had taken fire several times during the action, but at this moment her situation was awful. She was on fire both forward and aft; the flames were bursting up each hatchway; a large quantity of powder below exploded, and word was given that the fire was near the magazine. Thus surrounded by horrors, without any chance of saving the ship, Captain Porter turned his attention to rescuing as many of his brave companions as possible. Finding his distance from the shore did not exceed three quarters of a mile, he hoped many would be able to save themselves should the ship blow up. His boats had been cut to pieces by the enemies' shot, but he advised such as could swim to jump overboard and make for shore. Some reached it—some were taken by the enemy, and some perished in the attempt; but most of this loyal and gallant crew preferred sharing the fate of their ship and their commander.

Those who remained on board now endeavoured to extinguish the flames, and having succeeded, went again to the guns and kept up a firing for a few minutes; but the crew had by this time become so weakened that all further resistance was in vain. Captain Porter summoned a consultation of the officers of divisions, but was surprised to find only Acting Lieutenant Stephen Decatur M'Knight remaining; of the others some had been killed, others knocked overboard, and others carried below disabled by severe wounds. The accounts from every part of the ship were deplorable in the extreme; representing her in the most shattered and crippled condition, in imminent danger of sinking, and so crowded with the wounded that even the birth deck could contain no more, and many were killed while under the surgeon's hands. In the mean while the enemy, in consequence of the smoothness of the water and his secure distance, was enabled to keep up a deliberate and constant fire, aiming with coolness and certainty as if firing at a target, and hitting the hull at every shot. At length, utterly despairing of saving the ship, Captain Porter was compelled, at 20 minutes past 6 P.M. to give the painful order to strike the colours. It is probable the enemy did not perceive that the ship had surrendered, for he continued firing; several men were killed and wounded in different parts of the ship, and Captain Porter thinking he intended to show no quarter, was about to rehoist his flag and to fight until he sunk, when the enemy desisted his attack ten minutes after the surrender.

The foregoing account of this battle is taken almost verbatim from the letter of Captain Porter to the secretary of the navy. Making every allowance for its being a partial statement, this must certainly have been one of the most sanguinary and obstinately contested actions on naval record. The loss of the Essex is a sufficient testimony of the desperate bravery with which she was defended. Out of 255 men which comprised her crew, fifty-eight were killed; thirty-nine wounded severely; twenty-seven slightly, and thirty-one missing, making in all 154. She was completely cut to pieces, and so covered with the dead and dying, with mangled limbs, with brains and blood, and all the ghastly images of pain and death, that the officer who came on board to take possession of her, though accustomed to scenes of slaughter, was struck with sickening horror, and fainted at the shocking spectacle.

Thousands of the inhabitants of Valparaiso were spectators of the battle, covering the neighbouring heights: for it was fought so near the shore that some of the shot even struck among the citizens who, in the eagerness of their curiosity, had ventured down upon the beach. Touched by the forlorn situation of the Essex, and filled with admiration at the unflagging spirit and persevering bravery of her commander and crew, a generous anxiety ran throughout the multitude for their fate: bursts of delight arose when, by any vicissitude of battle, or prompt expedient, a chance seemed to turn up in their favour; and the eager spectators were seen to wring their hands, and uttered groans of sympathy, when the transient hope was defeated, and the gallant little frigate once more became an unresisting object of deliberate slaughter.

It is needless to mention particularly the many instances of individual valour and magnanimity among both the officers and common sailors of the Essex: their general conduct bears ample testimony to their heroism; and it will hereafter be a sufficient distinction for any man to prove that he was present in that battle. Every action that we have fought at sea has gone to destroy some envious shade which the enemy has attempted to cast on our rising reputation. After the affair of the Argus and the Pelican, it was asserted that our sailors were brave only while successful and unhurt, but that the sight of slaughter filled them with dismay. In this battle it has been proved that they are capable of the highest exercise of courage—that of standing unmoved among incessant carnage, without being able to return a shot, and destitute of a hope of ultimate success.

Though, from the distance and positions which the enemy chose, this battle was chiefly fought on our part by six twelve pounders only, yet great damage was done to the assailing ships. Their masts and yards were badly crippled, their hulls much cut up; the Phœbe, especially, received 18 twelve pound shot below her water line, some three feet under water. Their loss in killed and wounded was not ascertained, but must have been severe; the first lieutenant of the Phœbe was killed, and Captain Tucker, of the Cherub, was severely wounded. It was with some difficulty that the Phœbe and the Essex could be kept afloat until they anchored the next morning in the port of Valparaiso.

Much indignation has been expressed against Commodore Hillyar for his violation of the laws of nations, and of his private agreement with Captain Porter, by attacking him in the neutral waters of Valparaiso. Waiving all discussion of these points, it may barely be observed, that his cautious attack with a vastly superior force, on a crippled ship, which, relying on his forbearance, had placed herself in a most defenceless situation, and which for six weeks previous had offered him fair fight, on advantageous terms, though it may reflect great credit on his prudence, yet certainly furnishes no triumph to a brave and generous mind. Aware, however, of that delicacy which ought to be observed towards the character even of an enemy, it is not the intention of the writer to assail that of Commodore Hillyar. Indeed, his conduct after the battle entitles him to high encomium; he showed the greatest humanity to the wounded, and, as Captain Porter acknowledges, endeavoured as much as lay in his power to alleviate the distresses of war by the most generous and delicate deportment towards both the officers and crew, commanding that the property of every person should be respected. Captain Porter and his crew were paroled, and permitted to return to the United States in the Essex junior, her armament being previously taken out. On arriving off the port of New-York, they were overhaled by the Saturn razee, the authority of Commodore Hillyar to grant a passport was questioned, and the Essex junior detained. Captain Porter then told the boarding officer that he gave up his parole, and considered himself a prisoner of war, and as such should use all means of escape. In consequence of this threat the Essex junior was ordered to remain all night under the lee of the Saturn, but the next morning Captain Porter put off in his boat, though thirty miles from shore; and, notwithstanding he was pursued by the Saturn, effected his escape, and landed safely on Long Island. His reception in the United States has been such as his great services and distinguished valour deserved. The various interesting and romantic rumours that had reached this country concerning him, during his cruise in the Pacific, had excited the curiosity of the public to see this modern Sinbad; on arriving in New-York his carriage was surrounded by the populace, who took out the horses, and dragged him, with shouts and acclamations, to his lodgings.

The length to which this article has already been extended, notwithstanding the brevity with which many interesting circumstances have

been treated, forbids any further remarks on the character and services
of Captain Porter. They are sufficiently illustrated in the foregoing summary of his eventful life, and particularly in the history of his last cruise,
which was conducted with wonderful enterprise, fertility of expedient,
consummate seamanship, and daring courage. In his single ship he has
inflicted more injury on the commerce of the enemy than all the rest of
the navy put together; not merely by actual devastation, but by the
general insecurity and complete interruption which he occasioned to an
extensive and invaluable branch of British trade. His last action, also,
though it terminated in the loss of his frigate, can scarcely be considered
as unfortunate, inasmuch as it has given a brilliancy to his own reputation, and wreathed fresh honours around the name of the American sailor.

[December, 1814]

DEFENCE OF FORT M'HENRY

[These lines have been already published in several of our newspapers; they may
still, however, be new to many of our readers. Besides, we think that their
merit entitles them to preservation in some more permanent form than the columns
of a daily paper. The annexed song was composed under the following circumstances.—A gentleman had left Baltimore, in a flag of truce for the purpose of
getting released from the British fleet a friend of his who had been captured at
Marlborough. He went as far as the mouth of the Patuxent, and was not permitted
to return lest the intended attack on Baltimore should be disclosed. He was, therefore, brought up the bay to the mouth of the Patapsco, where the flag vessel was
kept under the guns of a frigate, and he was compelled to witness the bombardment of Fort M'Henry, which the Admiral had boasted that he would carry in
a few hours, and that the city must fall. He watched the flag at the fort through
the whole day with an anxiety that can be better felt than described, until the night
prevented him from seeing it. In the night he watched the bomb-shells, and at
early dawn his eye was again greeted by the proudly-waving flag of his country.]

Tune—ANACREON IN HEAVEN.

O! say can you see, by the dawn's early light,
    What so proudly we hail'd at the twilight's last gleaming,
Whose broad stripes and bright stars through the perilous fight,
    O'er the ramparts we watch'd, were so gallantly streaming?
        And the rockets' red glare, the bombs bursting in air,
        Gave proof through the night that our flag was still there—
            O! say, does that star-spangled banner yet wave
            O'er the land of the free, and the home of the brave?

On the shore, dimly seen through the mists of the deep,
    Where the foe's haughty host in dread silence reposes,

What is that which the breeze o'er the towering steep,
  As it fitfully blows, half conceals, half discloses?
    Now it catches the gleam of the morning's first beam,
    In full glory reflected now shines on the stream—
      'Tis the star-spangled banner, O! long may it wave
      O'er the land of the free, and the home of the brave.

And where is that band who so vauntingly swore
  That the havock of war and the battle's confusion
A home and a country should leave us no more?
  Their blood has wash'd out their foul foot-steps' pollution.
    No refuge could save the hireling and slave,
    From the terror of flight or the gloom of the grave;
      And the star-spangled banner in triumph doth wave
      O'er the land of the free, and the home of the brave.

O! thus be it ever when freemen shall stand
  Between their lov'd home, and the war's desolation,
Blest with vict'ry and peace, may the heav'n-rescued land
  Praise the power that hath made and preserv'd us a nation.
    Then conquer we must, when our cause it is just,
    And this be our motto—"In God is our trust!"
      And the star-spangled banner in triumph shall wave
      O'er the land of the free, and the home of the brave.

[March, 1815]

A BIOGRAPHICAL SKETCH OF THOMAS CAMPBELL

[This sketch was designed for a biographical preface to an American edition of Campbell's poems, and was originally published in that form some time ago. It has now been revised, corrected, and materially altered by the author.]

It has long been deplored by authors as a lamentable truth, that they seldom receive impartial justice from the world while living. The grave seems to be the ordeal to which their names must be subjected, and from whence, if worthy of immortality, they rise with pure and imperishable lustre. Here many, who have flourished in unmerited popularity, descend into oblivion; and it may literally be said, that "they rest from their labours, and their works do follow them." Here likewise, many an ill-starred author, after struggling with penury and neglect, and starving through a world which he has enriched by his talents, sinks to rest, and becomes a theme of universal admiration and regret. The sneers of the cynical, the detractions of the envious, the scoffings of the ignorant, are silenced at the hallowed precincts of the tomb; and the world awakens to a sense of his value, when he is removed beyond its patronage for ever. Monuments are erected to his memory, books are written in his praise, and thousands will devour with avidity the biography of a man, whose life was passed unheeded before their eyes. He is like some canonized saint, at whose shrine treasures are lavished, and clouds of incense offered up, though, while living, the slow hand of charity withheld the pittance that would have soothed his miseries.

But this tardiness in awarding merit its due, this preference continually shown to departed, over living authors, of perhaps superior excellence, may be attributed to a more charitable source than that of envy or ill nature. The latter are continually before our eyes, exposed to the full glare of scrutinizing familiarity. We behold them subject to the same foibles and frailties with ourselves, and, from the constitutional delicacy of their minds, and their irritable sensibilities, prone to more than ordinary caprices. The former, on the contrary, are seen only through the magic medium of their works. We form our opinion of the whole flow of their minds, and the tenor of their dispositions, from the writings they have left behind. We witness nothing of the mental exhaustion and languor which follow these gushes of genius. We behold the stream only in the fulness of its current, and conclude that it has always been equally profound in its depth, pure in its wave, and majestic in its career.

With respect to the living writers of Europe, however, we may be said, on this side of the Atlantic, to be placed in some degree in the situation of posterity. The vast ocean that rolls between us, like a space of time, removes us beyond the sphere of personal favour, personal prejudice, or personal familiarity. A European work, therefore, appears before us depending simply on its intrinsic merits. We have no private friendship, nor party purpose, to serve, by magnifying the author's merits; and, in sober sadness, the humble state of our national literature places us far below any feeling of national rivalship.

But, while our local situation thus enables us to exercise the enviable impartiality of posterity, it is evident we must share likewise in one of its disadvantages. We are in as complete ignorance respecting the biography of most living authors of celebrity, as though they had existed ages before our time; and, indeed, are better informed concerning the character and lives of authors who have long since passed away, than of those who are actually adding to the stores of European literature. A proof of this assertion will be furnished in the following sketch, which, unsatisfactory as it is, contains all the information we can collect, concerning a British poet of rare and exquisite endowments.

Thomas Campbell was born at Glasgow, on the 27th of September,

1777. He is the youngest son of Mr. Alexander Campbell, late merchant of Glasgow; a gentleman of the most unblemished integrity and amiable manners, who united the scholar and the man of business, and, amidst the corroding cares and sordid habits of trade, cherished a liberal and enthusiastic love of literature. He died at a very advanced age, in the spring of 1801, and the event is mentioned in the Edinburgh Magazine, with high encomiums on his moral and religious character.

It may not be uninteresting to the American reader to know that Mr. Campbell, the poet, has very near connexions in this country; and, indeed, to this circumstance may be in some measure attributed the liberal sentiments he has frequently expressed concerning America. His father resided, for many years of his youth, at Falmouth, in Virginia, but returned to Europe about fifty years since. His uncle, who had accompanied his father, settled permanently in Virginia, where his family has uniformly maintained a highly respectable character. One of his sons was district attorney under the administration of Washington, and died in 1795. He was a man of uncommon talents, and particularly distinguished for his eloquence. Robert Campbell also, a brother of the poet, settled in Virginia, where he married a daughter of the celebrated Patrick Henry. He died about the year 1808.

The genius of Mr. Campbell showed itself almost in his infancy. At the age of seven he possessed a vivacity of imagination, and a vigour of mind, surprising in such early youth. A strong inclination for poetry was already discernible in him; and, indeed, it was not more than two years after this that we are told "he began to try his wings." These bright dawnings of intellect, united to uncommon personal beauty, a winning gentleness and modesty of manners, and a generous sensibility of heart, made him an object of universal favour and admiration.

There is scarcely any obstacle more fatal to the full development and useful application of talent than an early display of genius. The extravagant caresses lavished upon it by the light and injudicious, are too apt to beget a self-confidence in the possessor, and render him impatient of the painful discipline of study; without which genius, at best, is irregular, ungovernable, and ofttimes splendidly erroneous.

Perhaps there is no country in the world where this error is less frequent than in Scotland. The Scotch are a philosophical, close-thinking people. Wary, and distrustful of external appearances and first impressions, stern examiners into the *utility* of things, and cautious in dealing out the dole of applause, their admiration follows tardily in the rear of their judgment, and even when they admire, they do it with peculiar rigidity of muscle. This spirit of rigorous rationality is peculiarly evident in the management of youthful genius; which, instead of meeting with enervating indulgence, is treated with a Spartan severity of education, tasked to the utmost extent of its powers, and made to undergo a long and laborious probation, before it is permitted to emerge into notoriety. The consequence is, an uncommon degree of skill and vigour in their writers. They are rendered diligent by constant habits of study, powerful by science, graceful by the elegant accomplishments of the scholar, and prompt and adroit in the management of their talents, by the frequent contests and exercises of the schools.

From the foregoing observations may be gathered the kind of system adopted with respect to young Campbell. His early display of genius, instead of making him the transient wonder of the drawing room, and the *enfant gaté* of the tea table, consigned him to the rigid discipline of the academy. At the age of seven he commenced the study of the Latin language under the care of the Rev. David Alison, a teacher of distinguished reputation in Scotland. At twelve he entered the university of Glasgow, and in the following year gained a bursary on Bishop Leighton's foundation, for a translation of one of the comedies of Aristophanes, which he executed in verse. This triumph was the more honourable, from being gained, after a hard contest, over a rival candidate of nearly twice his age, who was considered one of the best scholars in the university. His second prize exercise was the translation of a tragedy of Æschylus, likewise in verse, which he gained without opposition, as none of the students would enter the lists with him. He continued seven years in the university, during which time his talents and application were testified by yearly academical prizes. He was particularly successful in his translations from the Greek, in which language he took great delight; and on receiving his last prize for one of these performances, the Greek professor publicly pronounced it the best that had ever been produced in the university.

Moral philosophy was likewise a favourite study with Mr. Campbell; and, indeed, he applied himself to gain an intimate acquaintance with the whole circle of sciences. But though, in the prosecution of his studies, he attended the academical courses both of law and physic, it was merely as objects of curiosity, and branches of general knowledge, for he never devoted himself to any particular study with a view to prepare himself for a profession. On the contrary, his literary passion was already so strong, that he could never, for a moment, endure the idea of confining himself to the dull round of business, or engaging in the absorbing pursuits of common life.

In this he was most probably confirmed by the indulgence of a fond father, whose ardent love of literature made him regard the promising talents of his son with pride and sanguine anticipation. At one time, it is true, a part of his family expressed a wish that he should be fitted for the church, but this was completely overruled by the rest, and he was left, without further opposition, to the impulse of his own genius, and the seductions of the muse.

After leaving the university he passed some time among the mountains of Argyleshire, at the seat of Colonel Napier, a descendant of Napier Baron Merchiston, the celebrated inventor of logarithms. It is probable that from this gentleman he first imbibed his taste and knowledge of the military art, traces of which are to be seen throughout his poems. From Argyleshire he went to Edinburgh, where the reputation he had acquired at the university gained him a favourable reception into the distinguished circle of science and literature for which that city is renowned. Among others he was particularly honoured by the notice of Professors Stewart and Playfair. Nothing could be more advantageous for a youthful poet, than to commence his career under such auspices. To the expansion of mind and elevation of thought produced by the society of such celebrated men, may we ascribe, in a great measure, the philosophic spirit, and moral sublimity displayed in his first production, the Pleasures of Hope, which was written during his residence at Edinburgh. He was not more than twenty when he wrote this justly celebrated poem, and it was published in the following year.

The popularity of this work at once introduced the author to the notice and patronage of the first people of Great Britain. At first, indeed, it promised but little pecuniary advantage, as he unfortunately disposed of the copyright for an inconsiderable sum. This, however, was in some measure remedied by the liberality of his publisher, who, finding that his book ran through two editions in the course of a few months, permitted him to publish a splendid edition for himself, by which means he was enabled, in some measure, to participate in the golden harvest of his labours.

About this time the passion for German literature raged in all its violence in Great Britain, and the universal enthusiasm with which it was admired, awakened, in the inquiring mind of our author, a desire of studying it at the fountain head. This, added to his curiosity to visit foreign parts, induced him to embark for Germany in the year 1800. He had originally fixed upon the college of Jena for his first place of residence, but on arriving at Hamburgh he found, by the public prints, that a victory had been gained by the French near Ulm, and that Munich and the heart of Bavaria were the theatre of an interesting war. "One moment's sensation," he observes, in a letter to a relation in this country, "the single hope of seeing human nature exhibited in its most dreadful attitude, overturned my past decisions. I got down to the seat of war some weeks before the summer armistice of 1800, and indulged in what you will call the criminal curiosity of witnessing blood and desolation. Never shall time efface from my memory the recollection of that hour of astonishment and suspended breath, when I stood with the good monks of St. Jacob, to overlook a charge of Klenaw's cavalry upon the French under Grennier, encamped below us. We saw the fire given and returned, and heard distinctly the sound of the French *pas de charge* collecting the lines to attack in close column. After three hours' awaiting the issue of a severe action, a park of artillery was opened just beneath the walls of the monastery, and several wagoners, that were stationed to convey the wounded in spring wagons, were killed in our sight." This awful spectacle he has described with all the poet's fire, in his Battle of Hohenlinden; a poem which perhaps contains more grandeur and martial sublimity than is to be found anywhere else, in the same compass of English poetry.

Mr. Campbell afterwards proceeded to Ratisbon, where he was at the time it was taken possession of by the French, and expected, as an Englishman, to be made prisoner; but he observes, "Moreau's army was under such excellent discipline, and the behaviour both of officers and men so civil, that I soon mixed among them without hesitation, and formed many agreeable acquaintances at the messes of their brigade stationed in town, to which their *chef de brigade* often invited me. This worthy man, Colonel Le Fort, whose kindness I shall ever remember with gratitude, gave me a protection to pass through the whole army of Moreau."

After this he visited different parts of Germany, in the course of which he paid one of the casual taxes on travelling; being plundered among the Tyrolese mountains, by a Croat, of his clothes, his books, and thirty ducats in gold. About midwinter he returned to Hamburgh, where he remained four months, in the expectation of accompanying a young gentleman of Edinburgh in a tour to Constantinople. His unceasing thirst for knowledge, and his habits of industrious application, prevented these months from passing heavily or unprofitably. His time was chiefly employed in reading German, and making himself acquainted with the principles of Kant's philosophy; from which, however, he seems soon to have turned with distaste, to the richer and more interesting field of German belles-lettres.

While in Germany an edition of his Pleasures of Hope was proposed for publication in Vienna, but was forbidden by the court, in consequence of those passages which relate to Kosciusko, and the partition of Poland. Being disappointed in his projected visit to Constantinople, he returned to England in 1801, after nearly a year's absence, which had been passed much to his satisfaction and improvement, and had stored his mind with grand and awful images. "I remember," says he, "how little I valued the art of painting before I got into the heart of such impressive scenes; but in Germany I would have given any thing to have possessed an art capable of conveying ideas inaccessible to speech and writing. Some particular scenes were, indeed, rather overcharged with that degree of the terrific which oversteps the sublime, and I own my flesh yet creeps at the recollection of *spring wagons and hospitals—*

but the sight of Ingolstadt in ruins, or Hohenlinden covered with fire, seven miles in circumference, were spectacles never to be forgotten."

On returning to England he visited London, for the first time, where, though unprovided with a single letter of introduction, the celebrity of his writings procured him the immediate notice and attentions of the best society. His recent visit to the continent, however, had increased rather than gratified his desire to travel. He now contemplated another tour, for the purpose of improving himself in the knowledge of foreign languages and foreign manners, in the course of which he intended to visit Italy and pass some time at Rome. From this plan he was diverted, most probably, by an attachment he formed to a Miss Sinclair, a distant relation, whom he married in 1803. This change in his situation naturally put an end to all his wandering propensities, and he removed to Sydenham, in Kent, near London, where he has ever since resided, devoting himself to literature, and the calm pleasures of domestic life.

He has been enabled to indulge his love of study and retirement more comfortably by the bounty of his sovereign, who some few years since presented him with an annuity of 200*l*. This distinguished mark of royal favour, so gratifying to the pride of the poet, and the loyal affections of the subject, was wholly spontaneous and unconditional. It was neither granted to the importunities of friends at court, nor given as a *douceur* to secure the services of the author's pen, but merely as a testimony of royal approbation of his popular poem, the Pleasures of Hope. Mr. Campbell, both before and since, has uniformly been independent in his opinions and writings.

Though withdrawn from the busy world in his retirement at Sydenham, yet the genius of Mr. Campbell, like a true brilliant, occasionally flashed upon the public eye, in a number of exquisite little poems, which appeared in the periodical works of the day. Many of these he has never thought proper to rescue from their perishable repositories. But of those which he has formally acknowledged and republished, Hohenlinden, Lochiel, the Mariners of England, and the Battle of the Baltic, are sufficient of themselves, were other evidence wanting, to establish his title to the sacred name of Poet. The two last-mentioned poems we consider as two of the noblest national songs we have ever seen. They contain sublime imagery and lofty sentiments, delivered with a "gallant swelling spirit," but totally free from that hyperbole and national rhodomontade which generally disgrace this species of poetry. In the beginning of 1809, he published his second volume of poems, containing Gertrude of Wyoming, and several smaller effusions; since which time he has produced nothing of consequence, excepting the uncommonly spirited and affecting little tale of O'Connor's Child, or Love Lies Bleeding.

Of those private and characteristic anecdotes which display most strikingly the habits and peculiarities of a writer, we have scarcely any to furnish respecting Mr. Campbell. He is generally represented to us as being extremely studious, but at the same time social in his disposition, gentle and endearing in his manners, and extremely prepossessing in his appearance and address. With a delicate and even nervous sensibility, and a degree of self diffidence that at times is almost painful, he shrinks from the glare of notoriety which his own works have shed around him, and seems ever deprecating criticism, rather than enjoying praise. Though his society is courted by the most polished and enlightened, among whom he is calculated to shine, yet his chief delight is in domestic life, in the practice of those gentle virtues and bland affections which he has so touchingly and eloquently illustrated in various passages of his poems.

That Mr. Campbell has by any means attained to the summit of his fame, we cannot suffer ourselves for a moment to believe. We rather look upon the works he has already produced as specimens of pure and virgin gold from a mine whose treasures are yet to be explored. It is true, the very reputation Mr. Campbell has acquired, may operate as a disadvantage to his future efforts. Public expectation is a pitiless task-master, and exorbitant in its demands. He who has once awakened it, must go on in a progressive ratio, surpassing what he has hitherto done, or the public will be disappointed. Under such circumstances an author of common sensibility takes up his pen with fear and trembling. A con-sciousness that much is expected from him deprives him of that ease of mind and boldness of imagination, which are necessary to fine writing, and he too often fails from a too great anxiety to excel. He is like some youthful soldier, who, having distinguished himself by a gallant and brilliant achievement, is ever afterward fearful of entering on a new enterprise, lest he should tarnish the laurels he has won.

We are satisfied that Mr. Campbell feels this very diffidence and solicitude from the uncommon pains he bestows upon his writings. These are scrupulously revised, modelled, and retouched over and over, before they are suffered to go out of his hands, and even then, are slowly and reluctantly yielded up to the press. This elaborate care may, at times, be carried to an excess, so as to produce fastidiousness of style, and an air of too much art and labour. It occasionally imparts to the muse the precise demeanour and studied attire of the prude, rather than the negli-gent and bewitching graces of the woodland nymph. A too minute at-tention to finishing is likewise injurious to the force and sublimity of a poem. The vivid images which are struck off, at a single heat, in those glowing moments of inspiration, "when the soul is lifted to heaven," are too often softened down, and cautiously tamed, in the cold hour of correction. As an instance of the critical severity which Mr. Campbell exercises over his productions, we will mention a fact within our knowledge, concerning his Battle of the Baltic. This ode, as published, consists but of five stanzas; these were all that his scrupulous taste permitted him to cull out of a large number, which we have seen in manuscript. The rest, though full of poetic fire and imagery, were timidly consigned by him to oblivion.

But though this scrupulous spirit of revision may chance to refine away some of the bold touches of his pencil, and to injure some of its negligent graces, it is not without its eminent advantages. While it tends to produce a terseness of language, and a remarkable delicacy and sweetness of versification, it enables him likewise to impart to his productions a vigorous conciseness of style, a graphical correctness of imagery, and a philosophical condensation of idea, rarely found in the popular poets of the day. Facility of writing seems to be the bane of many modern poets; who too generally indulge in a ready and abundant versification, which, like a flowering vine, overruns their subject, and expands through many a weedy page. In fact, most of them seem to have mistaken carelessness for ease, and redundance for luxuriance: they never take pains to condense and invigorate. Hence we have those profuse and loosely-written poems, wherein the writers, either too feeble or too careless to seize at once upon their subject, prefer giving it a chase, and hunt it through a labyrinth of verses, until it is fairly run down and overpowered by a multitude of words.

Great, therefore, as are the intrinsic merits of Mr. Campbell, we are led to estimate them the more highly when we consider them as beaming forth, like the pure lights of heaven, among the meteor exhalations and false fires with which our literary atmosphere abounds. In an age when we are overwhelmed by an abundance of eccentric poetry, and when we are confounded by a host of ingenious poets of vitiated tastes and frantic fancies, it is really cheering and consolatory to behold a writer of Mr. Campbell's genius, studiously attentive to please, according to the established laws of criticism, as all our good old orthodox writers have pleased before; without setting up a standard, and endeavouring to establish a new sect, and inculcate some new and lawless doctrine of his own.

Before concluding this sketch, we cannot help pointing to one circumstance, which we confess has awakened a feeling of good will toward Mr. Campbell; though in mentioning it we shall do little more, perhaps, than betray our own national egotism. He is, we believe, the only British poet of eminence that has laid the story of a considerable poem, in the bosom of our country. We allude to his Gertrude of Wyoming, which describes the pastoral simplicity and innocence, and the subsequent woes of one of our little patriarchal hamlets, during the troubles of our revolution.

We have so long been accustomed to experience little else than contumely, misrepresentation, and very witless ridicule, from the British press; and we have had such repeated proofs of the extreme ignorance and absurd errors that prevail in Great Britain respecting our country and its inhabitants, that, we confess, we were both surprised and grati-fied to meet with a poet, sufficiently unprejudiced to conceive an idea of moral excellence and natural beauty on this side of the Atlantic. Indeed, even this simple show of liberality has drawn on the poet the censures of many narrow-minded writers, with whom liberality to this country is a crime. We are sorry to see such pitiful manifestations of hostility toward us. Indeed, we must say, that we consider the constant acrimony and traduction indulged in by the British press toward this country, to be as opposite to the interest, as it is derogatory to the candour and magnanimity of the nation. It is operating to widen the difference between two nations, which, if left to the impulse of their own feelings, would naturally grow together, and among the sad changes of this disastrous world, be mutual supports and comforts to each other.

Whatever may be the occasional collisions of etiquette and interest which will inevitably take place between two great commercial nations, whose property and people are spread far and wide on the face of the ocean; whatever may be the clamorous expressions of hostility vented at such times by our unreflecting populace, or rather uttered in their name by a host of hireling scribblers, who pretend to speak the senti-ments of the people; it is certain, that the well-educated and well-informed class of our citizens entertain a deep-rooted good will, and a rational esteem, for Great Britain. It is almost impossible it should be otherwise. Independent of those hereditary affections, which spring up spontaneously for the nation from whence we have descended, the single circumstance of imbibing our ideas from the same authors has a powerful effect in causing an attachment.

The writers of Great Britain are the adopted citizens of our country, and, though they have no legislative voice, exercise an authority over our opinions and affections, cherished by long habit and matured by affection. In these works we have British valour, British magnanimity, British might, and British wisdom, continually before our eyes, por-trayed in the most captivating colours; and are thus brought up in con-stant contemplation of all that is amiable and illustrious in the British character. To these works, likewise, we resort, in every varying mood of mind, or vicissitude of fortune. They are our delight in the hour of re-laxation; the solemn monitors and instructors of our closet; our com-forters in the gloomy seclusions of life-loathing despondency. In the season of early life, in the strength of manhood, and still in the weakness and apathy of age, it is to them we are indebted for our hours of refined and unalloyed enjoyment. When we turn our eyes to England, therefore, from whence this bounteous tide of literature pours in upon us, it is with such feelings as the Egyptian experiences, when he looks toward the sacred source of that stream, which, rising in a far distant country, flows down upon his own barren soil, diffusing riches, beauty, and fertility.*

Surely it cannot be the interest of Great Britain to trifle with such feelings. Surely the good will, thus cherished among the best hearts of a country, rapidly increasing in power and importance, is of too much consequence to be scornfully neglected or surlily dashed away. It most certainly, therefore, would be both politic and honourable, for those enlightened British writers, who sway the sceptre of criticism, to expose these constant misrepresentations, and discountenance these galling and unworthy insults of the pen, whose effect is to mislead and to irritate, without serving one valuable purpose. They engender gross prejudices in Great Britain, inimical to a proper national understanding, while with us they wither all those feelings of kindness and consanguinity, that were shooting forth, like so many tendrils, to attach to us our parent country.

While, therefore, we regard the poem of Mr. Campbell with complacency, as evincing an opposite spirit to this, of which we have just complained, there are other reasons, likewise, which interest us in its favour. Among the lesser evils, incident to the infant state of our country, we have to lament its almost total deficiency in those local associations produced by history and moral fiction. These may appear trivial to the common mass of readers; but the mind of taste and sensibility will at once acknowledge them as constituting a great source of national pride and love of country. There is an inexpressible charm imparted to every place that has been celebrated by the historian, or immortalized by the poet; a charm that dignifies it in the eyes of the stranger, and endears it to the heart of the native. Of this romantic attraction we are almost entirely destitute. While every insignificant hill and turbid stream in classic Europe has been hallowed by the visitations of the Muse, and

---

* Since this biographical notice was first published, the political relations between the two countries have been changed by a war with Great Britain. The above observations, therefore, may not be palatable to those who are eager for the hostility of the pen as well as the sword. The author, indeed, was for some time in doubt whether to expunge them, as he could not prevail on himself to accommodate them to the embittered temper of the times. He determined, however, to let them remain. However the feelings he has expressed may be outraged or prostrated by the violence of warfare, they never can be totally eradicated. Besides, it should be the exalted ministry of literature to keep together the family of human nature; to calm with her "soul-subduing voice" the furious passions of warfare, and thus to bind up those ligaments which the sword would cleave asunder. The author may be remiss in the active exercise of this duty, but he will never have to reproach himself, that he has attempted to poison, with political virulence, the pure fountains of elegant literature.

contemplated with fond enthusiasm; our lofty mountains and stupendous cataracts awaken no poetical associations, and our majestic rivers roll their waters unheeded, because unsung.

Thus circumstanced, the sweet strains of Mr. Campbell's muse break upon us as gladly as would the pastoral pipe of the shepherd, amid the savage solitude of one of our trackless wildernesses. We are delighted to witness the air of captivating romance and rural beauty our native fields and wild woods can assume under the plastic pencil of a master; and while wandering with the poet among the shady groves of Wyoming, or along the banks of the Susquehanna, almost fancy ourselves transported to the side of some classic stream, in the "hollow breast of Appenine." This may assist to convince many, who were before slow to believe, that our own country is capable of inspiring the highest poetic feelings, and furnishing abundance of poetic imagery, though destitute of the hackneyed materials of poetry; though its groves are not vocal with the song of the nightingale; though no Naïads have ever sported in its streams, nor Satyrs and Dryads gamboled among its forests. Wherever nature—sweet nature—displays herself in simple beauty or wild magnificence, and where-ever the human mind appears in new and striking situations, neither the poet nor the philosopher can ever want subjects worthy of his genius.

Having made such particular mention of Gertrude of Wyoming, we will barely add one or two circumstances connected with it, strongly illustrative of the literary character of the author. The story of the poem, though extremely simple, is not sufficiently developed; some of the facts, particularly in the first part, are rapidly passed over, and left rather obscure; from which many have inconsiderately pronounced the whole a hasty sketch, without perceiving the elaborate delicacy with which the parts are finished. This defect is to be attributed entirely to the self-diffidence of Mr. Campbell. It is his misfortune that he is too distrustful of himself; and too ready to listen to the opinions of inferior minds, rather than boldly to follow the dictates of his own pure taste and the impulses of his exalted imagination, which, if left to themselves, would never falter or go wrong. Thus we are told, that when his Gertrude first came from under his pen, it was full and complete; but in an evil hour he read it to some of his critical friends. Every one knows that when a man's critical judgment is consulted, he feels himself in credit bound to find fault. Various parts of the poem were of course objected to, and various alterations recommended.

With a fatal diffidence, which, while we admire we cannot but lament, Mr. Campbell struck out those parts entirely; and obliterated, in a moment, the fruit of hours of inspiration and days of labour. But when he attempted to bind together and new model the elegant, but mangled, limbs of this virgin poem, his shy imagination revolted from the task.

The glow of feeling was chilled, the creative powers of invention were exhausted; the parts, therefore, were slightly and imperfectly thrown together, with a spiritless pen, and hence arose that apparent want of development which occurs in some parts of the story.

Indeed, we do not think the unobtrusive, and, if we may be allowed the word, occult merits of this poem are calculated to strike popular attention, during the present passion for dashing verse and extravagant incident. It is mortifying to an author to observe, that those accomplishments which it has cost him the greatest pains to acquire, and which he regards with a proud eye, as the exquisite proofs of his skill, are totally lost upon the generality of readers; who are commonly captivated by those glaring qualities to which he attaches but little value. Most people are judges of exhibitions of force and activity of body, but it requires a certain refinement of taste and a practised eye, to estimate that gracefulness which is the achievement of labour, and consummation of art. So, in writing, whatever is bold, glowing, and garish, strikes the attention of the most careless, and is generally felt and acknowledged; but comparatively few can appreciate that modest delineation of nature, that tenderness of sentiment, propriety of language, and gracefulness of composition, that bespeak the polished and accomplished writer. Such, however, as possess this delicacy of taste and feeling, will often return to dwell, with cherishing fondness, on the Gertrude of Mr. Campbell. Like all his other writings, it presents virtue in its most touching and captivating forms: whether gently exercised in the "bosom scenes of life," or sublimely exerted in its extraordinary and turbulent situations. No writer can surpass Mr. Campbell in the vestal purity and amiable morality of his muse. While he possesses the power of firing the imagination, and filling it with sublime and awful images, he excels also in those eloquent appeals to the feelings, and those elevated flights of thought, by which, while the fancy is exalted, the heart is made better.

It is now some time since he has produced any poem. Of late he has been employed in preparing a work for the press, containing critical and biographical notices of British poets from the reign of Edward III. to the present time. However much we may be gratified by such a work, from so competent a judge, still we cannot but regret that he should stoop from the brilliant track of poetic invention, in which he is so well calculated to soar, and descend into the lower regions of literature to mingle with droning critics and mousing commentators. His task should be to produce poetry, not to criticise it; for, in our minds, he does more for his own fame, and for the interests of literature, who furnishes one fine verse, than he who points out a thousand beauties, or detects a thousand faults.

We hope, therefore, soon to behold Mr. Campbell emerging from those dusty labours, and breaking forth in the full lustre of original genius. He owes it to his own reputation; he owes it to his own talents; he owes it to the literature of his country. Poetry has generally flowed in an abundant stream in Great Britain; but it is too apt to stray among rocks and weeds, to expand into brawling shallows, or waste itself in turbid and ungovernable torrents. We have, however, marked a narrow, but pure and steady, channel, continuing down from the earliest ages, through a line of real poets, who seem to have been sent from heaven to keep the vagrant stream from running at utter waste and random. Of this chosen number we consider Mr. Campbell; and we are happy at having this opportunity of rendering our feeble tribute of applause to a writer whom we consider an ornament to the age, an honour to his country, and one whom his country "should delight to honour."

Washington Irving, 1809

An engraving by John de Mare from a portrait by John Wesley Jarvis.

[1803]

[LINES WRITTEN IN "THE TEMPLE OF DIRT"]

Here Sovereign Dirt erects her sable throne,
The house, the host, the hostess all her own.

[1805]

[VERSES WRITTEN ON THE LAKE OF LUCERNE]

Upon the placid bosom of the Lake
    I lie and sweetly dream the Hours away.
    Anon a Vision of approaching Day
Strikes on my Lids, and I awake
    To find 'tis but the Glimmering Ray
Of the false dawn: And I again partake
Of the Lethean Waters of the Lake,
    And sleep and dream throughout this night of May.
    Tomorrow must I up and to the Plow
    With Aching Back and labored sweating Brow,
In the Vineyard and Garden of the Lord to take
    My Place: But tonight I dream and sleep
And gently sigh, and drink long draughts and Deep
Of the Lethean Waters of the Lake.

[1806]

PASSAIC—A TRADITION

In a wild tranquil vale fringed with forests of green
Where nature had fashion'd a soft sylvan scene
The retreat of the ring dove, the haunt of the deer
Passaic in silence roll'd gentle and clear.

No grandeur of prospect astonished the sight
No abruptness sublime mingled awe with delight
Here the wild flowret blossom'd the elm proudly waved
And pure was the current the green bank that laved.

But the spirit that ruled o'er the thick tangled wood
And deep in its gloom fix'd his murky abode

149

Who lov'd the rude scene that the whirlwind deforms
And gloried in tempest and lightning and storms,

All flush'd from the tumult of battle he came
Where the red men encounter'd the children of flame
While the noise of the war whoop still rung in his ears
And the fresh bleeding scalp as a trophy he wears.

Oh deep was the horror and fierce was the fight
When the eyes of the red men were shrouded in night
When by strangers invaded, by strangers destroyed
They ensanguined the fields which their fathers enjoyed.

So the sons of the forest in terror retire
Pale savages chase them with thunder and fire
In vain whirls the war club, in vain twangs the bow
By thunder and fire are his warriors laid low.

From defeat and from carnage the fierce spirit came
His breast was a tumult—his passions were flame
Despair swells his heart, fury maddens his ire
And black scowls his brow o'er his eyeballs of fire.

With a glance of disgust he the landscape survey'd
With its fragrant wild flowrets its wide waving shade
Where Passaic meander'd through margins of green
So transparent its waters—its surface serene.

He rived the green hills, the wild woods he laid low
He turned the pure stream in rough channels to flow
He rent the rude rock the steep precipice gave
And hurl'd down the chasm the loud thundering wave.

A scene of strange ruin he scatter'd around
Where cliffs piled on cliffs in rude majesty frown'd
Where shades of thick horror embrown'd the dark wood
And the rainbow and mist marked the turbulent flood.

Countless moons have since roll'd in the long lapse of time
Cultivation has softened those features sublime,
The axe of the white man enlivened the shade
And dispell'd the deep gloom of the thicketed glade.

Yet the stranger still gazes with wondering eye
On rocks rudely torn and groves mounted on high

Still loves on the cliff's dizzy border to roam
Where the torrent leaps headlong embosomed in foam.

May 26th—1806.

[1806–1807]

ADDRESS OF COOPER ON ASSUMING THE MANAGEMENT
OF THE PARK THEATRE

In drowsy days of yore—those stupid times
Ere fashion sanctioned follies—varnished crimes;
When neither rigid laws nor cynic rules
Could check the increase of knaves—the growth of fools—
Old Thespis then, a shrewd, though laughing sage
Fell on a merry plan to cure the age,
Held up a polished mirror to their faces,
Shewed guilt his scowl—folly her queer grimaces.
Both shrunk ashamed their hideous forms to view,
And from the arch reproof a lesson drew.
This magic glass we have—but when we shew it
'Tis to amuse the curious throng who view it.
'Twere rude to hint in these enlightened days
The polished world could aught demand but praise.
Yet should some straggling vices lurk behind,—
We do not hold a mirror to the blind.
For your amusement on its surface clear,
We bid the Drama's varied train appear.

See, wrapped in brooding sorrow, Hamlet move—
The glare of courts he shuns—the joys of love—
Holds dread communion with the opening tomb,
And, shuddering, learns his sire's mysterious doom.
On fate's drear verge in awful thought revolves
The fearful plunge—half doubts and half resolves,
Yet pausing, fears to pass the gloomy bourne
Of that dark realm whence travellers ne'er return.

Here may the lover learn how sure and strong
The potent passion bears its course along.
What jealous doubts perplex Othello's brain—
What transports throb in youthful Romeo's vein.

Lo! mad Octavian shuns with sullen pride
The hated sun, in cavern glooms to hide—
Now calls to mind the days when fortune smiled,
And love, and hope, and joy his youth beguiled,
Then spurns the golden vision, welcomes care,
On sorrow gluts and banquets on despair.

Nor shall young lovers only here discern
Congenial souls, and useful lessons learn.
Here may our touchy sparks, who dare resistance
"And hold their honors at a wary distance,"
From ancient Pistol learn the valiant stride,
The frown ferocious secret fears to hide,
And when with furious air he eats the leek
The art to bluster, and with strut—to sneak.

"Plague on all cowards still," cries Mammoth Jack;
"Marry and amen—Bardolph, a cup of sack—"
Puffs under forty stone of solid mirth,
And, as he waddles, lards the trembling earth.

But would you mark how beams the mental ray,
How warms and animates the lifeless clay,
Note Leon's idiot speech and vacant stare,
His smile, and bashful look, and awkward air;
Then see this simplest of the idiot kind
Step forth in all the majesty of mind;
Assert himself, the husband's rights maintain,
And brave the power that would his honor stain.

Sometimes a harsher picture stands displayed
Where Brutus sternly waves the patriot blade
And Julius falls; or where our scenes disclose
The secret pangs that cursed ambition knows;
See fell Macbeth with Tarquin's stealthy stride
And cautious glance to Duncan's chamber glide,
Yet startled pause, while guilt unnerves his force,
To mark the air-drawn dagger's fatal course.

Success may crown ambition's daring blow,
The diadem may press the guilty brow,
Yet not the courtly buzz of regal state,
Where crowds of bowing lords obsequious wait,

Nor hosts of guards can chase those fiends away
That haunt his dreams by night, his thoughts by day.

What terrors agonize the tyrant's heart!
See from his couch the bloody Richard start!
Guilt breaks his slumbers, fear his sense confounds,
"Another horse!" he cries, "bind up my wounds!
Have mercy! Heaven—soft—'twas but a dream;"
Yet down his limbs cold drops of horror stream.

O, who that sees alarmed conscience roll
Her tide of terrors o'er the guilty soul,
But draws a lesson from the scene sublime,
Detests the culprit and abhors the crime.

Yet why thus bid dramatic phantoms pass
Like shadowy monarchs seen in Banquo's glass?
Vanish each tragic sprite—each comic elf,
And let the manager enact himself.
While hopes invite and anxious doubts assail
I've launched my bark and hope a favoring gale.
Why should I fear? When round I cast my eye,
I see a friendly shore, a cloudless sky.
(*Box.*—) A tranquil deep which every doubt beguiles,
A horizon of beauty, dressed in smiles.
And sure those smiles which cheered my former terrors,
Which beamed indulgence on my early errors,
Will not withdraw; nor censure's waves overwhelm
Our feeble vessel, now *I hold the helm*.

Some, too, I see—I speak with grateful pride—
Whose generous favor knows no ebbing tide;
In every changeful season still the same,
Still prompt to aid—to prize my humble name.
Friends whom my heart, with honest warmth, would greet,
And still shall honor, while its pulses beat.

(*Pit.*—) But lo! the critic tribe, a sapient band
Who full before me take their watchful stand;
Sages self-dubbed, who deign to teach the town
When to look pleased, or glum, to smile, or frown.

A precious set ye are—of motley hue,
Some arrant grumblers, faith, a crusty crew,—

Who blame in gross, in trivial points commend,
And often coin the fault you reprehend.
Some merry wags, who strike a careless stroke,
And crack an actor's crown to crack a joke.—
How shall I win your favor, asks a pause—
To your own humors I commit my cause.

(*Gallery.*—) Ye whose *high* wrath in rumbling thunder rolls
To fright lords', senators', and warriors' souls,
Distilled almost to jelly with their fears,
While your descending censures storm their ears;
Your right assumptive none shall dare disprove
To hoot when groves, chairs, tables *wrongly* move.
Shifters of scenes no more shall act amiss
Nor jumbling seas with towns provoke your hiss;
Musicians dread your ever ready hands,
And *John* shall *make his bow* at your commands.

But hold! the anchor's weighed, the sail's unfurled,
And sink or swim, we try the billowy world.
No time is left for prayers to wind or wave,
But *skill* must try the slender bark to save;
Then rouse, my steadfast soul. "Blow wind, come wrack,
At least, I'll die with harness on my back."

[1810]

SONG

Oh, turn, cruel fair one! nor slight a fond youth
Who would woo thee with tenderness, fervor and truth!
Tho' my fortune's but small, yet stern want I'm above,
And I'll swear that no swain is *more wealthy in love!*

In a shady, white cottage, embosom'd in trees,
Where boughs, lightly waving, invite the cool breeze,
My empire I've fixed,—and full green is my bower,
And pure is the wild brook that runs by my door.

Oh! there let me lead thee! for there shalt thou reign,
The cottage thy palace, the grove thy domain;
With a chaplet of roses and myrtle so green
I'll encircle thy brows, and proclaim thee my queen!—

A green bank shall form thy imperial seat;
And the fruits of each autumn I'll lay at thy feet;
Or on beds of sweet violets shalt thou recline;
And the tributes of spring shall thy temples entwine.

What queen could e'er boast of a tribute so fair?
Of a throne so serene? of a palace so rare?
Could reign more secure, and unrivall'd than thee?
Or could boast of a subject more faithful than me?

New York, Oct. 1810.

[1810?]

SIGNS OF THE TIMES

As Morris once stroll'd into Trinity Church,
He quickly discovered he'd got in a lurch;
For as soon as the minister eyes on him set,
"S'blood, Morris," says he, "but I'll give you a sweat."
　　　　　　　　　Down, down, down, Derry Down!

"This scapegrace, my breth'ren, who keeps such late hours,
And Broadway from the Park to the Battery scours,
Must not fancy, from me, he his wickedness hides,
Since they know up aloft when he frolics at Dyde's."—
　　　　　　　　　Down, down, down, Derry Down!

Then he talk'd very much 'bout the "SIGNS of *the Times*,"
And that *pulling them down*, was the vilest of crimes!
He that *pulls down a sign* should be laid fast in fetters,
Since 'tis plain that he hastens—*the downfall of letters!*
　　　　　　　　　Down, down, down, Derry Down!

In defense, Morris urg'd—tho' he frolick'd at night,
Yet, according to Scripture, he acted but right;
For *at night* he improved his time like the devil,
As very well knowing "the days," sir, "are evil."
　　　　　　　　　Down, down, down, Derry Down!

With respect to the sign, no defense need be made—
As he wish'd but to give *Mr. Cheesbrough* his trade—

So not caring just then the good folks to arouse—
He wisely *took down*, sir, *the name of the house!*
                    Down, down, down, Derry Down!

Far be it from him, sir, the peace to molest—
He meant, on the contrary, all for the best:—
And tho' he had shoulder'd the sign in his fun,
He was sure he had given *the firm a good run!*
                    Down, down, down, Derry Down!

[March 2, 1833]

[LINES WRITTEN AT STRATFORD]

Of Mighty Shakespeare's birth the room we see,
    That where he died in vain to find we try,
Useless the search:—for all Immortal He
And those who are Immortal never die.

Washington Irving.

Second visit. October 1821.

[1822]

WRITTEN IN THE DEEPDENE ALBUM

Thou record of the votive throng,
    That fondly seek this fairy shrine,
And pay the tribute of a song
    Where worth and loveliness combine,—

What boots that I, a vagrant wight
    From clime to clime still wandering on,
Upon thy friendly page should write
    —Who'll think of me when I am gone?

Go plow the wave, and sow the sand;
    Throw seed to every wind that blows;
Along the highway strew thy hand,
    And fatten on the crop that grows.

For even thus the man that roams
    On heedless hearts his feeling spends;

Strange tenant of a thousand homes,
   And friendless, with ten thousand friends!

Yet here, for once, I'll leave a trace,
   To ask in aftertimes a thought;
To say that here a resting-place
   My wayworn heart has fondly sought.

So the poor pilgrim heedless strays,
   Unmoved, through many a region fair;
But at some shrine his tribute pays,
   To tell that he has worshipped there.

WASHINGTON IRVING.

June 24th, 1822.

[1823]

TO MISS EMILY FOSTER ON HER BIRTH-DAY

'Twas now the freshness of the year
   When fields were green and groves were gay,
When airs were soft and skies were clear,
   And all things bloomed in lovely May—

Blest month, when nature in her prime
   Bestows her fairest gifts on earth—
This was the time, the genial time,
   She destined for her favorite's birth.

And emblems delicate she chose,
   Thy gentle virtues to bespeak—
The lily and the pale, pale rose
   She faintly mingled in thy cheek.

The azure of her noontide sky
   With dewy gleams of morn combining,
She took to form thy speaking eye
   With heaven's own blue serenely shining.

She bade the dawning's transient blush,
   The light and warmth of day revealing,

At times thy pallid beauty flush
    With sudden glows of thought and feeling.

But oh! the innate worth refined
    She treasured in thy gentle breast;
The generous gifts of heart and mind,
    They best can tell who know thee best.

Bloom on—bloom on—frank nature's child,
    Her favorite flower, her spotless one,
Still may she keep thee pure, unsoiled,
    Still fresh, though ever shone upon.

[1827]

THE DULL LECTURE

FRONTISPIECE.

Frostie age, frostie age!
Vaine all thy learning.
Drowsie page, drowsie page,
Ever more turning.

Younge heade no lore will heede,
Younge heart's a recklesse rover,
Younge beautie while you reade,
Sleeping dreames of absent lover.

[1830]

[¡AY DIOS DE MI ALMA!]

¡Ay Dios de mi alma!
Saqueisme de aquí,
¡Ay! que Inglaterra
Ya no es para mí.

¡Ay Dios de alta parte
La mejor del suelo,
Con quien se reparte
Gran parte del cielo!

Mira el desconsuelo,
Que yo paso aquí,
¡Ay! que Inglaterra
Ya no es para mí.

¡Ay Dios! que pecados
He yo cometido,
Que tan bien pagados
Y tan presto han sido;
Mas he merecido,
Pues que me partí
¡Ay! que Inglaterra
Ya no es para mí.

¡Ay, ay! que mi mal
Con mil males viene,
Es pena infernal
Que ningun fin tiene
Morir me conviene,
Pues grosero fuí:
¡Ay! que Inglaterra
Ya no es para mí.

Que el seso no pierda
Ningun hombre habrá,
Del bien que se acuerda
Y el mal en que está;
¡Ay Dios! baste ya
Saqueisme de aquí;
¡Ay! que Inglaterra
Ya no es para mí.

Washington Irving
London. Sept. 9th 1830.

[1855]

THE LAY OF THE SUNNYSIDE DUCKS.
HUMBLY DEDICATED TO
MISS FLORENCE JAFFRAY

By Sunnyside bower runs a little Indian brook,
    As wild as wild can be;

It flows down from hills where Indians lived of old,
   To the mighty Tappan Sea.

And this little brook supplies a goodly little pond
   Where the Sunnyside ducks do play;
Snowy white little ducks, with top knots on their heads,
   And merry little ducks are they.

And high up the hill stands fair Jaffray Hall,
   Where a mighty chief doth dwell;
And this little Indian brook flows through his lands
   And its own little rugged dell.

But the laird of Jaffray rose in his might,
   And he said to his wife, one day,
This little Indian brook is an idle little brook,
   And shall no longer have its way.

No longer shall it run down to Sunnyside pond
   Nor eke to the Tappan Sea.
I'll stop it with a dam and pump it up hill with a ram,
   And make it work for a living, said he.

It shall run in pipes about our garden and lawn
   Making jets and fountains clear,
It shall run up stairs and downstairs of Jaffray Hall
   And into your bathroom—my dear.

Then the Sunnyside ducks they quaked* with fear,
   And dolefully they did cry,
Oh laird of Jaffray spare our little brook
   Or we shall be left high and dry!

But soon it appeared that this brave little brook
   Defied the laird of Jaffray's skill;
For though he dammed the little brook and rammed
    the little brook,
   The little brook still ran down hill.

Then the Sunnyside ducks again plucked up heart
   And got over their quanda—*ry*
And the little brook still runs down to Sunnyside pond,
   And the mighty Tappan Sea.

* Qu: quacked?

Washington Irving, 1820

An engraving from a portrait by Gilbert Stuart Newton.

[THE FREYSCHÜTZ]

Act 1. Scene 1.

Enter Hunters &c.

All. Huzza—huzza! it's down! Andreas forever—
Huzza for the King of Sharpshooters!

Albert. Confusion! vanquished again, and by that braggart Andreas.
(*Strikes his forehead*)

Andreas comes forward with a swaggering air, followed by the crowd.

Chorus. Victoria &c

Albert. Am I then blind? or has this arm lost all its steadiness? Sure—
sure I never took a better aim—and yet continually to miss—
(*Rises & crosses the stage &c*)

Procession—& March
Song. Andreas.

Look at me and know your King Sir,
I'm the Lad a bird to wing Sir
Doff your hat, man, 'tis the law
Tell me, will you? ha! ha! ha!

Star on breast and plume in bonnet,
I'm the lad that shot and won it,
Doff your hat then 'tis the law—
What have you won?—ha! ha! ha!

Mighty sir, excuse one joking,
Ne'er to hit is quite provoking
You, who hit whate'er you saw
Quite chapfallen—ha! ha! ha!

or this

Mighty Sir, excuse our grinning
You're the lad, were sure of winning

163

Never miss'd whate'er you saw
Never? tell me—ha! ha! ha!

Albert. (*Springing up & seizing Andreas by the collar*) This is not to be endured—do you dare then to insult me Sirrah.

Andreas. 'Sblood man stand off—Can't ye take a joke and be hang'd to ye—
(*Scuffle & tumult of the hunters peasants &c*)

Christopher. (*Scrambling out of the affray*) To it boys—to it boys—support the King—support the King of the Sharpshooters!

Enter Conrad & Hunters

Conrad. Hey! what's all this—what thirty upon one, for shame—for shame—Ah you're here Master Andreas are you? Ah then it's no wonder—Wherever you are there's sure to be uproar & mischief—But Albert too—what does this mean?

Christopher. Nothing but sport Sir—nothing but sport—all in good humour—The lads have been shooting at the Target, for the yearly prize—Andreas has won so we are greeting him as King for the Year, according to custom—and as Albert has missed every time—why according to custom we were joking him a little, you know—but all in good humour—all in good humour!—

Andreas. Yes—but some people can't take a joke, that's all—some people can't bear being cut out, that's all—plague on't where's the use of getting into a passion? I don't get into a passion—

Christopher. Not when you win—that's pretty clear—

Andreas. And then if one is a better marksman—where's the use of quarrelling with him about it? I can't help it if I am a better shot—that's all—(*consequentially*)

Conrad. What do I hear? Who has missed every shot? Not Albert surely—What and surpassed by Andreas; it cannot be!

Andreas. May be not—may be not—may be one cannot shoot at all—May be one cannot hit a mark—ask him yourself—that's all—ask him yourself—but don't joke, or you'll put the gentleman in a passion that's all—

Conrad. Why Albert, is this true?

Albert. It is indeed too true. I have been continually unsuccessful—

Caspar. (*Aside*) Urian has kept his word! the magic spell acts bravely.

Conrad. Can it be possible—what, you, the surest marksman of the Forest thus to fail—But now I bethink me—you have not sent a single head of game to the Forest House for many days—what means this sudden change?

Albert. Indeed I know not—it seems as if all skill had left me—I feel cast down—disheartened—

Christopher. 'Ods blood Master Albert the case is plain—thou'rt spell bound. Some one has been practising witchcraft on thee—thou'rt spell bound as sure as thou'rt alive—

Conrad. A truce good Christopher to all such nonsense—

Christopher. Nonsense—Nay—nay—Master Grand Forester, there's more truth in these matters than you think for. My good old Grandmother who lived all her life in these forests, has told me many a story about the spells that used to be laid upon hunters to make them miss their aim—and then who has not heard of the Wild Huntsman?

Several Peasants. Ah—the Wild Huntsman! what of him?

Christopher. Hush—whisht—be quiet can't ye—is this a time and place to be gabbling so loud about him? Who knows but he is at your elbow this very moment?

Huntsman. But what of him good Christopher? I know you have a thousand stories to tell about him.

Christopher. But I'm in no story telling mood look ye—or I might tell you how I have heard him scowring through the woods like a storm at midnight—and clattering along in the air, with whoop & hound & horn—Well—well—be he what he may—goblin or wizard—they say he casts spells upon all that displease him, and gives magic balls to his favorites—

Hunter. Magic Balls—what are they?

Christopher. Why, balls that never miss the mark be it ever so far off—but then they say he always gives one ball that flies where he pleases & does mischief.

Caspar. Old wives' gossip! the slanders of bad marksmen, with which they seek to decry the skill of their betters—a quick eye & a steady arm—that's your only witchcraft.

Conrad. Enough of all this prattle—but hearken my good Albert. This sudden loss of skill distresses me. Recollect, tomorrow you shoot before the Duke for the place of Ranger of the Forest. I have staked my judgement on your success—Nay more in my confidence in your skill I have consented that your marriage with my daughter should immediately follow—Have a care then Albert. Remember that I hold a place which from earliest days has been hereditary in my family. I never can give my daughter's hand to any but the man who is to follow me in office. Tomorrow will determine whether or not you are that man. Should you fail tomorrow—think it not hard—but it is impossible the marriage should take place—

Albert. Tomorrow! Tomorrow—Is then my fortune—my love, my happiness all cast upon one chance—and I so luckless?

Conrad. I feel for you my son—would I had not been so confident—would that we could put the trial off, until this singular spell of ill fortune were past. But the Duke is punctilious and would think

we trifled with him—(*encouraging with cheery manner*) Rouse thee
then, Albert, shake off this heartless desponding mood, which is the
whole cause of thy ill luck—Rouse thee & be thyself, and the event
is certain!—And now Brother Huntsmen, remember—the place of
rendezvous for tomorrow's hunt is in the meadow by the mill—His
Grace will be there by sunrise—we'll show him sport I'll warrant
& make the forest echo with the music of our horns.

Chorus.

Conrad.   Now let's away—Albert—we'll go together—come be of good
heart man—Courage & success go hand in hand. (*Exeunt Conrad
& Albert*)
Peasant.   A worthy gentleman as ever breathed is our Grand Forester—
Christopher.   Why—yes—a worthy kind of dry virtuous man—but I
don't altogether relish your men of dry virtue—they're bad customers
to us publicans—give me a moist spongy old age—that soaks up
good liquor by the flaggon—that's the kind of virtue to thrive by—
Marian.   Oh Father, but then the Grand Forester's daughter, Miss
Bertha—what an angel she is—so kind, and affable—and so fond of
Mr. Albert too—
Caspar.   Aye—there's some of that witchcraft that your father prated
about—for sure the girl's bewitched to dote on such a spark as
Albert—a smooth tongued Sir, that takes the lead of all the stout
lads of the forest, and yet when it comes to the test cannot hit a
target.
Hunter.   Come Come Master Caspar, there's not a worthier fellow in all
Bohemia—he is a favorite with us all: and till lately he was the
very best of marksmen. Why he has failed heaven only knows—
Caspar.   (*aside*) I might give a reason for that too perhaps—
A Peasant Girl.   But we all know why Caspar is no friend of Albert—
Marian.   Oh yes, 'twas because Bertha rejected you for Albert, Caspar!
We've noticed that you've borne him a grudge ever since—
Caspar.   Pish—out on your nonsense! (*aside with bitterness*) Must I
be constantly thus stung with sneers, twitted with woman's taunts?
Sure of all nettles thorns & thistles there is no curse on earth so
teasing to the soul as woman's tongue.
                              (*exit into the Inn*)
Andreas.   (*comes bustling forward*) Come no more of this snapping &
wrangling—what the deuce, am I to have nothing but brawling on
the day of my coming to the Crown? Come Lads & lasses—I'm king
of the year and egad we'll have a merry reign of it, so strike up
music, every man to his partner, and hey for a dance to round all
off cheerily—

Dance—&c—

Exeunt

Enter Caspar from the Inn

Are they then gone? So—my spirit is free again. Curse on their piping & their dancing—their shallow, broad mouthed merriment— Ever more music—ever more frolick—as if 'twere done to mad me. And I must go about with evil luck, but fretting festering heart, a cursed being in a happy world—a lost one—a hopeless crawler upon earth—No matter, still I *am* on earth—Still still I breathe this cooling air of heaven—better be here however bad than *elsewhere*. But how to keep here that's the question—This very night my term of compact ends, and ere tomorrow's sun, this unknown being claims me for his own, unless I soothe him with another votary. Strange magic bond in which I have involved myself! Little did that dotard think when prating about magic spells, how near he touched upon the truth. The Wild Huntsman! inexplicable being! Still he has kept his word, and Albert spell bound by his arts is driven to despair. Thus far my project thrives. Yes yes. Albert is in the very state of mind that suits my purpose—now to work on him, to tempt him to the scene of incantation and throw him into the Wild Huntsman's power. But should he shun the snare! Some other victim must be had—no time is to be lost—why—a little wine and flattery will make an easy dupe of that poor — &c &c &c

Scene 2.

A room in the village Inn—a round table & chairs.
Andreas without—

Come, come along my boys. I tell you it's not too late—Odds blood, an't I King of the Sharpshooters—and Ranger of the Forest that is to be? (*Banging at the door—& forcing it open & swaggering into the room—*) Who dares to set up doors to keep out jolly fellows? 'Sblood when I'm Upper Forester as I mean to be in the fullness of time— we'll have no doors in the forest—

First Hunter. Enough good Andreas—come it's getting late—Old Christopher will give us no more wine—& we must be home—

Andreas. Enough—'Sblood man it's never enough while there's penny in pouch & bottle in cellar. 'Sblood an't I King of Sharpshooters? Mustn't I drink my rounds—and bring all the Inns in my dominion into proper order? Damme Sir I mean to rule by drinking and my court shall be composed of none but jolly red noses—Halloo! house! house! bottles! bottles! full bottles & be hanged to ye—

Second Hunter. Well, well—one bottle more Master Andreas—but it must be only one bottle—recollect how far we have to go—

Andreas. To go—who talks of going? Damme if any man shall go in my dominions—Every man shall be carried—House! house! bottles! bottles! I say—

Enter Marian.

What did you please to want Gentlemen?

Andreas. Want Gentlemen? No my dear we don't want Gentlemen but we have no objection to Ladies—So come my pretty Marian let's have a taste of your quality. (*kisses her*) Od's blood she smacks like her father's own wine—Aye & bounces too like a bottle of beer—Egad I must have another taste—(*She struggles*)

Marian. Let me alone—let me alone I say—you wild man of the woods!

(*Enter Christopher—*)

Christopher. Hoity toity—what's all this, who's making such a riot in the house?

Andreas. Who?—Why the King of Sharpshooters! Damme—going his rounds to taste all the old wine & young lips in the forest—

Christopher. What is it you Master Andreas?

Andreas. Me?—no it's not me—for they say I'm not myself today—but if I'm a man beside myself, why damme I must have double the quantity of wine—so bottles—bottles old Boy—

Christopher. Long life to you Master Andreas—You shall have wine as long as there is a bottle in my cellar—(*aside*) and a dollar in your pocket—

Andreas. And hark'ee old slabber chops—none of your damned thin cold Bohemian swampy stuff that lays a man's heart under water—but the juice of real old fiery Hungarian grapes; that kindles one up like touch wood—

Christopher. You shall have it—you shall have it Master Andreas—I know how to treat a good customer—There Marian—(*gives a key*) from the South side of the cellar—(*exit Marian*) Ah Master Andreas good luck to you—it did my heart good to see you carry off the prize today—I like to see jolly fellows succeed—it all comes of good drinking—there's nothing clears one's sight like good old wine—

First Hunter. Egad I never heard that before—

Christopher. It makes one see double at least—and that comes to the same thing I take it—

Andreas. 'Sblood—old Kit's right—and that's another reason for drinking hard tonight—that I may see better tomorrow—

(*enter Marian, with wine & glasses*)

So come bumpers—bumpers (*filling the glasses*) and here old Kit, you shall be my taster, to shew that there's no poison—

Christopher. (*Taking the glass—*) Ah bless your jolly heart—Well—
here's success to you tomorrow—

Hunters. (*take their glasses*)—Aye—Success to Andreas!

Andreas. Thank you my boys—Od's blood, if I become ranger we'll
have rare times on't—There [will] be a wet spell set in I'll warrant
you.

Christopher. Well I always wish success to good customers & jolly
drinkers—I've no idea of these steady fellows as they call men like
Albert—Their virtue is a pitiful dry quality and no friend to us
publicans—

Andreas. When I come to be upper forester, look you—as I mean to
be, now I've got my hand in—we'll have no virtuous men in these
parts—damme—None but jolly companions & hard drinkers—Come,
boys—a song—a song, in praise of jolly old wine—

Glee

(*—Enter Caspar during the chorus & stands on one side observing them
with malignant satisfaction*)

Caspar. Aye—here's my man—just in the proper vein too—flush'd to the
eyes with wine and vanity—Good evening comrades—I hope there's
no intrusion—you've drawn me hither by your merriment—for faith
you make the forest ring again—

Andreas. Ah Caspar! my cock of the woods. What at your old tricks—
owling in the dark? Come sit down here man—'Sblood you shall
drink scot & lot free, and for once be merry in honor of the King
of Sharpshooters!

Caspar. With all my heart, boy! think you I've no soul in me, because
I will not lend my company to all the riff raff of the forest? No—
give me boon companions like yourself—free hearted blades & lads
of pith & mettle and by the lord I'll drink with them till cock crow-
ing—

Andreas. Say you so? Why then you're my right hand man. Here's
Karl   and little Hans Handaside are talking of deserting me—
let 'em go, if they will—You & I'll too & too it together & 'sblood
we'll have a night of it—

Caspar. Agreed—and to begin I'll give you a toast—(*fills*) Here's
"Success to merry souls & sharpshooters"—

(*They all drink it*)

Andreas. Meaning me no doubt—thank ye—thank ye—'Sblood Land-
lord another bottle—(*Exit Christopher—*) This is amazing dry wine—
there's no keeping one's lips moist with it—

Hunter. And now comrade, before we go, let us have a parting song—

Come—that song you sung last night as we came thro the forest—
I dare say Caspar has never heard it—

Andreas.　What—my "Three joys of life"? You shall have it—Look you
Master Caspar I'm called a *Re-Raw* kind of a fellow—but I have
my creed, as this song will shew you—

Caspar.　I don't doubt it—and I like a random fellow that is irregular
according to method—So come—your three joys of life—

Song. Andreas.

(*After first Couplet they all applaud—*)

Caspar.　Aye—aye—all the ills of life vanish before the jolly god—So
come, I'll give you another toast (*fills round*)—"Here's to the heart
that fills as the bottle empties"—
They drink—

Andreas.　Meaning me, no doubt—thank ye—thank ye Caspar—'Sblood
who'd have thought you had been a lad of this mettle?

Caspar.　And now my boy at it again—I'll wager I guess your second
joy—or you're not the choice fellow I take ye for—
(*Andreas Sings second verse—*)

Caspar.　I was sure that would be it—Aye there's nothing after all like
the dear creatures, life's naught without 'em. Come I'll give you
another toast—"May the girl of your heart be as true as your rifle."
(*They drink*)

(*enter Marian with another Bottle*)

Andreas.　Thank ye, thank ye—Master Caspar—here's to the lasses—&
egad here's pretty Marian just in time to share the toast—(*Kisses
her, she resists*)—Old Kit, this daughter of yours is devilish hard on
the trigger & kicks like an old musket—

Christopher.　A young thing—a young thing—she'll know better by &
by—Go to girl—there's no harm now & then in a civil kiss—(*aside*)
from a good customer—(*exit Marian*)

Caspar.　Now Comrade, your third joy—
(*Andreas Sings—*)

Caspar.　A good finale, too—Women—wine—and play—give me your hand
Comrade—faith you are not merely the King of Sharpshooters—but
the King of good fellows into the bargain—

Christopher.　That's what he is—as my cellar can bear witness—and so
gentlemen with your leave I'll suggest to you one toast before you
break up—"May every Sharpshooter be able to pay his shot."

Andreas.　Out upon him! out upon him! a publican's toast! a publican's
toast! (*they drive him out in sport*)

First Hunter. Well comrade—it is getting late—'tis near eleven—We must be off—(*they rise*)

Caspar. What you will not leave us lads?

Second Hunter. We must—we have to be at the Hunting lodge early in the morning—The Duke will be on the ground soon after Sunrise.

Caspar. Well, ere you go—one round to the success of our friend here—and may tomorrow's trial make him Ranger of the Forest.

Hunters. With all our hearts—Success attend ye Andreas!
   (*exeunt—*)

Caspar. Oh never doubt—the place is his for certain—

Andreas. (*half drunk*) I'm not quite sure of that comrade, between ourselves—the more I drink it seems the more I doubt—this wine has potent reason in it—I begin to see clearly (*blinking a little*)—that fellow Albert's a devil of a marksman—

Caspar. And so are you—

Andreas. That's admitted friend—there's no disputing that—I'm King of Sharpshooters—that's enough.

Caspar. And Albert if you recollect did not get a single star today—

Andreas. That's true again—and no less strange than true—considering what a shot he is—

Caspar. I hear he has been unsuccessful for this week past—depend upon it—he's out of luck—he'll miss tomorrow.

Andreas. May be so—may be so—but I doubt it—I'm an unlucky dog and never won any prize in my life before today—but what care I if he does get the place of ranger—that for the place (*snaps his fingers*)—Damme I've got credit yet at some of the Inns—and when that's run out—why I'll off to the wars—there's rare living I'm told in camp—

Caspar. Aye rare living indeed—to lie on the ground, drink sour wine and be obliged to fall into the ranks instead of roving about like a deer of the forest. Why the place of Ranger would be the making of you—You might then be your own master—live like a prince—drink your six bottles a day—man—

Andreas. 'Sblood, that's true—there's sound reason in that—six bottles a day!

Caspar. Aye—and you might have "the laughing girl with roguish eye" that you were singing about just now—

Andreas. Fire & flints!—but I'd take up my quarters in old Kit's castle here—I'd marry Marian—& take all the bottles in the cellar into keeping!—

Caspar. Aye—or what say you to Bertha for instance—is not she a choice girl?

Andreas. Softly comrade—tender on that point if you please—You know I had a sneaking kindness for the girl—but this Albert cut us all out—No matter, that's an old affair—I've poured so many bottles on it that it's quite drowned—but you must not fish it up again—

Caspar. (*encreasing in earnestness*) And do you know so little of the sex; or do you think so meanly of yourself? Faith man the girl's within your reach—'tis your own fault if you don't make her yours—What made her give the preference to Albert?—a woman's vanity—he was the talk and boast of all the forest—the first of marksmen—Well, he has lost his skill—you've carried off the palm and been the Hero of the triumph—Shoot but tomorrow as you have today and you are Ranger of the Forest.

Andreas. Well and what then?

Caspar. What then? Why change of fortunes changes minds—you've plucked the feather out of Albert's cap that made him every thing in Bertha's eyes—Think you when she beholds you Ranger of the Forest—prais'd by the hunters, courted by the women—(*Andreas chuckles*)—turn round man, let me look at ye—Faith—the very fellow to please a woman's fancy—Zounds the case is clear—Albert will stand no chance against you—

Andreas. Well—supposing all this true—which I dare say it is—Do you not recollect that Bertha is engaged—positively engaged, man?

Caspar. And did ye not hear what Conrad said to Albert this evening, man? If he fails in the trial the engagement is at an end—for she can marry none but one who can succeed him in his hereditary office of Grand Forester—And will you not be the very man when you are ranger and first marksman? And will she not gladly make a merit of obedience and take the man her father chooses for her? To be sure she will—

Andreas. (*a little muzzy, but interested in the subject*) Faith the case grows clearer & clearer—but—there is only one little difficulty remains—

Caspar. None that I know of—

Andreas. I have not got the place you know—

Caspar. Oh for the place we can make *sure* of that.

Andreas. Make *sure* of it? How? (*A slight flash of lightning is seen thro the window—*)

Caspar. Why look ye—Andreas. A lad of spirit & mettle like yourself need never despair. It is because men flinch at difficulties that they fail—(*distant thunder is heard*)—Some are impeded in their course by *Virtue* (*sarcastically*)—some by *fear*—

Andreas. S'blood man, no one can accuse me of too much *virtue*—and as for *fear*—the Devil himself can't frighten me—(*A tremendous clap of thunder is heard—a flash of lightning—Urian glares in at the window & passes by*) Zounds! what was that? I thought some thing passed the window—

Caspar. I suppose the Devil heard you & had a mind to try your mettle—but I see comrade you are a little frightened—

Andreas. (*Swaggering—*) Frightened? What I? not I. 'Sblood an't I called Dare devil Andreas, all thro the forest?

Caspar. Well then, what say you to another glass? (*fills—*) Come here's to—the Wild Huntsman—eh? (*lightning*)

Andreas. With all my heart—damme I had always a kind of good feeling for that will o' the wisp fellow—and should like to join one of his hunting parties in the clouds.

Caspar. Faith you're the lad I took you for! (*taps him on the shoulder*) You *shall have* the place and the girl & the six bottles into the bargain, for you deserve them—You shall have them—I promise you & that's enough—

Andreas. 'Sblood you're one of the most promising fellows I've met with—but how will you keep your promise?

Caspar. Nothing more simple—Now I see you've courage—thus—you shall shoot tomorrow with magic balls—and then you know you cannot miss the mark—

Andreas. *Magic balls?*—Aye—aye—but where to get them?

Caspar. I can provide you. (*whispering*)

Andreas. (*growing grave & surprised—*) You Caspar?

Caspar. Aye lad—This night—this very night—It happens luckily that this night the moon's eclipsed—that is the only time to cast such balls—at midnight—at the very time when night & morning separate —I know all the spells—an ancient hunter taught me them—How lucky that the moon should be eclipsed tonight. I see you're born under a happy star—Come drink boy—you shall one day be Grand Forester—(*lightning*)

Andreas. 'Sblood how the lightning sizzes—

Caspar. Never mind—'twill serve to light us at our work—At twelve we cast the balls—You must assist me—at twelve precisely meet me in the Wolf's Glen—(*Tremendous Thunder*)

Andreas. In the Wolf's Glen? (*starting*) Why that's the very place where the Wild Huntsman prowls—aye & they say a whole legion of hobgoblins haunt that glen—

Caspar. Whether Saints or Goblins what is't to us? Are you not called Dare Devil Andreas thro the forest? (*sarcastically*)

Andreas. True, true—but can't we go together? (*a little anxious*)

Caspar. No—I must first prepare alone what's necessary for the purpose—

Andreas. Well then—at twelve I'll meet you—(*lightning*)

Caspar. And be silent—a single word would mar our hopes—

Andreas.   Depend upon me.

Caspar.   (*Going*) Till twelve—farewell—(*Exit Caspar*)

Tremendous Thunder

Andreas.   'Sblood this strange talk of Caspar has somewhat sobered me—I don't half like this business of the wolf's glen—not that I'm afraid—damme—Dare devil Andreas afraid? That would be a good joke—but I don't like this cooking in the night air—and I've not been long enough in the conjuring line to feel easy in it—Egad—I'll e'en have another pull at the bottle (*fills*)— if I am to be a conjuror damme it shall be a bottle conjuror—

Enter Christopher in nightgown & slippers.

Christopher.   What—still at it Master Andreas? Shall I bring you another Bottle?

Andreas.   No good Christopher—it's time for sober people like me to go home to bed—(*Looking out of the window—*) Zounds what a storm is gathering—Harkee good Christopher—no more wine, but a cloak good Christopher—a good mantle to keep out the rain— Your wine is dry wine good Christopher and I wish to keep it dry— So give me a mantle good Christopher to keep out the rain—I've no idea of making a flask of wine & water of myself—A dry body and a wet soul—that's my motto—So give me a mantle honest Christopher —'twere a pity good liquor should be spoiled.

(*During this* muzzy *speech Christopher goes & returns with a mantle—*)

Christopher.   Here's one for you Master Andreas—and a weatherproof one it is I'll warrant you—but don't fail to bring it back in the morning—

Andreas.   Never fear—Never fear—and now go to bed old man—go to bed—I hold it a shame that old men should keep such late hours— but what can be expected from a man that passes his whole life in a tavern?   (*exit—*)

Christopher.   (*looking after him*)—There he goes—one of the most rattling—roaring—rantum scantum fellows in the whole forest—One of your good for nothing chaps that's nobody's enemy but his own— he's a good drinker and that covers a multitude of sins—I love such fellows, I joy in them—May I never want such a friend—nor a bottle to fill him—But Marian! Marian!

Enter Marian—

Come—bustle—bustle girl—clear away the things & make all fast— it's time we were in bed—but hark'ee child—what a bother didst thou make this evening about nothing—

Marian.   Indeed father I can't abide that Andreas. He's always pulling one about—

Christopher.   Pooh—pooh child, he means no harm—mere bar-room romping—I'll have thee take care of thyself child; but be reasonably honest: there is virtue of all kinds—& suited to all conditions—Some stands all on end like a porcupine—and stings on every touch—that won't do for us—be thou as virtuous—but *reasonably* virtuous as befits the daughter of a publican and I'm content—

Marian.   (*goes to the window & shuts it*) Dear me how the wind begins to howl about the house—and there's such a whistling about the old forest trees—Father they say the Wild Huntsman has been seen lately—

Christopher.   Hush—hush—child—you must not talk on such subjects at night—We are too near the Wolf Glen to meddle with its concerns—I dare say the Wild Huntsman is a very worthy kind of gentleman if he does ride at nights—

Marian.   Lord father—they say he is the Devil himself—

Christopher.   Poo poo child—no such thing, & if he was—what's that to us? We publicans must learn to be civil to all kinds of people—& to give the devil his due—

Marian.   Will you help me out with the table father?

Christopher.   Stop—first let me count the bottles & keep good tally—One—two—three—four—five—six—so—(*Goes to the slate—*) Let me see—it has been rather a mellow night. Andreas is sometimes troubled with second sight in his cups—I've no doubt he saw double tonight & if so—why he enjoyed double the quantity of wine—So mark up twelve bottles—and now my girl—let's say prayers & to bed—

Exeunt—

Scene 3.

enter Albert.

Albert.   The hand of fate is sure against me. I am almost ready to turn driveller and believe in spells of witchcraft. What I, who scarcely knew what 'twas to fail—whose skill was proverbial among the greybeards of the forest—now to be surpassed, defeated—to lose all skill—now when every thing is at stake, fame, fortune, Bertha—oh tomorrow tomorrow!

Recitative & aria.

At the end throws himself on the bench at the door of the cottage & hides his face in his hands. Enter Caspar. Stands for some time unobserved by Albert, contemplating him with an air of malicious satisfaction.

Caspar.   What comrade! lost in thought!

Albert.   (*Starting up*) Caspar!

Caspar. What, has a little turn of ill luck sunk so deeply in your heart? Pshaw! give not way to melancholy, man! But how in the name of wonder happens it, that you the keenest marksman of the Forest should suffer such a paltry shot as Andreas to surpass you—nay that for seven days, you should not once have hit your mark?—Sure there must be some strange mysterious cause!—Have you an enemy?

Albert. None that I know of—why do you ask the Question?

Caspar. Look you comrade—you heard what that old babbler Christopher suggested—The old man thought some one had practised spells upon you—Our Warden is incredulous—but trust me **Albert** I have known such things—

Albert. Absurd. I never will believe such power exists—'tis contrary to common sense & reason.

Caspar. "Contrary to reason," aye ever since the world began that is the cry of all your would be wise men—"contrary to reason!" and what forsooth is reason? What but a feeble taper that just illumes a little space about you, while all beyond is a wide waste of darkness? Harkee comrade (*comes up to him &c*)—I am a solitary man —a little strange perhaps, and wayward in my humours. My pleasure is to walk these wilds alone—to lurk in shades & glens & the deep wood's dark bosom, where the loud babbling hound or saucy horn ne'er break the charm of silence—'Tis in these sacred haunts shy nature opes her mysteries, and to the musing eye of lonely mortals imparts strange secrets. These forest shades are full of wonders, could we read them rightly. In these my wanderings have I learnt some things you wise men scoff at as impossible—Believe me comrade there are things—aye—*there is a thing*—(*checks himself on observing an air of distrust in Albert*) How far think you may this rifle carry?

Albert. (*with a look of surprise*) As far I suppose as any other rifle— eight hundred or a thousand yards!

Caspar. And think you at that distance you could kill your game?

Albert. Preposterous! What mean you Caspar by such questions?

Caspar. (*without seeming to pay attention to the enquiry gazes upwards as if looking for something in air, crosses to the Proscenium, and returns muttering between his teeth*) Has he then deceived me? No! 'tis there indeed (*he returns hastily takes Albert by the arm & points upwards*) look there!

Albert. Where!

Caspar. There—directly over that tall black fir. (*with an air of satisfaction*) 'Tis the great night Vulture.

Albert. I see a black speck just against that rosy cloud—Ah! sure enough, it moves; it may be a night vulture for aught I can distinguish; but what of that!—

Caspar. (*Fetches Albert's rifle*) Here shoot at it!

Albert. Are you mad or do you deem me so? Why man 'tis near half a mile high, and now the cloud is fading I can scarcely see it—

Caspar. You will not shoot at it! Then mark—(*Goes to the back of the stage & shoots—a laugh in the air*) Look! here he comes—dost see?

Albert. I see a whirl & fluttering of wings in the midway gloom— (*A great eagle falls at his feet—he starts back with astonishment— gazes at it—then at Caspar—*)
Art thou some Devil clothed in human form? (*to Caspar*)

Caspar. (*affecting a careless air*) A simple hunter like thyself good comrade, but one, who, unlike thee, doubts not of every thing he cannot understand, nor measures nature's powers by scanty reason. (*He takes up the bird and examines it.*) 'Tis as I thought, the great night Vulture—and not ill shot 'i faith—the ball has struck just underneath the wing—Here (*to Albert*) you may get it stuff'd, and lay it at your mistress' feet—or let old Conrad hang it 'mongst the stag horns in his Hall. (*Albert takes up the vulture as if unconsciously, Caspar crosses, places one of the wing feathers in his hat, then turning suddenly to Albert*) By the bye—speaking of your mistress—tomorrow decides your loves & fortunes—'i faith good comrade you must shoot better than today or you stand little chance either for wife or office—

Albert. Why do you stab me with these cruel doubts; I fear indeed my case is hopeless!

Caspar. Nay not hopeless—not altogether hopeless—'tis true the chances are against you—your ill success of late has marr'd your confidence & then shooting for a mistress is not apt to make the hand most steady—the anxiety—the doubt—

Albert. Cease—cease & do not torture me—(*leans against a tree in despair*)

Caspar. Comrade I feel for your distress—indeed I do—Poor Bertha too! she who dotes on you! 'twill break her heart to see you fail. (*Albert evinces great agitation*) And yet this might be averted— means there are that would ensure success—but no—you'd never listen to them!

Albert. (*With surprize*) Means to *ensure* success? What means, Caspar?

Caspar. Oh nothing—nothing—idle talk—*contrary to reason*—you have never heard of charmed bullets—that are infallible?

Albert. I have—but hold it all for old wives' gossip.

Caspar. Ah like enough—like enough—*contrary to reason*—*contrary to reason*—what think you of my bringing down that vulture from the clouds?

Albert. Was then your rifle charged with such a ball? (*Caspar smiles*)
Speak I entreat you, was it such a ball?

Caspar. It was!—now think you—had you some such balls!

Albert. Have you then more of them?

Caspar. That was my last.

Albert. Caspar, don't trifle with me—I've too much at stake to bear
this trifling—

Caspar. I am no trifler comrade—Such balls are to be had—but on
conditions—that—no—'tis in vain—you'd never pay the price—

Albert. (*Impetuously*) What price? speak out! by heavens I'll not endure to have my mind disturb'd by hints and vague suggestions!

Caspar. You must engage—you must agree to certain terms—trifling
indeed to one whose life—*whose all* depends upon success—to one
whose soul like thine is bold & manly.

Albert. No flattery, proceed—proceed—

Caspar. Aye *bold & manly*—I say so without flattery. Did I not think
thee such I should have ta'en no interest in thy fate, but passed
thee by like this same rabble rout of hunters that I scorn. Comrade—
I speak of things too great for vulgar minds—of things that I have
learnt in these dark forests—believe me there are mysteries which
truly baffle all the force of reason—Such is the world of spirits. (*laying his hand on Albert's arm*) Now some weak natures tremble if
you but name a spirit!

Albert. (*steadfastly*) Speak out man! to the point—what is all this to
the purpose?

Caspar. ———— I know thee *brave* comrade—in *common* matters brave
—but are you as I deem you, above *vulgar* fears—say—dare you hold
communion with a spirit of air—a being of another world—who has
the power to grant the aid you seek for?

Albert. With whom!—what being!

Caspar. Thou hast heard of the Wild Huntsman.

Albert. I've heard of such a sprite—the phantom Hunter—the forest
chronicles are full of him. Some say it is the spirit of a cruel huntsman—doomed for his crimes to wander restless in the night—to ride
the storm and hunt about the world till doomsday—but these are
tales I heed not—

Caspar. Such a being there *is*!—mark me—*there is*—I speak not like
others, from report—*for I have seen him*—

Albert. (*With surprise*) Seen him! what is he then?—

Caspar. That I know not—a being wrapped in fear & mystery—of
powers vast, indefinite—but whether indeed a wizard of the earth—
or some embodied phantom of the air, some supernatural agent, is
more than I can say. He comes in gleams & shadows. He permits not

his nature nor his powers to be questioned—he must be summoned by ceremonies & incantations—

Albert. (*with horror*) And are such the means you would propose—and is this the aid you would invoke!

Caspar. (*hastily interrupting him*) Consider Albert how thou'rt situated—tomorrow is thy day of trial—tomorrow every thing depends upon a chance and that chance is against thee—What right hast thou to hope for better luck than what has dogged thee lately? Thinkst thou a fluttering heart, a faltering hand will guarantee success? I see thee foil'd, defeated—retiring midst the shrugs, the sneers, the taunts and scoffings of the vulgar throng of which thou'st had today a bitter foretaste—But what is worse—thy gentle Bertha—she whose whole soul is bound up in thy love—I see her too—in bridal robes—a mark for sneer & jesting—the nuptial wreath turn'd to a crown of scorn—the wedding preparations turn'd to mockery—I see the roses fading from her cheek—

Albert. Oh God! oh God!

Caspar. Well—I do not seek to torture thee—let us reverse the picture—With the balls I proffer thee thy fortune's sure—I see thee crowned with triumph, the lovely Bertha deck'd in smiles & flowers comes blushing to receive thee—the nuptial throng conducts thee to the altar—I see thy dwelling blessed with love and beauty—a little paradise of sweets around thee.

Albert. (*much moved*) But is this being you speak of good or evil?

Caspar. Pah! is this a time to stand on squeamish points? The happiness, the life of her *who loves thee* hangs upon the moment—An earthly paradise—a certainty of present bliss is offered to thee—Seize it and trust not to the uncertain future—So thou art happy think not of the means. Good spirit or bad, what is it to thee so that the gift be good? for good is good whether from heaven or hell.

Albert. (*Starting at the last words*) No gift is good that comes from evil power—nor can that power be good that walks in darkness—I wake as from a dream—How for a moment have I been beguiled, and laps'd in thought from the strict path of honour—Away, away! —I spurn thy proffered services—All magic means, if such there be —I scorn—On heaven and honest skill I rest my hopes nor seek by juggling arts to cozen fortune.

Caspar. Poor, feeble hearted wretch—I thought thou hadst more nerve & spirit—but thou art e'en a canting, virtuous driveller—fit only for the common rabble that I scorn—henceforth I leave thee to thy fortune. But mark me Sir. (*walks close up to him*) I've talk'd to you in confidence, because I wished to serve you—I have foolishly opened my soul to you—betray me, if you have the heart to do so; but recollect you must at the same time have the hand to answer it.

Albert. Away—away—thy offers and thy threats are equally contemptible—to heaven I leave thee—I do naught but scorn and pity thee—
Exit Caspar

Albert Solus.

Thank heaven he's gone—the very air seemed tainted with his presence—I blush to think that for a moment I should have listened to his temptings—What were success, gain'd by unworthy means? Nay what were Bertha's self, won by base arts? How could I e'er have borne her angel look! Her heavenly purity had been a ceaseless torment to me—Now can I clasp her to an honest heart and in her virtuous love find heaven on earth—But are there powers like this he talks of—that move unseen around us and control our fate? Away with anxious doubts and gloomy fears. If there are powers of darkness to befriend bad men, sure there are spirits of light that guard the virtuous—In such I put my trust to bear me through my trial.

Exit into the Cottage

[Act 2. Scene 1.]

Nina Counting—&c

Bertha. Nine o'clock & Albert not come yet—

Nina. At what time did he promise to come then?

Bertha. At eight precisely! Oh me—my heart is very heavy!

Nina. And all forsooth because your lover is an hour after his appointment!

Bertha. Nay Nina—I fear something has happened to him—He was always so punctual—

Nina. This comes of one's getting a character for punctuality—Give me a lover that never keeps an appointment—one that never comes when the door is open, but climbs into the window when I least expect him—one that never surprises me when he stays away & always surprizes me when he comes.

Bertha. Would my dear Nina I had thy light spirits—but in truth, I have a strange presentiment of evil—And then the Hermit spoke of some impending danger hanging over me—

Nina. Hanging over you, why it was that old picture hanging over you—and that fell just now—just as you had passed thro the door—it's a mercy it had not fallen on your head—it must have killed me—

Bertha. That is the picture of my Ancestor—the founder of our house—the first who had the place which my father holds of Hereditary Grand Forester—

Nina. Indeed—a worthy old gentleman! Pity he could not keep quiet however—

Bertha. There's some old saying about that picture which I do not recollect—'tis strange that it should fall for it was well secured—I'm almost tempted to believe it ominous—Would Albert were come —My mind misgives me Nina—

Nina. Lud my dear—I don't wonder at your being hipped a little—for two poor girls like us to be all alone in this great rambling house in the midst of the forest— —The evening too before your marriage, when one is so apt to be serious—and then, instead of a visit from your lover, to have your great grandfather popping upon you uninvited from the wall.—For my part I don't like such visitors—I'm for the young & the living.

(*Polacca*)

Heigh ho! I hope I shall one day marry a Forester—

Bertha. Why so Nina?

Nina. Because you know none but a forester's Bride may wear green trimmings—and I should so like to be married in such a pretty dress. Lord my dear, how fine you will look in your white & green, and your wreath of white roses! Well well—a forester for my money!

Bertha. Ah Nina you little think upon a Forester's life, so full of fatigue and danger—

Nina. Well my dear—what's a good man good for that can't face danger—Oh give me a lover that is always hunting—and chasing like another Nimrod—one that serenades me with the hunter's horn under my window—and never comes without a grinning wolf's head to lay at my feet—Lud—lud—how I should like a husband that was fond of the sport—racketting about the forest & breaking his neck every day in the year—

Bertha. Don't talk of dangers Nina—my mind runs on them too dismally already.—What *can* keep Albert?

Nina. Nay my dear Bertha, I only meant to cheer you by my gossip—Would you had not seen the Hermit—Come, cheer up, I must give orders that your father's breakfast be ready betimes in the morning —He goes early to the Hunt—I will be here again in a moment dear Bertha—

(*exit with a lamp*)

Bertha. Was that a footstep—! Alas no, he comes not—How tedious seem the moments of a lover's absence!

Recitative—

Albert appears at a window which is open—

Bertha. Albert! Albert! yes—'tis he!

Albert. My Bertha—(*embraces her*)

Bertha. Have you then come at last—why have you staid so long? I
 feared some evil had befallen you. You look pale & agitated. I'm
 sure some thing is wrong—Some danger has beset you—

Albert. Say rather some good fortune—Proceeding hither thro the
 forest a wolf of monstrous size rush'd from the thicket & would
 have crossed my path—but for once my aim was sure—I left him
 weltering in his blood—See here the trophy in my hat—(*Forcing
 a smile*) this is good luck my love—let's take it as an omen of success tomorrow—

Bertha. (*shaking her head doubtingly*) I hope it may be—but in sooth
 my mind is filled with fears—the Good Hermit too warns me of
 threatening dangers—And see, just as the clock struck seven, yon
 portrait of my ancestor, fell from its fastening on the wall & nearly
 crushed me.

Albert. Just as the clock struck seven! (*aside*) Most strange!—'twas
 then that Caspar brought the eagle from the cloud!

Bertha. What do you utter to yourself—!

Albert. Nothing my love—I feel harassed & weary—A little rest however will restore me—(*He throws his hat upon the table &c*)

Bertha. See—Albert see you have extinguished the light!

Albert. Never mind my love—the moon shines bright & clear—come
 sit by me and let our souls discourse—Methinks there's something
 in this quiet light that calms the breast—The moon is full and spreads
 its tender radiance o'er the forest—canst thou not draw a happy
 omen from it Bertha?

Bertha. Alas, this night the moon is in eclipse and when that happens,
 I've been often told, all evil things have power; they say it is a time
 of crimes and dangers—

Albert. Fond girl! the gossips of the forest have filled thee with these
 dreams—Believe me love these gentle lights of heaven that rule the
 night are all propitious to the lover's fortune—Be of good heart my
 girl—the heavens smile on us—tomorrow makes us one—and then
 we'll wear this broad fair moon out, to its last silver rim, in love
 and true happiness—

Bertha. Heaven grant it! (*pensively*) for oh, should any adverse fortune
 happen I feel 'twould break my heart—

enter Nina with light

Nina. What Albert here—and all in darkness? (*archly*)

Bertha. You forget 'tis moonlight—

Nina. Ah, true, the honey moon—the moon—the moon is every thing
 to you lovers—it seems to me as if this love was all a matter of
 moonshine—(*goes to the window—*) But see your moonshine will
 soon be at an end—there are clouds gathering over the distant hills
 and I heard just now a muttering of thunder—

Albert. 'Tis so indeed—how wild the southern sky looks—(*aside*) I must
away—in spite of all my efforts there is a sadness sets upon my
heart & sinks me in despondency—Farewell my love—

Bertha. What so soon Albert? Go not so soon—wait till the storm be
over—

Albert. 'Twill be too late, it is my night of watch. I have a round to
make deep in the forest.

Bertha. I do not like this roving thro the forest—You know the night's
unlucky and they tell fearful things about this forest—

Albert. Mere tales my girl—I am to meet a villager at the place where
the wolf lies—that I killed—He promised to assist me in carrying
home the spoil—

Bertha. Where does it lie? is it far off?

Albert. Down in the valley, near the wolf glen.

(*Terzetto*)

[Scene 2.]
Scene of Incantation.

Chorus &c &c
Urian—appear—appear—

———

Rock opens & Urian appears—(*P.S.* I should prefer that the goblin
should appear in some other manner than from the center of a
rock—this shoving aside of canvas—or trap door has too barefaced
a look of mechanism, for any good effect—These tricks always
appear paltry to me—Let him rise thro a trap door which is concealed by some small rocks—)

Urian. Wherefore am I summon'd?

Caspar. Mighty Spirit, I claim the fulfilment of thy promise, to grant
me three years more liberty.

Urian. Canst thou fulfill the condition?

Caspar. I can, I bring this night another votary.

Urian. What does he seek?

Caspar. Unerring balls.

Urian. Seven shalt thou cast—six for him—the seventh flies at my
direction.

Caspar. I crave that ball, as a reward for faithful service.

Urian. 'Tis thine—but have a care—mischief it must do—if not to
others—to thyself—

Caspar. I take the risk—for I know where to send it.

Urian. Remember—thy victim or thyself—! (*disappears—*) *Andreas
appears among the rocks* (omit the appearance of ghosts—they

always to my notion spoiled the grandeur of the scene of incantation—which ought to have a singleness in its nature—Something
magical—not *ghostly*. Besides, though they might be sent to warn
Albert—they would hardly trouble themselves about such a random
blade as Andreas—)

Caspar. (*looks up*) Ah—art thou there at last? Hasten it grows late!

Andreas. I come—I come—'Sblood this night air, and the walking alone
in these haunted woods have quite sobered me—(*descends the rocks
rapidly—enters onto proscenium. The moon is again partially observed—Andreas looks about him with a troubled & fearful air*)
Here am I—what am I now to do?

Caspar. (*taking the bottle from his pocket—*) First drink—the night
air's chill and damp—this will warm thee.

Andreas. (*drinks*) Egad, 'tis fire itself—it warms one's very marrow—

Caspar. (*aside*) That well may be—'tis from a strange distillery.
(*Snakes & other reptiles surround Andreas—he endeavours to drive
them off*)

Caspar. Thou'rt yet a novice—come within this circle—'tis a magic wall
between us and all evil spirits that reaches from the centre to the
firmament—The time approaches—fear not, whate'er thou seest or
hear'st—'Tis not without severest struggles that nature yields her
secrets up to us weak mortals.—Be silent now until thou seest me
fall & cry for aid—then call thyself. Else Andreas we are lost—(*He
points to the moon which is partially eclipsed*) See—this is the moment—the moon already is eclipsed—

NB—*Private note—*

(In the progress of the incantation let the uproar of the scene gradually
encrease—The apparition of the Wild Huntsman hounds &c in the air
[should] be at the sixth Ball—And at the seventh let the trees fall—rocks
roll on the stage &c &c—& the Wild Huntsman appear from behind a
rock &c &c &c—But omit the *phantasmagoria* of Bertha—Death &c which
in my opinion would give a commonplace character to the whole and
be a complete Bathos—The scene as an incantation may be made grand
and awful—but care must be taken to avoid all commonplace stage
trickery—such as rocks opening by slides—transparencies of queer faces
appearing on rocks as in the representation at Dresden &c &c—A little
use of white, blue, & red fires would heighten the effect—)

Act 3. Scene 1.

Morning

*The outside of a picturesque old Hunting Lodge in the Gothic style—
decorated with stag's horns over the Door &c. A latticed window with
a balcony before it, which projects considerably over the Stage & is*

supported by rustic columns, forming a kind of porch to a door. Forest Scenery in the background. The sound of hunting horns is heard from time to time in the distance.

Enter two of the Duke's Huntsmen.

First. A fine morning comrade after the storm—charming weather for the hunt—Who would have thought last night to have had such a day break? Faith I fear'd we should never see the sun again—

Second. The sun—no—nor the moon either! egad I thought the wind would have blown the very stars out. Did you ever hear such howling & whistling as it made among the forest trees?

First. And then the thunder, how it cracked and bellowed! I'll warrant comrade there's been pretty work on the east side of the mountain by the wolf's glen, the sky seemed all in a blaze of lightning in that direction—

Second. I came that way this morning—the blasts out of the glen have lain the forest trees before it as flat as bull rushes. The firs that grew among the cliffs are standing with their roots in the air. The brook that runs through the glen came roaring like a torrent—overflowed its banks and nearly drowned old Karl Brenner in his mill. The old man swears the Wild Huntsman was abroad and that he saw him and his hell hounds in full cry among the clouds. But hark! the horns are sounding at the hunting camp—something must be going on there—

Enter another Huntsman

Huntsman. What—lagging here & losing all the sport?

First Huntsman. What sport?

Huntsman. What sport! Why some of the sharpest shooting you ever saw—Don't you know that Albert and Andreas are shooting for the Ranger's place? You never saw so dead a match—three times have they each shot, and three times has each hit the mark.

First. What Andreas—so sharp a shooter? Who would have thought it! But heaven defend us from that scatter brained fellow becoming Ranger of the Forest, he would turn everything topsy turvy—But how came you to leave the ground while such sport was going on?

Hunter. Oh there's a respite for an hour—The Duke has ordered the target to be placed at double the distance so that it is next to impossible either should hit the centre, but who ever comes nearest to it on the next shot, wins the day.

First. Well—Albert's my man—

Second. And mine also—Ah here he comes!

Enter Albert Cheerily

Good morning comrade—glad to hear you're in such good shot this morning.

Albert. Thank ye my friends—the spell indeed seems broken—this trusty rifle (*shewing his rifle*) is once more true to its master—but the trial is not yet over—the next shot will probably be the deciding one.

Hunters.   Well good luck to ye—good luck to ye Comrade—   *Exeunt.*

Albert.   (*alone*) Now to tell my good luck to Bertha—Yonder's her window—what still closed & gloomy on a bridal morn? Oh let me cheer her with my own bright hopes. The day's success has put new life into me, my heart again beats light and cheerily and shares the freshness of this glorious morning—

Aria—

Bertha.   (*at the window*) Albert is that you?

Albert.   It is my love, but what—not yet prepared—and our nuptial hour so near at hand?

Bertha.   Alas Albert, I have not the heart to make preparations—whene'er I try to twine a bridal wreath, it seems as tho' it were my funeral garland—

Albert.   It is thy anxious mind that turns all things to portents. The night has been to every one a night of horror but see how sweet and holy is the morn—and know my girl once more I am myself; and every shot has been successful.

Bertha.   (*With eagerness*) Is the trial then over? Thank heaven! thank heaven!

Albert.   Not over—not quite over Bertha—The next shot will decide: but now I am myself again I feel a calm assurance of success.

Bertha.   Would the trial were quite over—Do not chide my weakness Albert—I am a poor timid girl, forgive me if my weak spirit clogs your bolder nature. Alas! there's something awful even in a wedding day! and this has been preceded by such omens!

Albert.   Still thinking of these omens. Come down my love & greet me with a smile. Come deck my breast with a gay white rose & trust me love we'll have a merry day of it.

Bertha.   I come—and with the rose I bring the Hermit's blessing—
(*She leaves the window—Enter Bertha below—approaches Albert with faltering hesitating manner & voice. In the course of the Duet he tries to reassure her—She looks up to him with doubting look as if seeking encouragement—but relapses into pensiveness & her air is thoughtful & unquiet.*)

Duet. Albert & Bertha

Bertha.   Ah me!

Albert.   Come—Cheer up my girl—the Bride's maids and village lasses will soon be here to hail you with the bridal song—and to conduct you to the duke's presence—who is in the Banquet tent. So brighten up—I cannot miss the mark when you're the prize. Come, the white rose in my hat—one brief smile & I'm sure of success.

Bertha.   (*twists a rose in his hatband in silence—places it on his head— looks in his face with a pensive smile—retires thoughtfully to the house Albert looking wistfully after her—when she reaches the door she turns, kisses her hand and exclaims:*) Success attend you Albert!

Albert.   It will—it will!—and now Andreas for the final trial—

(*Exeunt*)

[Scene 2.]

Enter Caspar

Three shots—all true to the mark—and with a skill that rivals even witchcraft! 'Tis plain the spell of Urian is over, and something holy blesses Albert's aim—Well then—to my last resort—All his balls exhausted, Andreas must now come to me for further aid—Three of the balls I've wasted in the air—only one now remains—the fatal *seventh*—that precious ball which Urian granted me, to fly & wherever I please—Enough—Albert, if thou must triumph—thy prize shall cost thee dear—

Enter Andreas hastily—

Andreas.   Casper well met! I've sought you all the forest over.

Caspar.   Well met at last then, comrade! I greet you on your luck—did I not tell you these Balls would do wonders?

Andreas.   Yes but i'faith all my ammunition's gone and you see, with all your infernal cookery Albert shoots as well as I—Hast any more balls? Give me the rest!

Caspar.   One more—only one more remains—the Seventh Ball—the rest I've used.

Andreas.   Hold comrade—Let me think a moment—said you not something about that ball's doing mischief? I don't like to meddle with that ball—

Caspar.   Pish—man! that's the very best of all—worth all the rest & therefore have I kept it to myself—it is endowed with wondrous power and returns to the owner's pouch however often he fires it— but had it ten times its power I'd give it thee for I've conceived a wondrous friendship for thee.

Andreas.   Say you so? Why then i'faith give me that ball & the day is mine!

Caspar.   Here it is, but do not fire until I give the signal—the ball depends upon my will.

Andreas. 'Tis well—Caspar when I am Ranger of the Forest you know
   where to look for a Venison pasty—a pretty girl and a jolly round
   bottle—

Exit

Caspar. Now for my master stroke—(*Horns sound cheerfully at a distance*) Aye, sound your horns, and fill the air with music—I for once
   can bear it. Yes, I can even join the nuptial throng and swell the
   strain that greets a rival's triumph—Aye—Aye—prepare your wreaths;
   bring forth the bride and strew her path with flowers—but have a
   care there [be] not a serpent under them! The seventh ball must
   fly at my command—*And Bertha's heart shall be its fatal mark!*—
   Bertha *thou'st slighted me*—enough—no hated rival shalt thou ever
   bless—thy wedding morn shall be a morn of horror—thy nuptial
   wreath shall be a funeral crown, thy bridal song shall be a death
   shriek!

(*exit*)

[Scene 3.]

Scene Bertha's Chamber—

Nina. Dear dear Bertha—for heaven's sake don't look so gloomy on
   your wedding morn—upon my word you frighten one—I had no
   idea marriage was such a terrible thing.—Why lud my dear 'twill
   soon be over, and then you'll think no more of it than all the other
   married folks one sees. Come, cheer up and I'll go get thee the
   wedding wreath that old Agatha has just brought from the village.
   You'll look as fine as a little queen—and then we'll be off to the
   hunting camp.

exit

Bertha. (*remains pensive & musing—clasps her hands & looks upwards
   with a sigh—*) Still—still this strange—this unaccountable forebod-
   ing presses on my heart—no—no—I'll not yield to it—There is a
   power above that watches over innocence.

(*Air—Und ob die Wolke*)

Oh me! Would that this day were happily over! What can it be
that thus weighs down my spirits & makes me feel more like a
victim than a bride? (*music*) Hark, the Bride maids are coming—
alas how strange it is—I feel more as if going to a sacrifice than
to a marriage altar—

(*Song & chorus—*)

Enter Nina.

Here it is—Here's the wedding wreath Bertha—Come no more dole-
ful looks, but dress your face in smiles, while I dress your head with
flowers—Come (*to the girls*) let's have your pretty chorus again
while I crown the bride—

(*While they sing she kneels before Bertha on the little stool—unties
the green ribband which fastens the Box & opens it—The girls who
are looking over as she opens the Box start back with expressions
of horror*)

Bertha.   Oh God! (*throws herself back with marks of alarm*)

Nina.   (*from whom the contents of the box were concealed by the lid*)
What's the matter?

(*Bertha takes the silver wreath out of the box—*) Oh Heavens! A
death wreath! this indeed is—(*checks herself*)—is not to be endured—
that stupid half blind old creature Agatha has brought a wrong
box from the shop through mistake! (*the girls look at each other
with an enquiring air—Bertha fixes her eyes on the silver wreath &
clasps her hands together with a look of despondency—Nina considers a moment—then quickly:*)

Come—away with this wreath! (*shuts it up in the box*) We must
have one however—come let us make one out of the white roses
which the good Hermit gave you.

Bertha.   Nay—these must I wear in my bosom—they have the hermit's
blessing.

Nina.   Ah but here remain enough beside—(*fetches the rest of the roses
&c seats herself & wreathes them &c*) Only see what a charming
wreath they make and how lovely they look! Now let us go—Come
sing girls—sing!

(*They repeat the chorus—but with a saddened tone—Exeunt*)

[Scene 4.]

Duke.   'Tis well—and now for the last trial of skill. Never did I see a
closer match, nor better shooting—I wish to be impartial, but some
how or other, Albert has my good will—I like not the saucy swaggering air of his opponent—and there's a pretty love story, whose
sequel hangs upon the fortune of the day—Conrad—

Conrad.   Your Grace?

Duke.   This is a worthy youth—this Albert—

Conrad.   A trustier heart my lord beats not in any bosom of Bohemia—
And for a shot—there's none could e'en match him in these forests—

Duke.   Still methinks he's met his match today—that strutting scapegrace keeps even shot with him—But where's your pretty daughter
Conrad?

Conrad. She will be here anon, my lord—I feared to bring her earlier to the field—her heart was too full of anxiety for the event of this trial—But now that Albert has his usual luck I fear no longer—

Duke. He has my hearty wishes—but when is the wedding good Conrad?

Conrad. This very day my lord—should Albert be successful. The shot that makes him Ranger of the Forest & proves him worthy to succeed me in my hereditary office gives him my daughter's hand—

Duke. He must succeed—Cupid will guide the ball—And now give signal with the horn for the candidates to make ready—

Caspar. Where can the Bride be lingering? I fear she will come too late for my plan—(*gets on a rock*) Ah—there I see her at a distance, with her wedding train winding through the trees—. Urian thou makest all happen pat to the purpose!

    —*Horns—Albert advances to the front of the Stage—pauses for a moment—Looks upward—lays his hand upon his heart—*"Now Bertha!" *Shoots—A shout—*"He has hit the mark! he has hit the mark! —Close to the centre!"

Conrad. 'Twill puzzle Andreas to equal that—

Andreas. (*coming forward—with a swaggering, self confident air—*) That's yet to be seen—Now magic, do your duty—'Sblood how heavy the ball feels in my hand—heavier than all the others put together— no matter it has the magic in it of ten thousand—so here goes— (*puts it in the rifle*) but first I must see Caspar give the signal, for unless he directs the ball it will miss the mark—[*Caspar gives the signal and Albert fires. Bertha falls to the ground.*]

Albert. (*Wildly*) Bertha! Bertha! My love, look up—Speak to your wretched Albert—. (*puts aside her hair which had fallen over her eyes*) She lives! She lives! Oh god oh god I thank thee!

All. She lives! She lives!

Bertha. My Father—My Albert!

Albert. But art thou wounded love?

Bertha. I scarce can tell—it seemed as if a flash of lightning struck me— I feel no pain, but I am wondrous faint—

Nina. Dear Bertha lean on me—(*They place her in the Duke's chair &c. Caspar is led tottering forward between two hunters*)

Hunter. My lord this man is wounded—the Ball has pierced him in the Breast.

Duke. How can that be, he stood not in the range of fire—Yet 'tis most true—the man is wounded—

Caspar. Stand off & let me gaze upon my victim—Ah, (*With malignant joy*) have I reach'd thy heart thou *scorner*? nay then I care not for myself—Now Albert take thy bride & boast thy triumph but spare

your pains—no power on Earth can save her—'twas a charm'd ball
and faithful to its errand—

Albert.   Horrible wretch, what has thou done?

Hermit.   (*Who has been near Bertha &c—*) Almighty providence I thank
thee—my prayers were heard—the lamb preserved from danger—See
here my friends (*pointing to the roses*)—these holy flowers have
saved her spotless heart—their leaves are scorched & withered—the
magic ball has struck them but being repelled by their sacred
power—has winged its mischief to the murderer's breast—

Caspar.   What—caught in my own snare—defeated—lost. And is thy
power so frail thou mighty spirit of air, that a poor rose can foil
thee? Must I then fall & pull no ruin with me? Ah trembling
coward (*to Andreas*)—thou at least must bear me company! (*Gasps*)
Let me get hence—the day grows black around me—the air is thick
& stifling—What sulphurous streams are those that choak me—stand
off and let me breathe—(*pants*) further—further—(*tears free his
bosom*) Oh—scorching—scorching—Hell is within me—Ah those
flames—those flames—Water! water!—plunge me in the fountain!
Ah Urian here? Oh let me live another year—a little—little month—
A day—an hour—Oh save me save me—(*Staggers among the crowd
& seizes upon one of the Hunters*)—

Hunter.   (*dismayed*) Heaven have mercy on thee—!

Caspar.   I have no hopes of heaven! (*falls & dies—*)

*Duke.   Horrible—Horrible—*haste—take this dreadful object from my
sight! Where is the Hunter Andreas?—(*Andreas, who has been
amazed & overwhelmed by the preceding events, comes forward
completely crestfallen.*)

Andreas.   Here my good lord—

Duke.   What was the meaning of those dreadful words which Caspar
uttered? Wert thou accomplice in his crime?

Andreas.   Alas my lord, I scarce know what to say. Last night, when
foolish with vanity & wine this man beset me—he talked to me of
magic balls by which I could make my fortune, and of the Wild
Huntsman—and so bewildered my poor brain that I agreed to meet
him in the Wolfglen where he cast these balls which I have used
today—

Duke.   Hast thou then dealt in magic?

Andreas.   I hope not my lord— I meant no such thing—whatever Caspar
meant—There were strange sights & sounds but then I crossed myself & prayed—I meant no harm today whate'er I've done—I hope I
have not sinned past all forgiveness.

Duke.   Thy free confession & thy penitence obtain my mercy—to this
good father's keeping I commit thee—follow his counsels—fast &
pray & seek to make thyself a better man—

Andreas. My lord I've had a lesson today that I shall not easily forget
—I feel that I am more an ass than I had any idea of—Henceforth
I renounce all vanity & vainglory—Wine women & play I abjure—
if bread & water have any efficacy I'll take them ten times a day—
Go on, holy father, I'll follow thee—(*aside going out*) 'Sblood I
long to be at my prayers, if it's only to pay the devil for the trick
he's played me.

exeunt—Andreas & Hermit

Duke. And now to turn our thoughts to Happier objects—Albert, be
thine the place of Ranger. Well hast thou won it by thy skill, but
still more by thy Virtue. (*To Conrad*) I know thy will, excuse me
if I play your part—(*Advances to Bertha & takes her hand which
he places in Albert's—*) Thus let me recompense thee lovely maid
for all thy troubles past—Continue to be virtuous my friends &
Heaven will bless you—

(*Tableau*)

[1823]

[ABU HASSAN]

[Act 1.]   Scene 1.

*Abu Hassan's chamber in the Palace of the Caliph. On one side a door,
leading to a Cabinet, with a grated opening over it; on the opposite side
a window. In the background two Divans. Fatima and Abu Hassan
seated on Cushions. Before them, a table with Bread & Water—(right
hand)*

Abu Hassan.

Dearest darling give me wine!

Fatima.

Neither red wine nor white Sir,
Mahomet forbids it quite Sir.

Abu Hassan.

Therefore give it a disguise,
Give Sherbet.

Fatima.

Oh, you mean water.

Abu Hassan.

No! for water is my death.
Turbot, dainty tit bits!

Fatima.

Gourmand!

Abu Hassan.

A nice pasty!

Fatima.

Here is bread.

Both.

Can such fare put one in spirits?
Can it give one heart to struggle?
Silent symptoms of my need,
Bread and water, Water, Bread!

Fatima.

Come, I'll sing the pretty ballad
"With Aurora's early beam."

Abu Hassan.

Wilt thou drive me to distraction?
        or
(To distraction will you drive me?)

Fatima.

No, 'twill lull thy hunger's rage.

Abu Hassan.

Dearest darling give me wine! &c

Abu Hassan.

A princely meal truly; Dry bread and—egad the mere word sticks in my
throat;—and, and Water! But such is the fate of us poor devils of husbands whose wives are more ambitious of ruling the roost on Parnassus
than in their Kitchens.

Fatima.

Mighty fine truly! You, the lord and master, revel and revel as long as
there is a Zechine in the house. I keep silence out of mere tenderness;

eat with you out of connubial fidelity, and how do you reward me for both–! Why instead of cursing your own palate you must clamour at my poor poetical talent. Truly you deserve to lose also the only jewel that you can yet call your own.

Abu Hassan.

What, have I yet a jewel left? My dearest Fatima let me embrace thee, and then run with it my dear girl, to the Pawn Broker's!

Fatima.

Thou shameless spendthrift. What—wouldst thou sell even the wife of thy bosom?

Abu Hassan.

Oh! What then! You, you are the jewel you talk of; in truth you are the only one that is likely to remain on hand, for since a wife can't be Set in a ring like any other jewel, I fear I should find but a bad market for you at the Jeweller's.

Fatima.

Ay—and yet there are folks, that are ready at any moment to lay all their wealth at my feet.

Abu Hassan.

Golden Fatima–? What, will any one lay his wealth at thy feet?—let him—I beseech you let him my girl—By the head of the Prophet I swear to thee it shall not be there long. But speak, who is the scoundrel that would make you untrue to me—and the fine fellow that would pay thy untruth so royally?

Fatima.

A man who had already a sneaking kindness for me before the unlucky moment that Zobeide gave my hand to a certain Abu Hassan. In one word, it is Omar, the Caliph's humble banker and Abu Hassan's overbearing creditor.

Abu Hassan.

Omar? impossible! What! can a usurer love women more than money?

Fatima.

If you will not believe me, at least believe this letter, which he ordered a slave to slip into my hands a few days since, as I went to the Bath.

Abu Hassan.

(*Reads.*) "Fairest Fatima! my heart burns with love for you. Extinguish these consuming flames, and take command over all my treasures. All that I possess is thine, and happy should I think myself if thou permittedst thy slave to kiss the dust beneath thy feet.   *Omar*"

Fatima.

Do you still doubt?

Abu Hassan.

And what answer hast thou sent him?

Fatima.

That I abhorred him; and that if he dared again to make his audacious proposal, my protectress the Sultana Zobeide should be instantly informed of it.

Abu Hassan.

Do not take it amiss of me, my very good little woman; but truly this speech hardly became a wife who had nothing to set before her husband but Bread and Water.

Fatima.

Do you speak seriously! What! shall I sell my honour?

Abu Hassan.

By no means—though thou mightest have led the would be purchaser a little by the nose, both to thine & mine advantage; and through a little cleverness thou mightest have spared my poor head a vast deal of hard and fruitless labour; for I assure thee, in spite of the exertions of all my five Senses, I cannot discover the art of making gold.

Fatima.

And yet there is no one to whom it is more indispensable; for none knows how to squander it more readily. My heart bleeds when I remember the costly marriage gifts of the Caliph and his spouse, that have vanished almost sooner than your love.

Abu Hassan.

Don't talk of things that we have had, but help me to think of some means by which we may supply their loss. (*after a moment's pause of reflection*) Do you think of nothing? What: shall a man's wit for once triumph over a woman's in devising stratagems? Now, make up your mind on the spot to die; and you will make me the happiest of husbands and thyself the happiest of wives!

Fatima.

Are you in your senses? I die! What a request!

Abu Hassan.

Shame on thee! hast thou forgotten the chaste Lucretia, and the unchaste Sappho who both killed themselves for mere trifles! And do I desire that thou shouldst plunge a dagger into thy bosom, or jump from the top of a precipice? No, I only ask thee to assume the mask of death; and I hope the mummery will bring thee more profit than fifth acts of twenty Tragedies, wherein twenty times as many heroes and heroines give up their mighty souls.

Fatima.

Oh that's quite another thing. A theatrical death gives me as much pleasure as a real one is my abhorrence.

Abu Hassan.

Good! However, now I think of it. Our joke would be more complete and help our circumstances more certainly if we both die—and as in cases of real death, it is commonly the wife that first buries the husband, so it is best that I begin. Look upon me therefore as a dead person. Howl and cry somewhat more than you would if I were really dead, tear thy garments, pluck out thy hair—

Fatima.

Why so? nay nay—

Abu Hassan.

At least seem to pluck it out—and hasten with dishevelled hair and streaming eyes, to thy powerful patroness.

Fatima.

I cannot as yet understand for the life of me, what this juggling is to lead to.

Abu Hassan.

Therefore let me expound. Zobeide, when she understands the cause of thy distress, will sympathize with thee in true goodheartedness; and, according to custom, will give thee a sum of money for funeral expences and a piece of Brocade for winding sheet. As soon as you return with your booty I will play the same part with the Caliph, and hope to find him no less free handed than you will his spouse.

Fatima.

(*Puts her dress in disorder*) Adieu my dear dead husband! I hope soon to see you awakened to a better life.

(*exit through door in flat*)

Scene 2.

Abu Hassan alone.

(*During the following speech he clears away the table.*) The Farce is begun, now fortune favour us that Zobeide may a second time shake over us the horn of plenty—Fifty Gold pieces will she give Fatima for certain—even so much will I get from the Caliph—together one hundred bright gold pieces. By the Great Prophet I'll not leave any good luck unenjoyed.

> But how to manage
> That I may spend the little yellow Shiners
> Like a good fellow?
> I'll give a fête champêtre,
> With song & dance first rate Sir,
> The foremost place shall my little wife have,
> A chaplet gay her brows adorning,
> And smiling like a bright May morning
> The empress of the feast appear.

> Ho! Slaves there!—bring wine,
> Then scatter roses in,
> And with her purple lip sweet
> Shall first Fatima sip it.

> So! set the goblet here!—
> Now dearest—to our welfare—
> And that it long may tell fair,
> Drink I this goblet clear.

> Today's the time for singing
> Therefore the guitars bring in
> Quick, quick, and do not stay,
> Through piping, singing, laughing
> And jolly goblets quaffing
> We while dull life away.

Oh Fatima my dearest,
Who to me so tender art,
Love Inviting joys delighting,
Care no more my bosom fills.

Around now my darling in light moving measure
Comes dancing with bright eyes all sparkling with pleasure.
Fine! Bravo!—Surpassing! She trips now more near
And slyly she gives a sweet kiss to her dear—
    Though should our project fail
    Why what cares she or I?

(*A noise at the centre door*)

Who's there?

Scene 3.

Omar appears at the head of Abu Hassan's creditors—

Abu Hassan.

Ah, here comes that cursed dun-visaged fellow Omar—the devil take him that he must pop in just at this moment to wake me out of my delightful dream.

Omar.

Do you not know me Abu Hassan?

Abu Hassan.

Since you call me by name it is pretty clear that at least you know me!

Omar.

Will you pay me?

Abu Hassan.

Pah! *Pay!*—what a cursed ungentlemanlike phraze. I wish to Allah the Caliph would have it struck out of the language—but who are these at your Heels?

Omar.

Your creditors—we have had a meeting and are decided—all of us— not to wait any longer.

Creditors.

Yes, that's what we are—

Abu Hassan.

Softly, softly—egad the whole pack is in excellent unison—You don't mean to hunt me down, do you?—Harkee! (*to Omar*) a little patience—keep off your hounds from my haunches—The money you shall have—as soon as I can get it—that is to say if not the whole, at least a part of your demand.

Omar.

We are not to be put off any longer—we'll have the whole!

Creditors.

Aye the whole—the whole!

Abu Hassan.

You're cursed unanimous—'Sblood this concord among creditors makes confounded bad music—Is this all your gratitude for the patronage of a man of my fashion? 'Sdeath, are you not content with my custom but you must have my money into the bargain?

Creditors.

Aye aye—the money—we'll have our money—the cash down—

Abu Hassan.

Well, well—if you will be so unreasonable I must try what I can do to appease you—My wife is just gone to the Sultana to procure a sum of money from her—as soon as she returns I shall go for the same purpose to the Caliph.

Omar.

These are mere evasions! If the Caliph was disposed to give you money he would have done so long since.

Abu Hassan.

My honest friend, it is damn'd uncivil in you to doubt my word—however, I was sure it would be so, because Fatima maintained the very contrary this morning.

Omar. (*attentive*)

Fatima? What did she say then?

Abu Hassan.

She praised your generosity & kindness.

Omar.

Yes, I am generous—or at least I can be so.

Abu Hassan.

Well, shew it then—

Omar.

Ah, but if *I* would wait—these would not.

Creditors.

No—no—we'll wait no longer.

Omar.

There, you hear—they are determined to throw you into prison.

Abu Hassan.

Fatima desired me to entreat you—

Omar.

Indeed!

Abu Hassan.

Most earnestly; she implored me most pressingly to tell you so.

Omar.

What can I do?

Abu Hassan.

Every thing!

Omar.

What do you want then?

Abu Hassan.

Longer credit.

Creditors—chorus.

Cash! cash! cash!
We will no longer linger,
But will the money finger,
Before you go to smash.

Abu Hassan.

Have patience, only one more day—only till Evening—sure that's nothing to ask—

Chorus of Creditors.

No! no! no!
Your note of hand is out Sir
And I must without doubt Sir
The first of all be paid.

Abu Hassan.

But look you now, my exceedingly worthy gentlemen, that is just the damn'dest difficulty in the world that I cannot pay you all first—and yet Mahomet forbid that I should show partiality and pay any one before the others. Omar, most gentlehearted of all Bankers, do render me some assistance.

Omar.

Not for any love of you—but for the sake of Fatima—

Abu Hassan.

Aye aye—for Fatima's sake be it.

Omar.

Poor woman—my heart bleeds for her that your thoughtlessness makes her so unhappy.

Abu Hassan.

Well, don't let your heart content itself with mere bleeding— (*aside*) egad I'll make your purse bleed too you rogue before I'm done with you.

Omar.

(*To the creditors*)

Come with me to my house, and I'll satisfy your demands. Are you contented?

Chorus of creditors.

Aye! aye! aye!

Omar.

And you too are contented?

Abu Hassan.

Aye! aye! aye! and you?

Omar.

Aye! aye! aye!

(*aside*)
I am right well contented
And eke right well intended,
    Slyly to sneak back here.

Abu Hassan.

(*aside*)
The scoundrel will repent it
That ever he has meant it
    To tamper with my dear.

Chorus of Creditors.

We all are well contented
And so our fears all ended,
    We take ourselves off clear.

(*Omar & the creditors retire thro centre door.*)

Scene 4.

Abu Hassan. (*alone—*)

Thanks to the Great Prophet I have got rid of this rabble rout of
creditors at such a cheap rate—the unreasonable wretches made a demand on me for goods the receipt of which is lost in remote antiquity—
Egad they have been long worn out, not merely from my back but from
my memory—I wonder how such men can have the conscience to
worry a gentleman for payment for things so long after he has enjoyed
them. Of all animals that infest the world I hate duns—they are the
natural enemies of all good fellows—I wish the whole race was extinct—
I'd have nothing in this world but giving and lending and spending—to
ask for pay should be a capital crime, and all notorious duns should be
hung in chains.

Scene 5.

Enter Fatima—thro centre door—

Your humble servant my dear corpse; and how have matters gone with
you since your death?

Abu Hassan.

Oh sadly sadly—I've not only been dead but damn'd into the bargain—
I've been most hideously tormented—a whole legion of imps have been
let loose upon me—

Fatima.

What do you mean?

Abu Hassan.

Creditors! Creditors! the worst of all tormentors—led by that arch fiend
Omar—'Sblood if these plagues are to follow a man into the other world,
a fine gentleman will literally be but a poor devil after all.

Fatima.

And how did you manage to get rid of the gang?

Abu Hassan.

How—why I paid them, to be sure.

Fatima.

What, without money?

Abu Hassan.

Certainly—where's the use of having wit if it is not to supply the place
of money? Any blockhead can pay with money; but give me the man
of talents that can pay with the coinage of his brains. Tho I must confess, you aided me in appeasing the monsters.

Fatima.

I! In what manner?

Abu Hassan.

Oh forsooth, the very thoughts of thy pretty face, and the hope of thy
smiles had as soothing an effect on the heart of old Omar as tho he had
heard the sound of my money ringing upon his counter.

Fatima.

But how were they brought to bear upon him?

Abu Hassan.

Why I told him you had praised his generosity, and had begged me to
cast myself upon it—

Fatima.

And you carried your point in an instant!

Abu Hassan.

Gloriously! The old Sinner laughed in his sleeve—leered with such a liquorish glance that I could have cut his throat—took all the creditors home with him—and while we are now talking of it he is paying all my debts.

Fatima.

There! Now say that I am not a jewel indeed, when you can raise money even upon the sight of me—See how much others are ready to give for the very hope of those smiles which are lavished on you in vain.

Abu Hassan.

Very true, very fine—but in the mean time my dear little wife—never think of carrying your smiles to market yourself—Let me, at least, have the pawning of them—but come let me hear your story—

Fatima.

Here you have a little foretaste of it—in the chink of these hundred gold pieces—(*chinks a purse at his ear*)

Abu Hassan.

A hundred! charming sound.

Fatima.

Zobeide heard my lamentations at a distance and came to meet me at the door of the antechambre. "What has happened to you?" said she. "Ah," cried I with broken voice, "what greater misfortune could happen to me than the loss of my beloved husband? Yes, dearest protectress, Abu Hassan, the poor Abu Hassan, he whom your majesty honoured with your favour and made happy with my hand—Abu Hassan is no more— He is dead, he is dead!"

Abu Hassan.

Faith, you move even me!—well, and what answer made she?

Fatima.

Why—after a long pause of silent sympathy the Sultana tried all she could to console me for my loss.

Abu Hassan.

Ah! you see what a treasure you have in me. How others know my value though you don't—Well! the good Sultana—bless her soul! did her best to console thee.

Fatima.

She did indeed—"My dear Fatima," said she, "thou hast lost one of the merriest of men—"

Abu Hassan.

Ah! dear good Sultana!

Fatima.

"But then," added she, "his jokes were growing sadly stale—"

Abu Hassan.

Hem! hem!

Fatima.

"No man could be more precious than he!"

Abu Hassan.

The good Zobeide!

Fatima.

"For he squandered away even more than belonged to him—"

Abu Hassan.

Phaw!

Fatima.

"He was of a loving disposition."

Abu Hassan.

Did I not tell thee so?

Fatima.

"For he made love to every woman he met with!"

Abu Hassan.

Nay nay—that's Scandal!

Fatima.

"Take him for all in all my dear Fatima," said she, "he was such a man as thou wilt not readily meet with again—"

Abu Hassan.

By the Prophet but the Sultana was in the right after all—

Fatima.

"But thou mayst meet with a better man any day in the week!"

Abu Hassan.

Out upon thee—baggage—this is all thy own joking. The Sultana is a woman of too great discernment to make such a Speech. But come, it is my turn to play the mourner, though I doubt whether the Caliph will think my loss worthy of such a heavy purse full of consolation, as the Sultana has given thee—

Fatima.

Perhaps not—though thy loss is ten times heavier than mine—but thou will display so little grief on the event that the Caliph will be more apt to censure thy indifference than to console thy affliction—

Abu Hassan.

Let me alone for weeping & whining. Where's the widower who could not weep to some tune, when he was to win by it a heavy purse & a piece of Brocade. It is thy business therefore to die & mine to cry—so have at it—

Fatima.

Well, well—this is all well enough in jest—but Allah preserve us dear Hassan from shedding any tears in earnest—

Abu Hassan.

Never my dearest little wife—our griefs shall all be imaginary—our pleasures only real—I have a stock of loving good humour in my heart, that shall bear us up let times go as they may—If thou dost shed a tear my girl, it shall only be for a moment, to give a brighter gleam to thy eye and freshen the roses on thy cheek—

Duetto.

Abu Hassan.

Never shalt thou sigh and languish,
   Thou belov'd & faithful heart,
But this breast shall spare thy anguish
   Seeking comfort to impart.

Fatima.

Tears love are like dew from heaven
   Under which affection blooms,

And the guardians of the flower
Faithfulness and Constancy.

Abu Hassan.

Prove this heart!

Fatima.

I know it well, love.

Abu Hassan.

Banish Jealousy and doubt.

Fatima.

Since within no errors dwell, love,
Sure there needs no watch without.

Both.

Forever then loving and wooing
Confiding in mutual truth,
'Tis the way thus, in billing & cooing
To heighten the joys of one's youth.

Fatima.

But come, don't let us waste any more time with singing and toying.
The Caliph must hear the news of my death from you, before he hears
of yours from Zobeide.

Abu Hassan.

Well, I'm off, but I must take care not to appear too miserable, that I
may act my part naturally—

exeunt severally

Act 2. Scene 1.

Fatima. (*alone*)

I would that Hassan were returned—I am impatient to learn what—
success he has met with from the Caliph. Well heaven be praised that
the man is not really dead. They call losing one's husband gaining one's
liberty, and yet a widow is expected to shed whole rivers of tears.

The nightingale ne'er grieves her
When from her cage set free,

Once more among the blossoms
    She sports from tree to tree.

One glance towards the window
    Where her late prison hangs,
Then loud she pours her rapture
    And fills the grove with joy.

She flaps her little pinions
    And far aloft doth soar
Through heaven's unclouded regions,
    Glad to be free once more.

But Abu Hassan with thee
    No pleasure have I ever,
Thou dearest, thou inspirest me,
    From thee I'd never sever.

I feel myself most bless'd & free
    When in thy gentle power,
And in this tender slavery
    I'd spend my latest hour.

Enter Omar (thro the center door) who looks cautiously round and advances when he finds Fatima is alone.

Omar.

Excuse me beautiful Fatima. I am looking for your husband.

Fatima.

He's gone to the Caliph.

Omar.

Ah—well, I'll take some other opportunity to speak with him. (*pretends to be going*)

Fatima.

As you please.

Omar. (*turning back*)

I would not wish to disturb you.

Fatima.

You are too good!

Omar.

Then I have nothing to expect from your lips but cruelties—

Fatima.

You know me but little Omar—I would not intentionally grieve any one.

Omar.

Did I not say so to myself, when Zelica brought back your answer to me?
No, said I to myself, she can't mean that in earnest. The expression
about the old goat and about complaining to Zobeide, these were only
figurative. He—he—he—Egad I guessed as much!

Fatima.

You have read my very soul.

Omar.

Aye, aye, I can read.

Fatima.

(*Significantly*) And write.

Omar.

And reckon.

Fatima.

But have you never reckoned without your host?

Omar.

No! no! I examine & re-examine all carefully.

Fatima.

My husband unluckily has not so much forethought.

Omar.

Ah! I have often pitied you in silence on that account.

Fatima.

He squanders every thing away.

Omar.

Blindly.

Fatima.

If he has any money—

Omar.

Away it must go!

Fatima.

If he has none—

Omar.

He borrows.

Fatima.

He eats!

Omar.

Drinks!

Fatima.

Gives away!

Omar.

Squanders.

Fatima.

What is left to me at last?

Omar.

Nothing.

Fatima.

Debts! It makes my heart ache when I think of the crowd of our creditors.

Omar.

The crowd is dispersed fair Fatima—one only remains—but not a hostile —hardhearted one.

Fatima.

Explain yourself more clearly.

Omar.

(Draws a pacquet of papers out of his bosom)

Mark this mighty mass of papers,
Bills of Taylors, butchers, bakers,
Pastry cooks and Mantua makers,
All these papers now are mine.

Fatima.

Ah thou givest me the vapours!
Will our fate then never brighten?
Seek no more my soul to frighten,
Saying all these bills are thine.

Omar.

Pluck up heart!

Fatima.

I will endeavour!

Omar.

Do you love me?

Fatima.

I'll hate thee never!

Omar.

Speak out free!

Fatima.

Trust not to show—

Omar.

Speak thy mind—

Fatima. (*pretending embarrassment*)

No—yes—no! no!

(*Aside*)   See how joy his visage flushes
                Sure he thinks I am his prize.
(*To Omar*) Ah kind Sir pray spare my blushes
                Read my answer in my eyes.

Omar.

(*Aside*)   Zounds, how joy my visage flushes
                 Sure the ninny is my prize.
(*To Fatima*) Ah how lovely are thy blushes
                 Thou'rt the idol of mine eyes.
                 Thou lov'st me! Thou lov'st me! my treasure!

Fatima.

I love thee? I love thee? nay! nay!

Omar.

Oh give me a foretaste of pleasure,
A morsel of pleasure today.

Fatima.

Alas sir—I am so embarrassed
I can not—

Omar.

      Oh take my advice,
A kiss when with love one is harassed
Puts all things to rights in a trice.

Fatima.

And thinkst thou I then would be better?

Omar.

Why surely thou canst not be worse.
Thy cash and thy credit all gone,
How canst thou these papers manage?

Fatima.

Those papers?

Omar.

(*lays them on the table*)
      They are all discharg'd.

Fatima & Omar.

Oh how joy his ⎱
Oh how joy my ⎰ visage flushes
Sure he thinks I am his ⎱
Sure the ninny is my ⎰ prey.
[*Fatima.*] Doting fool, these scornful blushes
Ever proud disdain betray.

———————

Omar. Pretty dear, how sweet kindling blushes
Ever secret love betray.

Fatima.

(*looking through the window, to the left.*) Oh dreadful!

Omar.

What is it?

Fatima.

We are both ruin'd!

Omar.

Say what is it!

Fatima.

My husband.

Omar. (into the cabinet)

Help Allah! Oh get me off—

Fatima.
(Locks the door on him & takes out the key)

Stay you there, you good for nothing old wretch—thy flames of love shall have a little damping before I've done with thee.

(Enter Abu Hassan, through the centre door)

What, are you already back, most distressed of Widowers? Let us see if your tears are as productive of a golden stream as mine—(*Speaks low to him*) The bird is caught.

Abu Hassan. (loud)

What bird?

Fatima. (Softly & pointing to the cabinet)

Omar. (*loud*) Where is the piece of Brocade and where the purse? (*softly*) There lie your accounts!

Abu Hassan.

(*Softly—*)Excellent! (*loud*)—Here are both—a heavy purse of a hundred gold pieces—and see what a piece of brocade! Now say whether I have not outdone you in the art wherein the strength of your sex consists—the art of crying!

Fatima.

A hundred gold pieces—a very pretty sum. Ah you see how the Caliph valued me—he knew that so heavy a loss needed great consolation.

Abu Hassan.

Yes truly, and there was another consolation he offered me—which dried my tears in a twinkling.

Fatima.

Ah! & pray what was that?

Abu Hassan.

Six beautiful Slaves! "Abu Hassan," said he—"loving, tender Abu Hassan
—thy heart is too kind & fond to be suffered to wither in loneliness—
Thou hast given a proof in thy fidelity to thy wife what a vast stock of
affection thou hast in thy disposition—Take now to comfort thee a Score
of the fairest of these Slaves just brought to my harem!"

Fatima.

A Score of beautiful Slaves!

Abu Hassan.

Do not alarm thyself my Dear—"No," said I—"Commander of the
Faithful, with a mighty potentate like thee, it is meet to have hundreds
of wives—I am a philosopher—I have learnt to moderate my desires.
Once indeed I should have thought a score of wives a score of blessings
—but now I am fain to content myself with half a dozen!" Oh nature,
nature, how easily art thou satisfied!

Fatima.

Half a dozen wives! Let them not come here though—or you'll find one
wife too many for you!—Ah, rogue!—rogue! I see by that twinkle of the
eye you are at your jokes again. (*softly*) By this time our prisoner must
be in a comfortable plight!

Abu Hassan.

(*softly*) True I had almost forgotten him—(*he goes towards the cabinet
—loud*) Where is the key of the Cabinet?

Fatima.

(*in a tone of Embarrassment—*) The—the Key?

Abu Hassan.

Aye—the key—open the door for me.

Terzetto—

Fatima.

I seek & seek the room all over
Where, where is the provoking key?

Abu Hassan.

Who knows but that some hidden lover
May here in snug concealment be!

Omar.

(*appears at the grated opening over the door*)

Oh dear! Now will he soon discover
That I am here, then woe to me!

Abu Hassan.

Yes were I e'er so cold of spirit
Yet would I feel suspicion here.

Fatima.

Trust me—your doubts I do not merit,
I feel a conscience pure & clear.

Omar.

Oh dear—I've lost all heart and spirit,
My knees together knock through fear.

Fatima & Abu Hassan.

The rogue is now with terror quaking
    And sees of hope no flatt'ring ray;
He'll never here again come raking
    If he this once can get away.

Omar.

My limbs are all with terror quaking
    I see of hope no flatt'ring ray;
Oh Allah! I give up all raking,
    Let me but this once get away.

Abu Hassan.

In yonder closet
There is a rival
From me conceal'd.
Give me the key then,
That I may seize him,
That I may squeeze him
Soon as his cowardly
Face is reveal'd.

Fatima. (*after a pause of thought*)

Sudden reflection
Is in my bosom
Just now awak'd.

You have the key love
From out the key hole
With you I'll wager
Taken away—

Abu Hassan.

If thou dost linger
I will break open
Bar, bolt & door.

Fatima.

Every corner
Have I examin'd,
But the vile key, dear,
On word and honour
Can I—
(*She lets the key fall to the floor as if through fear*)

Abu Hassan.

See here!

Omar.

Oh dear!

Fatima & Abu Hassan.

Thou art ⎱ done over
   He is ⎰
Should he thee ⎱ find,
Should I him ⎰
He has thee ⎱ to death giv'n over
I have him ⎰
And nought shall change my mind.

Omar.

I am done over
Should he me find,
He has me to death given over,
Oh what a murderous mind!

Fatima. (*looking out of the window,
quick and anxiously*)

See, the upper chamberlain Mesrour is hurrying hither—You can imagine
on what errand he comes.

Abu Hassan.

Hastens from the door which he was on the point of opening.

Quick. Quick; stretch yourself on this Divan, your feet towards Mecca; now let me cover you with the Brocade. So!—now he may come as soon as he pleases!

Abu Hassan sets himself down with a sorrowful countenance by Fatima's head—and from time to time wipes his eyes with a handkerchief.

Mesrour enters thro' centre door—Stops at the threshold and after a pause:

By the Great Prophet the Caliph has won the wager!

Abu Hassan.

(*Rises and approaches him.*) I kiss thy hand in all humility—Ah! (*sighs heavily*)

Mesrour. (*with sympathy*)

Poor Abu Hassan.

Abu Hassan.

Yes, so the dear soul called me herself—a few moments before her departure—Here convince yourself (*lifts the Brocade a little from Fatima's face*)

Mesrour.

Ah! Spare me the melancholy sight.

Abu Hassan.

The curtain falls! (*covers her with the Brocade*) As she is so shall I soon be; for I feel that my part is fast drawing to a close.

Mesrour.

Nay; be not so downhearted, Abu Hassan—none but a weak spirit suffers itself to be overcome by misfortune. The noble soul rises strengthened, like the flowers after a Storm—faith a young fellow like you may live to bury a dozen wives!

Abu Hassan.

The Storm is not yet over—Did not you say something about a wager?

Mesrour.

Certainly. The Commander of the Faithful informed Zobeide of Fatima's death; but she insisted it was you were dead. The Caliph was too sure of the fact to give up and Zobeide—she is a woman, and a Sultana into the bargain—How then could she be in the wrong?

Abu Hassan.

By the beard of the Great Prophet, I wish she was not—and that my dear Fatima were once more alive—though I must confess poor dear soul she did sometimes plague me a little.

Mesrour.

Ah she was a young thing—young and giddy—you must not remember her faults with censure. Well, at length the Caliph offered to bet, and the wager was closed with great heat on both sides—He sets his pleasure Garden against Zobeide's picture Palace.

Abu Hassan.

No one has more reason than I do to lament that the good lady should lose her picture Palace; but what are dead pictures in comparison with a living beauty like Fatima?

Mesrour.

She is dead. So much the worse for thee if thy grief is really from thy heart; but so much the better for the Caliph. I must hasten therefore to carry him the joyful tidings.

(*Abu Hassan accompanies him through the centre door.*)

Fatima.

(*Sits up*) I had hard work to keep from laughing. I'm glad he is gone—

Abu Hassan.

Ay, he's off as fast as his legs can carry him to take the pleasant tidings to the Caliph.

Fatima.

(*rising from the Couch*) Pleasant?

Abu Hassan.

I mean merely on account of the Wager.

Fatima.

Who knows whether he would not rather have lost it? But you owe me an inquiry and then a formal apology for your suspicion.

Abu Hassan.

I?

Fatima.

Yes, with respect to the Key and the Closet.

Abu Hassan.

(*After a moment's thought*) Well well, let that rest for the present; and now I am cool I must entreat you to pardon my fit of passion— Besides, we are not yet out of this scrape, for Zobeide will not be satisfied with the mere testimony of the upper Chamberlain. (*During this speech he approaches the window and suddenly stops before it.*) Here we have it! Quick—quick—make ready! (*he throws himself on the other Couch*)

Fatima.

Why what's the matter?

Abu Hassan.

Zemrud—the old nurse!

Fatima.

Who?

Abu Hassan.

Don't ask, but cover me with the brocade.

Fatima.

(*Spreads the Brocade over him, lays his turban on his face and then sits beside him.*) She does not come yet. (*listens*) Ah—I believe I hear her panting.

Air

Here lies! what miserable fate!

[Scene 2.]

Enter Zemrud—stands at the door astonished.

Fatima.

Ah is it you good Zemrud?

Zemrud.

(*without listening to her—*) Now this is too much! This Mesrour and his impertinence makes me mad! Did he not Swear that the living was dead and the dead was living? Now I am only curious to know what kind of death the Caliph will put him to.

Fatima.

You speak of the upper chamberlain, what has he said?

Zemrud.

What has he said? His scandalous tongue has murdered you. He swore by the Holy Tomb that it was not your husband but yourself that wast dead.

Fatima.

Would to Allah that I lay here instead of him.

Zemrud.

No, no—would to Allah no such thing! Better ten men should die than one single woman—What, wouldst thou that our protectress should lose thee and her picture palace at one blow?—nay that would be too much. But come—let me look at the worthy Abu Hassan for an instant that I may swear with a good conscience he is dead.

Fatima.

(*raises the Turban*) Since you wish it look here & weep—Here lies not merely Abu Hassan but Fatima also—her better self—the soul of her soul—

Zemrud.

Poor Abu Hassan. Poor Fatima—but bless me! why he looks just as if he were asleep—why he does not look at all like other worthy dead people—why I should hardly think him dead if I did not know it.

Fatima.

It is the same with me I'll assure you—I can hardly consider myself a widow—a widow—most wretched of all beings! (*weeps*)

Zemrud.

Ah well aday—well aday—(*weeps with Fatima—then suddenly in a common tone:*) There now I must go—the Sultana will be all impatience for my return—Nay, nay (*patting Fatima on the cheek*)—cheer up my child—cheer up—Never take the loss of one husband so much to heart—

Fatima.

Ah—but such a husband—

Zemrud.

Why truly he was a good personable man—a handsome man—but then he had his faults—I never could endure his nose—

Fatima.

His nose I confess was faulty—

Zemrud.

Oh abominable—but he was a tolerable looking man for all—and a good natured man, excepting that he was a little passionate.

Fatima.

Yes I must confess he was a little passionate.

Zemrud.

Oh he was fire & touchwood—a brush heap in a blaze—I never could abide his temper—but yet he was a good kind of a man—very merry— very fond of his joke—excepting that he sometimes joked a little out of season.

Fatima.

Yes I confess his jokes were sometimes ill timed.

Zemrud.

Oh intolerable. I never could bear his jokes—yet the man after all was well enough—but mercy on us—not a man for such a pretty young widow as you to break your heart about—Abu Hassan—pshaw! he was not the only man in the world—For instance there's the young ——— but no matter now—another time will do—we'll then speak of him and of twenty others. (*During this conversation Abu Hassan now & then peeps below, & shakes his fist from under the brocade, unseen by Zemrud.*) Now, farewell my dear child—but don't cry so much, it hurts the eyes. (*Going*) I can't get that accursed upper chamberlain out of my thoughts— But patience—patience! (*goes with Fatima through the center door—*)

[Scene 3.]

Abu Hassan. (*Sits up*)

Fire & furies! What it is to hear what's said of me after death! The cursed old babbling beldame with her young fellow—and twenty more! (*To Fatima*) Now who has the old woman nominated as my successor?

Fatima.

She was today more discreet & silent than common—but—between our- selves, I begin to wish that thou wert really dead, for I should be very sorry to be caught in a lie.

Abu Hassan.

A right womanlike conscientiousness, but our best wishes are not always fulfilled. Therefore prepare yourself in time, and be steadfast—and what is still more needful—be discreet—

Terzetto
Fatima. Abu Hassan. Omar.

Fatima.

    Now the mischief is quickly completing;
    From this scrape there's no longer retreating,
    Oh how my poor heart is beating
    Would the danger were well o'er.

Abu Hassan.

alter'd
measure

    Our farce now is quickly completing;
    None must think now of retreating,
    So away with all heart beating
    Soon the frolick will be o'er.

Omar.

    Now my misery is completing;
    From this trap there's no retreating,
    Oh I fear a hearty beating
    My poor back and shoulders o'er.

Abu Hassan.

    Come die bravely!
          Fatima. Can you joke me?

Abu Hassan.

    Pluck up heart!
          Fatima. My terrors choke me!
    How I tremble!
          Abu Hassan. You provoke me,
    Give these silly terrors o'er!
  (*March at a distance*)

Fatima.
       Hark! I hear a distant drumming!

Abu Hassan.
       Now be brave, your courage rouse!

Fatima.
  (*calling his attention to the sound*)
    Don't you hear?
Abu Hassan. (*goes to the window*)
             Aye! aye! they're coming!

Fatima.
  (*also at the window*)
    The Sultana!
          Abu Hassan. And her spouse!

Fatima. Abu Hassan. Omar.

Fatima.

    Dismal terrors quite o'ercome me,
    I've no longer heart nor head.

Abu Hassan.

    Let not terror quite o'ercome thee,
    Now's the time to task your head.

Omar.	Zounds how terrors overcome me!
	Never more I'll shew my head!
Abu Hassan.	Quickly, quickly dead and dumb be!
Fatima.	Ah already I'm half dead!
Abu Hassan.	Both must lie upon our death bed,
	Then completed will the Hum be!
Fatima.	Oh I'm in a mortal fright!
Abu Hassan & Omar.	Silence!—silence!

> *Abu Hassan.* Hush! good night!
>
> *All.* Hush! good night!

[Scene 4.]

The attendants of the Caliph & Zobeide enter and arrange themselves so that the two Couches remain in sight.

Chorus

> Bow your heads and lift your voices,
> Throw the doors all open wide;
> See he comes who all rejoices,
> Haroun with his beauteous bride!

At the end of the Chorus enter the Caliph, Zobeide, Mesrour & Zemrud; at the entrance of the Caliph all the attendants kneel. Mesrour points to the Divan on which Fatima lies and at the same time Zemrud points to that on which is Abu Hassan—Both approach them eagerly.

Caliph.

Now—look for yourself—have I been misinformed? (*Makes signs for the attendants to rise.*)

Zobeide.

How! have I lost my wager?

Caliph.

(*Starts back with astonishment—*) What do I see! both dead—Abu Hassan—my favourite Abu Hassan—Dead!

Zobeide.

My dear Fatima a corpse—oh lamentable!

Caliph.

This is one of the heaviest misfortunes that has ever happened to me. It surpasses even the loss of poor Zara, my favorite green monkey—Ah poor Abu Hassan—he was the most expensive favorite I ever had, I must confess, and cost me ten times as much as my poor Zara, that used to break all the china in the palace, but he was a *merry soul*—I would he were alive again.

Mesrour.

Commander of the Faithful, (*pointing to the table*) here lie papers which may throw some light upon his death—(*hands them to the Caliph*)

Caliph.

Mere accounts & notes of hand which Abu Hassan apparently had arranged before his death. Poor fellow—they say he kept his accounts admirably—the only trouble was he never discharged them—(*hands them to Zobeide—*)

[Zobeide.]

A very considerable amount—which must have exceeded the means of the young couple.

Caliph.

Ah! Abu Hassan had always a talent for the ways and means—No statesman could run in debt more intrepidly—But how to settle our wager—there's the perplexing point. Fatima told you of her husband's death—he told me of hers—which of them was first dead?

Zobeide.

Abu Hassan. And your pleasure garden is mine.

Caliph.

And I maintain that Fatima died first, & I condole with you on the loss of your beautiful picture gallery.

Zemrud.

What has the black babbler now to say for himself, did the wife or the husband die first?

Mesrour.

I say the very opposite of what you say—therefore I say the truth.

Zemrud.

I say that thou art not a knave.

Mesrour.

The first truth thou hast ever spoken, which I pay you for with my first lie; or rather, I give thee a threefold lie for a single truth, for I affirm thou hast yet three teeth in thy head.

Zemrud.

Commander of the Faithful, can you endure it that such a monster should abuse the Nurse of your Sultana? Cannot a worthy Gentlewoman lose a single tooth but what the most excellent knave must publish her misfortune to all Bagdad? If he is not hanged upon the spot I'll tear his eyes out.

Caliph.

Cease your quarrelling! None of us can decide who is in the right. But I hate uncertainty and I swear by the Great Prophet I will give a thousand gold pieces to whoever will prove who died first, Abu Hassan or his wife.

Abu Hassan. (sitting up)

Commander of the Faithful, I claim the reward, for I died first.

All. (except the Caliph & Zobeide, start back with dismay)

Allah preserve us!

Caliph & Zobeide.

What's this?

Abu Hassan.

Your favour only can waken me to life—if however thine eyes are turned upon me in anger—I am once more a dead man.

Caliph.

Rise and explain to me this riddle.

Abu ,Hassan. (Throws himself at the Caliph's feet)

The explanation is simple. The daintiness of my palate, wherewith my better half wonderfully sympathized, brought me thus early to the grave.

Zobeide.

But thy wife—?

Abu Hassan.

A friendly word from thee will also bring her back from the world of shadows.

Zobeide.

Fatima!

Fatima. (sits up—)

My protectress!

Zobeide.

Art thou awake?

Fatima.   (kneels before Zobeide)

If your eyes give me a pardon as a morning's salutation.

Caliph.

(*to Abu Hassan & Fatima*) Rise! Tell me then, how came you to resort to this whimsical project?

Abu Hassan.

Commander of the Faithful, thou and thy Spouse have overloaded us with benefits; which we have squandered away with merry hearts. The consequence was that we were compelled to have recourse to Userers; but at length these would lend no more and nothing remained for our miserable dinner but bread & water.

Caliph.

I understand! In this way you would inform us of your necessities—But how was it possible for you to pay off these Bonds?

Abu Hassan.

Sire they are not discharged. One of my Creditors, who persecuted Fatima with his love, brought these papers to her and offered them as the price for her favours.

Caliph.

Name the wretch to me!

Abu Hassan.   (opens the Cabinet & draws forth Omar)

Omar, thy Banker!

Omar.   (falling at the Caliph's feet)

Thy humbled slave!

Caliph.

Scoundrel! dar'st thou to steal into the dwelling of my favourite to destroy his domestic happiness? Thank my kindness that I do not punish thy offense with death—out of my sight! (*Omar sneaks off. To Mesrour:*) Order my treasurer to pay to Abu Hassan the thousand gold pieces.

Abu Hassan.

Commander of the Faithful, thou hast awakened me from the Grave— By this new favour you have acquired a double right to my gratitude.

Zobeide.

Zemrud—you must pay the like sum to Fatima. I will take care in future that your wants shall be supplied without a sham death—

Fatima.

I have not words to express my thanks.

Abu Hassan.

Am I not the shrewdest of all dead men? The simple folks let themselves be laid upon the Bier without any future object; but I knew well what I was about—I had not the slightest inclination to remain dead, but only died—to gain a living!

Finale

Happy happy is the dwelling
In which Haroun doth come,
Then loud his praises swelling
Sound Trump & Kettle drum.
or
Hail all Hail the happy dwelling
Into which the Caliph comes,
Then loud his praises swelling
Sound Trump & Kettle drums.

EDITORIAL APPENDIX

Textual Commentary,
Discussions, and Lists by
Wayne R. Kime

LIST OF ABBREVIATIONS

The following symbols have been used in the editorial apparatus to designate the manuscript and previously published texts of Irving's *Miscellaneous Writings*:

[CONTRIBUTIONS TO THE NEW-YORK *MORNING CHRONICLE*]

1A   New-York *Morning Chronicle*, December 24, 1803, p. 2 col. 5; December 30, 1803, p. 3 cols. 1–2.

[CONTRIBUTIONS TO *THE CORRECTOR*]

1A   *The Corrector*, nos. 2–10 (March 31–April 26, 1804).

"WE WILL REJOICE!!!"

1A   New-York *Evening Post*, May 14, 1804, p. 2 col. 5.

THE NEW-YORK REVIEW; OR, CRITICAL JOURNAL....

1A   *The New-York Review; or, Critical Journal.* New York: Inskeep & Bradford, 1809.

[REVIEW OF *THE WORKS . . . OF ROBERT TREAT PAINE*]

P   *The Works, in Verse and Prose, of the Late Robert Treat Paine. . . .* Boston: J. Belcher, 1812.
1A   *Analectic Magazine*, 1 (March 1813), [249]–66.
2A   *Spanish Papers*, II, [303]–24.

BIOGRAPHY OF CAPTAIN JAMES LAWRENCE

1A   *Analectic Magazine*, 2 (August 1813), [122]–39.
9A   *Spanish Papers*, II, [37]–58.

CAPTAIN LAWRENCE

1A   *Analectic Magazine*, 2 (September 1813), 222–23.
2A   *Spanish Papers*, II, 58–59.

THE LAY OF THE SCOTTISH FIDDLE: A TALE OF HAVRE DE GRACE

L   *The Lay of the Scottish Fiddle: A Tale of Havre de Grace.* New-York: Inskeep & Bradford, 1813.
1A   *Analectic Magazine*, 2 (September 1813), 223–30.

BIOGRAPHICAL NOTICE OF THE LATE LIEUTENANT BURROWS

1A   *Analectic Magazine*, 2 (November 1813), [396]–403.
4A   *Spanish Papers*, II, [60]–69.

BIOGRAPHICAL MEMOIR OF COMMODORE PERRY

1A   *Analectic Magazine*, 2 (December 1813), 494–510.
4A   *Spanish Papers*, II, [70]–90.

[LINES WRITTEN AT STRATFORD]

1A	"Washington Irving at Stratford-on-Avon," *The Albion*, N. S. 1 (March 2, 1833), 72 col. 1.
2A	"Scraps from the book kept at Stratford upon Avon," *New-York Mirror*, 11 (October 26, 1833), 136 col. 1.
3A	N. P. Willis, "A Note for the Reader," *Home Journal*, no. 724 (December 24, 1859), p. 2 col. 1.
4A	John H. Birss, "New Verses by Washington Irving," *American Literature*, 4 (November 1932), 296.

WRITTEN IN THE DEEPDENE ALBUM

1E	*Cornhill Magazine*, 1, no. 5 (May 1860), 582.
1A	PMI, II, 85–86.

TO MISS EMILY FOSTER ON HER BIRTH-DAY

1A	PMI, II, 152–53.
MSy	Manuscript journal of Emily Foster, pp. [123–24] (Beinecke Library, Yale University).

THE DULL LECTURE

1A	*The Atlantic Souvenir; Christmas and New Year's Offering. 1828*. Philadelphia: Carey, Lea, & Carey, [1827]. P. 294.
2A	*Irvingiana*, p. lxiii.

[¡AY DIOS DE MI ALMA!]

MSv	Author's manuscript, University of Virginia.

THE LAY OF THE SUNNYSIDE DUCKS

MSm	Author's manuscript, in the possession of Mrs. Florence F. Locke, Milton, Massachusetts.
1A	James T. Scharf, *History of Westchester County, New York*. 2 vols. Philadelphia: C. E. Preston, 1886. I, 239–40.
2A	Mrs. J. Borden Harriman. *From Pinafores to Politics*. New York: H. Holt & Co., 1923. Pp. 22–23.

[THE FREYSCHÜTZ]

MSn	Author's manuscript, Manuscript Division, New York Public Library

[ABU HASSAN]

MSn	Author's manuscript, Manuscript Division, New York Public Library

ARE	Author's Revised Edition of *The Works of Washington Irving*, 15 vols. (New York: George P. Putnam, 1848–1850)
Irvingiana	Evert A. Duyckinck, ed. *Irvingiana: A Memorial of Washington Irving* (New York: C. B. Richardson, 1860 [1859])
T	Twayne edition
Johnson	Samuel Johnson, *A Dictionary of the English Language*, 9th ed., 2 vols. (London: J. Johnson et al., 1806)
Walker	John Walker, *A Critical Pronouncing Dictionary* (London: G. G. J. and J. Robinson and T. Cadell, 1791)

Webster   Noah Webster, A *Compendious Dictionary of the English Language* (Hartford: Hudson and Goodwin, 1806)

The following further editorial symbols are employed throughout the editorial apparatus:

↑ ↓	Interlinear insertion
⟨ ⟩	Cancelled matter
[roman]	Editorial insertion
[*italics*]	Editorial comment
⟨? ?⟩	
or	Doubtful readings
[? ?]	
undeciphered	Unrecovered word. When more than one word is unrecovered, the fact is noted: e.g., "⟨*three undeciphered words*⟩"

EXPLANATORY NOTES

The numbers before all notes indicate page and line or lines respectively. Chapter numbers, chapter or section titles, epigraphs, author's chapter or section summaries, text quotations, and footnotes are included in the line count. The quotation from the text, to the left of the bracket, is the matter under discussion.

3.7 your friendly vindication of the "Rights of Actors"] An allusion to the "Letters of Jonathan Oldstyle" severally, and in particular to letter VI (January 17, 1803), in which "Andrew Quoz" first gives an eloquent defense of the prerogatives and immunities of actors, and "Jonathan Oldstyle" then comments: "From the tenor and conclusion of these remarks of my friend . . . they may not improperly be called the 'Rights of Actors.'"

3.11–12 "writ down in my duty,"] Adapted from *Hamlet*, I, ii, 222.

4.4 An old assembly room] "A large building, formerly a flour store, has been converted into a temporary theatre, for their [the players'] accommodation." ("Communication," New York *Morning Chronicle*, August 13, 1803, p. 3, col. 1).

5.26 the New-York leader] Probably G. K. Jackson, a New York music teacher who served as musical director at the Park Theatre. See the "Letters of Jonathan Oldstyle," letter IV (December 1, 1802).

5.30–31 "we sung *without warbling*, that defect common to modern singers! !"] "Warbling" was a style of singing in trills and quavers then in fashion. On September 30, 1803, "Thalia" wrote in the Albany *Centinel*, p. 2, col. 5–p. 3, col. 1, that the singing of Mrs. Seymour, an actress in the Old American Company, had been well received: "The *warbling* of modern stage singers has not been copied by her, and we cannot say we disapprove of it."

6.10 *An eminent Artist*] Joseph Delacroix, a New York pyrotechnician and candymaker. On August 3, 1803, the Albany *Centinel* published a "Communication" which began (p. 3, col. 2): "We are informed, that two gentlemen, eminent in the art of Pyrotechny . . . intend to gratify our citizens by a display of the effects of Gun-Powder, combined with other combustible ingredients. . . ."

6.13–14 "they swore in faith 'twas strange! 'twas passing strange!"] Adapted from *Othello*, I, iii, 160–61.

6.24 a certain fourth of July exhibition] On July 4, 1803, Joseph Delacroix had sought with disastrous results to mount a grand display of fireworks on a patriotic theme. See the New York *Evening Post,* July 3, 1803, p. 2, col. 1; New York *Morning Chronicle,* July 12, 1803, p. 2, col. 5.

6.26–27 a company of wooden puppets] A reference to the activities of a Mr. Maginnis, who is described in the New York *Morning Chronicle* for August 13, 1803, as "of puppet shew memory" (p. 3, col. 1). In March, 1804, Maginnis opened the Grove Theatre in New York, where for a short time he offered legitimate drama and other entertainments.

6.36 the *learned pig!*] According to contemporary advertisements, the "learned pig" was brought from England and purchased for $1000 by one "Mr. Pinchbeck," who displayed the animal's talents in several American cities at the turn of the nineteenth century. The pig appeared in Albany in 1797 and perhaps at other times. See also 36.11–12.

6.38–39 Cocker or Dilworth] Edward Cocker (1631–1675) was the author of two textbooks, *Arts Glory: or the Pen-Man's Treasury* (London, 1657?) and *Cockers Arithmetick* (London, 1664?), both of which were frequently reprinted in England and America for more than a century after their first publication. Thomas Dilworth (d. 1780) was also the author of two popular works, *The Schoolmaster's Assistant,* 2d ed. (London, 1774), and *The Young Book-keeper's Assistant* (London, 1765).

6.43 Mr. Hogg] John Hogg (d. 1814), an actor in the Old American Company and a member of that company's contingent in Albany.

7.3 *Major Sturgeon*] A character in Samuel Foote's farce *The Mayor of Garret* (1764).

7.26 Dr. Last] A shoemaker who passes an amusing examination for the degree of M.D. in Samuel Foote's *The Devil upon Two Sticks* (1768). Perhaps the allusion is also to Peter Irving, who was an M.D. and who, as editor of the New York *Morning Chronicle,* occupied the premises of the Old American Company during its absence in Albany.

7.29–30 "*sic tempora mutantur et* trumpery *mutantur idem.*"] "Thus change the times, and trumpery change[s] the same." Probably a misquotation of the concluding line in an article on the Albany expedition published in the New York *Morning Chronicle* for August 13, 1803, p. 3, col. 1: "*Sic tempora mutantur, et trumpery mutatur etiam.*" The Latin is probably an adaptation of Lucretius, *De Rerum Natura,* I, 76.

8.3 BEWARE OF IMPOSTORS!!] Some characteristic features of style: James Cheetham as a medical doctor (See "Letters of Jonathan Old-style," letter VII—January 22, 1803); men as animals (8.23); Aeolism (8.25–26); typographical variety; format of published advertisement; the slang "phiz," often used in the "Jonathan Oldstyle" series.

8.7 JAMES CHEETHAM] As the editor of the New York *American Citizen* (see 8.17) and the author of several pamphlets, Cheetham (1772–1810) zealously promoted the Clintonian faction of the Democratic party in the state of New York.

8.12 VIEW, NARRATIVE, NINE LETTERS] *A View of the Political Conduct of Aaron Burr, Esquire* (New York, 1802), *Narrative of the Suppression by Colonel Burr of the History* (New York, 1802), and *Nine Letters on the Subject of Aaron Burr's Political Defection* (New York, 1803), all by James Cheetham.

8.19 A REPLY TO ARISTIDES] James Cheetham, *A Reply to Aristides* (New York, 1804). See Explanatory Notes 8.23.

8.23 "the . . . race."] A close paraphrase of a passage in William P. Van Ness's *Examination of the Various Charges Exhibited Against Aaron Burr, Esq. . . . By Aristides* (New York, 1803), p. 52, characterizing Tunis Wortman, Irving's "OURANG OUTANG" (8.22).

8.28 the Baboon and Surrogate] Sylvanus Miller, surrogate for the city of New York.

8.39–40 Joe Gumption, Homefpun, &c. &c.] Apparently pseudonyms adopted by Sylvanus Miller for newspaper articles on political topics.

9.3 *BILLY LUSCIOUS.*] Some characteristic features of style: wordplay (9.15); illustrative literary quotations; typographical variety; men as animals; "political jugglers" (see "Letters of Jonathan Oldstyle," letter VI); justices as rogues (see 36.33–35, 37.1–2); "ragged regiment," a preferred phrase; burlesque professional titles (see 38.36).

9.8 *Billy Luscious*] William L. Rose, a New York attorney.

9.9 "*A Rose by any other name would smell as sweet.*"] Adapted from *Romeo and Juliet*, II, i, 43–44.

9.12 "clouds and thick darkness"] Possibly echoes of *Paradise Lost*, II, 264, or *Paradise Regained*, I, 41. However see Roth, *Washington Irving's Contributions*, p. 55, where Sterne's *Tristram Shandy* is identified as Irving's source.

10.9 the federal party] The Federalist party, then waning in power.

10.9 RIKER, SPENCER] Richard Riker, district attorney for the state of New York; Ambrose Spencer, a state senator.

10.12 CANDIDATE BOB] Robert L. Livingston, a member of a leading family in the state of New York. An article entitled "Candidate Bob" had appeared in the first issue of *The Corrector*, p. 3, cols. 1–2.

10.17 JOSEPH SURFACE, Esq.] A character in Sheridan's *School for Scandal*. The sheriff of New York in 1804 was Joseph Broad.

10.26 ARISTIDEAN GALLERY OF PORTRAITS.] Some characteristic features of style: Aeolism (10.38–39); attention to details of clothing; wordplay (11.4); "worthy" (11.5), a favorite epithet; "Knight of the burning house" (11.18—see 39.17).

10.31 Captain Skunk] John Swartwout, U.S. marshal for the district of New York, who in 1802 had fought a duel with De Witt Clinton.

11.2–3 The intimate friend . . . of our noble Captain Skunk] Probably Ambrose Spencer; see 11.4 and Roth, *Washington Irving's Contributions*, p. 61, n. 3.

11.9–10 An animal, very much resembling an Ourang-Outang] Tunis Wortman, clerk of the Mayor's Court.

11.16 Brother George, and a certain Bull-faced notary] George Clinton, brother of De Witt Clinton, and (perhaps) William L. Rose, who was a public notary. See *"muffin faced meddler"* (9.19).

11.21–22 a more *elevated* mark of distinction was intended him] James Cheetham was arrested in England in 1793 on charges of conspiracy to overthrow the government but was later released. He came to the United States in 1798. Irving portrays him as virtually a fugitive from justice.

11.39 *Till it son*] I.e., Thomas Tillotson, the secretary of state for New York.

12.4 THE CONGRESSIONAL FRACAS] Some characteristic features of style: mock heroic manner; illustrative literary quotations; quotation from "Snigger's Travels" (see 38.24–27); parody of the New York *American Citizen* (12.11–12); attention to the protagonist's "breeches"; man as animal; typographical variety.

12.9–10 D——— W——— C———] De Witt Clinton (1769–1828), the mayor of New York and an adherent of the Democratic (Jeffersonian) party.

12.10–11 "round unvarnished tale"] *Othello*, I, iii, 90.

12.18 appointed mayor of the city] In October, 1803, De Witt Clinton resigned his office as a U.S. senator to accept that of mayor of New York.

12.34 *tender-hearted Isaac's* brow] Isaac Clason, a director of the Manhattan Company, had recently won local notoriety for beating a German servant. See pp. 26–27.

13.10 General Dayton] Jonathan Dayton (1760–1824), soldier, was from 1799 to 1805 a U.S. senator from New Jersey.

13.27–28 Major P. Butler] Percival Butler (1760–1821).

13.36 S———t] John Swartwout; see Explanatory Notes, 10.31.

14.1 *Yahoo** MILLER] Sylvanus Miller; see Explanatory Notes, 8.28.

14.9 WARRIOR PURDY] Ebenezer Purdy, a state senator.

14.13 NED FERRIS] Benjamin Ferris, a public notary.

14.36 Snigger's Travels] An imaginary work, obviously modelled on *Gulliver's Travels*.

17.1 EBENEZER.] Some characteristic features of style: illustrative literary quotations; man as animal; real life as a theatric entertainment; ironic use of "honorable."

17.2–3 "But to ſay I know any good of him, were to ſay more than I know."] Possibly an adaptation of Timon's contemptuous dismissal of Alcibiades in *Timon of Athens*, III, iv, 56–57.

17.7 "ſeven-fold ſhield of tough bull hide"] Adapted from the description of Telamon's shield in Pope's *The Iliad*, VII, 267–68.

17.11 *"The lion preys not upon carcaſes."*] For a hypothetical identification of this proverb as a paraphrase from Edmund Burke's "A Letter to a Noble Lord" see Roth, *Washington Irving's Contributions*, p. 21, n. 34; p. 69, n. 3.

17.20–21 Jean Bon St. André] French revolutionist (1749–1815).

17.28–29 Our "moſt righteous judge," our "ſecond Daniel,"] Adapted from *The Merchant of Venice*, IV, i, 324, 335.

17.33 honest Lithgow . . . rejoicing . . . delights."] William Lithgow (1582–ca. 1645), Scottish traveler in Europe and the East. The quotation is adapted from his *Totall Discourse, of the Rare Adventures and Painefull Peregrinations* (London, 1632), pt. 1, p. ix.

18.7–8 "the crumbs . . . table."] Adapted from Luke 15:14.

18.20–21 "I had rather . . . dungeon,"] *Othello*, III, iii, 270–71.

18.24 "So much for Buckingham!"] Adapted from a speech by Gloster in Colley Cibber's *Tragical History of King Richard III. Alter'd from Shakespeare*, IV, iii.

18.26 TO TOBY TICKLER, ESQ.] Some characteristic features of style: format of a letter from a relative; politics as a play or farce; dignified first paragraph; wordplay (19.35); burlesque professional titles (19.37– see 38.37).

18.35 Mons. H. Carritat, *Libraire and Bibliothécaire*] Henry Carritat kept a circulating library and bookstore at the City Hotel, on Broadway, New York.

19.13–14 Meſſrs. C——n, L——n, L——s, S——r, and P——y] De Witt Clinton; John R. or Brockholst Livingston; Morgan Lewis (1754–1844), the Democratic candidate for governor of New York; Ambrose Spencer; Ebenezer Purdy.

19.15–16 the Hon. W——m D——g, and J——n W——h] William Denning, a director of the Manhattan Company and of the Bank of New York; John Woodworth, in 1805 attorney general of the State of New York.

19.17–18 "The character of . . . Jeremiah Sneak . . . Mr. Samuel Foote.] Jeremiah Sneak is the title character in Samuel Foote's farce *The Mayor of Garret* (1764).

19.23–24 M——n L——n, toad-eater to the honorable the C——f J——e and director of the M——n C——y] Maturin Livingston, described elsewhere in *The Corrector* (p. 6, col. 1) as "that convenient and obsequious tool of his more wealthy relatives"; Chief Justice Morgan Lewis (see Explanatory Notes 19.13–14); Manhattan Company.

19.37 D——— L———] Daniel Ludlow, president of the Manhattan Company.

19.41 Mr. J——s A——n] James Arden, a director of the Manhattan Company.

20.2–4 "Argus . . . thro'."] An adaptation from "No. III" in *Criticisms on the Rolliad. Part the First*; see the 8th ed. (London, 1788), p. 51. The allusion may be to Schuyler Livingston, who elsewhere in *The Corrector* (p. 39, col. 1) is described as a "gimblet-eyed jackanapes."

20.6 TO TOBY TICKLER, ESQ.] Some characteristic features of style: reference to earlier instalment (20.10–12); dignified first paragraphs; format of a letter from a relative; illustrative literary quotations; typographical variety; politician as comedian; biblical parallels (see 38.30–32).

20.27 Shakeſpeare Gallery] At 11 Park, New York. The offices of William Dunlap's Old American Company and David Longworth's printing house were located here.

20.30–31 a director diſtinguiſhed for his improved taste] Possibly Robert R. Livingston, a director of the New York Academy of Fine Arts who as U.S. minister to France had exerted himself in recent years to arrange for the transfer to the institution of plaster casts taken from great works of sculpture in the museums of Paris. In 1804 Livingston assumed the presidency of the Academy.

21.6–8 "———Shall fall . . . behind."] Adapted from *The Tempest*, IV, i, 151–56.

21.9–13 "We . . . . booty." Hen. IV.] Adapted from *Henry IV, Part I, II*, i, 80–91.

21.15 Autolicus] Autolycus, the peddler and "snapper-up of unconsidered trifles" in *The Winter's Tale*.

21.15–16 "I am . . . Tiber in it."] Adapted from *Coriolanus*, II, i, 51–52.

21.21–22 "And fee . . . a holy man."] Adapted from *Richard III*, III, vii, 98–99.

21.23–25 "'Tis . . . paw, &c."] These lines are adapted from the refrain of a song in act 2, scene 2 of George Colman the Younger's *Blue-Beard; or, Female Curiosity* (1798): "I strut as fine as any Macaw, / I'll change for down my bed of straw, / On perquisites I lay my paw, / I pour wine, slily, down my maw, / I stuff good victuals in my craw, / 'Tis a very fine thing to be Father-in-Law / To a very magnificent three tail'd Bashaw!"

21.27 Capt. Bobadil] A cowardly braggart in Jonson's *Every Man in His Humour*.

21.27–28 the tragi-comedy of the *bloody buſineſs*] Probably an allusion to De Witt Clinton's role in the events described above, pp. 12–16.

21.30–34 "And telling me . . . a warrior."] Adapted from *Henry IV, Part 1*, I, iii, 57–64.

21.35–38 "Why he . . . knocking."] Adapted from *Troilus and Cressida*, III, iii, 251–57.

22.2 *Spero meliora*] "I hope for better."

22.5–8 "–Beware . . . upon him."] Adapted from *Richard III*, I, iii, 289–93.

22.9–10 "I'll not meddle . . . it checks him."] Adapted from *Richard III*, I, iv, 137–40.

22.13–17 "The high permission . . . to others."] Adapted from *Paradise Lost*, I, 212–16.

22.18–21 "Gratiano . . . the ſearch."] Gratiano is a character in *The Merchant of Venice*, from which this passage is adapted (see I, i, 114–18).

22.22 Dicky Gofling] Apparently Richard Riker, who is portrayed elsewhere in *The Corrector* as a fawning sycophant; see Explanatory Notes, 10.9.

22.27–32 "I do remember . . . ſhut."] Adapted from *Romeo and Juliet*, V, i, 37–56.

23.3–9 "High . . . . diſplay'd."] Adapted from *Paradise Lost*, II, 1–10.

23.15 A———e S———r] Ambrose Spencer; see Explanatory Notes 10.9.

23.17–22 "———Moloch . . . at all;———"] Adapted from *Paradise Lost*, II, 43–48.

23.23–29 "The character . . . fiend."–Addiſon on Milton.] A very loose paraphrase of a passage in Joseph Addison's essay on Milton in *The Spectator*, no. 309 (February 23, 1712).

23.31 the hon. J——— A——g] General John Armstrong (ca. 1758–1843), an ally of De Witt Clinton. When Clinton assumed the mayoralty of New York, Armstrong was appointed a U.S. senator in his place.

23.33–24.3 "–On *th' other* . . . pleaſ'd the ear."] Adapted from *Paradise Lost*, II, 108–17.

24.6–14 "———The leaft . . . beatific:———" . . . "———than whom . . . itſelf:———"] Adapted from *Paradise Lost*, I, 679–84; I, 490–92.

24.20–26 "–A ſerpent . . . unſeen."] Adapted from *Paradise Lost*, II, 652–59.

24.29–35 "Which . . . in ruin."] Adapted from *Paradise Lost*, II, 299–305.

25.1 CHARACTERISTIC PORTRAITS] Some characteristic features of style: continuation of earlier instalment (25.3); literary quotations; typographical variety; associate objects of satire with "savages" (26.7–8—see 38.4–5); "eminent artists" (25.5–see 6.10).

25.7–16 "By the pricking . . . angry . . . *Hecate* . . . our art."]   *Macbeth*, IV, i, 44–45; III, v, 2–9.

25.19–25 "Thou . . . an aſs."]   Adapted from *As You Like It*, III, ii, 30–39, *Much Ado About Nothing*, IV, ii, 77–90.

25.27–28 "You . . . lantern."]   Adapted from *Much Ado About Nothing*, III, iii, 22–24.

25.30 Young Adam L——s, he that ſhot ſo true.]   Presumably the allusion is to Morgan Lewis; see also *Romeo and Juliet*, II, i, 13.

25.35–38 "*1ſt Judge* . . . Very like a whale."]   Adapted from *Hamlet*, III, ii, 393–99.

25.39 G——t L——n]   Gilbert Livingston (1742–?)?

26.1–6 "There . . . no dog bark."]   Adapted from *The Merchant of Venice*, I, i, 88–94.

26.9–10 "Yes . . . than I."]   Adapted from *Much Ado About Nothing*, III, v, 15–17.

26.14 ISAAC.]   Some characteristic features of style: wordplay (26.38); burlesque of learned manner; "ycleped," a favorite archaism; demeaning coined epithets (26.35); attention to "Galligaſkins" (27.4).

26.17–18 "Who . . . diſagree."]   Adapted from Pope, *Moral Essays*, Epistle III, 1.

26.18 Ainſworth, Lempriere and Walker]   Robert Ainsworth (1660–1743), author of a standard Latin dictionary; John Lempriere (1760–1824), author of a classical dictionary; John Walker (1732–1807), author of *A Critical Pronouncing Dictionary* (1791) of English.

26.36 *Argumentum Baculinum*]   Appeal to the rod; argument by force.

27.10 COL. BLUBBER]   Some characteristic features of style: illustrative literary quotations; typographical variety; attention to styles of dress; man as animal; "all the majeſty of" (27.27–see 4.30–31); "for a ſhew" (27.30–see 38.21).

27.11–15 "*What* . . . *fiſh*."]   Adapted from *The Tempest*, II, ii, 24–36.

27.16 Col. Blubber]   Possibly one Preserved Fish, of Flushing, who elsewhere in *The Corrector* is described as a "blubbering fellow, who has recently been imported into Queens' county" (p. 35, col. 1). This identification would account for all the wordplay on "fish" in the present article (e.g., 27.11–15, 28.6–7).

27.18–19 deſtroying the Merchant's Bank]   The Merchant's Bank was a Federalist-supported company which in 1803 and 1804 was seeking a charter from the New York state legislature. Despite powerful opposition, the bank was chartered in 1804.

28.6–7 "*Thou liest* . . . *monſter!*"]   Adapted from *The Tempest*, III, ii, 28–33.

28.8 TO TOBY TICKLER, ESQ.] Some characteristic features of style: format of a letter from a relation; man as animal; associate objects of satire with the vulgar populace; "with all the eagernefs of expectation" (28.19–20—see 4.1); "smoaking" (29.14—see 4.25).

29.3 Foh . . . imagination.] Adapted from *King Lear*, IV, vi, 131–33.

29.19 young Behrens] Herman Behrens, a German who had resided in New York since 1798, when he had arrived to claim the estate of a relation, Albright Behrens (d. 1797). Aaron Burr, who was administering the estate, was not at that time satisfied of Behrens' identity or of his claim, and the assets did not change hands. In April, 1804, Burr's enemies circulated a handbill reflecting discredit on him for his part in this affair. See *The Corrector*, p. 23, cols. 1–2.

29.24–25 Arnold, and Catiline] Benedict Arnold (1740–1801) and Lucius Sergius Catiline (108–62 B.C.,), both traitors to their countries.

30.9 ORIGINAL PICTURES] Some characteristic features of style: continuation of earlier instalment (30.11); illustrative literary quotations; objects of satire associated with Satan and his followers; "aukwardly" (31.7—see above, 4.26).

30.14–23 "Satan . . . fight."] Adapted from *Paradise Lost*, IX, 83–92.

30.33–38 "So . . . fcorn."] Adapted from *Paradise Lost*, X, 504–9.

31.1–2 S———— O————] Samuel Osgood (1748–1813), naval officer for the port of New York.

31.3–5 "Hypocrify . . . earth."] *Paradise Lost*, III, 683–85.

31.15–19 "Him . . . furprifed."] *Paradise Lost*, IV, 810–14.

31.25–33 "—Upftood . . . spake . . . Be . . . truth."] The first five lines are adapted from *Paradise Lost*, VI, 446–50; those remaining, from *Paradise Regained*, I, 427–30.

32.1–16 "They . . . fill'd."] Adapted from *Paradise Lost*, X, 564–70.

32.9 TO TOBY TICKLER, ESQ.] Some characteristic features of style: format of a letter; objects of satire associated with the vulgar populace; justices as rogues; "quiz," a favorite slang expression.

33.28 J———n W———t's] Possibly John Watts, a director of the Manhattan Company and an ally of the Livingston family.

33.38 RIGDUMFUNNIDOS] Rigdum-Funnidos is a character in Henry Carey's *Chrononhotonthologos* (1734).

34.1 TO TOBY TICKLER, ESQ.] Some characteristic features of style: continuation of earlier instalment (34.13–14); illustrative literary quotations; "The way to wealth" (35.27—see 46.9); "the learned pig" (36.11–12—see 6.36); burlesque series of academic titles (36.12–15—see 37.37).

34.24–25 the celebrated author of the "Redemptioners"] Isaac Clason; see 19.33 and Explanatory Notes, 12.34.

34.31–32 "the mafter ftring . . . him."]   Adapted from Nicholas Rowe, *Jane Shore* (1714), III, i, 238–39.

34.39–40 "Great genius . . . divide."]   Adapted from Dryden's *Absalom and Achitophel*, I, 163–64.

35.7 that *great man*]   Samuel Latham Mitchill; see Explanatory Notes, 36.12.

35.23 J——n B——me]   John Broome, the Democratic candidate for lieutenant governor of New York.

35.24 *"Non cuicunque datum eft habere nasum."*]   "It is not given to everyone to have a nose" (Martial, *Epigrams*, I, 42, 18).

35.25 "He wou'd or he wou'd not. . . ."]   A takeoff on the title of Colley Cibber's play *She Wou'd and She Wou'd Not* (1702).

35.27–28 "The way to wealth . . . faving a fortune"]   An allusion to Benjamin Franklin's collection of prudential maxims from *Poor Richard's Almanac*, "The Way to Wealth" (1758).

35.33–34 "——*Rem facias rem . . . modo rem.*"]   "Make money; if possible, honestly; if not, by any means whatever" (Horace, *Epigrams*, I, 1, 65).

35.40 A.G.S.D.]   "Attorney General Southern District" of the state of New York.

36.1–2 "The Loves of the Tygers," . . . from Dr. Darwin]   An allusion to Erasmus Darwin's "The Loves of the Plants" (1789), part 2 of *The Botanic Garden*.

36.12—— —— of Plandome]   Samuel Latham Mitchill (1764–1831), scientist and U.S. senator from New York.

36.28 Fredonia]   Samuel Latham Mitchill was well known at this time for his fruitless attempts "to introduce *Fredonia,* and *Fredes,* as descriptive of the United States and its citizens" (New York *Evening Post*, April 24, 1804, p. 2, col. 5).

36.38 RARE FUN! ! !]   Some characteristic features of style: typographical variety; men as animals; Aeolism; politics as a puppet show; objects of satire associated with filth.

36.42 MONKEY DICK]   Richard Riker; see Explanatory Notes, 10.9

37.4 OURANG OUTANG]   Tunis Wortman; see Explanatory Notes, 11.9–10.

37.11 YAHOO]   Sylvanus Miller; see Explanatory Notes, 8.28.

37.18 *Ferris*]   Benjamin Ferris; see Explanatory Notes, 14.13.

37.25 Young SLABSIDES]   According to Martin Roth (*Washington Irving's Contributions*, p. 119, n. 10), Richard Riker's brother.

37.34 (*To be continued.*)]   The final issue of *The Corrector* was published on March 26, 1804, the last day of the three-day state elections. Apparently further issues were contemplated should Aaron Burr win the governorship.

37.36 "*WE WILL REJOICE ! ! !*"]   Probably an allusion to Psalms 20:5, though Irving may have intended to parody a source nearer at hand. On February 15, 1803, p. 2, cols. 3–4, James Cheetham's *American Citizen* reprinted from the *American Mercury* a report of a "Republican Festival" recently celebrated, each of whose paragraphs began with the phrase "We Will Rejoice."

37.39 William Duane] Duane (1760–1835) was editor of the Philadelphia *Aurora*, the most powerful journalistic organ of the Democratic party. He was instrumental in organizing celebrations of the Louisiana Purchase in several cities. See the New York *Evening Post*, May 11, 1804, p. 2, col. 5; May 16, 1804, p. 3, col. 1.

37.39–40 Citizen Mooncalf] William Mooney (1756–1831), a founder of the Society of Tammany (see Explanatory Notes, 39.17–18), was Chairman of the Committee on Arrangements for the celebration Irving is describing.

38.15 Savages' Museum] The New-York Museum, operated by Edward Savage (1761–1817), housed an exhibition of works of art and curiosities of nature.

38.23 *****poke] Probably *shitepoke*, a term applied to a heron and sometimes to other birds. The origin of the term is the common vulgar word for excrement plus *poke*, a bag—from the bird's action when flushed.

38.37 Dr. Septon] Samuel Latham Mitchill (see Explanatory Notes, 36.12) performed experiments on mineral waters and formed a theory of the mineral action of a substance he called "septon."

38.39 *Fredon*] After "Fredonia"; see Explanatory Notes, 36.28.

39.1 the Judges] Probably a reference to Morgan Lewis (see Explanatory Notes, 19.13–14), who prior to his election to the governorship of New York was chief justice of the state Supreme Court.

39.12–14 *Louisiana . . . salt in the centre*] By designating these items of common country fare in his parody of phrases from Leviticus 20:24, "a land that floweth with milk and honey," Irving probably intends to ridicule the unsophisticated masses whom he describes as adherents of the Democratic party. He may also intend to mock the Louisiana Purchase as a measure supported by the Southern states, where the influence of Thomas Jefferson, a Virginian, was strong. In referring to "a huge mountain of salt" in the territory of Louisiana, Irving alludes to the unfounded rumor that such a mountain existed in regions of the Purchase yet unexplored. The Federalist controversialist Thomas Green Fessenden also refers in his *Democracy Unveiled; or, Tyranny Stripped of the Garb of Patriotism* (Boston, 1805), p. 101, to this "mount of salt, / Which late, 'tis said, in weather rainy, / Was melted in Louisiana."

39.15–16 citizen Cowdry . . . master Sammy, of certificate memory]   Jonathan Cowdry was an inspector of lumber; Samuel Cowdry, his son, was a New York lawyer. The latter is described as "of certificate memory" because he had attempted unsuccessfully to secure from a local citizen an affidavit concerning a supposedly incriminating "certificate" supposedly drawn up by Aaron Burr.

39.17–18 "Lo! the poor Indian,"]   Pope, *Essay on Man*, I, 99. The "Indian" was probably a member of the Society of Tammany, which took its name from a Delaware Indian chief and which was represented in the procession.

39.21–22 Bully Lowther]   Henry Lowther, a cartman.

39.24 JAMES DAGGERMAN]   James Cheetham (see Explanatory Notes, 8.7), the hatchet man for the New York Democratic party.

39.28–29 the *Mammoth Loaf* frolic of our worthy President]   In the New York *Evening Post* for April 2, 1804, p. 2, col. 5–p. 3, col. 1, appeared the first part of an anonymous sketch describing a celebration at Washington, wherein a "number of the sovereign people" carried into the capitol building "a *Mammoth Loaf of Bread*, about 12 feet in length, 2 feet in breadth, and of a suitable height." Welcomed by President Thomas Jefferson, the "*Man of the People*," the delegation proceeded to eat the mammoth loaf and other food, including wine and "cyder," the latter of which Jefferson selected "as being more congenial with the spirit of genuine republicanism." The "mutual congratulations" of this assembly became so loud that "the Senate in the adjoining room soon found it impossible to proceed in their debates." The article continued in a similar vein in the *Evening Post* of April 3, concluding with the assurance that "this mob procession was framed, if not originally at the desire, at least with the connivance of the President himself" (p. 3, col. 1).

40.9–10 a *Sentimental Philosopher*]   James Ogilvie (1760–1820), orator and elocutionist, the supposed compiler of the *Fragment of a Journal*.

40.15–16 Southey, Holcroft, Darwin, Smith, and Minshull]   Robert Southey (1774–1843), Thomas Holcroft (1745–1809), Erasmus Darwin (1731–1802), and Adam Smith (1723–1790) were all writers associated with Deism or radical political theories. John Minshull was a New York merchant who in 1803 and 1804, and perhaps afterward, wrote plays for the local stage. He was ridiculed by Irving and his friends, who nicknamed him "The Jocular Author."

40.20 a stinking little French proverb]   *Fragment of a Journal* concludes (p. 38): "*Qui se sent galeux se gale* / French Proverb." Translated, "He who feels himself scabby, let him scratch."

40.28 Godwin]   William Godwin (1756–1836), fictionist and philosopher of anarchical views.

41.12 Ironmonger] John Rodman (1775–1847), the author of *Fragment of a Journal*. For a biographical sketch see Charles H. Jones, *Genealogy of the Rodman Family*, (Philadelphia, 1886), pp. 53–55.

41.40 the portrait of Noah Webster to his spelling book] Webster's *Spelling Book*, often reprinted, originally formed the first part of his *Grammatical Institute of the English Language* (1783–1785).

42.39 the author of "The Pursuits of Literature;"] Thomas James Mathias (1754–1835), English critic, anthologist, poet, and translator, published *The Pursuits of Literature, or, What You Will: A Satirical Poem in Dialogue* in 1794. The work was reprinted several times in the decade that followed.

44.11 honest old Burton] Robert Burton (1577–1640), author of *The Anatomy of Melancholy* (1621).

44.19 *nil desperandum—risum teneatis amici*, and *fas ab hoste doceri*] "Nothing must be despaired of"; "could you help laughing, my friends?"; "it is allowable to learn from an enemy."

45.4 Dr. S———— and Mr. M————] Dr. Smith—see the Textual Commentary, note 72; John Minshull—see the same note and Explanatory Notes 40.15–16.

45.24–25 mounted on his Rosinante . . . in the far famed field of Montoil] See *Don Quixote*, pt. 1, bk. 1, chap. 2.

45.32–33 the poor Knight of the woful countenance] Don Quixote.

46.23–26 Tom Paine . . . the very passage that makes such contemptuous mention of his name] In *Fragment of a Journal* the Philosopher at one point reveals his godlessness as follows (pp. 16–17): "The *stuff* that Beattie, Paley, and Porteus have written about christianity, is now more read and admired, than the sublime effusions of the immortal Godwin, Holcroft, Volney or Tom Paine—many people now even study the gospels of Christ, for a system of morality . . . instead of the *limpid* stream of *pure, unadulterated* atheism. This is not the case in Virginia. . . ." Thomas Paine (1737–1809) was notorious as an atheist for the deistic speculations in his *The Age of Reason* (1794–1795).

47.28 a Butler and a Watson] Joseph Butler (1692–1752) was the author of *Analogy of Religion, Natural and Revealed, to the Constitution and Course of Nature* (1736); Richard Watson (1737–1816) was the author of an *Apology for Christianity* (1776) and of an *Apology for the Bible* (1796), the latter in reply to Thomas Paine.

48.26 "from nature up to nature's God,"] Adapted from Pope, *Essay on Man*, IV, 331.

51.6 "be all . . . here"] Adapted from *Macbeth*, I, vii, 5.

53.25–26 the Boston Theatre] A new theater was opened in Boston in 1793, and two years later Paine married an actress, Eliza Baker. At that time he was cast out by his father and took up the post of master of ceremonies to the theater.

54.24 "the grasshopper . . . burden."]   Adapted from Ecclesiastes 12:5.

55.11 "Where lonely want . . . die."]   Adapted from Samuel Johnson's "Verses on the Death of Mr. Robert Levet."

56.9 *Nullius addictus . . . magistri;*]   "Not pledged to swear to the words of any master."

56.21 *Parcere . . . superbos*]   "To spare the vanquished and subdue the proud."

57.32–35 "His delight . . . vacancy."]   A quotation from a passage near the conclusion of Samuel Johnson's *Life of Dryden.* See Johnson, *Works,* 12 vols. (London, 1820), IX, 423.

59.15–16 more touchingly . . . elegy of Gray]   See Thomas Gray, "Elegy Written in a Country Churchyard," stanza 9.

59.24 Sir Fopling Flutter]   A character in George Etherege's *The Man of Mode* (1676).

59.29–30 the Swiss peasant of Goldsmith]   See Oliver Goldsmith, "The Traveller," lines 177–98.

65.33 When the war was declared against Tripoli]   The Tripolitan War, or Barbary Wars, between the United States and the Barbary states began in 1801 and continued until 1805.

65.35–36 the hazardous exploit of destroying the frigate Philadelphia]   After the capture of the *Philadelphia* near Tripoli on October 31, 1803 (see 120.11–26), the ship was floated and moved to the harbor. It was in the process of being fitted out as a Tripolitan cruiser when an American party commanded by Stephen Decatur succeeded in cutting it from its moorings and burning it to the water's edge.

66.19–20 the squadron that cruised under Commodore Rodgers]   John Rodgers (1773–1838) was the ranking officer in the American naval service during the War of 1812. At the outset of the war Rodgers went to sea with a fleet of five vessels and extended his cruise as far eastward as the coast of Spain before returning to Boston, having captured eight merchantmen.

66.20 Lieutenant Morris]   Charles Morris (1784–1856) was executive officer of the *Constitution* during its engagement with the *Guerrière* in August, 1812.

67.12–13 Commodore Bainbridge, who commanded the Constitution]   William Bainbridge (1774–1853) was appointed in September, 1812, commander of a squadron consisting of the *Constitution,* of 44 guns, the *Essex* and the *Hornet.*

68.40–41 under a Cockburn . . . scenes of unpremeditated atrocity]   Rear Admiral George Cockburn (1772–1853) commanded the British naval squadron in Chesapeake Bay in 1813. Amid almost daily conflict with

U.S. militia and landing parties, he oversaw the burning and destruction of American government stores, especially at Havre de Grace, Georgetown, and Fredrickstown, all in Maryland.

69.13–14 the affair with the Leopard] The *Chesapeake*, under the command of James Barron (1768–1851), was attacked and captured in 1807, in time of peace, by the British ship *Leopard* because Barron refused to surrender three alleged British deserters. For his conduct in this affair Barron was court-martialed and deprived of his rank and pay for five years.

71.40 "don't surrender the ship!"] This speech, variously reproduced in different accounts, is the original of the motto "Don't give up the ship!"

79.14 their excesses at Havre de Grace] See Explanatory Notes, 68.40–41.

80.11–12 'The bigots . . . a crime;'] Walter Scott, *The Lay of the Last Minstrel*, Prelude, lines 7–8.

80.42 St. Hubert's breed] St. Hubert (d. 727) is the patron saint of huntsmen, so his "breed" is presumably the hunting dog.

84.2 Pompton stream] A stream in a rural area of northern New Jersey, a few miles west of the city of New York.

85.24 the great feats of John Paulding] Paulding (1758–1818) was one of the Americans who captured the British spy Major John André near Tarrytown, New York, in September, 1780.

89.20–21 On Mr. Hamilton's going into office] Paul Hamilton (1762–1816) was secretary of the U.S. Navy from 1809 to 1813.

91.32–33 his good conduct under Sir James L. Yeo, in the capture of Cayenne] In January, 1809, Captain James L. Yeo (1782–1818), later an English commodore, led four hundred men in an attack on the city of Cayenne, in French Guiana. After five weeks the place surrendered.

93.32–33 "Can such things be, and overcome us, like a summer cloud,"] *Macbeth*, III, iv, 111.

94.41–42 "troubled night" . . . "star of peace"] From Thomas Campbell's song, "Ye Mariners of England," stanza 4.

95.28 the embargo act] An act of Congress (1807) inspired by President Thomas Jefferson forbidding all international trade with American ports. It was intended as retaliation for English and French interference with neutral shipping.

96.20–21 the squadron under Commodore Chauncey] Isaac Chauncey (1772–1840) commanded the United States naval forces on the Great Lakes during the War of 1812.

96.38–39 captured . . . by Captain Elliot . . . under the very batteries of Malden] Fort Malden, or Fort Amherstburg, the British naval base on the Lakes during the War of 1812, was located on the lower Detroit River opposite the island of Bois Blanc. Early in the war Captain Jesse

Duncan Elliot (1782–1845) surprised and captured on Lake Erie, near this fort, the two British vessels *Detroit* and *Caledonia*.

98.22 "and the boldest holds his breath;"]   Adapted from Thomas Campbell's "The Battle of the Baltic," stanza 2.

103.15–16 an imitation of Nelson's letter after the battle of the Nile]   Admiral Horatio Nelson's letter from the ship *Vanguard*, August 3, 1798, to Admiral the earl of St. Vincent, K.B., commander in chief, began: "Almighty God has blessed his Majesty's Arms in the late Battle, by a great Victory over the Fleet of the Enemy, who I attacked at sunset on the 1st of August, off the Mouth of the Nile" (Sir Nicholas Harris Nicolas, ed., *The Dispatches and Letters of Vice Admiral Lord Viscount Nelson*, 7 vols. [London, 1845], III, 56).

105.37–38 "presented . . . a *very small portion*"]   No statement resembling Irving's "quotation" appears on the cover of either of the two copies of Holland's *Odes* consulted in the preparation of this edition (see p. 307). On the title page Holland is designated simply as "*Author of several Communications under the Signature of 'Orlando.'*"

107.26 "a world . . . shrunk shanks,"]   Adapted from *As You Like It*, II, vii, 159–60.

107.33 "needs . . . steep,"]   Thomas Campbell, "Ye Mariners of England," stanza three. The passage "her home . . . deep" (107.37) is quoted from the same source.

108.18–24 "the blue eyed Myra," . . . ". . . nectarous morning tide air."]   Irving quotes phrases from the following in Holland's *Odes:* "The Portrait: *To the Blue-Eyed Myra*," pp. 27–30; "To Rosa-Matilda," pp. 38–39; and "Song Set to Music by the Author, and Inscribed to Miss ❀❀ ❀❀," p. 33, from which latter the couplet is taken.

108.29–30 the style of Della Crusca. Gifford has long since brushed away all this trumpery.]   In his *The Baviad* (1794) and *The Maeviad* (1795) the English critic William Gifford (1756–1826) attacked a pretentious group of contemporary poets and dramatists which took its name from the Florentine Academy, or Accademia Della Crusca.

108.35–36 "brilliant pleasures," . . . "ardent kisses,"]   The first two phrases are quoted from Holland's "To Rosa-Matilda" *(Odes*, p. 39); the second two, from "To Marion" (pp. 34–35).

108.42 the modern Anacreon]   Thomas Moore (1779–1852), who in 1800 published a translation of Anacreon's odes into English verse. Byron called him "Anacreon Moore."

109.30 "roseate hues," and "ambrosial odours," and "purple mists,"]   These phrases are not to be found in Holland's *Odes*, but they are nonetheless not unrepresentative; for example, see "rosy beauties" (p. 27), "ambrosial clime" (p. 38).

109.35–110.2 "His . . . *sternest move.*"] Robert Burns, "Sketch" ("Hail, Poesie! thou nymph reserv'd!"), stanza eight.

110.12–13 like Nick Bottom's hero, . . . "slipt . . . fire!"] Nick Bottom is a weaver and the star actor in the playlet of "Pyramus and Thisbe" in *A Midsummer Night's Dream.* However, the passage within quotation marks is not to be found in the play.

111.3–4 the Tower Stamp] Apparently a reference to the authenticity of money or medals produced at the Tower of London.

113.1–32 "There . . . again!"] "Elegaic Lines. *Inscribed to the Memory of* Miss ANNA CLAUDIA BENNETT, *who Died on the 5th day of August, A.D. 1813, in the 17th year of her Age,*" *Odes*, pp. 31–33. The three concluding stanzas of the poem are omitted from Irving's quotation.

115.10–29 "Newstead! . . . former day."] The quoted passage comprises the last five stanzas of Byron's "Elegy on Newstead Abbey."

115.33–116.6 "Still . . . sinner."] The quoted passage comprises the tenth and eleventh stanzas of Byron's "To the Earl of Clare."

116.26–27 when he mentions Jeffrey] See *English Bards and Scotch Reviewers*, lines 438–539. Francis Jeffrey (1773–1850) was a co-founder with Sydney Smith of the *Edinburgh Review*, in which Byron's *Hours of Idleness* (1807) had been contemptuously reviewed.

119.1 Commodore Truxton] Thomas Truxton (1755–1822) commanded the U.S. frigate *Constellation* when in February, 1799, it captured the French frigate *L'Insurgente.*

119.4–5 Commodore Barron] Samuel Barron (ca. 1763–1910) who in 1805 assumed command of a United States squadron of ten vessels operating against Tripoli.

119.14 Commodore Talbot] Captain Silas Talbot (1751–1813) commanded the Santo Domingo station in 1799–1800.

119.37–38 The gallant and lamented Trippe] Lieutenant commandant John Trippe died at sea off Havana in July, 1810. At the time of his death he had command of the U.S. schooner *Enterprise.*

122.1 a Pharos] That is, a lighthouse—after the lighthouse built by Ptolemy Philadelphus on the island of Pharos, off Alexandria, Egypt.

123.26–28 Commodore Bainbridge's victorious action with the Java . . . the capture of the Hornet by the Montague] On December 29, 1812, Commodore William Bainbridge (see Explanatory Notes 67.12–13), in command of the *Constitution*, fell in with a large British frigate, the *Java*, off the coast of Brazil, and after a gun battle two hours in length captured her. The *Hornet* was not captured by the British ship *Montagu*; see 67.41–44. Shortly after escaping from the *Montagu* early in 1813, the *Hornet* fell in with the British brig *Peacock* and captured it, as described by Irving, 67.44–68.15.

125.3 the expected arrival of Commodore Hillyar]   James Hillyar (1769–
1843), who did arrive off Valparaiso (see 125.30–31), in command of
the British frigate *Phoebe*.

130.36 the affair of the Argus]   Shortly after the outbreak of war the
U.S. ship *Argus*, Captain Sinclair, of sixteen guns, was chased for
three days and nights by a British squadron, including two ships of
the line. The *Argus* escaped. See James F. Cooper, *The History of the
Navy of the United States of America* (Philadelphia, 1839), II, 180–81.

132.14 FORT M'HENRY]   On September 13, 1814, a British fleet in
Chesapeake Bay bombarded Fort McHenry, on a small island in Baltimore harbor. The bombardment did not result in surrender of the fort,
as the British had anticipated.

132.25 the   Admiral]   Vice-Admiral   Sir   Alexander   Forrester   Inglis
Cochrane (1758–1832) was in command of British naval forces along
the United States coast. For an account of the British naval attack on
Fort McHenry and Baltimore, see Francis F. Beirne, *The War of 1812*
(New York, 1949), pp. 309–20.

132.30 ANACREON IN HEAVEN]   A song by John Stafford Smith, often
used in patriotic lyrics of the era. Robert Treat Paine's "Adams and
Liberty" (see 53.36) was set to the same tune.

133.25–27 [This ... author.]]   The brackets are Irving's. This sketch
originally appeared in *The Poetical Works of Thomas Campbell* (Baltimore, 1810); see the Textual Commentary, pp. 311–12.

133.33–34 "they rest ... them."]   Revelations 14:13.

135.13–14 His uncle ... settled permanently in Virginia]   Archibald
Campbell, the uncle of the poet, took a D.D. at the University of Edinburgh, went out to Jamaica as a Presbyterian minister, and after several years settled in Virginia, where he acquired landed property to
which he gave the name "Kirnan." (William Beattie, ed., *Life and
Letters of Thomas Campbell* [London, 1849], I, 6).

136.14–15 Bishop Leighton's foundation]   Among other charities Bishop
Robert Leighton (1611–1684), the Scottish divine, founded bursaries
in the universities of Edinburgh and Glasgow.

137.10 Professors Stewart and Playfair]   Dugald Stewart (1753–1828),
professor of moral philosophy at the University of Edinburgh; John
Playfair (1748–1819), professor of mathematics at the same university.

137.35 an interesting war]   In July, 1800, the French, commanded by
Moreau, attacked and took Munich.

138.34–35 those passages which relate to Kosciusko, and the partition of
Poland]   See *The Pleasures of Hope*, pt. 1, lines 349–92. In 1794 a
national uprising of the Poles led by Thaddeus Kosciusko (1746–1817)
was defeated by Russia. Following the surrender of Warsaw, in Octo-

ber, 1795, the third partition of Poland was enacted, wherein Russia, Austria, and Prussia obtained portions of the country.

139.36–37 "gallant swelling spirit,"]   Possibly an adaptation of "Noble swelling spirits," *Othello*, II, iii, 58.

140.41 "when the soul is lifted to heaven,"]   Possibly a paraphrase of *Henry VIII*, II, i, 79: "And lift my soul to heaven."

146.12 "should delight to honour."]   Probably an adaptation of Esther 7:9: "The man whom the king delighteth to honour."

152.10 "And hold . . . distance,"]   Adapted from *Othello*, II, iii, 58.

152.15–16 "Plague . . . sack—"]   Adapted from *Henry IV, Part 1*, II, iv, 127–29.

152.21 Leon's idiot speech]   Leon, a character in Fletcher's *Rule a Wife and Have a Wife* (1624), was one of Thomas A. Cooper's finest parts, one which he had played in New York since 1798. (George C. D. Odell, *Annals of the New York Stage, Vol. 2, 1798–1821* [New York, 1927], p. 46).

153.6–7 "Another . . . dream;"]   Adapted from *Richard III*, V, iii, 178–79.

154.16 And *John* shall *make his bow* at your commands.]   One John Wilson presented a concert at the City Hotel in New York on January 20, 1807, which was reported in *Salmagundi* two weeks later. Wilson, according to "Anthony Evergreen, Gent.," "gave . . . infinite satisfaction by the gentility of his demeanor, and the roguish looks he now and then cast at the ladies, but we fear his excessive modesty cast him into some little confusion, for he absolutely forgot himself, and in the whole course of his entrances and exits, never once made his bow to the audience" (*Salmagundi*, ed. Evert A. Duyckinck [New York, 1860], p. 39). Apparently this person is the John alluded to.

154.21–22 "Blow wind . . . back."]   Adapted from *Macbeth*, V, v, 51–52.

155.12 Morris]   Possibly Lewis Morris Ogden (1783–1810), who had graduated with an A.B. from Columbia College in 1801 and was a student at law.

155.12 Trinity Church]   Trinity Church, founded in 1696, destroyed by fire in 1776 and rebuilt in 1790, was the largest and most fashionable place of Protestant worship in the city of New York.

155.20 Dyde's]   A public house in Park Row, in New York, near the Park Theatre.

158.26–159.28 ¡Ay . . . mí.]   The poem has been translated as follows: "Oh, God of my soul! Take me out of here. Oh, England is no longer for me. / Oh God of the higher region, the best of the earth, with whom a great part of heaven is shared, look at the grief which I endure here. Oh, England is no longer for me. / Oh, God! What sins I have committed which have been paid for so quickly and so well. But I deserved it. Therefore I left. Oh, England is no longer for me. / Oh, oh! That my affliction comes with a thousand torments. It is an infernal pain which has no end. Death is convenient to me, because I was foul. Oh, England is no longer for me. / There is probably no man who does not lose his mind who remembers goodness and [yet] exists in evil. Oh God! Take me out of here. Oh, England is no longer for me" (Richard E. Peck, "An Unpublished Poem by Washington Irving," *American Literature*, 39 [May 1967], 206).

181.23 Nimrod]   A mighty hunter, grandson of Ham (see Genesis 10).

188.32 *Und ob die Wolke*]   "And though the sky." The corresponding first line in Livius' *The Freyschütz* (1824) is "Though oft the sun be from us shrouded" (p. 50).

193.33 Zechine]   An obsolete gold coin of Italy and Turkey, first struck at Venice at the end of the thirteenth century.

196.6–7 the chaste Lucretia, and the unchaste Sappho who both killed themselves]   In Roman legend, Lucretia, the wife of Tarquinius Collatinus, was raped by one Sixtus. Having avowed her dishonor before her father, husband, and friends, she killed herself. Sappho (fl.600 B.C.), the Greek poetess of Lesbos, is fabled to have thrown herself into the sea because her advances had been rejected by the beautiful youth Phaon.

223.18 Haroun]   That is, the Caliph. In Hiemer's libretto for *Abu Hassan* he is also called "Harun."

Pierre M. Irving, *ca.* 1870
A photograph by N. S. Bowdish, Richfield Springs, New York.

TEXTUAL COMMENTARY

Included in the *Miscellaneous Writings* are all Washington Irving's completed works, published or unpublished, fragmentary or surviving in full, which if published during the lifetime of the author did not first appear as independent volumes. An unusually wide range of bibliographical information available concerning Irving's literary activities during his productive career of more than half a century has facilitated the effort to assemble a comprehensive collection of his miscellaneous prose works, poems, and plays.[1]

Of the mass of unpublished material which he left at his death in 1859 to his literary executor, Pierre M. Irving, only a small fraction is published here for the first time.[2] Some of these manuscript texts, in particular the journals, notebooks, and letters, Pierre drew upon rather extensively in his delegated biography, *The Life and Letters of Washington Irving* (1862–1863). Others, "The Chronicle of Pelayo," the first three chapters of "Chronicle of the Ommiades," "Chronicle of Fernan Gonzalez, Count of Castile," and "Chronicle of Fernando the Saint," he edited for publication in a posthumous gathering of Irving's miscellaneous

---

1. Of primary importance are Stanley T. Williams and Mary Allen Edge, comps. *A Bibliography of the Writings of Washington Irving: A Check List* (1936; reprinted New York, 1970), with its helpful listing of further bibliographic sources, pp. xiv–xix; the descriptive bibliography by William R. Langfeld and Philip C. Blackburn, *Washington Irving: A Bibliography* (1933; reprinted Port Washington, N. Y., 1968); Herbert L. Kleinfield, "A Census of Washington Irving Manuscripts," *Bulletin of the New York Public Library*, 68, no. 1 (1964), 13–32—reissued in the reprinted Langfeld-Blackburn volume; Jacob Blanck, *Bibliography of American Literature*, vol. 5 (New Haven, 1969)—cited hereafter as BAL; the *National Union Catalog: A Cumulative Author List* (1955–); and the *Union List of Serials in Libraries in the United States and Canada*, ed. Edna Brown Titus, 3d ed., 5 vols. (New York, 1965). An authoritative survey of the literature pertaining to Irving, by Henry A. Pochmann, is in *Fifteen American Authors before 1900. Bibliographic Essays in Research and Criticism*, ed. Robert A. Rees and Earl N. Harbert (Madison, 1971), pp. 245–61.

2. These works are "The Successors of Pelayo: Favila," Chapters IV–IX of the "Chronicle of the Ommiades," "Sir David Wilkie in Spain," and "The Village Curate." Several other items included here were published posthumously through the agency of persons other than Pierre M. Irving: they are "Verses Written on the Lake of Lucerne," "Song," "Signs of the Times," "Lines Written at Stratford," "¡Ay Dios De Mi Alma!," "The Lay of the Sunnyside Ducks," *The Freyschütz, Abu Hassan*, "My Uncle," "The Log House Hotel," "History of the Conquest of Mexico," and "Illustration to the Legend of Prince Ahmed."

writings, *Spanish Papers and Other Miscellanies, Hitherto Unpublished or Uncollected* (1866). As was the custom of his era, Pierre distributed many signatures and scraps of his late uncle's manuscript copy to admirers and to members of the Irving family. Yet he was nevertheless a wise steward of the author's literary remains, for he conducted this partial dispersal of manuscripts with a keen sense of priorities. The authoritativeness and range of the present edition of Irving's *Complete Works* is owing in no small part to the care taken by Pierre M. Irving to preserve for further study the primary manuscript evidence of his uncle's life and literary achievements.

Confronted, then, not only with an array of published works but with a wealth of manuscript texts for consideration as possible contents of the *Miscellaneous Writings*—the latter comprising research notes, translations, transcriptions, rejected or superseded drafts, unidentified fragments, and revised and unrevised copy of all descriptions—one is obliged at the outset to formulate working principles to define a "completed" work. No serious problem ordinarily arises in regard to items for which a combination of manuscript and printed copy survives, or in cases where a printed version only is known to exist. In the absence of evidence to the contrary, one simply assumes that if published during the author's lifetime a given writing is a completed one.[3] However, unpublished and posthumously published texts pose more serious problems of interpretation.

The physical appearance of an Irving manuscript does not in itself constitute a sure index of that text's being "complete" or only "in progress." Some manuscripts published during his lifetime, such as the one for "Newton the Painter," are minimally revised and appear to have been written hastily at a sitting; others, such as that for the *Knickerbocker Magazine* text of "Pelayo and the Merchant's Daughter," show signs of deliberate care, incorporating passages written at various times and including pages marked with as many as four different series of pagination. Most of Irving's printer's copy manuscripts are slipshod in punctuation and presented numerous editing problems; but a few, including the extant portion of "The Taking of the Veil, and The Charming Letoriéres" and the memoir of Washington Allston, were prepared with closer attention to detail. The diversity in appearance among the manuscript texts not known to have been published is just as great as that

3. There is no evidence to indicate that any of the present contents of the *Miscellaneous Writings* were first published during the author's lifetime without authorization and so might have been considered by him as incomplete. On the contrary, manuscript copy-texts are repeatedly encountered which Irving did authorize for publication despite his having prepared them in a hasty, even slovenly manner; see below, p. 256; Vol. II, pp. 411–12, 422–23.

among those which did appear in print. Thus it is impossible confidently
to conclude whether a particular text of an unpublished work is "complete" without taking into consideration Irving's compositional habits
at the time it was written and his intentions, if known, for that item. For
example, the surviving manuscripts of *The Freyschütz* and *Abu Hassan*,
the two plays he wrote in collaboration with Barham J. Livius in 1823,
may in themselves appear unfinished—including, as they do, untraceable
reference marks, cryptic abbreviations, and private notes for possible
revisions which were apparently never acted upon—but the evidence of
his cooperation with the English playwright suggests otherwise. The
manuscripts were working copies, consulted by each of the two men independently and probably also while at work together; and when Irving's
contributions to the collaborative effort were over, his much-revised texts
were simply set aside.[4] Nevertheless, because they do include the evidence of his final input into the experiments in play-adaptation, experiments to which he devoted serious attention over several months, the
two manuscript plays merit a place among his completed writings.

On the other hand, a number of texts unpublished during Irving's lifetime are omitted from the collection. These include early drafts set
aside and never taken up again,[5] transcriptions and narrative notes apparently made for future reference, superseded drafts, and other notes and
embryonic fragments.[6] Translations, including the anonymous one from
the French of François de Pons, *A Voyage to the Eastern Part of Terra
Firma* (1806), which the author prepared together with Peter Irving and
George Caines,[7] and the unpublished translated fragment of Fray Bernardino de Sahagún's *Historia General de las Cosas de Nueva España*, which
he wrote by himself as an aid to research, are not included. The previously unpublished texts included here are ones which, from textual and

4. Or possibly they were used for the preparation of fair copies by some other
person; see the respective Textual Commentaries, pp. 351, 366.

5. "Alonzo the Chaste and Alonzo the Catholic" (Virginia), "Don Garcia Fer-
nandez" (Virginia), "Wigs and Haircutting" (Manuscript Division, New York
Public Library), "William the Conqueror" (Berg Collection, New York Public
Library), "Polly Holman's Wedding" (Berg Collection, New York Public Library),
and "The Seven Sons of Lara" (Texas). The latter two works have appeared in
print; see Stanley T. Williams and E. E. Leisy, "Polly Holman's Wedding. Notes by
Washington Irving," *Southwest Review*, 19 (1934), 449–54, and William J. Scheick,
" 'The Seven Sons of Lara': A Washington Irving Manuscript," *Resources for Ameri-
can Literary Study*, 2 (1972), 208–17.

6. "Milton's Account of His Motives for Writing *Paradise Lost*" (Virginia),
"The Schooner Amistad" (Yale), "The Vindication of Christmas" (Virginia), and
Chapters X and following of "Chronicle of the Ommiades" (Columbia). The fullest
published listing of Irving's unpublished manuscripts available at present is H. L.
Kleinfield's "A Census of Washington Irving Manuscripts," pp. 21–28; see also the
index to STW.

7. See Williams and Edge, *Bibliography*, p. 152; STW, I, 75.

other evidence, appear to have received Irving's attention at a stage at least approaching completion. As he remarked in 1847 concerning his manuscript chronicles of medieval Spain, they are in a paradoxical state, "complete, though not thoroughly finished off."[8]

The same might in fact be said of most of the manuscript texts for the miscellaneous works Irving did see published during his lifetime. As a rule he was far from scrupulous in preparing accurate texts of these shorter works and was content for his editors to supply any nonsubstantive details which he found it easier not to bother with. Nor did he often express criticism of any of the several different house stylings imposed on his writings.[9] He expected "fair play," of course, and after the publication of his notice of Alexander Slidell's *A Year in Spain* in the *Quarterly Review* for February, 1831, he complained bitterly to the editor, J. G. Lockhart, about the omissions and other revisions Lockhart had made to his manuscript text.[10] It should be noticed, however, that his concern for the integrity of his commentary had not in this case impelled him to correct the proofsheets prior to publication. "Drudgery" of that sort he left to other persons; and with the single exception of his letter to H. R. Schoolcraft published in the *Literary World* for November 22, 1851, there is no indication that he ever revised, or even read, proofsheets for any of his miscellaneous works.

A second set of difficulties in defining the contents of the *Miscellaneous Writings* pertains to published articles which first appeared anonymously or pseudonymously and have since been attributed in whole or in part to Irving. Here again textual evidence proves inadequate by itself conclusively to confirm or disprove these traditional attributions. Manuscript texts for the works in question, most of which appeared in New York

8. Irving to Pierre M. Irving, [Sunnyside], April 14, 1847; PMI, IV, 15.

9. In a much-quoted letter to Henry Brevoort, Jr., in 1819, Irving complained mildly that the American edition of a section of *The Sketch-Book* then recently published "appears to be a little too *highly pointed.*" "High pointing," he continued after an intervening sentence, "is apt to injure the fluency of the style if the reader attends to all the stops." This would seem to be a clear criticism of the system of pointing imposed on his text, were it not that in the sentence separating the two comments he confessed that he was unsure "whether my manuscript was so, or whether it [was] the scrupulous precision of the printer" that had accounted for the unsatisfactory pointing (Irving to Brevoort, London, July 28, 1819; PMI, I, 425). The uncertainty about the punctuation in his own manuscript suggests that, even for *The Sketch-Book*, "scrupulous precision" in punctuating was not one of his own failings.

10. Ben H. McClary, "Washington Irving's Amiable Scotch Friends: Three Unpublished Letters to the John Gibson Lockharts," *Studies in Scottish Literature*, 4 (October 1966), 103.

in 1809 or before,[11] are invariably wanting. Evidence of stylistic or thematic affinities between writings supposed to be the youthful Irving's and those which he acknowledged is naturally of interest, but it is not conclusive. For example, at the outset of his career he was one of a "club" of "good humoured dashers"[12] who between 1802 and 1804 contributed articles under various pseudonyms to the New York *Morning Chronicle*. These persons wrote in virtually indistinguishable styles—perhaps, indeed, because they wrote in collaboration. Unless we possess evidence from outside a given *Morning Chronicle* article, such as an affirmation by Irving that he wrote it, or a rumor to that effect circulated within his family, we are on doubtful ground when we admit the work into the canon of his writings on the basis of stylistic features alone. Hence for each anonymous or pseudonymous work printed before 1815 and included in the present collection a discussion of the evidence warranting its attribution to Irving is given in the corresponding section of the Textual Commentary.[13] In all likelihood evidence for attribution of further anonymous writings to Irving will accumulate as the years pass.

TRANSCRIPTION AND COLLATION

Manuscripts adopted as copy-texts for titles in this collection have ordinarily been analyzed and transcribed in an unvarying sequence of steps: comparison of a photocopy of the text with the original; preparation of a typed transcription from the marked photocopy; collation of the transcription against the photocopy by a second Irving editor; rechecking of the transcription against the original manuscript.[14] Irving's slurred handwriting poses formidable difficulties in preparing a critical edition whose basic claim to definitiveness must rest on the accurate transcription of his manuscript texts. Paragraph indentations are often negligible, especially in the Spanish histories such as "The Successors of Pelayo.

11. For lists of works attributed to Irving, see Langfeld and Blackburn, *Washington Irving: A Bibliography*, p. 66; and Williams and Edge, *Bibliography*, p. 160.

12. "Communication," New York *Morning Chronicle*, August 4, 1803, p. 3, col. 2.

13. See the Textual Commentaries for the contributions to the New York *Morning Chronicle* and *The Corrector*, "We Will Rejoice! ! !," *The New-York Review*, "The Lay of the Scottish Fiddle," "Lord Byron," and "Defence of Fort M'Henry." Irving's two contributions to the New York *Morning Chronicle* are discussed in a single section of the Textual Commentary, as are his fifteen articles in *The Corrector*.

14. These procedures are in accordance with the *Statement of Editorial Principles and Procedures: A Working Manual for Editing Nineteenth-Century Texts*, rev. ed. (New York, 1972), pp. 1–4. In cases where the analysis and transcription of the copy-text manuscripts have followed sequences which differ from these, the differences are noted in the appropriate sections of the Textual Commentary. Ordinarily the exceptions relate to physical descriptions of the manuscripts supplied to the editor by other persons.

Favila," where he wrote using only the right five eighths of each page so as to leave space for subsequent insertions. In manuscripts written hastily, as was most often the case with briefer pieces such as the toast at the Booksellers' Dinner on March 30, 1837, it is frequently perplexing to distinguish (assuming that Irving himself made the distinctions) between a comma, a dash, a period, and a half-intentional dot marking a pause for thought. Decisions concerning unhyphenated compounds are often delicate as well, for in such words as "foothold" ("The 'Empire . . . West,'" II, 137.29) or "weathercocks" ("Communipaw," II, 123.16) he left spaces between the segments of the compounds only slightly shorter than between words he intended to appear separately. However, the most frequently encountered problem in deciphering the author's manuscript text stems from the whimsical and often indiscriminate manner in which he wrote capitals and lowercase letters. His upper- and lowercase formations of a, c, g, k, m, n, p, s, v, and w are often indistinguishable. Especially for a, c, and k, the size of a letter in relation to those surrounding it is not always a clear indication of whether a capital is intended. For letters other than the ten listed above the conformation is generally a reliable indicator of Irving's intention, but on the basis of size and shape one must conclude, for example, that he ordinarily wrote "Christendom" but sometimes "christendom" (as in "Chronicle of Fernan Gonzalez," II, 252.7, 252.10). That his practices of capitalization were not consistent is indicated by the presence in the same works of clearly decipherable usages such as "boar" and "Boar" ("The Chronicle of Pelayo," II, 187.28, 189.5), "friars" and "Friars" (Chronicle of Fernando the Saint," II, 316.33, 318.9).

If it were possible to specify with confidence the rules for capitalization which Irving followed at successive stages of his career, the task of transcribing the manuscript texts of his works would be simplified. Borderline words customarily capitalized might be given the benefit of the doubt and capitalized themselves, provided their initial letters were not in lowercase formations; and the converse procedure might apply to words customarily uncapitalized. However, the evidence of his practices throughout his lifetime is contradictory. As editor of the *Analectic Magazine* in 1813 and 1814, as a contributor to the *Knickerbocker Magazine* between 1839 and 1841, and as an author whose revised works were published in fifteen volumes between 1848 and 1850 by George Putnam, he either imposed or approved systems of editorial styling which dispensed with the capitalization of nouns except in rather sharply defined circumstances. Nevertheless, his own manuscripts reveal that from youth to age he continued fitfully to follow the obsolescent convention of capitalizing for emphasis; or perhaps rather, he adhered consistently to no discernible system at all.

In response to the chronic ambiguities and contradictions associated with Irving's scribal practices, the methods adopted by the editors of his *Journals and Notebooks* are followed here as providing rough guidelines for distinguishing between capital and lowercase letters.[15] Doubtful words *within a particular manuscript* which are ordinarily capitalized in that text are so transcribed, the only exceptions being cases in which the letters in question are clearly lowercase formations. Similarly, doubtful words customarily uncapitalized within the manuscript are so transcribed unless their initial letters are clearly shaped as capitals. This procedure does not obviate Irving's inconsistencies and is not intended to; it simply removes some possible discrepancies while introducing a minimum of new ones. Given the nature of the evidence, this is the most that can reasonably be expected. The checking of typed transcriptions against marked photocopies by second readers has probably been the most important and effective step in the attempt to conjoin knowledge of Irving's habits of penmanship with the consistent application of a method for deciphering his manuscripts.

For those works whose textual history includes one or more printed versions, multiple copies of each printed text have been consulted and are specified at the close of the respective Textual Commentaries. Unless indicated otherwise, the printed versions of the works comprising the *Miscellaneous Writings* appeared during Irving's lifetime in unique editions having only single impressions. Collation of the reprinted texts of various works against the original publications has led repeatedly to four gatherings of the author's uncollected writings, all of which merit at least brief comment.[16] The earliest, *Irvingiana: A Memorial of Washington Irving* (1860) was edited by Evert A. Duyckinck and appeared within four weeks of Irving's death. Four reprinted selections appeared in this testimonial volume,[17] none of which possesses textual authority independent of the original published version. Pierre M. Irving's research as author of the delegated *Life and Letters* of his uncle is reflected in eight items he reprinted in that work for their biographical

15. See "General Introduction to Journals," *Journals*, I, ed. Nathalia Wright, pp. xxi–xxv.

16. For a checklist of the several gatherings of Irving's selected works which appeared during his lifetime—none of which, however, contains material relating to the textual histories of writings in this volume, see Williams and Edge, *Bibliography*, p. 7.

17. These were *"Passaic—A Tradition,"* "The Dull Lecture," the dedicatory letter to Samuel Rogers in *Poems, by William Cullen Bryant* (1832), and "Correction of a Misstatement Respecting *Astoria.*" To avoid needless repetition in the Textual Commentary for the separate works, the copies of *Irvingiana* consulted in the preparaiton of this edition are listed here: New York Public Library (AN (Irving)); New-York Historical Society (PS/ 2085/ .17).

interest. Characteristically, Pierre indicated his sources for all eight selections, five of which had first appeared in New York newspapers. The reprinted texts show no signs of authorial revision and carry no independent textual authority.[18] The latest of the posthumous collections is *The Crayon Papers* (1883), a probably unauthorized gathering of articles reprinted from the *Knickerbocker Magazine*. Most of these had already been reprinted in *Wolfert's Roost and Other Papers, Now First Collected* (1855), Irving's own selective anthology of sketches chiefly from the same magazine. The remaining four titles, which are included in the present volume, had not. None of the reprinted *Crayon Papers* texts of these articles, in any of the several editions in which that collection appeared,[19] possesses textual authority independent of the first published version.

The most comprehensive and carefully prepared gathering of Irving's miscellaneous writings to appear after his death was *Spanish Papers*, edited by Pierre M. Irving. In the preface to this work Pierre explained that its "contents, in large measure, consist of the scattered productions of

18. These were "Written in the Deepdene Album," the dedicatory letter to Samuel Rogers in *Poems, by William Cullen Bryant* (1832), the address at the Irving Dinner, May 30, 1832, the letter to the Editor of the New York *American*, January 4, 1837, the letter to the editor of *The Plaindealer*, January 28, 1837, the letter to William Cullen Bryant, February 16, 1837, the toast at the Bookseller's Dinner, March 30, 1837, and the letter on International Copyright. Drawing upon the manuscript material Irving had entrusted to him, Pierre also included in the biography four previously unpublished works or fragments: these were the "Address of Cooper on Assuming the Management of the Park Theatre," "To Miss Emily Foster on Her Birth-Day," the account of a voyage up the Hudson River in 1800, and the account of a journey to Sackett's Harbor in 1814.

To avoid needless repetition, the copies of PMI consulted in the preparation of this edition are listed here: Volume I: Collection of the editor, penciled signature of "Phebe J. Rushmore" on flyleaf; collection of the editor, penciled signature of "E. E. Andrews" on flyleaf; collection of the editor, "National Edition," "Alice Bradford Library" written in ink on the flyleaf. Volume II: Collection of the editor, penciled signature of "E. E. Andrews" on flyleaf; collection of the editor, "Lucius & Carrie from Mother Christmas 1862" penciled on flyleaf; collection of the editor, "National Edition," "Alice Bradford Library" written in ink on the flyleaf. Volume III: Collection of the editor, bookplate of "L. P. Thompson" pasted upside-down on inside back cover; New York Public Library (AN).

19. The articles were "American Researches in Italy," "The Taking of the Veil, and the Charming Letoriéres," "Letter from Granada," and "Abderahman"; for Irving's revisions to the *Knickerbocker Magazine* text of the latter work see the Textual Commentary to "Chronicle of the Ommiades." To avoid needless repetition, the copies from editions of *The Crayon Papers* consulted in the preparation of this edition are listed here: (1) New York: J. W. Lovell, 1883–Lovell's Library, vol. 5, no. 249 (New York Public Library NBF p.v. 23 v. 3); (2) New York: J. B. Alden, 1883 (University of Chicago PS/ 2072/ C8/ 1883); (3) New York: James B. Millar & Co., 1884 (Toronto Public Library 827/ .I); (4) New York: William L. Allison, n.d. (University of Windsor PS/ 2060/ .A1/ 1880).

[Irving's] pen which it was his intention to have brought together and published in a collected edition.... He made some slight preparation towards this object ... but he left his purpose unfulfilled."[20] Probably Irving had spoken with Pierre about his wishes for this supplement to the Author's Revised Edition of his works. He had assisted his nephew in gathering information for use in the *Life and Letters*, ferreting out correspondence with old friends and offering suggestions for further research, and it seems natural that he would also discuss his uncompleted project with his literary collaborator and future literary executor. For example, on April 3, 1859, his seventy-sixth birthday, he called Pierre into his study and drew from his desk the manuscripts of his still-unpublished Spanish chronicles. Pierre made no comment on this incident in his journal entry for the day, although a notation immediately following the reference to the histories ("Spoke of now being able to tell me anecdotes, &c.") suggests that the preparation of the *Life and Letters* was a topic for conversation.[21] In light of their presence in *Spanish Papers*, one is tempted to speculate that on this day or some other Irving suggested the narratives of medieval Spain as eligible components of a future collection of his writings. At any rate we have Pierre's testimony in 1866 that the contents of *Spanish Papers* were published "in answer to repeated demands to make the collection of his writings complete," and also "in pursuance of [Irving's] intention."[22]

Whatever the "slight preparation" Irving made to the collection may have been, in editing *Spanish Papers* Pierre had access to the results of his uncle's preliminary activity and was aware of at least some of his intentions. In a preliminary note to the reprinted "Letters of Jonathan Oldstyle" he remarked that "in deference to the wishes of the author" he was including only the first five of the nine letters in the original "Oldstyle" series. He went on to say that Irving had "marked them as 'not to be reprinted,' when there was question of including [them] in a collective edition of his writings."[23] The pattern of Pierre's close relationship with his uncle over the twenty-five years preceding Irving's death suggests that he adhered elsewhere to the author's wishes, so far as they had been expressed.[24] *Spanish Papers* was thus produced under the most

20. "Preface by the Editor," in *Spanish Papers and Other Miscellanies, Hitherto Unpublished or Uncollected*, ed. Pierre M. Irving, 2 vols. (New York, G. P. Putnam, 1866), I, iii; hereafter cited as *Spanish Papers*.

21. Pierre M. Irving, Journal, 1859 (Berg Collection, New York Public Library).

22. "Preface by the Editor," in *Spanish Papers*, I, iii.

23. *Spanish Papers*, II, 10.

24. The relationship between Pierre M. Irving and his uncle is described by Wayne R. Kime in *Pierre M. Irving and Washington Irving: A Collaboration in Life and Letters* (Waterloo, Ont., 1977).

favorable auspices possible, given the circumstance of its posthumous publication. It was edited by a devoted relative of painstaking habits who was better informed than any other person concerning Irving's intentions for the collection. It was printed by the firm of John F. Trow, some of whose compositors—Messrs. Cummings, "J.S.G.," Hall, and Nelson —were familiar with the eccentricities of Irving's manuscript copy; and it was published by George Putnam, with whom he had enjoyed a remarkably smooth business relationship, and whose house style he had approved.[25] Aside from its textual significance, *Spanish Papers* is clearly of interest as a pendant to the Author's Revised Edition of Irving's works and as the final fruit of the collaborations between him and his nephew.

The collection is moreover of potential importance in a critical edition of Irving's miscellaneous writings, for the possibility exists that it includes substantive and accidental readings[26] which represent the wishes of the author expressed after the original publication of some of its contents. The deliberate manner in which it was produced—it was partially in type six months before the date of publication[27]—and the low incidence of typographical errors in it suggest that, in addition to being edited with care, the first edition of *Spanish Papers* incorporated whatever evidence of authorial revisions Pierre M. Irving had on hand. Only a fraction of the printer's copy submitted by Pierre has survived, but the textual history of the published work nevertheless lends weight to this hypothesis. Machine collations of four copies of the first volume—the only one which included previously unpublished titles—reveal the beginnings of plate deterioration as evidenced by broken types chiefly at the margins, but they show no resettings, corrections, or other signs of more than a single state within the first impression.[28] Machine collation of a copy of the

25. See the "Textual Commentary" to *Mahomet and His Successors*, ed. Henry A. Pochmann and E. N. Feltskog (Madison, Wisc., 1970), pp. 571, 599.

26. "Substantives" are the author's words; "accidentals" are his spelling, capitalization, punctuation, paragraphing, and word-division. Other bibliographic terms used here ("edition," "impression," "state") conform to the definitions by Fredson Bowers in *Principles of Bibliographical Description* (Princeton, 1949).

27. Pierre M. Irving to Edward J. H. Howell, April 8, 1866 (Historical Society of Pennsylvania). *Spanish Papers* was published in New York on September 12, 1866.

28. Patterns for the machine collations, which were performed under the direction of Professor Henry A. Pochmann, are as follows: *Spanish Papers*, vol. 1 (BAL 10201) University of Texas (Ir8/ SP1) vs. Texas (Ir8/ SP) reveals a single broken type unmatched in the latter copy, at 226.30 (purify); Texas (Ir8/ SP1) vs. St. Benedict's College (PS 2062/ A1/ 1866) reveals three unpecedented breaks in the latter copy, two adjacent to the right margin; Texas (Ir8/ SP1) vs. Denver Public Library (946.02/ I72 S1) reveals seven unprecedented breaks in the latter copy, chiefly at the margins. No punctuation is lost at the margins owing to type batter in any of the four copies.

first volume, first impression, against one from the second impression, of 1867, reveals alterations of data on the title page, thirty-nine broken types, one missing semicolon, and types repaired at three points, totaling five letters; but no other variations are present.[29] A further machine collation of the first volume in subsequent impressions made in 1869 and 1872 confirms the pattern of accumulating type damage with minimal resetting for repairs, but it reveals no introductions of emended readings.[30] Sight collations of three copies of the second volume, first impression, have been of no use in isolating changes to the plates, but they do reveal that no substantive or accidental variants occur among the copies of Irving's reprinted texts.[31] Sight collation of a copy of the second volume, first impression, against one from the first and only authorized English edition, published in 1866 from Putnam's stereotype plates by Sampson Low, Son, and Marston, of London, yields the same result, as does one against a copy from the second American impression of 1867.[32] Having prepared *Spanish Papers* for publication in 1866 with considerable care, Pierre M. Irving introduced no new readings into subsequent printings of the work.

In prefatory notes to the various sections of *Spanish Papers* Pierre

29. The pattern for the machine collation, performed under the direction of Professor Henry A. Pochmann, is Texas (Ir8/ SP1) vs. University of Wisconsin (PS/ 2052/ .I7). The revised title page reflects George Putnam's resumption of active direction of his publishing business shortly after the Civil War. The first impression includes a decorative crest above the information: "NEW YORK: / G. P. PUTNAM; HURD AND HOUGHTON. / 1866." The second impression (BAL 10380) is without the crest, and the publisher is given as "NEW YORK: / G. P. PUTNAM AND SON, 661 BROADWAY, OPPOSITE BOND STREET. / 1867."

30. The pattern for this machine collation of two copies from the "Riverside Edition," also made under the direction of Professor Henry A. Pochmann, is Texas (Ir8/ SP 1869) vs. Wisconsin (Y/ Ir8/ SP/ 1872). The former volume was published by George Putnam and Son; the latter, by J. B. Lippincott of Philadelphia. For the use of Putnam's plates by Lippincott, see the discussion in BAL 10201. An incorrect page-sequence in the 1869 text—314, 316, 315—is rectified in the 1872. The Lippincott edition reveals no resettings except to repair broken types, made at eleven points; but 102 new breaks occur in it, many of which occur at the ends of lines; and seven marks of punctuation are lost.

31. Copies of *Spanish Papers*, vol. 2, first impression, used for sight collation are as follows: National Library of Canada (PS/ 2052/ I7/ 1866) vs. New York Public Library (NBQ); and vs. Yale University (IW/ Ir8/ 866). The latter sight collation was made twice and independently.

32. Copies used for these sight collations are, respectively, as follows: National Library of Canada (PS/ 2052/ I7/ 1866) vs. Wisconsin (PS/ 2052/ I7/ 1866); and vs. University of Michigan (828/ I72Spa/ 1867). A spot collation of both volumes of *Spanish Papers* in the National Library of Canada copy against the York University copy (PS/ 2063/ A1/ 1867) of *Biographies and Miscellaneous Papers*, a pirated edition published in 1867 by Bell and Daldy of London, did not reveal substantive variants but did reveal that the type was entirely reset.

specified the publications from which the reprinted articles in the collection were derived. Sight collation of the original texts thus identified by him against the twenty-one items reprinted in *Spanish Papers* and also represented in the present collection indicates that a modest number of substantive changes were made.[33] Setting aside alterations of titles, corrections of misprints, and introductions of new misprints, forty substantive readings without precedent in the original texts occur in seventeen of the reprinted ones. Since Pierre was an experienced and conscientious proofreader one must assume that he authorized at least the majority of these emended readings; but who was originally responsible for their introduction, Pierre or his uncle? The surviving manuscripts of the Spanish chronicles, which served as printer's copy for the *Spanish Papers* texts, reveal that Pierre did not hesitate on occasion to make minor changes to Irving's narratives in order to avoid repetition, clarify relationships, or achieve economy or idiomatic usage according to contemporary standards. Of the substantive variants in the reprinted texts, thirty pertain to only one or two words in the originals, and they conform neatly to the patterns observable in Pierre's attentions to the manuscript narratives of early Spain. For example, in the reprinted "Biography of Captain James Lawrence" the phrase "funeral obsequies" is shortened to the equally descriptive "obsequies" (75.28); in "Biographical Notice of the Late Lieutenant Burrows" the phrase "a singular aversion" is shortened to the more general "singular aversion" (86.39); in Irving's self-review of *A Chronicle of the Conquest of Granada* the phrase "changeful as the wind" is altered, rather indifferently, to the perhaps more idiomatic "changeful as the winds" (II, 21.21); and in "Desultory Thoughts on Criticism" the construction "trust to" is shortened to form part of the simplified phrase "trust his own discernment" (II, 122.23). The meticulous, even finical attention evident in these instances

33. The articles reprinted in *Spanish Papers* and also included here are the review of *The Works* of Robert Treat Paine, "Biography of Captain James Lawrence," "Captain Lawrence," "Biographical Notice of the Late Lieutenant Burrows," "Biographical Memoir of Commodore Perry," the review of Edwin C. Holland's *Odes*, "Biographical Memoir of Captain David Porter," "A Biographical Sketch of Thomas Campbell," the self-review of *A Chronicle of the Conquest of Granada*, the review of Henry Wheaton's *History of the Northmen*, the letter to the editor of the *Knickerbocker Magazine* for March, 1839, "Sleepy Hollow," "National Nomenclature," "Desultory Thoughts on Criticism," "Communipaw," "Conspiracy of the Cocked Hats," "Letter from Granada," the 1850 memoir of Thomas Campbell, "The Catskill Mountains," "Conversations with Talma," and the memoir of Washington Allston.

To avoid needless repetition, the copies of *Spanish Papers* used for sight-collation of reprinted articles are listed here: Volume 1: University of Texas (Ir8/ SP1); National Library of Canada (PS/ 2052/ I7/ 1866); Volume 2: National Library of Canada (PS/ 2052/ I7/ 1866); New York Public Library (NBQ).

is characteristic of Pierre's editorial hand and thoroughly uncharacteristic of his uncle, who tended when revising printed copy to rewrite whole sentences or passages several words in length,[34] but seldom to make adjustments to single words. Four other of the forty substantive changes to the texts reprinted in *Spanish Papers* are omissions of footnotes, emendations which Pierre also made on occasion when editing the Spanish chronicles.

The six remaining alterations made to produce the reprinted texts stand out sharply in contrast to the ones just surveyed, for they are not uncharacteristic of Irving and could thus less improbably have originated in his "slight preparation" of the miscellaneous articles for publication together. The first of these, made to the "Biographical Memoir of Commodore Perry," is the omission of a particularly grisly detail pertaining to Commodore Barclay, Perry's British antagonist in a naval battle on Lake Erie. In the original text, published in the *Analectic Magazine* for December, 1813, Irving wrote that Barclay "was twice carried below, on account of his wounds, and had the misfortune to have his remaining hand shot away" (T 101.20–22). In *Spanish Papers* the statement was abridged to "was twice carried below, on account of his wounds." Evidently the emendation was motivated by concern for the sensibilities of the reader, but whether it was made by Irving or Pierre is impossible to say. The five other substantive variants occur in "Sleepy Hollow," an article first published in the *Knickerbocker Magazine* for May, 1839. Of these, four appear in a single sentence concerning Frederick Filipsen, one of the founders of the New Netherlands. Th original and the revised passages describing Filipsen and his wife are given below in parallel texts (see also II, 107.26–29):

Knickerbocker Magazine	*Spanish Papers*
Frederick Filipsen . . . reigned over a wide extent of this neighborhood, and held his seat of power at Yonkers; and his wife, Katrina von Courtlandt, of the no less potent line of the Van Courtlandts of Croton, who lorded it over. . . .	Frederick Filipsen . . . got the better of the native savages, subdued a great tract of country by dint of trinkets, tobacco, and *aqua vitae*, and established his seat of power at Yonkers,—and his wife, Katrina Van Courtlandt, of the no less heroic line of the Van Courtlandts of Croton, who in like manner subdued and occupied. . . .

Although in editing the Spanish chronicles Pierre M. Irving did revise

---

34. See the Textual Commentary to "Correction of a Misstatement Respecting *Astoria*" and "Chronicle of the Ommiades." See also the "Textual Commentary" to *Mahomet and His Successors*, ed. Pochmann and Feltskog, pp. 580–81, n. 13, and the "Textual Commentary" to *Astoria*, ed. Richard D. Rust (Boston, 1976), p. 403, n. 12.

passages of this length, his changes were generally extractive, to stream-line the text and to avoid redundancy.[35] On the other hand, the particu-larized elaboration made to produce the *Spanish Papers* version of the above passage is consistent with Irving's habits when going over his own printed works. It thus seems possible that Pierre submitted to the printers a copy of the *Knickerbocker Magazine* text of "Sleepy Hollow" bearing a few corrections by the author; but in the absence of such a copy the textual evidence relating to this lengthiest alteration of the articles reprinted in *Spanish Papers* seems less than conclusive. And for the contents of the collection taken as a group, the most liberal interpre-tation of the substantive variants observed between them and their texts as first published must be that Irving made only minimal adjust-ments to the works he selected for inclusion. His preparation of the mis-cellaneous collection of his writings seems to have consisted almost entirely of assembling the texts in their earliest printed forms.

The accidental readings in the reprinted *Spanish Papers* articles in-clude numerous and consistent variations from those in the earlier publications, reflecting the imposition of the Putnam house style.[36] In his later career Irving adopted what Henry A. Pochmann has termed a "settled policy (in so far as it can be reconstructed from available evi-dence, including author-corrected proof sheets and lists of corrigenda) of being meticulous about substantive matters (including spelling) but trusting the printer to supply whatever punctuation he neglected to incorporate in his manuscripts."[37] Another consistent practice was to revise the accidentals in printed copy only in conjunction with changes made to the substantive readings. From these observed procedures it follows that Irving was not responsible for the emended accidentals in the posthumous volumes. The Putnam style appears to have been applied in a continuous overlay, for there are no passages whose spell-ings or punctuation seem to reflect faithful adherence to a model, such as a scrap of manuscript, embodying conventions other than those regu-larly observed by the publisher. Unquestionably, in reading proof for *Spanish Papers* Pierre M. Irving devoted more attention to reviewing the accidental readings that his late uncle would have done; but from

---

35. Pierre's preparations of the Spanish chronicles for publication are summa-rized in the respective sections of the Textual Commentary. A similar pattern of revision was set in March, 1859, when at Irving's request he rehandled the con-cluding chapter of the *Life of George Washington*. Pierre wrote in his journal that he had improved it "mainly by omissions" (Journal, 1859–Berg Collection, New York Public Library).

36. For a practical description of the Putnam house style, see below, pp. 273–76.

37. Henry A. Pochmann, "Textual Commentary," in *Mahomet and His Succes-sors*, ed. Pochmann and Feltskog, p. 599.

the surviving printer's copy it seems that, like his uncle, he left the determination of accidentals mainly in the hands of the publisher and the firm of John F. Trow.

COPY-TEXTS

In order to formulate critical texts of Irving's miscellaneous writings the theory of copy-text as set forth by W. W. Greg is adopted as a useful basis for a rationale in making editorial decisions.[38] Ideally the manuscript that was used as printer's copy (or author-corrected proofs, if they alone survive) provides copy-text; when neither is extant, the printed version nearest the author's manuscript is selected. The contents of the *Miscellaneous Writings* represent a variety of textual situations, but for each item of the seventy-six included here the choice of copy-text has been made with the identical aim: to identify among available texts that version which, according to textual and historical evidence, comes closest to realizing the author's final intentions for the work in its original form. Printed versions are chosen in cases where manuscripts are not extant,[39] where manuscripts survive but do not represent Irving's latest wishes,[40] and where manuscripts survive in forms so fragmentary as to be of little use for establishing the full texts of the works

38. The theory is explained by Greg in "The Rationale of Copy-Text," *Studies in Bibliography*, 3 (1950–1951), 19–36.

39. These works are the contributions to the New York *Morning Chronicle*, the contributions to *The Corrector*, "We Will Rejoice! ! !," *The New-York Review*, the contributions to the *Analectic Magazine*, the lines written in "The Temple of Dirt," "Address of Cooper on Assuming the Management of the Park Theatre," "Song," "Signs of the Times," "Written in the Deepdene Album," "The Dull Lecture," the advertisement of an abridgement of *The Life and Voyages of Christopher Columbus*, the self-review of *A Chronicle of the Conquest of Granada*, the dedicatory letter in *Poems, by William Cullen Bryant* (1832), the review of Wheaton's *History of the Northmen*, "An Unwritten Drama of Lord Byron," "The Haunted Ship," the letter to the editor of the New York *American*, January 4, 1837, the letter to the editor of *The Plaindealer*, January 28, 1837, the letter to William Cullen Bryant, February 16, 1837, the letter as "Geoffrey Crayon" to the editor of the *Knickerbocker Magazine*, "Sleepy Hollow," the letter as "Hiram Crackenthorpe" to the editor of the *Knickerbocker Magazine*, "National Nomenclature," "Desultory Thoughts on Criticism," the letter on International Copyright to the editor of the *Knickerbocker Magazine*, "Letter from Granada," "American Researches in Italy," the 1850 memoir of Thomas Campbell, the remarks at the Cooper Memorial Meeting, the account of a voyage up the Hudson River in 1800, and the account of a journey to Sackett's Harbor in 1814.

40. Only the lines "To Miss Emily Foster on Her Birth-Day" fall into this category.

in question.[41] In the appropriate sections of this Textual Commentary an account is given for each item of all manuscript versions known to exist and of all printed texts published during the author's lifetime or after which possess some claim to authority. The variety and number of revisions made by Irving or other persons as the work passed from stage to stage are also summarized; and, on the basis of the textual history and the possible alternatives thus set forth, the choice of copy-text is then specified.

EMENDATIONS

No attempt is made to impose a single pattern of styling upon the range of Irving's miscellaneous works, which were written to serve a great many different purposes in several places at various times. Some of the author's practices, like himself, changed a good deal during his long career. Although in reviewing works which he prepared at successive periods one does reencounter certain characteristics of composition— often details such as a tendency not to hyphenate compound words, an inability to distinguish between "counsel" and "council," or the use of a semicolon (rather than a comma) to mark a distinct pause—these curiosities of Irving's practice do not occur with inevitable regularity and taken together do not in any case add up to a full system of styling. Bearing in mind his willingness to permit the final adjustments of his fugitive writings to be made by persons other than himself, it would be folly to attempt the formulation of a single "Irving style" for imposition on all his writings gathered here. In general, when a norm for Irving's practices is necessary to provide a basis for emendation at problematical points, it is derived from the work under consideration or the group of works (such as the contributions to *The Corrector*) of which it forms a part. Emendation is made when necessary to clarify ambiguities, rectify unintentional errors, achieve a reasonable degree of consistency in matters where an authorial preference is clearly evident, and supply details which the textual evidence indicates Irving would certainly have wished his editors to include. No attempt is made to impose consistency merely for its own sake, however; and unless particular intentions are readily discernible, the author's inconsistencies in practice are respected and permitted to stand. Emendations are kept to a minimum and reported in full.

41. These works are "Conspiracy of the Cocked Hats," "The 'Empire of the West,'" "The Taking of the Veil, and the Charming Letoriéres," and "History of the Conquest of Mexico."

TREATMENT OF SUBSTANTIVES

Precopy-text manuscript sources have at times been useful to confirm readings in the copy-texts and to provide bases for emendation, either in an indirect manner (for example, "The Chronicle of Pelayo," II, 190.18) or as direct authorities at points where errors were introduced into printed versions and overlooked by Irving in his subsequent revisions. More often than not, however, precopy-text sources are of greater utility for a general understanding of the ways in which particular works, such as "A Biographical Sketch of Thomas Campbell," "Conversations with Talma," or "Chronicle of Fernando the Saint," took shape rather than for the specific purpose of defining critical texts. Comparison of manuscript copy-texts against their printed sources, when known, occasionally does draw attention to errors which require correction ("Chronicle of the Ommiades," II, 232.6).

For manuscript copy-texts which have themselves undergone revision by the author and which, owing to his oversight or indecision, include two different readings at points where only one can properly form part of the final version (for example, *Abu Hassan*, 198.9), Irving's later choice is ordinarily adopted unless it introduces an error (as in *Abu Hassan*, 206.15). However, on occasion in tinkering with his text Irving wrote fragments of prospective changes which he did not follow through (*Abu Hassan*, 212.5); and in these instances the original statements are necessarily allowed to stand.

Some manuscript copy-texts include readings introduced by persons other than the author. These changes to Irving's texts are all identified and their authorship, if known, is indicated. For the majority of his manuscripts, such as those for his contributions to the *Knickerbocker Magazine*, he gave tacit permission if not an imperative direction for them to be corrected as necessary for publication. However, while it is true that his inattention to detail often necessitated revision by editors like Lewis Gaylord Clark of the *Knickerbocker Magazine*, it does not follow that Irving would have approved all their alterations of his texts. For example, in the anecdote of Admiral Harvey published in the issue for February, 1840, Clark altered "up home" to the more formal "up to their homes" (II, 135.7), and in so doing he removed from the vignette a bit of the rural tone Irving obviously intended. In "Communipaw," which appeared in the issue for September, 1839, Clark made an indifferent emendation of the phrase "with concern" to "with great concern" (II, 128.37), and in the same article he apparently authorized the omission from the published work of an entire 120-word postscript Irving had included in his manuscript. In such instances the author's own readings are restored unless they are erroneous. The two plays, *The Freyschütz*

and *Abu Hassan*, require a somewhat different approach to the determination of substantive readings, for their authorship was the result of
close consultation and collaboration. Unless Irving deleted the changes
or insertions made by his collaborator, John B. Livius, these emendations are ordinarily allowed to stand on the assumption that by not
canceling them he tacitly assented to their presence.

Readings in manuscript copy-texts are in general given preference
over those in printed texts which derive from them, unless, of course,
the manuscript is itself erroneous (for example, "The Catskill Mountains," II, 164.1, 165.25–26). Since Irving rarely played a part in the publishing process beyond submitting a manuscript, it follows that substantive
changes reflected in the first printed versions of his texts are rarely
authorial. The changes are usually owing to compositor's error ("Conversations with Talma," (II, 169.36) or simply to editorial preference
("Conversations with Talma," II, 168.22), and hence they have no place
in critical texts.

The predominant pattern in Irving's attentions to his miscellaneous
writings was to pay them little or no attention once they had appeared
in print. Exceptions do occur, as for example his adaptations of the
Knickerbocker Magazine texts of "Communipaw" and "Conspiracy of
the Cocked Hats" to a single new purpose.[42] In general, however, the
reprinted texts of the articles included here do not possess independent
textual authority. Beginning with the *Analectic Magazine* contributions
and continuing through the remainder of his career, Irving's writings
were reprinted, and sometimes even revised, without his approval and
in many cases probably without his knowledge. Accordingly, for both
manuscript and printed copy-texts substantive readings unique to the
reprinted versions are regarded as of at best doubtful significance.

Collation of copy-texts against the original passages for Irving's quoted
material in the articles on *The Works* of Robert Treat Paine, James Kirke
Paulding's *The Lay of the Scottish Fiddle*, Edwin C. Holland's *Odes*,
Henry Wheaton's *History of the Northmen*, and Irving's own *Chronicle
of the Conquest of Granada* reveal that in quotations he placed no
premium on absolute faithfulness to his sources. In the review of Slidell's
A Year in Spain, the text of which work he had himself edited, he presumably did intend to quote accurately, although in the manuscript he merely
indicated passages for quotation by writing the first few words and
adding a page reference. Elsewhere, however, he altered the "quoted"
lines to suit the contexts of his own discussions, and at one point in the
review of Wheaton's *History* (II, 71.6–13) he virtually rewrote a passage
several sentences in length. Unless they introduce outright errors, Irving's

42. See the Textual Commentary to "Communipaw," II, 412–15.

inaccurate quotations are allowed to stand on the assumption that they represent his wishes. This principle is also observed for other works such as the contributions to *The Corrector*, where his loose quotation paraphrases of diverse literary sources are of a piece with the freewheeling obliviousness to convention which characterizes these works generally.

TREATMENT OF ACCIDENTALS

No attempt is made to "Americanize" Irving's spelling nor to render it consistent throughout. There is no indication that at any period during his lifetime he relied upon the prescriptions of a single lexicographer, English or American. During the period of his apprenticeship in New York he was no doubt conscious of the authority of Dr. Johnson's *Dictionary*, but he could not have remained unaffected by Noah Webster's attempt in his *Compendious Dictionary of the English Language* (1806) to systematize native American usage. A further possibility is that he relied upon John Walker's *Critical Pronouncing Dictionary of the English Language* (1791), which had reached a second American edition by 1806 and was frequently reprinted thereafter. The fact is, however, that adherence to a particular authority was probably as far beyond his powers as it lay outside his interests. He was not only an inconsistent speller but also a poor one.[43] Hence if any of his spellings is to be found in Johnson, Webster, or Walker, or if it listed in the *Oxford English Dictionary* as in contemporary use, it is allowed to stand, even if the word is spelled differently at another point in the same work. On the other hand, if a clear preference is evident within that work, the preferred spelling is adopted throughout. Apostrophes are added when necessary to possessives and contractions, the various configurations of conjoined S and *t* are normalized to "St.," and periods are added to this and other abbreviated forms of address such as "Mr." and "Lieut." Proper names are regularized to consistent spellings if a preference is evident or if there is danger that the names used are not clearly recognizable as referring to the same person (for an extreme example, see "Chronicle of Fernan Gonzalez," Discussions of Adopted Readings, II, 243.34).

Words at the beginnings of sentences or statements are capitalized, but at other points capitalizations or emendations to lowercase forms are made only in accordance with Irving's clearly preferred usage in the work or group of works concerned. Place-names are ordinarily capi-

43. A more detailed discussion of Irving's spelling habits and the dictionaries he may at times have relied upon is in Henry A. Pochmann's "Textual Commentary" to *Mahomet and His Successors*, ed. Pochmann and Feltskog, pp. 607–9. See also the "Textual Commentary" to *Astoria*, ed. Richard D. Rust, pp. 407–8.

talized; and in accordance with Irving's usual practice military, civil, and religious titles are also capitalized when they are used as parts of proper designations. Exceptions to the latter procure, justified by the occasional consistent departures from the author's own rule, are reported as they occur.

As we have seen, Irving's punctuation in his manuscripts was often slipshod. Frequently he neglected to punctuate at the end of a line or after an interlineation, apparently assuming that the pause usually indicated by a comma, dash, or semicolon was implied by the position of the preceding word or phrase along the line or above it. He often neglected to revise punctuation on either side of cancellations and substitutions which necessitated adjustments, and when writing fluently he was much less inclined to insert punctuation near the left margin, when just beginning a new line, than he was just after reaching its midpoint. According to Henry A. Pochmann, his practice was "guided less by grammatical rules or syntactical principles than by what seeems to be a kind of half-visual, half-oral sense for supplying punctuation . . . [and thereby] indicating a pause, placing a shade of emphasis, or supplying a special nuance of meaning whether covered by the rules or not."[44] This is an apt summary for the manuscript texts which Irving prepared with care, but for the miscellaneous writings it requires the qualification that his obliviousness to "the rules" was not seldom the result simply of neglect.

An effort is therefore made to distinguish between marks of punctuation in manuscript copy-texts resulting from error or obliviousness and those reflecting a legitimate though slightly unorthodox intention. In order to correct some classes of Irving's recurrent oversights or omissions through inattention, periods are regularly supplied to conclude sentences,[45] quotation marks are added to signify direct quotations, commas are added to separate quotations from the commentary, and end-of-line punctuation is supplied as required. In themselves, Irving's mild eccentricities of pointing create no difficulties; they are even welcome, as betokening a degree of care on his part. However, those copy-texts casually prepared and requiring emendation do pose problems for the establishment of critical versions, for they necessitate a working familiarity with Irving's current practices to provide a rationale for the departures from faulty copy-text readings that the emendations entail. The contrast between the manner in which the four manuscript

44. Pochmann, "Textual Commentary" to *Mahomet and His Successors*, ed. Pochmann and Feltskog, pp. 580–81.

45. If a sentence in a copy-text ends with a dash or a double dash the original punctuation is emended to a period unless there is clear evidence that the dash or dashes represent Irving's intention.

texts of the Spanish chronicles were emended for publication in *Spanish Popers* and the manner in which they are treated here should serve to typify the approach throughout the volume to the emendation of accidentals in semicompleted manuscript copy-texts.

Irving revised and partially rewrote his narratives of early Spain in the spring of 1847, as a respite from "muddling" over his printed works to prepare them for reprinting in a uniform edition. Accordingly, he pursued his "amusing occupation" in a desultory manner, with marked inattention to editorial detail. At the close of this interlude he informed Pierre M. Irving that, having sketched in "the frame and part of the finish of an entire new work," he intended to "put it by to be dressed off at leisure."[46] However, he never did return to his series of partially completed chronicles, and at his death it devolved upon Pierre to give the works their final preparations for publication. Collations of the manuscript texts as revised and corrected by Pierre against the published narratives reveal that, as with the articles reprinted in *Spanish Papers*, he authorized George Putnam to impose the usual house styling on the series of posthumous writings. On the basis of these collations some of the principles observed by Putnam's editor, or printers, for the emendation of Irving's accidentals may be inferred; and taken together, the principles constitute a rough practical definition of the Putnam style.

Setting aside corrections of errors and normalizations of proper names, most of the regularizations of Irving's spellings were made according to a few readily formulable rules: (1) compound words: (a) a hyphen is added to compounds written by the author as two words ("after ages," "light horsemen"), or, (b) a compound written by the author as two words ("day light," "strong hold") is printed as one; (2) *-our* spellings, often though not always employed by Irving, are altered to *-or* ("armour," "valour"); (3) internal *-z-* spellings are altered to *-s-* ("enterprize," "partizans"); (4) Irving's *e-* or *-e-* spellings are altered to *i-* or *-i-* ("encrease," "despatch"); (5) Irving's obsolescent spellings are modernized ("shew " to "show"; 'traytor" to "traitor"); (6) arbitrary changes are made from preference of one of two acceptable contemporary usages ("chasten'd" to "chastened"; "afterward" to "afterwards"; "suspence" to "suspense").[47]

The inconsistent capitalization in the manuscripts was regularized in

46. Irving to Pierre M. Irving, [Sunnyside], April 14, 1847; PMI, IV, 15–16.
47. Putnam's practices for emendations of spelling conform to the prescriptions in *Webster's Unabridged Dictionary*, which appeared in 1848 and became the norm for the Author's Revised Edition of Irving's works. A full accounting of changes made in *Spanish Papers* to the spelling and the hyphenation of compound words in the manuscript of "The Chronicle of Pelayo" is provided in the Textual Commentary to that work, notes 385 and 386.

Spanish Papers according to principles, most of which are also clear:
(1) lowercase to capital: (a) a designation of title or rank employed
as part of a proper name is capitalized ("count," "grand master"); (b)
words associated with the Christian faith are usually capitalized ("apostle," "holy sepulchre");[48] (c) the first word of a direct quotation a full
sentence or more in length is capitalized. Emendations from Irving's
capitals to lowercase letters were far more numerous than in the other
direction: (2) capital to lowercase: (a) a designation of title or rank not
used as part of a proper name is emended to lowercase ("archbishop,"
"queen"); (b) a foreign word immediately followed by a definition is
rendered lowercase ("adalid," "genetes"); (c) capitalized words within
a sentence which are not proper names and do not fall into categories
noted above as ordinarily altered from lowercase to capital are emended
to lowercase.[49] Foreign words written without underlining by Irving are
printed in italics rather than roman type ("duelo" to "*duello*"; "Te deum
laudamus" to "*Te Deum Laudamus*").

Emendations of the punctuation in Irving's manuscripts took the forms
of insertions or substitutions far more often than deletions, and they were
usually made to internal punctuation—commas, semicolons, and colons.
Setting aside simple corrections of errors, the situations in which changes
to the author's pointing were most frequently made were these (the
square brackets in the several examples enclose the changes incorporated
in *Spanish Papers*, I). Commas were (A) added (1) before, after, or
before and after participial, adverbial, or prepositional constructions:
"The illustrious son and mother remained together six weeks[,] enjoying each other's society[,] after which they separated." (405.22–23);
"Now[,] at this time[,] there was . . ." (335.12); ". . . sallying forth, sword
in hand[,] upon the wall[,] they gained . . ." (383.3–4); (2) before a
relative or other subordinate clause: ". . . the mountain cliffs[,] which
so long had echoed nothing but lamentations, . . ." (235.8–9); ". . . but
to press on and gain the victory[,] for he had slain the King of Navarre."
(306.3–5); (3) following any coordinated element within a sentence:
"His father Gonzalvo Nuñez died in 903[,] and his elder brother Rodrigo
in 904[,] without issue . . ." (279.18–19); ". . . a tile, either falling from
the roof of a tower, or sportively thrown by one of his companions[,]
struck him in the head . . ." (356.26–28); (4) before "and" separating mul-

48. As an example of Putnam's inconsistency in capitalizing words associated
with the Christian faith, see the Textual Commentary to "Chronicle of Fernando
the Saint," note 472.
49. A full accounting of changes made in *Spanish Papers* to the capitalization
in the manuscript of "The Chronicle of Pelayo" is provided in the Textual Commentary to that work, notes 387 and 388.

tiple verbs in a sentence having a simple subject: "... she embraced Pelayo with mingled tears and kisses[,] and proclaimed him as her long-lost son." (219.3–5); (5) separating appositives: "Fernan Gomez de Pudiello[,] a stout cavalier, who . . ." (370.21–22); ". . . and lies buried with his queen[,] Gaudiosa[,] in the church . . ." (244.6–7); (6) after the second item in a list of three: ". . . the heads of stags, of wolves[,] and wild boars . . ." (214.5–6); (7) before and after a logical connective: ". . . Magued[,] however, did not await his coming . . ." (242.13); ". . . and feared[,] moreover[,] that. . . ." (343.7); ". . . those[,] therefore[,] who. . . ." (378.11). Commas were (B) deleted (1) preceding a subordinate clause: ". . . proclaim far and wide among the mountains [ ] that Pelayo. . . ." (233.30–31); (2) following any coordinated element within a sentence: ". . . a good prince, who shall reside within it[ ] and devote himself entirely to its prosperity . . ." (253.13–14); "If you will amend your ways in this respect[ ] and remedy the past . . ." (304.8–9); (3) separating subject and verb: "One of the first to join his standard[ ] was . . ." (266.17). Commas were (C) emended (1) to a semicolon separating the major elements of a compound sentence: "The latter was sent in chains to the castle of Gordon[;] but the count was carried to Leon . . ." (329.24–25); (2) to a colon introducing a direct quotation: ". . . he paused and said[:] 'Señor Perez, . . ." (422.18–19).

Semicolons were (A) added separating the major elements of a compound sentence: "The case required bold measures, combined with stratagem[;] so he confided in her . . ." (293.30–294.1). Semicolons were (B) emended (1) to a comma, (a) before a relative or other subordinate clause: ". . . . squadron after squadron of swarthy Arabs spurred into the valley[,] which was soon whitened . . ." (237.11–13); ". . . he repaired to Toro and entered the chivalrous order of Santiago[,] that he might gain the indulgences . . ." (363.6–8); (b) before a participial construction: ". . . the Castilians were hardly pressed[,] being so inferior in number." (308.29–30); separating multiple verbs in a sentence having a simple subject: "The Moors were silenced by this reply[,] and prepared . . ." (446.29); separating the major elements of a compound sentence: ". . . the king and his court came to receive her[,] and their nuptials were celebrated . . ." (365.24–25); (e) separating items in a list or parallel sequence: "Some came to serve the king[,] others out of devotion to the holy faith[,] some to gain renown . . ." (384.12–14); (2) to a comma followed by a dash, separating interpolated explanatory material from the text preceding it: ". . . he shared the rest with God, devoting a large part to the Church, and to the relief of souls in purgatory[,–] a pious custom, which he ever after observed." (282.22–25).

Colons were emended (A) to a semicolon, (1) separating parallel constructions: "It was a city of great splendor and wealth[;] situated in the midst of a fertile country . . ." (411.17–18); (3) separating the major elements of a compound sentence: "They will have the advantage if they attack us[;] but if we attack them . . ." (305.14–16); (B) to a comma followed by a dash, introducing a direct quotation: ". . . it was affixed at night to a column in the public square, with this inscription[,–] 'Thus Abderahman . . .'" (266.27–28). Single quotation marks were invariably altered in *Spanish Papers* to double quotation marks.

From the above examples it will be seen that neither Irving nor the persons responsible for the punctuation of the *Spanish Papers* texts regulated themselves by mechanical rules inflexibly applied. The author did and did not include commas before subordinate clauses, and the *Spanish Papers* text does and does not emend his usages, depending on the contexts in which they occur; similarly Irving used a comma, a dash, a colon, or no punctuation at all to introduce a quotation, while in *Spanish Papers* a comma followed by a double dash, or a colon are on various occasions employed. The imposition of the Putnam style was thus a selective application of definable guidelines to Irving's texts, made by the editor or compositors on the basis of their judgment of the author's intentions in particular situations,–or in cases of error their notions of what his wishes should have been.[50]

The process rendered Irving's erratic manuscripts continuous in styling with his works issued from Putnam's presses during the last decade of his career, and it thereby realized an aim of which he would probably have approved in general. At the same time, however, the regularization of the manuscripts produced texts with a much heavier system of pointing than the author had employed, and it involved numerous departures from his legitimate and consistently expressed wishes. For example, the modernization of spellings such as "chaunt" to "chant" or "relique" to "relic" divested the chronicles of some of the archaic flavor Irving intended should characterize his "legendary" narratives of Old Spain. The printing in lowercase of words not ordinarily capitalized by Putnam several times ran counter to Irving's considered intentions (for example, see the Discussions of Adopted Readings concerning "Countess" and "Stout Prior" in "Chronicle of Fernando the Saint," II, 297.24, 318.17). And the relatively dense punctuation in *Spanish Papers* resulted in a prose style less fluent than in the author's own text.[51] The following

---

50. A classified list including multiple examples of characteristic emendations in *Spanish Papers* to the punctuation in the manuscript texts of the four Spanish chronicles is on file at the University of Texas. Also on file are documented lists of changes in *Spanish Papers* to the spelling and capitalization of all four manuscript texts.

parallel versions illustrate how the *Spanish Papers* system affected the texture and pace of his prose (see also II, 316.28–33):

Manuscript	*Spanish Papers*
The alarm was given in the camp and six sturdy friars sallied forth on foot, with two cavaliers, in pursuit of the marauders. The Prior himself was roused by the noise; when he heard that the beeves of the Church were in danger his ire was kindled and buckling on his armour he mounted his steed and gallopped furiously to the aid of his friars, and the rescue of his cattle.	The alarm was given in the camp, and six sturdy friars sallied forth, on foot, with two cavaliers, in pursuit of the marauders. The prior himself was roused by the noise; when he heard that the beeves of the Church were in danger his ire was kindled; and buckling on his armor, he mounted his steed and galloped furiously to the aid of his friars, and the rescue of his cattle.[52]

In short, the *Spanish Papers* texts reflect both in their corrections of errors and in their departures from Irving's usages the philosophy of editing adopted by Pierre M. Irving, under whose supervision they were produced: Pierre seems to have regarded his task as insofar as possible to *fulfill* his late uncle's imperfectly expressed intentions.

The twentieth-century editor's aim in producing critical texts of these works is different, for the primary emphasis is placed upon accurately *representing* Irving's own wishes, so far as he expressed them. A conservative bias regarding emendation is implicit in this aim. Within such a general limitation it remains possible, on the combined basis of manuscript evidence and the precedent of Irving's practices during his later career, to justify certain editorial procedures, such as the regularization of footnote form and even the interpolation of chapter numbers and chapter headings. More problematical, however, are the specific cruxes that present themselves from sentence to sentence and require the formulation of a procedure for emending the accidentals, particularly the internal punctuation, of manuscript texts which in Irving's phrase are "complete, though not thoroughly finished off." In this edition emendations of accidentals which are judged to be necessary are made on the practical basis of the author's observed habits within the suite of manuscript chronicles and also in his other Spanish histories, chiefly *Legends of the Conquest of Spain* (1835), *Mahomet and His Successors*

---

51. For examples of similar changes to Irving's prose style wrought by the imposition of "high pointing" on his manuscript text, see the "Textual Commentary" to *Astoria*, ed. Richard D. Rust, pp. 405–6.

52. Cancellations and line-divisions are not included in the transcription of the manuscript passage.

(1849), and the Author's Revised Edition of *A Chronicle of the Conquest of Granada* (1850).[53] Commas, for example, are supplied to complete pairs, to separate appositives, to separate independent clauses, and to mark pauses either following introductory constructions or before subordinate expressions; but they are supplied in only a modest fraction of the instances in which these situations occur, and then at points where the evidence suggests Irving would have approved the changes and would have been unsatisfied were they not made. The result of this approach, conjoining what the author wrote with a minimum of regularizations and other emendations warranted by textual precedent, is a group of texts appreciably less regular and self-consistent than those which appeared in *Spanish Papers* but in every respect representing more faithfully Irving's instincts and his final expressed wishes. A more particular accounting of the varieties of emendation undertaken in pursuit of this aim for each of the four chronicles is provided in the appropriate section of the Textual Commentary.

TEXTUAL HISTORIES, DISCUSSIONS OF ADOPTED READINGS, AND TABLES

Each section of this Textual Commentary setting forth the textual history of a particular work or group of works concludes with a listing of the manuscript and printed versions of that item which possess textual authority and are drawn upon as sources for the present critical edition. A key to identifying symbols used in referring to manuscript and printed sources is given on pages 229–32. Owing to the differences in textual history and textual evidence at hand for the various writings in the collection, differing combinations of tables summarizing changes made to the copy-texts, rejected substantive readings, and rejected precopy-text

53. The appropriateness of the histories on Spanish topics published and reprinted during Irving's lifetime as norms for the posthumously published chronicles is evident from the author's conception of all his Spanish histories, legends, and chronicles as forming parts of a single series. In a letter to the Reverend H. Coppée dated October 20, 1862, Pierre M. Irving explained that while living in Spain in 1826 and 1827 his uncle had "projected a series of writings illustrative of the Moorish domination in Spain." Pierre continued: "That plan, if carried out, would have resulted in a chain of Chronicles, linking the 'Legends of the Conquest of Spain' with Fray Antonio Agapida's 'Conquest of Granada'; and including 'Mahomet and His Successors' as introductory,—the whole series would have formed a wild and varied, but compact and complete department of history. . . . His preparations, however, for the fulfillment of his plan were altogether fragmentary" (Historical Society of Pennsylvania).

readings are required from work to work. The tables included for each item, and the content and degree of coverage therein, are reported in the appropriate section of the Textual Commentary immediately preceding the summary of collation procedures for that work.

Following this comprehensive textual discussion, the textual evidence for the seventy-six works is arranged in five lists: Discussions of Adopted Readings; List of Emendations; List of Rejected Variants; List of Rejected Precopy-text Variants; and List of Compound Words Hyphenated at End of Line. The Discussions of Adopted Readings describe particular textual problems at points signified by asterisks in the several tables. As well, these discussions include explanations of the editor's decisions whether to emend the copy-text at points not recorded in the tables. The List of Emendations is a complete record of all changes made by the editor to the original copy-texts. The List of Rejected Variants provides a record of variants in texts which originated after the copy-texts. The List of Rejected Precopy-Text Variants provides a record of variants in texts which antedate the copy-texts and are not incorporated in the text of the present critical edition. The List of Compound Words Hyphenated at End of Line includes all compound or possibly compound words that are hyphenated at the end of a line in the copy-texts or in the Twayne edition. Each word is listed in its editorially accepted form. Within all five lists, information concerning the several works is arranged by page and line in the same order as are the texts themselves.

At a minimum the textual histories, Discussions of Adopted Readings, and tables provide the evidence necessary for an interested reader to reconstruct the final version of each copy-text in its entirety. For Parts III and V, the plays and the Spanish chronicles, limitations of space render it impracticable to reproduce in addition the hundreds of canceled passages included in the manuscript copy-texts; but for Parts I, II, IV, and VI this information is included in the tables as well. Records of cancellations within all manuscript copy-texts are on file together with other collation data at the University of Texas.

Although Irving's texts are faithfully and critically rendered, ordinarily no attempt is made to reproduce exactly the so-called appurtenances of the text—such details as the precise arrangement of preliminary matter, lineation, and capitalization. However, in order to achieve some degree of continuity a small number of normalizations are made by the editor. Titles and subtitles of all works are given in full capitals, in roman or italic type as the textual evidence may dictate; the period, if any, following each title is deleted. For untitled works titles are supplied and enclosed within brackets. For prose writings except the plays, the first word of each article is treated as the beginning of a paragraph. The first word of each item is capitalized and its remaining letters are lowercase.

Taken together, the Introduction, Textual Commentaries, tables, and Discussions of Adopted Readings should enable the reader to examine and consider the bases on which all editorial decisions were made in the process of establishing critical texts, and thereby to see the relationships that exist among the versions of the works included here–from the author's earliest manuscript notes, where they survive, to reasonably close approximations of what he intended his miscellaneous writings to be.

[CONTRIBUTIONS TO THE NEW YORK *MORNING CHRONICLE*]

The attribution to Irving of the two letters from "Dick Buckram" to "Andrew Quoz" is made primarily on the strength of his affirming in 1859 that the phrases "its spires glittering with tin, and its hospitable boards smoking with sturgeon," quoted by Gulian C. Verplanck in a tale entitled "Gelyna; A Tale of Albany and Ticonderoga, Seventy Years Ago,"[54] were in fact taken from a work of his own about Albany. The article, he told Pierre M. Irving, had been "written for the *Chronicle*"– that is, his brother Peter Irving's New York *Morning Chronicle*.[55] The first of Buckram's letters to Quoz, which appeared in the *Morning Chronicle* for December 24, 1803, does include references to "the majestic domes and tin steeples" of Albany and to an impromptu *"sturgeon feast"* enjoyed by the citizens of the city. Buckram's second letter, published in the *Morning Chronicle* for December 30, is a continuation of the first, rounding out his account of a dramatic troupe's recent trials amongst the "Albanians." For purposes of attribution, the two letters may be considered in effect a single work. Published in the *Morning Chronicle*, where the "Letters of Jonathan Oldstyle" had appeared a few months before; recounting the adventures of William Dunlap's Old American Company, whose performances at the Park Theatre in New York had

54. "Gelyna" originally appeared in a gift-book edited by Verplanck, *The Talisman for MDCCCXXX* (New York, 1829), pp. 302–35. It was reprinted in the *Home Journal*, no. 735 (October 22, 1859), pp. 1–2. Irving's remark about his authorship of the lines quoted by Verplanck was prompted by his reading the tale in the latter publication. For further discussion of "Gelyna" in relation to another of Irving's early works, his review of *Fragment of a Journal of a Sentimental Philosopher* (New York, 1809), see below, pp. 288–89.

55. Pierre M. Irving, Journal, 1859, p. [158] (Berg Collection, New York Public Library).

been the predominating subject matter in the "Oldstyle" letters;[56] and replete with literary quotations, abstruse local allusions, puns, and other comic devices characteristic of the youthful Washington Irving,[57] these two letters are certainly his own.

No manuscript versions of the letters are known to survive, and the *Morning Chronicle* texts were not reprinted during the author's lifetime. The newspaper texts are thus the inevitable choices as copy-text. Our knowledge of Peter Irving's editorship of the *Morning Chronicle* is slight, but the paper was apparently edited by him alone.[58] It is unlikely that his twenty-year-old brother Washington played any part, beyond the stage of manuscript preparation, in preparing the letters for the press. On the other hand, the *Morning Chronicle* was from day to day not at all given to displays of typographical vivacity—for example, multiple exclamation marks and full capitals, or italics, for emphasis—such as appear in Irving's letters. Probably therefore the accidentals in the works as published in the newspaper reflect the author's wishes rather than a style imposed on his composition by Peter or the printer.[59]

In the preparation of this edition a handwritten transcription of the texts in a copy of the *Morning Chronicle* owned by the New-York Historical Society was collated twice and independently against the texts in a copy of the newspaper owned by the Library of Congress.

The source of the text is the New York *Morning Chronicle*, December 24, 1803, p. 2, col. 5; December 30, 1803, p. 3, cols. 1–2.

See Discussions and Lists pp. 371–72, 392–93.

[CONTRIBUTIONS TO *THE CORRECTOR*]

Our knowledge of the manner in which *The Corrector* was edited and printed is extremely slight. Peter Irving, who continued to edit the

56. See the following "Oldstyle" letters in the Twayne edition: III (December 1, 1802), IV (December 3, 1802), V (December 11, 1802), VI (January 17, 1803), VII (January 22, 1803), VIII (February 8, 1803).

57. See Wayne R. Kime, "Washington Irving and the 'Extension of the Empire of Freedom': An Unrecorded Contribution to the *Evening Post*, May 14 1804," *Bulletin of the New York Public Library*, 76 (1972), 224–25.

58. See Lenoard B. Beach, "Peter Irving's Journals," *Bulletin of the New York Public Library*, 44 (August, 1940), 595–96; Wayne R. Kime, "Pierre M. Irving's Account of Peter Irving, Washington Irving, and the *Corrector*," *American Literature*, 43 (March, 1971), 110–13.

59. Each of the two letters is preceded by the phrase "FOR THE MORNING CHRONICLE / ———." In the present text these introductory headings are treated as editorial insertions rather than as parts of the articles and are therefore omitted.

New York *Morning Chronicle* from March 28 to April 26, 1804, while *The Corrector* was being published, was quite possibly assisted in supervising the latter work by one or more of his Burrite associates.[60] However, the numerous typographical errors which mar the text of *The Corrector* suggest that the work was hastily prepared; and it may be that, obliged to edit the newspaper by himself, Peter Irving was unable to give it the careful attention he customarily gave to the *Morning Chronicle*. Of his brother Washington's role as a contributor to *The Corrector* we know only what he told Pierre M. Irving in 1859: that when Peter invited "persons of wit and genius" to join him in mounting a campaign to "check the licentiousness of the [New York] press," and incidentally to promote the political aspirations of Aaron Burr, Washington "was not slow in cracking his lance in response"; and that, while some "of the severest sarcasms in the Corrector came from his pen," the subject matter of his productions was not of his own choosing. "They would tell me what to write," he recalled of his unnamed coadjutors, "and then I'd dash away."[61]

Although Irving's recollection of his own early writings was usually sharp, his comment of 1859 on this episode was so brief and generalized that it need not be taken as applying to all his contributions to *The Corrector*. Nevertheless, the possibility it raises—that the anonymous articles presented here as by Irving alone were in some sense collaborative efforts—requires some notice. The author was in 1804 neither a Burrite nor, apparently, a strong adherent of any political party, and he would certainly have needed some coaching in order to mount the appropriate corrective attacks upon the persons and policies inimical to the cause of Aaron Burr. Moreover, as a member of a "knot of wits" who contributed humorous articles to the local newspapers, he may also have received assistance in his enterprise from such cronies as John Furman, Alexander Beebee, Elias Hicks, and James Kirke Paulding. On these grounds, there-

60. In correcting proofs of a biographical notice of Peter Irving intended for publication in Evert A. and George L. Duyckinck's *Cyclopædia of American Literature* (New York, 1855), Irving wrote the following note on a slip of paper which he pasted onto a sheet of proof containing an account of Peter's editorship of *The Corrector*: "I think this paragraph had better be omitted. My brother was not the editor of the Corrector which was a chance medley affair, thrown together occasionally by different hands" (Manuscript Division, New York Public Library). However, Irving may have made his notation out of a wish to dissociate his family's name from the entire political controversy surrounding the New York gubernatorial campaign of 1804.

61. These comments from part of an account of the incident prepared by Pierre M. Irving for the *Life and Letters* but subsequently withheld from that work. See Wayne R. Kime, "Pierre M. Irving's Account of Peter Irving, Washington Irving, and the *Corrector*," *American Literature*, 43, no. 1 (March, 1971), 108–14.

fore, attribution of articles in *The Corrector* to Irving alone must be tentative. The task of specifying which articles were his own is made still more difficult by the nature of the articles themselves. The traditional techniques of burlesque, invective, and parody which characterize the satiric portions of *The Corrector* were staples of political satire in American newspapers of the period. Rudolph Bunner's erroneous supposition that William Coleman had written for the New York *Evening Post* an anonymous article which was in fact Irving's (see p. 287) points up the likelihood that in 1804 the young author had not yet developed a satiric manner which clearly set him apart from his contemporaries.

Recognizing these complications, in 1968 Martin Roth selected forty-five articles, including items from each of the ten issues of *The Corrector*, and published them as *Washington Irving's Contributions* to the newspaper. Roth justifies his proposed attributions by stylistic evidence drawn from a comparative study of Irving's writings—letters, journals, and published works—between 1802 and 1809. In footnotes to his selections he provides a helpful list of the recurrent motifs, turns of phrase, sources of quoted material, and other features of style which account for his choices—thus affording the interested reader an opportunity to evaluate for himself the likelihood that individual works may convincingly be regarded as Irving's. In an introduction to the collection, Roth admits that one serious limitation is inherent in his method, namely, "the strength of an attribution is obviously proportional to the length of a piece." Inevitably a shorter selection, which Irving may in fact have written, tends merely on account of its brevity to appear doubtfully attributed. Nevertheless, in the face of this difficulty Roth includes several brief items which he regards as characteristic of the author. The "shorter pieces," he notes, "are under-attributed and must remain so."[62]

In preparing this edition I have adopted methods of selecting aritcles from *The Corrector* for attribution to Irving which are in some respects more conservative than the ones described above. First, I have not employed the journals and letters as sources for comparison with these published writings. On July 24, 1804, only three months after *The Corrector* ceased publication, Irving wrote from Bordeaux to his friend Elias Hicks: "If I should think any thing I was writing would be published, it would put such a constraint upon my letters that they would become an intolerable burden to me." A natural inference from this statement (designed to discourage Hicks from publishing any of his European observations) is that he did not write to himself or his correspondents as he did for publication. It follows that by joining the "public"

---

62. Roth, *Washington Irving's Contributions to the Corrector* (Minneapolis, 1968), p. 40.

and the "private" writings for comparison with certain published works possibly to be attributed to Irving, one may be inviting confusion. A second difference in methodology is that, whereas Martin Roth included the anonymous *Salmagundi* papers (1807–1808) and the *History of New York* (1809) as legitimate sources for comparison to articles in *The Corrector*, I set aside these productions of the somewhat more mature author and confine myself to the nine "Letters of Jonathan Oldstyle" (1802–1803) and three other works almost contemporaneous with *The Corrector*—Irving's two *Morning Chronicle* articles, December 24 and 30, 1803 (pp. 3–7), and his *Evening Post* contribution, May 14, 1804 (pp. 37–39)—which had not yet been established as his at the time Roth published his study. The article in the *Evening Post* seems particularly useful for comparison to *The Corrector*, for it was a direct outgrowth of the political controversy in which the latter newspaper had played a significant part. One further principle adopted here for the evaluation of stylistic similarities is identical to that observed by Roth: in the case of articles serialized in *The Corrector* (for example, the series of "CHARACTERISTIC PORTRAITS"), strong evidence of Irving's hand in one installment must be considered as in some degree extending its force to the others. If in doubt about the merits of an attribution, I have excluded rather than included the article in question.

Despite this conservative bias and the differences of method noted above, the conclusions I have reached are notably similar to those of Martin Roth. Fifteen anonymous or pseudonymous articles from *The Corrector* are included here, all of which appear in the Roth volume. In addition, I have discovered thirty-five other titles in the newspaper which, with varying degrees of cogency, may be considered as possibly by Irving; and of these latter works, thirty are included in the Roth collection.[63] The close similarity between the two sets of proposed attri-

---

63. In the following list of possible contributions by Irving to *The Corrector*, the original page- and column-number for each item, if included in the Roth collection, is followed by the number assigned it there; if not included in that collection, it is followed by an asterisk: "It would make a pretty register," p. 3, col. 1 (Roth, no. 1); "CANDIDATE BOB," p. 3, col. 1 (Roth, no. 2); "SYLVANUS AND DANIEL," p. 6, col. 1 (Roth, no. 3); "COLONEL BLUBBER," p. 6, col. 3 (Roth, no. 5); "MAJOR PURDY'S OBSEQUIES," p. 7, col. 1 (Roth, no. 6); "ISAAC," p. 7, col. 1 (Roth, no. 7); "FOR THE CORRECTOR," p. 8, col. 1 (Roth, no. 10); "A Horrid Tale" p. 8, col. 2 (Roth, no. 11); "TO TOBY TICKLER, ESQ.," p. 12, col. 2*; "CHUCKLEHEAD BOB," p. 14, col. 3 (Roth, no. 13); "JUDAS.," p. 18, col. 3*; "BAROMETER MITCHELL.," p. 18, col. 3*; "PROMOTION.," p. 19, cols. 1–2 (Roth, no. 16); "THE COALITION.," p. 20, col. 1 (Roth, no. 18); "TO TOBY TICKLER, ESQ.," p. 22, col. 3*; "DAVY," p. 23, col. 3 (Roth, no. 20); "BOB *again*.," p. 23, col. 3 (Roth, no. 21); "THE OLD FOX, AND THE OURANG-OUTANG," p. 27, col. 3 (Roth, no. 25); "FOR THE CORRECTOR," p. 28, col. 1 (Roth, no. 26); "FOR THE CORRECTOR," p. 28, cols. 1–2 (Roth, no. 27); "Five Cents Reward!!," p. 31, col.

butions suggests that, while absolute confidence as to their authorship remains impossible of attainment, the articles from *The Corrector* included here are thoroughly characteristic of the early style of Washington Irving. Ultimately the decision whether to attribute a particular article to Irving must remain an individual judgment, to be made upon careful comparison of the pertinent texts.[64]

No manuscript version of any article published in *The Corrector* is known to survive. No portion of *The Corrector* is known to have been reprinted during Irving's lifetime. Accordingly, the newspaper itself is adopted as copy-text for the articles tentatively identified as his contributions to it.[65]

The necessarily hypothetical attribution to Irving of articles published in *The Corrector* places a constraint upon editorial emendation of the copy-text except for the correction of obvious lapses in styling, typographical errors, and misspellings.[66] Our uncertainty as to the authorship

---

3 (Roth, no. 30); "I am preparing a *pickle* ...," p. 35, col. 1 (Roth, no. 33); "TULLY MAGPIE," p. 35, col. 2 (Roth, no. 34); "BILLY LUSCIOUS," p. 35, col. 3 (Roth, no. 35); "CHEETHAMANA.," p. 36, col. 1 (Roth, no. 36); "FOR THE CORRECTOR.," p. 36, cols. 2–3 (Roth, no. 37); "CITIZEN W.," p. 38, col. 2 (Roth, no. 38); "DAVY.," p. 38, col. 3 (Roth, no. 39); "OLD CUPID.," p. 39, col. 1 (Roth, no. 40); "SCHUYLER," p. 39, col. 1 (Roth, no. 41); "THE DILEMMA, AN ELECTIONEERING STORY.," p. 39, cols. 2–3 (Roth, no. 43); "Cheetham had the impudence ...," p. 39, col. 3 (Roth, no. 44); "Fat Ferris ...," p. 39, col. 3 (Roth, no. 45); "TO TOBY TICKLER, ESQ.," p. 40, col. 3*.

64. In order to afford some indication of the rationale for selecting the articles included here from *The Corrector*, entries in the Explanatory Notes, corresponding to the title-line for each item, set forth principal similarities between it and the "Jonathan Oldstyle" series, the *Morning Chronicle* articles, and the *Evening Post* article.

65. Page-line references to the articles as published in *The Corrector* are as follows: "BEWARE OF IMPOSTORS ! !" (issue 2 (March 31, 1804), p. 6, cols. 2–3); "BILLY LUSCIOUS." (issue 2, p. 7, cols. 1–2); "ARISTIDEAN GALLERY OF PORTRAITS." (issue 3 (April 4, 1804), p. 11, col. 3); "THE CONGRESSIONAL FRACAS, A TRUE STORY." (issue 4 (April 7, 1804), p. 15, cols. 1–3); "EBENEZER." (issue 5 (April 11, 1804), p. 18, cols. 2–3); "TO TOBY TICKLER, ESQ." (issue 5, p. 19, cols. 2–3); "TO TOBY TICKLER, ESQ." (issue 6 (April 14, 1804), p. 22, cols. 1–3); "CHARACTERISTIC PORTRAITS, *Lately added to the Shakespeare Gallery. (Continued.)*" (issue 7 (April 18, 1804), p. 26, col. 3–p. 27, col. 1); "ISAAC." (issue 7, p. 27, col. 2); "COL. BLUBBER." (issue 7, p. 27, cols. 2–3); "TO TOBY TICKLER, ESQ." (issue 8 (April 21, 1804), p. 30, col. 3–p. 31, col. 1); "ORIGINAL PICTURES *For the Pandemonian Gallery.* (Continued.)" (issue 8, p. 31, cols. 1–2); "TO TOBY TICKLER, ESQ." (issue 9 (April 24, 1804), p. 33, col. 2–p. 34, col. 1); "TO TOBY TICKLER, ESQ." (issue 9, p. 34, cols. 1–3); "RARE FUN ! ! !" (issue 10 (April 26, 1804), p. 39, cols. 1–2).

66. In two instances the problem arises of defining the exact point at which an article begins. "EBENEZER." (17.1–18.25) is preceded in *The Corrector* by the

of any single piece—whether by Irving, Irving in collaboration with others, or entirely by others—renders it indefensible to consider the fifteen selections as a unit for the purpose of a thoroughgoing regularization of accidentals. The accidentals in the articles included here are in several respects erratic. For example, the capitalization of nouns other than the names of persons and places follows no consistent rule (Ourang-Outang, 11.9–10; OURANG-OUTANG, 14.19; ourang-outang, 22.4; Ourang-outang, 29.13), and the names of persons are variously abbreviated (for example, De Witt Clinton: D. W., 14.30; D. W——'s, 16.1; D—— W——t C——n, 19.19; D. W. C., 25.6; D W——t, 32.31; D—— W——t, 32.35). Commas and dashes appear to be used interchangeably; more than one spelling is employed for some words (ecſtacy, 16.16, extacy, 9.37; carcass, 12.20, carcaſe, 37.20; ſteadfaſt, 13.3, ſtedfaſt, 18.13); direct quotations are only occasionally enclosed in quotation marks; and preterit endings are rendered either *-ed* or *-'d* according to no discernible principle of selection. Provided that the copy-text is not in error and poses no serious and apparently unintentional inconsistencies or problems of interpretation, emendation of its accidentals is in general not undertaken. Like the frequent slang expressions, the lavish heterogeneity of type styles, and the casual treatment, verging onto paraphrase, of "quoted" literary sources, the latitudinarian principles of spelling, capitalization, and punctuation observed in these selections lend an air of racy irreverence, of cavalier indifference to convention, which is an essential ingredient in the satiric style of *The Corrector*. Some questionable readings may be the results of lax editorial supervision; others may have been introduced as the result of Irving's probably hurried preparation of copy; but the problem of disentangling authorial, editorial, and compositorial intention and error is largely insoluble. Except in special circumstances the aim of realizing Irving's intention for his contributions to his brother's experiment in corrective journalism is best served by allowing the copy-text to remain as it stands.

Thus, the minimal procedures for automatic regularization specified in the introduction to the Textual Commentary (pp. 279–80) are adopted here, but with a single exception. The titles of the several articles vary widely in length, type style, and format; in their free experimentation with visual effects they are of a piece with the bodies of the works themselves, and so they are integral to Irving's total expression from item to item. They are not regularized but are presented as they first appeared in *The Corrector*.

---

phrase "FOR THE CORRECTOR," and "TO TOBY TICKLER, ESQ." (18.26–20.5) by the word "COMMUNICATION." These introductory headings are treated as editorial insertions and hence omitted.

In the preparation of this edition the following collations of *The Corrector* have been made: (1) a xerox version of the New-York Historical Society copy collated with a microfilm print of the copy owned by the Boston Athenaeum; and (2) the above xerox copy collated with the Library of Congress copy (Rare Books JK/ 2311/ .C7) and with the Yale University copy (AN 33/N5 + C81—wanting issues 8 and 10).

The source of the text is *The Corrector*, nos. 2–10 (March 31–April 26, 1804) (New York: S. Gould).

See Discussions and Lists pp. 372–73, 393–94.

"WE WILL REJOICE!!!"

The attribution of this anonymous newspaper article to Irving is based primarily on his recollections in 1859 of its contents and his claim at that time that it had been a work of his own. On April 11, 1859, having recently completed the concluding volume of the *Life of George Washington*, the elderly author relaxed in his study and related to Pierre M. Irving an amusing anecdote of his early career. At "about the time of Jefferson's *Inauguration*," he recalled, his friend Rudolph Bunner had quoted to him "a certain article in the *Evening Post*" in proof of the "genius" of William Coleman (1766–1829), the editor of that New York daily newspaper. The article, he said, had been one written to ridicule a "Democratic procession," and it had included an "allusion to the cassiwary," a description of one "Van Zandt with his prize feathers," and a quotation of Revelations 6:8: "And I looked, and behold a pale horse: and his name that sat on him was death, and Hell followed with him." When Bunner had praised this obviously extravagant piece as the work of Coleman, Irving continued, he had exclaimed in reply, "Oh! that is mine!" to which Bunner had returned, "I'm sorry for it—you could do without it—he needed it."[67] The text of *"WE WILL REJOICE!!!"* in the *Evening Post* for May 14, 1804, matches almost exactly Irving's description of it fifty-five years afterward.[68]

No manuscript version of the article is known to exist; and because the work was not reprinted during the author's lifetime, the *Evening Post* text is necessarily adopted here as copy-text. No information is available as to the manner in which the article was prepared for the

67. Pierre M. Irving, Journal, 1859, p. [28] (Berg Collection, New York Public Library). The contribution to the *Evening Post* went unmentioned in PMI.

68. The article has been reprinted, with a discussion of the political context in which it appeared, by Wayne R. Kime in "Washington Irving and the 'Extension of the Empire of Freedom': An Unrecorded Contribution to the *Evening Post*, May 14, 1804," *Bulletin of the New York Public Library*, 76 (1972), 220–30.

press. However, William Coleman was seventeen years Irving's senior and had edited the *Evening Post* singlehandedly since its inception in October, 1801; there is no reason to suppose he would have required, nor any likelihood that he would have solicited the author's assistance in making final preparations of the manuscript for the printer. On the other hand, the lavish experimentation with typography in the copy-text—for example, italicized capitals in the title, roman capitals in the reference to the "GRAND PROCESSION" (38.8), and a combination of both type styles and cases in another title, " 'LOUISIANA CONQUERED *by an Ass—laden with gold!*' " (37.41), was not at all characteristic of the staid *Evening Post* style; these features, like the multiple exclamation marks, the multiple asterisks, and the capitalization for emphasis also conspicuous in the text, are characteristic of Irving's youthful style and probably represent his own wishes rather than a set of procedures imposed on his text by Coleman.

In the preparation of this edition a xerox copy of the *Evening Post* text owned by the New York Public Library has been sight collated with the following additional copies: Library of Congress; New-York Historical Society; Yale University (Folio AN33/ .N5/ .N469).

The source of the text is the New York *Evening Post*, May 14, 1804, p. 2, col. 5.

See Discussions and Lists pp. 373–74, 394.

THE NEW-YORK REVIEW; OR, CRITICAL JOURNAL

According to Stanley T. Williams the single issue of the *New-York Review*, which has more than once been ascribed to Irving alone, was probably the joint effort of Irving, his elder brother William, and James Kirke Paulding—the trio who had recently collaborated in writing the *Salmagundi* papers—assisted perhaps by others of the New York literati who had been offended by remarks in John Rodman's *Fragment of a Journal of a Sentimental Philosopher* (1809).[69] Gulian C. Verplanck, one of Rodman's targets and an acquaintance of Irving, appears years later to have taken sole credit for the authorship of the review. Under the pseudonym of "Francis Herbert," Verplanck commented in 1829, in a work entitled "Gelyna; A Tale of Albany and Ticonderoga Sixty Years Ago," that "some good folks, especially in New-York and Philadelphia, have no notions about [Albany] but those derived from the old traditionary jokes upon its ancient Schepens and Schoutens, its burly Burgomasters, its seventeen-petticoated beauties, 'its spires glitter-

69. STW, I, 125, 412, nn. 106, 111.

ing with tin, and its hospitable boards smoking with sturgeon.*'" In a
note to the passage, he added: "I quote from an anonymous jeu d'esprit
of my own, written when I was very young. It had great currency in the
day of it, but now sleeps undisturbed, as it deserves to do. I quote it only
to take this occasion to make the *amende honorable* to my Albany
friends."[70] Verplanck appears to be alluding in "Gelyna" to the *New-
York Review*, published twenty years earlier, for the passage he quotes
concerning the steeples and the sturgeon of Albany almost exactly
duplicates one in the satiric pamphlet (see 46.16–17).[71] He may thus
be taken at his own word as probably having played some part in the
production of the review. Considering, however, that Rodman's *Fragment of a Journal* included the abbreviated names of a great many
persons thus alluded to,[72] it is quite possible that the two Irvings and

70. *The Talisman for MDCCCXXX* (New York, 1829), p. 303.

71. It should be noted, however, that Irving was not himself impressed by
Verplanck's statement. In 1859, coming by chance upon the passage in "Gelyna"
concerning Albany, he immediately informed Pierre M. Irving that (as the latter
recorded the observation in a notebook) the "quotation in the piece about Albany—
Sturgeon—claimed by F[rancis] H[erbert]" was in fact "*his*—written for the Chronicle" (Berg Collection, New York Public Library). The article in the New York
Morning Chronicle which the elderly Irving had in mind was the first of two he
had contributed to that newspaper in December, 1803, describing in extravagant
fashion the excursion to Albany of a company of actors; see pp. 3–7.

72. A copy of the *Fragment of a Journal* owned by the University of Pittsburgh
Library includes an additional sheet of manuscript identifying the personages alluded to in the work. A transcription follows:

The initials	supposed to mean
D—	C. D. Colden Esq.
K—	Anthy Bleecker Esq.
P—	G VerPlanck
T—	Wash[n] Irving
D[r] MacN.	D[r] M[c] Neven
D[r] S—	D[r] Edw[d] Miller
D[r] S—	D[r] Smith professor of Anatomy
M[r] W—	W[m] Johnson Esq.
Mrs.—	M[rs] Randolph, daughter of M[r] Jefferson
M[r] V—	P. C. VanWyck—recorder of the City
D—	J. Dennie Esq.
B—	C B Brown Esq.
D[r] S—	D[r] Smith—much known as a declaimer in the [out wards?]
M[r] M—	M[r] Minshull—a miserable pretender to literature
M[r] C—	Cooper, the Actor

In "James Ogilvie and Washington Irving," *Americana*, 35 (July 1941), 441, Richard B. Davis notes that the copy of the *Fragment of a Journal* owned by the Boston
Public Library includes marginal identifications of persons whose names are

Paulding were joined in their verbal annihilation of Rodman by still other willing hands.[73]

On the strength of Irving's participation in preparing the *New-York Review*, Stanley T. Williams has suggested that "sections" of the work "should probably be included in any collected edition" of the author's writings;[74] but it is neither practicable nor desirable to excise passages from the review for tentative attribution to Irving alone. Unlike a work such as *The Corrector*, this anonymous pamphlet is not a mosaic of discrete contributions by various hands but a unified effort, a statement carefully paced and organized and developing a coherent argument in respect to its topic. The consensus that Irving played at the very least a leading part in its composition is itself a sufficient warrant for the review's being included in unmutilated form among his miscellaneous writings.

No manuscript version of the work is known to exist. Because it is not known to have been reprinted, the first edition becomes copy-text.

We have no information concerning the manner in which printer's copy for the *New-York Review* was prepared, whether the printing was supervised, or whether proofs were read. Irving's recent displeasure with the editorial liberties taken with his manuscripts by "Duskie Davie" Longworth, the printer of the *Salmagundi* papers, would suggest in this

---

abbreviated in the work. "Mr. D—" is identified as "C. D. Colden," "P—" as "G. Verplanck," and "T" as Irving. The Boston Public Library copy identifies "Mr. C—" as "Mr. Cabel" [Joseph C. Cabell] rather than Thomas A. Cooper, as in the University of Pittsburgh copy.

A copy of the *Fragment of a Journal* owned by the New-York Historical Society (copy 1) includes marginal notations which duplicate some of those noted above and add still other persons to the list of those who may have joined Irving in his counterattack on John Rodman. The following identifications are made:

Page, line	Name	Handwritten Identification
7.1	Mr. D———'s	Colden's
7.16	Haughterston	Flatherson
8.16	P.	Paulding
9.2	Dr. L.	Miller
12.19	Mrs. Y's	Douglass
12.27	Dr. Mac N.	Niven
14.8	Dr. A.	Abercrombie
17.11	M———o	Jefferson
17.21	Mr. W.	Johnson
19.25	D.	Dennie

73. In "Ogilvie and Irving," p. 439, n. 47, Davis speculates that the brochure was "possibly the work of several members of the group."

74. STW, I, 125.

case an attitude of vigilance on his part toward the labors of Inskeep & Bradford, who later in 1809 were the printers for the first edition of *A History of New York*. At any rate, on the score of general appearance (if not freedom from typographical error) he would have been well satisfied with the *New-York Review*.[75] In some respects the accidentals in the pamphlet are not mutually consistent. For example, a comma is on a few occasions used to separate subject from object, with the result of enforcing a slight pause in the reading of a relatively elaborate sentence (43.23, 45.2, 46.8). Elsewhere, on occasion, a semicolon is employed with similar effect following a participial or adverbial phrase or a relative clause (40.29, 41.41, 42.36, 44.32). However, such exceptional usages as do occur often appear to be devices subtly to alter rhythm and emphasis; and because they are not grossly inconsistent with contemporary usage, they ordinally require no emendation.

In the preparation of this edition a xerox copy of the *New-York Review* text owned by the New-York Historical Society (AP 2/ .N, copy 1) was sight collated with a second copy owned by the New-York Historical Society and with a xerox copy of the text owned by the Boston Public Library (A4470.28/ Pph. v. 3/ 21754).

The source of the text is *The New-York Review; or, Critical Journal* (New York: Inskeep & Bradford, 1809).

See Discussions and Lists pp. 374–75, 395.

[REVIEW OF *THE WORKS...OF ROBERT PAINE*]

Irving's review of the *Works* of Robert Treat Paine was first published in the *Analectic Magazine*, 1 (March 1813), [249]–66. It was reprinted by Pierre M. Irving in *Spanish Papers*, II, [303]–24, under the title "Robert Treat Paine." Aside from its altered title, the *Spanish Papers* text includes only a single substantive variant from the original, a clear misprint (see Rejected Variants, 61.35). A few of its accidental variants from the earlier text—the regularization to a consistent "Mr. Paine" of Irving's earlier usage of either "Mr. Paine" or "Mr. P," and the alteration of his sentencing at two points (see Emendations, 51.5, 57.39)— fall outside the pattern of a consistently imposed Putnam house style,[76]

---

75. The work was neatly printed on paper of medium quality, 8¼ x 6¼ inches, and sold possibly with a paper wrapper. No doubt to lend it the appearance of an actual and established periodical—which it was not, since it appeared in only a single issue subtitled "TO BE CONTINUED AS OCCASION REQUIRES"—the pamphlet was marked conspicuously on its title page "March 1809" and was paged, not from 1 upward, but from 103 to 119.

76. See the Introduction to the Textual Commentary, pp. 273–76.

but the posthumously reprinted text reveals no definite evidence of authorial revision.

Irving's editorship of the *Analectic Magazine* began with the first issue, that of January, 1813 (the publication had previously been known as *Select Reviews*). The proprietor, Moses Thomas of Philadelphia, had engaged him at a generous annual salary to select and arrange articles for reprinting from contemporary foreign journals, as well as on occasion to secure original contributions. Irving was for a time extremely pleased with his new occupation. On January 2, 1813, he explained to his friend Henry Brevoort, Jr., that performing the editorial duties would be a "pastime and employment of idle hours. I am handsomely paid, and the work is no trouble."[77] Presently, however, it developed that his employed wished him as part of his responsibilities to write articles for the magazine. He somewhat reluctantly assented to this modification of the arrangement,[78] and the review of Paine's *Works* was the first of his productions to appear in the *Analectic Magazine*.

Although he edited this Philadelphia magazine throughout 1813 and 1814, Irving does not appear during this period to have spent a large proportion of his time away from New York. The manner in which he could have supervised the printing of the work thus comes into question, if indeed he did so. His comment to a friend in December, 1812, that he had just "written to Philadelphia that I would not consent to have a fool's cap put on my head" seems to refer to a stipulation he had made as to the manner in which the *Analectic Magazine* was to be produced. Quite possibly, being jealous of his leisure time and impatient of tedious tasks, he was determined to have as little as possible to do with the final preparation of the monthly issues. In the same letter he expressed a determination to retain sole editorial control ("... if they intended to interfere in the conduct of the work, I should decline having anything to do with it"), but he added that the matter of seeing each issue through the press was a chore he did not covet: "I think Job was a trifle out when he wished that his enemy had written a book; had he wished him to be obliged to print one, he would have wished him a curse indeed!"[79] Throughout his association with the *Analectic Magazine* Irving apparently did retain sole responsibility for the selection of its contents. He may also have corrected proofs from time to time. In the absence of any indication that the printer went against his wishes, we must assume in general that the magazine was produced from month to month as he intended it. More particularly, in the absence of manuscript evi-

77. PMI, I, 294.

78. STW, I, 136–37; see also PMI, I, 290.

79. Irving to James Renwick, Washington, December 18, 1812; PMI, I, 290.

dence or any other evidence to the contrary, we must assume in general that the printed versions of his own contributions realized his intentions for them.

In his capacity either as author or as editor, Irving undertook in his review of Paine's *Works* thoroughly to revise the accidentals in the passages he quoted from that volume. He tampered extensively with the biographical sketch which precedes the writings of the poet and with the poems themselves. He deleted punctuation, chiefly the commas used liberally by Paine, on twenty-three occasions; altered punctuation, chiefly from semicolon to comma, on eight; altered spellings from "-or" to "-our" on three; altered spellings on fourteen; altered capitalization, chiefly from capitals to lowercase letters, on twenty-four; altered paragraphing, usually by the deletion of paragraph breaks, on five; altered the spacing between lines of verse on six; altered words in italics to roman type on one; and altered words in roman to italic type on two. At three points (see Precopy-Text Variants, 54.36, 56.29–30, and Discussions of Adopted Readings, 62.14–30) he revised the text of Paine's *Works* so as to fit it into the context of his own discussion. At two others (see Emendations, 56.39, 63.2) either his own or the printer's errors resulted in obviously unintentional changes to the quoted text. In general, however, his emendations must be regarded as results of a conscious effort either to bring the quoted passages into a form consistent with his personal tastes or to cause them to conform to an *Analectic Magazine* style. The latter possibly is the less likely, both because the magazine can hardly be said to have boasted a well-formulated style,[80] and because Irving's instinct for consistency was neither so strong nor so erratic as on this unique occasion to have impelled him to undertake the regularization out of a zealous sense of editorial responsibility.[81] Of course, the alterations may have been made without his knowledge or

80. It may be noted, however, that Irving's revision of passagees from Paine's *Works* did bring them into consistency with certain conventions followed consistently in the *Analectic Magazine*: specifically, "-our" spellings, the absence of internal capitalization except for proper nouns and other words conventionally capitalized (such as "Christian"), and the printing in italics of quotations from foreign languages.

81. Wholesale emendation of this sort occurs in no other review article published by Irving. The manuscript of his review of Alexander Slidell's *A Year in Spain* (II. 30–57) reveals that he did not even bother to transcribe the quoted passages from that work into his text, but merely indicated to the printer the page numbers and the first few words of the passages he wished to include. The relatively small number of variants between passages from Henry Wheaton's *History of the Northmen* quoted in Irving's review of that work (II, 61–86) and the original publication indicates that he probably followed a procedure similar to the one he had recently adopted for *A Year in Spain*.

consent; but on the available evidence we must assume that his intention in this review was not to quote with absolute faithfulness. We must regard his "improvements" of Paine as part of the intellectual labor which contributed to the making of his review.

Because no manuscript version of the review is known to exist, and because there is no convincing evidence that Irving ever revised the work as first published, the *Analectic Magazine* text is adopted here as copy-text. Substantive variants and accidental variants of particular interest between the copy-text and the *Spanish Papers* text, and also between corresponding passages of the copy-text and Paine's *Works*, are reported in the tables which follow.[82]

Late in his extended review (63.5–6) Irving indicates concern for the limitations of space. Because this constraint may have been responsible for his occasional alteration of spacing between lines of Paine's verse from double to single spaces, the poet's own spacing is restored in this edition (see Emendations, 58.41–59.1). Regularization has been undertaken for one other class of accidentals. After his first three references to Robert Treat Paine as "Mr. Paine" (51.1, 51.11, 52.21), Irving refers to the poet as either "Mr. Paine" or "Mr. P." The name is used, in all, sixteen times in the essay, eight with the full spelling, eight in abbreviated form. Because Irving's usual procedure as a reviewer—in his notices of Holland's *Odes*, his own *Conquest of Granada*, Slidell's *A Year in Spain*, and Wheaton's *History of the Northmen*—is to refer to an author by his full surname rather than in an abbreviated form, his references to "Mr. P." are emended to "Mr. Paine" (see Emendations, 52.32).

In the preparation of this edition the following collations have been made: (1) a xerox copy of the *Analectic Magazine* text owned by the Toronto Public Library (M/ 051/ .A 54) sight collated with the following additional copies: New-York Historical Society (XN/ AP 2/ .A 48, copy 1); New York Public Library (*DA); (2) the xerox copy of the *Analectic Magazine* text sight collated twice and independently with the text in a copy of *Spanish Papers* owned by the National Library of Canada; (3) a xerox copy of the above *Spanish Papers* text sight collated with the following additional copies: New York Public Library; Yale University Library (Iw/ Ir8/ 866); (4) two collations of the xerox copy of the *Analectic Magazine* text with *The Works . . . of Robert Treat Paine*: one using the Yale University Library copy (Iv/ P 17/ B812); one using the New York Public Library copy (NBG).

---

82. A full accounting of substantive and accidental variants between the passages quoted in the copy-text from Paine's *Works* and the original passages is on file at the University of Texas

The sources of the text are *The Works, in Verse and Prose, of the Late Robert Treat Paine* (Boston: J. Belcher, 1812); (2) *Analectic Magazine*, 1 (March, 1813), [249]–66; (3) *Spanish Papers*, II, 303–24.

See Discussions and Lists pp. 375–76, 395–96, 435, 443.

BIOGRAPHY OF CAPTAIN JAMES LAWRENCE

Irving's memorial sketch of James Lawrence, the first of his four accounts of the lives of American naval heroes, was published in the *Analectic Magazine* for August, 1813, pp. [122]–39. It was promptly reprinted in an anonymous volume entitled *Biography of James Lawrence, Esq. . . . Together with A Collection of the Most Interesting Papers Relative to the Action Between the Chesapeake and the Shannon, and the Death of Captain Lawrence, &c. &c.* (1813), pp. [9]–55,[83] where it is referred to as "copied from the Analectic Magazine" (p. 61). Excepting alterations of accidentals, five substantive variants each limited to a single word,[84] and three superadded footnotes,[85] the *Biography* text is a faith-

---

83. (New-Brunswick: L. Deare). The preface to this volume is dated September 20, 1813 (p. 8). Following a few pages of explanatory material appended to Irving's text, the editor of the *Biography* wrote: "N.B. The preceding notes were in type before the Analectic Magazine for Sept. was received . . ." (p. 60). The *Biography* was thus in the process of printing within one month after Irving's memoir had appeared.

84. The substantive variants are as follows:

Analectic Magazine (Page, line)	Twayne edition (Page, line)	Analectic Magazine (Reading)	Biography (Reading)
127.5	68.9	Americans	American
129.12	69.38	strangers	stangers
136.21	75.29	ceremonials	ecremonials
137.29	76.25	would be	will be
138.5	76.32	sailor	sailors

85. The first two notes, which appeared at points corresponding to Irving's references to Commodore Bainbridge (70.3) and to the *Bonne Citoyenne* (70.8), refer the reader respectively to Notes A and B "at the end of this Biographical Sketch" (p. 29). The third note appears at a point corresponding to the word "sisters" (74.26). Signed "EDITOR," it adds the detail that Lawrence "was also the prop and consolation of a single sister who has been many years in a delicate state of health" (p. 44). Notes A and B (pp. 56–58) correct statements in the *Analectic Magazine* article. The first is introduced as follows: "In justice to the memory of Capt. Lawrence, it is proper to state that his biographer must have been misinformed upon the subject of Commodore Bainbridge's remonstrating with Capt. L. against risking an engagement with the Shannon" (p. 56). Note B is

ful reprinting of the original; it reveals no evidence of revision by the author. Irving's memoir was reprinted a second time in 1813, in a more extensive anonymous compilation entitled *An Account of the Funeral Honours Bestowed on the Remains of Capt. Lawrence and Lieut. Ludlow* (1813), pp. 17–32. In that work it is preceded by qualified praise of "*Mr. Irvine*" as a biographer:

> *In copying from the Analectic Magazine, a Biography of Captain Lawrence, written by the erudite scholar and accomplished gentleman who is editor of that publication, we regret the appearance of numerous errors in point of fact. A production the eloquence of which does so much honour to the talents of the author, we dared not mutilate, and having appended such notes as were considered necessary to correct these mistakes, it is printed entire. The genius and taste of Mr. Irvine have been directed to the Biography of many of our Naval heroes, and the specimens of elegant composition in this department, to which his pen has given birth, are highly honorary to the literary character of the country.*[86]

Except for freely altered accidentals and nine brief substantive variants,[87] with eleven superadded notes to correct Irving's supposed errors, *An*

---

preceded by a similar statement and is followed by a letter (pp. 59–60) from Bainbridge to the secretary of the navy explaining the circumstances of Lawrence's challenge to the *Bonne Citoyenne*. Irving was to touch upon the points raised in both these discussions in his additional comments on James Lawrence published in the *Analectic Magazine* for September, 1813; see p. 78.

86. *An Account* (Boston: J. Belcher, 1813), p. 17. The statement that Irving had written biographies of naval heroes other than Lawrence was of course incorrect. However, biographical sketches of military worthies contributed by James Kirke Paulding had by this time begun to appear in the *Analectic Magazine*; see A. L. Herold, *James Kirke Paulding, Versatile American* (New York, 1926), p. 43.

87. The substantive variants are as follows:

Analectic Magazine (Page, line)	Twayne edition (Page, line)	Analectic Magazine (Reading)	An Account (Reading)
124.19	66.8	an adventurous	the adventurous
125.4	66.28	the frigate Philadelphia	the Philadelphia
126.15	67.29	and from which	from which
126.34	68.1	24th February	24th of February
127.5	68.9	Americans	American
133.12	73.4	among	by
133.30	73.20	nation	nations
134.21	74.4	had been	he had
138.35	77.23	hem	them

Account is, as it purports to be, a faithful reprinting of the *Analectic Magazine* text. It reveals no evidence of authorial revision.[88]

In 1814 the biography of Lawrence was again reprinted, in a work edited by Benjamin Folsom and entitled *A Compilation of Biographical Sketches of Distinguished Officers in the American Navy* (1814), pp. 67–89. The Folsom version omits the *Analectic Magazine* text corresponding to 64.16–32, 72.42–73.27, and 76.16–77.38 (The question . . . uninjured.); it also omits Irving's note at the point corresponding to 71.2. It includes two notes which have no precedent in the *Analectic Magazine*, both providing supplementary details; for, like the editor of *An Account*, Folsom found it necessary to flesh out Irving's sketch with additional information.[89] No evidence exists that Irving was in any way involved with the revision of his text for publication in Folsom's *Compilation*. As in the case of the two 1813 reprintings, his memoir of Lawrence was being drawn upon by Folsom as a suitable means of swelling the tide of patriotic feeling generated by events in the war. The same is to be said of a fourth reprinting, anonymously produced, entitled *Naval Biography, or Lives of the Most Distinguished American Naval Heroes of the Present Day* (1815), pp. 44–70. The *Naval Biography* version reproduces the full *Analectic Magazine* text and reveals no substantive variants from it. Still another reprinting in 1815, in a volume compiled by Isaac Bailey and entitled *American Naval Biography*, pp. [104]–25, is acknowledged there as from the *Analectic Magazine*. Excepting a corrected misprint, a revision of a single word obviously the result of the editor's or the printer's tinkering, and two further clusters of changes—one intended to bring the two-year-old text up-to-date, the other toning down through omission one of Irving's conciliatory

---

88. At one point, however, it does betray the editor's impatience with what he evidently regarded as Irving's obliviousness to historical accuracy. A note to the author's statement that Commodore Bainbridge and others had attempted to dissuade Lawrence from encountering the *Bonne Citoyenne* (70.3–6) began with an abrupt disclaimer: "Nothing can be wider from the truth than this declaration" (*An Account*, p. 24). Irving's admittedly hasty preparation of the sketch (see "Captain Lawrence," 78.7–9) had resulted in errors which probably justified the testiness of this patriotic editor.

89. In addition, at the conclusion of his truncated but otherwise faithful reprint (no substantive variants occur in the passages included), Folsom included a note introducing a narrative chiefly of the return of the bodies of Lawrence and Ludlow to Boston and New York for funeral services and interment: "The foregoing [he wrote in reference to the *Analectic Magazine* text] was written and published soon after the interment of Lawrence and Ludlow. The following is subjoined to render the biography more perfect" (*A Compilation* [Newburyport: The Compiler, 1814], p. 89).

comments about England, the Bailey version includes no substantive variants from its original.[90]

In 1820 the sketch of James Lawrence was included by John M. Niles in his *The Life of Oliver Hazard Perry. With an Appendix Comprising Biographical Sketches of the Late General Pike and Captain Lawrence,* pp. [338]–59. Here the article is again acknowledged as from the *Analectic Magazine,* but since the two most extensive variant readings between the magazine text and the one in *American Naval Biology* appear in the Niles volume exactly as they do in *American Naval Biography,* the 1815 collection would appear to be Niles' immediate source. However, in addition to incorporating the corrected misprint of Isaac Bailey and to including a printing error of his own, at two other points Niles made unprecedented minor substantive changes—one involving one, the other three words in the original; he also dropped two footnotes, and at three points near the conclusion of the reprinted article he omitted passages of Irving's commentary ranging from a fragment of a sentence to two sentences in length.[91] Quite possibly all these

90. In the order specified, the substantive variants in *American Naval Biography* (Providence: H. Mann, 1815) are as follows:

Analectic Magazine (Page, line)	Twayne edition (Page, line)	*Analectic Magazine* (Reading)	*American Naval Biography* (Reading)
127.5	68.9	Americans	American
139.12	77.37	do but	would but
135.17–18	74.34–35	is now ... yet to learn	has at length recovered from a long a dangerous confinement; but has now learned
137.1–4	75.44–76.3	outdone; but ... friendship.	outdone.

91. Excepting those variants between the text in *The Life of Oliver Hazard Perry* (Hartford: William S. Marsh, 1820) and that in the *Analectic Magazine* which duplicate those shown in the preceding note, the substantive variants between the two versions, in the order specified, are as follows:

Analectic Magazine (Page, line)	Twayne edition (Page, line)	*Analectic Magazine* (Reading)	*The Life of Oliver Hazard Perry* (Reading)
128.11	69.3	Evans	Evens
136.1	75.11	may sooth	sooth
138.30	77.19	now	in future wars
130.38–39	71.42–43	*The ... authentic.	[omitted]
137.33–40	76.37–44	*In this ... sailors.	[omitted]
137.28–30	76.24–26	claim; the ... more.	claim.
138.16–19	77.6–9	The ... fortune.	[omitted]
139.4–13	77.29–38	What ... uninjured.	[omitted]

omissions were made owing to considerations of cramped space alone; but it may be noticed that as a result of Niles' streamlining Irving's text is appreciably more truculent in tone than as originally composed. As it stands in revised form, it leads neatly into the concluding article of *The Life of Oliver Hazard Perry*, a discourse written by John M. Niles himself and entitled "A View of the Present Naval Force of the United States; Its Increase, and Its Future Prospects."

The biography of Lawrence was published once more, under the title "Captain James Lawrence," in *Spanish Papers*, II, [37]–58. Except for changes in certain classes of accidentals reflecting imposition of the Putnam house style,[92] and in addition seven minor substantive variants— two corrections of misprints (see Emendations, 68.9, 77.23), a new misprint (see Rejected Variants, 74.21), and four other changes characteristic of the scrupulous editorial hand of Pierre M. Irving (see Emendations, 72.19; Rejected Variants, 72.7, 72.8, 75.28), the *Spanish Papers* text is a faithful reprinting of the original publication. As Irving's literary executor Pierre may possibly have had access to a copy of the *Analectic Magazine* minimally revised by the author; but this possibility is remote. The *Spanish Papers* text includes no convincing evidence of authorial revision.

Because no manuscript version of the biography of James Lawrence is known to exist, and because the original *Analectic Magazine* text appears never to have undergone revision by the author, the first edition of the work is adopted as copy-text. Substantive variants, and accidental variants of particular interest, between the copy-text and the *Spanish Papers* text are listed in the tables which follow.

In the preparation of this edition the following collations have been made: (1) a xerox copy of the *Analectic Magazine* text owned by the Toronto Public Library (M/ 051/ .A48) sight collated with the following additional copies: New-York Historical Society (XN/ AP 2/ .A48); New York Public Library (*DA); (2) a collation of the above xerox copy with the text in *Biography of James Lawrence, Esq.* owned by the Yale Univesity Library (Z/ Ir8/ 1813); (3) a collation of the xerox copy with the text in *An Account of the Funeral Honours* owned by the New York Public Library (IAG p. v. 170, no. 7); (4) a collation of the xerox copy with the text in *A Compilation of Biographical Sketches* owned by the New-York Historical Society (XN/ E 353/ .F67), and with a second copy owned by the Yale University Library (Za/ Ir8/ 813C); (5) a collation of the xerox copy with the text in *Naval Biography* owned by the Library of Congress (Office/ E 353/ .N28); (6) a collation of the xerox copy with the text *American Naval Biography*

92. See the Textual Commentary, pp. 273–76.

owned by the Library of Congress (Office/ E 353/ .B16) and with
a second copy owned by the University of Delaware (E 353/ .B16);
(7) a collation of the xerox copy with the text in *The Life of Oliver
Hazard Perry* owned by the Library of Congress (E 353/ .1/ .P4N58)
and with a second copy owned by the New-York Historical Society
(CT/ .P464N6); (8) a collation of the xerox copy with the text in
Spanish Papers owned by the National Library of Canada, made twice
and independently; (9) a sight collation of a xerox copy of the above
Spanish Papers text with the following additional copies: New York
Public Library; Yale University Library (Iw/ Ir8/ 866).

The sources of the text are (1) *Analectic Magazine*, 2 (August, 1813),
[122]–39; and (2) *Spanish Papers*, II, [37]–58.

See Discussions and Lists pp. 376–77, 396–97, 435.

CAPTAIN LAWRENCE

Irving's explanation of his methods in gathering material for the "Biography of Captain James Lawrence" was first published in the *Analectic
Magazine* for September, 1813, pp. 222–23. It was reprinted in none
of the patriotic compilations of military memoirs which during the
next two years included the "Biography," but Pierre M. Irving did
include it in *Spanish Papers*, II, 58–59, as an untitled addendum to that
work. As in the case of the "Biography," the *Spanish Papers* text includes accidental variants from that in the *Analectic Magazine* reflecting
the imposition of the Putnam house style,[93] but it is otherwise a faithful reprinting of the original. Except for the omitted title it includes no
substantive variants from the earlier text, and it reveals no evidence of
authorial revision. Because no manuscript version of "Captain Lawrence" is known to exist and there is no evidence that Irving revised
the original text, the *Analectic Magazine* version is adopted as copy-text.

In the preparation of this edition the following collations have been
made: (1) a xerox copy of the *Analectic Magazine* text in a copy owned
by the Toronto Public Library (M/ 051/ .A54) collated with the following additional copies: New-York Historical Society (*XN*/ AP 2/ .A48),
New York Public Library (*DA); (2) the xerox copy collated twice
and independently with the text in a copy of *Spanish Papers* owned by
the National Library of Canada; (3) the xerox copy of the above
Spanish Papers text sight collated with the following additional copies
of *Spanish Papers*: New York Public Library; Yale University Library
(Iw/ Ir8/ 866).

93. See the Textual Commentary, pp. 273–76.

The sources of the text are (1) *Analectic Magazine*, 2 (September, 1813), 222–23; and (2) *Spanish Papers*, II, 58–59.

See Discussions and Lists p. 397.

THE LAY OF THE SCOTTISH FIDDLE:
A TALE OF HAVRE DE GRACE

The review of James Kirke Paulding's *The Lay of the Scottish Fiddle* (1813), published in the *Analectic Magazine* for September, 1813, pp. 223–30, is specified by Pierre M. Irving as one of his uncle's contributions to that work.[94] Although Stanley T. Williams refers to it in the *Life* as Irving's, in their *Bibliography* he and Mary A. Edge note only that it is "sometimes ascribed" to him.[95] In *Washington Irving: A Bibliography*, William R. Langfeld and Philip C. Blackburn list the work without comment as one of the author's contributions to the *Analectic Magazine*.[96] It is in fact almost certainly his. Even though the notice is too brief to support by itself a confident attribution on stylistic grounds, one may reasonably assume that Irving would have reviewed an anonymous work just published by his old comrade "Jim" Paulding, who was then contributing generously to the *Analectic Magazine*. The editorial "we" employed conspicuously in the review—see 79.6–7, 79.22, 79.27—appears not to be merely a conventional mode of editorial self-reference but specifically to denote the individual or individuals into whose hands *The Lay* was put "at a late period," and who copied from it "a few extracts, hastily made, as specimens of the nature and merits of the work." Since Irving held sole control over the contents of the *Analectic Magazine* and was thus responsible for all copy published in it, he would seem of necessity the author of the few paragraphs preceding the extracts from Paulding's poem.[97]

The quotations in the review include no substantive variants from the corresponding sections in Paulding's poem, but in taking his "extracts" Irving did use a free hand with the accidentals of *The Lay of the Scottish Fiddle*. Between the quotations and the original thirty-nine accidental variants occur, thirty of which involve the addition (fifteen) or

94. PMI, I, 299.
95. STW, I, 138, 415, n. 48; *Bibliography*, p. 164.
96. *Washington Irving: A Bibliography*, p. 55.
97. Nevertheless, we need not take too seriously his professions of haste. If he wished, he could easily enough have had access to Paulding's work prior to its publication. His ostensibly hurried manner of noticing the volume may indeed have been a means of suggesting that the anonymous author of *The Lay* was receiving no special treatment at the hands of the *Analectic Magazine*.

deletion (fifteen) of commas. On the assumption that, as editor of the *Analectic Magazine*, Irving saw his own articles into print as he wished them to appear, the emended accidentals in the quotations are allowed to stand unless they create serious ambiguities or are clearly in error.

Because the review has not been reprinted and no manuscript version of it is known to exist, the *Analectic Magazine* version is adopted as copy-text. Accidental variants of particular interest between the copy-text and corresponding passages in *The Lay of the Scottish Fiddle* are reported in the tables which follow.[98]

In the preparation of this edition the following collations have been made: (1) a xerox copy of the *Analectic Magazine* text in a copy owned by the Toronto Public Library (M/ 051/ .A54) sight collated with the following additional copies: New-York Historical Society (*XN*/ AP 2/ .A48); New York Public Library (*DA); (2) the above xerox copy collated with the copy of *The Lay of the Scottish Fiddle* owned by the New-York Historical Society (PS 2527/ .L3/ 1813), and with a micro-card edition of the same work (American Antiquarian Society copy).

The sources of the text are (1) *The Lay of the Scottish Fiddle: A Tale of Havre de Grace* (New York: Inskeep & Bradford, 1813), and (2) *Analectic Magazine*, 2 (September, 1813), 223–30.

See Discussions and Lists pp. 397–98, 443.

BIOGRAPHICAL NOTICE OF THE LATE
LIEUTENANT BURROWS

Irving's sketch of the life of Lieutenant William Burrows was first published in the *Analectic Magazine* for November, 1813, pp. [396]–403. Shortly thereafter it was included by Benjamin Folsom, under the title "Lieut. William Burrows," in *A Compilation of Biographical Sketches of Distinguished Officers in the American Navy* (1814), pp. 123–32. With the exception of a single misprint ("allotted" corresponding to 87.15 appears as "alotted") and three alterations of spelling, the reprinted text duplicates the original. The *Analectic Magazine* biography was also reprinted, under the title "Lieutenant Burrows," in an anonymous collection of previously published works, *Naval Biography, or Lives of the Most Distinguished American Naval Heroes of the Present Day* (1815), pp. 134–44. The *Naval Biography* text omits Irving's first three para-

---

98. A full reporting of the variants between the pertinent portions of the two texts is on file at the University of Texas.

graphs (86.6–30), an asterisk at a later point and the footnote to which it refers (90.35, 90.38–44), and the first three sentences in the paragraph following (91.10–14). No reason for the omission of these particular passages is apparent, except possibly a desire to exclude material which did not pertain directly to Burrows' life history. The essay was the final item in *Naval Biographies,* and its appearance there in slightly condensed form may have been the result of a need to conserve space. Aside from the omissions, the *Naval Biographies* text includes no substantive variants from the original. Neither it nor the Folsom *Compilation* reveals any evidence of authorial revision.

Irving's biographical sketch was published once more, under the title "Lieutenant Burrows," in *Spanish Papers,* II, [60]–69. Aside from alterations of accidentals, including the printing of ships' names in italics, to bring the text into conformity with the Putnam house style,[99] a corrected misprint and one other substantive variant characteristic of the editorial hand of Pierre M. Irving (see Rejected Variants, 86.39), the *Spanish Papers* text is a faithful reprinting of the original. This version of the Burrows biography reveals no substantial evidence of authorial revision.

Because no manuscript version of the work is known to exist and there is no evidence to suggest that Irving revised it after its first publication in the *Analectic Magazine,* that version is adopted as copy-text. Substantive variants, and accidental variants of particular interest, between the copy-text and the *Spanish Papers* text are listed in the tables which follow.

In the preparation of this edition the following collations have been made: (1) a xerox copy of the *Analectic Magazine* text owned by the Toronto Public Library (M/ 051/ .A54) sight collated with the following additional copies: New-York Historical Society (XN/ AP 2/ .A48); New York Public Library (*DA); University of Michigan; (2) the above xerox copy collated with the text in *A Compilation of Biographical Sketches* owned by the New-York Historical Society (XN/ E 353/ .F7), and with an additional copy owned by the Yale University Library (Za/ Ir8/ 813C); (3) the xerox copy collated with the text in *Naval Biography* owned by the Library of Congress (Office/ E 353/ .N28); (4) the xerox copy collated twice and independently with the text in a copy of *Spanish Papers* owned by the National Library of Canada; (5) a xerox copy of the above *Spanish Papers* text sight collated with the following additional copies: New York Public Library; Yale University Library (Iw/ Ir8/ 866).

99. See the Textual Commentary, pp. 273–76.

The sources of the text are (1) *Analectic Magazine*, 2 (November, 1813), [396]–403; and (2) *Spanish Papers*, II, 60–69.

See Discussions and Lists pp. 377, 398, 436.

BIOGRAPHICAL MEMOIR OF COMMODORE PERRY

Irving's sketch of the life of Oliver Hazard Perry was first published in the *Analectic Magazine* for December, 1813, pp. 494–510. Not long afterward, portions of it were reprinted by Benjamin Folsom, under the title "Com. Oliver Hazard Perry," in *A Compilation of Biographical Sketches of Distinguished Officers in the American Navy* (1814), pp. 132–47. The Folsom version omits the *Analectic Magazine* text corresponding to 92.18–95.5 ("In ... inspire.") and 101.27–102.13 ("We ... force."), and the portions included in it reveal a variety of accidental variants and one substantive variant from the original ("Oliver" at a point corresponding to 95.6 appears in *A Compilation* as "Com. Oliver"); but with these exceptions it is a faithful reprinting. The sketch was also reprinted in 1815, under the title "Commodore O. H. Perry," in *Naval Biography; or Lives of the Most Distinguished American Naval Heroes of the Present Day*, pp. 70–95; immediately following the sketch of Perry in this work, the *Analectic Magazine* is cited as the source of the text.[100] Except for accidental variants and its altered title, the *Naval Biography* text is a faithful reprinting of the original. Neither it nor the Folsom *Compilation* reveals evidence of authorial revision.

The biography of Perry was reprinted once more, under the title "Commodore Perry," in *Spanish Papers*, II, [70]–90. Except for changes in accidentals to bring the text into conformity with the Putnam house style,[101] the correction of misprints, and three other substantive variants (see Rejected Variants, 98.6, 101.21–22, 103.21), the *Spanish Papers* text is a faithful reprinting of the original. Interestingly, the grisly detail in the *Analectic Magazine* text that Commodore Barclay, the British commander, "had the misfortune to have his remaining hand shot away" (101.21–22) is omitted from *Spanish Papers*. It is possible that Pierre M. Irving made this deletion at the behest of his late uncle, though no evidence is available to support such a speculation. More likely the emendation is the result of Pierre's own cautious sense that,

---

100. Irving's biographies of three naval worthies—James Lawrence, William Burrows, and O. H. Perry—were reprinted in *Naval Biography* (Pittsburgh: R. Patterson, 1815); but the *Analectic Magazine* is specifically cited as the source only of the Perry text. No citations whatever are provided for the other two titles.

101. See the Textual Commentary, pp. 273–76.

if preserved, the original reading might prove needlessly distressing to the readers of *Spanish Papers*.

Because no manuscript version of the work is known to exist, and no evidence suggests that Irving ever revised his original text, the *Analectic Magazine* version is adopted as copy-text. Substantive variants, and accidental variants of particular interest, between the copy-text and the *Spanish Papers* text, are listed in the tables which follow.

Certain of Irving's accidentals in the copy-text, such as his tendency to employ a colon merely to enforce a significant pause in the reading of a sentence (93.7, 93.13, 97.8), his failure to capitalize the names of federal enactments (95.28, embargo act), agencies (navy, army), and offices (95.43, secretary of the navy), and his tendency to insert a comma between subject and object (95.14) strike the modern reader as odd, if not incorrect. However, they appear so consistently in his contributions to the *Analectic Magazine* that they must be assumed in general to represent his intentions. Except at points where they create serious ambiguity, they require no emendation. On two occasions, Irving refers to Lake Erie simply as "the Lake" (96.37, 97.2); at another, as "Erie" (104.42); and at two others, as "Lake Erie" (96.35, 105.11); but because his meaning is clear in each instance, his several terms are all permitted to stand.

Some emendations have been made to Irving's lists (97.26–36 and 98.1–9) of the American and British naval squadrons on Lake Erie. In each of these he abbreviates the word "Schooner" to "Sch.," and in the list of American forces he abbreviates "Commodore" to "Com.," "Captain" to "Capt.," and "Midshipman" to "Mid." He may have employed the abbreviations to preserve a neat appearance in the tabular lists, but they are not really necessary for that purpose; and because the words are invariably spelled in full elsewhere in the article, they are emended for consistency.

In the preparation of this edition the following collations have been made: (1) a xerox copy of the *Analectic Magazine* text in the copy owned by the Toronto Public Library (M/ 051/ .A54) sight collated with the following additional copies: New-York Historical Society (XN/ AP 2/ .O48); New York Public Library (*DA); (2) the above xerox copy collated with the text in the Folsom *Compilation* owned by the New-York Historical Society (XN/ E 353/ .F67) and with a second copy owned by the Yale University Library (Za/ Ir8/ 813C); (3) the xerox copy collated with the text in *Naval Biography* owned by the Library of Congress (Office E 353/ .N28); (4) the xerox copy collated with the text in a copy of *Spanish Papers* owned by the National Library of Canada, twice and independently; (5) a xerox copy of the above *Spanish Papers* text sight collated with the texts in the following additional copies: New York Public Library; Yale University Library (Iw/ Ir8/ 866).

The sources of the text are (1) *Analectic Magazine*, 2 (December, 1813), 494–510; and (2) *Spanish Papers*, II [70]–90.

See Discussions and Lists pp. 377–78, 399, 436.

ODES, NAVAL SONGS, AND OTHER OCCASIONAL POEMS. BY EDWIN C. HOLLAND, ESQ. CHARLESTON

The review of Edwin C. Holland's *Odes* (1813) was first published in the *Analectic Magazine* for March, 1814, pp. 242–52. It was reprinted, under the title "Edwin C. Holland," in *Spanish Papers*, II, [325]–38. Except for the altered title and a single other substantive variant characteristic of Pierre M. Irving's concern for economy and clarity (see Rejected Variants, 106.8), the *Spanish Papers* version is a faithful reprinting of the original. It includes emended accidentals reflecting the imposition of the Putnam house style,[102] but it reveals no evidence of authorial revision.

As he had in his notices of the *Works* of Robert Treat Paine and Paulding's *Lay of the Scottish Fiddle*, Irving freely altered the accidentals in the passages he quoted from Holland's poems. Setting aside from consideration the brief phrases he adapted from the verse to the context of his own discussion—identified in the tables which follow—the two passages quoted from "The Pillar of Glory" (111.10–19, 111.26–35) and that from "Elegaic Lines. *Inscribed to the Memory of* MISS ANNA CLAUDIA BENNETT ..." (113.1–32) include together sixty-three variants from their originals, of which fully fifty-two are alterations of capitals to lowercase letters. In the absence of evidence to the contrary, we must assume that, either as editor or author of the review, or both, Irving intended his text to include these alterations of Holland's poems.

Because no manuscript version of the review is known to survive, and there is no evidence that the work as first published was ever revised by Irving, the *Analectic Magazine* text is adopted as copy-text. Substantive variants, and accidental variants of particular interest between the copy-text and the appropriate passages in Holland's *Odes*,[103] and between the copy-text and the *Spanish Papers* reprinting, are listed in the tables which follow.

102. See the Textual Commentary, pp. 273–76.
103. A full accounting of variants between the copy-text and the corresponding passages in Holland's *Odes* is on file at the University of Texas.

In the preparation of the edition the following collations have been made: (1) a xerox copy of the text in the *Analectic Magazine* owned by the Toronto Public Library (M/ 051/ .A54) sight collated with the following additional copies: New-York Historical Society (*XN*/ AP 2/ .A48); New York Public Library (*DA); University of Virginia (*AP 2/ .A48); (2) the above xerox copy collated with the appropriate passages in the copy of Holland's *Odes* owned by the New-York Historical Society (PS 3/ .H) and with a second copy owned by the Library of Congress (Office PS 1939/ H 804/ 1813); (3) the xerox copy collated twice and independently with the text in the copy of *Spanish Papers* owned by the National Library of Canada; (4) a xerox copy of the above *Spanish Papers* text sight collated with the following additional copies: New York Public Library; Yale University Library (Iw/ Ir8/ 866).

The sources of the text are (1) *Odes, Naval Songs, and Other Occasional Poems*, by Edwin C. Holland, Esq. (Charleston: For the Author, 1813); (2) *Analectic Magazine*, 3 (March, 1814), 242–52; and (3) *Spanish Papers*, II, [325]–38.

See Discussions and Lists pp. 378–79, 399, 436, 443–44.

LORD BYRON

The sketch of Byron's career to 1814, published in the *Analectic Magazine* for July of that year, pp. 68–72, has never been reprinted, even though it was ascribed to Irving by Pierre M. Irving and subsequently by Stanley T. Williams.[104] Because no manuscript version of the work is known to exist, the *Analectic Magazine* version is adopted as copy-text.

Irving's interest in Byron is reflected elsewhere in his miscellaneous writings: see "An Unwritten Drama of Lord Byron," II, 88–90; "Conversations with Talma," II, 172–73.

In the preparation of this edition a xerox copy of the *Analectic Magazine* text owned by the Toronto Public Library (M/ 051/ .A54) has been sight collated with the following additional copies: Columbia University (051/ An 1); New-York Historical Society (*XN*/ AP 2/ .A48); New York Public Library (*DA).

The source of the text is the *Analectic Magazine*, 4 (July, 1814), 68–72.

See Discussions and Lists pp. 379, 399.

104. PMI, I, 299; STW, I, 138, 415, n. 48. However, in their *Bibliography*, Williams and Edge refer to "Lord Byron" as only "sometimes ascribed to Irving" (p. 164). The work is included without comment by Langfeld and Blackburn in *Washington Irving: A Biography*, p. 56.

BIOGRAPHICAL MEMOIR OF
CAPTAIN DAVID PORTER

The biographical sketch of Porter first appeared in the *Analectic Magazine* for September, 1814, pp. 225–43. It was reprinted once during the author's lifetime, in the anonymous *Naval Biography, Consisting of Memoirs of the Most Distinguished Officers of the American Navy* (1815), pp. 249–74. The text in this patriotic compilation shows no evidence of authorial revision. It incorporates one correction of a misprint in the *Analectic Magazine* version, includes three unprecedented misprints of its own, and also a fourth variant in spelling from Irving's text which may be a misprint,[105] but no other substantive variants from the original.

The sketch was reprinted by Pierre M. Irving, under the title "Captain David Porter," in *Spanish Papers*, II, [91]–114. Except for changes in accidentals reflecting the imposition of the Putnam house style,[106] the later text includes only five substantive variants from the original besides its altered title: one the correction of a misprint (see Emendations 119.17) and the other limited to single words (see Rejected Variants, 117.40, 118.10, 119.2, 127.1). It includes two further emendations of accidentals in the earlier text, both characteristic of Pierre M. Irving's editorial hand (see Emendations, 121.34, 131.10–11), but it reveals no convincing evidence of authorial revision.

Because no manuscript version of the work is known to exist, and there is no evidence of authorial revision, the *Analectic Magazine* text is adopted as copy-text. Substantive variants, and accidental variants of particular interest, between the copy-text and that in *Spanish Papers* are recorded in the tables which follow.

The biography of Porter frequently reveals Irving's tendency to employ the colon to mark a pause rather than particularly to introduce the words following it (118.27, 120.15, 126.29, 130.19), and the semi-

---

105. In the order specified, the substantive variants between the original text and that in *Naval Biography* (Cincinnati: Morgan, Phillips & Co., 1815) are as follows:

Analectic Magazine (Page, line)	Twayne edition (Page, line)	Analectic Magazine (Reading)	Naval Biography (Reading)
227.1	119.17	faking	taking
225.14	118.10	command of	command [*blank*]
239.33	129.22	advised	a[*blank*]ed
242.31	131.35	landed	lande[*blank*]
226.23	119.1	Truxton	Truxtun

106. See the Textual Commentary, pp. 273–76.

colon as an introductory mark of punctuation (121.40); but since as a contributor to the *Analectic Magazine* he is consistently casual in distinguishing between the functions proper to the two marks, his unusual usages are allowed to stand. His methods of indicating days of the month are inconsistent: at some points he follows the pattern observable at 123.6–7–"3rd of July" (see also 120.12, 123.34), but at others the one at 117.40–"1st February" (see also 125.22). Because the differing usages create no ambiguity and reflect no clear preference, they are both allowed to stand. Irving's manner of writing numbers is also inconsistent: ordinarily he spells them as words, but not infrequently he uses numerals instead. He tends in this sketch, as in the "Biographical Memoir of Commodore Perry" (pp. 92–105), to employ numerals when itemizing data of the forces in naval conflict (see 126.12–19, 130.10–12, 130.43–131.3). Even in these passages, however, he appears to adopt either form almost at random. For example, at 131.2 he refers to "18 twelve pound shot," but at 126.18–19 to "ten 18 pound carronades and ten short sixes." It appears likely that in thus specifying the number of guns of various ratings he deliberately alternated between numerals and words when two numbers were juxtaposed so as to avoid confusion. In any case, his usages create no ambiguities and require no regularization.

In the preparation of this edition the following collations have been made: (1) a xerox copy of the *Analectic Magazine* text owned by the Toronto Public Library (M/ 051/ .A54) collated with a microprint text of the *Naval Biography* version (American Antiquarian Society copy); (2) the xerox copy of the *Analectic Magazine* text sight collated with the following additional copies: New-York Historical Society (*XN*/ AP2/ .A48); New York Public Library (*DA); (3) the above xerox copy collated twice and independently with the text in a copy of *Spanish Papers* owned by the National Library of Canada; (4) a xerox copy of the above *Spanish Papers* text sight collated with the following additional copies: New York Public Library; Yale University Library (Iw/ Ir8/ 866).

The sources of the text are (1) *Analectic Magazine*, 4 (September, 1814), 225–43, and (2) *Spanish Papers*, II, [91]–114.

See Discussions and Lists pp. 379, 399, 436–37.

DEFENCE OF FORT M'HENRY

This brief item was first published in the "Poetry" section of the *Analectic Magazine* for December, 1814, pp. 433–34. It has not previously been ascribed to Irving, but the bracketed introduction to Francis Scott Key's lyric is very probably his work. While stylistic considerations are of no use in the attribution of so brief a work as this single paragraph, two historical details, taken together, make out a fairly conclusive case. The first is that, as (apparently) the sole editor of the *Analectic Magazine*, Irving was responsible for its entire contents—including, presumably, the unusual interpolated comments here cast in the editorial "we."[107] The second is that, in reprinting Key's verses, he was transforming into editorial policy an opinion he had expressed a few months before in his review of Edwin C. Holland's *Odes* (see pp. 105–14): the need of encouraging the creation and dissemination of original American patriotic songs rather than ones transparently derived from those of Great Britain. Which of the "several" American newspapers was Irving's source for the text of Key's lyric is unknown.

Because no manuscript version of "Defence of Fort M'Henry" is known to exist and the published work has not been reprinted, the *Analectic Magazine* version is adopted as copy-text.

In the preparation of this edition a xerox copy of the *Analectic Magazine* text owned by the Toronto Public Library (M/ 051/ .A54) has been sight collated with the following additional copies: Columbia University (051/ An 1); New-York Historical Society (*XN*/ AP 2/ .A48); New York Public Library (*DA).

The source of the text is the *Analectic Magazine*, 4 (December, 1814), 433–34.

See Discussions and Lists pp. 379, 400.

A BIOGRAPHICAL SKETCH OF THOMAS CAMPBELL

The original impetus for Irving's sketch of Campbell was a request he received in 1810 from Archibald Campbell, a brother of the Scottish poet, to promote the publication in America of the recently completed *O'Connor's Child*. Irving offered the work to a Philadelphia bookseller, Charles I. Nicholas, who with his partner agreed to undertake it provided he would select other poems to be included in the volume and

---

107. Given our scanty knowledge of the process by which issues of the *Analectic Magazine* were prepared, it does not seem justified simply to attribute to Irving all bracketed interpolations published in the magazine during his editorship. As, for example, in the case of the explanatory paragraph preceding the reprinted text of Leigh Hunt's "Memoir of Me" in the issue of July, 1814, p. 73, such necessary glosses may well have been supplied by persons who first brought the articles to Irving's attention; or, they may have beeen written by another person with whom he occasionally shared editorial duties.

in addition write an introduction to it. He assented; and after gathering a few particulars from Archibald Campbell, including passages from the poet's letters, he worked them up hurriedly into a brief biography.[108] This version of the sketch was well received both in England and in the United States, but it gave Irving little satisfaction. Years later he told Pierre M. Irving that it had been "written against the vein," and that the process of composition had been "up hill work."[109]

In its early form the biography first appeared, under the title "A Biographical Sketch of the Author," in a two-volume edition of the collection Irving had engaged to prepare, *The Poetical Works of Thomas Campbell*, I, [vii]–xliii. The work was produced as a joint venture by several persons or firms, all of whose names appeared on the title page. However, the imprint varies from copy to copy because each bookseller issued the book with his own name and location listed prominently at the head of the imprint, as for example: "PRINTED FOR PHILIP H. NICKLIN & Co., BALTIMORE. / Also, For D. W. Farrand and Green, Albany; D. Mallory & Co., / Boston; Lyman and Hall, Portland; and E. Earle, / Philadelphia. / Fry and Kammerer, Printers. / 1810." The copies comprising this edition appear to be from a single impression, revealing no variants whatever in the text of Irving's introduction. We therefore have no sure means of determining the sequence in which the five issues of the work were produced.[110] Probably they were intended to be offered for sale simultaneously. According to Langfeld and Blackburn, this method of cooperative publication by several booksellers was seldom attempted in the United States in 1810.[111]

A further experiment was undertaken by the same firms when, also in 1810, they produced a one-volume edition of *The Poetical Works of Thomas Campbell* in which Irving's sketch appeared, pp. [7]–41. In contrast to the two-volume edition, its successor was paged in Arabic rather than Roman numerals and included twenty-six rather than twenty-three or twenty-four lines to a full page.[112] However, in all other respects—type style, line length, spacing, and punctuation—the texts of Irving's sketch in the two editions are identical. It would appear that

108. PMI, I, 253; STW, I, 121; *Irvingiana*, p. viii; "[Memoir of Thomas Campbell]," II, 157–60.

109. PMI, I, 253.

110. Langfeld and Blackburn have noted that the name "Nicklin" is spelled thus in some copies of the Albany issue and "Nickilin" in others. "Since there was a correction," they add, "it would seem the copies with the error are earlier" (*Washington Irving: A Biography*, p. 13).

111. *Washington Irving: A Biography*, p. 14.

112. Langfeld and Blackburn note as well that "the contents of the one-volume edition is that of the two-volume edition, but differently arranged" (*Washington Irving: A Bibliography*, p. 14).

subsequent to printing the sheets for the two-volume edition, the printers simply altered the lineation and page-numbering of the original, inserted new signatures, and printed a single impression of the one-volume edition. In 1811, having recruited another set of firms for a reprise of his enterprise of multiple publication, Philip H. Nicklin of Baltimore produced a *"Second American Edition"* in the one-volume format.[113] This publication has a freshly designed title page, but the text of Irving's introduction to it is identical in every respect to that in the one-volume edition of 1810. It is possible that the one-volume publications dated 1810 and 1811 are in fact separate issues of a single impression made *before* the two-volume of 1810, but the likelihood is that, having first published the two-volume and then the one-volume edition, Nicklin kept the types for the latter work intact until a fresh impression was warranted.[114]

In March, 1815, "A Biographical Sketch of Thomas Campbell," "revised, corrected, and materially altered by the author," appeared in the *Analectic Magazine,* pp. 234–50. Irving had resigned his editorship of the magazine in December, 1814, when its publisher, Moses Thomas, was in dire financial straits; and he may have sent the revised sketch as a helpful courtesy to his former employer, whom he admired and considered to have been unfairly used by his associates. At any rate it seems unlikely that, under the circumstances, he received more than token payment for his contribution. Probably, in fact, he had made the revision less from financial motives than from a lingering dissatisfaction with the 1810 version. Peter Irving, whose "pure and classic"[115] taste he valued, had found fault with the essay in its original form. A previously unpublished letter from Peter, which Pierre M. Irving at one time intended to include in the *Life and Letters,* suggests that the fraternal disapproval may have played a major part in effecting Irving's determination to revise. "I perceive that the materials have been scanty," Peter

---

113. Nicklin's co-publishers in this venture were E. Sergeant, New York; A. Finley, Philadelphia; D. Mallory & Co., Boston; Joseph Cushing, Baltimore; Joseph Mulligan, Georgetown; James Kennedy, Sen., Alexandria; John R. Jones, Richmond; and Caleb Emerson, Marietta, Ohio.

114. Although in this discussion I have described the precedence of the two-volume and one-volume editions of the *Poetical Works* in accordance with the order unanimously specified by Williams and Edge in *Bibliography,* Langfeld and Blackburn in *Washington Irving: A Bibliography,* and Jacob Blanck in BAL, V, 14, it must be noted that collations performed in the preparation of this edition have not warranted revision of the statement by Langfeld and Blackburn (reiterated by Blanck) that there "is no means to establish any priority, either among the imprints, or between the one- and two-volume editions" (*Washington Irving: A Bibliography,* p. 14).

115. PMI, I, 220. The phrase is Pierre M. Irving's.

wrote from Europe shortly after the 1810 version had appeared; "but the accompanying observations by which they are amplified cannot be considered irrelevant to the subject, and have much of intrinsic merit to recommend them." He continued, however, in a more critical vein: "I perceive . . . that you join in the popular hue & cry against German literature and censure the people of Great Britain for travelling from their own libraries to a languishment after foreign crudities and the splendid absurdities of the German muse. It was some time ago the fashion among the ⟨English⟩ writers of this century to rail against the absurdity of sending their young men to travel over the continent and imbibe foreign follies, &c. instead of staying at home in this best of all possible little islands, feeding themselves with beef and plum pudding, breaking their necks at fox chases, and becoming body & soul true born Englishmen. I think the two recommendations should go together."[116] After quoting this passage, Pierre M. Irving commented that when Irving prepared the *Analectic Magazine* version of the eassy he "would seem to have expunged the passages which had called forth the strictures of his brother."[117]

Although Stanley T. Williams has characterized Irving's revision of the 1810 version of the sketch as "slight,"[118] in fact it was painstaking and quite thorough. An accounting of the substantive variants between the two-volume 1810 and the *Analectic Magazine* texts is given in the tables which follow, but it will be useful to specify here the varieties of revisions which resulted in the later version. At four points passages containing the "observations" with which, as Peter Irving had perceived, the 1810 sketch had been "amplified" are deleted (see Precopy-Text Variants, 134.19, 134.24–25, 134.39, 135.34); these are generalized reflections on authorship and literary fashion. At five other points Irving's rather pungently phrased opinions on various topics, such as "the race of booksellers," are dispensed with (see Precopy-Text Variants, 135.41, 136.6, 137.22, 137.28, 139.25); and elsewhere the originally ample quotations from the letters of Thomas Campbell are deleted, abbreviated,

116. Berg Collection, New York Public Library. For further commentary on Irving's frequent reliance on the literary judgments of his elder brother, see Leonard B. Beach, ed. "Peter Irving's Journals," *Bulletin of the New York Public Library*, 44 (August, 1940), 594–95, 598.

117. Berg Collection, New York Public Library. Pierre M. Irving's published comment on the *Analectic Magazine* version, which omits mention of the correspondence between the author and Peter Irving, is in PMI, I, 299.

118. STW, I, 415, n. 47. It should be noted that, in *Bibliography*, p. 98, Williams and Edge cite the biographical sketch of Campbell as appearing in two works which do not include it: *Specimens of the British Poets*, ed. Thomas Campbell, 7 vols. (London: John Murray, 1819); Thomas Campbell, *The Pleasures of Hope and Other Poems* (New York, 1822).

or rendered into condensed paraphrase (see Precopy-Text Variants 138.5, 138.27–31, 139.6). The sequence of material in the *Analectic Magazine* is almost unchanged from the 1810 text (an exception is the commentary on the private characteristics of authors; see 134.12–16 and Precopy-Text Variants, 134.24–25); in general, Irving confined himself to selecting material to be excised and to rewriting what remained. He did add material—chiefly two passages commenting on Campbell's extreme sensitivity to criticism of his own works (140.43–141.5, 144.29–145.8), and also a footnote discussing the applicability in a time of war of a remark in the 1810 version that the interest of England lay in cultivating the affections of Americans (143.32–45)—but as the following passages from the two texts will suggest, he essentially rewrote portions of the earlier essay with attention to both manner and matter:

Poetical Works	*Analectic Magazine*
He is represented as being extremely studious, but at the same time social and lively in his disposition, highly prepossessing in his appearance and of engaging and courteous manners. His circle of acquaintance is of the most polished and enlightened kind, and in this his great colloquial powers and a peculiar talent for recitation, make him a distinguished favourite. In domestic life he appears to no less advantage; a kind husband, a tender parent, and an affectionate son; in a word, few men, who have been brought up in studious and literary seclusion, unite to such brilliant endowments, such gentle and endearing qualities of the heart.	He is generally represented to us as being extremely studious, but at the same time social in his disposition, gentle and endearing in his manners, and extremely prepossessing in his appearance and address. With a delicate and even nervous sensibility, and a degree of self diffidence that at times is almost painful, he shrinks from the glare of notoriety which his own works have shed around him, and seems ever deprecating critiscism, rather than enjoying praise. Though his society is courted by the most polished and enlightened, among whom he is calculated to shine, yet his chief delight is in domestic life, in the practice of those gentle virtues and bland affections which he has so touchingly and eloquently illustrated in various passages of his poems.[119]

Irving gave careful consideration in 1815 to questions of syntax, diction, and punctuation. The revised essay reveals a marked tendency to substitute semicolons for commas, to employ commas where none had previously appeared, and to add hyphens to compounds earlier printed as either one or two words. Years later Irving was to refer deprecatingly to his production of 1810 as written "in great haste" and "slight and im-

---

119. *Poetical Works*, 2 vols. (1810), I, xxxi; *Analectic Magazine*, 5 (March, 1815), 242. Other emendations to reflect the passage of five years since the original version had appeared are noted in Precopy-Text Variants 135.20, 139.17.

perfect."[120] He evidently intended in 1815 to distill from it a work with which he would be better satisfied.

Following its appearance in the *Analectic Magazine*, the revised memoir was reprinted in 1815, under the title "A Biographical Sketch of the Author," in *The Poetical Works of Thomas Campbell. Comprising Several Poems Not Contained in Any Former Edition*, pp. [1]–24. In this edition the publisher Edward Earle (or whoever was responsible for Irving's text as it stands) freely altered the accidentals of the essay, corrected two typographical errors in the magazine text,[121] introduced two of his own,[122] and made eleven other substantive emendations besides deleting a prefatory note (133.25–27) explaining the history of the text.[123] One substantive change in the Earle edition is of the reading "some few years since" to "about three years since" (see 139.17). In-

120. See "[Memoir of Thomas Campbell]," II, 157. The *Analectic Magazine* text exists in two states. The copies owned by the New-York Historical Society and the Toronto Public Library have the reading "ɔorrectness" at 243.38 (T 141.11); in the copies owned by the New York Public Library and the University of Virginia the inverted type is righted and replaced. Other typographical errors are common to all four copies. In the tables which follow no distinction is made between the two states except at Emendations 141.11.

121. The corrections made in *The Poetical Works* (Philadelphia: E. Earle, 1815) of typographical errors in the magazine version are as follows:

Analectic Magazine (Page, line)	Twayne edition (Page, line)	*Analectic Magazine* (Reading)	(Earle, 1815) (Reading)
242.24	140.8	critiscism	criticism
243.38	141.11	ɔorrectness	correctness

122. The typographical errors introduced by Earle are as follows:

Analectic Magazine (Page, line)	Twayne edition (Page, line)	*Analectic Magazine* (Reading)	(Earle, 1815) (Reading)
235.5–6	134.13	familiarity	familarity
240.24	138.27	unprofitably	unprofitable

123. The substantive variants are as follows:

Analectic Magazine (Page, line)	Twayne edition (Page, line)	*Analectic Magazine* (Reading)	(Earle, 1815) (Reading)
235.22	134.28	A	An
237.9	135.41	This	The
241.11	139.5	attentions	attention
241.24–25	139.17	some few years since	about three years since
242.14	139.43	bleeding."	bleeding," published in the following collection.
243.16	140.35	produce	produce a
243.29	141.3	a large number	about a dozen
244.1	141.13	to be	to have been

terestingly, the emended reading duplicates that in Irving's 1810 text—
and therefore reintroduces an error of chronology which the author
had corrected in his revision of five years afterward. This curious dupli-
cation between the undated Earle volume and Irving's original sketch
is one of several similar instances which suggest that in revising the
work Earle had before him a copy both of the *Analectic Magazine* text
and of the earlier one as well.[124] In any case, it is virtually certain that
Irving, who departed for his seventeen-year sojourn in Europe on May
25, 1815, played no part in making the further revisions incorporated
in the Earle edition.

Edward Earle included the sketch in a subsequent edition of Campbell's *Poetical Works* produced in a manner similar to that adopted in
1810 by Philip H. Nicklin of Baltimore. That is, he caused the types of
the undated edition to be partially reset, altering the page numbers to
Roman numerals, retaining thirty-four lines per page but lengthening
each line from 2 3/8 to 2 1/2 inches by means simply of shifting type
already set into slightly larger chases, and adding a new title page.
The latter edition includes in its imprint: "PHILADELPHIA:/ PUB-
LISHED BY EDWARD EARLE. / William Fry, Printer. / 1815.";
the former includes none of this data. With few exceptions, two of
which establish the priority of the editions,[125] the texts of Irving's essay
in the two Earle publications are identical.

Reprints of the biography of Campbell appeared on several occasions
subsequent to the Earle editions, but Irving played no part in any of

---

246.30	143.33	have been changed by a war	are changed and we are now at war
246.32	143.35	as	as of
248.1	144.24	character of the literary author	literary character of the author
249.26	145.37	well calculated	calculated

124. Readings in the Earle volume emended from the *Analectic Magazine* text
and duplicating those in the 1810 version are as follows:

Analectic Magazine (Page, line)	Twayne edition (Page, line)	Analectic Magazine (Reading)	1810 and (Earle, 1815) (Reading)
237.34	136.19	prize exercise	prize-exercise
244.7	141.18–19	loosely-written	loosely written
244.9	141.20	chase	chace

125. At a point corresponding to 138.77, the undated Earle edition includes
the erroneous reading "unprofitable"; in the dated edition the word is corrected
to "unprofitably." At a point corresponding to 144.35, the undated edition includes the awkward reading "pen it"; in the dated edition this is altered to "pen,
it"—the *Analectic Magazine* reading. Two further accidental variants between
the two editions are caused by Earle's alterations of line length.

them. In 1821 the sketch was included in *The Poetical Works of Thomas Campbell*, the "*First complete American Edition*", pp. [ix]–xxxiii. Clearly derived from the Earle text,[126] that of 1821 omits as no longer pertinent the footnote concerning the relations in 1815 between the United States and England (143.32–45), but except for further alterations of a few accidentals it is a faithful reprinting of the Earle text. Under the title "A Biographical Sketch of Thomas Campbell, Esq. by Geoffry [sic] Crayon, Gent.," Irving's biography was published in an English periodical, *Bolster's Quarterly Magazine*, 1 (January, 1826), 28–39. The source of this reprinted (that is, pirated) item is cited in *Bolster's* as "an American edition of the poems of Mr. Campbell, printed, ten years ago, at Philadelphia" (p. 28)—one of the Earle editions.

In 1841 the sketch was again reprinted, almost certainly without authorization, this time by William L. Stone in his *The Poetry and History of Wyoming*, pp. [ix]–xxiv.[127] Acknowledging in his "Preface" the assistance of various persons, Stone wrote that "in addition to all, Mr. WASHINGTON IRVING has kindly furnished a biographical sketch of the author of Gertrude [of Wyoming]" (p. viii). Stone's clear suggestion is that Irving had prepared the essay specifically for publication in this work. In fact, what appeared as the initial item in Stone's anthology was a mangled version of the 1810 text marred by omissions,[128]

126. A selective list of readings shared between the Earle editions and that of 1821 (Philadelphia: Edward Parker), and differing from those in the *Analectic Magazine* text, will indicate the derivation of the Parker version:

Analectic Magazine (Page, line)	Twayne edition (Page, line)	Analectic Magazine (Reading)	Earle and Parker (Reading)
235.22	134.28	A	An
241.23–24	139.17	some few years since	about three years since
242.9	139.37–38	rhodomontade	rodomontade
242.14	139.43	bleeding."	bleeding," published in the following collection.
248.1	144.24	character of the literary author	literary character of the author

127. (New York and London: Wiley & Putnam, 1841). Stone (1792–1844), for a time the editor of the New York *Commercial Advertiser*, is best remembered as the defendant in James Fenimore Cooper's successful suit in response to slanderous public criticism of his works.

128. The following passages in the 1810 version, which may be pieced together by reference to the Twayne text and the table of Precopy-Text Variants, are omitted by Stone:

Poetical Works 2 vols. (1810)	Inclusive Text	Twayne edition
xii.8–11	He ... character	135.5–7 Text

transpositions,[129] casual rephrasings,[130] and additions to that work. The penultimate paragraph of Stone's piracy will exemplify the latter class of that editor's revisions. Irving's claim in the sketch that a fraternal friendship ought to be maintained between England and the United States was not in accordance with Stone's views. He therefore set aside the author's remarks and proceeded to generalize in a manner befittting his own truculent nationalism:

> As we before remarked, the lapse of thirty years has materially impaired the cogency of the foregoing remarks. The acrimony and traduction of the British press produced the effect apprehended, and contributed to hasten a war between the two nations. That war, however, made us completely a nation, and destroyed our mental dependence on England forever. A literature of our own has subsequently sprung up and is daily increasing with wonderful fecundity; promising to counteract the undue influence of British literature, and to furnish us with productions in all departments of taste and knowledge, illustrative of our country, its history and its

xii.14–17	country; ... America	135.9–11 Text
xii.24–xiii.2	He ... eloquence	135.17–18 Variants
xiii.17–xiv.11	There ... satisfy.	135.29–34 Text and Variants
xiv.12–xvi.3	Perhaps ... Scotland.	135.35–136.13 Text and Variants
xviii.11–13	Nothing ... auspices.	137.10–11 Text
xxvi.10–xxvii.20	These ... hands.	139.6 Variants (beginning with "These" at the outset of the new paragraph)
xxxi.6–21	Of the ... heart.	139.44–140.13 Text and Variants
xxxi.22–xxxv.4	That Mr. Campbell ... his own.	140.14–141.34 Text and Variants
xliii.5–22	But ... honour."	145.31–146.12 Text and Variants

129. The following passages shifted or transposed by Stone are cited for the interested reader:

Poetical Works 2 vols. (1810)	Stone, Poetry and History
xiii.6–9 and xv.24–xvi.3	xii.29–33—the two passages juxtaposed
xxxi.3–5, xxxiv.15–18, and xliii.5–23	xxiv.6–22—the three passages incorporated into Stone's final paragraph

130. The following passages thoroughly revised by Stone are cited for comparison by the interested reader:

Poetical Works 2 vols. (1810)	Stone, Poetry and History
xii.3–8	xii.12–16
xiii.12–16	xiii.2–7
xvii.1–xix.19	xiii.24–xiv.29
xxix.3–xxx.5	xix.9–18
xxx.11–23	xix.24–30

people, and in harmony with our condition and the nature of our institutions.[131]

There is no evidence that Irving ever alluded to the gross liberties taken by Stone with the text of his youthful essay, or indeed that he ever looked into *The Poetry and History of Wyoming*. It is certain, however, that he would neither have authorized nor have approved this use of the work. Ironically, in 1845 Stone's text was itself drawn upon and slightly revised by the Reverend Rufus W. Griswold, for publication in *The Poetical Works of Thomas Campbell, Complete*, pp. v–xv.[132]

Pierre M. Irving reprinted the sketch once more, under the title "Thomas Campbell," in *Spanish Papers*, II, [115]–35. With the exception of changes to accidentals reflecting the imposition of the Putnam house style,[133] the correction of typographical errors, and four substantive alterations characteristic of Pierre M. Irving's cautious editorial hand, the *Spanish Papers* text is a faithful reprinting of that in the *Analectic Magazine*.[134] It reveals no evidence of authorial revision.

No manuscript version of any text of Irving's sketch of Thomas Campbell is known to exist. Because he regarded his earliest published version as hasty and inadequate, revised it with care for publication in the *Analectic Magazine* five years later, left it untouched thereafter, and authorized Pierre M. Irving to include the "revised, corrected, and materially altered" version in a posthumous collection of his miscellaneous works, the *Analectic Magazine* text is adopted as copy-text. Substantive variants between the copy-text and the sketch in the Baltimore issue of the two-volume edition of the 1810 *Poetical Works* are recorded in a

131. *Poetry and History*, pp. xxiii–xxiv. Other passages added to the 1810 text by Stone may be found in *Poetry and History* at xix.31–xx.12, xxiv.10–16.

132. (Philadelphia: Lea and Blanchard). Besides altering a few words and spellings in the Stone text, Griswold substituted for the final paragraph in *Poetry and History* a lengthier one of his own, summarizing the career of Thomas Campbell from 1810 until his death in 1844. Although this paragraph is enclosed in brackets, it follows immediately upon Irving's already much-revised text and hence lends the misleading impression that it is an authorial addendum.

133. See the Textual Commentary, pp. 273–76.

134. Irving's prefatory note explaining the history of the text prior to its publication in the *Analectic Magazine* (T 133.25–27) is deleted by Pierre M. Irving as being redundant; see his editorial note in *Spanish Papers*, II, [36]. For the other substantive emendations see Rejected Variants, 134.20, 134.38, 146.4. Three typographical errors in the *Analectic Magazine* text are corrected in *Spanish Papers*; see Emendations, 140.8, 141.11, 144.30. One new one is introduced; see Rejected Variants, 139.12. The *Spanish Papers* text is followed by a paragraph of editorial explanation and then by the reprinted text of Irving's untitled "[Memoir of Thomas Campbell]," which had first appeared in 1850; see II, 157–60.

table of Precopy-Text Variants.[135] Substantive variants, and accidental variants of particular interest, between the copy-text and the *Spanish Papers* text, are recorded in a table of Rejected Variants.

In the preparation of the edition the following collations have been made: (1) a xerox copy of the *Analectic Magazine* text owned by the Toronto Public Library (M/ 051/ .A54) sight collated with the following additional copies: New-York Historical Society (*XN*/ AP 2/ .A48); New York Public Library (*DA); University of Virginia (*AP 2/ .A48); (2) the above xerox copy collated three times and independently with the text in *Poetical Works* (2 vols., 1810), Baltimore issue, owned by Yale University (Za/ Ir 8/ 810) and once with an additional copy owned by the New York Public Library (*KL Campbell, copy 2); (3) a xerox copy of the Yale University text of *Poetical Works* (2 vols., 1810) collated with the following copies of *Poetical Works* (1810): Yale University, Albany issue (Za/ Ir8/ 1810d); New York Public Library, Baltimore issue (*KL, copy 2); (4) the above xerox copy of the Yale University *Poetical Works* (2 vols., 1810) sight collated with the text in *Poetical Works* (1811) owned by New York Public Library, Baltimore issue (NCM); (5) the xerox copy of the *Analectic Magazine* text (see no. 1) collated with the following copies of *Poetical Works* (Philadelphia: E. Earle, 1815): Yale University (Za/ Ir8/ 815B); University of Delaware (PR/ 4410/ A2/ 1815); Library of Congress (PR/ 4410/ .A2 / 1815); (6) the xerox copy of the *Analectic Magazine* text collated with the *Poetical Works* (Philadelphia: Edward Earle, 1815) text: Yale University (Za/ Ir8/ 815); New York Public Library (NCM); (7) the xerox copy of the *Analectic Magazine* text collated with the *Poetical Works* (Philadelphia: Edward Parker, 1821) text owned by Yale University (Za/ Ir8/ 815 cb); (8) a xerox copy of the Yale University *Poetical Works* (Earle, 1815) text collated with the *Bolster's Quarterly Magazine* text owned by Yale University (Za/ ZB/ 62); (9) the xerox copy of the Yale University *Poetical Works* (2 vols., 1810) text (see no. 2) collated with the following copies of the *Poetry and History of Wyoming* text: Yale University (Ck 19/ 333); New York Public Library (ISD); (10) the Yale University *Poetry and History of Wyoming* text collated with the text in the *Poetical Works*, ed. Griswold (Philadelphia, 1845), owned by Yale University (WB/ 53380); (11) the xerox copy of the *Analectic Magazine* text collated twice and independently with the *Spanish Papers* text owned by the National Library of Canada; (12) a xerox copy of the above *Spanish Papers* text sight col-

---

135. Except as noted above, the texts of the biographical sketch in the two pre-copy-text editions are identical. A full accounting of variants between the copy-text and the Baltimore issue of the *Poetical Works* text is on file at the University of Texas. Collation data for the other texts consulted are also on file.

lated with the following additional copies: New York Public Library; Yale University (Iw/ Ir8/ 866).

The sources of the text are (1) *The Poetical Works of Thomas Campbell*, 2 vols. (Baltimore: Philip H. Nicklin [&c., &c.], 1810), I, [vii]–xliii; (2) *Analectic Magazine*, 5 (March, 1815), 234–50; and (3) *Spanish Papers*, II, [115]–35.

See Discussions and Lists pp. 380, 400–01, 437, 444–52.

[LINES WRITTEN IN "THE TEMPLE OF DIRT"]

No manuscript version of this couplet is known to exist. Probably there never was one, since, according to Pierre M. Irving, his uncle had "scribbled" the lines "over the fireplace" of the house in upstate New York which he and his companions had named "The Temple of Dirt."[136] The lines were first published after Irving's death in PMI, I, 51, which is adopted as copy-text. In the preparation of this edition the texts in three copies of PMI in the possession of the editor have been compared.

The source of the text is PMI, I, 51.

[VERSES WRITTEN ON THE LAKE OF LUCERNE]

These lines are ascribed to Irving on the authority of Joseph C. Cabell, his traveling companion during 1805. On May 10 of that year the two young men crossed Lake Lucerne together while on their way from Rome to Paris. Although in his own journal entry for the day Irving makes no mention of writing verses,[137] Cabell copied into an undated section of his own journal a short poem which he entitled "Verses by Mr Irving written on the Lake of Lucerne"; and there is no reason to doubt his attribution.[138] Irving's poem was not published during his lifetime,[139] and no other manuscript copy of it is known to exist. The

136. PMI, I, 51; *Journals*, I, 16.

137. *Journals*, I, 378–84.

138. Cabell's transcription, written in pencil on one side of a sheet of light blue laid paper 4⅞ x 7¼ inches in size, is on page 176, volume 7 of the unpublished Cabell journals. The eight volumes of journals, covering the years 1802–1806, and a collection of letters to and from Cabell throughout his lifetime, form part of an extensive collection of Cabell family papers acquired by the University of Virginia in 1948.

139. Richard B. Davis published the verses for the first time in his essay, "Washington Irving and Joseph C. Cabell," in *English Studies in Honor of James Southall Wilson* (Charlottesville, 1951), pp. 12–13.

manuscript journal, extant at the University of Virginia, is hence adopted as copy-text.

The source of the text is the manuscript journal of Joseph C. Cabell, at the University of Virginia.

See Discussions and Lists pp. 380–81, 401.

PASSAIC—A TRADITION

A holograph manuscript text of this poem, dated "May 26*th*–1806," is owned by the Library of Congress; it is the earliest known manuscript of a completed literary work by Irving.[140] Written neatly in ink on both sides of a single sheet of heavy linen paper 7⅞ x 9⅝ inches in size, it is clearly a copy of an already completed draft of a poem. Its forty-eight lines of verse include only five minor cancellations.[141] Both the color of ink in which these changes were made, and their placement along or above the lines where they occur, suggest that they are adjustments made by Irving as he wrote out the manuscript text. Perhaps to lend a bit of elegance to his copy of the poem, at the left margin below each quatrain he wrote two short diagonal slashes in the space separating it from the next stanza. The manuscript includes three marks in pencil, apparently not written by Irving. Two of these are mere clarifications of his handwriting, the other an emendation of a single word (see Emendations, 149.31).

The care with which Irving wrote out this copy, and also the fine paper on which it is written, suggest that he may have intended to give it to someone, possibly a lady. On May 26, 1806, the same date he appended to the manuscript text, Irving wrote to his friend Gouverneur Kemble that, having returned to New York, he had now "quietly set down under petticoat government. There's a touch of the poetic for you. Inspired by the sublimity of the subject, I find my eyes begin once more to rise from the melancholy slough into which they have been plunged."[142] Clearly, as he wrote to Kemble poetry, "sublimity," and his lady friends, were in Irving's mind. Quite likely he sent the extant manuscript of *"Passaic—A Tradition"* either to Kemble, his comrade in recent excursions along the Passaic River in New Jersey, or to

140. The manuscript is accompanied by a note, signed by Irving's nephew Pierre Paris Irving, which reads: "The only poetical piece of Washington Irving's in his own handwriting." However, another Irving poem, "The Lay of the Sunnyside Ducks," is extant in manuscript form; see pp. 339–41.

141. See Emendations, 149.26, 149.31, 150.9, 150.16, 150.20.

142. PMI. I. 171.

someone in New York, under whose "petticoat government" he now found himself.

Two features of the accidentals in the Library of Congress manuscript require particular mention. First, the text is only minimally punctuated. Except for a single comma (150.32), no punctuation is included at the end of the first three lines in any of the twelve quatrains. Punctuation within the lines is somewhat less spare, but in general Irving was scrupulous to conclude each quatrain with a period,[143] to add diagonal slashes between stanzas, and to omit as much punctuation as reasonably possible from within stanzas. Since he wrote the manuscript with a degree of care, one must assume the scanty punctuation in many of its lines to be his considered intention. A second notable detail is that, despite the neat appearance of the manuscript, Irving's spelling of preterit forms of verbs knows no law: he mades no discernible distinction between forms ending "-ed," "-d," or "-'d." At other points his odd spellings (for example, "Dispair" for "Despair," 150.17) simply reveal the lapses in orthography that were to plague him all his life; but the preterit verbs in the manuscript seem to reflect not uncertainty but indifference to a single standard.

The poem was first published, under the title "From the Passaic Album," in a New York magazine, the *Weekly Visitor; or, Ladies' Miscellany* for September 27, 1806, p. 370. It was introduced by a letter to the editor from "C. W.," who wrote that, having recently visited Passaic Falls "and received ample gratification from the sublimity of the scene," he had "transcribed the following handsome production of a young gentleman of this city" from "the 'PASSAIC ALBUM' at Major Godwin's." This album was kept by one Abraham Godwin at his public house along the river, between the town of Newark and the falls, as a repository for the sentiments of guests.[144] The identity of "C. W." is unknown, but there is no apparent reason why his account of his transcribing the poem should not be taken as true. Irving apparently played no part in supervising this first printing of the work.

The poem next appeared in a magazine published in Schenectady, New York, *The Pastime. (A Literary Paper)* for May 28, 1808, pp. 27–28. It was entitled (similarly to the Library of Congress manuscript) "PASSAIC FALLS ... A TRADITION," and was preceded by a note: "[These beautiful lines were taken from the Album, kept at a public-house near Passaic Falls, New Jersey.]" No evidence suggests that Irving was associated with this second publication of his verses in any way, other than

143. He did omit one period, at a point corresponding to 150.22.
144. Eugene L. Huddleston, "Washington Irving's 'On Passaic Falls,'" *American Notes & Queries*, 4 (1965), 51–52.

that he was the author of the manuscript text from which the poem was taken. Evidently Godwin's album provided ample grist for the mills of contemporary magazine editors.

The same album was the acknowledged source of the third published text of Irving's verses, in a Boston weekly, *The Ordeal: A Critical Journal* for May 13, 1809, pp. 298–99. Here the poem is untitled and, like the two published texts preceding it, undated; but it is signed "TOBINUS." That pseudonym—possibly a sentimental takeoff on "Toby Tickler," the fictional editor of *The Corrector*[145]—may or may not have been affixed by Irving to his original album contribution. At any rate, the introductory comments in *The Ordeal* include the observation that the verses are "supposed to have been written by one of the authors of 'Salmagundi.'"[146] Since the *Weekly Visitor* had also indicated in general terms its awareness of the poem's authorship, it seems likely that in his album contribution—which has since been lost—Irving identified himself, if not by name, then by some easily recognizable pseudonym.

The three first printed texts of the poem, all derived from a single manuscript no longer extant and none prepared for publication under the supervision of the author, share many features in common. All are forty-eight lines in length, consisting of twelve quatrains arranged in an order identical to those in the Library of Congress manuscript, and recounting the same mythic tale of the creation of a sublime landscape by a passionately sorrowful spirit of the forest who is identified with the vanishing Indian races. However, each printed version differs from the others in many smaller features—not only in accidentals but in substantive readings up to several words in length. As an example of the variations between these three texts, their differing versions of the line corresponding to 150.33, in the manuscript "The axe of the white man enlivened the shade," are given below: (1) *Weekly Visitor*: "The axe of the white man has lightened the shade"; (2) *The Pastime*: "The axe of the white-man enliven'd the shade"; (3) *The Ordeal*: "The axe of the white man, has lighted the shade." In light of inconsistencies such as these, the faithfulness of all three published texts in reproducing the poem in the Godwin album must be regarded as doubtful.

On the other hand, some readings shared. in common by all three magazine texts differ from those at corresponding points in the Library of Congress manuscript, thus suggesting that the texts in the album and the surviving manuscript were not identical. For example, in the manu-

145. See p. xx and the Textual Commentary to Irving's contributions to *The Corrector*, p. 281–82.

146. "Poetry," p. 297. In their prefatory comment the editors go on to attack a rival magazine, the *Monthly Mirror*, for its strictures on *Salmagundi*, in which they profess to discover "genuine though playful excellence."

script version corresponding to 149.31, the penciled substitution of "that" for Irving's "who" corresponds to a consistent "that" in the magazines; at 151.2 the manuscript "embosomed" parallels a consistent printed "embosom'd." We thus have available as textual evidence, in addition to the Library of Congress manuscript, three unfaithful copies of a manuscript whose relationship to the surviving one is unknown (but may have preceded it),[147] and whose text probably differed at some points from it.

The poem was printed a fourth time, under the title "Lines Written at the Falls of the Passaick," in *The Port Folio* for May, 1814, pp. 487–89. Nothing is known for certain of the circumstances surrounding its publication in *The Port Folio* except that, in the issue for June, the editors of the magazine wrote a fulsome acknowledgment to "our much-admired correspondent" for his "elegant stanzas on the falls of the Passaic," indicating their willingness to include in subsequent issues any further works which might "flow from his pen." That Irving should thus be designated a "correspondent" suggests that he himself had supplied a copy of the poem. Quite possibly he did so. Although they were competitors, *The Port Folio* and the *Analectic Magazine*, the latter of which Irving was then editing, were by no means rivals.[148] In May, 1814, *The Port Folio* began publication under the supervision of a new editorial board, and it would not be surprising if they had solicited from Irving a contribution suitably to grace their first issue.

However this may be, it is apparent that the text of the poem in *The Port Folio* derives neither from the extant manuscript—which shows no signs of having been used as printer's copy—nor from any of the previously printed versions. In addition to a variety of accidental and brief substantive variants from each of the earlier texts, that in *The Port Folio* includes in one line a substantive reading which differs from all the others (see Rejected Variants, 150.10). The textual evidence is not conclusive, but the poem in *The Port Folio* appears to be based upon a third manuscript, now lost, whose relation to the first two is unknown. Irving was living in New York in May, 1814, and played no part in the final preparations in Philadelphia for the republication of his poem.

The work was printed a fifth time, under the title "On Passaic Falls. Written in the Year 1806," in *The Atlantic Souvenir; Christmas and New*

147. Irving's comment to Gouverneur Kemble on May 26, 1806, the date he wrote on the evidently copied Library of Congress manuscript, that he had just returned to the city suggests that his visit to Major Godwin's public house may have occurred before that time. It remains true, of course, that he could have written his verses in Godwin's album at any time before September 27, 1806, when they were first published.

148. See Introduction, pp. xxix–xxx.

Year's Offering. 1827, pp. 146–48. Because Irving was then living in Spain, he played no part in the final preparations of the poem for publication. He may indeed have authorized its appearance in this popular gift-book, whose publishers, Carey and Lea, had two years previously brought out the first American edition of *Tales of a Traveller*. There is no definite evidence that he did so, but it may be noticed that another of his poems, "The Dull Lecture," appeared in *The Atlantic Souvenir* for 1828, and that later in the latter year Carey and Lea agreed to lease for seven years the copyright to four of his back works.[149] These details lend plausibility to the suggestion that Irving or his agent supplied a copy of the Passaic poem to the publishers, either at their request or as an unsolicited favor.

Although in length and subject matter it is identical to the earlier texts, the *Atlantic Souvenir* poem differs from those versions in several respects other than its title and the signature, "WASHINGTON IRVING," appended to it. For example, it includes eighteen substantive variants from the Library of Congress manuscript, eleven of which involve substitutions of single words, such as "thunder" for "tempest" (150.2), "mark" for "marked" (150.30). Three of the remaining variants form a complex of two full lines (149.32–150.1):

Library of Congress Manuscript	*Atlantic Souvenir*
And deep in its gloom fix'd his murky abode	And had fixed in its glooomy recess his abode,
Who lov'd the rude scene that the whirlwind deforms	Loved best the rude scene that the whirlwinds deform,[150]

The minor substantive variants between these two texts resemble the somewhat finical revisions evident in collations of the Library of Congress manuscript with the other printed versions. The forty-three variants in punctuation between the two texts, which include no cancellations of any kind but thirty-one added commas, are also representative: in each case the printed texts are punctuated more liberally than the manuscript. The variants in spelling are representative as well, reflecting the consistent imposition in *The Atlantic Souvenir* text of conventions different from those followed in the manuscript. For example, preterit endings, anarchic in the manuscript, are printed according to clear and almost

149. PMI, II, 280.

150. Unless otherwise indicated, the additional substantive variants may be found at the following points in Rejected Variants: 149.31 (Emendations), 150.1, 150.2, 150.11, 150.14, 150.18 (Emendations), 150.24, 150.28, 150.29, 150.30, 150.31; 150.21 (Rejected Variants and Emendations), 150.22, 150.26, 150.29.

consistently observed principles: "-d" is ten times altered to "-'d", "-ed" is four times altered to "-'d", and "-'d" is three times altered to "-ed."[151] In short, the *Atlantic Souvenir* text reveals a sprinkling of substantive variants and numerous variants in accidentals from the Library of Congress manuscript, both of which classes are characteristic of the deviations between the manuscript and other printed texts.

However, the *Atlantic Souvenir* text affords no evidence that it derives from any of the printed versions. Rather, the patterns of variants between it and the preceding texts suggest that it derives from a source independent of them. As an instance of the lack of agreement betweeen the six texts reviewed thus far, their versions of a single line, corresponding to 150.21, are given below: (1) Library of Congress manuscript: "Where Passaic meanderd thro margins of green"; (2) *Weekly Visitor*: "Where Passaic meanders through margins of green"; (3) *The Pastime*: "Where Passaic meander'd through margins of green"; (4) *The Ordeal*: "Where Passaick meanders through margins of green"; (5) *The Port Folio*: "Where Passaick meanders in silence unseen"; (6) *The Atlantic Souvenir*: "Its river meand'ring through margins of green." The likelihood is that the source of the *Atlantic Souvenir* poem is a manuscript, now lost, written either "in the Year 1806" as the title specifies, or afterward. However, the relationship of such a manuscript to the one extant at the Library of Congress is undeterminable. All that is finally clear is that, even if the *Atlantic Souvenir* text was authorized for publication by Irving, he did not supervise the printing process. The substantives of the poem as published are thus of doubtful origin and the accidentals of severely limited authority.

The sixth printed text of the poem which appeared during the lifetime of the author is in Samuel Kettell's *Specimens of American Poetry*, II,173–74, where it was entitled "The Falls of the Passaic." Whether Irving authorized Kettell to include the poem in his anthology of verse is unknown; but since he was still living in Europe at the time *Specimens* appeared, he clearly played no part in editing and proofreading the text of his own work. The Kettell text differs significantly from all those which precede it. Four stanzas—corresponding to 150.7–18 and 150.27–30—in the earlier versions are omitted, and in the lines that remain variants from all the earlier versions occur. The inference is inescapable that Kettell relied upon a fifth manuscript copy of the poem (four of which are now lost), either prepared by Irving or copied by another person.

---

151. The *Atlantic Souvenir* text did include one "-'d" spelling ("roll'd," corresponding to 150.31); nine other variants in spelling occur between the manuscript and the *Atlantic Souvenir* text.

The Kettell text of "The Falls of the Passaic" formed the basis for several subsequent reprintings of the work during Irving's lifetime, none of which possesses independent textual authority.[152] We are thus presented with a situation in which Irving certainly wrote two manuscript versions of the poem (the Library of Congress manuscript and the entry in Godwin's album) and possibly as many as five, but only one of which is extant. None of the printed versions is based directly upon the surviving manuscript; those (in the *Weekly Visitor, The Pastime,* and *The Ordeal*) which purport to be "copied" from Godwin's album are obviously unreliable; and the three other versions of the poem published during Irving's lifetime and possessing any claim to independent textual authority (*The Port Folio, The Atlantic Souvenir,* and Kettell's *Specimens*), are all of dubious value, deriving as they do from unknown sources and having been prepared for publication by persons other than the author.

Despite the complex textual history of the poem, the choice of copy-text for this edition is inevitable: the Library of Congress manuscript clearly constitutes the best available evidence of Irving's intention for the work. Indeed, although he may well have been responsible for many of the variants noticed between the copy-text and the printed versions, the manuscript is the only certain evidence we possess of his intentions. Thus, despite its sparse punctuation, which may be owing to haste in writing out an almost-fair copy, the manuscript is emended only sparingly, in cases of ambiguity, clear indication of the author's contrary

152. In 1834 the poem was included in *Selections from the American Poets* (Dublin: W. F. Wakeman; London: Simpkin and Marshall, and Richard Groombridge; Edinburgh: Frazer & Co.), pp. 261–62. The *Selections* version includes only a single substantive variant from the one in Kettell's *Specimens*—"who" for the earlier "that" at a point corresponding to 149.31—and the same single variant from Kettell occurs in two other reprinted texts thus quite possibly derived from the 1834 *Selections: The Gems of American Poetry* (New York: A. & C. B. Edwards, 1840), pp. 105–6, and *American Melodies,* comp. George P. Morris (New York: Linen and Fennell, 1841), pp. 48–49. In 1837 Charles Fenno Hoffman reprinted Samuel Kettell's text in *The New-York Book of Poetry* (New York: George Dearborn), pp. 105–6. Hoffman reproduced the *Specimens* text with almost absolute faithfulness: the two versions differ in only two accidental readings and in no substantives. *The New-York Book of Poetry,* or else Kettell's *Specimens,* was the source for two further reprintings: the first, in *The Poets of America,* ed. John Keese (New York: S. Coleman, 1840), pp. 194–95, includes no substantive variants from Kettell or Hoffman; and the second, in Mrs. Caroline M. Kirkland's *Garden Walks with the Poets* (New York: G. P. Putnam, 1852), pp. 242–43, includes one—"streams" for the earlier "stream" at a point corresponding to 150.24. Finally, Evert A. Duyckinck included the poem, acknowledged as from *The New-York Book of Poetry,* in *Irvingiana,* p. lxiii; the posthumous reprinting includes no substantive variants from its source.

preferences, or outright error. In accordance with Irving's own habits and with correct usage, one variety of automatic regularization is undertaken in addition to those in effect throughout this volume: preterit endings spelled "-d" in the copy-text are emended to "-'d." As appurtenances to the text, serving only in a redundant manner to indicate extra spacing, the double flourishes between stanzas of the copy-text are not reproduced.

In the tables which follow this discussion the texts in the *New-York Book of Poetry* and *Irvingiana*, which have no authority, are not represented. In addition to cancellations within the copy-text, all substantive variants, and accidental variants of particular interest, between the copy-text and the first six printed versions of the poem are recorded. Collation records showing all variants between the copy-text and subsequent printed texts are on file at the University of Texas.

In the preparation of this edition the following collations have been made: (1) a typed transcription of the Library of Congress manuscript collated twice and independently with the text in a microfilm copy of the *Weekly Visitor* belonging to the New-York Historical Society, and once with a second copy owned by the Library of Congress (AP 2/ .L274); (3) the typed transcription collated twice and independently with the text in a microfilm copy of *The Pastime* belonging to the New-York Historical Society (AP 2/ .P), and once with a second copy owned by the Library of Congress (Rare Books AP 2/ .A2P3); (3) the typed transcription collated twice and independently with the text in a microfilm copy of *The Ordeal* belonging to the Library of Congress (AP 2/ A2O7/ 2d set); (4) the typed transcription collated twice and independently with the text in a microfilm copy of *The Port Folio* belonging to the Library of Congress (AP 2/ P 85/ Office), and once with a second copy, owned by the New York Public Library (*DA); (5) the typed transcription collated twice and independently with the text in the copy of *The Atlantic Souvenir* owned by Yale University (Ia 107/ At 635), and once with a second copy owned by the New York Public Library (NBA); (6) a xerox copy of the Yale University *Atlantic Souvenir* text collated with the text in a copy of Kettell's *Specimens* owned by Yale University (Is 55/ t 829), in a second copy owned by the University of Toronto (PS 586/ K3), and in a third copy owned by the New York Public Library (NBH); (7) the typed transcription collated twice and independently with the text in a copy of *The New-York Book of Poetry* owned by the New York Public Library (NBH); (8) the typed transcription collated twice and independently with the Yale University copy of Kettell's *Specimens*; (9) a xerox copy of the text in the New York Public Library's copy of *The New-York Book of Poetry* sight collated with the following additional copies: University of Delaware (PS 548/ N7 H6/ 1837); University of Virginia (PS 548/ .N7H6); (10) the above xerox copy of *The New-York Book of Poetry*'s text collated with the text in *Selections from the American Poets* (1834) owned by the Library of Congress (PS/ 586/ .S4); (11) the above xerox copy of *The New-York Book of Poetry*'s text collated with the text in *The Gems of American Poetry* (1840) owned by the New-York Historical Society; (12) the above xerox copy of *The New-York Book of Poetry*'s text collated with the text in *The Poets of America* (1840) owned by the University of Texas (811.08/ K258p) and with a second copy owned by the University of Delaware (Spec/ PS 586/ .K25/ 1840); (13) the above xerox copy of *The New-York Book of Poetry*'s text collated with the text in *American Melodies* (1841) owned by the Library of Congress (PS 586/ .M6) and with a second copy owned by the University of Delaware (Spec/ PS 586/ .M6/ 1841); (14) the above xerox copy of *The New-York Book of Poetry*'s text collated with that in *Garden Walks with the Poets* owned by the University of Texas (821.08/ K 635G); (15) the above xerox copy of *The New-York Book of Poetry*'s text collated with that in two copies of *Irvingiana*.

The sources of the text are (1) Author's manuscript, Library of Congress; (2) *Weekly Visitor; or, Ladies' Miscellany*, 4, no. 43 (September 27, 1806), 370 [error for 384], cols. 1–2; (3) *The Pastime. (A Literary Paper)*, 2, no. 2 (May 28, 1808), 27–28; (4) *The Ordeal*, 1, no. 19 (May 13, 1809), 298–99; (5) *The Port Folio*, n.s., 3, no. 5 (May, 1814), 487–89; (6) *The Atlantic Souvenir; Christmas and New Year's Offering. 1827* (Philadelphia: Carey & Lea, [1826]), pp. 146–48; (7) *Specimens of American Poetry*, ed. Samuel Kettell, 3 vols. (Boston: S. G. Goodrich & Co., 1829), II, 173–74.

See Discussions and Lists pp. 381, 401–02, 437–39.

ADDRESS OF COOPER ON ASSUMING THE MANAGEMENT OF THE PARK THEATRE

According to Pierre M. Irving, who first published a text of this poem in PMI, I, 204–8, Irving had "attempted, but left incomplete, an address for the opening" of the Park Theatre in New York for the season of 1806, when Thomas A. Cooper became its lessee and manager. Pierre noted that the manuscript of the work, since lost, was endorsed in Irving's handwriting "Address of Cooper on assuming the management of the Park Theatre"—that is, in 1806—but he added that the lines were spoken by Cooper on the night of September 9, 1807, a year later.[153]

153. PMI, I, 204.

Probably, therefore, the manuscript was a draft begun in 1806 and completed in 1807. Since no manuscript version of the poem is known to exist, and since the work was unpublished during the lifetime of the author,[154] the PMI version is adopted here as copy-text.

In the preparation of this edition the texts in three copies of PMI in the possession of the editor have been compared.

The source of the text is PMI, I, 204–8.

See Discussions and Lists pp. 381–82, 403.

SONG

This poem was first published, under the title "Song. / From Manuscript, by Washington Irving," in Gabriel Harrison's *Life and Writings of John Howard Payne* (1875), p. 397. Since Irving and Payne were well acquainted by October, 1810, the date printed immediately following the poem in the Harrison volume, and since in later years the two authors became close friends, it is not surprising that an Irving manuscript, or a copy of one, should have been among Payne's papers at his death in 1852. Thus, although no manuscript of the poem is known to survive, there is no reason to doubt Harrison's attribution. In the preparation of this edition the texts of the poem in the following copies of Harrison's *Life and Writings*, which is adopted as copy-text, have been compared: New-York Historical Society (PS/ 2533/ .H3); New York Public Library (MWES (Payne, J.)); Yale University (Iw/ P 293/ +S875H).

The source of the text is Gabriel Harrison, *The Life and Writings of John Howard Payne* (Albany: J. Munsell, 1875), p. 397.

See Discussions and Lists pp. 382, 403.

SIGNS OF THE TIMES

This poem was first published, preceded by a note explaining the circumstances of its composition,[155] in Gabriel Harrison's *Life and Writings of John Howard Payne* (1875), p. 398. Although, according to Harrison, Irving wrote the lines "on a leaf of a Psalm-Book," neither that book nor any other manuscript text of the poem is known to survive.

154. The poem was reprinted from PMI in *Opening Addresses*, ed. Laurence Hutton, Publications of the Dunlap Society, no. 3 (New York, 1887), pp. 22–26. The reprinted text has no textual authority.

155. See Introduction, pp. xxxiii–xxxiv.

Since Irving and Payne were well acquainted in New York before the latter departed for Europe in 1813, it is not surprising that this humorous song, filled with references to landmarks in the city, should have been among Payne's papers at his death in 1852. There is no reason to question Harrison's attribution of the work to Irving. In the preparation of this edition the texts of the poem in the following copies of the *Life and Writings*, which is adopted as copy-text, have been compared: New-York Historical Society (PS/ 2533/ .H3); New York Public Library (MWES (Payne, J.)); Yale University (Iw/ P293/ +S875H).

The source of the text is Gabriel Harrison, *The Life and Writings of John Howard Payne* (Albany: J. Munsell, 1875), p. 398.

See Discussions and Lists p. 403.

[LINES WRITTEN AT STRATFORD]

John H. Birss reported in 1932 that, in the house at Stratford-on-Avon where Shakespeare was born, there hung a framed manuscript on which was written, in Irving's hand, a quatrain of verse preceded by a first draft. Birss supplied a transcription of the entire text, noting that he had been informed that the manuscript had been presented to the Trustees and Guardians of Shakespeare's birthplace in 1870.[156]

A text of Irving's lines had appeared in print almost a century before Birss announced his discovery, however. The verses were first published in an anonymous article entitled "Washington Irving at Stratford-on-Avon," *The Albion*, March 2, 1833. The author of this brief account, who identified himself as an American and who wrote *"For the Albion,"* explained that he had visited Stratford in August, 1832, and had found at Shakespeare's birthplace "an Album or Register kept for visiters to inscribe their names," in which was a quatrain by Irving. The four lines of verse which he went on to quote differ only in accidentals from the final draft of the lines transcribed by John H. Birss.

A few months later the lines were published a second time in another New York weekly miscellany, the *New-York Mirror* for October 26, 1833. Again in this article, also anonymous, the quoted verses differ only in accidentals from the transcription by Birss of Irving's final draft. The *New-York Mirror* article is entitled "Scraps from the book kept at Stratford upon Avon. / From the letter of a friend in London." Because

---

156. Birss, "New Verses by Washington Irving," *American Literature*, 4 (November, 1932), 296. The first draft is as follows: "Great Shakespeare's b / [*line omitted*] / The house of Shakespeare's birth we here may see, / That of his death we find without a trace / Vain the inquiry, for Immortal he."

the article also includes commemorative lines written at Stratford by the American actor-playwright James H. Hackett, and because the American author of the earlier article in *The Albion* remarked that while at Stratford he had jotted down not only Irving's lines but those of "several others" as well, the possibility arises that the two magazine contributions of 1833 were written by the same person.

Shortly after Irving's death, N. P. Willis published in the *Home Journal* for December 24, 1859, a "chance-saved scrap of paper" written, he claimed, in September, 1835, during a visit to Stratford, and including Irving's quatrain, copied from the "book" of the landlady at the Red Lion inn of that town.[157] The quatrain thus introduced by Willis differs in only a single one-word substantive variant, and in accidental variants, from the Birss transcription. Willis would seem a likely candidate as the unknown author of the two articles in which the verses had earlier appeared—except that he had not even set foot in England until June 1, 1834,[158] and so could not possibly have transcribed the original Stratford quatrain for publication in *The Albion* and the *New-York Mirror*. At any rate, whoever the author or authors of the two 1833 articles may have been, no evidence suggests that Washington Irving himself was directly involved in the publication of either of those texts.

As deriving immediately from the author, and as providing the most complete text available, the transcription by John H. Birss—which in all probability reproduces the same manuscript original as formed the basis for the published versions that appeared between 1833 and 1859—is adopted here as copy-text.[159] All variants between it and the printed texts are reported in the tables which follow.

In the preparation of this edition the following collations have been made: (1) the Birss transcription collated twice and independently with the text in *The Albion* owned by the University of Texas (f051/ Al 14); (2) the Birss transcription collated with the text in the *New-York Mirror* owned by the University of Texas (051/ N48m) and by the

157. In the same issue of the *Home Journal*, p. 1, Willis reprinted an account of a visit he had made to Stratford "in 1836" (*sic*). Probably this article had originally appeared in the *New-York Mirror*, to which Willis had directed weekly letters between 1832 and 1836. However, it is clear from his comments that the visits described in the reprinted article and in the note introducing Irving's verses were the same; and in the latter commentary the day in Stratford is noted precisely from his "memorandum-book": September 18, 1835.

158. Henry A. Beers, *Nathaniel Parker Willis* (Boston, 1890), p. 130.

159. Professor Ralph M. Aderman kindly made plans to consult the original manuscript while in England in 1975, working on behalf of the Irving edition. However, his studies in the archives of John Murray and Sons, Ltd., London, prevented him from making the trip to Stratford. The Birss transcription, which purports to be exact, must thus stand in lieu of a new one.

New-York Historical Society; (3) the Birss transcription collated twice and independently with the text in the *Home Journal* in the possession of the editor.

The sources of the text are (1) "Washington Irving at Stratford-on-Avon," *The Albion*, n.s. 1 (March 2, 1833), 72, col. 1; (2) "Scraps from the book kept at Stratford upon Avon," *New-York Mirror*, 11 (October 26, 1833), 136, col. 1; (3) N. P. Willis, "A Note for the Reader," *Home Journal*, no. 724 (December 24, 1859), p. 2, col. 1; (4) John H. Birss, "New Verses by Washington Irving," *American Literature*, 4 (November, 1932), 296.

See Discussions and Lists pp. 382, 403, 439.

WRITTEN IN THE DEEPDENE ALBUM

This poem, of which no complete manuscript text survives, was first published shortly after Irving's death, in the *Cornhill Magazine* for May, 1860. Entitled "Written in the Deepdene Album" and followed by the author's signature and the date "*June 24th*, 1822," it was accompanied by no further comment. Yet that it was in fact the work of Irving is indicated by several details. First, during June, 1822, he did spend a few days at Deep Dene, Surrey, as the guest of its owner, Thomas Hope; the poem was no doubt his contribution to an album Hope kept on hand as a repository for the sentiments of his many visitors. Second, Pierre M. Irving reprinted the *Cornhill Magazine* text in PMI, in juxtaposition with a letter Irving had written from Deep Dene on June 21, 1822, expressing to his sister Mrs. Catharine Paris his wishes "to enjoy the affection of my relatives while living, and leave a name that may be cherished by the family when my poor wandering life is at an end."[160] The similarities of sentiment between the letter and the poem dated three days later suggests that the verses are Irving's own rather than, as was the case on occasion, ones appropriated by him from the published works of another.[161] The attribution is confirmed by early drafts of two stanzas, the third and fourth, of the published poem, extant in a

160. PMI, II, 85.
161. In 1832, having declared to Emily Foster that "it was impossible for him to be less in a writing mood," Irving copied into her scrapbook Sir Egerton Brydges' "Echo and Silence"; see PMI, IV, 405–6. Miss Foster seems to have assumed the poem was Irving's own, but he had copied it into his own book of extracts from Brydges' *Recollections of Foreign Travel* (London, 1825), II, 20–21; see *Journals*, III, 714–15. For further discussion of Emily Foster's misattribution, see Francis P. Smith, "Washington Irving, the Fosters, and Some Poetry," *American Literature*, 9 (1937), 228–32.

notebook Irving entitled "Notes, Extracts, &c / at various dates"; see *Journals*, III, 744. The nine lines in the notebook clearly represent an early stage of composition and are of no use for establishing a critical text;[162] nevertheless, they do establish Irving's authorship of the published poem.

The text published in PMI differs from the first printed version in minor respects. It omits the signature at the close, moves the dateline to a point immediately beneath the title, alters two spellings, and introduces seven variants in punctuation; but clearly these changes are the results either of the imposed Putnam house style or the particular wishes of Pierre M. Irving. The textual authority of the PMI text derives solely from that published in the *Cornhill Magazine*. The earlier version is accordingly adopted as copy-text. Substantive variants between the two texts are reported in the tables which follow; a full collation record is on file at the University of Texas.

In the preparation of this edition the following collations have been made: (1) a xerox copy of the *Cornhill Magazine* text owned by the University of Toronto (AP 4/ C 76) compared with two additional copies owned by York University (AP 4/ C 8); (2) the above xerox copy collated with the texts in three copies of PMI in the possession of the editor.

The sources of the text are (1) the *Cornhill Magazine*, 1, no. 5 (May, 1860), 582; and (2) PMI, II, 85–86.

See Discussions and Lists pp. 404, 439.

TO MISS EMILY FOSTER ON HER BIRTH-DAY

Irving wrote these verses on May 3 and 4, 1823, and on the latter day he sent them to Emily Foster's mother with a note enjoining her, if she thought best, to "slip them into the stove, that convenient altar, and sacrifice them as a burnt-offering to appease the Muses"; they remained unpublished during his lifetime. Their first appearance in print was in PMI, where Pierre M. Irving introduced them with the observation that, as "it was but rarely that Mr. Irving kindled into poetry, the reader may not object to see this further specimen of his rhymes."[163] A second text of the poem is in Emily Foster's manuscript journal, extant

---

162. Five lines (and one additional, a false start) were thoroughly revised in the corresponding *Cornhill Magazine* text. For example, "Scatter thy seed to every wind" in the early draft became "Throw seed to every wind that blows" (156.29); and in the remaining three lines three other substantive variants occurred.

163. PMI, II, 151–52; the poem appeared on pp. 152–53.

in the Yale University Library; she transcribed the work into her entry for May 4, 1823, pp. [123–24].[164] No manuscript version in Irving's own hand is known to survive. The PMI text of the poem, which is preceded by Irving's note to Mrs. Foster transmitting it, is entitled "To Miss Emily Foster on Her Birth-Day"; Emily Foster's transcription is entitled "Washington Irving 1823." Both versions consist of seven quatrains, and aside from their different titles they reveal only two substantive variants (see Rejected Variants, 158.2, 158.9). Accidental variants between the two texts include six variants in spelling and twenty-six in punctuation.

Since Irving's own manuscript is missing, the fact that Emily Foster's transcription forms part of a manuscript that antedates Pierre M. Irving's printed text is irrelevant to the choice between them as prospective copy-texts: both are one step removed from what the author wrote. In preparing PMI, Pierre obviously had before him a manuscript version of the poem, along with Irving's letter to Mrs. Foster. Quite possibly, in fact, he used the same manuscript the author had sent to the Fosters forty years before. On at least one other occasion the Fosters returned to Irving a written communication he had sent them, which latter manuscript was in Pierre's possession at the time PMI was published.[165] The fact that Emily decided to transcribe Irving's offering into her journal lends weight to the possibility that Irving's birthday poem was to be returned. Moreover, that the substantives in her text and Pierre's are almost identical suggests their common derivation from a single source.

For several reasons, the verses as published in PMI seem probably to approximate Irving's original wishes more closely than those in Emily Foster's journal. First, Pierre's title is a much likelier choice than "Washington Irving 1823," which Emily no doubt wrote as a kind of identifying reference title rather than as part of her transcription. Second, the physical appearance of the verses in the published text, with the second and fourth lines of each stanza slightly indented, is consistent with Irving's habits as revealed in two of the three poems for which manuscript evidence is available;[166] in her transcription Emily Foster

164. The manuscript journal has been edited and published by Stanley T. Williams and Leonard B. Beach as *The Journal of Emily Foster* (New York, 1938); the transcribed poem appears on pp. 131–32.

165. The manuscript was an autobiographical narrative Irving had addressed to Mrs. Foster on June 19, 1823, explaining why he was not married. Pierre M. Irving published a portion of it in the PMI, I, 224–27. The full text of Irving's confession is in STW, II, 255–62.

166. "¡Ay Dios de mi alma!," pp. 158–59, and "The Lay of the Sunnyside Ducks," pp. 159–60. In the manuscript of *"Passaic—A Tradition,"* pp. 149–51, Irving did not indent alternate lines.

began all the lines flush with the left margin. Third, the accidentals in PMI, even though presumably normalized in accordance with the Putnam house style, are probably more consistent with those in Irving's original manuscript than the text in the Foster journal. It is reasonable to suppose that in writing out verses which had taken him at least two sittings to complete, and which he intended to offer as a birthday gift to a young lady he deeply admired, he would have prepared his manuscript with care.[167] However, Emily Foster's transcription clearly reflects a certain casualness, either on Irving's part, or, more probably, on her own. Her text of the verses is consistent in some features of spelling and punctuation with her lax habits in these matters as revealed in the rest of her journal. For example, she wrote "&" much more often than "and" (her text five times employs the abbreviation, whereas that in PMI uses the fuller form). Similarly, she tended to end sentences with dashes; and contrary to Irving's habits as a poet, at two points she ended stanzas wiith dashes rather than the periods which appear at the corresponding points in PMI. In short, her transcription of the poem is a "Fosterized," just as Pierre's printed text is probably a "Putnamized" version, quite possibly of the identical manuscript. Manuscript evidence relating to Irving's other poems, the biographical evidence of his regard for Emily Foster and his care in preparing the poem for her, and the punctilious manner in which he presented the verses to her mother, all suggest that the fully spelled and conventionally punctuated PMI text is more in keeping with his original wishes than the comparatively careless transcription by Emily Foster. Accordingly, the PMI version is adopted here as copy-text. A full accounting of substantive and accidental variants between the two texts is given in the tables which follow.

In the preparation of this edition the following collations have been made: (1) the text in the manuscript journal of Emily Foster collated against the transcription of it in the published *Journal of Emily Foster*, pp. 131–32; (2) the published *Journal* text collated twice and independently with the text in a copy of PMI in the possession of the editor; (3) the PMI text sight collated with the texts in two additional copies of PMI in the possession of the editor.

The sources of the text are (1) PMI, II, 152–53, and (2) the manuscript journal of Emily Foster, pp. [123–24] (Beinecke Library, Yale University).

See Discussions and Lists pp. 404, 440.

---

167. The manuscript of "The Lay of the Sunnyside Ducks," Irving's offering to a five-year-old neighbor girl in 1855, is neatly written, carefully punctuated, and devoid of the abbreviated spellings he often employed.

THE DULL LECTURE

These verses, of which no manuscript text is known to survive, were first published in a gift-book prepared by the firm of Carey, Lea, & Carey, *The Atlantic Souvenir; Christmas and New Year's Offering. 1828*, p. 294. The poem took its title from an engraving of a painting by G. S. Newton which was reproduced opposite the title page of the volume. Because Irving was in Spain at the time *The Atlantic Souvenir* appeared, he played no part in the actual printing process. Probably he had authorized the publishers, with whom he was then in treaty for rights to produce a collected edition of his works, to include this minor accompaniment to Newton's picture if they wished. The poem was not reprinted during the author's lifetime, but it was included by Evert A. Duyckinck in *Irvingiana*, p. lxiii, with an inaccurate note that it was taken from Charles Fenno Hoffman's *New-York Book of Poetry* (1837), in which it had not appeared.[168] The *Irvingiana* text clearly derives from that in *The Atlantic Souvenir*, but it is altered in several ways. Most notably, Irving's archaic spellings are at ten points emended to contemporary ones. Other changes include indenting alternate lines, the omission of the subtitle and of Irving's signature at the end of the poem, and five additional emendations of accidentals. Whether authorized by Duyckinck or effected by the printer of this hastily produced volume of miscellanea, the altered readings in the *Irvingiana* text carry no textual authority. The *Atlantic Souvenir* version of the poem is thus adopted as copy-text. Substantive variants and variants in spelling between it and the *Irvingiana* text are recorded in the tables which follow.

In the preparation of this edition the following collations have been made: (1) a xerox copy of the *Atlantic Souvenir* text owned by Yale University Library (Ia 107/ At 635 v.3) sight collated with a copy owned by the New York Public Library (NBA); (2) the above xerox copy collated with the text in two copies of *Irvingiana*.

The sources of the text are *The Atlantic Souvenir; Christmas and New Year's Offering. 1828* (Philadelphia: Carey, Lea, & Carey, [1827]), p. 294, and (2) *Irvingiana*, p. lxiii.

See Discussions and Lists pp. 404, 440–41.

---

168. The erroneous citation was printed as a note to the title of a section in *Irvingiana*, "Two Poems by Washington Irving," p. lxiii. The second of the two selections, "The Falls of the Passaic," had in fact been included in Hoffman's anthology; see above, p. 328, n. 152.

[¡AY DIOS DE MI ALMA!]

A holograph manuscript of this poem, which remained unpublished during Irving's lifetime,[169] is owned by the University of Virginia. Written with care in black ink on both sides of a sheet of heavy cream-colored paper 5½ x 8⁹⁄₁₆ inches in size, the text includes not a single cancellation. Followed by his signature and the dateline "London. Sept. 9ᵗʰ 1830," Irving's poem in Spanish was evidently his contribution to a guest-book or an album or scrapbook from which it has since been separated.[170] There is no reason to suppose it was not of his own composition. The University of Virginia manuscript is adopted here as copy-text.

The source of the text is the author's manuscript at the University of Virginia.

See Discussions and Lists p. 404.

THE LAY OF THE SUNNYSIDE DUCKS

A holograph manuscript copy of this poem, which remained unpublished during Irving's lifetime, is in the possession of a descendant of the author's brother Ebenezer Irving, Mrs. Florence F. Locke of Milton, Massachusetts.[171] The manuscript text is written with (for the elderly Irving) considerable care, in dark brown ink, on a single sheet of paper folded at the center to form a booklet of four pages, each 6½ x 8 inches in size.[172] The manuscript is nearly a fair copy and evidently represents a late stage, if not indeed the final stage, of composition. On the second and third pages (the fourth is blank) the text includes only two can-

169. It was first published by Richard E. Peck in his note, "An Unpublished Poem by Washington Irving," *American Literature*, 39 (May 1967), 204–7.

170. Both sides of the sheet on which the text is written include oval sepia smudges, approximately four inches high, as if they had been pressed against engravings. As filed at the University of Virginia, the manuscript is accompanied by another loose sheet of paper identical to it in size, type, and smudging. On one side of this latter sheet, written in ink, is a sixteen-line poem which begins "O not for me, O not for me / Is England's gloomy scenery!" and is signed "John Bowring" and dated "London July 7. 1831." At the bottom of this page is a penciled note: "From Mrs. Roosevelt's scrap book. (Put with W Irving)."

171. Mrs. Locke has kindly made the manuscript available for study in the preparation of this edition.

172. The paper, now yellowed and slightly foxed, has in the upper-left-hand corner on the first page an embossed monogram with "Paris" printed across the device. No marks but Irving's appear, except a penciled "Washington Irving" written in an unknown hand at the bottom of the third page.

cellations, each of a single word, and one interlineation. The first page reveals ampler evidence of Irving's propensity for minor tinkering with works he had "completed." At one point almost an entire line is canceled and a substitution inserted above it, and elsewhere four less extensive alterations are made.[173] Whether this slightly corrected manuscript is the one the author sent in 1855 to his young neighbor Miss Florence Jaffray, or whether he wrote out a fresh copy and sent that to her, is unknown.

The poem was first published in James T. Scharf's *History of West-chester County, New York* (1886), I, 239–40, where it formed part of a letter furnished to the author by Edward S. Jaffray, the "Laird of Jaffray Hall" in Irving's poem. As it appeared in the *History*, the text of the work included six substantive variations from the extant manuscript. Of these, four involved single words, one involved a transposition of two words, and the last was the omission of a footnote.[174] As an indication that the variant readings in this printed text may have been departures from Irving's intention, it may be noted that none of the variants in the Jaffray poem corresponded to the text on the first page of the extant manuscript, which Irving had slightly revised; all corresponded to the second and third pages, which in the manuscript are virtually fair copies and appear thus to embody his considered wishes. Moreover, of the six variants at least one was a clear error: for "eke" in the manuscript "No longer shall it run down to Sunnyside pond / Nor eke to the Tappan Sea" (corresponding to 160.15–16), the published text substituted "e'en"—an absurdity, since the topographical level of the Tappan Sea was *below* Sunnyside pond.

The poem was next published in Mrs. J. Borden Harriman's *From Pinafores to Politics* (1923), pp. 22–23. Mrs. Harriman, a niece of Florence Jaffray, appears to have based her text upon the version in her grandfather's letter to J. T. Scharf. Her introduction of Irving's verses closely parallels Jaffray's prefatory comments, and her remarks immediately following the poem also echo his.[175] Mrs. Harriman's text

173. In the order specified in the two preceding sentences, see Emendations, 160.29, 160.31, 160.29; 160.3; 159.36, 160.1, 160.2, 160.3.

174. In the order specified, see Rejected Variants, 160.11, 160.11, 160.16, 160.34; 160.14; 160.36. Jaffray's text included five spellings different from those in the extant manuscript, and four variants in capitalization. For each of the three speeches by characters in the poem, Jaffray supplied pairs of single quotation marks. His text also includes double quotation marks, all without precedent in the manuscript, preceding the first, third, and fourth lines of its title, at the beginning of each of the nine stanzas, and at the end of the final stanza; it includes fifteen other accidental variants, two pertaining to type style and the remainder to punctuation.

175. For example, after quoting "The Lay of the Sunnyside Ducks" each author introduced a reply to it prepared supposedly by Florence Jaffray. Edward S. Jaffray

of "The Lay of the Sunnyside Ducks" includes five substantive variants from the extant manuscript, and these readings duplicate four of the six substantive variants from the manuscript in the Jaffray text. The only substantives in the earlier version not reproduced by Mrs. Harriman are the incorrect "e'en"—which is restored to "eke"—and a transposed reading which is also restored to the original order (160.14). That the later printed text should thus return to the one in Irving's manuscript is of some interest, for it raises the possibility that Mrs. Harriman had access to a textual authority other than her grandfather's letter— either the extant manuscript or else another, which latter his since disappeared. Although that may indeed have been the case, the weight of the evidence suggests it was not. The substitution of "eke" for "e'er" in the context of the poem was after all a natural one, since the latter word obviously required correction. Moreover, the accidentals in Mrs. Harriman's text closely resemble those in the Jaffray version.[176] Except for the two substantive variants between it and the earlier printed poem, Mrs. Harriman's version demonstrates no claim to textual authority independent of the Jaffray text.

As the latest available evidence of Irving's own wishes for the poem, the manuscript in the possession of Mrs. Florence F. Locke is adopted here as copy-text. This manuscript may not have been used by Edward S. Jaffray in preparing his letter for J. T. Scharf or by Mrs. Harriman in preparing her version; but on the other hand, it may well have been a textual authority for one or both of the printed versions. A full accounting is given in the tables which follow of the variants between the manuscript and printed versions; variants within the copy-text are also recorded in full.

In the preparation of this edition the following collations have been made: (1) a xerox copy of the text in Scharf's *History* owned by the

---

wrote: "To this [i.e., Irving's poem] Florence (with some assistance, as you may suppose) returned the following answer:" Mrs. Harriman's comment was: "Aunt Florence's reply, I suspect, was written by grandfather." As if to suggest that she was quoting from memory, Mrs. Harriman added: "Bits of it I recall ran as follows." However, her text of the sixty-one-line "Reply to the Lay of the Sunny-side Ducks" includes only a single one-word substantive variant from the version of the poem Jaffray had published almost forty years before ("But" for earlier "And," line 8).

176. For example, all four of the variants in capitalization between the poem in *From Pinafores to Politics* and the manuscript duplicate those between the Jaffray text and the manuscript; like Jaffray, Mrs. Harriman enclosed the three direct quotations within the poem in single quotation marks and the work as a whole in double quotation marks; and in addition, two variants in spelling and four others in punctuation between her text and the manuscript were identical to the variants between the manuscript and the verses quoted in Edward S. Jaffray's letter.

University of Delaware (F/ 127/ .W5/ S3) sight collated with an additional copy owned by the New-York Historical Society (F 127/ .W553); (2) a typed transcription of the manuscript collated twice and independently with the above xerox copy; (3) a xerox copy of the text in *From Pinafores to Politics* owned by the New-York Historical Society (CT/ .H2973A3) sight collated with an additional copy owned by the New York Public Library (AN (Harriman, F.)); (4) the typed transcription of the manuscript text collated twice and independently with the above xerox copy of the *From Pinafores to Politics* text.

The sources of the text are (1) the author's manuscript, in the possession of Mrs. Florence F. Locke, Milton, Massachusetts; (2) James T. Scharf, *History of Westchester County, New York*, 2 vols. (Philadelphia: C. E. Preston, 1886), I, 239–40; (3) Mrs. J. Borden Harriman, *From Pinafores to Politics* (New York: H. Holt & Co., 1923), pp. 22–23.

See Discussions and Lists pp. 382, 404–05, 441–42.

[*THE FREYSCHUTZ*]

On January 13, 1823, then at Dresden, Irving began his daily journal with a notation that he had been "Busy with Col Livius about the songs & music of the Freischutz."[177] Livius, the amateur composer and dramatist, who since Irving's arrival in Dresden the previous November had become his frequent companion, had himself come to the German city in order if possible to purchase from Karl Maria von Weber the score of his famous opera, *Der Freischütz* (1821), and the right to adapt it for presentation on the English stage.[178] Probably owing to the influence of various literary personalities whom he assiduously cultivated, Livius was successful. Recognizing Irving's enthusiasm for amateur stage representations, his familiarity with dramatic literature, his impatience at having no literary project immediately at hand, and perhaps also the future usefulness of his established reputation, Livius encouraged him to become, like himself, an adapter of plays. Why, indeed, should they not collaborate in adapting *Der Freischütz*? Despite Irving's as yet modest proficiency in German, in January they began doing so. Probably they returned to the lyrics from time to time until May 20, when Irving left Dresden in company with another friend,

177. *Journals*, III, 112.
178. Percival R. Kirby, "Weber's Operas in London, 1824–1826," *Musical Quarterly*, 32 (July, 1946), 333–53; "Washington Irving, Barham Livius, and Weber," *Music and Letters*, 31 (April, 1950), 133–47, esp. p. 140.

Lieutenant John Cockburn, for a month's tour of Silesia and Bohemia.[179]

In the course of this journey Irving gave what was apparently his most sustained and serious attention to translating and adapting the play. Cockburn took ill in Prague; and between May 30 and June 4, to pass the time while his companion recuperated, he wrote and revised a translation of the libretto of *Der Freischütz* by Friedrich Kind (1768–1843).[180] Irving's interest in the opera must have remained thoroughly aroused during the remainder of his tour with Cockburn, for he saw it performed on two occasions before his return to Dresden on June 26.[181] Probably the period between that date and mid-July, when he left Dresden permanently, was the one of his closest collaboration with Livius in preparing a saleable text of the libretto,[182] but Irving kept up an active interest in the work for some time afterward. In October, then in Paris, he dispatched John Howard Payne to London with a manuscript of the *Freischütz* text to be offered to the theaters, and in the same month he sent texts of *Freischütz* lyrics to Livius, who was at Weimar. In December he advised Payne not to give himself "any trouble" further about marketing the work,[183] but he continued to follow Livius' separate negotiations in the months that ensued. From August to October, 1824, he assisted Livius in making final revisions to the play, which was then about to be produced and published in London. Although it appeared under Livius' name only, the published *The Freyschütz* was demonstrably—its songs excepted—the product in large part of the collaborations between Livius and Irving more than a year earlier.[184]

Irving's own text of the translated libretto remained unpublished during his lifetime.[185] The sole surviving evidence of his intentions for the work, as modified at a few points by Livius, is a manuscript owned by the Manuscript Division, New York Public Library (hereafter cited as NYPL). The manuscript, which consists of sixty-two sheets of unlined paper of various textures, ranging in size from 4½ x 8¼ to 4⅞ x 7¼ inches, includes text written on 107 sides; that is, seventeen sheets include text

179. *Journals*, III, 113, 169, n. 55.

180. *Journals*, III, 169–70. See *Friedrich Kind's Theaterschriften*, 4 vols. in 2 (Grimma, 1827), IV, 234–332; further citations of the Kind libretto refer to this text. For a discussion of the folklore origins of the opera, see Felix Hasselberg, *Der Freyschütz: Friedrich Kinds Operndichtung und ihre Quellen* (Berlin, 1921).

181. Walter A. Reichart, *Washington Irving and Germany* (Ann Arbor, 1957), p. 198.

182. *Journals*, III, 181; Reichart, *Washington Irving and Germany*, p. 123.

183. Thatcher T. Payne Luquer, "Correspondence of Washington Irving and John Howard Payne," *Scribner's Magazine*, 48 (October, 1910), 478.

184. See below, pp. 346–51, 354–55.

185. It was edited and published in 1924 by George S. Hellman under the title *The Wild Huntsman* (Boston: The Bibliophile Society).

on one side only.[186] Representing two separate drafts of the work, a few associated notes, and a fragment of the "hints" Irving wrote to Livius for the introduction to the 1824 *Freyschütz* text, this conglomerate manuscript sheds helpful light on stages of the collaboration between the two playwrights.[187] It provides the primary basis for an account of the genesis of Irving's own text between May and July, 1823.

The fable of *Der Freischütz*, as embodied in the libretto by Friedrich Kind, is as follows. Caspar, a hunter who has sold his soul to the Black Hunter—that is, the Devil—has almost reached the time of reckoning when he must forfeit his life. Max, another forester, hopes to marry Agathe, daughter of Cuno, the hereditary Forest Warden to Ottokar, Prince of Bohemia. However, the fulfillment of his wishes depends upon his success in a contest of marksmanship, to be held the following day, to determine the successor to Cuno: should he win, Agathe's hand is his. Sensing his anxiety, Caspar tempts Max to a meeting deep in the forest that midnight, where Samiel, the Black Hunter, will cast for him magic bullets whose supernatural qualities will enable him to win the next day's competition. Caspar has been slighted by Agathe and intends not only to sacrifice Max to the Black Hunter, as a substitute offering for himself, but also to see that Agathe is killed the next morning by one of the magic bullets. Max meets Agathe that night but invents an excuse for the journey he must make into the forest. Later he meets Caspar at the appointed place, the "Wolfschlucht" or "Wolf's glen," and a horrific scene of incantation ensues. Samiel forges six magic bullets for the use of Caspar; but a seventh, he warns, must fly in whatever direction he himself ordains.

At the competition the next morning Max, using the charmed bullets, shoots with unerring accuracy; but so does Kilian, a wealthy farmer, his principal rival for the post of Forest Warden. On the seventh shot, using the bullet set aside by the Black Hunter for his especial use, Max hits the mark; but not before his bullet has by providential aid glanced harmlessly off Agathe and then passed through the body of Caspar, inflicting a mortal wound. Kind's libretto ends here, with Agathe and Max looking forward to a happy life together, and joining in a final chorus:

186. The manuscript is irregularly paged by Irving and Livius. In the consistent system of pagination assigned it by the New York Public Library, the following pages include text on one side only: 16, 18, 25, 30, 32, 35, 36, 47–49, 51–54, 56, 57, 62.

187. Pages 55 and 55v ("verso") of the manuscript include text which does not pertain to *Der Freischütz*. The former, numbered 120, includes dialogue, written in ink by Irving, between two characters from an unknown play; their names are abbreviated "Les." and "Car." On page 55v are written two sums which apparently relate to the collaborative authorship of Irving and Livius on this unknown work.

Ja lasst uns zum Himmel die Blicke erheben,
Und fest auf die Lenkung des Ewigen bau'n;
Wer rein ist von Herzen, und schuldlos von Leben,
Darf kindlich der Milde des Vaters vertrau'n![188]

In his initial draft of the play, which he wrote out on forty-eight
sheets of paper (thirty of which are included in the extant manuscript),
Irving altered the names of almost all Kind's characters, reconceived the
central figure of Max, suitor to Agathe, and added two new characters:

Kind	*Irving*
Ottokar, Prince of Bohemia	The Duke
Cuno, Forest Warden	Conrad
Agathe, His Daughter	Bertha
Annchen, a Young Servant	Nina
Caspar ⎱ Foresters	Caspar ⎱ Foresters
Max ⎰	Albert ⎰
Samiel, the Black Huntsman	Urian, the Wild Huntsman
Kilian, a Rich Farmer	Andreas, a Roistering Braggart
Hermit	Hermit
Hunters	Hunters
	Christopher, a Tavernkeeper
	Marian, His Daughter

In Irving's version, Albert is proof against the temptations of Caspar,
whom he senses to be evil. Caspar is thus forced to tempt Andreas,
who has drunk too liberally at the tavern of Christopher, enticing him
by the prospect of using the magic bullets to gain the hand of Marian,
and in addition a daily ration of six free bottles of her father's wine.
Albert still makes his (now poorly motivated) journey into the forest
late at night, but it is Andreas who together with Caspar meets Urian
at the Wolf's glen.

Irving arranged his first draft in the following three-act structure.
Act 1, scene 1: *Afternoon*: Andreas vaunts at his recent successes in
marksmanship and taunts Albert for his uncharacteristic failures. Albert
is anxious about the outcome of tomorrow's contest; scene 2: *Early evening*: Nina and Bertha visit a holy hermit who gives them a bunch of
white roses to be woven into a bridal wreath for Bertha; scene 3: *Evening*: Caspar soliloquizes about his predicament and attempts to tempt
Albert, but he is unsuccessful. Act 2, scene 1: *9 P.M.* Bertha and Nina
at home, awaiting Albert. Albert arrives, comforts Bertha in her anxiety

188. Kind, *Der Freischütz*, IV, 316.

about the outcome of tomorrow's contest, and excuses himself to go into the forest to meet "a villager at the place where the wolf lies—that I killed"; scene 2: *Later in the evening*: Andreas carouses at Christopher's tavern. Caspar enters, succeeds in tempting him to witness the forging of the magic bullets at midnight, so as to use them the next day; scene 3: *Midnight*: The scene of incantation. Act 3, scene 1: *Morning*: Bertha and Albert meet outside the hunting lodge. She has a "presentiment" of evil, but he comforts her and then departs to join the contest; scene 2: *At the contest*: Albert has fired six shots successfully, and Caspar recognizes with consternation that "something holy blesses Albert's aim." Andreas requests the fated seventh ball, which Caspar intends for Bertha's heart, and is given it; scene 3: *Bertha's chamber*: Bertha prepares herself to attend the conclusion of the contest. She expresses her faith in providence; scene 4: *At the contest*: Andreas' seventh ball strikes and stuns Bertha but pierces the breast of Caspar, who dies. Andreas confesses his part in the forging of the magic bullets. He is contrite and is referred by the Duke to the holy hermit as a penitent. The Duke places Bertha's hand in Albert's, and the play concludes with a tableau.

In preparing this first draft Irving did not include lyrics corresponding to the various songs in the opera, but he indicated them (*"Aria," "Recitative,"* and so on) at the points where they were to be inserted. He did write texts of at least two songs and fragments of two more on unnumbered pages following the draft; but in light of his and Livius' attention to the songs earlier in 1823, it is by no means certain that he made an attempt to translate the other lyrics.[189]

As was his frequent failing, Irving paged his draft of the play irregularly, sometimes skipping a page, sometimes assigning no pagination whatever to entire scenes. It is not surprising, therefore, that when he submitted his work to Livius for inspection, the latter found it necessary for his own reference to assign consecutive page numbers to the work as a whole. For convenience, Irving's acts and scenes, his pagination, and Livius' pagination in watery red ink are set forth below as they cor-

---

189. Page 50 of the NYPL manuscript includes a crude translation of a "Cavatina" sung by Agathe/Bertha in act 3, scene 3 ("Und ob die Wolke"; see 188.32, and Kind, *Der Freischütz*, IV, 299). The translation is further described by Hellman in *The Wild Huntsman*, p. 98, n. 1. On page 51 of the NYPL manuscript Irving wrote a portion of a duet between Bertha and Nina in act 2, scene 1, parts of which he had attempted to translate on pp. 47–49 ("Schelm, halt fast!"; see Kind, *Der Freischütz*, IV, 268–70); on page 52 he wrote a translation of another portion of the duet, a few lines of which he had attempted to set down on page 50v. Page 53 includes an early version of a song by Andreas and the hunters in act 1, scene 1 ("Schau der Herr mich an als König!"; see 163.16–164.2, and Kind, *Der Freischütz*, IV, 243–44).

respond to the pages in the extant manuscript. The letter v in the right column signifies "verso"; "[n.n.]" signifies "no number."

Act, Scene	Number of Pages	Irving's Pagination	Livius' Pagination	NYPL Pagination
II, 1	9	[n.n.], 2, [n.n.]	18–22	58–62v
II, 2	22	1, [n.n.], 2–12, [n.n.], 13–17, [n.n.], 18, [n.n.]	23–34	7–18
III, 1	8	1–8	36–39	26–29v
III, 2	4	[n.n.], 10–12	40–42	30–32
III, 3	2	[n.n.]	43	33–33v
[III, 4] Scene Last	8	[n.n.]	44–48	34–38v
Song	1	[n.n.]	1	53
Song	2	[n.n.]	2–3	51–52

The entire first act of this draft (Livius' pp. 1–17), the scene of incantation (Livius' p. 35), and any songs on pages numbered by Livius above "3" are missing from the manuscript.[190]

Except for his pagination in faint red ink, Livius' marks on the extant portions of the draft were few. Possibly this was because, with Irving on hand, Livius could discuss his reactions to the text with the manuscript before them both. In any case, besides his pagination he made only two notations in the extant portions of the draft, both queries of single words.[191]

Perhaps as a result of his consultation with Livius, Irving made a few minor adjustments of his own, using dark ink. These included nineteen substantive revisions—ten involving cancellations and substitutions, six cancellations only, and three additions only. However, he does not appear to have regarded his revisions to the first draft as final touches to a work almost completed. Rather, they were apparently incidental to a larger notion in his mind even as he wrote them: a major reorganization of the play, altering it still more significantly from the Kind libretto. It is by no means certain that he undertook this revision at the instance of Livius, who in fact was to publish under his own name a play almost identical in organization to his first draft. But whether or

190. The original contents of the first act have been inferred from the extant portions of the original draft, the full extant text of the revised version, the full text of Livius' *The Freyschütz*, and the text of Kind's libretto, from which all the others were derived.

191. Livius underlined the words "lovelorn" and "luck" in a subsequently superseded passage (NYPL manuscript, p. 28, lines 10, 12).

not Livius encouraged him to prepare it, Irving's revised version was, so far as available textual evidence indicates, to represent his final intention for his own text of *The Freyschütz*.

Even though the contents of the lost first act of the original draft may be inferred with some confidence, it is of course impossible to specify how thoroughly Irving revised those portions of it which corresponded to the later version. By analogy between the first act of the final version and the third, for which early and late drafts of three scenes are extant, it would appear that the changes may not have been extensive. The chief difference between the revised first act (NYPL, pp. 1–25) and the one it superseded is clearly that, whereas Caspar's successful temptation of Andreas had earlier occurred in act 2, scene 2, *after* his failure to tempt Albert in act 1, scene 3, here it occurs before that confrontation; without bothering even to rewrite it, Irving simply shifted the successful temptation of Andreas to become the second scene of the first act. Thus, at the close of act 1, scene 1 (NYPL, pp. 1–6v), in which Andreas vaunts over his success thus far and derides Albert for his want of shooting skill, Irving now causes Caspar in soliloquy to outline his plans:

The Wild Huntsman! / inexplicable being! ↑⟨Fearful Urian⟩↓ Still he has kept his / word, and Albert spell bound by his / arts is driven ⟨almost⟩ to despair. Thus far / my project thrives. ⟨Hes in⟩ ↑Yes yes. Albert is in↓ the very state / of mind that suits my purpose—now / to work on ⟨his sinking hopes,⟩ ↑him,↓ ⟨and⟩ ↑to↓ temp[t] / him to the scene of incantation and throw / him into ⟨Urians⟩ ↑the Wild huntsmans↓ power. But should he / shun the snare! Some other victim must / be had—no time is to be lost—why ⟨aye⟩ / —a little wine and flattery will make an / easy dupe of that poor—&c &c &c[192]

192. The series of asterisks clearly indicates, in Irving's usual manner of doing so, that at this point the continuation of Caspar's speech is to be drawn from a manuscript already drafted. It seems virtually certain that he intended the first draft of Caspar's soliloquy, now missing, to conclude the scene. The text of the corresponding speech by Caspar in Livius' *The Freyschütz* (London, 1824), pp. 10–11, closely resembles Irving's. Even though the published text is not Irving's, he did participate in its composition. The continuation of Caspar's speech in the version published by Livius is thus given here as the closest available approximation of Irving's wishes for the conclusion of his first scene: "But Wilhelm [i.e., Irving's Albert], Wilhelm is my game. In gaining him I serve two purposes—appease the claims of my terrific creditor, and gratify this gnawing worm within, that craves and craves for vengeance. He, my rival—my favoured, hated rival! my safety will be doubly dear, if purchased with his ruin. Well, well, there's yet enjoyment, e'en for me, on earth: if, like a spider, I must crawl about this flowery world, yet, like a spider, will I weave my web and brew my poison. . . ."

Using "wine and flattery" to good advantage, in the following scene (NYPL, pp. 7–18) Caspar ensnares the foolhardy Andreas. The revised third scene (NYPL, pp. 19–25) portrays his unsuccessful temptation of the virtuous Albert.[193] Apparently dropped from the revised version is a counterpart to the original second scene, in which Bertha and Nina visit the holy hermit.

Act 2 of the revised play begins as before, with an interview between Bertha and Albert interrupted by the latter's appointment with a "villager" to retrieve the carcass of a wolf Albert has slain. For this scene Irving used the identical pages he had first shown to Livius. However, for the scene of incantation—earlier the third, now the second scene in the act—he wrote out a new version (NYPL, pp. 39–40v) expanded from the lost original text,[194] including careful stage directions and a further *"Private note"* to Livius concerning the manner in which the supernatural machinery accompanying this weird event ought to be presented.[195]

For act 3, as indicated above, Irving wrote revised drafts for each of the first three scenes; he did not alter their sequence, nor, apparently, did he include in them material which in the first draft had formed part of the earlier acts. His revisions to scenes 1 (NYPL, pp. 41–43v) and 2 (NYPL, pp. 36, 46v, 44v) consisted chiefly of the rephrasings from sentence to sentence which it was his custom to undertake, at times almost as an amusement. The early and later versions of scene 3 (NYPL, pp. 44, 45, 45v) are also similar up to the point following the indicated *"Song & chorus—"* (see 188.38) where Nina brings a supposed "wedding wreath" to her distraught mistress. However, the continuation of the scene, which had a precedent in Kind's libretto,[196] Irving had for some reason omitted from the first draft. Quite possibly, having decided to omit the scene in the early version portraying the interview between Bertha, Nina, and the hermit, he now included this later passage, with

193. The manuscript of Irving's *Abu Hassan* owned by the Manuscript Division, New York Public Library, includes on one page [16a] a fragmentary speech by Albert which may have formed part of the first draft of act 1, scene 3. A transcription follows: "*Alb.* I've heard of such a being—Some say it/ is the ↑restless↓ spirit of a hapless mortal, ↑doomd↓ ⟨who⟩ for/ his ⟨misdeeds is doomed to hunt the air and⟩/ ride the storm, and" (compare 178.32–35).

194. Apparently in the first draft the full scene had been written on the missing page 35 in Livius' sequence. In Kind's libretto the scene of incantation includes little dialogue, consisting primarily of careful description of the necessary stage effects; see *Der Freischütz*, IV, 292–94.

195. That Irving should thus have included such a note (184.26–37), clearly addressed to Livius, in the text of his revision suggests that whatever his ultimate plan for the manuscript may have been, his immediate intention was to use it as a contribution to the cooperative effort with Livius.

196. Kind, *Der Freischütz*, IV, 303–6.

its reference to the white roses received from the holy hermit, as a means of introducing that character at secondhand—thus rendering less unnatural his presence in the final scene.[197] Showing a characteristic instinct for economizing his own exertions, Irving adapted the text of that concluding scene to his revised draft without bothering to rewrite it. The revised version of the play reveals no evidence of further attempts to translate the lyrics which occurred at intervals throughout Kind's libretto.

Having completed his new draft, Irving scanned the patchwork manuscript, entering corrections to four scenes using dark ink of a shade identical to that he had used in his desultory corrections made before undertaking the revision.[198] The dark-ink emendations included twenty cancellations, the lengthiest of twenty-one words; twelve cancellations and substitutions, the lengthiest of which involved deleting twenty-three words and adding nineteen; four brief additions, and a few miscellaneous marks.

Irving's final attentions to the revised text, which he gave it prior to submitting the manuscript to Livius' inspection, were made in pencil to the play as a whole. Here, while he was clearly concerned with minor economies and adjustments of phraseology, he was also interested in his friend's reactions to more general features of the work—entire speeches, and indeed, the new arrangement of scenes. Thus, in addition to seventeen cancellations (one of twenty-three, one of twenty-four words), five brief insertions, and fourteen substitutions, at four points he solicited Livius' opinion, designating the passages in question by encircling them, by underlining them with series of dashes, or by writing vertical lines at appropriate points in the left margin.[199] Whether Irving was still in Dresden at the time he wrote these corrections and queries, or whether instead he mailed the manuscript to Livius, is unknown. Certainly it is clear that he was interested to learn his collaborator's reaction to the manuscript.

197. The portrayal of Nina's discovering a death wreath enclosed by accident in a package intended to contain a bridal bouquet is also formally appropriate; see 188.13–15.

198. Because three of these scenes—I, 2; II, 1; III, 4—are adapted from the earlier version, the possibility exists that the dark ink corrections to their texts, summarized here together with the similar corrections to the fourth scene so marked—I, 3—were written before Irving even began writing the final draft. However that may be, it remains that he subjected all four scenes to a close review, pen in hand, and that he did not revise at least one of them until after he had begun the final draft.

199. See Discussions of Adopted Readings, 172.40–173.2, 178.19–26, 187.31–38, 190.41–43. At a point corresponding to 188.11–12, the second line of the following passage is underlined with a series of dots and is cancelled, all in pencil: ⟨I'm the/ <Urian ↑Now↓ for my master stroke⟩>"

The revised text affords no clear indication, however, that Livius gave it the close attention Irving seems to have anticipated. The final draft includes only eleven marks by Livius, all but one in the text of the first act: two brief stage directions on the first page, seven minor alterations of from one to four words, and two "stet"s in terse response to Irving's queries.[200] While it is possible that the two men discussed the new draft thoroughly before Irving left Dresden, thus rendering textual marks by Livius unnecessary, the scarcity of his notations raises doubts as to the degree of his interest in this contribution to the project. By the fall of 1823 Livius had on hand a text of the play which he was attempting independently of his collaborator to place with a London theater. Possibly by the time Irving had completed his reshaping of the libretto, Livius had already satisfied himself with a text based upon his friend's first draft, which he had studied with care. At any rate, while the published fruit of the collaboration, *The Freyschütz; or, The Wild Huntsman of Bohemia* by "BARHAM LIVIUS, Esq.," was to reveal the pervasive influence of Irving's hand, Irving's own final draft appears from textual evidence to have been almost entirely his own composition.

In the fall of 1823, through the agency of John Howard Payne, Irving attempted without success to sell a text of the adapted libretto to the theaters. On November 12 he reported to Payne that a copy of the work sent him (apparently rejected) by John Miller, the London publisher, had been received, and the following month he directed Payne to abandon his marketing efforts as "only time and trouble thrown away." Meanwhile, he sought to follow the more persevering negotiations of Livius, who sent a "corrected copy" of the work to John Kemble, manager of the Covent Garden Theatre.[201] On December 28 Livius informed another acquaintance that "Mr. Kemble has written to me in the most kind & flattering way respecting the piece which I sent him . . . and expressed an *anxious wish 'to venture it.'* "[202] The following May, Livius wrote Irving that the work would definitely be produced the next season— that is, in the fall; and on August 27, 1824, shortly after the two had met again in Paris after a year apart, Irving recorded in his journal that "Livius tells me . . . the Freischutz is to be brought out . . . with great Splendor." Interestingly, he added immediately afterward: ". . . get the MS: from him."[203] In accordance with Irving's wishes, Livius had him-

200. See Emendations, 163.4, 163.14, 166.7, 169.2, 171.4, 173.39, 178.14, 178.25, 179.3; Discussions of Adopted Readings, 172.40–173.2, 187.31–38.

201. Luquer, "Correspondence of Irving and Payne," p. 472.

202. Livius to Karl August Böttiger, Berlin, December 28, 1823; in Walter A. Reichart, "Washington Irving's Friend and Collaborator: Barham John Livius, Esq.," *PMLA*, 56 (June, 1941), 523.

203. Reichart, "Irving's Friend and Collaborator: Livius," p. 525; *Journals*, III, 386.

self arranged for the production and publication of Weber's adapted opera; but once these matters were attended to, Irving resumed active co-partnership. Whether he and Livius had agreed on a financial arrangement to share the fruits of their cooperative effort is unknown. Certainly by his active participation in the final preparations of the libretto more than eighteen months after he had begun work on it, Irving displayed a more than casual interest in the success of the enterprise.

The "MS:" he had been given by Livius was not, of course, the prompter's copy for use at Covent Garden; the opera was produced there on October 14, and Kemble would have needed a complete manuscript on hand well before that time in order to arrange for performances of the "Splendor" he evidently had in mind. Rather, the manuscript was eventually to serve as printer's copy of the edition of the libretto which John Miller had agreed to publish. Between August 27 and October 11 Irving noted in his journal every few days that he had "looked over" or "corrected" parts of the play. That his suggestions were taken quite seriously by Livius is suggested by a comparison of the "hints for Livius' introduction to Freischütz," which he wrote on October 6, and which survive in fragmentary form, and portions of the published work.[204] Irving's hastily written commentary on the play as one distinct in conception from Kind's libretto, written in ink on one side of two pages numbered 2 and 3, comprises pages 56 and 57 in the NYPL manuscript. A transcription of the fragmentary manuscript "hints" appears below, beside Livius' rather literal adaptations of them. Irving's manuscript begins amid a discussion of defects in Kind's portrayal of Max, the hunter who succumbs to the temptations of Caspar yet ultimately wins the hand of his loved one:

Irving	*The Freyschütz*, pp. vi–vii.
twelve months. In fact the audience / is ⟨ultim⟩ ultimately left in doubt how / far he had committed himself in his / half sealed dealing with the fiend. / Whether he was to be saved or Damned, / or whether indeed, ↑from his weakness & indecision of character,↓ he were worthy of / either. /	yet the audience are left in doubt whether, though he gain his wife, he has not lost his soul, and they go away quite at a loss to determine whether he be ultimately to be saved or damned; or, indeed, whether he be worthy of either.
In the present Drama the Hero is made / to rise superior to temp-	Attempt has been made in the present Opera, to obviate this glaring defect, so far at least as was possible, in writing a drama

204. *Journals*, III, 402, 413.

tation; to spurn / at all base & underhand means of / securing success, and by his steadfastness / & faith to merit & receive the protection / of heaven. /

⟨The Another character is made to yield / to temptation, and by⟩ /

⟨The Another Another⟩ To carry on the / supernatural part of the story however / another person is made to yield to temp-/-tation & to seek the assistance of infernal / agency. ⟨This is For this an ignorant / fellow is chosen, puffed up by vanity / of transient success,⟩ and ⟨wa⟩ / He is represented as inflated by the / vanity of temporary success & the moment / of successful temptation is when he is / in the midst of dissolute revelry. ⟨He / yields however but a blind & blundering / spirit, not inherently really / bad, and⟩ /

The character of Caspar, ⟨the self-sold⟩ / the hunter who has sold himself to the / fiend, & who seeks to gain a respite by / furnishing fresh victims, has been / heightened and extended. ⟨to⟩ A more / poetical tone has been given to it, as / more suited to a being who ⟨who⟩ holds / communion with the invisible world, / ⟨and has been able to penetrate into the⟩ / and is familiar with such terrible agencies— /

A more vague ⟨& indistinct⟩ character / also has been given to the ⟨supernatural / being⟩ machinery of the fable

under the trammels of music already composed. It has been endeavoured to describe the hero of the piece inflexible in virtue—firm in resisting temptation, and spurning all base and sinister means of obtaining success; his confidence in Providence remains unshaken, and his steadfastness and constancy meet with their merited reward.

To carry on the supernatural part of the story, another character has been introduced, whose dissolute habits render him a fitter victime of seduction: he is taken in a moment of riot and revelry, and falls an easy dupe to the flattery and artifice of the tempter.

To the character of the hunter, who is in league with the evil spirit, it has been attempted to give somewhat of a more wild and poetic tone of colouring, as better suited to a being who is supposed to hold converse with the invisible world, and who is familiar with supernatural agencies.

A veil of uncertainty has been thrown over the evil power invoked and he appears shrouded in the fanciful and picturesque superstition of *"the Wild Huntsman,"* that favourite hero of the forest legends of Germany.

It would surely be unfair to Livius to propose on the basis of this sample that he virtually allowed Irving to dictate to him; the two men must

have discussed the play enough times to ensure a meeting of minds
at least on their general aims, which are described here. At the same
time it must be said that, besides adding flesh to the frame supplied
him by Irving's notes, Livius wrote nothing in this fragment of the
introduction to make it conceptually his own.

Of course Livius was placing his name alone on the title page in
deference to Irving's no doubt repeatedly expressed wish to remain
anonymous. He would have been pleased publicly to share responsibility for the play with "Geoffrey Crayon," but Irving would not have
it. The best Livius was able to do for his collaborator was, near the
close of the introduction, to take "the opportunity of stating the obligation he is under to [a] friend, whose name, were he permitted, it
would be his pride and his pleasure to declare, for various valuable
hints and emendations." Livius did not neglect to express gratitude to
"the manager of the theatre" nor to "the performers" of the play—in
short, to anyone who had been involved in writing or producing his
adaptation; but he singled out only one person by name: James R.
Planché, a popular playwright who had made some changes to the
text to prepare it for presentation at Covent Garden. "For whatever of
poetic merit this opera may possess," he wrote, "the author is beholden
to his friend, Mr. Planché. . . ."[205] But this profession of indebtedness
appears to have been a toadying gesture rather than an avowal of
genuine sentiment, for on October 22 Livius read to Irving what the
latter described as "a very conceited ungentlemanlike letter from Planche
about Freyschutz." The letter, in which Planché apparently took credit
for a greater portion of the libretto that Livius was prepared to grant,
seemed to Irving so unfair that the immediately "wrote letter to Miller
in [Livius'] behalf."[206] However lavish his ritual expressions of gratitude
to others, Livius evidently felt that *The Freyschütz* was essentially a
creation of himself and Irving.

In the absence of Livius' manuscript of the play, a precise estimate
of the proportionate contributions by him and Irving to the published
work is impossible to make. However, comparison of Irving's manuscripts with *The Freyschütz* reveals that, while Livius' phraseology was
pervasively influenced by that of his friend, it was not so nearly identical with that in the first or the later version as to suggest plagiarism
or even unquestioning acceptance of Irving's preferences. Similarly, while
Livius' general conception of the plot as revised from the Kind libretto
was identical with Irving's, he did not arrange it in the manner textual

205. Livius, *The Freyschütz*, p. viii.

206. *Journals*, III, 413. For Planché's account of his part in the Covent Garden
production, see his *Recollections and Reflections*, rev. ed. (London, 1901), p. 54, note.

evidence reveals to have been Irving's latest intention. As noted above, he followed a sequence of acts and scenes identical with that in Irving's first draft. Moreover, while his characterizations were identical with Irving's, to several characters he assigned names different from those adopted by his collaborator:

Irving	*Livius*
The Duke	Ottokar, Baron of Hohenwalde
Nina	Lina
Albert	Wilhelm
Urian (or, the Wild Huntsman)	The Wild Huntsman
Andreas	Killian

Unlike Irving, in the scene of incantation (act 2, scene 3) Livius portrays the actual casting of the seven magic bullets, specifying in his stage directions the necessary visual accompaniments (*Freyschütz*, pp. 37–43).

Probably the most striking divergence between Irving's manuscript and Livius' published text occurs at the conclusion of the two plays. As summarized above, Irving's final scene ends on a positive note consistent with that sounded by Kind: Caspar is dead, Bertha and Albert are about to be married, and Andreas is conditionally forgiven by the Duke. In contrast, omitting the other elements of Irving's concluding scene, Livius presents a chilling portrayal of Caspar being overcome by the Wild Huntsman (p. 55):

Caspar. Ha! caught in my own snare!—Defeated!—Lost!—Must I then fall, and drag no ruin with me? Let me go hence—the day grows dark—the air is thick and stifling!—Stand off, and let me breathe! Further!—further!—Hark!—what sounds!—'Tis the cry of hell-hounds!—He comes!—He comes!—I am beset!—Off!—Off!—They tear me!—Save me! Save me from their fangs!

[*He rushes towards a groupe of Hunters, who are standing before the tree. They fly from him with horror—he staggers and supports himself by clinging to a projecting, withered branch. The stage darkens, the thunder rolls, the tree disappears, and the figure of the Wild Huntsman is seen in its place, grasping* CASPAR *by the hand that seized the withered branch, which has become the arm of the Demon. A terrible crash of thunder follows, the Huntsman disappears with* CASPAR. *The stage becomes rapidly light again, and the curtain falls upon a general picture.*

Whether Irving preferred this grisly climax to his own thorough tying-up of loose ends—or whether indeed he was instrumental in drafting it, cannot of course be determined; certainly he was by October, 1824, familiar with the whole of Livius' final text.

Livius claimed in his introduction to *The Freyschütz* that to "preserve entire and uninjured the delicate and beautiful structure of [Weber's] music has been the object of the author's chief attention and anxiety" (p. vii). This remark may have been intended in part as a politic compliment to the famous composer whose score Livius had purchased, but probably also it was not devoid of truth. Livius was something of a musician, fancied his own skill as a composer of lyrics,[207] and accurately judged that the primary claim to memory of Weber's opera was its music. What part, then, did Irving play in drafting the sixteen songs which punctuate the text of *The Freyschütz?* Unfortunately, the evidence is too slight to warrant confident speculation: Irving's early draft included two attempts to translate Kind's lyrics and fragmentary translations of two more; his final version included the text of only one song, and that not closely resembling the corresponding text in Livius' play (pp. 2–3). On the basis of the almost total absence of lyrics from Irving's text, as edited by George S. Hellman and published as *The Wild Huntsman,* Percival R. Kirby and Walter A. Reichart have concluded, in the words of the latter, that "Irving had not been so much concerned with those portions of the opera that were to be sung."[208] Quite possibly this was so. It should be noted, however, that for *Abu Hassan,* Irving's other play prepared in collaboration with Livius, Professor Kirby concluded on the basis of somewhat fuller evidence that throughout their adaptation of that opera "each man helped the other, [and] their work represents, in general, a joint effort." In January and again in October, 1823, by his own account Irving was busy translating the songs, and only the songs of *Der Freischütz.* It may be true that, as Professor Kirby expresses it, Livius "was superior to Irving when it came to fitting singable works to music,"[209] but the latter appears to have made whatever contributions he could. If he was more interested in the play proper than in its music, he was surely not unaware that the plot was too flimsy to stand by itself. He would have agreed with the remark of Livius in his introduction to *The Freyschütz* that, revising Kind's libretto, one could hope only to have "remedied some of the most glaring defects in

207. *The Journal of Emily Foster,* pp. 115–16; Kirby, "Irving, Livius, and Weber," p. 143.

208. Reichart, *Washington Irving and Germany,* p. 130; Kirby, "Irving, Livius, and Weber," p. 143.

209. Kirby, "Irving, Livius, and Weber," p. 147.

the original piece, which appeared... a worthless **Drama**, embalmed in immortal Music" (p. vii).

The Freyschütz, as published in 1824—possibly with emendations by Planché[210]—was thus the result of a close collaboration at intervals between Irving and Livius. The extant manuscript notes and drafts of the libretto represent stages in that collaboration, but they also represent at least a fraction of Irving's independent contributions to the cooperative venture. The revised manuscript draft of the work, which exists in complete form except for the lyrics whose placements are indicated in it, is the latest available evidence of Irving's own intentions for the play and it therefore adopted as copy-text.[211] Having written this draft, Irving may afterward have agreed with Livius' decision to return to the arrangement of acts and scenes in the fragmentary first version, but there is no compelling reason to suppose he did. He clearly conceived of the second version forming part of the New York Public Library manuscript as a useful and substantial contribution to the joint task of adaptation, not an idea to be dismissed lightly. It seems reasonable to suppose that, if he had strongly disagreed with any of Livius' few emendations to the manuscript of the final version he would have restored his own readings as the more effective. Accordingly, unless subsequently canceled by Irving, Livius' infrequent changes to the manuscript are considered to form parts of the copy-text as the author intended it; but the authorship of each such emendation is noted at the appropriate point in the List of Emendations.

Because Irving's manuscript was working copy intended first for review by Livius and only possibly afterward by a prospective producer or publisher,[212] in writing it he revised as he proceeded and was far from scrupulous in supplying punctuation, avoiding abbreviations, and otherwise taking pains to prepare what might be considered finished copy. The copy-text includes hundreds of corrections in Irving's hand alone, chiefly brief substitutions (e.g., 164.4 ⟨borne⟩ endured—) or dele-

210. Irving's letter to John Miller, the publisher of *The Freyschütz*, which he wrote upon reading Planché's insulting letter to Livius, appears to have been a testimony in favor of Livius as the sole author of the work, presumably as a contradiction of Planché's claims.

211. For convenient reference, the pages in the NYPL manuscript which serve as copy-text are listed here: Act I. Scene 1 (1–6v); Scene 2 (7–18); Scene 3 (19–25); Act. II. Scene 1 (58–62); Scene 2 (39–40v); Act III. Scene 1 (41–43v); Scene 2 (46, 46v, 44v); Scene 3 (44, 45, 45v); Scene 4 (34–38v).

212. In view of his wish to remain anonymous as a collaborator with Livius, Irving's intention ever to submit a manuscript in his own handwriting to a theater manager or publisher must remain in doubt. The manuscript of *The Freyschütz* returned him by John Miller in November, 1823, may well have been a copy prepared by another person.

tions of false starts, but often rewritings of entire speeches, and on one occasion the cancellation and rewriting of a full page (168.2–13).[213] Limitations of space render it impracticable to list all canceled passages in the List of Emendations; those only are set forth which reveal in an economical fashion the textual situation necessitating an editorial decision (e.g., see Emendations, 167.29–30), provide textual bases for Discussions of Adopted Readings (Emendations, 182.44–183.2), or pertain to revisions by Livius.[214] A full list of canceled passages within the copy-text is on file at the University of Texas.

The aim in emending the copy-text has been to produce a critical version which reflects the peculiar circumstances surrounding the composition of the play while at the same time it serves conveniently as reader's copy. A conservative approach to the emendation of accidentals is implicit in this intention. While the avoidance of thoroughgoing revisions of Irving's accidentals results in a text far from "finished" or even in all respects self-consistent, it on the other hand yields a relatively just impression of the author's actual achievement in the manuscript.

Some regularizations are undertaken, chiefly to correct errors, dispel ambiguities, and achieve consistency in matters where Irving seems to have intended it. His habits throughout the play of employing dashes to separate statements within speeches,[215] and of neglecting to capitalize the first words of statements which might be interpreted as new sentences, are respected. However, when he clearly did intend to begin a new sentence the appropriate capitalization is supplied (Emendations, 165.12), and when he concluded a statement with no punctuation whatever a period is ordinarily supplied (Emendations, 165.36). When a dash or other punctuation concludes a statement which the context indicates Irving intended as a question or an exclamation, the appropriate punctuation is again supplied (Emendations, 163.6, 163.11). End-of-line punctuation within sentences is provided on a few occasions as required (Emendations, 166.18).

213. Page 13v in the manuscript is blank except for a brief, all but indecipherable notation in dark ink of the shade Irving used to enter revisions in four scenes of the final version of the play. A tentative transcription follows: "Check up double score / 3 nos interpag pags and polishd." The note may refer to the songs in *The Freyschütz*, the lyrics to which Livius probably wrote—as he did for *Abu Hassan* —on the "score" of the opera he had purchased from Weber. In Irving's manuscript of *Abu Hassan*, Livius entered the numbers—the "nos" of the various songs—prominently at the appropriate points, so as to "interpage" the libretto with the score and lyrics.

214. Substantive and accidental readings inadvertently left uncanceled by Irving are listed in single entries (see Emendations, 165.4, 170.40).

215. In the Twayne text Irving's single dashes in the copy-text are printed as one-em dashes. Spacings on either side of the dashes are closed up.

Irving's carelessness in punctuating, probably owing both to haste and to an intimate familiarity with the material which obviated the necessity for scrupulous pointing, is fully equaled by his inattention to correct or consistent spelling. Most of his abbreviations, such as the ubiquitous "&" for "and," or "thro" for "through," are left unemended as causing no ambiguities or serious awkwardness, but apostrophes are added when necessary to the possessive forms of nouns (Emendations, 167.20–21), contracted forms of verbs (Emendations, 164.1), and other unapostrophized contractions. Irving's habits of capitalizing within sentences were capricious and are allowed to remain so, except that the proper names and titles "Wild Huntsman," "Grand Forester," "Ranger of the Forest," and "King of [the] Sharpshooters" are consistently capitalized in accordance with what appears to have been his intention (Emendations, 165.10, 166.12, 167.28, 167.36–37). Abbreviated names of characters preceding speeches by them are spelled in full (Emendations, 164.8, 164.30, 164.35, 164.36, 164.37), and all such introductory names are italicized and followed by periods (Emendations, 164.11, 168.17). Stage directions, usually but not invariably underlined in the manuscript, are made consistent in this regard: all are italicized (Emendations, 163.14).

The source of the text is the author's manuscript, Manuscript Division, New York Public Library.

See Discussions and Lists pp. 382–87, 405–20.

[ABU HASSAN]

Three months after they began to collaborate in translating and adapting the libretto of Karl Maria von Weber's popular opera *Der Freischütz,* Irving and his friend Barham Livius took up a second Weber opera, *Abu Hassan.* From April 20 to May 18, 1823, the two men worked intensively on their translation of the one-act libretto of *Abu Hassan* by Frank Karl Hiemer.[216] On fourteen days during that period Irving reported in his journal that he was engaged in the translation; and, indicating the closeness of the collaborative effort, in ten of these entries he mentioned either that he and Livius had worked together or that he had worked just before or after seeing Livius.[217] Conditions for the experi-

216. Weber's *Singspiel* was first performed in 1811. See Hiemer, *Abu Hassan* (Leipzig, n.d.), and a later edition wherein the libretto is partially incorporated with the piano score, *Abu Hassan von C. M. v. Weber* (Leipzip, 1961) ["Unveränderter Neudruck des 1877 in der Edition Peters erschienenen Klavierauszuges"].

217. Irving, *Journals,* III, 141–53. The ten entries referred to are those for April 21, 24, 25, 26, and May 2, 3, 6, 11, 15, 18.

ment in joint authorship were favorable, and progress was rapid. On April 25 Irving noted that he had "finishd rough translation of Abu Hassan," and the very next day, probably as an aid to translating its ten songs, he listened to Livius playing on a piano the music to the opera. On May 18, two days before he set out with another acquaintance for a five-week tour of Bohemia and Silesia, he wrote in his journal that he had completed the "alterations in Ab. H" and had called at Livius' home immediately afterward,[218] possibly to leave off the manuscript or to discuss it. This journal entry concludes the recorded history of Irving's co-authorship of *Abu Hassan*.

A manuscript representing at least a substantial proportion of his input into this second venture with Livius, and serving as the primary basis for our understanding of the manner in which the translated libretto took shape, is extant in the Manuscript Division, New York Public Library (hereafter, NYPL). Written in brown ink on both sides of sheets of medium-weight unlaid paper approximately 4¾ x 7⅞ inches in size, the bound manuscript is seventy-nine pages in length, all but two of which pages include text pertaining directly to Irving's preparation of *Abu Hassan*.[219] The queries and reference notes scattered throughout its length, and the numerous minor revisions entered in it by both Livius and Irving, suggest that in 1823 it served as a focus for continuing mutual attention.

The first stage in Irving's adaptation of the Hiemer libretto resulted in a manuscript sixty-one pages in length, divided into thirteen scenes.

---

218. *Journals*, III, 143, 153.

219. One page, assigned number 30-A in the sequence in which the manuscript is bound, includes four lines of text rejected from a draft of *The Freyschütz*; see above, p. 349. The second page, numbered 77-A, consists of brief notes written by Livius and apparently concerning possible revisions to the manuscript text of *Abu Hassan*.

The manuscript is accompanied by a handwritten endorsement by George S. Hellman explaining in general terms its provenance. According to Hellman, the manuscripts of both *The Freyschütz* and *Abu Hassan* "had been preserved by Capt. Livius, to whom Irving had given [them]; and finally [Hellman] located them in England." A second page of endorsement, signed with the initials "M H [J?]" (various readers have also identified the final letter as a G or an F). It reads: "This was given to Henry by C. S. Forster—C. S. F. understood from Capt. J. B. Livius that the Manuscript is the writing of Washington Irving—" Possibly "Forster" was a misspelling for "Foster." While at Dresden collaborating with Livius, Irving had been on even closer terms of friendship with members of the Foster family, to whom Livius was related. Both the Foster and the Livius families resided in Bedfordshire; and in the summer of 1824 Irving visited at each home. For an account of Livius' family history and early career, see Walter A. Reichart, "Washington Irving's Friend and Collaborator: Livius," pp. 514–19; Kirby, "Irving, Livius, and Weber," pp. 136–37.

Incorporated with this draft were ten revised scenes or portions of scenes, often written on unnumbered sheets of paper but in each case keyed to the proper points for insertion by a "vide" or "v" in the upper-right-hand corner of the first revised page, followed by the appropriate page number in the original sequence of pagination. It will be convenient at this point to summarize in tabular form the contents of the extant portions of the original draft in relation to the pagination of the NYPL manuscript as a whole. Page numbers for the latter manuscript are listed in the two columns at the right; "[n.n.]" signifies "no number":

Scene Number	Irving's Pagination	Original (Superseded) Passage	Revised Passage	Revised Passage NYPL	Inclusive Passage NYPL
1	1.1–10.5				1.1–10.5
2	10.6–13.8				10.6–13.8
3	13.9–14.24, 13.1–19.5	13.9–14.24	13.1–14.21	15.1–16.21	13.9–21.5
4	19.6–22, 21.1–20	19.6–22	21.1–20	23.1–20	21.6–22, 23.1–20
5	20.3–24, 22.1–32.26	20.3–24	22.1–16	24.1–16	22.3–24, 24.1–35.26
		26.1–27.4	23.1–25.13	25.1–27.13	
		25.1–[26].11	28.1–30.20	30.1–32.20	
6	⟨26⟩33.1–27.9				36.1–37.9
7	27.10–35.23				37.10–45.23
8	36.1–43.9 [Pages 38, 40 missing]	36.20–22, 37.1–13	[n.n.].1–24, [n.n.].1–23	47.1–48.23	46.1–49.13, 52.1–54.9
9	43.10–45.26				54.10–56.26
10	[n.n.].1–24, 47.1–26, [n.n.].1–3				57.1–59.3
11	49.1–51.19 [Page 50 missing?]	[n.n.].1–25	[n.n.].1–[n.n.].8	62.1–64.8	60.1–65.19
		51.1–14	[n.n.].8–18	64.8–18	
12	52.1–54.26				66.1–68.26
"Last Scene"	55.1–61.23	[n.n.].1–22, 57.1–22	[n.n.].1–28, [n.n.].1–22	71.1–28, 72.1–22[220]	69.1–77.23

220. The page-line numbers in the NYPL sequence of pagination for the ten superseded passages in Irving's draft are 13.9–14.24; 21.6–22; 22.3–24; 28.1–29.4; 33.1–34.11; 46.20–22, 49.1–13; 61.1–25; 65.1–14; 70.1–22; 73.1–22. These early versions are in general thoroughly reworded and expanded in the revised drafts, reflecting Irving's concern to flesh out the libretto by adding repartee between his few characters.

Irving's first draft appears to be extant in full except for the missing pages 38 and 40 in his pagination, in scene 8, and possibly page 50, in scene 11.[221] Perhaps because he wished Livius to consider both versions of certain passages he had rewritten, he deleted only seven of the ten original versions.[222] He was apparently concerned about the slightness of the action portrayed in *Abu Hassan*—the plot was an elaboration of a single brief passage in one of the *Arabian Nights Entertainments*[223]—for even at this stage he was considering the notion of adding material and dividing the libretto into two acts. Between the canceled fourth and fifth scenes, at the bottom of page 21 and the top of page 22 in the NYPL series of pagination which is adopted henceforward, he wrote a note to Livius expressing his intentions in the matter: "—Here I propose to introduce the Scene at the Seraglio [–] 2d act must open with a short Scene in which Hassan apostrophises." However, the revised fourth scene, in which Abu Hassan speaks alone concerning his hatred of creditors, is the only extant approximation of the addition he had in mind. Quite likely Irving never did write the "Scene at the Seraglio."

At this point he turned over the manuscript to Livius for review. Of course, as the above table of pagination eloquently testifies, simply arranging the work, with its interrupted or overlapping page sequences and its several pages not numbered at all—not to mention the ten re-written passages, some so indicated and some not—posed a challenge even to a person familiar with the libretto. Accordingly, to smooth his own way Livius renumbered the manuscript pages in faint red ink throughout, beginning at Irving's first oversight, the incorrect "13" at NYPL page 15. Consistently with his practice of using this shade of ink for purposes of reference and identification only,[224] Livius wrote

221. In the NYPL sequence of pagination, Irving's original page 37 is page 49, his page 39 is page 50, and his page 41 is page 52. Since the present NYPL pages 50–52 include the text of a lyric which Irving revised later in the process of manuscript preparation (see pp. 363–65), it seems likely that the missing two pages may have included a text of the lyric which was subsequently discarded. In the NYPL pagination, Irving's original page 49 is page 60, his page 51 is page 65. Irving wrote "vide P 50" on NYPL page 62, "v p. 50" on NYPL page 64, and obviously wrote page 63 as part of a three-page substitute text. Page 61, which is canceled by a single diagonal slash, is an early version of the revised text on page 62 (T 220.9–25); it is not numbered, but it may have been Irving's original page 50.

222. For the page-line numbers of the ten first drafts, see note 5. Those which Irving did not delete occur at pages 13.9–14.24; 33.1–34.11; and 46.20–22, 49.1–13.

223. See *The Thousand and One Nights*, trans. Edward W. Lane, 3 vols. (London, 1883), II, 313–34.

224. The manuscript libretto of *The Freyschütz* and three pages of translated songs for that opera by Irving are assigned separate series of pagination by Livius in the same red ink he employed here. Livius wrote no alterations to that text in red ink.

only two other red ink notations in the manuscript. The first was a nine-word cancellation in a passage which was to receive the attention of Irving and himself more than once afterward.[225] The second, in response to his friend's note about dividing the play into two acts, he wrote at the top of page 36, at the beginning of scene 7. Here he inserted a note expressing agreement with Irving's basic idea but proposing a different point as the one where the supplementary scene ought to occur ("here the new scene is introduced to finish the act"). Also at this point he wrote a series of bars across a diagonal cancellation of a speech made by Irving, and in the left margin beside the speech he added a series of dots and another note: "To begin the 2ᵈ act." The available textual evidence indicates that Irving acceded to this alteration of his earlier plan.

Livius now went through the manuscript a second time, revising it in pencil. His penciled emendations, which are not numerous,[226] may seem to indicate that he gave the work only a cursory review, but probably this was not the case. Irving was close at hand for discussion of mooted points, and many of his own subsequent revisions may have been made on the basis of such conversations. Certainly Irving's revisions to the text in pencil and ink, including reference marks beside problematical lines (particularly in the lyrics) requiring further thought, indicate careful attention to detail. Livius' penciled revisions reveal an interest in stage directions and in act-scene divisions. Elaborating on his notes in red ink at the top of page 36, he canceled Irving's "Scene 6.," substituted beneath it the designation "Act II Scene 1," and wrote in the right margin a nineteen-word introduction to a speech by Fatima which he had restored from Irving's cancellation (see Discussions of Adopted Readings, 207.27–28). On the following page, prompted apparently by a concern to avoid a staccato succession of inconsequential and not really distinct scenes, he deleted Irving's designation "7 Scene." and wrote a minor emendation to the stage direction immediately beneath it. His further penciled marks included entering the appropriate numbers of songs from Hiemer's libretto at points in the manuscript where Irving had not included full texts for them, another brief alteration of a stage direction, and eight additional changes involving passages from one to four words in length.

The next stage of Irving's attention to the manuscript, a portion of which he quite possibly gave it in company with Livius, when the two worked together on the songs, resulted in numerous minor emen-

225. See Discussions of Adopted Readings, 219.5–6.

226. However, from page 1 through page 35 of the manuscript he wrote many penciled clarifications of Irving's slurred hand.

dations and reference marks of several kinds, all in pencil. The twenty-four reference marks—of which, significantly, twenty-two pertain to the texts of the translated lyrics—include fifteen "x" marks in the margins beside lines in songs, three vertical lines in the margins beside mooted speeches, and occasional parentheses, encirclings, and under-linings. The pattern of special attention to the songs is also apparent in Irving's thirty-five substantive alterations in pencil, fully twenty-eight of which involve minor adjustments to the lyrics. Reflecting the con-sultative process of which these revisions formed a part, four of Irving's substantive "emendations" of the songs are in fact alternative readings from four to seven words in length, written above or beside the phrases in question. Apparently in response to Livius' redefinition of scene 6 as act 2, scene 1, on page 36, below the speech of Fatima which he had earlier canceled by a diagonal dash, Irving indicated by penciled bars across the continuation of the slash that a portion of a song by Fatima was also to be restored. In similar fashion, on page 73 he added penciled bars to a diagonal slash across a full page previously canceled in favor of the revised version on page 72. At the bottom of page 72 he wrote and encircled the word "stet," indicating that parts of both versions were to be used in combination for the final text (see Discussions of Adopted Readings, 224.27–225.10).

At some point, pehaps when he had canceled by diagonal ink slashes the two restored passages just discussed, Irving had written similar summary cancellations over three songs and a portion of one other.[227] Although these marks appear to be outright deletions, they were prob-ably intended to signify that the designated lyrics or parts needed re-working. It is of course possible that, recognizing in a version indepen-dently prepared by Livius a text superior to his own, Irving did delete these passages as inferior contributions to the eclectic final text; but it is nevertheless evident that he continued to work with care on the lyrics even after he had "canceled" them. All but one of the lyrics thus sum-marily stricken out include penciled emendations and reference marks indicated careful adjustments; and the exception is the "Finale" on page 77, for a single quatrain of which Irving had already written two alternative versions. Unlike the revisions and queries in the remainder of

227. The songs entirely canceled occur in the NYPL manuscript on pages 36.13–27, 37.1–9 (T 207.31–208.17); 41.19–42.27 (T 210.28–211.21); 77.14–23 (T 227.18–27). The first of these is the song described in the paragraph above as having been partially restored by Irving. In that instance he wrote pencil bars across the diagonal slash on page 36 but not across the slash on the next page. Probably he neglected to do so through oversight. The portions of songs partially canceled are on pages 35.1–16 (T 207.3–16), 52.1–53.13 (T 216.1–31).

the manuscript, the pencil marks associated with these passages were written by Irving only.[228]

Having looked through the full text with close attention to the songs, Irving added a new set of pagination in pencil at the bottom-right-hand corner of each sheet (1–41; bringing the series of pagination originally used in arranging the work to three), and once more turned his manuscript over to Livius.

Livius' notations in dark ink to the now-much-revised *Abu Hassan* suggest his view that the project had reached a point where some finishing touches might properly be applied. On the other hand, possibly because he planned to have the work copied by a person in whose intelligence he felt confidence, he took few pains to render the manuscript self-consistent or to expand abbreviations, supply punctuation, or write explanatory notes of a sort necessary to make it truly finished copy. No dark ink emendations of Irving's text occur before page 46 of the manuscript, the beginning of the original (and at the point still so designated) "8*th* Scene." From here to page 58 Livius made twenty-two substantive alterations, of which twelve pertained to stage directions or scene numbers (he canceled the scene numbers for scenes 8, 9, and 10), and seven involved changes of one or two words in length only. From page 59 to page 77 he wrote only a single emendation, a minor adjustment of syntax. On pages 1–59 he had entered at the appropriate points beginning Irving's songs a series of identifying numbers from 1 to 8, correlating them with the first eight of the ten songs in Hiemer's libretto (see Emendations, 192.25). For some reason, however, he failed to assign numbers to the two songs following page 59, the carefully drafted "Terzetto" on pages 67–68 and the "Finale." This inattention to the final eighteen pages of the manuscript—Livius also failed to assign new numbers to scenes 11, 12, and Irving's "Last Scene.," which now formed parts of an interrupted sequence—may have been owing to simple carelessness, but Livius was of methodical habits, and in a matter involving an investment he had already made—the purchase of Weber's score—and hoped to recoup, this theory is not very plausible. Either he thought Irving's text simply not worth his trouble—also implausible in light of his use of some of his friend's lyrics and his subsequent collaborations with him in preparing *The Freyschütz*—or, more likely, he left

228. A further index of Irving's attention to the songs at this intermediate stage of composition is that the manuscript includes two lyrics, the first portion of a "Terzetto" on pages 50–51 (T 214.28–215.36) and the full text of another "Terzetto" on pages 67–68 (T 222.5–223.10), which are unique (excepting pages 1–14) in not including Livius' pagination in red ink, and which were thus almost certainly drafted after Irving had written his first version. The latter of these song texts includes ten revisions and other marks in pencil.

to another person, such as a copyist, the carrying out of his clearly indicated intentions for numbering the remaining scenes and songs.

Livius' dark ink corrections to the manuscript are the latest textual evidence of collaboration on the play between him and Irving. The latter does not mention *Abu Hassan* in his journals after his return to Dresden on June 26, 1823; nor, unlike the case of *The Freyschütz*, is there any indication that during the fall, after the two men had separated, they made further revisions to the text which they communicated to each other by mail. Although in November Irving delegated John Howard Payne to offer "as from Livius" a text of the work to Elliston, manager of Drury Lane, a month later he washed his hands even of that negotiation by proxy.[229] On meeting Livius in Paris, in August, 1824, he found him "employed about Abu Hassan for french stage"; but he showed no interest in joining the new project.[230]

In the meantime, Livius had done what he could to place a version of *Abu Hassan* with one of the London theaters. He had carefully written the lyrics for the ten songs of the opera into the score of the work which he had purchased directly from Weber.[231] He may also have possessed a recopied and regularized draft of Irving's text, or else a draft representing his own somewhat different wishes. In the absence of such manuscripts, the form in which he offered the adapted opera to the managers must remain in doubt, except that presumably he did send round the marked score he had been at such trouble to prepare.[232] At any rate, on December 30, 1823, Livius reported to Karl August Böttiger that he had not been able to dispose of the work and had "determined to *lay it by*."[233] Thus deferred, Livius' plans for the work never came to fruition.

Professor Percival R. Kirby, of the University of the Witwatersrand, South Africa, possessed in 1950 the score of *Abu Hassan* with lyrics en-

229. Thatcher T. P. Luquer, "Correspondence of Washington Irving and John Howard Payne," *Scribner's Magazine*, 48 (October, 1910), 472, 478.

230. *Journals*, III, 385. He returned a manuscript of *Abu Hassan* on September 6 (p. 392), so he may at least have looked over his friend's work.

231. Kirby, "Irving, Livius, and Weber," p. 144.

232. Immediately after indicating to Payne his wishes as to the manner in which the latter was to offer *Abu Hassan* for sale, on November 12, 1823, Irving reminded him before he left London "to ask once more for the music at Burchills" (Luquer, "Correspondence," p. 472). Possibly a marked copy of the score for *Abu Hassan* had been in his possession. See also PMI, II, 171.

Possibly too, the text of the play Irving had wished Payne to offer to Elliston of Drury Lane was in fact the manuscript now extant in the NYPL. But this seems somewhat doubtful in light of Irving's wish not to be identified as a collaborator in the authorship of the work; his handwriting was, after all, distinctive and readily identifiable.

233. Reichart, "Irving and Livius," pp. 523–24.

tered onto it by Livius. In an article on the collaborations of Irving and Livius, Kirby presented in summary form the results of his collation of Livius' lyrics with those in Irving's manuscript, as edited by George S. Hellman and published in 1924 by the Bibliophile Society.[234] Although he provided only a small fraction of Livius' text—fifteen lines— his description of the marked score and his collation of it with the Hellman edition afford helpful insight into an important part of the collaboration in preparing *Abu Hassan.* Hellman included eight of the ten lyrics Irving wrote or began to write in the NYPL manuscript, omitting only the eighth, of which Irving appears to have written only two lines, one canceled,[235] and the tenth, the "Finale." Hellman included only a fragment of the fourth song, omitting the latter portion "canceled" by a diagonal ink slash.[236]

Professor Kirby's comparison of the Irving text thus selectively included by Hellman with the Livius score yielded the following results. Irving's fragmentary fourth lyric and the corresponding portion in Livius' manuscript are according to Kirby "very close"; the two texts of the third, sixth, seventh, and ninth songs—the latter two based upon Irving's rewritten texts—are "practically identical." On the other hand, the first, second, and fifth lyrics in the two texts, though obviously based upon the same German song, are "almost entirely different." On the evidence, Kirby regards Livius as "superior to Irving when it came to fitting singable words to music"; but with regard to the fundamental question of assigning responsibility for producing the texts of the songs, he concludes: "The basic translation may well have been completed jointly, after which Livius, the better musician, revised his copy later on, but did not communicate his changes to his collaborator. I . . . prefer to consider that each man helped the other, and that their work represents, in general, a joint effort."[237]

Irving's manuscript makes it clear that he drafted and revised his own lyrics; there is no evidence whatever, of a textual sort at least, that

234. *Abu Hassan by Washington Irving (Hitherto Unpublished),* ed. Hellman (Boston, 1824).

235. According to Kirby, this song, a dirge, "was not composed by Weber until March 1823, and not performed in public until August 30th of that year" ("Irving, Livius, and Weber," p. 146). Kirby infers that Livius could not have obtained a copy of the song until September, but the two lines in Irving's manuscript, representing at least a fragment of a translated text, suggest otherwise. Weber was, after all, in Dresden at the time when Irving and Livius were at work on *Abu Hassan.*

236. The eight songs or fragments of songs reproduced by Hellman in his *Abu Hassan* may be found on pp. 23–24, 32–33, 38, 49, 50–51, 54–57, 61–64, 73–75.

237. Kirby, "Irving, Livius, and Weber," pp. 144–47. On the other hand, Walter A. Reichart expressed the view in *Washington Irving and Germany* that Irving "was not concerned with the music and interested himself only in rendering the German

Livius played a part in the revisions he made. On the other hand, as described by Kirby the Livius score makes it equally clear that Livius regarded Irving's efforts as contributions, sometimes acceptable and sometimes not, to their joint effort. It should moreover be noticed that the sixth and seventh lyrics in the libretto, parts of which Irving "canceled" but continued to revise, but full texts of which were included by Hellman in his edition of *Abu Hassan*, are practically identical to the songs in Livius' final version. This detail indicates strikingly that, whatever Irving may have thought of the lyrics, Livius regarded them as by no means canceled. Almost certainly therefore, the diagonal "cancellations" of songs and other passages in the manuscript are properly to be construed, not as deletions, but as reference marks indicating a need for further study and possible revision (see Discussions of Adopted Readings, 207.3–16). Of course, the wide divergence reported by Kirby between the two texts of the first, second, and fifth songs suggests that, once the collaboration on *Abu Hassan* was over, Livius kept on revising independently. Even were the Livius lyrics available for study, they would thus not be especially useful for the purpose of establishing a critical text of Irving's own contributions to the collaboration. As integral parts of the NYPL manuscript, the lyrics drafted and revised by Irving himself afford us the latest available evidence of his wishes for these portions of the developing text.

As written and revised by Irving, and as reviewed and at some points revised by Livius, the NYPL manuscript represents Irving's latest known wishes for the libretto as a whole, and it is therefore adopted here as copy-text.[238] The conditions of close collaboration under which the work was prepared, and also the absence in the manuscript of marks

---

text into English" (p. 133). For convenience, page-line references to the ten songs or fragments of songs included in the present edition are listed here:

Song Number	Twayne edition
1, Duet	192.25–193.25
2, Air	197.15–198.10
3, Chorus	200.25–201.8
4, Duet	206.27–207.16
5, Air	207.31–208.18
6, Duet	210.28–212.31
7, Terzetto	214.28–216.31
8, Air	219.23–24
9, Terzetto	222.5–223.10
10, Finale	227.18–27

238. For convenience, page-line references to the portions of the NYPL manuscript which serve as copy-text are listed here: Act 1. Scene 1 (1.1–10.5); Scene 2

by Irving challenging the moderate number of emendations made to it by Livius, indicate (though they do not prove) that Irving regarded the work as it stands to be the product of their combined wishes. Accordingly, in the instances where the final state of the text incorporates changes by Livius, those readings are considered to form parts of the copy-text. However, each instance of an accepted reading introduced by Livius is identified in the List of Emendations, and Irving's superseded reading is also recorded and identified.

Because both men regarded the manuscript as working copy only, the copy-text is not only much revised but is under-punctuated and often characterized by abbreviated spellings, omitted carets, inconsistent capitalization, and other irregularities. The text includes hundreds of cancellations and corrections in Irving's hand alone, and limitations of space render it impracticable to list all deleted passages in the List of Emendations. Those only are set forth which reveal in an economical fashion the textual situation necessitating an editorial decision (e.g. Emendations, 207.25), provide textual bases for Discussions of Adopted Readings (Emendations, 204.8–9), or pertain to revisions by Livius.[239] A full list of canceled passages within the copy-text is on file at the University of Texas.

The aim in emending the copy-text has been to produce a critical version which reflects the peculiar circumstances surrounding the preparation of the play while at the same time it serves conveniently as reader's copy. A conservative approach to the emendation of accidentals is implicit in this intention. While the avoidance of thoroughgoing revisions of Irving's accidentals results in a text far from "finished" or even in all respects self-consistent, it on the other hand yields a relatively just impression of the author's actual achievement in the manuscript.

Some regularizations are undertaken, chiefly to correct errors, dispel ambiguities, and impose consistency in matters where Irving's intention is reasonably clear. His tendency throughout the play to separate statements within speeches by dashes, and even to avoid capitalizing the first words of statements which could be interpreted as beginning new sentences, is respected. However, when he clearly did intend to begin a new sentence, the appropriate capitalization is supplied (Emendations, 197.17). When he concluded a statement with no punctuation whatever,

---

(10.6–13.8); Scene 3 (13.9, 15.1–21.5); Scene 4 (23.1–20); Scene 5 (24.1–27.13, 29.5–32.20, 34.12–35.26); Act II. Scene 1 (36.1–59.3); [Scene 2] (60.1–24, 62.1–64.18, 65.14–19); [Scene 3] (66.1–68.26); [Scene 4] (69.1–22, 71.1–72.11, 73.1–77.23).

239. Substantive and accidental readings inadvertently left uncanceled by Irving are listed in single entries (Emendations, 192.28, 194.12).

a period is supplied (Emendations, 192.32). Similarly, when the context indicates than an exclamation or a question is intended and Irving's punctuation is inappropriate or entirely lacking, suitable punctuation is supplied (Emendations, 192.26, 193.21). Quotation marks are added at appropriate points (Emendations, 195.2–5), and end-of-line punctuation omitted from the manuscript is inserted as required (Emendations, 192.31).

As might be expected given the essentially unpublic nature of the manuscript text, Irving was no less inattentive to accurate spelling in it than he was to precise punctuation. Most of his abbreviations, such as *"thro"* (202.17, 202.30, 208.19) or *"thro'"* (217.8) for "through" are left unemended as creating no ambiguities or serious awkwardness, though some, such as *"astonishmt"* (228.29), are expanded (in this case, to *"astonishment"*). Variant spellings of the same words, such as *"centre"* (217.8) and *"center"* (221.25), are allowed to stand if both were in contemporary usage. Apostrophes are added to the possessive forms of nouns (Emendations, 192.20), contracted forms of verbs (Emendations, 193.23), and other contractions such as "bless'd" (Emendations, 208.15). Irving's capricious habits of capitalizing within sentences are permitted to remain in evidence, except that the proper names or titles "Allah," "Caliph," "Commander of the Faithful," "Great Prophet," and "Prophet" are consistently capitalized in accordance with his usual practice (Emendations, 198.26, 198.27, 214.10–11, 197.13, 194.21).

A few features of the play's format are regularized. Irving's abbreviations of the names of characters preceding speeches by them are spelled in full (Emendations, 192.30, 193.4, 199.16, 217.20, 220.3, 224.22, 224.24), italicized if not underlined in the manuscript (Emendations, 192.33), and followed by a period (Emendations, 192.27). In accordance with the author's usual practice in the copy-text, designations of speakers written on the same lines as the beginnings of the speeches themselves are shifted to the lines above (see Emendations, 198.15–16; Discussions of Adopted Readings, 198.16–199.22). Stage directions not underlined in the manuscript are italicized (Emendations, 192.20–24), and those not enclosed in parentheses, if at variance from Irving's usual procedure at points similar to those where they occur, are parenthesized (Emendations, 213.19, 217.12). Act-scene numbers are presented in a consistent form: "Act" (if necessary) followed by an arabic number and a period; "Scene" followed by an arabic number and a period (Emendations, 197.7).

The source of the text is the author's manuscript, Manuscript Division, New York Public Library.

See Discussions and Lists pp. 387–91, 420–34.

DISCUSSIONS OF ADOPTED READINGS

These notes present the rationale for editorial decisions to emend, or not to emend, the copy-text. To the left of the bracket are the page, line, and reading of the Twayne text; to the right the commentary.

A key to identifying symbols used in referring to manuscript and printed texts is given on pages 229–32.

[CONTRIBUTIONS TO THE NEW YORK *MORNING CHRONICLE*]

3.28 Albany–Albany!] Elsewhere in the copy-text Irving employs a period followed by a double dash to separate distinct yet closely related sentences; see 5.23, 5.28, 6.12, 7.23. However, he also combines distinct statements within single sentences, separating them by semicolons (see Discussions of Adopted Readings, 4.24) or dashes (6.40, 7.7). In the present instance, which resembles that at 7.7, the pause enforced by the dash lends a tone of reflectiveness. The juxtaposed references to Albany might well form parts of two separate sentences; but they need not, since the two parts of the present sentence are not distinct, both dealing with the subjective responses of the actors upon their approach to the city. Irving's usage is thus allowed to stand.

3.34 We] Although uncapitalized words follow exclamation marks elsewhere in the copy-text—see 3.28, 6.32, 7.8—they occur only when the punctuation follows ejaculations such as "Lord!" The situation here is different. "Such . . . munificence." (3.33–36) might properly stand as a single sentence were "we" preceded by a dash separating it from the exclamation mark; for an example of Irving's use of the dash to this effect (but without the complication of the exclamation mark) see 4.15. As it stands, however, the statement is awkward and inconsistent with Irving's usual practice; see 3.30, 5.38, 6.17, 6.36. The "we" is thus emended to "We."

4.24 buckles;] The copy-text reading—"buckles,"—is inappropriate in its context and inconsistent with Irving's usage. Elsewhere he separates related yet complete statements within a sentence by a semicolon—see 4.21, 4.34—or on occasion by other marks of punctuation (see Discussions of Adopted Readings, 3.28). Irving clearly intends a significant pause after "buckles," which completes the itemization of Dick Buckram's costume; the latter part of the sentence, dealing with the "tobacco pipe" carried by him as a suitable accoutrement, is presented as an addendum.

7.4 Hogg] The copy-text is not without usages of commas which to modern taste appear eccentric—see especially 4.7, 6.22, 6.39—but in this case the reading is almost certainly an error. The sentence is divided into three parallel subject-verb statements, separated by commas, which summarize the smooth results of the actors' latest shift to increase their audience. The copy-text reading—"Hogg,"—interferes with the tripping rhythm Irving obviously wishes, and it is thus emended.

7.24 not material] The copy-text reading, "material," makes no sense. Irving's intention is to say that, since both theatrical companies and newspapers aim at "the instruction and amusement of the public," the use of the theater as a printing office during the absence of the actors made no real difference—"was not material in its nature."

[CONTRIBUTIONS TO *THE CORRECTOR*]

9.22 Handbills] The series of three "&c." preceding this word in 1A brings the statement to a generalized close; "handbills" begins a further account of Billy Luscious' campaign for patrons. The two sentences need not necessarily be considered distinct, except that the series of abbreviations intervenes between them. Run-on sentences do occur elsewhere in *The Corrector*—see 8.15, 10.37, 11.5, 29.36–37—but the series of "&c." ordinarily signifies the end of a sentence; see 19.19, 37.33. Thus on the assumption that "hand-bills" is intended to begin a new sentence, it is capitalized.

9.25 *price.*] The 1A reading, wherein a colon concludes a sentence, occurs at the end of a line and may be a printer's error; but at 11.29 a colon having no introductory function concludes a sentence within a printed line. If a colon followed by a capitalized word serves a specifically introductory function, it is allowed to stand; see Discussions of Adopted Readings, 10.32. In the present case and at 11.29 it does not and so is emended to a period.

10.32 circumstances: This] Here and at two other points, 20.26 and 33.27–28, Irving employs the colon in its traditional introductory function, but in a somewhat unorthodox manner he follows it with a capitalized word (at 20.26 a dash intervenes, at 33.27–28 a new paragraph follows the colon). Since in each case what is introduced is either a fragmentary sentence or a body of material extending beyond a single sentence, the colon as employed does not assume the function of a period. Hence at these points the colons and capitalized words following them are permitted to stand.

11.12 For] Although not capitalized in 1A, this word evidently begins a new sentence, as it certainly begins a statement distinct in content from the one preceding. Irving's frequent use of "&c." within sentences may have caused the printer to assume that the words immediately following did not require capitalization.

11.38 can you] The syntax in this speech (11.36–39) is awkward and possibly garbled by the printer. Irving intends to portray the old man as informing his son that the soil is so poor as to promise "benefit" only through hard work. This aim would be better served if "you" and "can" in 1A were transposed, which is the emendation made.

21.8 wreck] The misquotation of *The Tempest*, IV, i, 156, "Leave not a rack behind," may well be intentional, to portray "The Aristocratic Compact" as an incipient shambles or wreck. No emendation is made.

26.32 trading] In view of Irving's emphasis in this sentence on Isaac's thorough education, "training" would seem a better word than "trading." However, the intention may be to suggest that Isaac has used his classical knowledge to gain preferment, "traded" on it. No emendation is made.

29.42–43 Perhaps . . . allowance).] It is unclear whether this sentence is intended as a speech of Bickerstaffe Tickler in reply to the "pert jackanapes" or as an aside addressed to his correspondent. But even if it, or part of it, were a self-quotation, the copy-text does not afford a precedent for supplying quotation marks to enclose it; see 11.14–15, 11.24–26, 11.28–29.

30.26 No. 1.] The period following the numeral, though awkward, is probably intentional; see 31.24.

30.32 hifs . . . Sneak] The misleading syntax, which suggests that Satan is greeted with a hiss by Jeremiah Sneak rather than that Sneak is the painter of a picture portraying the fiend's greeting in Pandemonium, may well be a deliberate association of Sneak with Satan's followers.

32.33 Mats] No apostrophe is supplied because the diary is purportedly the production of a semiliterate person.

37.18 The Greasy Porpoise, *Ferris*,] The 1A reading is probably a printer's error. Irving apparently intends to place the name and the epithet in apposition, as in a parallel passage a few lines below, 37.25.

"WE WILL REJOICE!!!"

38.22 its head] The copy-text reading, "his head," creates an apparently unintentional confusion between the ostrich—the "it"—and the member of the audience—the "he," who is commenting on its appearance. The emendation to "its" is necessary for clarity.

39.8–9 countenance] The incorrect plural "countenances" creates no serious ambiguity, since the context makes clear that all the spectators showed by their countenances the "ridicule and contempt" they felt, but it is so clearly erroneous that it seriously distracts the attention. An emendation seems necessary to correct the error.

THE NEW-YORK REVIEW

39.30–33 THE . . . *PHILOSOPHER*"] The title is taken from the title page of the pamphlet. That Irving intended it to serve as the title of the review is indicated on the first page of the text proper, where, above the citation of the work under consideration (39.34–38), the short title "THE NEW-YORK REVIEW; &C." appears, followed by a decorative rule. The inaccurate reference on the title-page to "*FRAGMENTS OF THE JOURNAL . . .*" is emended to correct form, which Irving employs in his bibliographical citation.

40.10–11 Journal, in which the Philosopher] Irving occasionally capitalizes nouns for emphasis in this work (see "Ironmonger," 41.12, "Journalist," 45.13) and almost invariably capitalizes "Philosopher" when the word refers to the supposed author of the *Fragment*; see Emendations, 43.37. The former usages have ironic overtones consistent with Irving's aims, and the latter are also the results of his intention to give ironic prominence to the individual under discussion. The capitalizations are allowed to stand.

41.30 A smart, vapouring] Here and at another point in the review (47.44) Irving punctuates as sentences what are in fact sentence fragments. In each case he is characterizing an individual in detail, and the effect of the omitted verbs is to fix, or "freeze" the subjects as for scrutiny. No emendation is made in either case.

42.27 Christianity] Here and at 47.36 "christianity" is spelled in the copy-text with an initial lowercase letter, and at 47.21 "christian" is spelled with similar disregard for traditional usage. The latter word is once capitalized (41.31), but with that exception the two words are employed on these three occasions only. Possibly the deviation from traditional usage was intentional—a device further to exasperate John Rodman, who in his *Fragment of a Journal* had portrayed himself as a zealous adherent of the Christian faith; see Discussions of Adopted Readings, 45.20. More likely, however, it was unintended. the words in question are invariably capitalized in Irving's other published works, and the stance of orthodoxy adopted in this pamphlet is so firm as to preclude the obvious slighting of Christianity which would be implied by the lowercase *c*. The lowercase readings are thus emended.

42.40–41 anti-Jacobin and anti-Godwinian] Although "Godwinians"

(44.34, 47.13) and "Godwinism" (43.16–17) are invariably capitalized, in this single use of "Godwinian" as part of a compound the word is uncapitalized; "jacobin" appears in the review only once, at this point. The *OED* cites a single instance of "jacobin," from Byron's *Don Juan*, but the capitalized form was clearly prevalent in the early nineteenth century; the *OED* gives only the capitalized form of "Godwinian." In accordance with contemporary usage and Irving's usage elsewhere in the copy-text, the latter parts of the two compounds are capitalized.

43.37 pretensions] Irving clearly intends "pretensions" to be taken collectively so as to agree in number with "instance" and "is" earlier in the sentence. The construction is awkward but its meaning is clear; no emendation is made.

45.20 critick.—We] In view of Irving's two earlier comments on the use of dashes in Rodman's *Fragment*—see 42.14–16, 44.43—it seems likely that the multiple dashes here and at 45.23, 45.26, and 45.31, which have no substantive function, are included to parody Rodman.

48.23 formerly.—True] The word "formerly" concludes a statement characterizing the social effects of the Philosopher's activities; "true" begins a separate comment. In similar situations elsewhere (45.20, 45.23, 45.26, and 48.20) the multiple dashes between sentences are preceded by periods and followed by capitalized words. The copy-text reading is in this instance so awkward as almost certainly to be the result of a printer's error; it is emended to conform to Irving's otherwise consistent usage.

[REVIEW OF *THE WORKS . . . OF ROBERT TREAT PAINE*]

51.24 After leaving college, we] Irving tended throughout his career to begin sentences in this ambiguous manner, with an implied or assumed reference to a person other than the subject of his sentence; here the reference is to Paine, although the syntax would suggest "we" had left college. See also 53.39–40.

52.33 Federal politics] As it stands in the copy-text, this term may be taken to mean either the politics of the federated United States or the politics of the Federalist party. Since Robert Treat Paine had been an ardent Federalist, the latter meaning was no doubt Irving's intention. The 2A reading is thus adopted for clarification.

55.14 Robert] The poet was in fact named at birth Thomas Paine. His elder brother, the original Robert Treat Paine, Jr., died in 1798 of yellow fever; and out of respect for his father the younger brother three years later petitioned the Massachusetts state legislature to change his name. Moreover, as a Christian and a Federalist the poet had no wish to be confused with Thomas Paine, the Deist and advocate of universal democracy. Irving was aware of Paine's name-change—it is discussed in the "Biography" section of the poet's *Works*, p. xvii—and no doubt misnamed him through oversight.

56.28 —"He] Elsewhere in the review Irving sets off from his text quotations more than five lines in length, after a full stop indicated by either a period or a colon. In the present instance, where he introduces a lengthy quotation using a double dash, his intention appears to cause quotation and commentary to flow together. Possibly he was concerned at this point that his essay should not take on the appearance of a patchwork of other persons' opinions. At any rate, because the unusual format appears to suit his intentions, no emendation for consistency seems appropriate.

62.14–30 "Remote . . . obey!"] In quoting from Paine's ode (*Works*, pp. 243–44), Irving omits the first three stanzas—each of which, like those he does include, ends with a two-line refrain which he also omits: "Rise, Columbia, brave and free, / Poise the Globe, and bound the Sea!" Following the first stanza, in the original text the refrain is in each case abbreviated "Rise, Columbia, &c." Irving's line of asterisks, 62.26, is to indicate the omission of a stanza, the penultimate in Paine's poem.

BIOGRAPHY OF CAPTAIN JAMES LAWRENCE

65.9 between the age of thirteen and fourteen] Apparently Irving means "in the thirteenth year, before the age of fourteen." See the identical construction below, 65.24–25.

65.23 navy department] Irving's failure to capitalize words in the names of federal agencies or offices, such as "Navy," "Secretary of the Navy," or "Congress" may seem unusual to modern taste; however, the consistency with which he spelled these words with lowercase letters bespeaks a clear intention. Irving does not capitalize a title or a rank unless it appears together with the name of an individual. Thus he refers to "the rank of post captain" (68.44) or a "first lieutenant" (66.27), but to "Lieutenant Ludlow" (72.5), "Captain Thomas Tingey" (65.27).

68.1 24th February] Irving's usual practice in this work is to insert "of" between the abbreviated date and the name of the month following it; see 64.33, 67.41. In this instance, he may have departed from the usage in order to avoid a series of three interconnected prepositional phrases, a construction he seldom permitted himself. The copy-text reading is allowed to stand.

69.22 family:] Here and on four other occasions—69.36, 70.14, 72.20,

76.24–Irving employs the colon in an unorthodox manner: not to draw attention to the words which follow, but simply to enforce a pause, in the manner of a semicolon. At one point (66.40) he employs a semicolon where a colon might be thought more appropriate; but elsewhere (70.7) a colon does conclude a specifically introductory clause. Irving seems not to have made definite distinctions between the functions proper to the semicolon and colon.

BIOGRAPHICAL NOTICE OF THE LATE LIEUTENANT BURROWS

86.7 countrymen:] Irving's tendency not to distinguish carefully between the functions appropriate to semicolon and colon is much in evidence in this work. At three points (86.8, 86.40, 87.2) he employs the semicolon at the close of a statement drawing particular attention to the matter which follows. At four others (86.7, 87.5, 87.14, 92.9) the colon is used apparently to enforce a significant pause. But these reversed functions for the two forms of punctuation are not observed consistently; the stately pace of the sketch is owing largely to Irving's use of multiple semicolons within sentences. Like the insertion of a grammatically superfluous comma between subject and object (see 88.11, 91.13), Irving's allotment of overlapping functions to semicolon and colon is characteristic of his *Analectic Magazine* contributions.

90.31 14 guns] Irving regularly uses numerals to indicate the number of guns on warships. See *Letters of Washington Irving to Henry Brevoort, Jr.*, ed. George S. Hellman (New York, 1918), p. 358.

91.8 –sufficient . . . he should] The run-on sentences following the dash are awkward, but Irving evidently intends them to constitute together a single formulation of the bearing proper to a military victor. No ambiguity is present and no emendation is required.

BIOGRAPHICAL MEMOIR OF COMMODORE PERRY

94.13 long-suffering] Webster, Walker, and Johnson all spell this compound "longsuffering"; however, the *OED* lists both "longsuffering" and "long-suffering" as in nineteenth-centry usage, quoting from Irving's *Adventures of Captain Bonneville* as an example of the latter. Irving's usage in the copy-text, "long suffering," conveys a literal meaning somewhat different from the one he intends, which is "patient endurance of provocation or trial."

96.23 the whole of the crews] The reference is to the entire body of sailors comprising the crews of the several gunboats under Perry's command. Irving's usage would be unambiguous if he had not a few sentences above referred to Perry as "disciplining his crew"—the same

group of men (96.10). However, since the confusing effect of this
inconsistency is mitigated by the clear reference at the beginning of
the sentence to "the honest tars under [Perry's] command," the reading is permitted to stand.

97.5 fourth of August]   Irving's consistent procedure in this biography
(see, for example, 97.10, 97.13) is to indicate days of the month using
the ordinal number (e.g. fourth) followed by "of" followed by the
name of the month. This differs from his almost consistent practice
in his memoirs of Lawrence and Porter, where he abbreviates the
ordinal (e.g. 4th). However, since the dates are presented clearly in
all three texts, the two systems are allowed to stand in the respective
works.

97.37 the enemy]   Irving is inconsistent in his use of "enemy" and
its inflected forms to denote the combined British forces encountered
by Perry. At four points (97.37, 100.1, 100.21, 100.28) he refers to
"the enemy" as a collective noun to which the singular pronoun "he"
(or "his" or "him") is appropriate; and his use of "the foe" (99.11)
also suggests that to be his intention. However, on another occasion
(100.17), he combines the singular noun with a plural verb form
"were"; and on two others (99.22, 101.12) with the plural pronoun
"their"; and at four points elsewhere (98.35, 98.41, 99.6, 101.1), referring to the same military force opposing Perry, he employs the plural
"enemies' " and follows it with plural pronouns. In short, he was apparently unable to decide whether to refer to the British forces as a
single combined unit or as several ships or groups of men. His usages
are not mutually consistent, but neither are they grammatically incorrect taken individually. Because they create no serious ambiguities,
the various forms of "the enemy" are left unemended.

ODES . . . BY EDWIN C. HOLLAND

105.25–26 —we find, moreover]   This review stands out among Irving's
Analectic Magazine contributions for his frequent use in it of the
dash. In the present instance it separates two complete, syntactically
parallel statements, a function appropriate to the semicolon. At other
points, such as 108.11, 112.15, it serves an introductory purpose ordinarily assumed by the colon. In another, 114.2, it might aptly be replaced by either a semicolon or a period; and in another, 112.33–34,
a series of three dashes might naturally be replaced by three periods.
In these and in the four other instances where it is used—105.34,
107.12, 108.25, and 112.2–the dash serves purposes which in Irving's
usage overlap with the functions proper to other marks of punctuation. The unique purpose served in this article by the double dash

appears to be temporal rather than strictly grammatical. By enforcing a pause, it accentuates the moods either of judicial deliberation or, more frequently, of tongue-in-cheek irony, which characterize the review.

111.21 "halo and lustre of story"]   Although this phrase is altered from the original in H only in its capitalization, the immediately following quotation, "wave of the ocean" (111.21–22), is almost wholly invented by Irving. For the convenience of the reader in considering Irving's comments in this passage, the first four lines in stanza two of Holland's "Naval Song. The Pillar of Glory" (H, p .19) are given here: "The Ocean, ye Chiefs, (the Reign of Glory, / where Fortune has destin'd Columbia to reign,) / Gleams with the Halo and Lustre of Story, / That curl round the Wave, as the Scene of her Fame!"

LORD BYRON

114.19 university of Cambridge]   Irving's intention appears not to specify the proper name of the university Byron attended but to signify it by referring to its location. Hence "university" is left uncapitalized.

BIOGRAPHICAL MEMOIR OF CAPTAIN DAVID PORTER

131.10–11 Valparaiso. Waiving]   While Irving often separates two gramatically complete statements by a semicolon rather than a period (see for example 131.37–42), in this case the construction is not characteristic, because it conjoins statements not closely related in subject matter. The first part of the sentence, beginning "Much indignation," sets up a general situation which Irving discusses at some length— not only in the second part, but in the two sentences following. The phrase "waiving all discussion of these points" suggests that a full statement of the "points" has just been completed and that a quasi-judicial analysis of them—a different matter—is to begin. The differing aims of the two parts of the sentence, and the larger context of which they form parts, justify the emendation.

DEFENCE OF FORT M'HENRY

132.19 in a flag]   A more appropriate preposition would seem to be "under." However, the context does make it clear that the "gentleman" had left Baltimore protected by a flag of truce, so no emendation is made.

A BIOGRAPHICAL SKETCH OF THOMAS CAMPBELL

136.13–14 university of Glasgow] Irving appears to be indicating the location of the university rather than designating it by its proper name. See "college of Jena," 137.32; "Lord Byron," 114.19. Hence "university" is not capitalized.

137.15 the Pleasures of Hope,] The quotation marks in 9A clarify a slight ambiguity in Irving's first preference to *The Pleasures of Hope*, the first word of which has traditionally often been capitalized. However, Irving evidently regarded "Pleasures of Hope" as an adequate title—see 138.32—and used the article preceding it only to draw attention to the poem; see 139.23.

139.42–43 O'Connor's Child, or Love Lies Bleeding.] Except for the omitted quotation marks, the emended reading duplicates 9A and reflects Irving's otherwise consistent practice in 3A of capitalizing all words in titles of literary works unless they are conjunctions, articles, or prepositions not following a colon or semicolon. The quotation marks are omitted for consistency with the author's practice elsewhere in 3A; see 137.15, 139.31–32, 139.32, 139.40, 141.1.

143.31 Muse] Elsewhere in 3A Irving leaves "muse" uncapitalized; see 136.44, 144.4, 145.27. However, in those instances he is referring specifically to Campbell's own source of poetic inspiration. His reference in the present passage to "the visitations of the Muse," the source of all poetry, is thus different in kind from the other three. All four references had been uncapitalized in 1A. That this single capitalization of "Muse" occurs in 3A is thus an indication that the author intended the capital letter to mark his more general personification.

144.24 literary character of the author] The 3A reading is inappropriate to its context. Irving is introducing an anecdote about the composition of "Gertrude of Wyoming" not in order to exemplify the character of "the literary author" as a species but rather to suggest the "literary character" of Campbell, the author of the poem. Edward Earle noticed this confusion, possibly the result of a printer's error, and emended the reading to the one adopted here; see Textual Commentary, note 126. As corroboration of the above description of Irving's intentions at this point see 144.29–30, where he specifies his anecdote as an instance of a single characteristic, "the self-diffidence of Mr. Campbell."

[VERSES WRITTEN ON THE LAKE OF LUCERNE]

149.12 dawn: And] The use of a colon rather than a semicolon to mark a pause between coordinated constructions, and the following it with a capitalized word, is not uncharacteristic of Irving's early style. Here and at 149.18 the colon also introduces a description of an action. The construction creates no serious ambiguity and so is left unemended.

149.14 this night of May.] In MSv the phrase reads "this / night of May"—breaking off when Cabell ran out of room on one line and resuming halfway across the line below. The same situation occurs with "sweating / Brow," (149.16), "Lord / to take" (149.17), and "draughts / and Deep" (149.19). The configuration of the text appears to be owing, not to Irving's intentions, but to Cabell's limitations of space. The broken lines are treated as four single lines.

PASSAIC–A TRADITION

150.18 scowls his brow] The MSw reading "scowls his brows" is clearly incorrect. If "brows" refers to the spirit's eyebrows, then the noun should be allowed to stand and the verb emended to "scowl," as in 2A. If "brows" is an error for "brow," then "scowl" should be retained and the number of the noun emended. The latter course would more likely realize Irving's intention. In the preceding line, singular verbs are twice associated with singular nouns; "scowls his brow," a parallel phrase, continues the pattern. Moreover, eyebrows do not scowl; brows do.

150.21 through margins of green] The MSw spelling, "thro," is not authorized in the dictionaries. The 6A reading, which lacks a comma at the end of the line, is selected in keeping with Irving's practice of omitting punctuation at the ends of the first three lines of each stanza.

150.32 softened] The MSw spelling, "softned," is not authorized in the dictionaries. The emended spelling is adopted· in preference to "soften'd" because Irving clearly intended an "-ed" ending; see 150.30, 150.33. The emended spelling is preferred to "soft'ned" because there is no authority for the latter in the sources of the text, and because Irving did not drop a medial *e* elsewhere in MSw except at 149.29 (flowret) and 150.20 (flowrets).

ADDRESS OF COOPER ON ASSUMING THE
MANAGEMENT OF THE PARK THEATRE

153.30–31 name. / Friends] The period after "name" renders the two following lines a grammatical fragment—a situation unique in 1A. However, Irving elsewhere in his early writings used similar constructions as frames for thumbnail character sketches; see Discussions of Adopted Readings, 41.30, to the *New-York Review*. No emendation is made.

154.8 fright ... souls] Although "lords, senators, and warriors'" are arranged as parallel modifiers of "souls," the confusion of objectives and possessive enforces a pointless distinction: paraphrased, "to fright lords, senators, and the souls of warriors." Irving intends to say that the souls of all three groups are frightened; hence "lords" and "senators" are emended to possessives.

SONG

154.25 cruel] As it appears in 1A, "cruel" may be taken either as modifying "one," as an adverb modifying "turn," or as an elliptical participle ("being cruel"). However, Irving is addressing the lady in a conventional manner, as a reluctant maiden, a "cruel fair one." For clarity the comma following "cruel" in 1A is deleted.

[LINES WRITTEN AT STRATFORD]

156.16 Second ... 1821.] The "W.I." in 4A is deleted as redundant. According to Birss, in the manuscript the signature "Washington Irving." appears to the right of the quatrain and the dateline below it. Signature and dateline are arranged here to conform to Irving's usual practice in signing his poems.

THE LAY OF THE SUNNYSIDE DUCKS

160.13–18 This ... living,] In MSm Irving encloses none of the three direct quotations in the poem within quotation marks. Because he drafted the manuscript with care and punctuated it at most points elsewhere in a deliberate manner, these three omissions are probably not oversights. They create no problems of interpretation and so are allowed to stand.

[THE FREYSCHÜTZ]

163.2 [THE FREYSCHÜTZ]] MSn is untitled. In his seventeen references to the work in his journals, Irving adopted a variety of spellings: "Freischütz," "the Freischütz" (2) "the Freischutz," "Freischutz," "Freyschütz," "the Freyschutz," "the Freyschtz," "Freyschutz" (8), and "Freyschts." In a letter to John Howard Payne he refers to the play as "the Freyschütz." He would appear to have preferred the *y* spelling of "Freischütz" and "The" to "Der."

163.3 Act 1.] At most points in MSn at the beginnings of scenes, between stanzas of songs, and before and after the abbreviated indications of points where songs were to be inserted, Irving allowed extra space between the lines of his text. In accordance with his practice the spacing is widened preceding the following lines: 163.4, 163.10, 163.11, 163.14, 163.16, 163.20, 166.8, 166.9, 167.1, 167.2, 167.24, 167.25, 167.27, 169.15, 169.16, 170.8, 170.10, 175.27, 175.34, 175.35, 180.18, 180.19, 181.12, 181.38, 183.14, 184.38, 184.39, 186.38, 187.12, 187.13, 188.17, 188.18, 188.32, 188.33, 188.38, 189.1, 189.30, 189.31.

163.29–164.2 Mighty . . . ha!] In MSn this quatrain is enclosed at the left by a brace ({), which Irving may have added to draw attention to it as an alternative reading. It is omitted as unnecessary.

165.31–39 Ranger . . . place–] This passage, which continues a speech begun on the preceding page of MSn, is written flush with the left margin. It is indented here in accordance with Irving's usual practice. The same situation occurs at points corresponding to 167.11–16, 168.2, 169.13–14, 169.27–30, 173.4, 178.22–23, 179.6–16, 179.41–44, 182.7–8, 182.23, 185.13–14, 185.32–34, 187.14–21, 188.34–37, 189.14–19, 190.43–191.2, 191.43–44.

169.16 (–Enter Caspar . . . & stands] The confusion of imperative and indicative moods renders this stage direction awkward, but its meaning is clear nonetheless; no emendation is made.

169.32 Karl [blank space]] Irving never got around to supplying a surname.

169.33 too & too it] Apparently this is a slang term for "overindulge." "Two and two it" might seem more natural, but Irving has clarified his spelling of both instances of "too" in pencil, indicating that the unusual phrase was his intention.

172.40–173.2 the Devil . . . not] In MSn this passage, on pages 14 and 14v, is first deleted in ink by a series of horizontal lines and a sweeping x stroke (p. 14), but then its eleven lines of text are underlined with penciled dashes, to indicate that its appropriateness is to be reconsidered. Near the bottom of p. 14 Livius wrote in pencil "stet." Because Irving does not appear to have dissented from his collaborator's opinion, the passage is included here.

175.18 Marian. Will . . . father?] Irving first intended this speech to follow Christopher's discourse on "reasonable virtue" (174.44–175.5), but upon deciding to extend the scene he canceled Marian's response, wrote "See p 34" above it, and on the following page wrote the lines corresponding to 175.6–17. He then hastily added a shorthand version of the speech of Marian—"Marian will you help me out with the / table &c"—and beneath it the notation "See opposite *." The asterisk referred to the speech of Christopher on the first page (175.19–24), which closes the scene. In the present text Marian's speech follows the canceled version, not the shorthand copy which Irving added for easy reference.

176.17–18 darkness]   Immediately following "reason!'" (176.15), Irving added a vertical bar in MSn to signify the beginning of a mooted passage. In the left margin at the bottom of page 19v he wrote a wiggly line and beside it "Qu"; on the second line of the next page he added a second vertical bar, signifying the end of the mooted passage. The word "darkness" concludes the portion of Caspar's speech which he subsequently decided to retain.

176.35 *Proscenium*]   Irving's "PS" at first appears cryptic but in its context is much less so. Since Caspar *"crosses to"* it and then *"returns"* from it to Albert, it is clearly some part of the stage, or proscenium. The careful description of Caspar's movements is of a piece with Irving's attention in MSn to matters of stagecraft.

178.19–26 I speak . . . *Caspar.*]   This passage, on pp. 22, 22v in MSn, is encircled in pencil, as to query its being retained. No deletion marks occur except the one accompanying Livius' one-word substitution (Emendations, 178.24–25). Because the full passage is allowed to stand in MSn it is given here.

178.31 huntsman.]   Whether in this speech Caspar is making an affirmation or asking a question is uncertain. Irving's punctuation is left unchanged.

182.4–5 Proceeding . . . a wolf]   This is one of the more memorable instances of Irving's tendency to create confusion by writing constructions having improper antecedents. The statement cannot be clarified without rephrasing and is allowed to stand.

182.44–183.3 *Albert . . . love—*]   Irving first wrote the speech in a brief form, but after adding a further exchange between Albert and Bertha (183.4–7) he deleted it, preceded it with the asterisk, and wrote the expanded speech included here beneath the text of the exchange which properly followed it. He indicated the position of the revised speech by encircling it, drawing a line connecting it to the point at which the canceled speech began, and adding an asterisk before " Tis."

183.16–17 [Scene 2.] / *Scene of Incantation.*]   The scene number is supplied for the convenience of the reader, but Irving's own designation is retained as being descriptive and as indicating the name by which he and Livius referred to it; see 184.27, 184.33.

183.21 *Urian*]   In MSn the name is deleted in pencil but no substitution is made. "Urian" is used throughout the scene, and at this point the stage direction makes no sense unless some name is included; *"Urian"* is hence restored.

183.20–25 (*P.S.* .... rocks—)] In MSn Irving's note is set off from the text by a heavy line in ink from the initial parenthesis to the left margin, a wavy vertical line in the left margin curving to the right just below the final line, and another wavy line following "rocks –" which latter doubles as a right parenthesis.

183.41–184.5 (omit ... Andreas—)] Because square brackets are employed in T only to enclose editorial insertions, Irving's brackets are emended to parentheses. He drew attention to his note on stage management in two ways not reproduced here. First, above and to the left of "omit" he drew the conventional sketch ☞; second, he underlined the second and third lines of the eight-line passage with wavy lines in ink, and in the left margin he added a similar line extending the length of the passage and curving to the right below the bottom line.

184.9 *onto proscenium.*] The "*o.p.*" forms part of a stage direction—more specifically, a direction for the movements of a character onstage. The "*p.*" may thus be taken with some confidence as an abbreviation for "*proscenium*"; see Emendations, 176.35. The "*o.*" is only slightly more doubtful. Irving's setting for this scene clearly includes a pile of rocks above and behind Caspar, from which Andreas "*descends*" to him as he comes out of hiding. Either "*on*" or "*onto*" seems plausible as the full form of Irving's abbreviation—the latter more so, since it agrees idiomatically with "*descends*," defining a picture he apparently had in his mind, of the stage ("*proscenium*") nearest the audience and the rocks behind and above that free space.

184.27–37 (In ... effect—)] As in his other notes addressed to Livius (see 183.20–25, 183.40–184.5), Irving wrote a wavy line in the left margin beside these comments.

184.29 [should] be] The MSn reading is lacking a verb to complement "be." "Should" is interpolated rather than "to" because Irving's practice elsewhere in his "*Private note*" is to write complete sentences.

185.4 *Huntsmen*] In Act 1, scene 2 the "Huntsmen" are called "Hunters." In the present scene both terms are employed, and because they introduce no real confusion both are permitted to stand.

187.31–38 *Andreas* ... thee.] In MSn this exchange is marked in pencil with a large *x* as for deletion, but it is encircled in pencil, in Irving's usual manner of querying whether it should be retained; see Discussions of Adopted Readings, 172.40–173.4, 178.19–26. Written in pencil in the left margin, apparently by Livius, is the direction "stet." Because this notation seems to represent the latest opinion of Irving and Livius as to the suitability of the passage, the exchange is included here.

189.13 *Bertha takes the silver*] Irving first wrote "*Bertha*" flush with
the left margin, intending to introduce a speech by that character,
and then wrote "*Taking*" as the first word of a stage direction pertaining to it. On second thought, however, he decided to continue the
preceding speech by Nina and to use the stage direction relating to
Bertha within it. Hence "*Bertha*" and the words following it are indented here, in accordance with Irving's usual practice.

190.6 successful. The]   As it stands in MSn, the force of Conrad's explanation that victory in the shooting contest is a precondition of Albert's
winning the hand of Bertha is lost. As emended, the passage includes
a pause consistent with Irving's apparent intention in introducing the
anxiously disinterested formulation of Conrad.

190.11 *Caspar.*]   At this point in MSn Irving wrote in the left margin
a conspicuous reference mark which corresponds to another on the
following page, at the beginning of a speech by Caspar. He clearly
intended Caspar's speech (190.11–14) to be inserted at this point.

190.15–18 *—Horns . . . centre!*"]   Irving's practice in this passage of dis-
pensing with formal indications of the speakers' names, either at the
left margin or in stage directions immediately above the speeches
concerned, is unique in MSn. However, the identities of the speakers
are clear, and their dialogue is carefully set apart by quotation marks
from the contents of the stage direction. Except as noted in the List
of Emendations, the passage is allowed to stand as Irving wrote it.

190.35–36 *chair &c. Caspar . . . hunters*)]   Irving first wrote a right
parenthesis following "&c" and at the beginning of the next line
"*Caspar–*," to introduce a speech by that character. But, deciding to
defer the speech, he amalgamated a stage direction concerning Caspar with the one he had just written describing the attentions given
Bertha. In doing so, he neglected to cancel the parenthesis following
the original stage direction and to underline the added words.

190.41–43 Ah . . . myself—]   In the left margin of MSn Irving wrote in
pencil a series of doodles indicating concern whether the passage
ought to be retained.

191.25 Andreas?]   Either inadvertently or more probably for reference
as a kind of catch phrase, Irving repeated the final sentence of the
Duke's speech on the top line of the following page of MSn.

191.25 *—(Andreas, who*]   Irving first intended to begin at this point a
speech by Andreas; he thus wrote at the left margin an extended dash,
the name "Andreas" to identify the speaker, and a left parenthesis to
begin a stage direction preceding the speech. Upon deciding to use
the "Andreas" as part of the stage direction, he neglected to move

the left parenthesis. An indentation is made in accordance with Irving's usual practice for stage directions.

[ABU HASSAN]

192.18] [ABU HASSAN]] MSn is untitled, but Irving's consistent (though sometimes abbreviated) references in his journals to the work as "Abu Hassan," the title of Weber's opera and Hiemer's libretto, indicate that he assumed the work would be known by that name. See *Journals*, III, 141–55 passim, 385, 392.

192.19 [Act 1.] Scene 1.] In MSn the scene designation appears below the initial description of the setting, 192.20–24. In accordance with Irving's usual practice the positions are reversed here so that the description of the chamber and that of Fatima and Abu Hassan in it (192.22–24, *Fatima . . . water−*) form parts of a single stage direction.

192.20 *Abu Hassan's*] In accordance with Irving's usual practice in MSn of allowing extra space between lines before and after songs, between act-scene numbers and stage directions and speeches beginning scenes, the spacing preceding the following additional lines is widened: 192.18, 192.19, 193.26, 197.7, 197.8, 197.15, 197.24, 197.28, 197.32, 198.1, 198.11, 198.13, 198.14, 198.15, 200.25, 201.1, 201.4, 201.5, 202.5, 202.16, 202.17, 202.18, 202.29, 202.30, 206.27, 206.33, 207.17, 207.25, 207.26, 207.31, 208.3, 208.7, 208.11, 208.15, 208.19, 208.21, 210.28, 212.32, 214.28, 214.29, 216.32, 219.23, 219.24, 221.26, 221.27, 222.5, 222.7, 222.36, 223.11, 223.12, 223.14, 223.15, 223.19, 227.18, 227.19.

193.27 truly; Dry] The use of the semicolon to serve the introductory purpose ordinarily assigned the colon is not uncharacteristic of Irving and so is allowed to stand here, as creating no real confusion.

195.19 seriously!] The exclamation might as appropriately be a question, and Fatima's outburst probably was intended to have an interrogatory tone. But the exclamation mark is written clearly in MSn and is not actually erroneous; it is allowed to stand. See also 196.7.

198.3–4 Love . . . fills.] Irving canceled two lines with diagonal strokes of a pencil and wrote in the left margin beside them a penciled reference mark which corresponded to one at the bottom of the same page in MSn. Beside the latter mark he wrote in pencil the passage given here.

198.13 Scene 3.] At this point in MSn Irving moves from his original text to an interpolated revised passage on a different page (NYPL, p. 15). The first scene designation appears above the superseded earlier text; the second, above the revised passage, Irving canceled as redundant.

198.16–199.22 Ah . . . Caliph.] Contrary to Irving's usual practice, speeches in this passage, which occupies two pages in MSn, are indented after their first lines. See also Emendations, 198.15–16. In conformity with the predominating format of MSn, the speeches are printed flush with the left margin. The same alteration of format is made at 203.1–204.15, 204.31–206.26, 213.22–214.27, 220.9–221.22, 223.23–224.6, 224.27–225.15, 225.18–227.17.

201.31–202.4 Aye! . . . aye!] This series of exclamations by various persons is written at the center of the manuscript page, as if it formed part of a lyric to be sung. However, it constitutes a part of the introduction to the song which ends the scene (202.5–15) rather than part of the song itself. Irving was not always scrupulous about the placement of speeches on the manuscript page (see the preceding discussion); quite possibly he indented the exclamations simply because he was writing the names of the characters to whom the speeches were assigned at the center of the page and saw no need to deviate far from that point. The speeches in this passage are printed flush with the left margin.

202.6 And . . . intended,] The alternative, rejected reading is written in pencil at the bottom of the page. Although MSn includes no specific indication of preference, Irving appears to have been content with his original line as he emended it. "Slyly" is the first word in the line following, and he would not have repeated it, as the alternative reading would have made him do.

204.8–9 *Fatima.* / There!] Irving wrote the canceled beginning of this speech as the final line of a page in MSn only about three eighths filled. His parenthetical note at the top of the next page (NYPL, p. 27) makes clear that the speech of Fatima is to follow that of Abu Hassan (204.4–7) which immediately precedes the cancellation.

204.16–17 *Fatima.* / Here . . . foretaste] Irving wrote his fragmentary speech, followed by the reference note "*vide p. 22,*" on the final line of a half-filled manuscript page which included a revised portion of the scene (204.8–15). Having completed this passage, he intended the original text of the scene to be resumed. Fatima's original speech follows a canceled version on the comments of Abu Hassan, 204.13–15, on a subsequent page of MSn (NYPL, p. 29).

206.27 *Duetto.*] The first reference to the song to follow concludes a revised portion of the scene and serves as a note to indicate the point at which the original text, on a different page of the manuscript (NYPL, p. 34), is to be resumed. For Livius' "Nº 4" see Emendations, 192.25.

207.3–16 *Abu* . . . youth.] These lines are "canceled" in MSn by a single diagonal stroke of the pen. They are restored here because, as discussed in the Textual Commentary, pp. 364–65, 368, in most cases a "cancellation" of this kind only signifies the need for further attention to the passages affected. Passages similarly canceled, but which revisions, series of dashes written across the canceling strokes, considerations of context, or a combination of these reveal that Irving considered parts of his text, are 207.25–208.10, Act . . . more.; 208.11–18, But . . . hour.; 210.28–211.21, Dost . . . no!; 213.4–8, Say . . . off–; 216.1–31, You . . . mind!; 219.23–24, *Air* . . . fate!; 227.18–27, *Finale* . . . drums.

207.27–28 I . . . Caliph. Well] The placement of "I . . . Caliph.," which is written in pencil by Livius, is indicated by an asterisk above the canceled original first sentence of Fatima's speech, by Irving. Livius' second asterisk appears at the beginning of his interpolation, in the lower-right margin.

207.31–208.2 The . . . tree.] The second and fourth lines of this quatrain, which in MSn are indented a space equal to the others, are further indented in accordance with Irving's practice in the succeeding stanza.

208.13 dearest] In MSn this word is partially underlined in pencil, either half-consciously while reviewing the text, or to indicate the necessity of a substitution.

212.23–24 Oh . . . flushes] Irving did not repeat "Oh how joy" in MSn corresponding to 212.24, but a blank space below the first line indicates clearly that the phrase is to be understood as sung by both characters. Hence, as in 212.25–26, the two lines are given in full to the left of the brace, to make clear that Omar and Fatima sing simultaneously.

212.25–26 Sure . . . prey.] In MSn Irving first wrote a brace following "I" in 212.25 and "ninny" in 212.26; he then wrote a vertical bar (to indicate a brace) following "his" and "my." The first brace is omitted, as an error corrected but not canceled. Rather than rewriting "Sure" beneath the first line, Irving wrote a dash to indicate its forming a part of Omar's speech as well; for clarity, the dash is converted here to the word it represents.

212.33–213.6 Oh . . . husband.] Having completed his text of the duet between Fatima and Omar (210.28–212.31), in which he had departed from his usual procedure of beginning new speeches at the left margin (rather than, for example, center page to indicate that the speech about to begin is the second half of a line in the lyric), for these few lines Irving continued to begin speeches wherever he pleased—even though, as the Hiemer libretto makes clear, the song was over. The speeches are arranged here in the format ordinarily adopted in MSn.

213.7 (*into the cabinet*)] This stage direction is adapted from part of a canceled one six lines below in MSn. In adding the left parenthesis, Irving connected it to a line leading to a point beside the speech designation *"Omar.,"* thus indicating its new placement.

216.23 find] Irving first wrote a brace following "he" in 216.23 and "I" in 216.24, but on completing the two lines (216.23 and 216.24) which shared only the word "find," he wrote another brace just to its left. The first such symbol, written over on both lines, is omitted here. A brace written prematurely and then written over also occurs following "has" and "have" in 216.25, 26.

219.5–6 and now . . . Besides,] The first cancellation ⟨I . . . to⟩, the third ⟨my . . . passion⟩, and the fourth ⟨Besides⟩ are in Livius' faint red ink; the final substitution, the canceled "But," is also in red. Apparently, having canceled these portions of Irving's text, Livius wrote his revision of the first portion of the speech (see Emendations, 219.4). Using the same dark ink, he then wrote a bold *x* over the combined cancellation. (A part of the *x* crosses the substituted passage, but it appears not to apply to it.) However, upon further thought of his own, Irving decided to restore the original passage. Penciled in the left margin beside it is a wavy line and, written from bottom to top, "sic." This notation is interpreted here to mean "stet"—"let it stand"— because, the text having already been at least twice deleted, a further signal of an intention to delete it would be unnecessary. The text is presented here as it stood before Livius made his revisions in red ink.

221.23 Now . . . child–] The initial reading concludes a revised portion of the scene (220.9–221.23) which Irving interpolated into his earlier version; the reading serves as a reference note to indicate the point at which the original text is to be resumed. On the following page of MSn (NYPL, p. 65), much of the original speech of Zemrud is deleted; the cancellation ends at this point, where Zemrud begins to say her farewell.

222.5–223.10 *Terzetto* . . . night!] Irving departs in the Terzetto from the practice he observes at most points elsewhere in MSn, of designating the names of characters assigned individual speeches above, rather than along the lines in which the speeches begin. See Emendations, 198.15–16, Discussions of Adopted Readings, 198.16–199.22. By this method he retains in some measure the appearance of a lyric, written in stanzas, while at the same time indicating that the song constitutes a continuation of the dialogue. The text is written with care, and its format was clearly not adopted through happenstance; a similar, briefer departure in a song from the usual above-the-line format may be found at 212.27–31. The format is allowed to stand as Irving adopted it.

222.11 Our ... completing;]   The word order Irving decided upon is
indicated by the penciled numerals above the line; the cancellation
and the substitution below the line are also in pencil. The capitalization is emended in accordance with Irving's indicated intention.

222.11–14 Our ... o'er.]   The brace to the left of this stanza, in pencil,
is apparently to separate the text from the stage direction (222.13–14).
A vertical line is also written in pencil beside the preceding stanza
(222.7–10), but it appears to have been a sign that the lines required
revision.

222.36 *Fatima. Abu Hassan. Omar.*]   This stage direction is repeated
in MSn from the point corresponding to 222.5 because, as in 222.7–18,
a passage is beginning in which the three characters sing simultaneously. Lines 222.37–223.10 are a translation of the "Chor" or "Chorus"
in Hiemer's libretto, a coda to the Terzetto.

224.27–225.10 *Zemrud ... out.*]   Following the speech of the Caliph
(224.24–26), the same page in MSn (NYPL, p. 72) includes an interchange between Zemrud and Mesrour and an additional speech by
Zemrud; these constitute together a revision and condensation of the
material on the next page (224.27–225.10). Irving's original text on
the latter page was "canceled" by a single diagonal slash in ink, indicating a need for revision. But Irving subsequently added a series of
penciled bars across the slash, indicating that the text was to be restored. Also in pencil, he wrote in the left margin "stet." His penciled
notation below the revised text, "See also next page," seems thus to
mean either that Irving was himself unsure which of the Zemrud-
Mesrour interchanges to adopt, or that a portion of the new text—that
preceding the duplicated interchange—was to be used together with
the text on the following page. The latter interpretation is made here.
Certainly the penciled restoration of the original text was made at
a late stage of Irving's attention to the manuscript. Probably it was
written upon his reviewing the revised version and deciding it was
inferior to the original.

LIST OF EMENDATIONS

In this list are summarized all emendations of the original copy-texts. The numbers before each entry indicate the page and line. Chapter numbers, chapter or section titles, epigraphs, chapter-summaries, texts, quotations, and footnotes are included in the line count. Only running heads are omitted from the count.

The reading to the left of the bracket is the reading of the Twayne edition, and is an accepted emendation of the copy-text. The source of that reading is identified by symbol after the bracket. The readings after the semicolon include the rejected reading of the copy-text and any other text in which it appears, together with further alternatives which may occur. The swung (wavy) dash ∼ represents the same word, words, or characters that appear before the bracket, and is used chiefly in recording punctuation variants. The caret ∧ indicates that a mark of punctuation is omitted. T signifies that a decision to emend or not to emend has been made on the authority of the editor of this edition.

If explanatory comments are needed, editorial remarks follow the entry in italics. If more explanation is required than can conveniently be inserted in the List of Emendations, the entry is preceded by an asterisk and the necessary comments appear following the same page-line reference in the Discussions of Adopted Readings.

A key to identifying symbols used in referring to manuscript and printed texts is given on pages 229–32.

[CONTRIBUTIONS TO THE NEW-YORK *MORNING CHRONICLE*]

3.4	*TO . . . QUOZ*] T; To Mr. Andrew Quoz. 1A
*3.34	We] T; we 1A
4.10	meagre] T; maugre 1A. *Irving's intention is clearly "meagre" or "meager," but his spelling has no authority in the dictionaries, which define "maugre" as an adverb or conjunction meaning "in spite of." The spelling "meagre" is adopted as closer to the copy-text. The same emendation is made at 7.11.*
4.13	lightning] T; lightening 1A. *See* 4.32–33
*4.24	buckles;] T; buckles, 1A

4.33   moment's] T;   moments 1A. *Possessive*
5.23   conk-shell.—] T;   ~-~ₐ—/ A. *Probably a printer's er-*
                ror. See 5.28,6.12,7.23, where in 1A the punctuation at
                the ends of lines is as emended here
*7.4   Hogg] T; ~, 1A
*7.24   not material] T;   material 1A

[CONTRIBUTIONS TO *THE CORRECTOR*]

8.22   preparing] T; prepairing 1A
*9.22   Handbills] T; handbills 1A
*9.25   price.] T; ~: 1A. *A colon is also emended to a*
                period at 11.28.
9.34   rope's-ends] T; ropes-ends 1A. *Apostrophes are added*
                to possessives at the following additional points: 25.4,
                27.19, 27.27, 27.32, 27.33.
10.4   witticisms] T; witticims 1A
10.36   timbers.] T; ~ — 1A. *End of sentence*
*11.12   For] T; for 1A
11.35   it.] T; ~, 1A. *Comma occurs at the end of a line and*
                is evidently a misprint
*11.38   can you] T; you can 1A
12.3   AMATEUR] T; AMATUER 1A
14.9   warrior] T; warior 1A
14.14   fried,] T; ~. 1A. *Misprint*
17.21   St. André] T; St. Andié 1A
17.24–25   St. George—and] T; ~ ~-~ 1A. *Emendation reflects*
                usual practice in 1A to introduce a concluding phrase;
                see 17.17, 17.21
18.21   And live] T; "~ ~ 1A. *Quotation mark redundant; see*
                18.20
19.3   *Raiſonnée*] T; *Raiſounée* 1A
19.17   No. 2.] T; No. 2.– 1A
19.41   *With*] T; *with* 1A. *Misprint; see 19.14*
19.42   Capt.] T; capt. 1A. *See 21.27, 29.18*
20.4   thro' and thro'] T; ~ ~ thro 1A. *Emended for consis-*
                tency; see 31.5
20.9   irreſiſtibly] T; irreſiſtably 1A
21.4   background] T; back ground 1A. *No authority in dic-*
                tionaries
21.4   D. W. C.,] T; D. W. C.ₐ 1A. *For clarity the two por-*
                tions of the double attribution require separation
25.18   Dogberry] T; Dogbery 1A

26.22	States] T; Siates 1A
26.29	academy] T; aca-/my 1A
26.36	*Baculinum*] T; *Bacalinum* 1A
26.38	Spanish] T; Sqanish 1A
27.38	polls] T; poles 1A. *No authority in dictionaries; see 36.40, 37.19*
28.11	uncle] T; unele 1A
28.30	introductory] T; iutroductory 1A
28.38	breathe] T; breath 1A. *No authority in dictionaries*
29.25	Catiline] T; Cataline 1A
29.39	lofing] T; loofing 1A. *Misspelling*
31.10	reprefentation] T; reprefeutation 1A
31.15	intent] T; inteut 1A
31.34–35	connoiffeurs] T; conoiffeurs 1A. *Probably a misprint; see 30.24*
32.6	fill'd."] T; fill'd.ₐ 1A
32.17	unintelligible] T; uninteligible 1A
35.3	Peftle] T; Pef-/ftle 1A
35.4	Doric] T; doric 1A. *Johnson, Walker, and Webster afford no useful information, but OED invariably capitalizes the word*
35.21	"New . . . Authors."] T; '~ . . . ~." 1A
35.24	cuicunque] T; qaocunque 1A
35.35	in] T; iu 1A
36.5	accompaniment] T; accompanyment 1A
36.31	*Columbia*] T; *Colambia* 1A
36.37	wave."] T; ~.ₐ 1A. *Quotation mark completes a pair.*
37.12	incog] T; in cog 1A. *No authority in dictionaries*
*37.18	The GREASY PORPOISE, *Ferris*,] T; ~ ~ ~. ~ₐ 1A
37.25	ran] T; run 1A. *"Run" was not in contemporary usage as past tense form*
37.30	*meddler*] T; *medler* 1A. *No authority in dictionaries; see 9.19*

"WE WILL REJOICE ! ! !"

38.3	*distinction*] T; *dinstinction* 1A. *Obvious misprint*
38.17	cocks' tails] T; cocks tails 1A. *See "buck's tail," 38.43*
*38.22	its head] T; his head 1A
38.42	floundering] T; flounding 1A
*39.8–9	countenance] T; countenances 1A
39.12	Canaan] T; Canan 1A. *Misprint*

THE NEW-YORK REVIEW

*39.30–33   THE...ENTITLED *"FRAGMENT OF A JOURNAL
              ...PHILOSOPHER"*] T; ~...~ *"FRAGMENTS
              OF THE JOURNAL...~."* 1A

39.38   *pp. 38.*] T; *pp.*   1A. *1A reading is apparently an in-
              complete notation of the number of pages in the work
              under consideration*

39.39   Among] T; AMONG 1A

40.22–23   cumbrous] T; cumberous 1A. *No authority in diction-
              aries*

41.27   portray] T; pourtray 1A. *No authority in dictionaries.
              The same emendation is made at 45.29.*

41.34   paring] T; pareing 1A. *No authority in dictionaries*

*42.27   Christianity] T; christianity 1A. *The same emendation
              is made at 47.21 (christian), 47.36*

42.29   These] T; these 1A. *The exclamation mark preceding
              "these" concludes a statement; "these" begins a dis-
              tinct statement, properly a sentence, and is thus capi-
              talized*

42.38   noticing] T; noticeing 1A. *No authority in dictionaries*

*42.40–41   anti-Jacobin and anti-Godwinian] T; ~-jacobin ~
              ~-godwinian 1A.

43.37   Philosopher] T; philosopher 1A. *On the ten other oc-
              casions when the word is used in reference to the
              supposed author of the* Fragment, *it is capitalized. It
              is emended here for consistency*

44.23   razors] T; rasors 1A. *No authority in dictionaries*

48.9–10   consider] T; eonsider 1A

*48.22   formerly.—True] T; ~ₐ—true 1A

48.30   Why] T; why 1A. *The series of questions in this para-
              graph, each beginning "Why" or "Was it necessary,"
              suggests that "why" was also intended to be capi-
              talized here*

49.7   hung] T; hang 1A. *Misprint*

49.15   pamphlets] T; phamplets 1A

49.20   hardware] T; hard ware 1A. *Emended for consistency;
              see 42.32, 45.7*

[REVIEW OF *THE WORKS...OF ROBERT TREAT PAINE*]

49.30   [REVIEW...*PAINE*]] T; ROBERT TREAT PAINE.
              2A. *In 1A the citation of the work under review
              (49.31–33) serves as a title. The essay is separated*

by a rule from the heading "ORIGINAL REVIEW."

49.34 In] T; IN 1A; Iɴ 2A

51.5 such] 2A; Such 1A. *In 1A the word appears at the be-*
ginning of the bottom line of a page. Possibly the
printer failed to notice that he had concluded the pre-
ceding line with a colon rather than a period

52.32 Mr. Paine] 2A; Mr. P. 1A. *See Textual Commentary.*
The same emendation is made at 52.40, 53.8 53.14,
57.7 (P.'s), 57.16, 61.21, and 63.30

*52.33 Federal politics] 2A; federal ~ 1A

*55.14 Robert] T; Thomas 1A, 2A

56.39 only] P; daily 1A, 2A. *A misquotation*

57.39 similitudes. Such] 2A; similitudes—such 1A. *In construc-*
tions of this kind, at the point where a general formu-
lation is followed by a specific instance, Irving's usual
practice is to begin a new sentence with "Such"; see
57.12

58.41–59.1 page./ [*space*] / So] P; page./ So 1A, 2A. *See the Text-*
ual Commentary. Spaces are inserted between lines of
quoted verse at the following additional points:
60.33–34, 60.39–40, 61.2–3, 61.6–7, 61.14–15

59.18 commonplace] 2A; commonplaced 1A. *No authority in*
dictionaries; see "Odes . . . by Edwin C. Holland,"
110.8

61.20 Pp. 165–66] T; P. 165 1A; −P. 165 2A. *Incorrect page-*
reference

63.2 may'st] P; may'st thou 1A, 2A. *Error in transcription*

63.4 soul!"] 2A; ~!ₐ 1A. *Second quotation mark of a pair*

BIOGRAPHY OF CAPTAIN JAMES LAWRENCE

64.13–15 BIOGRAPHY . . . LAWRENCE] T; ~ . . . ~. 1A;
CAPTAIN JAMES LAWRENCE. 9A

66.12 No. 6,] 9A; No. 6. 1A. *Irving probably intended a*
comma. His frequent though not invariable practice
was to precede a relative clause by a comma; see
66.16, 66.24

67.29 lay] T; laid 1A, 9A. *Irving never did distinguish very*
carefully between the various forms of "lie" and "lay,"
and his usage in the copy-text is inconsistent. At two
points (67.44, 69.10) he employs forms of "lie" in
reference to ships at anchor, but at two others forms
of "lay" (67.29, 69.26). In nautical usage "to lay" is

defined as "to place oneself in a specified position"; but Irving means "to remain stationary, as at anchor or becalmed"—a definition of "lie." Thus "laid" is here emended to "lay," and "laying" at 69.26 to "lying." See also Emendations, 72.19

68.9 American] 9A; Americans 1A. *Misprint*

68.17 2] T; two 1A. 9A. *Elsewhere in the biography Irving employs numerals when describing the complements of guns aboard fighting ships; see 67.42, 67.44, 68.15*

68.18 inshore] T; in shore 1A, 9A. *No authority in dictionaries; OED lists "inshore" and also "in-shore" as in nineteenth-century usage*

69.8 Captain] T; Capt. 1A, 9A. *Irving's practice elsewhere in the work is to spell in full the military titles of persons with whose names they are used; see 68.12, 68.28, 68.42. The same emendation is made at 69.18.*

69.41 lieutenant] 9A; lieu-/ ˄enant 1A. *Blank type*

71.3 1st] 9A; first 1A. *Irving's invariable practice elsewhere in the work is to spell the day of the month using a numeral or numerals followed by an abbreviation (as, "1st"); see 63.44, 67.41, 68.1*

72.19 lying] 9A; laying 1A. *Irving's confusion between "lie" and "lay" was apparently noticed and corrected by Pierre M. Irving*

77.23 them] 9A; hem 1A. *Misprint*

CAPTAIN LAWRENCE

78.2 CAPTAIN LAWRENCE] T; ~ ~. 1A; [no title] 2A

78.3 Since] T; SINCE 1A, 2A

78.5 Captain] T; Capt. 1A, 2A. *Because Irving's practice in the "Biography" is almost invariably to spell the title in full when employing it as part of a proper name, the three instances of "Capt."—see also 78.7, 78.22— are emended to "Captain" for consistency. For the same reason the reference to Lawrence as "L." (78.7) is emended to "Lawrence"*

THE LAY OF THE SCOTTISH FIDDLE: A TALE OF HAVRE DE GRACE

79.3 A TALE OF HAVRE DE GRACE] T; A TALE OF HAVRE DE GRACE. 1A.

79.4 little] T; LITTLE 1A

80.8   'the . . . tailors,'] T; "~ . . . ~," L, 1A. *Emended for*
            consistency; see 79.32, 85.28. *The same emendation is*
            made at 80.11–12 (The . . . crime;)

80.12   Had] T; "~ L, 1A. *Quotation mark redundant; see*
            80.11

81.34   X.] L; X∧ 1A. *Emended for consistency*

82.39   gaze,] L; ~. 1A. *The copy-text reading, probably a*
            misprint, truncates a sentence in L and causes the
            six lines following it to comprise a fragmentary sen-
            tence

84.32   stone.] L; ~: 1A. *Irving's punctuation, which joins into*
            a single sentence statements which Paulding wrote as
            two sentences, misleadingly causes the reader to as-
            sume that "the legend on the stone" is about to be
            set forth

BIOGRAPHICAL NOTICE OF THE LATE
LIEUTENANT BURROWS

86.4–5   BIOGRAPHICAL . . . BURROWS] T; ~ . . . ~. 1A;
            LIEUTENANT BURROWS. 4A

86.6   It] T; Iт 1A, 4A

86.31   Lieutenant] 4A; Lieut. 1A. *Irving's spelling of military*
            titles in reference to specific persons is not consistent
            in this sketch. He twice writes "Lieut." (86.31, 90.25)
            and twice "Lieutenant" (86.5, 91.41); *he twice desig-*
            nates individuals as "Captain" (87.20, 91.28), *but*
            once as "Capt." (89.40). *The predominant usage in*
            the four military biographies is to spell the titles in
            full; hence the two references to "Lieut." and the
            to "Capt." are emended to the expanded readings for
            consistency

86.38   likewise kept] 4A; likewis ekept 1A

88.28   carelessness] 4A; carelesness 1A. *Possibly a misprint*

90.9   inshore] T; in shore 1A, 4A. *No authority in diction-*
            aries; the OED lists "inshore" and also "in-shore" as
            in nineteenth-century usage

90.15   weather-gage] 4A; weathergage 1A. *No authority in dic-*
            tionaries; the OED lists "weather-gage" or "weather-
            gauge" as in nineteenth-century usage. The former is
            adopted as closer to Irving's original spelling

BIOGRAPHICAL MEMOIR OF COMMODORE PERRY

92.15–17	BIOGRAPHICAL . . . PERRY] T; BIOGRAPHICAL MEMOIR OF COMMODORE PERRY. 1A; COMMODORE PERRY 4A
92.18	In taking] T; IN TAKING 1A; IN taking 4A
*94.13	long-suffering] T; long suffering 1A, 4A
97.26	Commodore] T; Com. 1A, 4A
97.27	Captain] T; Capt. 1A, 4A
97.29	Schooner] T; Sch. 1A, 4A. *The same emendation is made at 98.4, 98.7*
97.33	Midshipman] T; Mid. 1A, 4A
104.43	extends] T; extend 1A, 4A. *Emendation for grammatical consistency with the singular subject "forest"; in 1A "extend" occurs at the end of a line and may be a misprint*

ODES . . . BY EDWIN C. HOLLAND

105.13–14	*ODES . . . CHARLESTON*] T; *Odes, Naval Songs, and other occasional Poems. By Edwin C. Holland, Esq. Charleston.* 1A, 2A
105.15	small] 2A; SMALL 1A
107.18	maladroitly] T; mal-adroitly 1A, 2A. *No authority in dictionaries; the* OED *notes no hyphenated form but lists "maladroitly" as an example of nineteenth-century usage*
108.20	cloud's] H; clouds 1A, 2A. *See Precopy-Text Rejected Variants,* 108.20–21
111.1	sung] T; sang 1A, 2A. *No authority in dictionaries*
113.1	"There] 2A; ⊼There 1A. *Initial quotation mark omitted through oversight*

LORD BYRON

114.6	LORD BYRON] T; ~ ~. 1A
114.7	Among] T; AMONG 1A

BIOGRAPHICAL MEMOIR OF CAPTAIN DAVID PORTER

117.36–38	BIOGRAPHICAL . . . PORTER] T; BIOGRAPHICAL MEMOIR OF CAPTAIN DAVID PORTER. 1A; CAPTAIN DAVID PORTER. 3A
117.39	David Porter] T; DAVID PORTER 1A; DAVID PORTER 3A
119.11	Leogane] 3A; Leogan 1A. *Two contemporary encyclo-*

pedias, Rees' *(1819) and the* Metropolitana *(1818–1849), employ the 3A spelling exclusively*

119.17   taking] 3A; faking 1A. *Misprint*

121.31   brig] 3A; Brig 1A. *The 3A reading brings Irving's usage into conformity with his practice elsewhere in the work; see 119.8, 125.34–35*

121.34   colony. He] 3A; ~: ~ 1A. *Apparently a misprint*

123.13   seven feet of water] T; seven feet water 1A, 3A. *The unidiomatic construction is probably an error*

129.31   Acting] 3A; acting 1A. *In capitalizing this portion of a military title which forms part of a proper name, the 3A reading brings the text into conformity with Irving's practice elsewhere in 1A*

*131.10–11   Valparaiso. Waiving] 3A; ~; waiving 1A

DEFENCE OF FORT M'HENRY

132.14   M'HENRY] T; ~. 1A

132.25   M'Henry] T; M'Henry 1A

A BIOGRAPHICAL SKETCH OF THOMAS CAMPBELL

133.24   A . . . CAMPBELL] T; A BIOGRAPHICAL SKETCH OF THE AUTHOR. 1A; *A Biographical Sketch of Thomas Campbell.* 3A; THOMAS CAMPBELL. 9A

133.28   It] T; Iт 1A, 3A, 9A

136.14   Bishop] 9A; bishop 1A, 3A. *Emendation reflects Irving's usual practice in this work—see 136.12, 137.2—and in his other* Analectic Magazine *contributions*

137.10   Professors] 9A; professors 1A, 3A. *Irving's usual practice is to capitalize ranks and titles when using them as parts of proper names*

*139.42–43   O'Connor's Child, or Love Lies Bleeding] T; "O'Conner's ~, ~ ~ lies bleeding," 1A; "~ ~, ~ ~ lies bleeding." 3A; "~ ~, ~ ~ ~ ~." 9A

140.8   criticism] 9A; critiscism 3A. *1A wanting; see Precopy-Text Rejected Variants, 139.44–140.13*

141.11   correctness] 1A, 9A; ɔorrectness 3A. *See Textual Commentary, note 120*

*144.24   literary character of the author] T; character of the literary author 3A, 9A. *1A wanting; see Precopy-Text Rejected Variants, 144.23–24*

144.30   misfortune] 9A; misfortuue 3A. *1A wanting; see Precopy-Text Rejected Variants, 144.29–145.8*

145.26   Mr. Campbell] 9A; Mr. C. 3A. *1A wanting; see Precopy-*
              Text Rejected Variants, 145.23–27. Elsewhere in 3A
              Irving invariably spells the name of the poet in full.
              This exception may be owing to the abbreviated
              name's appearing at the end of a printed line

[VERSES WRITTEN ON THE LAKE OF LUCERNE]

149.6   [VERSES . . . LUCERNE]]T; Verses by Mr Irving
              written on/ the Lake of Lucerne/ ———— MSv
149.8   away.] T; ~ₐ MSv. *The word occurs at the end of a line*
              and concludes a sentence; a period is also supplied at
              the end of 149.14
149.11   'tis] T; tis MSv. *No authority in dictionaries*
149.13   Lethean] T; Lythian MSv. *No authority in dictionaries*
              for either "Lythian" or "Lythean" at 149.20. The
              emended spelling is the only one listed in OED as
              ever in use
149.16   Brow,] T; Brow. MSv. *What is given here as a period in*
              MSv may be a comma; the penciled handwriting is
              very faint. A comma is necessary to avoid creating a
              virtually meaningless fragment in the two lines
              following

PASSAIC–A TRADITION

149.22   *PASSAIC–A TRADITION*] T; *Passaic — a tradition —*
              MSw; *FROM THE PASSAIC ALBUM.* 1A; PASSAIC
              FALLS . . . A TRADITION. 2A; [*wanting*] 3A;
              LINES/Written at the Falls of the Passaickₐ 4A; ON
              PASSAIC FALLS./ WRITTEN IN THE YEAR 1806.
              5A; THE FALLS OF THE PASSAIC 6A
149.24   fashion'd] 1A, 2A, 3A, 5A, 6A; fashiond MSw; fashioned
              4A. *Apostrophes are added to abbreviated preterit or*
              participal forms at the following additional points:
              149.26, 149.29, 150.3, 150.4, 150.19, 150.21, 150.26,
              150.27, 150.28, 150.29
149.26   Passaic in silence] 2A, 4A, 5A, 6A; Passaic ⟨its waters⟩
              ↑in silence↓ MSw; ~, ~ ~, 1A; ~ₐ ~ ~, 3A
149.26   and] 2A, 4A, 5A, 6A; & MSw, 1A, 3A. *In accordance*
              with Irving's predominant usage in MSw, the same
              emendation is made at 150.30
149.31   that] 1A, 2A, 3A, 4A, 5A, 6A; ⟨that⟩ ↑who↓ MSw. *The*

deletion and substitution in MSw is in pencil by an unknown hand apparently not Irving's

149.31　　o'er] 1A, 3A, 4A, 5A, 6A; oer MSw; in 2A. *MSw spelling not authorized in dictionaries; see also* Emendations, 150.18

150.2　　lightning] 1A, 3A, 5A, 6A; lightening MSw; light'ning 2A; ∼, 4A. *MSw spelling not authorized in dictionaries*

150.2　　storms,] 4A; ∼. MSw, 2A; storm, 1A; storm; 3A; storm. 5A; storm∧ 6A. *The quatrain 149.31–150.2 forms a fragmentary sentence; the period at its close is inappropriate*

150.9　　invaded,] 1A, 2A, 3A, 4A, 5A; ⟨by⟩ ↑invaded↓∧ MSw; [*6A wanting*]. *Evidently Irving's error in copying. The caesural comma is added because Irving includes similar punctuation elsewhere in MSw—149.25, 150.13, 150.17, 150.23—and the printed texts are unanimous in including it*

150.16　　breast] 1A, 2A, 3A, 4A, 5A; ⟨heart⟩ breast MSw; [*6A wanting*]

150.17　　Despair] 1A, 2A, 3A, 4A, 5A; Dispair MSw; [*6A wanting*]

*150.18　　scowls his brow] 1A, 5A; ∼ ∼ ∼, 4A; ∼ ∼ brows MSw, 3A; scowl ∼ brows 2A; [*6A wanting*]

150.18　　o'er] 1A, 2A, 3A, 4A, 5A; ore MSw; [*6A wanting*]

150.20　　With] 1A, 2A, 3A, 4A, 5A, 6A; With⟨e⟩ MSw

150.21　　meander'd] 2A; meanderd MSw; meanders 1A, 3A, 4A, 6A; meand'ring 5A. *See* Emendations, 149.24

*150.21　　through margins of green] 6A; thro ∼ ∼ ∼∧ MSw; ∼ ∼ ∼ ∼, 1A, 3A, 5A; thro' ∼ ∼ ∼, 2A; in silence unseen, 4A

150.22　　serene.] 1A, 2A, 3A, 4A, 5A, 6A; ∼∧ MSw

150.29　　embrown'd] 1A, 2A, 3A, 4A; embrownd MSw; embrown 5A; [*6A wanting*]. *See* Emendations, 149.24

*150.32　　softened] 1A, 4A, 6A; softned MSw; soften'd 2A, 3A, 5A

151.1　　cliff's] 4A, 5A, 6A; cliffs MSw, 2A; cliff'[*blank type*] 1A; cliffs' 3A. *Context calls for singular possessive*

151.3　　May 26th–1806.] T; ∼ 26ᵗʰ – ∼. MSw; [*wanting*] 1A, 2A, 4A, 6A; TOBINUS. 3A; WASHINGTON IRVING∧ 5A

ADDRESS OF COOPER ON ASSUMING THE
MANAGEMENT OF THE PARK THEATRE

151.5 6   ADDRESS . . . THEATRE] T; Address of Cooper on assuming the management of the Park Theatre 1A

151.19   'Twere] T; ∧Twere 1A. *No authority in dictionaries*

152.15   "Plague . . . still,"] T; ~ . . .~,∧ 1A. *Elsewhere in 1A— at 152.10, 153.6-7, 154.21-22—direct quotations are enclosed in quotation marks; for consistency the appropriate punctuation is added here and in the continuation of the speech, 152.16 (Marry . . . sack—)*

153.6   wounds!] T; ~!" 1A. *End quotation mark premature and redundant*

*154.8   fright lords', senators', and warriors' souls] T; ~ lords∧, senators∧, ~ warriors' ~ 1A

SONG

154.24   SONG] T; SONG./ FROM MANUSCRIPT, BY WASHINGTON IRVING. 1A

*154.25   cruel] T; ~, 1A

SIGNS OF THE TIMES

155.11   TIMES] T; ~. 1A

155.12   Trinity Church] T; ~ church 1A. *Capitalized as part of a proper name*

155.18   And] T; "~ 1A. *Quotation mark deleted as unnecessary; see 155.17. The same emendation is made at the beginning of 155.19, 155.20*

155.24   fetters,] T; ~. 1A. *Evidently a misprint; the word precedes a subordinate clause concluding a single statement which comprises the contents of the quatrain*

154.27   frolick'd] T; frolic'd 1A. *No authority in dictionaries. The OED specifies "frolicked" and cites "frolicking" from Salmagundi*

[LINES WRITTEN AT STRATFORD]

156.10   [LINES . . . STRATFORD]] T; [*omitted*] 1A, 2A, 4A; LINES BY WASHINGTON IRVING AT STRATFORD. 3A

*156.16   Second visit. October 1821.] T; October, 1821." 1A; [*omitted*] 2A, 3A; W.I. Second visit. October 1821. 4A

WRITTEN IN THE DEEPDENE ALBUM

156.18 WRITTEN . . . ALBUM] T; Written in the Deepdene Album./———— 1E; WRITTEN IN THE DEEP DENE ALBUM./ *June* 24, 1822. 1A

156.19 Thou] 1A; THOU 1E

TO MISS EMILY FOSTER ON HER BIRTH-DAY

157.14 TO . . . BIRTH-DAY] T; ~ . . . ~-~. 1A; Washington Irving 1823 MSy

158.7 child,] MSy; ~ₐ 1A. *The word concludes a phrase in apposition to two others in the following line*

THE DULL LECTURE

158.12 LECTURE] T; ~. 1A, 2A

158.16 Frostie] 2A; FROSTIE 1A

158.23 lover.] 2A; ~./ WASHINGTON IRVING. 1A. *The 1A reading is less a signature, as in an album contribution, than simply a means of identifying the author; the name is hence omitted as unnecessary*

[¡AY DIOS DE MI ALMA!]

158.25 [¡AY . . . ALMA!]] T; [*wanting*] MSv.

159.3 ¡Ay!] T; ¡Ay¡ MSv. *The inverted punctuation following the exclamation is in error*

159.12 mí.] T; ~./ Ay MSv. *Irving added a catchword at this point, in the lower right margin; it is omitted as unnecessary*

159.30 Sept. 9th] T; ~ 9ᵗʰ MSv

THE LAY OF THE SUNNYSIDE DUCKS

159.32–35 THE . . . JAFFRAY/ ————] T; The Lay of the Sunnyside Ducks./ humbly dedicated to/ Miss Florence Jaffray/ ———— MSm; "THE LAY OF THE SUNNYSIDE DUCKS./ "*Humbly Dedicated*/ to/ "*Miss Florence Jaffray* 1A; [2A *wanting*]

159.36 By . . . runs] T; By ↑⟨Through⟩↓ Sunnyside ⟨there⟩ ↑⟨bowers,⟩ ↑bower↓ ⟨dell⟨s⟩ there⟩↓ runs MSm; "~ . . . ~ 1A, 2A. *See* Rejected Variants, 1.5

160.1 It . . . hills] 1A, 2A; It ⟨comes⟩ ↑flows↓ down from ⟨the⟩ hills MSm

160.2   To the mighty] 1A, 2A; ⟨And fl ↑⟨flows⟩↓ leaps into the⟩ ↑To the mighty↓ MSm

160.3   And . . . little] 1A, 2A; ⟨On its way it visits the Sunny-side⟩ ↑And this little brook supplies a goodly little↓ MSm

160.16   Sea.] 1A, 2A; ∼∧ MSm. *Punctuation necessary; the subject changes in the next line*

160.17   I'll] 1A, 2A; Ill MSm

160.22   dear.] 1A, 2A; ∼; MSm. *This ends a direct quotation and a stanza; Irving ordinarily supplies a period at similar points*

160.28   Jaffray's] 1A, 2A; Jaffrays MSm

160.29   For though he] 1A, 2A; ↑For though↓ He MSm

160.29   rammed] 1A, 2A; ⟨he⟩ rammed MSm

160.31   The] 1A, 2A; ⟨But⟩ the MSm

160.35   Sea.] 1A; ∼∧ MSm; ∼! 2A. *Irving would have been more likely to omit a period through oversight than an ex-clamation mark*

[THE FREYSCHÜTZ]

*163.2   [THE FREYSCHÜTZ]] T; [*omitted*] MSn

163.3   Scene 1.] T; Sc. 1∧ MSn

163.4   *Enter Hunters &c.*] T; ————/ Enter Hunters &c./ ———— MSn. *The stage direction is by Livius. Emendation reflects Irving's usual practice (see* Em-endations, 163.14)

163.5   it's] T; its MSn. *The same emendation is made at* 164.12, 167.27, 167.33, 167.35, 168.20, 172.2, 174.14, 174.40, 180.37, 192.6

163.6   Sharpshooters!] T; ∼∧ MSn. *The word concludes a series of exclamations. Exclamation marks are sup-plied in place of dashes or other indicated punctua-tion (*∧ *denotes no punctuation) at* 164.9, 164.29, 166.32, 168.13, 168.17, 169.3, 170.39, 170.39, 170.39, 170.40, 171.8, 173.10, 174.37, 174.37, 175.33∧, 176.33, 177.5, 171.8, 173.12, 174.37, 174.37, 175.33∧, 176.33, 177.5, 178.10, 178.11 *period,* 179.34∧, 181.18, 181.37, 181.40 *after "he,"* 182.20∧, 182.35, 184.6∧, 185.8, 185.11 *period,* 185.21, 185.40, 187.15, 187.24∧, 187.28, 187.34, 187.40∧, 188.10, 188.11, 188.33, 188.33, 189.16∧, 189.20, 189.27∧, 189.28, 190.14, 190.17∧, 190.17∧, 190.18, 190.29∧, 191.13, 191.18 *after "fountain,"* 191.25. *See also* Emen-dations, 163.23, 167.39–40

163.10   *Chorus Victoria &c*] T; CHORUS. VICTORIA &c MSn.
              Irving's underlining appears to have been a form of
              emphasis or a half-conscious flourish as he considered
              what was to follow; the emended reading reflects his
              usual practice; see Emendations, 163.14. *Other pas-*
              sages underlined twice in MSn and italicized here are
              as follows: 163.15 *Andreas,* 164.10 *Conrad & Hunters,*
              165.10 *Peasants,* 175.36 *Enter Caspar,* 184.6 *Caspar,*
              184.26 *Private note,* 187.13 *Caspar,* 189.1 *Enter Nina,*
              190.18 *Close to the centre,* 191.4 *Hermit . . . &c,* 191.23
              I . . . heaven

163.11   steadiness?] T; ~. MSn. *Question marks are supplied in*
              place of dashes or other indicated punctuation (∧
              denotes no punctuation) at 164.23, 164.26, 164.28,
              164.28, 164.34, 164.40, 165.9∧, 165.10, 165.12, 165.13,
              165.14, 165.22∧, 165.41 *period,* 166.33 *period,* 166.39,
              167.4, 167.29, 167.30, 167.36∧, 167.38, 168.3, 168.16,
              168.19, 169.23∧, 169.27, 169.31, 170.3, 170.15, 171.3,
              171.33, 172.4, 172.7, 172.12, 172.20, 172.22, 172.25,
              172.26, 172.34 *after* "it," 172.42, 173.3, 173.3, 173.5,
              173.15, 173.19, 173.21∧, 173.33∧, 173.36, 173.37∧,
              173.38∧, 174.12, 174.13, 174.31, 175.16, 175.18, 176.5
              period, 176.7, 176.18, 176.32 *period,* 176.37, 177.2,
              177.6, 177.10∧, 177.37∧, 177.38, 177.40, 177.44 *period,*
              178.1∧, 178.2 *period,* 178.10, 178.29 *period,* 179.10
              period, 179.25, 179.30, 180.7, 180.8, 180.12, 180.21,
              181.29, 182.1, 182.38, 183.4, 183.13, 183.13∧, 183.30∧,
              183.32∧, 184.6∧, 185.7, 185.10 *period,* 185.25∧, 185.29,
              185.31, 185.34∧, 186.21 *period,* 187.25 *period,* 187.28,
              187.32, 187.39, 188.35, 189.36, 189.42, 190.5, 190.11,
              190.42, 191.3, 191.12, 191.12, 191.25, 191.30, 191.30,
              191.37∧

163.14   *Procession—& March*] T; Procession – & March MSn.
              This stage direction is by Livius. Stage directions, or
              indicated portions thereof, not underlined in MSn are
              italicized at 163.15 *Song,* 164.7 *&c,* 164.10 *Enter,*
              165.10 *Several,* 166.10–11, 166.36 *exit,* 167.1, 167.25–
              26, 167.29–30 *& . . . room,* 168.12, 168.24, 168.31,
              168.32, 168.41, 168.42, 169.1, 169.3, 169.15, 169.35,
              169.37, 169.39, 170.8–9, 170.11, 170.13, 170.18, 170.22,
              170.23, 170.25–26, 170.29, 170.30, 170.32, 170.40, 171.2,
              171.9, 171.11, 172.34–35, 172.41–43, 173.5, 173.6,

173.10, 173.19 *Magic*, 173.20, 173.21, 173.28, 173.37, 173.38, 174.2, 174.9, 174.11, 174.15, 174.23–24, 175.20, 175.36 *hides*, 177.8 *he*, 179.3, 180.17, 180.19 *Nina*, 180.19 *&c*, 181.35, 181.38, 181.41 *her*, 182.7–8, 182.10, 182.15, 182.35, 182.37, 183.18, 183.40, 184.40–185.3, 186.38 *Albert & Bertha*, 187.13 *Enter*, 189.4, 190.12, 190.24, 190.36 *is . . . hunters*, 190.41–42, 191.6, 191.16, 191.20–21, 191.23, 191.25–27, 192.5, 192.8, 192.12–13, 192.16

163.18   'tis] T; tis MSn. *The same emendation is made at* 163.22, 172.5, 176.37, 176.41 'Tis, 172.2, 181.2, 181.40, 182.39, 183.37 'Tis, 184.14, 184.15, 184.18, 187.15 'Tis, 188.1, 'Tis, 189.31 'Tis, 190.39

163.21   I'm] T; Im MSn. *The same emendation is made at* 165.16, 168.21, 171.11, 171.16, 171.23, 171.27, 175.5, 181.10, 187.5

163.23   ha! ha! ha!] T; ~ – ~ – ~ₐ MSn. *Irving intends these exclamations to repeat the pattern at the end of the stanza above* (163.19), *where he carefully includes three exclamation marks. The same pattern is imposed at* 163.27 (MSn ha ha – ha –) *and* 164.2 (MSn ha – ha – ha –)

163.26   whate'er] T; whateer MSn. *The same emendation is made at* 164.1, 184.20, 191.40

163.30   You're] T; Youre MSn. *The same emendation is made at* 164.12 you're, 185.42 you're; *see also* Emendations, 170.17

164.1   miss'd] T; missd MSn. *Contracted preterit and participial forms ending in -d are apostrophized at* 164.5, 172.15, 177.16, 177.27, 178.11, 179.10, 179.14, 179.15, 179.20, 179.34, 180.7, 182.5, 183.27, 185.7, 190.42, 191.1. *Apostrophes are added to other contracted verb forms at* 166.14, 168.15 (who's *for* MSn whose), 170.20, 170.28, 173.25, 175.4, 179.11, 179.19, 182.35, 183.7, 184.13, 184.21, 186.5, 187.26, 187.32. *Multiple emendations of unapostrophized verb forms are listed in the following entries:* Emendations, 163.5, 163.18, 163.21, 163.30, 164.11, 164.13, 164.21, 164.21, 164.22, 164.23, 164.32, 165.3, 166.6, 166.9, 166.21, 166.30, 166.40, 167.6, 167.36, 169.2, 169.12, 170.17, 172.8, 173.30, 174.3

164.5   'Sblood] T; Sblood MSn. *The same emendation is made at* 167.30, 167.36, 168.39, 169.33 'sblood, 169.38, 170.14,

171.34, 173.5, 173.16, 173.29, 174.4, 184.7, 190.21
(MSn S'blood), 192.5

164.8   *Christopher.*] T; *Christoph*~ MSn. *Abbreviations of this
character's name preceding speeches by him are
emended to the full spelling at* 164.15, 164.24, 165.1,
165.5, 165.11, 165.16, 165.23, 166.13, 174.44, 175.10

164.11   *Conrad.*] T; ~∧ MSn. *Periods are inserted or substituted for dashes, or other punctuation as indicated,
following the italicized names of characters introducing speeches at the following points:* 164.8, 164.21,
164.24, 164.25, 164.28, 164.36, 165.10, 165.11, 165.14,
165.26, 165.40, 166.12, 166.25, 166.28, 166.29, 166.30,
166.32, 166.37, 167.35, 168.8, 168.13, 168.15, 168.17,
168.19, 168.20, 168.23, 168.26, 168.30, 168.36, 168.37,
168.39 *comma*, 169.1, 169.3, 169.4, 169.7, 169.18, 169.22,
169.26, 169.31, 169.35, 169.38, 169.41, 170.3, 170.6,
170.10, 170.14, 170.16, 170.19, 170.24, 170.28, 170.31
comma, 170.33, 170.36, 170.39, 171.1, 171.3 *comma*,
171.6, 171.8, 171.10, 171.11, 171.15, 171.16, 171.18,
171.19, 171.21, 171.34, 171.36, 171.41, 171.43, 172.3,
172.19, 172.21, 172.28, 172.31, 172.32, 172.36, 172.40,
173.1, 173.3, 173.5, 173.7, 173.10, 173.14, 173.20,
173.21, 173.22, 173.29, 173.30, 173.36, 173.39, 173.41,
173.42, 174.4, 174.12, 174.14, 174.25, 174.28, 174.32,
174.42, 175.6, 175.10, 175.14, 175.15, 175.18, 175.19,
175.40, 176.14, 176.30, 176.32, 176.34, 176.42, 177.1,
177.11, 177.24, 177.26, 177.37, 177.39, 177.41, 178.3,
178.5, 178.6, 178.8, 178.16, 178.24, 178.26, 179.17,
179.18, 179.25, 179.38, 180.20, 180.21, 180.22, 180.23,
180.25, 180.27, 180.32, 180.35, 180.38, 180.41, 181.1,
181.5, 181.14, 181.15, 181.19, 181.21, 181.28, 181.30,
181.36, 181.40, 181.41, 182.1, 182.4, 182.10, 182.17,
182.18, 182.20, 182.21, 182.26, 182.29, 182.35, 182.38,
182.39, 182.40, 183.1, 183.4, 183.6, 183.10, 183.13,
183.14, 183.30, 183.31, 183.32, 183.33, 183.34, 183.36,
183.37, 183.39, 184.6, 184.7, 184.12, 184.14, 184.15,
184.18, 185.11, 185.31, 185.35, 185.39, 185.40, 185.44,
186.4, 186.5, 186.11, 186.14, 186.17, 186.21, 186.23,
186.25, 186.29, 186.39, 187.6, 187.10, 187.23, 187.24,
187.29, 187.31, 187.34, 187.39, 187.41, 188.1, 188.19,
188.28, 189.1, 189.10, 189.11, 189.23, 189.25, 189.31,
189.36, 189.37, 189.38, 189.40, 190.1, 190.4, 190.6,

190.9, 190.11, 190.20, 190.27, 190.30, 190.31, 190.32, 190.33, 190.35, 190.37, 190.39, 190.41, 191.3, 191.4, 191.10, 191.22, 191.24, 191.28, 191.29, 191.31, 191.37, 191.38, 191.42, 192.1, 192.9

164.11   what's] T; whats MSn. *The same emendation is made at* 168.15, 173.39, 175.15, 181.21, 189.12 What's

164.13   Wherever] T; Whereever MSn. *Not in contemporary usage*

164.13   there's] T; theres MSn. *The same emendation is made at* 165.5, 166.20, 166.25, 167.35, 168.43, 169.19, 169.40, 170.19, 170.29, 171.16, 171.27, 171.34, 175.7, 181.1 There's, 182.22, 185.12, 185.35, 186.27, 189.39

164.14   mean?] T; ~.? MSn. *The period was probably a slip of the pen*

164.21   can't] T; cant MSn. *The same emendation is made at* 164.5 Can't, 164.22, 164.26, 165.11, 172.41, 173.38, 174.42, 181.21

164.21   that's] T; thats MSn. *The same emendation is made at* 164.22, 164.24, 164.27, 164.31, 164.33, 165.28, 166.16, 167.11, 168.39, 170.36 That's, 171.16, 171.17, 171.27, 171.34, 172.1, 173.13, 173.33, 174.21, 174.34, 190.21 That's

164.22   where's] T; wheres MSn. *The same emendation is made at* 164.25, 189.41

164.23   don't] T; dont MSn. *The same emendation is made at* 164.32, 166.14, 168.8, 170.6, 172.5, 174.5, 174.7, 174.26, 178.6, 181.5, 181.10, 181.28 Don't, 185.28 Don't, 187.32, 188.19

164.27   (consequentially)] T; ⟨⟨⟩~∧ MSn. *The right parenthesis, if any, is obscured beneath binding tape; the emended reading reflects Irving's usual practice. Readings supplied where the MSn text has been lost in this manner or by cropping the pages are summarized here. For each item the truncated MSn reading is given:* 165.36 family∧, 166.1 manner∧, 167.19 temp, 168.22 −bottle, 169.23 dark∧, 169.23 shal, 170.20 creature∧, 171.34 reaso, 172.1 matter∧, 172.1 bott, 172.3 i, 172.6 mad, 173.19 wher, 176.11 know, 176.14 worl, 176.16 illum, 179.14 wreat, 179.19 crown, 182.42 wil, 184.27 wou, 187.1 mai, 187.10 Andr, 187.31 momen, 189.23 bosom∧, 190.8 give, 190.17 *mark*∧, 190.20 *swaggering*∧, 190.23

thousa, 190.25 h, 190.29 thee$_\wedge$. *See also* Emendations, 188.10

164.30 *Andreas.*] T; *And.* MSn

164.32 you'll] T; youll MSn. *The same emendation is made at 188.25 You'll*

164.35 *Albert.*] T; *Alb.* MSn. *Abbreviations of this character's name preceding speeches by him are emended to the complete spelling at* 175.28, 176.12, 176.39, 176.42, 177.2, 177.7, 177.30, 178.1, 178.4, 178.10, 178.15, 178.30, 178.32, 178.39, 179.3, 179.24, 179.31

164.36 *Caspar.*] T; *Casp.* MSn. *Abbreviations of this character's name preceding speeches by him are emended to the complete spelling at* 176.8, 176.14, 176.34, 176.40, 177.1, 177.4, 177.11, 177.32, 177.43, 178.3, 178.5, 178.8, 178.12, 178.16, 178.31, 178.37, 178.40, 179.5, 179.25, 179.38, 183.28, 183.31, 183.33, 183.36, 183.39

164.37 *Conrad.*] T; *Con.* MSn

164.42 disheartened] T; disheartned MSn

165.3 thou'rt] T; thourt MSn. *The same emendation is made at* 179.5

165.4 *Conrad.*] T; ⟨Conrad⟩-/ ∼. MSn. *Dashes and other indicated punctuation inadvertently left uncanceled within or at the end of deleted passages in MSn occur before the following words*: 166.29 Albert, 168.19 Christopher, 168.37, It, 169.13 Come (*two dashes*), 170.27 kicks, 176.6 Have, 176.18 Harkee, 178.35 storm, 179.6 is (*comma*), 179.20 the lovely, 180.25 *Bertha*, 181.22 like (*two dashes*), 182.2 Some, 182.20 Come, 184.20 fear, 187.30 used, 188.12 Bertha, 190.33 it

165.10 Wild Huntsman] T; wild ∼ MSn. *The emended spelling, which occurs in MSn at points corresponding to* 165.9, 167.16, *and* 184.30, *is adopted at the following additional points*: 173.9, 173.34, 175.12, 185.20 (MSn, wild Huntsman); 167.20–21, 178.31, 184.28 (MSn, Wild huntsman); 175.8, 191.33–34 (MSn, wild huntsman)

165.12 Who] T; who MSn. *Words at the beginning of sentences are capitalized at the following additional points*: 165.34, 166.32, 167.30, 168.26, 169.31, 169.39, 170.16 (MSn, & *to* And), 171.16, 172.1, 172.3, 172.12, 172.16, 172.22, 172.26, 173.36, 174.6, 175.16, 176.6, 177.2, 177.4, 178.24, 178.43, 179.25, 180.9, 181.25, 182.15,

182.29, 183.3, 183.4, 184.4, 184.6, 185.7, 185.32, 185.33, 186.21, 188.35

165.26   wives'] T; wives MSn. *The same emendation is made at* 177.41

165.36   family.] T; ~∧ MSn. *See* Emendations, 164.27. *Periods are also supplied at the following points*: 165.44, 166.19, 166.35, 167.24, 167.35, 168.10, 169.6, 170.20, 170.38, 171.5, 171.31, 172.10, 173.3, 173.9, 173.20, 174.1, 174.42, 175.26, 175.36, 175.36, 175.38, 176.13, 176.40, 177.13, 177.18, 177.33, 177.41, 178.21, 179.23, 179.41, 180.31, 181.11, 181.29, 182.2, 182.14, 183.7, 183.31, 183.33, 183.35, 184.9, 185.30, 185.43, 186.3, 186.27, 186.30, 187.4, 187.30, 187.38, 188.21, 188.31, 189.1, 189.24, 190.36, 190.38, 191.27, 192.10

165.36   daughter's] T; daughters MSn. *The same emendation is made at* 190.8

166.5   tomorrow's] T; tomorrows MSn. *The same emendation is made at* 167.12, 171.7

166.6   sunrise] T; sunrize MSn. *No authority in dictionaries*

166.6   I'll] T; Ill MSn. *The same emendation is made at* 169.5, 169.29, 169.33, 169.35, 170.11, 170.16, 170.20 (MSn, ill), 170.37, 171.27, 173.41, 174.8, 174.26, 178.10, 185.11, 192.4 (MSn, ill), 192.5

166.7   the ... horns] T; ⟨our⟩ ↑the↓ music – of/ our horns MSn. *The cancellation and interlineation, and "of our horns," are by Livius.*

166.9   let's] T; lets MSn. *The same emendation is made at* 168.10 (MSn, lest), 175.24, 182.8, 189.4

166.10–11   *Conrad & Albert*] T; Con & Alb. MSn

166.12   Grand Forester] T; grand ~ MSn. *See* 165.5, 166.17, 177.24, 180.40. *The same emendation is made at* 173.29–30 (MSn, grand forester)

166.17   Forester's] T; Foresters MSn. *The same emendation is made at* 181.15 forester's, 181.19

166.18   she is–so] T; ~ ~∧/ ~ MSn. *Dash separates introductory comment from series of parallel phrases elaborating on it. End-of-line punctuation omitted from MSn is supplied after the indicated words at the following additional points*: (*dash*) 167.5 dancing; (*comma*) 171.29 ground, 177.19 crosses, 177.19 hat, 179.34 Away, 182.33 rim, 188.35 Hark, 192.5 father;

(*dash*) 179.18 thee, 184.16 *Andreas*, 187.29 remains; (*semicolon*) 176.43 moves

166.21   girl's] T; girls MSn. *The same emendation is made at 172.4*

166.30   'twas] T; ∧twas MSn. *The same emendation is made at 182.15, 191.1*

166.30   Albert,] T; ∼∧ MSn. *Comma supplied for clarity*

166.33   woman's] T; womans MSn. *The same emendation is made at 172.6, 172.17*

166.40   we'll] T; well MSn. *The same emendation is made at 167.32, 169.12, 169.34*

167.6   'twere] T; twere MSn. *The same emendation is made at 174.22*

167.12   ere] T; e'er MSn. *Irving means "before"*

167.13   soothe] T; sooth MSn. *No authority in dictionaries*

167.20–21   Huntsman's] T; huntsmans MSn. *Apostrophes are added to possessive forms at 168.27, 176.21, 177.14, 181.23, 184.41, 185.29, 186.7, 187.1, 187.36, 188.19, 191.9. Multiple emendations of unapostrophized possessives are listed in the following entries: Emendations, 164.5, 165.26, 165.36, 166.5, 166.17, 166.23, 168.10, 168.11, 168.39, 170.39, 172.13, 172.14, 173.32, 181.37, 185.4, 186.32*

167.24   Scene 2.] T; ∼∧ MSn. *Emendation reflects Irving's more frequent practice; see 163.3, 184.38. A similar emendation of "III* ᵈ" to "3." is made at 175.26*

167.25   A] T; – A MSn. *The dash is omitted as serving no purpose*

167.25   *Inn—a*] T; Inn∧ a MSn. *Punctuation is necessary to separate these distinct elements of the stage direction*

167.28   Ranger of the Forest] T; ∼ ∼ ∼ forest MSn. *See 165.31. The same emendation is made at 185.33, 188.1; also (MSn ranger of the forest) at 171.7, 172.10, 172.14–15, 190.7*

167.29–30   (*Banging . . . room—*)] T; (*Banging at/ the door –*) ↑& forcing it open & swaggers into the room –)↓ MSn. *Interlineation forms part of stage direction; the emendation to "swaggering" is necessary to avoid garbled syntax*

167.33   *First Hunter*] T; *1ˢᵗ* ∼ MSn. *Emendation reflects Irving's usual practice; see 185.5, 185.11. The same*

	emendation is made at 168.36 (MSn, 1.), 171.1 (MSn, 1)
167.36	an't] T; ant MSn. *See* 167.28. *The same emendation is made at* 173.5 (MSn, an't)
167.36	King of Sharpshooters] T; king $\sim$ $\sim$ MSn. *Emended for consistency; see* 167.28, 168.17, 170.34, 171.16–17
167.36–37	Sharpshooters? Mustn't] T; $\sim_\wedge$ ⟨&⟩ must-/ 'nt MSn. *Irving neglected to complete his revision after deciding to end the sentence*
167.39–40	Halloo! house! house! bottles! bottles!] T; $\sim - - \sim - - \sim -/$ $\sim - - \sim -$ MSn. *Emended in accordance with Irving's revision of an almost identical passage a few lines below; see* Emendations, 168.5–6
168.1	*Second Hunter*] T; 2^d $\sim$ MSn. *Emendation reflects Irving's usual practice; see* 185.8, 185.15. *The same emendation is made at* 171.4 (MSn, 2)
168.2	bottle–] T; $\sim_\wedge$ MSn. *Punctuation is necessary to avoid ambiguity*
168.2	recollect] T; reccollect MSn. *The same emendation is made at* 165.30 Recollect, 171.18, 172.20, 179.44, 181.2
168.4–5	House! house! bottles! bottles!] T; $\sim! - \sim! - \sim!/$ $\sim!$ MSn. *The first two exclamation marks were apparently intended as substitutions for the dashes, which are omitted*
168.8	Gentlemen?] T; $\sim - ?$ MSn. *The question mark is written above the dash, apparently as a substitution*
168.10	Od's blood] T; Ods' $\sim$ MSn. *No authority in dictionaries. The emended spelling and "odds blood"—see* 167.27— *are listed by the* OED *as in contemporary use; the former is adopted here as the closer to what Irving wrote. The same emendation is made at* 169.4 (MSn, Ods)
168.11	father's] T; fathers MSn. *The same emendation is made at* 181.32, 191.43
168.17	*Andreas.*] T; Andreas – MSn. *Names of characters not underlined in MSn when preceding speeches by those characters are italicized at* 168.36, 170.16, 170.19, 170.39, 173.16, 173.19, 174.2, 176.40, 183.1, 183.13, 183.14, 186.32, 190.35, 191.42, 192.9
168.26	damned] T; damnded MSn
168.27	Bohemian] T; bohemian MSn. *No authority in dictionaries*

168.35   one's] T; ones MSn. *The same emendation is made at* 169.40, 180.27, 184.14

168.39   Kit's] T; Kits MSn. *The same emendation is made at* 171.38

169.1   Well–] T; ⟨your a wet soul –⟩ ~ – MSn. *The cancellation is by Livius*

169.2   here's] T; heres MSn. *The same emendation is made at* 169.20, 169.31 Here's, 169.35 Here's, 170.11 Here's, 170.24, 170.25, 173.5, 174.25 Here's, 189.2 Here's

169.5   There [will] be] T; There be MSn. *Something has been omitted; "will" is supplied as appropriate to the prediction*

169.12   I've] T; Ive MSn. *The same emendation is made at* 172.1, 173.14, 174.7, 175.22, 178.32, 179.41, 182.27, 187.18, 187.23, 187.30, 191.40, 192.1

169.15   *Glee*] T; ———/ Glee/——— MSn. *Irving's reference to the song is italicized as a stage direction*

169.19   comrades–I] T; ~ᴧ ~ MSn. *A lengthy canceled passage intervenes between the two words; Irving neglected to supply punctuation*

169.31   man.] T; ~, MSn. *Irving neglected to revise punctuation after canceling the remainder of his sentence*

169.33   'em] T; ᴧem MSn

169.39   *Exit*] T; Exit. MSn. *Irving neglected to delete period after extending stage direction*

170.8   *Song. Andreas*] T; Songᴧ Andreas. No. 12 – MSn. *The reference number is omitted as without significance for this text in itself*

170.9   *first*] T; 1ᵗ MSn. *Emended for consistency; see also* Emendations, 170.18, 184.29

170.11   ⟨*fills round*⟩–] T; ⟨fills round⟩ᴧ MSn. *The dash separates the stage direction from the dialogue and marks a pause before Caspar's toast. Dashes are supplied in similar situations at* 171.13, 172.16, 172.39, 176.18, 191.7, 191.13

170.17   you're] T; your MSn. *The same emendation is made at* 173.10, 173.14, 173.26, 187.4

170.18   *second verse*] T; 2ᵈ vrse MSn. *Emended for consistency*

170.23   *Bottle*)] T; Bottleᴧ MSn. *Irving neglected to add the right parenthesis. The same emendation is made at* 181.35, 189.19; *see also* Emendations, 188.16

170.24   Thank ye,] T; ~ ~∧ MSn. *The comma avoids an awkward conjunction of the reiterated acknowledgment*

170.24   Master] T; master MSn. *See* 168.30, 170.4

170.39   publican's] T; publicans MSn. *The same emendation is again made at* 170.39

170.40   *in sport)*] T; in sport)/ *Andreas* – this is always the MSn. *Andreas' fragmentary speech was inadvertently left uncanceled by Irving when he deleted the remainder. Substantive readings thus left uncanceled within or at the ends of deleted passages occur in MSn as indicated, preceding the parenthesized words:* 172.7 the *(the talk),* 174.9 of *(the bottle),* 181.21 *Nina . . . the (Nina),* 182.2 evil – *(I'm),* 191.32 a *(foolish)*

171.1   *Hunter*] T; Hunters MSn. *Obvious error*

171.4   lodge] T; ⟨camp⟩ ↑lodge↓ MSn. *The cancellation and interlineation are by Livius*

171.27   wars–] T; ~∧ MSn. *Irving deleted an "and" but neglected to supply punctuation in its place*

171.29   lie] T; lye MSn

172.1   No matter] T; no ~ MSn. *Irving canceled the beginning of this sentence as first drafted, but he neglected to capitalize "no"*

172.6   Albert?–] T; ~ – MSn. *The dash is retained to mark a pause*

172.8   you've] T; youve MSn. *The same emendation is made at* 172.12

172.13   Albert's] T; Alberts MSn. *The same emendation is made at* 171.14 (MSn, alberts), 177.1, 185.39, 187.16, 192.13

172.14   Bertha's] T; Berthas MSn. *The same emendation is made at* 180.8, 188.11, 188.18

172.20   engaged, man] T; ~∧ ~ MSn. *See* Emendations, 172.21–22

172.21–22   evening, man] T; ~ – ~ MSn. *Irving's "dash" may be a slurred comma*

172.43   thought] T; tho^t MSn

172.44   passed] T; pass MSn. *Context requires past tense*

173.3   (Swaggering–)] T; ∧Swaggerg –∧ MSn. *Parentheses reflect Irving's usual practice at the beginning of speeches; a similar emendation is made to the stage direction at* 187.6–9

173.3   Frightened] T; Frghtened MSn

173.11–12	bargain] T; bargan MSn
173.24	separate] T; seperate MSn
173.30	'twill] T; twill MSn. *The same emendation is made at* 177.33, 183.5 'Twill, 188.21
173.32	Wolf's] T; Wolfs MSn. *The same emendation is made at* 173.33, 174.5 wolf's, 181.24 wolf's, 185.13 wolf's
173.36	Are] T; are MSn. *Word forms part of an interlineation at the beginning of a line and is clearly intended to begin a sentence*
173.37	Andreas] T; Andrias MSn
173.38	True, true] T; ↑True∧↓ True MSn. *Comma marks a reflective pause*
173.39	must first] T; ~ ↑~↓ MSn. *The interlineation is by Livius*
174.4	of Caspar] T; of ~ ~ MSn. *The first "of" forms part of an interlineation and is redundant*
174.6	afraid] T; affraid MSn. *The same emendation is made again at* 174.6
174.9	e'en] T; een MSn. *The same emendation is made at* 189.39
174.11	*slippers*] T; slipper MSn. *Obvious error*
174.23	muzzy] T; *muzzy* MSn. *Since the word forms part of a stage direction which is emended to italics, it is emended instead to roman type*
174.35	he's] T; hes MSn. *The same emendation is made at* 174.42
174.44	child, he] T; ~∧ ~ MSn. *The spacing in MSn indicates that Irving intended a pause*
175.8	forest trees–] T; ~.:/ ~ – MSn. *Irving neglected to cancel his punctuation after deciding to add a word*
176.2	melancholy, man] T; ~∧ ~ *Punctuation necessary for clarity*
176.26–27	comrade] T; comerade MSn
176.35	air,] T; ~∧ MSn. *Punctuation necessary to separate the coordinated phrases*
*176.35	*Proscenium*] T; PS MSn
177.5	Look!] T; *Casp.* ~ – MSn. *The identification of the speaker is omitted as redundant. Irving neglected to delete it after canceling an intervening speech by Albert*
177.8	(A great] T; ∧~ ~ MSn. *Irving forgot to include the left parenthesis; the same emendation is made at* 189.6

177.10	Art] T; *Alb.* ~ MSn. *The identification of the speaker is omitted as redundant*
177.42	Ah] T; A MSn. *Irving misspelled the mild exclamation*
178.9	that—] T; ~ — MSn. *Longer dash signifies the extended pause Irving intends*
178.12	terms] T; tirms MSn
178.14	thine] T; ⟨yours⟩ ↑thine↓ MSn. *The cancellation and interlineation are by Livius*
178.25	the purpose?] T; the ⟨balls we/ spoke of –⟩ purpose. MSn. *The cancellation and the substituted word "purpose" are in pencil, the latter certainly by Livius*
178.31	hast] T; has MSn. *Following "Thou," the MSn reading is not idiomatic; see 179.7*
178.32	Hunter—] T; ~∧ *Dash is second of a pair*
179.3	*(with horror)* And] T; ↑(with horror)↓ And MSn. *The interlineation is by Livius*
179.9	heart,] T; ~∧ MSn. *Irving neglected to add a comma to replace one in a deleted phrase immediately following*
179.25–26	happiness,] T; ~∧ MSn. *The comma marks a pause*
179.29	bad,] T; ~∧ MSn. *The comma marks a pause*
179.35	proffered] T; proferred MSn
180.12	control] T; controul MSn
180.17	*Cottage*] T; Cottage / [*space*]/⟨*end of Act 1.*⟩ MSn. *Irving's concluding note, apparently for his own reference, is omitted as unnecessary*
180.18	[Act 2. Scene 1.]] T; [*omitted*] MSn
180.19	*Counting*] T; *Countg* MSn
180.20	o'clock] T; Oclock MSn
180.22	eight] T; 8 Msn. *See 180.20, 182.11*
180.34	impending] T; empinding MSn
181.13	Heigh ho!] T; NINA – ~ ~! MSn. *Indication of speaker omitted as unnecessary*
181.26	sport—racketting] T; ~ ∧ ~ MSn. *Irving deleted an "and" but failed to supply the necessary punctuation to replace it*
181.37	lover's] T; lovers MSn. *The same emendation is made at 182.31*
182.13	fastening] T; fastning MSn
182.18	harassed] T; harrassed MSn
182.24	o'er] T; oer MSn
182.33	broad fair moon out,] T; ↑~ ~ ~ ~–↓ MSn. *Comma*

reflects Irving's usage in canceled phrase superseded by the interlineation

182.37   (archly)] T; ∧∼∧ MSn. Parentheses necessary to sep-
              arate speech from stage direction, Irving's usual prac-
              tice. The same emendation is made at 182.41, 183.39,
              189.13

183.1–3   Albert . . . love–] T; ALBERT – *⟨'Tis so indeed – I
              must   away – before/   the   storm   comes   on –⟩/ . . ./
              Albert* . . . love – MSn.

183.4   so soon] T; soo ∼ MSn

183.6   too] T; to MSn

*183.16–17   [Scene 2.]/ Scene of Incantation,] T; Scene of Incanta-
              tion. MSn

*183.21   Urian] T; ⟨Urian⟩ MSn

183.28   Spirit, I] T; ∼. ∼ MSn. Irving almost certainly intended
              only a slight pause

*183.41–184.5 (omit . . . Andreas–)] T; [omit . . . Andreas –] MSn

184.4   Albert] T; Max MSn. Irving inadvertently employed the
              name assigned this character in Kind's libretto

184.8   sobered] T; sobred MSn. No authority in dictionaries

*184.9   onto proscenium.] T; o.p. MSn

184.9–10   observed . . . air)] T; observed) . . . air∧ MSn. Irving ne-
              glected to cancel the parenthesis after deciding to
              extend the stage direction

184.11   Here] T; And. ∼ MSn. The identification of the speaker
              is omitted as redundant

*184.29   [should] be] T; be MSn

184.29   sixth] T; 6th MSn. See 184.29, 187.19, 187.30; and Emen-
              dations, 167.33

184.31   Bertha] T; Birtha MSn

184.36–37   &c– . . . effect–)] T; &c –) . . . effect –∧ MSn. After ex-
              tending his note, Irving neglected to shift the posi-
              tion of the parenthesis

184.40   Gothic] T; gothic MSn. In contemporary usage ordinar-
              ily capitalized

185.4   Duke's] T; Dukes MSn. The same emendation is made
              at 187.3 duke's, 190.35

185.11   thunder, how] T; ∼∧ ∼ MSn. Comma marks a pause
              after the introductory phrase

185.25   Huntsman.] T; Hunts. MSn. The same emendation is
              made at 185.27

186.14	Albert, I] T; ~∧ ~ MSn. *Irving clearly intended a pause after the mild exclamation*
186.14	whene'er] T; wheneer MSn
186.32	Hermit's] T; Hermits MSn. *The same emendation is made at 189.23 hermit's*
187.4	Come,] T; ~∧ MSn. *See 187.1, 188.23*
187.9	*exclaims:*] T; ~∧ MSn. *The final portion of the stage direction is specifically introductory*
187.17	exhausted,] T; ~∧ MSn. *Pause follows the introductory phrase*
187.20	Albert,] T; ~∧ MSn. *Pause follows the apostrophe*
187.34	*Caspar*] T; *Andreas* MSn. *Obvious oversight*
187.39	that] T; the ↑that↓ MSn. *The interlineation clearly represents a proposed alteration*
188.10	there [be]]T; there MSn. *The word following "there," if any, has been obscured in the binding process; see* Emendations, 164.27
188.15	shriek] T; shreik MSn
188.16	(*exit*)] T; (*exit*; MSn. *Irving apparently thought of continuing the stage direction but, abandoning the idea, neglected to add the parenthesis*
188.17	[Scene 3.]] T: [*omitted*] MSn
188.24	village.] T; ~: MSn. *On deciding to continue the sentence Irving neglected to alter his punctuation*
188.29	Still—still] T; ~ ∧ ~ MSn. *Irving intended a slight pause; see 188.30*
188.29–30	foreboding] T; forboding MSn
188.32	(*Air . . . Wolke*)] T; (~ . . . ~) (4) MSn. *The appended number is omitted as serving no purpose here*
188.36	sacrifice] T; sacrafice MSn
189.13	Oh Heavens!] T; Nina – ~ ~! MSn. *The identification of the speaker is omitted as redundant; see* Discussions of Adopted Readings, 189.13
189.19	quickly:] T; ~ – MSn. *The final portion of the stage direction is specifically introductory*
189.30	[Scene 4.]] T; Scene Last (p 14)/ (After *Grand* Chorus) MSn. *Irving's scene designations are omitted as being in effect reference notes for a particular draft of the play*
189.31	skill.] T; ~, MSn. *Irving canceled his original conclusion to the sentence but neglected to revise the punctuation*

190.5   Conrad?] T; ~. – MSn. *The period was added in pencil, perhaps as a substitution*

*190.6   successful. The] T; ~ – the MSn

*190.11   *Caspar.*] T; */ *Caspar – MSn

190.13   trees–.] T; ~ – [?,?] MSn. *Irving's comma may be a slurred period. At any rate, a period is called for at this point*

190.17–18   *mark!–Close*] T; mark –" "CLOSE MSn. *Irving neglected to delete quotation marks after deciding to extend the speech; he intended his underlining swipe of the pen to include "mark"*

190.25–26   [*Caspar . . . ground.*]] T; [*omitted*] MSn. *Editorial interpolation necessary for continuity*

*190.35–36   *chair &c. Caspar . . . hunters)*] T; chair &c)/ Caspar – 〈Tottering〉 is led tottering forward between two hunters) MSn

190.41   Ah,] T; ~∧ MSn. *Slight pause seems intended following mild exclamation*

191.16   breathe–] T; ~∧ MSn. *Added dash consistent with Irving's practice in this speech*

*191.25   Andreas?] T; ~ –/ *Duke* – Where is the hunter Andreas – MSn

*191.25   ———(*Andreas*, who] T; ———Andreas (who MSn

191.38   Caspar] T; Andreas MSn. *Obvious error*

191.43   counsels] T; councils MSn

192.9   Albert,] T; ~∧ MSn. *At this solemn moment Irving certainly intends a pause*

192.13   recompense] T; reccompense MSn

[ABU HASSAN]

*192.18   [ABU HASSAN]] T; [*omitted*] MSn

*192.19   [Act 1.] Scene 1.] T; 〈Act〉Scene 1. MSn

192.20–24   *Abu . . . Water–*] T; Abu . . . Water – MSn. *Emendation reflects Irving's usual practice. Stage directions or indicated portions of them are also italicized at 197.4, 197.9, 198.14, 201.23, 202.30 Enter Fatima, 207.24, 208.19 Enter, 208.20 advances, 210.27, 211.24, 213.13 Enter, 214.19, 216.15, 216.32 looking out of, 218.22, 218.27, 219.9–10 he . . . himself, other Couch, 220.25, 220.29, 221.21–22, 221.24, 222.13–14, 223.13 Couches, 227.18*

192.20   *Hassan's*] T; Hassans MSn. *The same emendation is made at* 194.28 Hassan's, 198.14. *Apostrophes are supplied to possessives at* 193.17, 194.7, 195.33, 195.34, 208.9, 218.11 (MSn, Zobiedes), 224.20, 226.8. *Multiple emendations of possessives are listed in* Emendations, 194.28, 195.33, 201.18, 207.16

192.23   *Cushions.*] T; Cushions∧ *Irving's punctuation, if any, was lost when the page in MSn was cropped. Additional readings truncated due to cropping or obscured beneath the binding of MSn are as follows*: 194.21 prophe, 198.6 pleasure∧, 199.6 deman, 204.18 chink, 207.28 Caliph∧, 209.9 figurati, 204.18 rogue., 216.34 imagin, 217.33 Zobei, 220.30 Nev, 220.34 personabl, 221.28 deat, 227.2 punis

192.25   *Abu Hassan.*] T; N° 1 ~ ~. MSn. *Livius' number-designation serves no purpose for the present manuscript in itself and is omitted. Similar ommissions of indicated notations by Livius occur at* 197.15 N° 2, 200.26 N° 3, 206.27 N° 4, 207.31 N° 5 [*and in faint red ink on the right side of the page:*] Aria N° 5, 210.28 N° 6, 214.28 N° 7, 219.24 N° 8

192.26   wine!] T; ~∧ MSn. *Exclamation marks are supplied, or substituted for indicated punctuation, at* 193.25, 199.10 *dash*, 213.8 *dash*, 213.23, 214.18 *period*, 216.31 *period*, 217.10 *period*, 217.21, 220.10, 220.25, 221.18 *dash*, 221.25, 221.28, 222.28, 223.8, 223,8, 223.29 *period*, 223.30, 227.2, 227.17 *period*

192.27   *Fatima.*] T; ~∧ MSn. *Periods are supplied or substituted for other punctuation after the names of characters preceding speeches by them at* 192.30, 192.33, 193.1, 193.4, 193.6, 193.8, 193.15, 193.18, 193.22, 193.24, 193.26, 193.31, 194.5, 194.8, 194.16, 194.25, 194.30, 195.6, 195.14, 195.18, 195.26, 196.3, 196.23, 196.28, 198.19, 199.9, 199.30, 200.1, 200.5, 200.9, 200.13, 200.15, 200.17, 200.21, 200.25, 201.4, 201.15, 201.19, 201.26, 201.30, 201.32, 202.3, 202.8, 202.12, 204.8, 204.16, 205.10, 205.16, 205.26, 206.13, 206.28, 206.33, 207.6, 207.9, 207.12, 207.17, 207.26, 208.21, 208.23, 208.28, 208.30, 208.32, 209.1, 209.3, 209.5, 209.10, 209.14, 209.16, 209.18, 209.20, 209.22, 209.24, 209.28, 209.30, 210.1, 210.3, 210.5, 210.7, 210.9, 210.11, 210.13, 210.15, 210.17, 210.19, 210.24, 210.26, 211.1, 211.6, 211.8, 211.14, 211.16, 211.18, 211.20, 211.26, 211.32,

212.1, 212.4, 212.7, 212.19, 212.22, 212.30, 212.32, 212.34, 213.1, 213.3, 213.5, 213.7, 213.9, 213.17, 213.30, 214.1, 214.7, 214.29, 214.32, 215.1, 215.8, 215.14, 215.19, 216.5, 216.9, 216.16, 216.18, 216.20, 216.28, 216.32, 217.1, 217.14, 217.16, 217.20, 217.25, 217.32, 218.7, 218.16, 218.21, 218.28, 218.30, 219.1, 219.3, 219.11, 219.13, 219.15, 219.19, 219.29, 220.1, 220.7, 221.3, 221.27, 221.31, 222.6 *following* "Fatima," 222.7, 222.15, 222.20, 222.22, 222.24, 222.27, 222.29, 222.31, 222.33, 222.35, 223.23, 223.26, 223.31, 224.9, 224.27, 224.30, 224.32, 225.1, 225.5, 225.11, 225.16, 225.25, 225.27, 225.30, 225.32, 226.3, 226.9, 226.18, 226.29, 226.31, 227.5, 227.8, 227.11, 227.13

192.28   red wine] T; ↑~ ~↓ wine MSn. *Irving neglected to cancel the redundant "wine." Substantives inadvertently left uncanceled in MSn occur as indicated in parentheses before the words shown at the following points*: 211.4 (heart) Seek, 211.11 (me) me, 212.6 (So) can

192.30   *Abu Hassan.*] T; *Abu H:* MSn. *Abbreviations of this character's name preceding speeches by him are emended to the full spelling at* 194.11, 194.19, 194.30, 195.1, 195.8, 195.14, 195.20, 195.31, 196.5, 196.16, 196.25, 196.31, 198.15, 198.21, 198.25, 199.1, 199.11, 199.18, 199.26, 199.32, 200.3, 200.11, 200.15, 200.19, 200.23, 201.1, 201.9, 201.17, 202.1, 202.8, 203.1, 203.7, 203.13, 203.17, 203.30, 204.3, 204.12, 204.19, 204.29, 204.34, 205.6, 205.10, 205.14, 205.18, 205.22, 205.26, 205.31, 206.3, 206.13, 206.21, 207.3, 207.7, 207.21, 213.17, 213.22, 213.30, 214.1, 214.9, 214.21, 214.26, 214.32, 215.5, 215.14, 215.24, 216.5, 216.16, 216.20, 217.1, 217.11, 217.16, 217.22, 217.30, 218.3, 218.12, 218.23, 218.28, 218.33, 219.3, 219.13, 219.17, 222.1, 222.11, 222.19, 222.21, 222.24, 222.28, 222.31, 222.35, 222.39, 223.3, 223.5, 223.8, 223.9, 225.27, 225.32, 226.12, 226.21, 226.26, 227.5, 227.13. *Similar emendations within stage directions or speeches occur at* 198.20, 220.20, 226.10

192.31   disguise,] T; ~∧/ MSn *End-of-line commas omitted in MSn are supplied after the indicated words at* 193.13 need, 193.32 master, 196.22 garments, 197.20 have, 197.21 adorning, 197.24 wine, 197.25 in, 197.34 stay,

198.1 dearest, 198.2 art, 198.3 delighting, 210.13 Omar,
202.14 ended, 206.35 blooms, 207.10 love, 207.14
truth, 207.32 free, 208.4 hangs, 208.9 regions, 208.12
ever, 208.13 me, 208.16 power, 210.28 papers, 211.4
frighten, 212.1 pleasure, 212.8 advice, 212.15 gone,
215.9 merit, 215.12 spirit, 215.28 then, 215.29 him,
216.11 examin'd, 216.23, 24 find, 216.30 over, 217.3
Divan, 220.29 Nay, 222.2 conscientiousness, 222.12 retreating, 222.16 retreating, 222.37 me, 222.39 thee,
223.5 bed, 223.19 *Caliph*, 224.25 first, 225.2 spoken,
227.20 come, 227.25 comes

192.32   Sherbet.] T; ∼∧ MSn. *Periods are supplied at the ends
of sentences or speeches at* 192.23, 192.34, 193.23,
194.29, 195.33, 197.2, 197.9, 197.14, 198.4, 198.6, 198.31,
199.6, 199.22, 199.33, 200.8, 200.10, 201.25, 202.7,
202.11, 202.16, 202.28, 203.14, 204.7, 204.20, 204.23,
206.32, 207.6, 207.20, 207.28, 207.30, 208.2, 208.10,
208.26, 208.31, 209.9, 209.13, 209.17, 209.21, 210.31,
211.23, 211.28, 212.10, 212.14, 212.25, 26, 212.28 (MSn
betray,), 212.31, 213.16, 213.20, 213.29, 213.32, 214.27,
215.10, 215.27, 216.27, 216.35, 217.12, 217.21, 218.6,
218.9, 218.19, 218.29, 218.32, 219.8, 219.21, 219.22,
219.26, 220.20, 221.5, 221.21, 221.22, 222.14, 222.38,
223.25, 223.34, 224.5, 224.16, 224.23, 224.26, 225.4,
226.8, 226.17, 226.24, 227.2, 227.12, 227.22, 227.27

192.33   *Fatima*] T; Fatima MSn. *Names of characters preceding
speeches by them and not underlined in MSn are
italicized at* 193.1, 193.15, 193.24, 193.26, 193.31,
194.19, 196.16, 197.3, 198.19, 201.1, 206.1, 212.22,
221.15, 223.33, 224.22, 224.24

192.34   Oh,] T; ∼∧ MSn. *A slight pause seems intended*
193.4   *Fatima.*] T; *Fatim:* MSn. *Abbreviations of this character's name preceding speeches by her are emended
to the full spelling at* 194.32, 195.10, 195.18, 195.26,
196.3, 196.13, 196.28, 203.5, 203.15, 203.22, 203.28,
204.1, 204.8, 204.16, 204.21, 204.31, 205.3, 205.8,
205.12, 205.16, 205.20, 205.24, 205.28, 206.1, 206.9,
206.18, 207.5, 207.9, 208.23, 209.10, 209.22, 209.26,
209.30, 210.3, 210.7, 210.11, 211.8, 211.12, 211.16,
211.20, 212.11, 212.17, 213.1, 213.5, 213.19, 213.27,
213.33, 214.16, 214.24, 214.29, 215.8, 218.26, 218.30,
219.1, 219.19, 220.1, 220.7, 220.15, 220.23, 220.31,

221.1, 221.6, 221.13, 222.7, 222.20, 222.22, 222.27, 222.29, 222.23, 222.37, 223.4, 223.7, 227.11

193.16   Come, I'll] T; ↑(*Come, Ill*)↓ I will MSn. *The parentheses indicate only that alternative matter is enclosed; see* Emendations 194.7. *The underlining seems to indicate preference for the later reading. The apostrophe is added to form "I'll" at* 197.13, 197.18, 201.24, 201.28, 211.13, 216.3, 220.24, 223.2, 225.10

193.21   me?] T; ∼ₐ MSn. *See* 193.19. *Question marks are supplied, or substituted for indicated punctuation, as follows:* 194.10 *period,* 194.24, 196.24 *dash,* 197.17, 198.20, 199.14 *dash,* 199.15 *dash,* 200.18 *period,* 201.33, 202.32 *dash,* 203.12 *period,* 203.19 *dash,* 203.23 *exclamation mark,* 203.29 *period,* 204.25 *period,* 204.30 *period,* 209.6 *dash,* 209.19 *period,* 211.3, 212.16, 213.14 *period,* 213.34, 214.31 *comma,* 217.31, 218.2 *period,* 218.15 *period,* 218.31 *dash,* 219.16 *dash,* 220.2 *period,* 220.12, 221.30 *period,* 224.29 *period,* 225.7 *period,* 225.9 *period,* 226.6, 226.11, 226.20 *period,* 227.14 *period*

193.23   'twill] T; twill MSn. *Apostrophes are supplied to contracted verbs, or contractions including verbs, at* 197.32 (*MSn* To days), 198.12 (*MSn* Whose), 203.18, 211.30, 214.17, 221.24, 222.40, 226.32. *Multiple apostrophized contractions are listed in* Emendations 193.16, 195.32, 196.14, 199.8, 201.24, 203.2, 211.31, 221.19, 221.28

194.2   palate] T; tongue (Qu. *palate*) MSn. *The underlining apparently indicates preference for the alternative reading*

194.7   Pawn Broker's!] T; Jewellers!/ (Qu *Pawn Brokers*) MSn. *The underlining appears to signify Irving's preference; see* Emendations, 193.16, 194.2

194.12   of; in truth] T; ∼ – /; ∼ ∼ MSn. *Dash forms part of a canceled passage and was inadvertently allowed to stand by Irving. Punctuation thus left uncanceled in MSn occurs before or after the indicated words as shown:* 197.16 (, may), 207.28 (–! Well), 215.11 (– / *Omar.*), 216.12 (, dear), 216.14 (I – –), 221.18 (– Hassan), 221.27 (*up,*), 221.28 (, Fire)

194.21   Prophet] T; prophe MSn. *See* Emendations, 192.23.

	Capitalization reflects Irving's usual practice; see 205.32, Emendations, 197.13
194.22	speak,] T; ~∧ MSn. *A pause seems intended before the question*
194.27	Zobeide] T; Zobiede MSn
194.28	Caliph's] T; Caliphs MSn. *The same emendation is made at 225.27 Caliph's, 226.29*
195.2–5	"Fairest . . . Omar"] T; ∧~ . . . ~∧ MSn. *Pairs of quotation marks are also supplied at* 204.23, 204.24, 204.24–28, 205.4, 205.4–5, 205.9, 205.9, 205.13, 205.17, 205.21, 205.25, 206.2, 214.2, 214.2–6, 214.10, 214.10–14
195.15	me,] T; ~; MSn. *Irving neglected to revise his punctuation after he had added the introductory clause*
195.21	mightest] T; mightst MSn. *See* 195.23
195.32	Don't] T; Dont MSn. *The same emendation is made at* 199.2 don't, 201.23 don't, 205.1 don't, 219.18, 221.23 don't
195.33	*moment's*] T; *moments* MSn. *The same emendation is made at* 219.4
196.14	that's] T; thats MSn. *The same emendation is made at* 198.33, 201.2, 205.27
196.33	distress,] T; ~∧ MSn. *Second comma of a pair*
196.34	thee] T; the MSn. *Oversight*
197.7	Scene 2.] T; *Scene 2ᵈ*∧ MSn. *For further emendations of Irving's act-scene numbers see* Emendations, 198.13, 202.29, 207.25, 208.19, 213.11, 217.8, 218.21, 219.25, 221.26, 223.11
197.13	Great Prophet] T; great ~ MSn. *See* 217.10, 225.13. *The same emendation is made at* 202.19 (MSn, great prophet), 218.4
197.17	Like] T; like MSn. *Words are capitalized at the beginnings of sentences or lines of verse at* 203.19, 204.9, 206.24, 210.28, 213.16, 213.23, 214.13, 214.19, 214.22, 219.31, 221.28, 223.29
197.18	fête champêtre] T; fete champetre MSn
197.24	Slaves there] T; *Slaves there* MSn. *Underlined in pencil for further consideration*
197.26	sweet] T; (~) MSn.*The penciled parenthesis signifies a need for further attention*
197.27	sip it.] T; ~ (it.) MSn. *The penciled parenthesis calls attention to an imperfect rhyme between "it" and "sweet" in the line above*

198.9   fail] T; (founder?) fail MSn. *The parentheses and "fail"
             are in pencil, indicating a substitution*

*198.13   Scene 3.] T; 3ᵈ sᴄᴇɴᴇ∧/ . . . / ⟨3 Scene⟩ MSn.

198.15–16   *Abu Hassan./* Ah,] T; *Ab H.* Ah, MSn. *In accordance
             with Irving's usual practice in MSn, the designation
             of the speaker is moved to the line above the speech
             here and at* 198.19, 198.21, 198.23, 198.25, 198.29,
             198.32, 199.1, 199.7, 199.9, 199.11, 199.16, 199.18,
             203.1, 203.5, 203.7, 203.11, 203.13, 203.15, 203.17,
             203.22, 203.24, 203.28, 203.30, 204.1, 204.3, 204.8,
             204.12, 204.31, 204.34, 205.3, 205.6, 205.8, 205.10,
             205.12, 205.14, 205.16, 205.18, 205.20, 205.22, 205.24,
             205.26, 205.28,, 205.31, 206.1, 206.3, 206.9, 206.13,
             206.18, 206.21, 212.17, 213.22, 213.27, 213.30, 213.33,
             214.1, 214.7, 214.9, 214.16, 214.21, 214.24, 214.26,
             218.7, 220.9, 220.15, 220.19, 220.23, 220.26, 220.31,
             220.33, 221.1, 221.3, 221.6, 221.8, 221.13, 221.15,
             223.23, 223.26, 223.28, 223.31, 223.33, 224.6, 224.9,
             224.17, 224.22, 224.24, 224.30, 224.32, 225.1, 225.5,
             225.11, 225.18, 225.20, 225.22, 225.25, 225.27,
             225.30, 225.32, 226.1, 226.3, 226.5, 226.7, 226.9,
             226.12, 226.18, 226.21, 226.25, 226.27, 226.29, 226.31,
             227.5, 227.8, 227.11, 227.13

198.26   Allah] T; allah MSn. *See* 213.8, 215.22, 220.10. *The
             same emendation is made at* 206.19, 220.8

198.27   Caliph] T; caliph MSn. *Also capitalized at* 206.6

199.8   we'll] T! well MSn. *The same emendation is made at*
             199.17, 221.20

199.16   *Creditors.*] T; *Cred.* MSn

199.27   damn'd] T; ⟨cursed⟩ ↑dam⟨d⟩nd↓ MSn. *The deletion of
             "cursed" and the interlineation are by Livius. An
             apostrophe is also added to "damnd" at* 203.2 *and
             "damndest" at* 201.11

201.4   *Chorus of Creditors*] T; ᴄʜᴏʀᴜs ᴏꜰ ᴄʀᴇᴅɪᴛᴏʀs MSn.
             *Stage directions and speech designations, or indicated
             portions of them, underlined twice in MSn are itali-
             cized at* 201.15, 204.21, 208.21, 208.30, 210.24, 210.26,
             212.19, 214.28, 215.33 *Fatima – after*, 217.8 *Mesrour*,
             217.14 *Mesrour*, 218.26, 219.26 *Enter Zemrud*, 220.27
             Abu Hassan, 223.23, 223.26, 225.18 *All*

201.13   render me] T; render ↑me↓ MSn. *The interlineation is
             by Livius*

201.18　　　　　Fatima's] T; Fatimas MSn. *The same emendation is made at* 217.7 *Fatima's,* 217.19 *Fatima's,* 217.33

201.23　　　　　let your] T; your MSn. *Irving accidentally included "let" in a cancellation*

201.24　　　　　I'm] Im MSn. *The same emendation is made at* 223.7

*202.6　　　　　And ... intended,] T; And ⟨what is more,⟩ ↑eke right well↓ intended,/ ... / But slyly I intend it MSn

202.19　　　　　rout] T; route MSn

202.24　　　　　enjoyed] T; ↑ceased↓ enjoyed MSn. *The interlineation, possibly an abandoned substitution of "ceased to enjoy," is by Livius; by itself it does not suit the context*

202.30　　　　　Scene 5.] T; 5 Scene_∧ MSn

203.2　　　　　I've] T; Ive MSn. *The same emendation is made at* 203.3

203.9　　　　　'Sblood] T; _∧Sblood MSn

203.14　　　　　them,] T; ~_∧ MSn. *Comma clarifies*

203.16　　　　　What,] T; ~_∧ MSn. *Slight pause seems intended after the mild exclamation*

204.5　　　　　liquorish] T; licquorish MSn. *No authority in dictionaries*

*204.8–9　　　Fatima./ There!] T; ⟨Fat. There—and yet you doubted whether⟩/ (after *paying all my debts*)/ Fat_∧ There! MSn

204.15　　　　　pawning of them] T; ~ ↑~↓ ~ MSn. *The interlineation is by Livius*

*204.16–17　Fatima./ Here ... foretaste] T; Fat. Here you have a little foretaste &c / *vide p. 22*/ ... / *Fat:*/ Here you have a little foretaste MSn

204.23　　　　　you?" said she.] T; you_{∧∧}/ said she? MSn. *Irving wrote the question mark belatedly*

204.24　　　　　Ah,] T; ~_∧ MSn. *Comma separates interrupted quotation from commentary. Commas are also supplied for this purpose at* 205.4, 205.29, 214.2, 214.10

205.27　　　　　Scandal] T; ⟨s⟩Scandal MSn. *The "S" is written over the "s" in pencil, probably by Livius*

205.29　　　　　all ... Fatima,"] T; all" my dear Fatima_∧ MSn. *The quotation mark is obviously misplaced*

206.15　　　　　was] T; ~ ↑were↓ MSn. *The ungrammatical interlineation, probably based on a misreading of Irving's hand, is by Livius*

206.25   for a moment,] T; ↑~ ~ ~ᴧ↓ MSn. *Comma marks*
                pause before lengthy infinitive phrase

*206.27   *Duetto.*] T; Duetto/ . . ./ N° 4 *Duetto.* MSn

206.30   belov'd] T; belov⟨e⟩d MSn

207.6   well, love] T; ~ᴧ ~ MSn. *See* 207.10

207.16   one's] T; ones MSn. *The same emendation is made at*
                207.29, 207.29

207.24   *exeunt severally*] T; ⟨exit thro center door⟩ ↑exeunt sev-
                erally↓ MSn. *The deletion and substitution are by*
                Livius

207.25   Act 2. Scene 1.] T; ⟨Scene 6.⟩/ Act II Scene 1 app.
                in H. House MSn. *The cancellation and the remaining*
                text are in pencil by Livius. The abbreviated scene-
                designation is omitted as unnecessary, probably hav-
                ing been intended as a private reference note

*207.27–28   I . . . Caliph. Well] T; ⟨Away ⟨you⟩ with your saucy
                jokes⟩ – ! ↑*↓/ * I . . . Caliph./ Well MSn

207.31   ne'er] T; neer MSn

208.7   She] T; ⟨And⟩ ↑She↓ MSn. *The deletion and substitu-*
                tion are by Livius

208.12   have I ever,] T; have I everᴧ ↑has ever[living?]↓ MSn.
                Interlineation rejected as failing to conform to rhyme-
                scheme

208.15   bless'd] T; blessd MSn

208.19   *Enter Omar*] T; ⟨7 Scene.⟩/ ⟨Fatima.⟩ Enter *Omar* MSn.
                The deletions and "Enter" are by Livius

208.20   *advances*] T; ⟨enters⟩ ↑advances↓ MSn. *Deletion and*
                substitution by Livius

208.24   He's] T; He's ⟨has⟩ MSn. *The deletion and the "'s"*
                are by Livius

209.8   goat] T; ⟨Fawn⟩ ↑goat↓ MSn. *The deletion and substitu-*
                tion are by Livius

209.27   He squanders] T; He Squanders MSn. *"He" is added in*
                the left margin; Irving neglected to alter the "S"

209.31   money–] T; ~ᴧ MSn. *See* 210.4

210.29   butchers,] T; ~ – MSn. *The dash may be a slurred*
                comma; the emendation reflects Irving's pactice else-
                where in the stanza

210.30   Mantua] T; Mantau MSn

211.27   (*Aside*)] T; (*Aside* –) MSn. *Irving intended this stage*
                direction and that at 211.22 to be identical

211.31   Thou lov'st me! Thou lov'st me!] T; *You love me, you*

	love me ↑~ ~ ~! ~ lovst ~!↓ MSn. *Irving's later choice is adopted, being consistent in its use of "thou" with the preceding lines. Apparently the underlining signifies a need for revision*
212.5	Alas sir] T; I know not ↑~ ~↓ MSn. *Irving attempted unsuccessfully to adapt the superseded "I know not" in the following line*
212.9	harassed] T; harrassed MSn
212.14	worse] T; wors MSn
212.27	[*Fatima.*]] T; [*omitted*] MSn. *Necessary to indicate the speaker of the following two lines. See* 212.30
212.27	fool,] T; ~∧ MSn. *See* 212.30
*213.7	(*into the cabinet*)] T; *hurries* (*into the cabinet* – (⟨*right hand*⟩) MSn.
213.11	Stay] T; ⟨8ᵗʰ *Scene*/ Fatima. Abu Hassan. Omar in the/ cabinet – –⟩/ *Fatima* (⟨*to herself*⟩) / Stay MSn. *The first deletion is by Livius. The designation of the speaker is omitted here as redundant*
213.11	nothing old wretch–] T; ~ ↑~ ~↓ – MSn. *The interlineation is by Livius*
213.12	I've] T; ⟨Ive⟩ ↑I've↓ MSn. *The deletion and correction are by Livius*
213.12	thee.] T; ⟨you⟩ ↑thee↓. MSn. *The deletion and substitution are by Livius*
213.13	*Enter*] T; ⟨*To*⟩ ↑Enter↓ MSn. *The interlineation is by Livius*
213.19	(*Softly*] T; ∧~ MSn. *Beginning parentheses are added at* 214.25, 216.32, 226.27; *end parentheses are added at* 220.28, 224.13
213.31	truly,] T; ~∧ MSn. *A pause seems intended*
214.5	disposition] T; ⟨temperament⟩ ↑disposition↓ MSn. *The interlineation is by Livius*
214.6	harem] T; haram MSn
214.10–11	Commander of the Faithful] T; commander ~ ~ ~ MSn. *See* 217.33, 224.7. "*Faithful*" *in this epithet is capitalized at* 227.6
214.11	thee, . . . meet] T; thee, it is meat ↑meet↓ MSn. *The comma and the interlineated correction are by Livius*
214.15	nature, how] T; ~∧ ~ MSn. *A pause seems proper following the repeated apostrophe*
214.19	(*softly*)] T; (⟨*aside*⟩ ↑softly↓) MSn. *The deletion and*

substitution are by Livius. The identical pattern of emendations occurs at 214.22

214.22–23   (he . . . loud)] T; (⟨loud⟩) ⟨Come Go⟩ he goes towards ⟨the/ door of⟩ the cabinet –) ↑(loud)↓ MSn. The "he" is by Livius; the parentheses following "cabinet –" and preceding "loud" are omitted as unnecessary

214.25   Embarrassment] T; Embarrasst MSn

215.6   Yes] T; Yes ∧ [sic] MSn. Apparently Irving thought better of an interlineation

215.9   me–] T; ∼ ∧ MSn. See 215.12; a pause seems intended

215.16   flatt'ring] T; flattring MSn. The same emendation is made at 215.21

215.16   ray;] T; ∼∧ MSn. See 215.21

215.29   seize] T; sieze MSn

215.32   reveal'd] T; reveald MSn

215.33   Fatima.] T; ————/ FATIMA. MSn. The line above the speech designation is apparently a half-conscious flourish made as Irving considered the line to follow

216.32–33   (looking . . . anxiously)] T; ⟨who at the end of the/ Terzetto had gone to ↑looking out of↓ the window, ⟨speaks/ the following⟩ (quick and anxiously) MSn. The interlineated "looking out of" is by Livius; the parenthesis preceding "quick" is omitted as unnecessary

216.34   See, the] T; See∧ The MSn. "See" is written in the left margin by Livius

216.34   Mesrour] T; Mezrour MSn

217.3   Quick.] T; Ab. H. / Quick MSn. The speech designation is omitted as redundant

217.8   Mesrour] T; ⟨9th Scene⟩/ MESROUR MSn. The scene-designation is deleted by Livius

217.9   pause:] T; ∼∧ MSn. The stage direction is specifically introductory. Colons are added in similar situations at 220.28, 227.3

217.12   (Rises . . . him.) I] T; Rises and approaches him∧/ I MSn. In accordance with Irving's usual practice in stage directions immediately preceding speeches, parentheses are also supplied at 217.14, 219.20–21, 221.7, 222.29, 226.3

217.20   Mesrour.] T; Mes: MSn. Abbreviations of this character's name preceding speeches by him are emended *to the full spelling at 217.25, 217.32, 218.7, 218.16, 224.6*

217.26 downhearted,] T; ∼∧ MSn. *Comma marks a pause*

218.8 giddy–you] T; ∼ ∧ ∼ MSn. *The spacing and the context in MSn indicate a pause is intended*

218.9 Well, at] T; well, At MSn. *Irving added "well" in the left margin, intending it to begin the sentence*

218.20 *accompanies*] T; *accompanys* MSn

218.21 *Fatima.*] T; ⟨10ᵗʰ *Scene/* FATIMA. *Shortly after Abu Hassan/ Omar in the closet.*⟩/ *Fatima* (setting up) MSn. *The deletion and the stage direction are by Livius; tahe latter is omitted because it virtually duplicates one in the next line by Irving*

218.22 I'm ... gone–] T; ⟨⟨*(to Abu/ Hassan as he enters)* Is he gone? so he's gone at las[t] ↓I'm glad he is gone ————↑ MSn. *The deletion and interlineation are by Livius. The extended dash appears to be merely a flourish*

218.24 he's off] T; ⟨he hies⟩ ↑he's off↓ MSn. *The deletion and substitution are by Livius*

218.27 (*rising ... Couch*)] T; ⟨*with some feeling as she rises/ from the Divan*⟩ (raising from the Couch) MSn. *The deletion and substitution are by Livius, whose "raising" is emended as ungrammatical*

218.32 for your suspicion.] T; ⟨–⟩ for your suspicion∧ MSn. *The deletion and the added phrase are by Livius*

219.2 Yes, with] T; ∼∧ ∼ MSn. *Cancellation intervenes between the two words*

219.4 Well well, ... present] T; ⟨No, no – the [*two words illegible*] may rest quiet⟩; ↑Well well∧ let that rest for the present↓ MSn. *The deletion and interlineation are by Livius*

*219.5–6 and now ... Besides,] T; and now/ ⟨I am cool I must entreat you to⟩ pardon/ ⟨the passion⟩ ⟨my fit of passion⟩ – ⟨Besides⟩ ↑⟨But⟩↓, MSn

219.6 scrape,] T; ∼∧ MSn. *Comma marks a pause preceding the dependent clause*

219.9–10 (*he ... Couch*)] T; (⟨*lies down*⟩ ↑he throws himself↓ on the ⟨*Divan*⟩ ↑other ⟨c⟩Couch↓) MSn. *The deletions and interlineations are by Livius*

219.12 Why what's] T; Why Whats MSn. *"Why" is added in*

> *the left margin; Irving neglected to revise his cap-*
> *italization*

219.21   Ah—] T; ⟨tho⟩Ah ⟨– tho⟩ – MSn. *"Ah" and the dele-*
tions are by Livius

219.25   [Scene 2.]] T; *11ᵗʰ Scene.* MSn

220.3   Zemrud] T; *Zem.* MSn. *Abbreviations of this character's*
name preceding speeches by her are emended to the
full spelling at the following points: 220.9, 220.19,
220.26, 220.33, 221.3, 221.8, 221.15

220.5   Holy Tomb] T; ~ tomb MSn. *Emendation reflects Irv-*
ing's usual practice for place-names

220.29   —cheer] T; ₍ₐ₎~ MSn. *Irving probably regarded the*
pause as supplied by the intervening stage direction

221.19   there's] T; theres MSn. *Also emended at* 222.16, 224.20

221.22   Zemrud] T; Zemroud MSn

*221.23   Now . . . child—] T; Now/ farewell my child &c/ . . ./
~ . . . ~ – MSn

221.26   [Scene 3.]] T; *12 Scene*₍ₐ₎ MSn

221.28   what's] T; whats MSn. *Also emended at* 225.22 What's

222.4   discreet—] T; ~ –/ Trio MSn. *The designation of the*
song is omitted as unnecessary; see 222.5, *whose text*
begins the following page in MSn

222.10   o'er] T; oer MSn. *Also emended at* 222.14, 222.18,
222.25

                                          3   1   2   4   5

*222.11   Our . . . completing;] T; Now our farce is ⟨fast⟩
                                        6
↓quickly↑ completing₍ₐ₎ MSn

222.15   completing;] T; ~₍ₐ₎ MSn. *See* 222.7

222.28   brave,] T; ~₍ₐ₎ MSn. *A slight pause seems intended*

222.32   they're] T; they'r MSn

222.37   o'ercome] T; oercome MSn. *The same emendation is*
made at 222.39

223.2   Never more I'll] T; How shall I dare ↓ Never more Ill↑
MSn. *Irving's penciled substitution is adopted here*
as representing the later opinion

223.3   Quickly, quickly] T; ~₍ₐ₎ ~ MSn. *Context seems to re-*
quire a slight pause before the repetition

223.3   dead and dumb be!] T; ~ ~ ~ ~! ↑lie ⟨thee⟩ down
here↓ MSn. *Original reading accepted because Irving*
apparently abandoned the idea of revising; note the
rhyme between 223.1, 223.3

223.5   Both . . . our] T; *Stretch thyself upon thy* ↑Both must lie
     upon our↓ MSn. *The underlining apparently signifies a need for revision*

223.9   night] T; Night MSn. *The capital "N" is little larger than a lower-case "n"; Irving's clear intention to write "night" in the identical next line warrants the emendation*

223.11   [Scene 4.]] T; Last Scene∧ MSn. *The scene number is supplied to complete the numerical series*

223.15   Bow . . . voices,] T; Bow your ↑⟨thy⟩↓ head⟨s⟩ and lift your ↑⟨the⟩↓ voice⟨s⟩, MSn. *Irving tentatively revised the line, abandoned his idea, but neglected to restore the "-s" endings; see 223.17*

223.17   See . . . rejoices,] T; See He comes who ⟨every heart⟩ ↑all↓ rejoices, MSn. *"See" is added in the left margin; "every heart" is encircled, apparently to indicate need for the substitution*

223.19–20   *At . . . Zemrud; at*] T; (*At . . . Zemrud*∧) *at* MSn. *Parentheses omitted as unnecessary; moreover, Irving neglected to delete the latter one on deciding to extend the stage direction*

223.29   *astonishment*] T; *astonishmt* MSn

223.30   Hassan—] T; ∼∧ MSn. *Dash is second of a pair*

224.1   poor Zara, my] T; ↑∼ ∼∧↓ ∼ MSn. *Comma separates appositives*

224.2–3   had, . . . confess,] T; ∼∧ . . . ∼∧ MSn. *Pauses separate the aside from the main statement*

224.7   Faithful,] T; ∼∧ MSn. *Comma marks a pause following the direct address. The same emendation is made at 225.6, 225.17, 226.13, 227.6*

224.7   *pointing*] T; *pointg* MSn

224.13–14   *Zobeide*—)/ [*Zobeide.*]] T; *Zobeide* –∧ MSn. *Probably through oversight, Irving caused the final word of a stage direction to do double duty as a speech designation; the missing right parenthesis is supplied and the speech designation added*

224.19   could] T; coud MSn

224.19   how] T; now MSn. *Irving's "n" may be an "h," and the context indicates he meant "how"*

224.22   *Zobeide.*] T; *Zob.* MSn

224.23   And] T; & MSn. *Emended to avoid confusion at beginning of sentence*

224.24	*Caliph.*] T; Cal. MSn. *An abbreviation of the title preceding a speech by this character is also emended to the full spelling at 226.25*
225.3	truth, for] T; ~∧ ~ MSn. *The comma marks a pause and separates clauses*
225.17	reward,] T; ~∧ MSn. *Comma marks pause before subordinate clause*
225.18	*Zobeide,*] T; ~∧ MSn. *Comma dispels awkwardness*
225.29	palate,] T; ~∧ MSn. *Comma is first of a pair*
226.7	*kneels*] T; *knees* MSn. *An error; see 226.10*
226.23	love,] T; ~∧ MSn. *Second comma of a pair*
227.17	to gain a living!] T; ⟨to live⟩! to gain a living∧ MSn. *The deletion and the text following the exclamation mark are by Livius*
227.27	Sound] T; Soundin MSn. *Irving apparently thought of altering "Sound" to "Sounding," then gave up the idea*

LIST OF REJECTED VARIANTS

This list provides a historical record of variants in texts which originated after the copy-texts.

The numbers before each entry indicate the page and line numbers. The reading to the left of the bracket indicates an accepted reading; its source is indicated by symbol after the bracket. The reading which follows the semicolon is a rejected one, the sources of which are identified by symbol. An asterisk preceding the page number refers the reader to the Discussions of Adopted Readings.

A key to identifying symbols used in referring to manuscript and printed texts is given on pages 229–32.

[REVIEW OF *THE WORKS . . . OF ROBERT TREAT PAINE*]

55.2	for ever] 1A; forever 2A
61.35	following] 1A; follow 2A

BIOGRAPHY OF CAPTAIN JAMES LAWRENCE

67.42	Montagu 74,] 1A; Montagu, 74, 9A. *Possibly Pierre M. Irving regarded the 1A designation of a vessel rated as carrying seventy-four guns as ambiguous, but the 9A reading does not clarify matters*
72.7	The comparatively] 1A; Owing to the comparatively 9A. *The 9A reading makes explicit a logical relation clearly implied in 1A*
72.8	decks] 1A; deck 9A. *The 9A reading probably represents an emendation by Pierre M. Irving to bring Irving's description of the ship into consistency with "deck" at 72.5. However, at 71.25 the term "upper decks" is used. Irving appears to use "deck" when designating the location of a single person, "decks" when speaking of the ship itself*
74.21	warming] 1A; warning 9A
75.28	funeral obsequies] 1A; obsequies 9A. *The 9A reading dispels a redundancy in 1A; however, "funeral obsequies" was an idiomatic expression*

BIOGRAPHICAL NOTICE OF THE LATE
LIEUTENANT BURROWS

86.39   a singular] 1A; singular 4A. *The indefinite article, while not unnecessary, may be dispensed with without materially altering the sense*

90.31   majesty's] 1A; Majesty's 4A. *Irving's failure to capitalize this reference to the king of England was perhaps a calculated slight*

BIOGRAPHICAL MEMOIR OF COMMODORE PERRY

92.24   enthusiasm] 1A; enthusiam 4A

98.6   3] T; 3 guns 4A. *The addition in 4A was necessary because the tabular list of forces extended onto a new page*

99.1   birth deck] 1A; berth-/deck 4A. *Webster prescribes the spelling "birth" under the definition "convenient room, place to lodge in"; see also "Biographical Memoir of David Porter"* 129.26

101.21–22   wounds, and . . . shot away.] 1A; wounds. 4A

103.21   "it had] 1A; "It has 4A. *The 4A reading duplicates that included in the full quotation above,* 103.10–11. *Clearly motivated by a desire to achieve consistency, it is probably the work of Pierre M. Irving*

ODES . . . BY EDWIN C. HOLLAND

106.8   some few years] 1A; some years 2A

106.11   muse] 1A; Muse 2A. *The same variant occurs at* 106.19, 110.22 (muses), 110.24, 112.26

110.21   chastness] 1A; chasteness 2A. *Walker prescribes "chastness" as the proper spelling*

BIOGRAPHICAL MEMOIR OF CAPTAIN DAVID PORTER

117.40   1st February] 1A; ~ of ~ 3A

118.10   the Active] 1A; Active 3A. *Irving does not ordinarily employ the article before a ship's name; see* 118.25, 123.9. *3A makes his usage consistent.*

119.2   the Insurgent] 1A; Insurgent 3A

119.11   Bite] 1A; Bight 3A. *Webster lists "bite" as the proper spelling of the word meaning "inlet or creek"*

123.24   majesty's] 1A; Majesty's 3A. *See "Lt. William Burrows,"* Rejected Variants, 90.31

124.37	groupe] 1A; group 3A. *Johnson, Walker, and Webster all specify "group" as the proper spelling (Webster also permits "groop"); but the* OED *lists "groupe" as in contemporary usage. The same variant occurs at* 125.11
127.1	28th March] 1A; ~ of ~ 3A
129.7	halser] 1A; hawser 3A. *Walker prescribes the 1A spelling; the same variant occurs at* 129.11

A BIOGRAPHICAL SKETCH OF THOMAS CAMPBELL

133.25–27	[This . . . author.]] 3A; [*omitted*] 9A
134.20	follow] 3A; followed 9A
134.38	authors] 3A; the authors 9A
*136.13	university] 3A; University 9A
*137.15	the Pleasures of Hope,] 3A; the "Pleasures of Hope," 9A
139.12	1803] 3A; 1603 9A
146.4	rocks] 3A; the rocks 9A

PASSAIC—A TRADITION

149.24	nature] MSw, 1A, 2A, 3A, 5A, 6A; Nature 4A
149.30	bank] MSw, 1A, 2A, 5A, 6A; banks 3A, 4A
149.32	And . . . abode] MSw, 6A; ~ . . . ~. 1A; ~ . . . ~; 2A; ~ . . . ~, 3A, 4A; And had fixed in its gloomy recess his abode, 5A
150.1	Who lov'd] MSw, 1A, 2A, 3A, 4A; ~ loved 6A; Loved best 5A
150.1	rude] MSw, 1A, 2A, 3A, 4A, 5A; wild 6A
150.1	scene] MSw, 1A, 2A, 3A, 5A, 6A; scenes 4A
150.1	whirlwind deforms] MSw, 4A; ~ ~, 2A; whirlwinds deform, 1A, 5A, 6A; whirlwinds deform 3A
150.2	tempest] MSw; tempests, 2A; thunder 3A; thunder, 1A, 5A, 6A; thunders, 4A
150.3	from] MSw, 2A, 3A, 4A, 5A, 6A; with 1A
150.5	While the] MSw, 1A, 2A, 3A, 5A, 6A; The 4A
150.5	noise] MSw, 1A, 3A, 4A, 5A, 6A; yell 2A
150.5	rung] MSw, 1A, 2A, 3A, 5A; rang 4A, 6A
150.6	the fresh] MSw, 1A, 2A, 3A, 6A; ~ ~, 5A; a fresh 4A
150.6	wears] MSw, 2A, 5A; bears 1A, 3A, 4A, 6A
150.7	Oh] MSw; Oh, 1A; Oh! 2A, 3A, 4A, 5A; [6A *wanting*]
150.8	red men] MSw, 1A, 3A, 4A; red-men 5A; white-man 2A; [6A *wanting*]

150.8   shrouded] MSw, 1A, 3A, 4A, 5A; shaded 2A; [6A *wanting*]

150.10   fields] MSw, 3A, 4A, 5A; ~, 2A; field 1A; [6A *wanting*]

150.10   which their fathers] MSw, 1A, 2A, 3A, 5A; their fore-fathers 4A; [6A *wanting*]

150.11   So] MSw; Lo! 1A, 2A, 3A, 4A, 5A; [6A *wanting*]

150.12   Pale savages] MSw, 2A, 5A; *Pale* ~ 1A, 3A; *Pale savages* 4A; [6A *wanting*]

150.14   By] MSw, 2A, 4A, 5A; With 1A, 3A; [6A *wanting*]

150.14   his warriors] MSw, 1A, 2A, 3A, 4A; the ~ 5A; [6A *wanting*]

150.16   passions were] MSw, 1A, 2A, 3A, 5A; passion was 4A; [6A *wanting*]

150.17   heart,] MSw, 1A, 3A, 4A, 5A; breast— 2A; [6A *wanting*]

150.20   flowrets] MSw; ~, 2A; flowers, 1A, 3A, 5A, 6A; flowers and 4A

150.20   wide waving] MSw, 2A, 3A; ~ – ~ 1A, 5A, 6A; wide spreading 4A

150.21   Where Passaic] MSw, 1A, 2A, 6A; Where Passaick 3A, 4A; Its river 5A

150.22   So transparent] MSw, 1A, 2A, 3A, 4A, 6A; Transparent 5A

150.22   waters—] MSw; ~, 2A, 3A, 4A, 6A; ~— 5A; surface, 1A

150.22   surface] MSw, 2A, 3A, 4A, 5A, 6A; waters 1A

150.24   turned] MSw; turn'd 1A, 2A, 5A; taught 3A, 6A; bade 4A

150.24   pure] MSw, 3A, 4A, 6A; smooth 1A, 2A; still 5A

150.25   rock] MSw, 6A; ~. . . . 1A; ~, 2A, 3A, 5A; rocks, 4A

150.26   loud thundering] MSw, 2A; thundering 1A, 3A, 4A, 5A, 6A

150.28   Where cliffs] MSw, 1A, 3A, 5A; ~ ~, 2A; ~ cliff 4A; [6A *wanting*]

150.28   on cliffs] MSw, 1A, 3A, 5A; ~ ~, 2A; ~ cliff 4A; [6A *wanting*]

150.28   rude] MSw, 1A, 2A, 3A; stern 4A; wild 5A; [6A *wanting*]

150.29   shades] MSw, 1A, 2A, 3A, 4A; shadows 5A; [6A *wanting*]

150.29   thick horror] MSw, 2A, 3A; deep horror 1A; thick foliage 4A; horror 5A; [6A *wanting*]

150.30   marked] MSw; mark'd 1A, 2A, 3A, 4A; mark 5A; [6A *wanting*]

150.31   since] MSw, 2A, 3A, 4A, 5A, 6A; now 1A

150.31	roll'd] MSw, 2A, 3A; roll[*blank type*]d 1A; pass'd 4A; ~— 5A; rolled 6A
150.31	in the] MSw, 1A, 2A, 3A, 4A, 6A; in this 5A
150.32	those features] MSw, 1A, 2A, 3A, 5A, 6A; the fractures 4A
150.33	axe] MSw, 1A, 2A, 3A, 5A, 6A; care 4A
150.33	enlivened] MSw; enliven'd 2A, 5A; his lightened 1A; has lighten'd 4A, 6A; has lighted 3A
150.34	deep] MSw, 1A, 2A, 3A, 5A, 6A; dark 4A
150.34	of the thicketed] MSw, 3A, 5A, 6A; ~ ~ thicketted 1A, 2A; from the thicket and 4A
150.35	Yet] MSw, 1A, 2A, 3A, 5A; But 4A, 6A
150.36	rocks] MSw, 1A, 2A, 3A, 4A, 5A; the rocks 6A
151.1	loves] MSw, 1A, 2A, 3A, 5A, 6A; delights 4A
151.1	border] MSw, 2A, 4A, 5A; borders 1A, 3A, 6A

[LINES WRITTEN AT STRATFORD]

156.11	Of] 2A, 3A, 4A; "~ 1A
156.11	Mighty] 4A; mighty 1A, 2A, 3A
156.11	Shakespeare's] 4A; Shakspeare's 1A, 2A, 3A
156.11	birth] 1A, 3A, 4A; *birth,* 2A
156.11	see,] 2A, 4A; ~; 1A, 3A
156.12	That] 2A, 3A, 4A; *That* 1A
156.12	died] 4A; ~, 1A, 3A; *died* 2A
156.12	try,] 1A, 4A; ~;* 2A; ~. 3A. *In 2A a note appears at the bottom of the page:* "*The house in which Shakspeare died has long since been pulled down."
156.13	search:—] 4A; ~— 1A, 3A; ~!— 2A
156.13	for] 1A, 2A, 4A; ~, 3A
156.13	all Immortal He 4A; *all immortal* he, 1A; all immortal he! 2A; all immortal he, 3A
156.14	those] 1A, 2A, 4A; they 3A
156.14	are Immortal] 4A; *are immortal* 1A; are immortal 2A, 3A
156.14	die.] 1A, 3A, 4A; ~! 2A
156.15	Washington Irving.] 4A; WASHINGTON IRVING, 1A; WASHINGTON IRVING 2A; [*omitted*] 3A

WRITTEN IN THE DEEPDENE ALBUM

157.12	*June 24th,* 1822] 1E; [*omitted*] 1A. *But see* Emendations, 156.18

TO MISS EMILY FOSTER ON HER BIRTH-DAY

157.16	green and] 1A; ~, & MSy
157.17	soft and] 1A; ~, & MSy
157.17	clear,] 1A; ~_∧ MSy
157.18	May—] 1A; ~. MSy
157.19	month,] 1A; ~_∧ MSy
157.20	earth—] 1A; ~, MSy
157.21	genial time,] 1A; ~ ~_∧ MSy
157.22	birth.] 1A; ~_∧ MSy
157.23	chose,] 1A; ~_∧ MSy
157.24	bespeak—] 1A; ~_∧ MSy
157.25	lily and] 1A; ~, & MSy
157.25	pale, pale] 1A; ~_∧ ~ MSy
157.26	cheek.] 1A; ~_∧ MSy
157.27	noontide] 1A; noon tide MSy
157.28	combining,] 1A; ~_∧ MSy
157.30	shining.] 1A; ~— MSy
157.31	blush,] 1A; ~_∧ MSy
157.32	light and] 1A; ~, & MSy
157.32	revealing,] 1A; ~_∧ MSy
158.2	and feeling] 1A; or ~ MSy
158.3	oh!] 1A; ~_∧ MSy
158.4	breast;] 1A; ~_∧ MSy
158.5	and mind,] 1A; &~_∧ MSy
158.7	Bloom on—bloom on—] 1A; ~ ~, ~ ~, MSy
158.8	flower,] 1A, ~_∧ MSy
158.8	one,] 1A; ~_∧ MSy
158.9	keep] 1A; guard MSy
158.10	upon.] 1A; ~— MSy

THE DULL LECTURE

158.13–15	————/ FRONTISPIECE. /———— 1A; [omitted] 2A
158.17	Vaine] 1A; Vain 2A
158.19	Ever more] 1A; Evermore 2A
158.20	Younge heade] 1A; Young head 2A. *The same variant occurs at* 158.21, 158.22
158.20	heede] 1A; heed 2A
158.21	recklesse] 1A; reckless 2A
158.22	beautie] 1A; beauty 2A
158.22	reade] 1A; read 2A

158.23 dreames] 1A; dreams 2A

THE LAY OF THE SUNNYSIDE DUCKS

159.36 By] MSm; "~ 1A, 2A. *Double quotation marks without precedent in the copy-text appear also in 1A at 160.3, 160.7, 160.11, 160.15, 160.19, 160.23, 160.27, 160.32, 160.35. A double quotation mark without precedent in MSm appears in 2A at 160.35*

159.36 brook] MSm, 1A; Brook 2A

160.1 old,] MSm; ~∧ 1A, 2A

160.4 play;] MSm, ~— 1A; ~, 2A

160.5 Snowy white] MSm, 2A; Snowy-white 1A

160.5 ducks,] MSm; ~∧ 1A, 2A

160.5 top knots] MSm; top-knots[1] 1A; topknots 2A; *The superscript in 1A refers to an explanatory note*

160.5 heads,] MSm, 1A; ~∧ 2A

160.7 Hall] MSm, 2A; ~, 1A

160.8 dwell;] MSm; ~, 1A; ~∧ 2A

160.11 But] MSm; And 1A, 2A

160.11 laird] MSm, 1A, Laird 2A

160.11 rose] MSm; arose 1A, 2A

160.11 might,] MSm; ~∧ 1A, 2A

160.12 wife,] MSm; ~∧ 1A, 2A

160.12 day,] MSm, 2A; ~,— 1A

*160.13–18 This . . . living,] MSm; '~ . . . ~,' 1A, 2A. *Direct quotations at 160.19–22 and 160.25–26 are also enclosed in pairs of single quotation marks in 1A and 2A but not in MSm*

160.13 brook is] MSm, 1A; ~, ~ 2A

160.13 brook,] MSm, 1A; ~∧ 2A

160.14 shall no longer] MSm, 2A; no longer shall 1A

160.16 eke] MSm, 2A; e'en 1A

160.17 stop it] MSm, 1A; ~ ~, 2A

160.17 dam] MSm; ~, 1A, 2A

160.17 ram,] MSm, 1A; ~∧ 2A

160.19 lawn] MSm, 2A; ~, 1A

160.20 clear,] MSm; ~; 1A; ~. 2A

160.21 up stairs] MSm, 1A; upstairs 2A

160.21 downstairs] MSm, 2A; down stairs 1A

160.21 Hall] MSm, 1A; ~, 2A

160.22 bathroom—] MSm; bath-room, 1A; ~, 2A

160.23   quaked*] MSm; quacked 1A; quaked 2A. *See* Rejected
                Variants, 160.36

160.23   fear,] MSm, 1A; ~_∧ 2A

160.25   Oh laird] MSm; Oh! Laird 1A; Oh Laird 2A

160.25   brook] MSm, 1A; ~, 2A

160.28   laird] MSm; Laird 1A, 2A

160.28   skill;] MSm, 2A; ~, 1A

160.29   brook and] MSm; ~, ~ 1A, 2A

160.30   brook,] MSm, 1A; ~_∧ 2A

160.32   heart] MSm, 1A; ~, 2A

160.33   quanda-*ry*] MSm; quanda-ry. 1A; quanda—*ry*, 2A

160.34   down] MSm; on 1A, 2A

160.34   pond,] MSm; ~_∧ 1A, 2A

160.36   *Qu: quacked?] MSm; [*omitted*] 1A, 2A

LIST OF PRECOPY-TEXT REJECTED VARIANTS

This list provides a record of variants in texts which antedate the copy-texts and which are not incorporated in the present critical texts.

The numbers before each entry indicate page and line numbers. The reading to the left of the bracket indicates an accepted reading; its source is indicated by symbol after the bracket. Any reading which follows the semicolon is a rejected one, the sources of which are identified by symbol. An asterisk preceding the page number refers the reader to the Discussions of Adopted Readings.

A key to identifying symbols used in referring to manuscript and printed texts is given on pages 229–32.

[REVIEW OF *THE WORKS . . . OF ROBERT TREAT PAINE*]

54.36	during] 1A, 2A; During P. *In P, "During" begins a paragraph immediately following "consolation" in the passage quoted above, 54.31–35. Irving has altered the capitalization to suit his convenience*
56.29–30	their continuous indulgence] 1A, 2A; the continuous indulgence of his habits P
62.19	Peace and, her offspring, Arts be thine] 1A; ~ ~, ~ ~, arts ~ ~ P. *Irving has clearly capitalized (and more explicitly personified) "Arts" in order to render this awkward line less confusing. Another attempt at the same result is made in 2A: "Peace, and her off-spring Arts, be thine"*

THE LAY OF THE SCOTTISH FIDDLE: A TALE OF HAVRE DE GRACE

82.18	whip-poor-will] 1A; whip-per-will L
82.30	Nature! Goddess] 1A; nature! goddess L

ODES . . . BY EDWIN C. HOLLAND

108.18	"the blue eyed Myra,"] 1A, 2A; "The Portrait: *To the Blue-Eyed Myra.*" H. *A title of a poem in H, pp. [27]–30*

108.18	"Rosa Matilda,"] 1A, 2A; "To Rosa-Matilda." H. *The title of a lyric in H, pp. 38–39*
108.19	"lucid . . . breasts,"] 1A, 2A; Mine be the maid, whose lucid vest/ But faintly veils the snowy breast, H. *Adaptation from "To Rosa-Matilda," H, p. 38*
108.19	"satin sashes,"] 1A, 2A; Now the satin sash is seen, H. *Adaptation from "The Portrait," H, p. 28*
108.19–20	"sighs . . . perfume,"] 1A, 2A; From thy lip's luxuriant glow,/ Sighs of rosy perfume flow, H. *"The Portrait," H, p. 29*
108.20–21	"trembling . . . seen,"] 1A, 2A; Like the trembling Eve-star beam,/ Through some light cloud's glory seen— H. *"The Portrait," H, p. 28*
108.23	—"The sweetest] 1A; Than the sweetest H. *"Song Set to Music by the Author, and Inscribed to Miss *** ***," H, p. 33*
108.35	"hours of bliss,"] 1A, 2A; The lovelier hour of bliss H. *"To Rosa-Matilda" H, p. 39*
108.36	"ardent kisses,"] 1A, 2A; I thought I felt thy ardent kiss H. *"To Marion," H, p. 35*
*111.21	"halo and lustre of story"] 1A, 2A; Halo and Lustre of Story," H
113.2	die] 1A, 2A; dye H. *The* OED *lists both spellings as in nineteenth-century usage*

A BIOGRAPHICAL SKETCH OF THOMAS CAMPBELL

133.25–27	[This . . . author.]] 3A; [*wanting*] 1A
133.28	deplored by authors] 3A; admitted 1A
133.28	they] 3A; authors 1A
133.29	living.] 3A; ~∧ 1A. *This error persists in all copies of precopy-text editions consulted*
133.30	to which] 3A; to which in a manner 1A
133.32–33	who . . . popularity,] 3A; who through the caprice of fashion, the influence of rank and fortune, or the panegyrics of friends, have enjoyed an undeserved notoriety, 1A
133.33	said, that] 3A; said∧ 1A
133.36	which he] 3A; he 1A
133.37	a theme] 3A; an object 1A
134.4	thousands] 3A; mankind 1A
134.8	miseries] 3A; necessities 1A

134.10   departed, over living authors,] 3A; departed authors, over living ones∧ 1A

134.11–12   attributed . . . ill nature.] 3A; ascribed to more charitable motives than those of envy and illnature. 1A

134.12–16   The latter . . . caprices.] 3A; [*wanting*] 1A

134.16–17   The former . . . works.] 3A; Of the former we judge almost exclusively by their works. 1A

134.19   writings . . . behind.] 3A; volumes they have left behind; without considering that these are like so many masterly portraits, presenting their genius in its most auspicious moments, and noblest attitudes, when its powers were collected by solitude and reflection, assisted by study, stimulated by ambition and elevated by inspiration. 1A

134.21   fulness] 3A; spring-/tide 1A

134.23   career] 3A; course 1A

134.24–25   With . . . placed] 3A; Living authors, on the contrary, are continually in public view, and exposed to the full glare of scrutinizing familiarity. Though we may occasionally wonder at their eagle soarings, yet we soon behold them descend to our own level, and often sink below it. Their habits of seclusion makes them less easy and engaging in society than the mere man of fashion, whose only study is to please. Their ignorance of the common topics of the day, and of matters of business, frequently makes them inferior in conversation to men of ordinary· capacities, while the constitutional delicacy of their minds and irritability of their feelings, make them prone to more than ordinary caprices. At one time solitary and unsocial, at another listless and petulant, often trifling among the frivolous, and not infrequently the dullest among the dull. All these circumstances tend to diminish our respect and admiration for their mental excellence, and show clearly, that authors, like actors, to be impartially criticized, should never be known behind the scenes.
                Such are a few of the causes that operate in Europe to defraud an author of the candid judgment of his countrymen, but their influence does not extend to this side of the Atlantic. We are placed, 1A

134.28   A] 3A; An 1A

134.39   literature.] 3A; ∼. Few think of writing the anecdotes of a distinguished character while living. His
intimates, who of course are most capable, are prevented by their very intimacy, little thinking that
those domestic habits and peculiarities, which an
every day's acquaintance has made so trite and familiar to themselves, can be objects of curiosity to all
the world besides. Thus then we, who are too distant to gather those particulars concerning foreign
authors, that are circulated from mouth to mouth in
their native countries, must content ourselves to remain in almost utter ignorance; unless perchance
some friendly magazine now and then gives us a
meagre and apocryphal account of them, which
rather provokes than satisfies our curiosity. 1A

134.40   this assertion] 3A; these assertions 1A

135.17–18   He ... eloquence.] 3A; He is still remembered and extolled by the Virginians as a man of rare and uncommon eloquence. 1A

135.20   the year 1808.] 3A; two years since. 1A

135.34   erroneous.] 3A. ∼. He shines for awhile in that period
of youth, when error is excused by inexperience, and
when we look for talents rather than knowledge—
but the ignorance that is pardonable in youth is contemptible in manhood, and insupportable in age.
Thus the world first seduces him from the thorny
path of instruction, intoxicates him by its adulation,
and having thus entailed ignorance and conceit upon
him for ever, abandons him in disappointment at his
not realizing those expectations, which its own blan-
dishments have incapacitated him to satisfy. 1A

135.41   muscle.] 3A; ∼. It is not the exclamation of "lo here a
prophet! and there a *prophet!*" or "here a *genius!*
and there a *genius!*" that can throw them into those
universal paroxysms of delight and infatuation, which
often prevail in other parts of the united kingdom. 1A

136.6   schools.] 3A. ∼. By these means they have acquired
their preeminent rank in the literary world, over
which they exercise a severe but salutary sway; acting as guardians of public morals, promoters of useful knowledge, and austere censors of the press. 1A

136.18   scholars] 3A; Latin scholars 1A

137.12   expansion of mind and elevation of thought produced]
          3A; ardour and elevation of mind awakened 1A

137.22   publisher, who,] 3A; publisher. The race of booksellers,
          who, like "dull weeds" have thrived and fattened,
          since time immemorial, on the banks of Helicon, have
          notwithstanding much reformed in these latter days.
          They still grow wealthy. and wax fat, it is true, but
          authors do not as uniformly starve: so that while the
          former make immense profits for the extreme trouble
          of selling a book, the author is generously allowed a
          tolerable recompense, in addition to the great pleas-
          ure of writing it. It was Mr. Campbell's good luck to
          encounter some bookseller of this conscientious class,
          who$_\wedge$ 1A

137.28   the universal enthusiasm] 3A; the literary world was
          completely infatuated by the brilliant absurdities of
          the German muse. The English are in literature what
          the Israelites of yore were in religion, a wayward,
          erring race, ever ready to stray from the paths of
          truth, and follow after strange idols and monstrous
          doctrines. To no nation has the clear light of reason
          been more abundantly imparted, to none have the
          immutable laws of criticism been more fully ex-
          pounded and exemplified, nor does any nation pos-
          sess libraries so replete with every thing that can
          instruct the understanding, delight the fancy and
          gratify the taste; yet no nation is more prone to turn
          from this wholesome aliment of the mind, this "man-
          na "sent down from heaven," and languish after for-
          eign and pernicious crudities.
          The universal enthusiasm 1A

137.28   it] 3A; this new species of literature 1A

138.5   sight."] 3A; sight. My love of novelty now gave way
          to personal fears. I took a carriage in company with
          an Austrian surgeon back to Landshut," &c. 1A

138.10   Mr. Campbell afterwards] 3A; From Landshut Mr.
          Campbell 1A

138.22   Croat] 3A; scoundrel croat 1A

138.27–31   His . . . belles-lettres.] 3A; "My time at Hamburgh," he
          observes, in one of his letters, "was chiefly employed
          in reading German, and, I am almost ashamed to con-
          fess it, for twelve successive weeks in the study of

Kant's Philosophy. I had heard so much of it in Germany, its language was so new to me, and the possibility of its application to so many purposes in the different theories of science and belles-lettres was so constantly maintained, that I began to suspect Kant might be another Bacon, and blamed myself for not perceiving his merit. Distrusting my own imperfect acquaintance with German, I took a disciple of Kant's for a guide through his philosophy, but found, even with all this *fair play*, nothing to reward my labour. His metaphysics are mere innovations upon the received meaning of words, and the coinage of new ones convey no more instruction than the distinction of Dun Scotus and Thomas Aquinas. In belles-lettres the German language opens a richer field than in their philosophy. I cannot conceive a more perfect poet than their favourite Wieland." 1A

139.6   society . . . however,] 3A; ~. The following brief sketch which he gives of a literary club, in London, will be gratifying to those who have felt an interest in the anecdotes of Addison and his knot of *beaux esprits* at Button's coffee house, and Johnson and his learned fraternity at the Turk's head.–"Mackintosh, the Vindiciæ Gallicæ was particularly attentive to me, and took me with him to his convivial parties at the King of Clubs, a place dedicated to the meetings of the reigning wits of London, and, in fact, a lineal descendant of the Johnson, Burke, and Goldsmith society, constituted for literary conversations. The dining table of these knights of literature was an arena of very keen conversational rivalship, maintained, to be sure, with perfect goodnature, but in which the gladiators contended as hardly as ever the French and Austrians in the scenes I had just witnessed. Much, however, as the wit and erudition of these men pleases an auditor at the first or second visit, this trial of minds becomes at last fatiguing, because it is unnatural and unsatisfactory. Every one of these brilliants goes there to shine; for conversational powers are so much the rage in London, that no reputation is higher than his who exhibits them. Where every one tries to instruct there is in fact but little instruction; wit, paradox, eccentricity, even absurdity, if delivered rapidly and facetiously, takes priority in these societies of sound reasoning and delicate taste. I have watched sometimes the devious tide of conversation, guided by accidental associations, turning from topic to topic and satisfactory upon none. What has one learned? has been my general question. The mind, it is true, is electrified and quickened, and the spirits finely exhilarated, but one grand fault pervades the whole institution; their inquiries are desultory, and all improvement to be reaped must be accidental."

These sentiments will perhaps surprise and disappoint the generality of readers, who will naturally suppose, that an association of men of quick parts and congenial tastes must be productive of the most refined and unalloyed pleasure. But in fact, conversation, to be truly agreeable, requires that the parties should be severally at their ease, less ambitious to please than willing to be pleased. Now, in a circle where the members have each a character for wit and learning to sustain, and their merits are nearly on a par, there will inevitably be a spirit of jealousy and rivalship among them. If one is lucky enough to make a successful sally, his neighbour, instead of cordially enjoying it, is tasking his invention to produce something better; considering it as a partial eclipse of his own lustre, which his credit requires him to outshine. Thus every man is constantly on the alert; anxious to excel, fearful of being surpassed; the brain is condemned to restless activity, while the social feelings of the heart lie almost entirely dormant. Conversation, instead of taking an easy and natural flow, and winding like a refreshing stream, through the mazes of science and literature, is constantly directed out of its course and forced into capricious turns and unnatural *jets d'eau* of great show but little utility. The mind becomes fatigued by constant flashes of wit, which dazzle rather than delight; and we grow weary of a conversation where there is nothing solid to gratify the understanding, and where the incessant poignancy almost sets the

teeth on edge. Indeed, these keen encounters cannot
but prove fatiguing to the parties themselves; no one,
however expert at attack and defence, would ever
choose to remain long with associates in whose company he must always have his weapons in his hands.

The friendship of Mrs. Siddons was another acquisition, of which Mr. Campbell spoke with great pleasure; and what rendered it more gratifying was its
being unsought for. It was the means of introducing
him to much excellent society in London. "The character of that great woman" he observes, "is but little
understood, and more misrepresented than any living
character I know, by those who envy her reputation,
or by those of the aristocracy, whom her irresistible
dignity obliges to pay their homage at a respectful
distance. The reserve of her demeanour is banished
towards those who show neither meanness in flattering her, nor forwardness in approaching her too familiarly. The friends of her fireside are only such as
she *talks to and talks of* with affection and respect."

The recent visit of Mr. Campbell to the continent
1A

139.17   some few years] 3A; about three years 1A

139.25   writings.] 3A; ~. In his politics he ranks with the con-
                stitutional whigs, a party little known in this country,
                for it has neither power, magnitude, nor turbulence
                sufficient to make much noise even in Great Britain.
                It is composed of moderate men, lovers of liberty and
                order, and sincerely attached to their country and
                its constitution. This party holds a middle stand
                between the two great ones, the friends of the court
                and the democrats; who are distracting Great Britain
                by their dissensions. If any thing, it leans a little, in
                the present crisis of affairs, towards the popular side.
                This explanation of Mr. Campbell's political senti-
                ments may serve to obviate the stigma of court hire-
                ling, too readily applied to such as experience the
                favours of the crown. 1A

139.43   Bleeding.] T; bleeding," published in the following col-
                lection. 1A

139.44–140.13   Of . . . poems.] 3A; Of the familiar habits and personal
                peculiarities of Mr. Campbell, which constitute the

kind of information most sought after by the admirers of an author, we know but little. He is represented as being extremely studious, but at the same time social and lively in his disposition, highly prepossessing in his appearance and of engaging and courteous manners. His circle of acquaintance is of the most polished and enlightened kind, and in this his great colloquial powers and a peculiar talent for recitation, make him a distinguished favourite. In domestic life he appears to no less advantage; a kind husband, a tender parent, and an affectionate son; in a word, few men, who have been brought up in studious and literary seclusion, unite to such brilliant endowments, such gentle and endearing qualities of the heart. 1A

140.35	fastidiousness] 3A; a fastidiousness 1A
140.43–141.5	As . . . oblivion.] 3A; [*wanting*] 1A
141.7	to injure] 3A; even to injure 1A
141.13	to be] 3A; to have been 1A
141.20	chase, and hunt] 3A; chace, and like true huntsmen pursue 1A
141.29	cheering] 3A; charming 1A
142.8	censures of many narrow-minded writers,] 3A; censures and revilings of a host of narrowminded writers, 1A
143.1	Egyptian experiences,] 3A; Egyptian, 1A
143.4	fertility.*] 3A; fertility.ʌ 1A. *See* Precopy-Text Rejected Variants, 143.32–45
143.25	acknowledge them] 3A; acknowledge it, 1A
143.29	native.] 3A; native inhabitant. 1A
143.31	Muse] 3A; muse 1A
143.32–45	*Since . . . literature.] A; [*wanting*] 1A
144.2	associations] 3A; feelings 1A
144.23–24	circumstances . . . author.] T; 3A; remarks on its merits. They are of a kind that commonly escapes the notice of the careless, and indeed require an attentive perusal to be properly appreciated. 1A
144.24–29	The story . . . finished.] 3A; The story is not sufficiently developed and amplified, and from this circumstance many have inconsiderately pronounced the whole a hasty sketch, without perceiving the great attention that has been paid to the finishing of the parts. 1A
144.29–145.8	This . . . incident.] 3A; [*wanting*] 1A

145.8	It] 3A; In fact, it 1A
145.11–12	readers; . . . qualities] 3A; readers, who are commonly led away by those glaring qualities in writing 1A
145.13	force and] 3A; strength, beauty, and 1A
145.14	a practised . . . estimate] 3A; accuracy of eye, to be sensible to 1A
145.15	consummation] 3A; the consummation 1A
145.16–17	whatever . . . and is] 3A; the more glowing and powerful qualities are 1A
145.21–22	will . . . Campbell.] 3A; will, we have no doubt, consider the Gertrude of Mr. Campbell, as an additional proof of the variety of his talents. 1A
145.23–27	Like . . . muse.] 3A; [wanting] 1A
145.27–30	While . . . thought,] 3A; He has shown in his former works, that he possesses the power of firing the imagination and filling the mind with sublime and awful images, while in this he has evinced his skill in those tender strokes of art, 1A
145.30	exalted] 3A; delighted 1A
145.31–146.2	It . . . country.] 3A; We have been told that he once contemplated a poem, descriptive of the scenery and manners of the Highlands of Scotland, and that the little fragment of Lochiel was one of the episodes connected with the original plan. Judging from that exquisite specimen, the highest expectations might be indulged, with regard to the rest of the work, and we earnestly hope it has not been abandoned. The splendid productions of Walter Scott have already shown what treasures of feudal romance, local fiction, and peculiar character, are to be found among the Scottish mountains, and how deliciously they may be interwoven into verse by the hand of genius. The theme selected by Mr. Campbell would not only be rich in the same kind of legendary lore, and original description, but would also be calculated to light up that spirit of patriotic enthusiasm, which is the noblest inspirer of the poet.
	But whatever may be the subject he may choose, we feel confident that modern literature cannot but be greatly benefited by the varied powers, the amiable morality, and above all, the critical correctness of his muse. 1A
146.12	one whom] 3A; whom 1A

LIST OF COMPOUND WORDS
HYPHENATED
AT END OF LINE

List I includes all compound or possible compound words that are hyphenated at the end of a line in the copy-texts. In deciding whether to retain the hyphen or to print the word as a single word compound (without the hyphen) or as two words without the hyphen, the editor has based his decision first on the use of each compound word elsewhere in the copy-text; or second, when the word does not appear elsewhere in the copy-text, on Irving's practice in other writings of the period; or finally, if the word does not appear in Irving's other writings of the period, on contemporary usage. Each word is listed in its editorially accepted form after the page-line number of its appearance in the Twayne text.

List II presents all compounds, or possible compounds, that are hyphenated or separated as two words at the end of a line in the Twayne text. They are listed in the form in which they would have appeared in the Twayne text had they been printed in midline.

LIST I

6.40	every one	44.39	likewise
8.29	*hydrophobia*	46.10–11	New-York
9.29	six-penny	47.38	outrages
9.36	gangway	52.3–4	understand
10.34	broadsides	53.23	newspaper
13.38	gunpowder	54.24	grasshopper
20.22	fellow-citizens	54.29	premature
28.29	chairman	57.27	ill-regulated
29.18	ſo-often	66.38	however
29.41	freeholders	69.7	New-York
38.11	broomsticks	71.16	companion-way
40.43	gentleman	78.10	ourselves
41.2	undertaken	92.35	countrymen
41.25	shop-boy	94.9	themselves
41.27	well dressed	94.28	himself

95.7	Newport	120.3	whenever
96.9	himself	120.13	ill-fated
101.11	overboard	124.23	throughout
103.27	firebrand	132.28	bomb-shells
103.37	himself	135.36	close-thinking
106.1	snow-storm	136.36	himself
107.31	highwaymen	136.42	overruled
108.33	heartless	144.19	where-ever
108.37	love-sick	184.32	commonplace
109.33	deep toned	198.16	dun-visaged
112.19	good-humoured	221.14	sometimes

LIST II

3.24–25	without	77.22–23	overwhelming
4.36–37	New-York	87.43–44	ringleader
11.6–7	horse-whip	88.2–3	himself
11.9–10	Ourang-Outang	90.20–21	broadside
26.25–26	*Harry-Strides*	91.41–42	twenty-ninth
34.32–33	however	99.17–18	throughout
37.4–5	however	108.36–37	cold-blooded
38.9–10	tatter-de-malion	117.20–21	bookshops
39.4–5	notwithstanding	129.3–4	hopeless
39.19–20	bobtail	129.22–23	overboard
40.43–44	gentleman-usher	131.28–29	passport
41.13–14	without	140.19–20	taskmaster
41.15–16	blacksmith's	141.18–19	loosely-written
42.14–15	praiseworthy	142.23–24	well-informed
44.44–45.1	mantlepieces	144.29–30	self-diffidence
46.10–11	New-York	181.24–25	wolf's head
46.17–18	forthwith	185.18–19	overflowed
51.2–3	sunshine	187.32–33	something
52.3–4	understand	191.39–40	myself
53.27–28	Notwithstanding	194.28–29	overbearing
58.19–20	sometimes	221.32–33	ourselves
67.15–16	Notwithstanding	225.7–8	Gentlewoman
67.31–32	twenty-four	227.14–15	themselves
72.35–36	shot-holes		

INDEX